DATE DUE

		MAR 0 6 2001
	OCT 2 4 2003	
FEB 2 0 2004	MAY 0 8 2006	

GAYLORD   #3523PI   Printed in USA

CHILD ABUSE

A Medical Reference

Second Edition

CHILD ABUSE

A Medical Reference

Second edition   *1992*

Edited by

Stephen Ludwig, M.D.

Professor
Department of Pediatrics
University of Pennsylvania School of Medicine
Division Chief
Department of General Pediatrics
Children's Hospital of Philadelphia
Education Coordinator
SCAN Inc.
Philadelphia, Pennsylvania

Allan E. Kornberg, M.D.

Assistant Professor
Departments of Pediatrics and Emergency Medicine
State University of New York at Buffalo School of Medicine
    and Biomedical Sciences
Division Chief
Division of Emergency Medicine
Children's Hospital of Buffalo
Buffalo, New York

Churchill Livingstone
New York, Edinburgh, London, Melbourne, Tokyo

Library of Congress Cataloging-in-Publication Data

Child abuse : a medical reference / edited by Stephen Ludwig, Allan E.
  Kornberg. — 2nd ed.
    p. cm.
    Rev. ed. of: Child abuse and neglect. 1981.
    Includes bibliographical references and index.
    ISBN 0-443-08722-9
    1. Battered child syndrome. 2. Child abuse.   I. Ludwig, Stephen,
date.   II. Kornberg, Allan E. III. Title: Child abuse and
neglect.
    [DNLM: 1. Child Abuse. WA 320 C5340025]
RA1122.5.C48 1992
614'.1—dc20
DNLM/DLC
for Library of Congress   91-36285
                                                                  CIP

Second Edition © Churchill Livingstone Inc. 1992
First Edition © Churchill Livingstone Inc. 1981

Distributed in the United Kingdom by Churchill Livingstone, Robert Stevenson House,
1–3 Baxter's Place, Leith Walk, Edinburgh EH1 3AF, and by associated companies,
branches, and representatives throughout the world.

Accurate indications, adverse reactions, and dosage schedules for drugs are provided in
this book, but it is possible that they may change. The reader is urged to review the package information data of the manufacturers of the medications mentioned.

The Publishers have made every effort to trace the copyright holders for borrowed material. If they have inadvertently overlooked any, they will be pleased to make the necessary
arrangements at the first opportunity.

Acquisitions Editor: *Robert A. Hurley*
Copy Editor: *Bridgett Dickinson*
Production Designer: *Charlie Lebeda*
Production Supervisor: *Christina Hippeli*

Printed in the United States of America

First published in 1992   7 6 5 4 3 2 1

We dedicate this book to our wives
Zella Ludwig and Ramsey Fountain, M.D.

Contributors

Marylou Barton, J.D.
Professor of Criminal Law, York College of Pennsylvania, York, Pennsylvania; Chief Deputy Attorney General, Child Abuse Prosecution Assistance Unit, Office of the Attorney General of Pennsylvania, Harrisburg, Pennsylvania

Joseph E. Bernat, D.D.S., M.S.
Associate Professor and Chairman, Department of Pediatric Dentistry, State University of New York at Buffalo School of Dental Medicine; Chief, Department of Pediatric Dentistry, Children's Hospital of Buffalo, Buffalo, New York

Karen Blount, R.N.
Director of Nursing for Critical Care, and Chairperson, Child Advocacy Team, Children's Hospital of Buffalo, Buffalo, New York

Derek A. Bruce, M.D.
Associate Clinical Professor, Department of Neurosurgery, University of Texas Southwestern Medical Center at Dallas Southwestern Medical School; Director, Department of Pediatric Neurosurgey, Pediatric Neurosurgical Institute, Humana Medical Center, Dallas, Texas

Ann Wolbert Burgess, R.N., D.N.Sc.
Professor, Department of Psychiatric Mental Health Nursing, University of Pennsylvania School of Nursing, Philadelphia, Pennsylvania; Associate Director of Nursing Research, Department of Health and Hospitals, Boston City Hospital, Boston, Massachusetts

Cindy W. Christian, M.D.
Clinical Assistant Professor, Department of Pediatrics, University of Pennsylvania School of Medicine; Assistant Physician, Department of Pediatrics, Children's Hospital of Philadelphia, Philadelphia, Pennsylvania

Katherine Kaufer Christoffel, M.D., M.P.H.
Professor, Departments of Pediatrics and Community Health and Preventive Medicine, Northwestern University Medical School; Attending Physician, Departments of General and Emergency Pediatrics, Children's Memorial Hospital, Chicago, Illinois

Pierre Coant, M.D.
Clinical Instructor, Department of Pediatrics, State University of New York at Buffalo School of Medicine and Biomedical Sciences; Fellow, Department of Pediatric Emergency Medicine, Children's Hospital of Buffalo, Buffalo, New York

Arthur Cooper, M.D.
Associate Professor, Division of Pediatric Surgery, Columbia University College of Physicians and Surgeons; Chief, Department of Pediatrics, Pediatric Surgical Critical Care, Harlem Hospital Center, New York, New York

Daniel L. Coury, M.D.
Associate Professor, Department of Clinical Pediatrics, Ohio State University College of Medicine; Director, Continuity Clinic, and Chief, Department of Behavioral Developmental Pediatrics, Children's Hospital, Columbus, Ohio

Allan R. De Jong, M.D.
Clinical Professor, Department of Pediatrics, Jefferson Medical College of Thomas Jefferson University; Director, Pediatric Sexual Abuse Program, Thomas Jefferson University Hospital, Philadelphia, Pennsylvania

Paul M. Diamond, M.D.
Clinical Affiliate, Department of General Pediatrics, Children's Hospital of Philadelphia, Philadelphia, Pennsylvania; Pediatrician and Child Abuse Consultant, Department of Pediatrics, Pediatric Practices of Northeastern Pennsylvania, Honesdale, Pennsylvania

Robert Goode, M.D.
State Medical Examiner, New Jersey State Medical Examiner Office; Clinical Associate Professor, Department of Pathology, University of Medicine and Dentistry of New Jersey School of Medicine, Newark, New Jersey

Margaret R. Hammerschlag, M.D.
Assistant Professor, Department of Pediatrics, State University of New York Health Science Center at Brooklyn; Attending Physician, Departments of Pediatrics and Infectious Diseases, Kings County Hospital Center, Brooklyn, New York

Carol R. Hartman, R.N., D.N.Sc.
Professor, Department of Psychiatric Nursing, Boston College of Nursing, Chestnut Hill, Massachusetts

John L. Hunt, M.D.
Professor, Department of Surgery, University of Texas Southwestern Medical Center at Dallas Southwestern Medical School; Co-Director, Department of Surgery, Parkland Memorial Hospital Burn Unit, Parkland Memorial Hospital, Dallas, Texas

Charles F. Johnson, M.D.
Professor, Department of Pediatrics, Ohio State University College of Medicine; Director, Child Abuse Program, Children's Hospital, Columbus, Ohio

Mireille B. Kanda, M.D.
Assistant Professor, Department of Child Health and Human Development, George Washington University School of Medicine and Health Sciences; Director, Division of Child Protection, Children's National Medical Center, Washington, D.C.

Allan E. Kornberg, M.D.
Assistant Professor, Departments of Pediatrics and Emergency Medicine, State University of New York at Buffalo School of Medicine and Biomedical Sciences; Division Chief, Division of Emergency Medicine, Children's Hospital of Buffalo, Buffalo, New York

Stephen Lazoritz, M.D.
Assistant Professor, Department of Pediatrics, State University of New York at Buffalo School of Medicine and Biomedical Sciences; Director, Department of Pediatrics, Erie County Medical Center, Buffalo, New York

Alex V. Levin, M.D.
Instructor, Department of Ophthalmology, Jefferson Medical College of Thomas Jefferson University, Instructor, Department of Pediatric Ophthalmology, Wills Eye Hospital; Clinical Affiliate, Departments of Ophthalmology and Pediatrics, Children's Hospital of Philadelphia, Philadelphia, Pennsylvania

Stephen Ludwig, M.D.
Professor, Department of Pediatrics, University of Pennsylvania School of Medicine; Division Chief, Department of General Pediatrics, Children's Hospital of Philadelphia; Education Coordinator, SCAN Inc., Philadelphia, Pennsylvania

Francis C. Mezzadri, M.D.
Clinical Assistant Professor, Departments of Pediatrics and Medicine, State University of New York at Buffalo School of Medicine and Biomedical Sciences; Pediatric Emergency Specialist and Maternal Medicine Consultant, Departments of Pediatrics and Internal Medicine, Children's Hospital of Buffalo, Buffalo, New York

Lavdena A. Orr, M.D.
Assistant Professor, Department of Pediatrics, George Washington University School of Medicine and Health Sciences; Assistant Medical Director, Division of Child Protection, Children's National Medical Center, Washington, D.C.

Mary Owen, M.D.
Clinical Assistant Professor, Departments of Pediatrics and Emergency Medicine, State University of New York at Buffalo School of Medicine and Biomedical Sciences; Attending Physician, Division of Emergency Medicine, Children's Hospital of Buffalo, Buffalo, New York

Gary F. Purdue, M.D.
Associate Professor, Department of Surgery, Unversity of Texas Southwestern Medical Center at Dallas Southwestern Medical School; Co-Director, Department of Surgery, Parkland Memorial Hospital Burn Unit, Parkland Memorial Hospital, Dallas, Texas

Sarah A. Rawstron, M.B., B.S.
Assistant Professor, Department of Pediatrics, State University of New York Health Science Center at Brooklyn; Active Attending Physician, Departments of Pediatrics and Infectious Diseases, Kings County Hospital Center, Brooklyn, New York

Lucy Balian Rorke, M.D.
Clinical Professor, Departments of Pathology and Neurology, University of Pennsylvania School of Medicine; Neuropathologist, Department of Pathology, Children's Hospital of Philadelphia; Forensic Neuropathologist, Office of the Medical Examiner, Philadelphia, Pennsylvania

Mimi Rose, J.D.
Senior Attorney, American Prosecutors Research Institute, National Center for Prosecution of Child Abuse, Alexandria, Virginia

Anthony L. Rostain, M.D.
Assistant Professsor, Departments of Psychiatry and Pediatrics, University of Pennsylvania School of Medicine; Medical Director, Pediatric Consultation-Liaison, Department of Psychiatry Service, Philadelphia Child Guidance Clinic, The Children's Hospital of Philadelphia, Philadelphia, Pennsylvania

Robert Schwartz, J.D.
Visiting Associate Professor, Haverford College, Haverford, Pennsylvania; Executive Director, Juvenile Law Center, Philadelphia, Pennsylvania

Toni Seidl, R.N., A.C.S.W., L.S.N.
Social Work Supervisor and Lecturer, Department of Social Work Field Cabinet, University of Pennylvania School of Medicine; Child Abuse Coordinator, Department of Social Work, Children's Hospital of Philadelphia, Philadelphia, Pennsylvania

Wendy E. Shumway, M.D.
Clinical Instructor, Department of Psychiatry, University of Pennsylvania School of Medicine; Child Psychiatry Resident, Department of Child Psychiatry, Philadelphia Child Guidance Clinic, The Children's Hospital of Philadelphia, Philadelphia, Pennsylvania

Brian S. Smistek
Director, Department of Medical Photography and Television, Children's Hospital of Buffalo, Buffalo, New York

Betty S. Spivack, M.D.
Assistant Professor and Chief, Division of Pediatric Critical Care, Department of Pediatrics, University of Connecticut School of Medicine, Farmington, Connecticut; Director, Pediatric ICU, Department of Pediatrics, Hartford Hospital, Hartford, Connecticut

Leonard E. Swischuk, M.D.
Professor of Radiology and Pediatrics, Director, Division of Pediatric Radiology, University of Texas Medical Branch at Galveston, Galveston, Texas

Josephine Ross Welliver, M.D.
Assistant Professor, Department of Pediatrics, State University of New York at Buffalo School of Medicine and Biomedical Sciences; Associate Director, Division of Emergency Medicine, Children's Hospital of Buffalo, Buffalo, New York

E. Peter Wilson, M.B., B.S., M.P.H.
Associate Clinical Professor, Departments of Pediatrics and Emergency Medicine, University of Pennylvania School of Medicine; Senior Physician, Department of General Pediatrics, The Children's Hospital of Philadelphia; Executive Director, SCAN, Inc., Philadelphia, Pennsylvania

Preface

The care of children who have been abused or neglected is a complex multidisciplinary venture that demands the skills of professionals from medicine, nursing, social work, education, psychology, law, law enforcement, and other child advocacy disciplines. Even for those in the health science disciplines there are many demanding roles and responsibilities, including recognition of abuse, reporting, short-term crisis intervention, and long-term treatment. As health care professionals, we must also provide some of the scientific underpinnings for understanding and treating abuse.

Child abuse is not a new phenomenon. Care of abused children is also not new, and in the United States it can be traced through social work history into the nineteenth century. However, medical attention to the plight of abused and neglected children is relatively recent. The 1960s marked the medical community's discovery of "child abuse." In the 1970s, physicians were alerted to the signs of abuse and the requirement to report suspected abuse. In the 1980s, the emergence of sexual abuse recognition and reporting was seen. Also the 1980s brought forth several research attempts at more in-depth understanding of how abuse occurs, how it is best recognized, its effective treatments, and its long-term outcomes. In the 1990s we are beginning to see the emergence of the "Science of Abuse."

There have been many excellent textbooks written in the field of abuse and neglect. Some of these concentrate on only one aspect of child abuse such as law enforcement, social work, or mental health. Other texts reflect the multidisciplinary nature of child abuse by covering several areas. Norman S. Ellerstein, M.D., the editor of the first edition of *Child Abuse and Neglect: A Medical Reference*, recognized the need for a text focusing on the medical aspects of child abuse and neglect. We have attempted to follow in his tradition with this second edition and to bring the science up-to-date.

As pediatricians, pediatric emergency medicine specialists, and child advocates, we recognized the need for an updated reference on clinical aspects of child abuse. This edition begins with general topics including definitions, etiology, epidemiology, history, and the multidisciplinary approach to child abuse and neglect. A unique and forward-looking chapter on the biomechanics of child abuse is also included. Next are sections on physical abuse, sexual abuse, neglect, and psychologic abuse with in-depth chapters on the manifestations of the different forms of abuse. The final section covers forensic issues including the court and judicial system, forensic pathology findings, foster care, and medical photography. Eight appendices are also included at the end of the book.

Is that burn accidental or suspicious for child abuse? Is it medical neglect for parents to not give prescribed anticonvulsants to their child? What causes the damage found in the shaken baby syndrome? What physical findings are suggestive for sexual molestation? How does the clinician and pathologist approach the possibility of homicide in the infant who appears to be a victim of sudden infant death syndrome (SIDS)? What dental findings suggest child abuse? This book can help answer these and many other questions.

Our hope is that physicians, dentists, and nurses will find this reference useful in its broad coverage of child abuse and neglect. Although pediatricians, family practitioners, emergency physicians, surgeons, radiologists, and pathologists may be the physicians most likely to see a victim of child abuse, nearly every medical specialist may be confronted with a case of child abuse in their clinical practice.

We believe that this text can also be useful to mental health professionals, child protection workers, social workers, attorneys, judges, law enforcement officials, and other non-health professionals who struggle with clinical issues. Most of the text, tables and figures are comprehensible to professionals who primarily work in non-medical fields. A glossary is also provided as one of the appendices to assist these readers.

We are fortunate to have gathered a large number of contributors with a vast knowledge of the field of child abuse and neglect. This reference benefits from both their considerable experience and extensive review of the literature. It is our hope that the victims of child abuse and neglect will also benefit from the publication of *Child Abuse: A Medical Reference*.

Stephen Ludwig, M.D.
Allan E. Kornberg, M.D.

Acknowledgments

My interest in child abuse has been part of a wider curiosity about families and how they function in society. Child abuse in all its subforms is a severe manifestation of family dysfunction, and thus, serves as a negative marker for a much broader multifaceted human function—the rearing of our young. I am very grateful to my own parents and my sister for instilling this curiosity in me. This curiosity has caused me to examine my own family structure and function as an adolescent and young adult and has also taught me many positive lessons for my own role as husband, father, and physician.

When professionally looking at the families of others, one cannot help but also to examine one's own. To that end, I have been most blessed in meeting and marrying Zella Ludwig, who has been my partner in this work, as in all that I have done, for more than 25 years. Susannah, Elisa, and Aubrey, my daughters, also have my never-ending gratitude for their support and understanding of my parenting abilities and of my demanding professional life.

In addition, I wish to acknowledge my colleagues. Those who have worked at my side in the child abuse program at the Children's Hospital of Philadelphia and at the Supportive Child Adult Network, Inc. for 17 years—Cathy Sharrar, Toni Seidl, Tony Mauro, Peter Wilson, Alex Levin, Cindy Christian, Cindy Briede, Paul Diamond, and the late Catherine Harris. In addition, there have been countless medical students, pediatric residents, fellows, nurses, family workers, Child Protection Service workers, lawyers, and law enforcement agents who have been with me on home visits, by the patient's bedside in the hospital, in the multidisciplinary team meetings, and in the courtroom.

My thanks also to my colleagues in the Emergency Department at the Children's Hospital of Philadelphia who enabled me to gain expertise as a child advocate; these include Fred Henretig, Gary Fleisher, Richard Ruddy, Steve Selbst, Doug Baker, Cathy Shaw, Lou Bell, Ben Silverman, Jane Lavelle, and Jackie Maller. My admiration to Fran Klass who aided in the editing of the manuscript and to Kim Loretucci, Carol Bader, and Bridgett Dickinson at Churchill Livingstone.

Working with Allan Kornberg has been an honor and a pleasure. He has been a consummate co-editor and a friend. I look forward to continuing our friendship and working relationship. Finally, my unmeasurable thanks to Rose Beato, my work partner for more than 13 years. Her hard work and loyalty have been a treasure.

What appears on the pages that follow is the amalgam of what all whose names are listed above, and many whose names I have forgotten, have taught me. They have given me a valuable and useful gift that I wish to share with our readers and ultimately with the children and families they serve.

Stephen Ludwig, M.D.

Norman S. Ellerstein, M.D., the editor of the first edition of *Child Abuse: A Medical Reference,* taught me much of what I know in the field of child abuse and neglect. His untimely death gave me the sad honor of co-editing this second edition. Dr. Ellerstein left extremely large shoes to fill in caring for and teaching about abused children in a scientific yet compassionate way. I also thank his widow, Ellen, who has been extremely supportive of this project.

Betty S. Spivack, M.D., during her many years in Buffalo, served as both my colleague and teacher in the field of clinical child abuse. I gained much from her knowledge and dedication and was deeply honored to include her chapter, Biomechanics of Nonaccidental Trauma, in this book.

Lucy Wargo, librarian at the Children's Hospital of Buffalo, greatly assisted me in my research of this topic as well as in several of my other projects. My secretaries, Cindy Sitterle,and Janet Lathrop, were invaluable, both by their direct assistance with this book and their support of my professional endeavors.

I would also like to thank the emergency nurses, the pediatric housestaff, and the physicians on the staff of the Children's Hospital of Buffalo. Their assistance with patient referrals and their insight into the issues of child abuse were indispensable. My two fellows in pediatric emergency medicine during the writing of this book, Pierre Coant, M.D., and Bohdan Dejneka, M.D., expertly performed most of the child protection consults. Their analysis and insightful questions contributed to my knowledge of child abuse and neglect.

I am grateful to the children and their parents who were an essential part of my research in the field of clinical child abuse. I hope that the experience I gained while caring for these children will allow me and others to reduce the potential suffering of children who follow.

I thank my parents for their love, guidance, and confidence in me.

My wife, Ramsey, has been extremely supportive of this project, and tolerant of the many evenings and weekends I spent writing this book. I dedicate this book to her in recognition of our love.

Allan E. Kornberg, M.D.

Contents

Section VI: Legal/Forensic Aspects

Appendices

Defining Child Abuse: Clinical Mandate— Evolving Concepts

Stephen Ludwig

WHAT IS CHILD ABUSE?

It may seem odd that a book that covers the topic of child abuse and neglect in great depth begins with so basic a question. On one hand, the answer seems simple, since we have all seen many children who have suffered extensive trauma inflicted by a parent or person acting in a parental role. We know what abuse is, because we have seen it all too many times, and we are able to recognize it. It is hoped that recognition directly translates to reporting abuse to the proper authorities. On the other hand, the precise definition of abuse remains elusive and difficult to grasp. What some consider abusive, others find normal and acceptable parenting. Certainly, what some health care personnel report as abuse, others tend not to see and not to report. Child abuse is a complex set of parental behaviors and child responses. It is a multifaceted personal, familial, community, and societal phenomenon. Before we delve into recognizing specific injuries, reporting, and managing abuse, it is important to consider the definitions of abuse and the complexity of the term *child abuse*.

Although this chapter explores the complexity of defining the term *child abuse*, there must be a clearly stated caution. As health care providers, we *must* report abuse. The complexity and changing nature of abuse definitions should never be used as an excuse for failing to report. The problems in defining abuse must be considered and understood; they are not a reason to shrink from our duty to protect children. Definitions may vary between individuals and change over time. Our requirements to report suspected abuse are mandated by state law and must be followed.

Legal Definition

To easily answer the question, "What is abuse?" the reply may be that "Abuse is what the law says it is." Child abuse is defined by each state's civil and criminal laws. Although many state child abuse laws are modeled after federal legislation, each varies from the model and from each other. Most laws define abuse by subcategorizing it into one of four types: physical, sexual, neglect, or emotional/psychological. The Pennsylvania law uses the following definitions.

Child Abuse

Serious physical or mental injury that is not explained by the available medical history as being accidental, or sexual abuse or sexual exploitation, or serious physical neglect of a child under 18 years of age if the injury, abuse, or neglect has been caused by the acts or omissions of the child's parents, or by a person responsible for the child's welfare, or an individual residing in the same home as the child, or a paramour of a child's parent. No child shall be deemed to be physically or mentally abused for the sole reason he is in good faith being furnished treatment by spiritual means through prayer alone in accordance with the tenets and practices of a recognized church or religious denomination by a duly accredited practitioner thereof or is not provided specified medical treatment in the practice of religious beliefs, or solely on the grounds of environmental factors which are beyond the control of the person responsible for the child's welfare such as inadequate housing, furnishings, income, clothing, and medical care.

Serious Bodily Injury.   Serious bodily injury is injury that creates a substantial risk of death or causes serious permanent disfigurement or protracted loss or impairment of the function of a body member or organ. Serious bodily injury (1) causes the child severe pain; (2) significantly impairs the child's physical functioning, either temporarily or permanently; and (3) is accompanied by physical evidence of a continuous pattern of separate, unexplained injuries to the child.

Sexual Abuse.   Sexual abuse is defined as any of the following when committed on a child by a perpetrator.

1. Statutory rape: sexual intercourse with a child who is less than 14 years of age by a person 18 years of age or older.
2. Involuntary or voluntary deviate sexual intercourse: intercourse by mouth or rectum or with an animal.
3. Sexual assault: sexual involvement, including the touching or exposing of the sexual or other intimate parts of a person, for the purpose of arousing or gratifying sexual desire in either the perpetrator or subject child.
4. Incest: sexual intercourse with an ancestor or descendant by blood or adoption—brother or sister of the whole or half blood, or an uncle, aunt, nephew, or niece of the whole blood.
5. Promoting prostitution: inducing or encouraging a child to engage in prostitution.
6. Rape: sexual intercourse by force or compulsion.
7. Pornography: includes the obscene photographing, filming, or depiction of children for commercial purposes; or the obscene filming or photographing of children or showing of obscene films or photographs to arouse or gratify sexual desire in either the perpetrator, subject child, or viewing audience.

Serious Physical Neglect.   Serious physical neglect is a physical condition caused by the acts or omissions of a perpetrator that endanger the child's life or development or impair physical functioning. Serious physical neglect is the result of prolonged or repeated lack of supervision or failure to provide essentials of life, including adequate medical care.

Serious Mental Injury.   Serious mental injury is a psychological condition as diagnosed by a physician or licensed psychologist caused by the acts or omissions—including the refusal of appropriate treatment—of the perpetrator that (1) render the child chronically and severely anxious, agitated, depressed, socially withdrawn, psychotic, or in reasonable fear that his life or safety is threatened or (2) seriously interfere with the child's ability to accomplish age appropriate developmental and social tasks.

This law is atypical in the sense that the term *serious* is used. State laws vary in detail. For example, some list specific acts such as leaving a young child alone in a motor vehicle, while others are more general in their definitions. States vary even in their definition of who is a child. Appendix B lists the characteristics of each state law and demonstrates state-to-state variation. It is important to realize that most state child abuse laws were enacted in the mid to late 1960s. Most states have revised their laws two or three times since then. The first model national legislation was formulated in the 1970s. The history of using laws to define child abuse is a recent phenomenon. Laws are constantly under interpretation and revision by case law. Thus, even the definitions of abuse in a specific geographic region are subject to change at any time.

Institutional Definitions

Beyond legal definitions of abuse, we are also subject to institutional or operational definitions. These definitions are determined by institutional policy or procedure. At The Children's Hospital of Philadelphia, we define (and therefore report) child abuse accordingly. All teachers at Elsewhere School must follow a set policy when reporting abuse. Institutional policy may modify the definition of abuse. What is abuse in the institution may not be abuse in another. There may be one state law in a given state but hundreds or thousands of institutional policies. Although all institutions are bound to follow state laws, the practical

interpretation of that legality may vary among institutions.

Personal Definitions

Taking the definition to a third level, there are personal definitions. Indeed, when it comes to either mandated or unmandated reporters of abuse, each individual may have personal definitions of acceptable parental behaviors. When a specific set of circumstances meets a person's definition of abuse, then that person will act accordingly and report abuse. It is this personal definition of abuse that prompts specific action.

People vary in their personal definitions. Some of the factors that may account for this variance include: (1) family background and rearing, the experience of rearing children, socioeconomic status, religious/racial/cultural factors, surrounding environment, and other subjective factors. Since there is wide variation in parenting styles, there is wide variation in the personal definition of acceptable parenting. In any group of people, no matter how homogenous they appear to be, there will be differences among them. Figure 1-1 shows, inside the circle, parenting behaviors that are now considered acceptable. Those outside the circle are clearly unacceptable. However, some items are partially inside and partially outside. These are behaviors over which people are divided, some accepting, others not. When reporters are in the process of making real-life decisions, a number of subjective factors come into play. For example, a woman leaves her 5-year-old alone in their apartment for 1 hour to take food to a sickly neighbor. She returns from her good deed and the child is fine. The same mother leaves the same aged child for the same period of time in the same apartment. However, this time she goes to a bar and while she is there, a fire

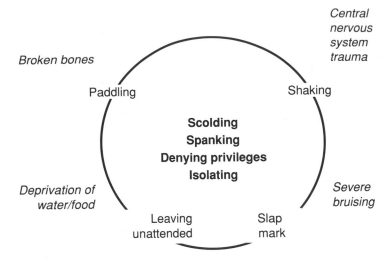

Fig. 1-1. Range of acceptable, unacceptable, and variable discipline practices.

erupts in her apartment building. Her 5-year-old child is burned. In the second situation, our subjective personal definition of abuse might have us see the woman as neglectful.

How much spanking is permissible? How much intimidation of a child is acceptable? These are a few of many such questions that get at the nature of our personal definition of abuse. It is no wonder that a professional reporter and a parent may not agree on what is abusive.

WHY IS IT DIFFICULT TO DEFINE ABUSE?

There are at least three levels of definition of abuse at any time: the legal, the institutional, and the personal. In addition, there are other factors that make the definitions difficult and nonuniversal.

Evolving Concepts Over Time

The positive side of examing child abuse is that the rights of children are examined. Children's rights have evolved

over time, similar to those of other minority groups such as women, blacks, homosexuals, and others. Thus, at the turn of the century, there was no legal obligation or social expectation to rear children without inflicting serious physical injury. There were no requirements to educate children. There were no reasons to keep children out of the work force. Children were viewed as property. During the twentieth century, a significant body of children's rights has been developed. Children's rights are in a state of dynamic tension with parental rights and family rights as shown in Figure 1-2. For most family members, these rights are usually in balance and harmony. However, at times, these rights clash. Chil-

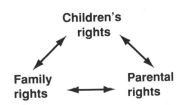

Fig. 1-2. State of dynamic tension between child, parental, and family rights.

dren clearly have rights that supersede their parents' rights. Child abuse is one such situation.

Child abuse as a concept has evolved over time and will continue to evolve. What was considered to be normal child care practice 50 years ago may now seem abusive. The way our children are treated today may be viewed as abusive by future generations. A historical view of child abuse is presented in Chapter 8.

Evolving Concepts Over Space

Definitions of abuse are not universal over space, just as they have not been over time. What is abusive in one locale may be normal in another. Parents in other parts of the world may do things to their children that we would consider painful and disfiguring. Similarly, many parents around the world would be appalled at the rigorous schedule of school and after school activities and the myriad of stimulators that we may push on our children, in the name of education. There are many cross-cultural and subcultural differences in defining abuse.

Defining Abuse by Parental Behavior

It is difficult to define abuse based on parental behavior. Parents may behave in a certain way, with no resultant physical or psychological harm to their child. However, on another day, that same parental behavior may result in extreme injury. When parental behavior as a way of defining abuse is examined, the concept of intent comes into play. Intent may be conscious or unconscious. To an outside observer looking at an injured child, it may be impossible to fully determine parental intent. From the child's perspec-

tive, intent may not be the issue. The injury, the pain, the morbidity, or the mortality is the same. An overstressed father may become so angry with his son that he may pick him up and throw him onto the floor injuring his brain or killing him. The same parent with the same stress level and the same seeming intent may throw his child onto a sofa. In the second example the child laughs and scampers away unharmed. Parental behavior and intent may be difficult or impossible to determine and should not be used in defining abuse.

Defining Abuse by Extent of Injury

The aforementioned example indicates that abuse cannot be defined by the extent of injury. A child with five broken bones is not more abused than the child with one. The child who has been sexually abused many times may not be as damaged as one who has experienced a one-time violation. The criminal justice system has particular difficulty in coping with this notion. The degree of abuse injury does not correlate with the amount of force used or resulting quantity or quality of physical injury.

Use of "Child Abuse" as a Medical Diagnosis

At times, the semantic use of the term *child abuse* is limiting. "Child abuse" is used as if it were a diagnostic term, like meningitis or pneumonia. In reality, it is a category of disorders like infectious diseases or metabolic disorders. The term is used to describe many different parental and child states. For example, child abuse refers to the child who is beaten, tied up, tortured, and murdered in a very extreme way. It is also used to describe a parent with "good" values who abuses a child in a moment of frustration. Child abuse may also be defined as the inaccessible medical care for 10 to 13 million children in the United States. As research and understanding improve, we will be better able to understand abuse not only as a disease, but as a specific form of abuse to which a specific treatment can be applied. Our level of understanding is primitive and our nosology imprecise.

DEFINING ABUSE

With all the aforementioned difficulties in defining abuse, the process of defining and reporting happens daily. The best working definition of abuse must be established, lest children go unreported and sustain more severe or fatal injuries. I view the definition of abuse as a symptom of family dysfunction in which the child sustains injury, be it physical, emotional, developmental, or sexual, rather than looking for "good parents" versus "bad parents." Examine the normal family functions shown in Table 1-1. Families may be dysfunctional either in underprovision or overprovision of needs. Column one shows the function of a family, column two lists the effects of underprovision, and column three shows the negative effects of overprovision. One can see where the various child abuse definitions fit in.

Table 1-1.   Child Abuse as Seen as Part of Family Functions and Dysfunctions

Task	Dysfunctional Inadequacy	Dysfunctional Excess
Supplying physical needs		
Protection	Failure to protect, child abuse	Overprotection and overanxiety
Food	Underfeeding, failure-to-thrive	Overfeeding, obesity
Housing	Homelessness	Multiple residences, "yo yo/vagabond" children
Health care	Medical neglect	Excessive medical care, Münchausen syndrome by proxy
Providing developmental behavioral, emotional needs		
Developmental and cognitive stimulation	Understimulation, neglect	Overstimulation, "hot housing," parental perfectionism
Guidance—approval and discipline	Inadequate approval, overcriticism, psychological abuse	Overindulgence, "spoiled child"
Affection, acceptance, intimacy	Inadequate affection, emotionl neglect, rejection, hostility	Sexual abuse, incest
Socialization		
Intrafamilial relationships	Attentuated family relationships, distanced parents	Parenting enmeshment, overinvolved relationships
Extrafamilial, community relationships	Boundless families, deficiency in training in extrafamilial relationships	Insular families, excessive restriction from extrafamilial relationships

(From Ludwig and Rostain,[4] with permission.)

When injury occurs and it can be demonstrated or when injury results from a parental dysfunction either by acts of omission or commission, then the definition of abuse has been met. Although there are difficulties in establishing a universal definition of abuse, we must act based on the here and now.

BARRIERS TO SEEING ABUSE

Beyond the many problems of defining abuse, there may be individual barriers to seeing abuse. These include denial, fear of consequences, overidentification, and acceptance of stereotypes.

Denial is the primary barrier. The human condition is such that the thought of an adult injuring a child is repugnant. Many individuals simply cannot believe that abuse occurs. Professionals who are parents themselves or those who have sustained contacts with children understand that a child can be provocative and incite aggressive responses from an adult. However, most adults are horrified by a parent's loss of control that results in injury.

Some professionals do not recognize abuse because they fear the consequences of recognition. Recognizing abuse means reporting it. Recognizing abuse may result in parental confrontation, in court appearance, in community response, and in lost time from work or leisure time. All of these fears may consciously or unconsciously prevent a potential reporter from recognizing abuse. A third pitfall to the recognition of abuse occurs when reporters perceive abusers to be like themselves. When someone of our own background, race, intellectual level, or neighborhood abuses a child, it may be difficult to see that as abuse. When the alleged perpetrator is different from us in personal characteristics, it becomes somewhat easier. Fourth, some professionals have created a stereotype of how an abusive parent should look and act. When a parent defies this stereotype, the professional may not see the parent as abusive. For example, the stereotype may be that abusive patients are secretive, avoid detection, and wish to continue to abuse their child unchecked. When a parent has beaten or injured a child significantly, and is sorry about its occurrence, the professional may not accept this behavior as abuse. The parent is not fulfilling the stereotype; thus, abuse did not occur. All of these mechanisms are barriers to defining, recognizing, and reporting abuse. Chapter 2 has detailed additional reasons why some physicians are reluctant to report suspected incidents of child abuse.

DEMOGRAPHICS OF ABUSE

The true incidence of abuse is unknown. There are data on the number of reports, substantiated reports, and deaths, but all are underestimates. The Pennsylvania statistics for the years 1974 to 1989 are shown in Table 1-2.

In 1988, the federal government provided some natural incidence statistics. These are shown in Figures 1-3 to 1-6. In any study of incidence, there are limitations to sampling techniques. Much abuse still occurs in the privacy of the child's home and is never publicized.

SUMMARY

Child abuse is a social concept that continues to evolve as children's rights are recognized by society. How we define

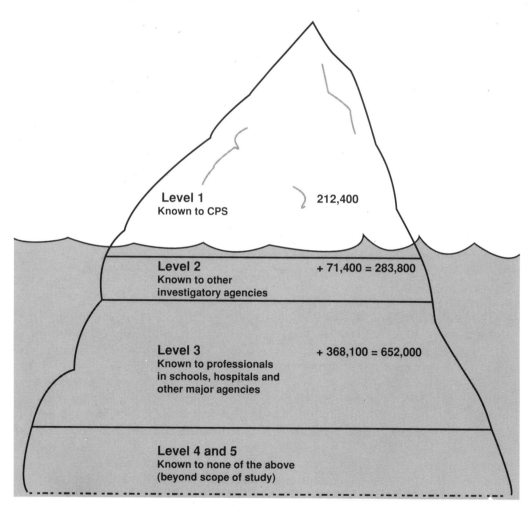

Fig. 1-3. Conceptual presentation of the recognition of "in-scope" maltreated children: an iceberg. (From U.S. Department of Health and Human Services.[5])

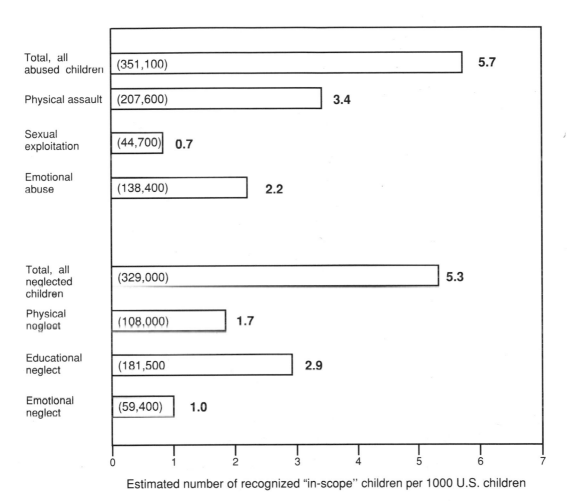

Fig. 1-4. National incidence rates and incidence numbers by major form of child maltreatment. The estimated number of children in each category is presented in parentheses. The total of all abused children is less than the sum of these subcategories because some children experienced more than one form of maltreatment. (From U.S. Department of Health and Human Services.[5])

Table 1-2. Forms of Abuse—Percent Pennsylvania Substantiated Reports, 1976 to 1990

Year	No. of Cases	Physical (%)	Sexual (%)	Mental (%)	Neglect (%)
1976	3872	64.0	9.0	4.0	23.0
1977	6183	65.0	10.0	4.0	21.0
1978	5961	61.0	11.0	3.0	25.0
1979	4304	66.0	15.0	2.0	17.0
1980	4133	65.0	21.0	2.0	12.0
1981	4689	64.0	25.0	2.0	10.0
1982	5119	61.0	27.0	2.0	10.0
1983	5623	60.0	33.0	1.0	6.0
1984	7429	53.0	41.0	1.0	5.0
1985	10,993	44.0	50.0	1.0	5.0
1986	10,170	44.0	51.0	1.0	5.0
1987	10,491	44.0	52.0	1.0	5.0
1988	11,385	45.0	49.0	1.0	5.0
1989	11,780	43.0	51.0	1.0	5.0
1990	12,013	43.0	52.0	1.0	4.0

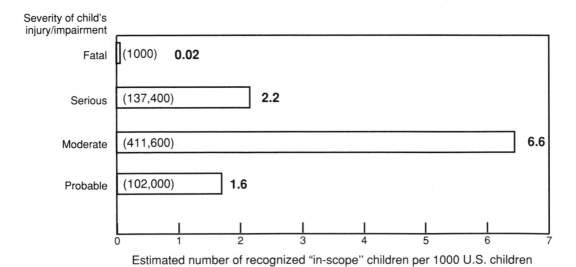

Fig. 1-5. National incidence rates and incidence numbers by severity of maltreatment related injury or impairment. The estimated number of children in each category is in parentheses. (From U.S. Department of Health and Human Services.[5])

Age of child

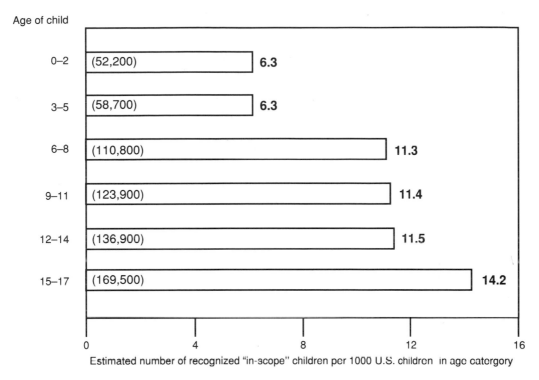

Estimated number of recognized "in-scope" children per 1000 U.S. children in age catergory

Fig. 1-6. National incidence rates and incidence numbers by age of maltreated children. The estimated number of children in each category is in parentheses. Age of child was reported on 99 percent of the "in-scope" children. The age distribution of the missing 1 percent was assumed to be identical to the reported 99 percent. (From U.S. Department of Health and Human Services.[5])

"abuse" has a great impact on our recognition of it. In turn, reporting abuse and incidence data depend on an individual's personal definition of abuse and willingness to get involved in child protection. There are barriers that prevent us from seeing abuse, and these need to be overcome by all who are legally mandated to report abuse. Knowing what those barriers and blocks are may be helpful to overcoming them. Undoubtedly, a child will be abused today. Although our concepts and understanding of abuse are in transition, we need to recognize, report, and protect that child.

SUGGESTED READINGS

1. American Medical Association: Diagnostic guidelines concerning child abuse and neglect. JAMA 254:796, 1985
2. Hampton RL, Newberger EH: Child abuse incidence and reporting by hospitals: significance of severity class, and race. Am J Public Health 75:56, 1985
3. Ludwig S: Child abuse: causes and solution. p. 61. In Luten RL (ed): Problems in Pediatric Emergency Medicine. Churchill Livingstone, New York, 1988
4. Ludwig S, Rostain A: Family dysfunction. In Levine MD, Carey WB, Crocker AC,

Gross RT (eds): Developmental and Behavioral Pediatrics. WB Saunders, Philadelphia, 1991

5. U.S. Department of Health and Human Services—National Center for Child Abuse and Neglect—Executive Summary: National Study of the Incidence and Severity of Child Abuse and Neglect. DHHS Pub No (OHDS 81-30329), 1988

6. Waller AE, Baker SP, Szocka A: Childhood injury, deaths: national analysis and geographic variations. Am J Public Health 79:310, 1989

7. Wilkerson AE: Rights of Children. Temple University Press, Philadelphia, 1974

2

Recognizing and Reporting Child Abuse

Allan E. Kornberg

We, as a society, have recognized that children are helpless against physical injury, sexual molestation, and neglect caused or allowed to occur by a child's parent or other legal guardian, unless third parties intervene. Parental rights are broad but not absolute. To protect children, all states have a child protective system in place. This system generally begins with a mandatory reporting law for certain professionals likely to encounter abused children, with voluntary reporting encouraged by others. Emergency protective custody is available for children in imminent danger. Many states have a central register to accept reports of possible child abuse and to collect data. A child protective service exists to protect children, investigate reports, and assist families to rehabilitate. The judiciary has a family court system that supervises abusing families and can order foster placement, or even the abrogation of parental rights, when necessary. The criminal court system can be used to prosecute perpetrators of a crime.

The first medical report in the modern era describing intentional trauma to children was by Caffey, a radiologist, noting the association between multiple long-bone fractures and subdural hematomas in children without a history of trauma. Other radiologists confirmed these findings in the ensuing years with little effect on the practice of medicine or law. Kempe et al. changed this inattention in 1961 at a symposium on *The Battered Child* at the annual meeting of the American Academy of Pediatrics, and published the following year.

Kempe's work gained national attention in both lay and professional publications. In 1963, the Children's Bureau, a part of the federal government's then Department of Health, Education, and Welfare, developed a model law for states to use in the development of their own child protective acts. Within a few years, all states had a law based on the federal model. Subsequent federal legislation, including the Child Abuse Prevention and Treatment Act of 1974, used eligibility for federal grants to encourage states to expand their child protective acts, specifically to include sexual abuse and neglect as well as physical abuse. The Child Abuse Prevention, Adoption, and Family Services Act of 1988 established the National Center on Child Abuse and Neglect, and continued the federal tradition of encouraging state compliance with national principles of child protective legislation by providing grant eligibility to those states meeting federal guidelines.

This chapter reviews reporting requirements for cases of possible child abuse, the struggle between under- and overreporting, how to discuss mandated reporting with families, and how to protect a child in danger. Also considered are false allegations and the reluctance of physicians and other professionals to report possible child abuse. No attempt is made to provide an encyclopedic review of child protective legislation in every state. Although certain central principles are common to the laws of most states, each state has its own specific child protection act. Also, laws change over time. It is the responsibility of all professionals working in a field in which the discovery of child abuse may occur as part of their duties, to be familiar with local and state statutory requirements.

LEGAL REQUIREMENTS TO REPORT

Most states require professionals working with children to report cases of suspected child abuse. Other states require all citizens to report. Physicians have been the first and foremost target of mandatory reporting statutes, since they are the most likely to see injured children and most able to distinguish child abuse and neglect from other conditions, by virtue of their training and experience. Other health professionals frequently included in mandatory reporting statutes are nurses, dentists, optometrists, chiropractors, podiatrists, and psychologists and other mental health workers. Some states even include Christian Science practitioners. Other persons frequently required to report are teachers and school officials, social service workers, child care workers, police officers, and the staff of the district attorney's office.

In general, the reporting requirement of state law supercedes the privileged communication that may otherwise exist between professional and patient or client. One controversial area involves the reporting of possible child abuse, particularly sexual abuse, when a psychiatrist or psychologist hears a confession from an adult patient. Berlin, a psychiatrist, attempted to distinguish between the propriety of mandated reporting for health professionals when the patient is an adult perpetrator versus a child victim. He believes that requiring a report based on an adult psychiatric patient's description of abuse of a child by the patient will exert a chilling effect on such patients coming forward. This theoretically will prevent mental health professionals from learning of "minor" abuse, and will interfere with their ability to treat the perpetrator before more serious abuse is committed. However, the same logic brought to an extreme, could be used to attack mandated reporting by a physician caring for an intentionally injured child, so as not to discourage the parent from seeking medical attention for the injury. State laws vary regarding the obligation of mental health workers to report abuse described by their adult patients.

In most states, failure of a mandated reporter to notify authorities of suspected child abuse is frequently punishable by criminal penalties, usually at the misdemeanor level. However, prosecution is rarely, if ever, entertained for the violation of mandatory reporting statutes. A mandated reporter may be the defendant in a negligence action for failure to report. For example, if a physician does not report a child with injuries likely to have been caused by an abusive parent, that physician may be subject to malpractice action if further injuries occur. Statute aside, the ethical imperative to report for a physician or other mandated reporter aware of child abuse is apparent.

Mandated reporters are in general given statutory immunity from litigation for making a report that is eventually unfounded, as long as the report was made in good faith. Most states generally presume the mandated reporter is acting in good faith. Over the last two decades, this protection has been found to be virtually complete.

In most jurisdictions, mandated reporters are only required to make reports known to them in their professional or official capacity. A physician who witnesses abuse in a public place is not required to make a report. However, that physician is certainly encouraged to make a voluntary report, just like any other good citizen. Not surprisingly, reports by mandated professionals tend to be substantiated more often than those reported by the public. Faller found that nearly one-half of reports by professionals required to report were proven, versus only one-third by the public. In the same study, anonymous lay reporters had a higher incidence of unfounded cases than nonprofessionals who gave their name.

Given suspected child abuse, should the report be made to child protective services or to the police? If the reporter believes that the child's parent or other legal guardian committed child abuse, then child protective services should be notified. Many states have a toll-free central number for making a report. Similarly, if parents or legal guardians knowingly allowed a child to be placed or to remain in a situation where child abuse or neglect occurred, child protective services should be called. If a child is the victim of a crime not perpetrated by a parent or guardian, the appropriate police agency should be notified.

Several situations regarding the appropriate agency to which a report should be made deserve additional clarification. Re-

gardless of whether a report is made to child protective services, most jurisdictions require a police report from physicians for gunshot wounds, stabbings, suspicious deaths, and the like. Nothing in the child protective statute obviates the need for a police report. Similarly, if a child is the victim of a severe assault likely to have been caused by a parent, involving the police early raises the likelihood of finding the perpetrator, identifying witnesses, and preserving evidence. These are issues sometimes ignored by health professionals and other noninvestigatory mandated reporters. Thus, joint child protection and police reports are sometimes most appropriate.

In many jurisdictions, reports of rape and sexual assault are left to the discretion of the victim or guardian, not the health professional. As a minimum, the physician or nurse should encourage the collection of evidence so that if prosecution is agreed to later, evidence is available. Nothing in a statute giving a parent the right to refuse police notification for pediatric sexual molestation interferes with the health worker's duty to report the case to child protective services, if the sexual assault may have been perpetrated by the child's parent or guardian.

Some states also require mandated reporters to notify child protective services if the abuse was committed by others, besides the parent or guardian, who are legally responsible for the child. This may include other adults living in the household, relatives who are regularly found in the home, babysitters, or employees of state youth and mental hygiene facilities. Certainly, if parents or guardians knowingly allow their children to remain in a setting where child abuse is known to occur, a report is indicated.

Can mandated reporters allow others to make required reports on their behalf? Institutions such as schools and hospitals usually have a protocol for filing a report, and generally only one report is necessary. If a physician has reason to believe child abuse has occurred, that physician usually reports the case. If the child is immediately referred to another physician, for example, a child abuse consultant or pediatric emergency physician for further management, the referring physician may allow the accepting physician to make the necessary report. It remains the responsibility of the referring physician to ensure that a timely report is made, or to personally make such a report. Sometimes, a physician sees a child and is unsure if child abuse is the appropriate diagnosis. In this situation, it is legitimate to leave the decision regarding reporting to a physician who is expert in recognizing child abuse.

REPORTING THRESHOLD

Under- Versus Overreporting

State reporting laws do not require mandated reporters to be convinced that child abuse or neglect has transpired in order to make a report. Physicians and other mandated reporters are required to make a report if they have "reasonable cause to suspect," "cause to suspect," or "cause to believe" that a child has been abused or maltreated, according to various state acts. Less conviction is required than "probable cause" on the part of the reporter. If a mandated reporter suspects that child abuse has occurred but cannot prove it, a report is still required.

State Laws
State child protective acts were passed to protect defenseless children (see Appendix B). Parents are generally deemed to be the best and most appropriate advocates for their children. Parental discretion is broad, but not absolute. Society has recognized that for child protection to succeed in the face of parental abuse or neglect, a report by a third party must first be made. The child victim usually cannot institute self-protection. Thus, reporting laws countenance some good faith overreporting at the expense of avoiding underdetection.

The law recognizes that physicians and other mandated reporters cannot always be certain that child abuse has occurred. They are simply required to permit the child protection system to investigate further, so that children at risk can be safeguarded. Most studies demonstrate that 50 to 70 percent of reports filed by mandated professionals are later substantiated. Of the unsubstantiated reports, some were false reports, and the others were real cases of abuse and neglect with insufficient proof obtained.

False Reports
Families can be harmed when a false allegation of child abuse is made. Arguments and marital strife can occur when a spouse is concerned that abuse is occurring within the family. Children may sometimes even be placed in foster care temporarily when child abuse is reported, though as yet unfounded. False accusations can be particularly stressful when made in reference to sexual molestation. Family tension may be very high in this setting. In the case of false allegations in an institution or day-care center, jobs may be lost and businesses may close, even if the accusation is eventually unsubstantiated.

Silverman describes the formation of a group of persons, mainly parents, who were victims of false child abuse accusations. They call themselves VOCAL, victims of child abuse laws. Silverman points out that they are not victims of child abuse laws, but of their implementation. Mandated reporters, particularly medical and criminal justice individuals, ought to remain open-minded to dialogue on justified grievances related to child protection laws. Due process, confidentiality, expunging records on clearly unfounded cases, and other safeguards of fundamental fairness for parents and others should be vigorously defended. Nonetheless, American society, represented by its elected legislatures in all 50 states, recognizes the importance of protecting defenseless abused children. Third party notification of a suspected abuse case by mandated professional reporters is frequently the first line of defense for abused children. Mandated reporters with "reason to suspect" child abuse or neglect should, and are of course obliged to, report.

Clinical Markers of Abuse

There are certain clinical markers that are suggestive of child abuse. Many of the chapters in this book discuss in detail specific findings noted in child abuse and neglect. Certain historical features are frequently prominent in a variety of maltreatment cases. Typically, the history given does not fit the injuries seen. For example, bruises are noted on a child's forearms and back. The history given is that the child ran forward, tripped, and fell. Usually with that history, anterior bruises are noted. Posterior and forearm ecchymoses suggest a defensive posture during an assault. Or severe red-blue bruising is noted by the physician and the history given is a fall 1 week ago. These are fresh bruises, and could not have occurred 1 week before. Sometimes the history given describes developmental skills that a child could not have obtained yet. For example, a 4-month-old infant cannot climb up on a table and therefore could not be accidentally injured after falling off a table in that situation.

Parents attempting to conceal abuse will typically give different histories to different health professionals. Injuries blamed on other young siblings are also suspect. Seeking delay in obtaining medical care, although not pathognomonic for abuse, is suspicious. A past history of other unexplained injuries is worth noting, and review of previous emergency department and inpatient records can be a valuable exercise.

Most abusive injuries can also occur accidentally. There are some findings that are virtually pathognomonic of abuse, including loop marks, adult human bite marks, immersion burns, and metaphyseal corner fractures. Nonorganic failure to thrive is pathognomonic of parental deprivation/child neglect. Other findings that are typically found in abused children should generally be reported, and are near certain markers of child abuse unless another plausible explanation is discovered, including sexually transmitted diseases in prepubertal non-neonates, fractures of different ages, rib and long-bone fractures in infants, scapulae and sternal fractures in children without a severe accidental mechanism of trauma, skull fractures more complicated than short, linear ones in infants allegedly falling less than 4 ft, retinal hemorrhages, absent hymen in young girls, and isolated posterior fourchette injuries.

Any child is at risk for child abuse and neglect, regardless of parental status and finances. A 1988 national incidence study of child abuse and neglect by the Children's Bureau did find that families with incomes below $15,000 per year exhibited four times the reported incidence of physical and sexual abuse, and eight times the incidence of neglect, than other families. Nonetheless, abuse occurs at all socioeconomic levels. Mandated reporters are bound legally and ethically to have their reporting threshold activated when they have "reason to suspect" that child abuse has been committed. Dr. Norman Ellerstein, the editor of the first edition of this textbook, would begin every lecture on child abuse and neglect to a new audience with a slide that simply stated "trust no one—assume nothing."

APPROACHING THE FAMILY

It is the obligation of any physician examining a child, who is about to make a report for possible child abuse, to notify the family in attendance of the need to make a report. This is one of the more difficult tasks facing any physician, especially an inexperienced physician. Above all else, be truthful. Ethically, telling the truth is mandatory. In a practical way as well, it is better for the parents to be able to trust what a physician says, regardless of their initial emotional response, than to doubt the candor of subsequent health-care and other workers because they were misled initially.

The physician must not allow personal feelings to affect the form and substance of the presentation to the family. Demonstrating anger and hostility toward the family is not appropriate. Neither is a nonchalant attitude, based on previous negative perceptions of the workings of the judicial system, acceptable. The clinician should approach the family in a confident manner, controlling personal anxieties.

The physician must not be accusatory, especially when unsure that child abuse has occurred, only that there is reason to suspect that it has been committed. Also, given that the patient is the victim of intentional trauma or some other type of child abuse or neglect, the physician does not know the identity of the perpetrator. For example, the physician should not say to a parent "You must have injured your child," but rather, "The injuries I have examined do not appear to have been caused by an accident."

Several reactions are frequently observed when parents are notified that a report to the child protective services will be made. Some parents cry or otherwise appear distressed. Others demonstrate little outward emotion, seeming matter-of-fact regarding the issue at hand. Another group is quite angry, sometimes furious, that a report is being made. The physician should guard against responding to the parents' sentiments by becoming angry or defensive. It is important to maintain objectivity, and to help the family to understand what is happening. The physician should not attempt to assess the likelihood of the parents' being the perpetrators of the injuries noted, based on their emotional response. Irate parents are not automatically guilty parents. Those falsely accused have every reason to be incensed. The physician's job is to care for and protect the child, report the suspected abuse, and communicate with the family, not to sit in judgment. If the parents become argumentative or accuse the physician of victimizing them, the physician needs to state that the diagnosis is based on medical training and experience. It is proper and frequently helpful for the physician to remark that the report is mandated by law, that the law does not offer a choice in the matter, and that the physician would be guilty of a crime if the report is not made.

The parents should be given a general description of what is likely to transpire. The role of the child protection worker should be explained. If it seems likely that the child will be hospitalized or placed in temporary foster care immediately, the family should be made aware of this possibility. If the police have not been called, the parents may be told that no one is being accused of a crime at that time. Deferring to child protective workers to provide much of this explanation is appropriate, given their onsite availability.

Physicians are frequently concerned regarding their right to order laboratory studies, radiography, and medical photography for the suspected child abuse victim if the parents refuse. Parents rarely refuse. On the occasions when there is initial resistance, most families can be encouraged to consent after being told that cooperation is in their best interest. In some states, the law gives authority to hospital personnel and child protective and law enforcement workers to obtain these studies without parental consent. If necessary, a judge can order that the necessary studies be performed.

Sometimes the adult who brings a child for medical attention for an intentional injury is aware that child abuse has occurred but is not prepared to admit this, or to name the perpetrator. The person who committed the abuse in this setting is usually a close family member. A common scenario is a child who is brought to an emergency department or other medical facility by the mother, with injuries caused by the child's father, mother's husband, or mother's boyfriend. Some of these women are also the victims of domestic violence. McKibben et al. found that 59 percent of mothers whose children were child abuse victims were themselves victims of violence perpetrated by their husbands or boyfriends. It should not be surprising to note an association between different types of family violence. It is appropriate to ask mothers in this setting if they are also being attacked. Many women who otherwise will not admit to being victimized may verbalize their exploitation during the immediate crisis period when their child has also been assaulted and is the subject of an investigation. As domestic violence involves adult victims, it is generally not subject to mandatory reporter statutes. Nonetheless, the victim can be encouraged to report her situation to criminal justice personnel. Many hospitals have protocols for dealing with domestic violence victims. The woman should also be offered temporary protective shelter. The child can then be placed in a safe environment with the mother, instead of being placed in foster care. Simultaneously, the mother-child family unit is maintained, and both are protected from further physical or sexual assault.

PROTECTING THE CHILD

Some child abuse victims presenting to a physician require immediate placement in a safe environment. Generally, only a judge can order foster placement or removal of parental rights. In some jurisdictions, child protective workers have the authority to place a child under protection in an emergency situation until the next business day, when a judge will hear the case. Some abused children need to be admitted to the hospital because of the severity of their injuries, which would require admission for trauma management, even if they were accidental. Even in these situations, it is appropriate to have child protective services and a judge place a holding order enforcing hospitalization regardless of parental wishes. This protects the child and hospital from a parent who initially agrees to hospitalization, but then attempts to have the child discharged against medical advice.

Not every child abuse victim requires immediate protection. For example, if a school age child presents with bruising on the buttock secondary to being repeatedly struck by the hand of an angry parent who is now remorseful, a report is appropriate, but immediate action may not be necessary. If the perpetrator has been arrested or the nonabusing parent has a safe residence provided by relatives or friends for the child victim and the nonabusing parent, the physician may feel comfortable that the child's immediate needs have been met by simply reporting the abuse without advocating emergent placement.

On the other hand, there are some children who require immediate removal from the home even if the injuries noted would not otherwise necessarily require hospitalization. An infant with an unexplained long-bone fracture would appear to be at risk for subsequent disabling or even life-threatening force. A child victim of intrafamilial rape where the perpetrator has not yet been identified or removed from the home needs emergent protection. Frequently, the parent in attendance is willing to accept hospitalization for a few days. Parents who are initially resistant can usually be encouraged to accept this option. Concurrent with "voluntary" hospitalization should be the acquisition of a temporary child protection order. Frequently, the parent will find hospitalization less threatening than temporary foster placement, although for the child who does not require hospitalization for medical indications, this decision is reached by the child protective system, frequently with input from the physician.

When parents refuse emergent removal from the home, it is always desirable to gain their cooperation, if possible. This agreement is preferable, as it will reduce the adversarial nature of subsequent attempts at treatment. If the parent rejects this approach or attempts to leave the medical facility with the child, decisive action is required. States typically give authority to child protection workers and police to take temporary custody of a child pending a court appearance. Many states also give physicians and hospitals temporary civil authority in these circumstances, pending the availability of those with formal police power, to temporarily take custody of a child believed to be in imminent danger to life or health. Familiarity with local statutes and hospital policy is important.

FALSE ALLEGATIONS

Occasionally, knowingly false reports of maltreatment are made to a child protection registry. This behavior is exceedingly rare on the part of mandated reporters. Most statutes that protect mandated reporters from civil and criminal liability for unsubstantiated reports qualify this immunity to reports made "in good faith." Thus, a report known to be false made by a mandated reporter as retribution for other issues, to coerce a family into a specific behavior pattern, or for any other malevolent purpose, may be subject to penalties.

Malicious false reports are generally uncommon, but they are occasionally made by voluntary reporters. They may, however, be made by mentally disturbed individuals. As most jurisdictions investigate anonymous allegations of child abuse by voluntary reporters, this gives persons the opportunity to harass neighbors, business associates, or other acquaintances. This behavior is contemptible, since, aside from triggering an investigation of the innocent, it casts aspersions on the child protection statutory structure.

Child Custody Disputes

Recently, contested allegations of sexual abuse have become a frequent part of child custody battles by divorced parents. These accusations often involve young children, usually girls, who are unable or unwilling to describe the alleged molestation to a physician. The child's parent tells the physician what the child is said to have told the parent. The child's physical examination is generally unrevealing. Some of these children are undoubtedly the victims of sexual assault. However, malicious reports of other unacceptable conduct such as alcoholism, illicit drug use, or other antisocial behavior sometimes take place in family court custody battles, given the hatred between some former spouses and the stakes involved. It would not seem extraordinary that deliberately false allegations of sexual abuse may sometimes occur also. Another scenario involves separated or divorced parents who allege sexual abuse in good faith, when no abuse has occurred. For example, a child spends the weekend with her father. She returns to her mother morose and taciturn. Mother asks what her father did with her. The child describes being bathed, and after maternal prompting, answers that she was touched all over. Her father was simply appropriately caring for his young daughter by bathing her, behavior that was certainly acceptable when the family was intact. Her reserved affect is secondary to the stress between her parents. Given the anger and lack of trust between the parents, mother presumes the worst and consults her attorney, who suggests having the child examined.

The importance of thorough chart documentation for all patients, especially suspected child abuse victims, is well known to physicians. Aside from carefully documenting physical examination findings and pertinent negative findings, a meticulous recording of historical data is extremely important. Memories fade, and the chart is the physician's only legal record. Indicating what was said, in quotes when possible, is very helpful. In addition, indicating who said what and whether the child directly described molestation, is important.

Some allegations of sexual abuse by one divorced parent regarding the other are certainly true. Paradise et al. found, in a consecutive series of 31 sexual abuse complaints lodged against a parent, that the incidence of the report being substantiated was higher when custody or visitation rights were not an issue. Nonetheless, she found a high incidence of verification that the original complaint was valid in each group, 95 percent when custody was not involved versus 67 percent when it was an issue. These data certainly suggest that reports of sexual abuse during custody battles should be taken seriously, although only 31 total complaints were studied, 12 involving custody or visitation. The ability of these data to be generalized requires independent corroboration.

Do Children Ever Lie

Do children alleging sexual abuse ever lie? It seems intuitive to most health care and mental health workers that prepubescent children describing molestation, particularly in a graphic, anatomic way, are telling the truth. Certainly most of these descriptions are valid. Everson and Boat and others describe the validation of the preponderance of these descriptions. Yates and Musty describe how children can describe sexual molestation that never occurred by being persuaded by one parent in a custody battle or being cajoled by an overzealous child protection worker. Yates and Musty also describe how a child may misunderstand terms such as *making love*, thinking this means *liking a lot*. Children can also share in the perceptions and fantasies of the adult making an accusation. Finally, a child, just like an adult, may erroneously report sexual or other abuse based on the child being mentally ill. Most allegations of sexual abuse by children are authentic. However, a professional who naively believes that "children never lie" will find sexual abuse whenever it is alleged. Conversely, unreasonable doubt of every allegation of abuse by a child will lead to missing real cases. As in all professional matters, thoughtful clinical judgment is the appropriate response.

Is a physician, faced with a parent alleging sexual abuse by a former spouse, with a nonverbal child, and with no other evidence of abuse, obliged to make a report? Characteristic of most difficult questions is the absence of a simple answer. The physician should remain objective and, if based on the clinical evidence, has "reason to suspect" sexual abuse, a report should be made. It is not mandatory for the physician to report every case of this nature. Frequently, the parent simply wants a physical examination performed and recorded at the advice of their counsel. The physician should be thorough, being careful to neither miss stigmata of molestation nor to overcall variants of normal not necessarily indicative of abuse. If custody and visitation are already being considered by a family court judge, the appropriateness and importance of a physician's report at this juncture is questionable.

PHYSICIAN RELUCTANCE TO REPORT

Physicians as mandated reporters are required to report all suspected cases of child abuse and neglect. Nonetheless, several considerations sometimes impede proper reporting of cases. Some physicians hesitate to report because they are uncomfortable with their training and experience in cases of child abuse. While it is suitable for all clinicians who may see an abused child to become familiar with this syndrome, the law does not require being absolutely sure that abuse has occurred, only that it is suspected. Physi-

cians should in general be better able to consider whether injuries have occurred accidentally or intentionally than other mandated reporters.

Saulsbury and Campbell have described misgivings regarding making a report by physicians apprehensive about testifying in court. Appearance in court is time consuming and infrequently appreciated. However, many court officers are willing to attempt to schedule testimony for busy physicians at as convenient a time as possible. Of course, this is not always feasible. Many physicians are fearful of testifying because of negative experiences in court from malpractice litigation. Although some child abuse proceedings are adversarial in nature with cross-examination, the physician is not on trial. The physician is there as an expert testifying on behalf of an injured child, and courts tend to be appreciative and respectful. Fear on the part of a physician for being named in litigation as a defendant after making a good faith report is unjustified.

Physicians and other mandated reporters sometimes express an unwillingness to place a report because "they (child protection, social welfare, the courts, etc.) don't do anything about child abuse," even when identified. Negative experiences of their own or other physicians' patients reported for abuse, returned to their parents, and subsequently abused again reinforce this attitude. However, the physician may not have been aware of the entire case, and good frequently comes from identifying abusive parents even if the child is not placed. Additionally, every situation, regardless of how clear the abuse may seem initially, has the potential to have pertinent information discovered subsequently.

A physician may incorrectly delay reporting child abuse because, although suspicious that a patient is a victim, the identity of the perpetrator has not been established. The law asks for a report when child abuse or neglect is suspected. The physician is not expected to identify the likely perpetrator, and delay in filing a report under these circumstances is incorrect.

Sometimes there is institutional pressure to avoid reporting child abuse, for fear of negative publicity or other perceived damage. This is more commonly a problem for educators, employees of residences for the disabled, and day-care workers, than for nurses and physicians. A mandated reporter who is an employee of an organization should become aware of institutional policy for reporting child abuse. For example, a jurisdiction may require only one standard report from the school, hospital, or home, instead of several reports from individual mandated reporters. Nonetheless, statute requires that the individual professional mandated reporter shall make a report when child abuse is suspected. It is inappropriate to be overruled by superiors and administrators when the mandated reporter has reason to believe that child abuse has occurred. For example, if a professional nurse has a well founded belief that child abuse has occurred, and the child's own physician insists that a report not be made for whatever reason, that nurse has the right and obligation to file a report. In situations where there is an honest professional difference of opinion, consultation from the hospital's child abuse consultant may be helpful.

One of the more difficult situations for a physician is when child abuse or neglect is suspected within a family known to that physician for many years. The obligation to report remains. It would not be proper to attempt to manage this condition unilaterally without making a report. The involvement of others with expertise different from that held by most physicians is required. The physician should honestly explain the clinical situation, explain to the family what to expect and why a report is necessary, and then file the report. Usually, it is still possible to maintain a professional relationship with the family, but sometimes it is not. The incidence of losing other patients once it is known that the physician reported a family for possible child abuse is greatly exaggerated.

There are many reasons for physicians to be reluctant to report child abuse. It is one of the most difficult tasks facing health professionals, particularly when the patient and parents are well known to them. Nonetheless, both the law and ethical standards are clear. If child abuse is suspected, reservations must be overcome, and a report must be made.

SUGGESTED READINGS

1. Baum E, Grodin MA, Alpert JA et al: Child sexual abuse, criminal justice, and the pediatrician. Pediatrics 79:437, 1987
2. Berlin FS: Laws on mandatory reporting of suspected child abuse. Am J Psychiatry 145:1039, 1988
3. Caffey J: Multiple fractures in the long bones of infants suffering from chronic subdural hematoma. AJR 56:163, 1946
4. Ellerstein NS: Child Abuse and Neglect: A Medical Reference. 1st Ed. Churchill Livingstone, New York, 1981
5. Everson MD, Boat BW: False allegations of sexual abuse by children and adolescents. J Am Acad Child Adolesc Psychiatry 28:230, 1989
6. Faller KC: Unanticipated problems in the United States child protection system. Child Abuse Negl 9:63, 1985
7. Kempe CH, Silverman FN, Steele BF et al: The battered child syndrome. JAMA 181:17, 1961
8. Krugman RD: Advances and retreats in the protection of children. N Engl J Med 320:531, 1989
9. Leake HC, Smith DJ: Preparing for and

testifying in a child abuse hearing. Clin Pediatr 16:1057, 1977

10. McKibben L, De Vos E, Newberger EH: Victimization of mothers of abused children: a controlled study. Pediatrics 84:531, 1989

11. Paradise JE, Rostain AL, Nathanson M: Substantiation of sexual abuse charges when parents dispute custody or visitation. Pediatrics 81:835, 1988

12. Saulsbury FT, Campbell RE: Evaluation of child abuse reporting by physicians. Am J Dis Child 139:393, 1985

13. Silverman FN: Child abuse: the conflict of underdetection and overreporting. Pediatrics 80:441, 1987

14. Study of national incidence and prevalence of child abuse and neglect. National Center on Child Abuse and Neglect, U.S. Department of Health and Human Services, 1988

15. Wong DL: False allegations of child abuse: the other side of the tragedy. Pediatr Nurs 13:329, 1987

16. Yates A, Musty T: Preschool childrens' erroneous allegations of sexual molestation. Am J Psychiatry 145:989, 1988

3

Etiology and Prevention of Abuse: Societal Factors

Cindy W. Christian

Child abuse and neglect is often believed to be a problem of industrialized nations, since in this setting children do not have economic value, and their lives are not of religious or cultural importance. However, as reflected in the literature and media coverage children throughout the world are being mistreated in both industrialized and less developed countries. Child abuse takes many forms. In some societies, children are sold by their parents for prostitution. In others, children may live and work in unsafe and unsanitary conditions and are sometimes left to die after birth if they are not the desired sex. The ways in which children are harmed differ among nations, in part owing to variability in cultural norms, child rearing practices, and societal attitudes toward children.

American children are privileged in many ways. They live in a country with vast resources, whose government is elected by the people, and whose people believe that they value and love their children. Unfortunately, there are many indications that America neglects its children. The United States ranks 19th in the world in infant mortality. Our resources are not allocated for children's needs. Our

children live in increasingly violent, impoverished, and unhealthy conditions. This chapter explores societal contributions to child abuse and neglect, focusing on the violence that pervades our children's lives and the ways in which American policies and laws fail to ensure a healthy and safe beginning for millions of American children.

INJURY AND VIOLENCE

American children experience unnecessary morbidity and mortality owing to intentional and accidental injuries. Although pockets of children throughout the world face extraordinary danger, among industrialized nations, childhood death rates are highest in the United States, almost exclusively because of injury and violence. The United States has high rates of recorded childhood homicide and higher teenage suicide rates than most other industrialized countries. In fact, injury and violence are the leading causes of death in childhood, and result in more deaths than all natural diseases combined in children aged 1

25

through 19 years. While this high mortality is a result in part of success in decreasing mortality from infectious diseases, the statistics highlight the impact that accidents and violence have on American children. Motor vehicle accidents cause almost one-half of childhood deaths, followed by homicide, suicide, drowning, pedestrian injuries, and fires (see Ch. 5).

The morbidity and mortality caused by injuries do not affect all children equally. While injury causes 40 percent of deaths in young children (ages 1 to 4 years old), by late adolescence (15 to 19 years old) it accounts for almost 80 percent of deaths. Minority children are also faced with higher morbidity and mortality rates. In general, injury death rates among black children are 1.3 to 2 times, and may be as much as 5 times, the rates of those for white children. While the death rates from suicide and motor vehicle accidents are higher among white children, homicide, residential fires, drowning, and pedestrian vehicle collision death rates are higher for black children.

Homicidal Deaths

Homicide is one of the 10 leading causes of death among poor and minority children in urban cities, particularly among infants and late adolescents. In the latter group, homicide ranks third after accidents and suicide. Although more than one-half of all children murdered are white, murder rates for black children greatly exceed those of white children. There is evidence to suggest that socioeconomic status accounts for much of this difference. Childhood homicide rates have more than doubled over the past 25 years, and there is no indication that this trend is abating. Adolescents are experiencing violence at extremely high rates.

For example, Gladstein and Slater report that almost one-fourth of the adolescents surveyed in an urban medical clinic in Maryland had witnessed a murder, and almost three-fourths knew someone who had been shot.

Firearm Homicides

The methods by which children are murdered vary according to age. While only 10 percent of murdered children younger than 5 years old are killed by firearms, guns are the leading means of homicide for victims older than 11 years old. Over the past 30 years, homicide rates from methods other than firearms have increased by 85 percent, while firearm homicides have increased by 160 percent, and handgun homicide rates have quintupled (handguns account for the majority of firearm homicides). Between 1960 and 1980, homicide rates have increased most rapidly among 5- to 9-year-old children. Children are either intentionally murdered, or are often unintentionally shot or killed by guns. A report in the *Journal of the American Medical Association* reviewed unintentional deaths by firearms in California between 1977 and 1983. Eighty-eight children younger than 14 years old were accidentally killed by either themselves or other children, usually while playing with guns they had found. Easy accessibility to the guns, their resemblance to toys, and weapon malfunctions were all factors that contributed to these accidental deaths. Children are increasingly the victims of nonfatal gunshot wounds. A recent retrospective review of 34 gunshot wounds, both fatal and nonfatal, in urban children younger than 10 years old found that approximately one-third of the children were accidentally shot by themselves or other children, and another one-third were unintended victims of domestic violence. A significant number of urban children, sometimes the younger siblings of gang members, were murdered by adolescents of opposing gangs, often as a gang retaliation. Childhood homicides committed by other children are not limited to urban gang wars. Increasing numbers of juveniles are being arrested for murder. For example, between the years 1983 and 1988, murder arrests for children younger than 14 years old increased by almost 30 percent. In 1989, a 10-year-old Pennsylvania boy was charged as an adult in the fatal shooting of a 7-year-old girl. This boy allegedly loaded his father's hunting rifle and shot the girl from a bedroom window. The prosecution of this boy as an adult highlights an increasingly frustrating issue: how should we deal with young criminals who are violent and whose numbers are increasing.

The Debate Over Gun Control. Because guns are used in the majority of homicides, many Americans argue that eliminating the availability of firearms, especially handguns, would have a significant and positive impact on homicide rates and shootings. There is heated debate concerning gun control laws. Opponents of gun control argue that Americans have the right to bear arms and to own guns for personal protection. They argue that restrictions will have minimal effect on homicide rates because individuals will do whatever is necessary to secure a gun and that without guns, homicide rates will increase by other methods. Furthermore, they argue that cities such as New York City and Washington, D.C., which have the strictest gun control laws, have the highest violence rates. What opponents of gun control fail to mention is that the majority of guns found in those cities are illegally secured. Advocates of gun control laws reason that many homicides occur as a result of assaults during domestic arguments. Since regional handgun ownership parallels the homi-

cide rates involving firearms, gun control in contiguous locales would cause a decrease in such deaths.

Eliminating young children's access to firearms might prevent significant pediatric morbidity and mortality; however, limiting gun access in an effort to lower homicide rates remains a controversial issue. Until recently, scientific research in this area has been limited. To examine the question of whether handgun regulation limits homicide, a 1988 *New England Journal of Medicine* study by Sloan et al. compared homicide rates in Seattle, Washington and Vancouver, British Columbia, two cities with similar socioeconomic conditions but very different handgun regulations. The authors found that despite similar overall rates in criminal activity and assault, the relative risk of death by homicide was significantly higher in Seattle, the city with more lenient handgun regulations and more firearm ownership. Homicide rates by means other than guns were not significantly different in the two cities. The authors concluded that limiting access to handguns may decrease homicide rates. Opposing the argument that guns are necessary for citizen self-protection, the authors found that justifiable homicide and homicides explainable by self-defense accounted for less than 4 percent of the total in each city. A retrospective review of 398 firearm deaths in Washington state, published in the *New England Journal of Medicine* by Kellerman and Reay, examined the epidemiology of deaths involving firearms kept in the home. Of the 398 deaths, only 2 involved an intruder being shot while burglarizing a home. For every justifiable homicide, 1.3 people died of accidental shooting, 4.6 died as a result of a criminal homicide, and 37 committed suicide, questioning the safety of keeping firearms in a home in the name of self-protection.

PREVENTION OF INJURIES AND VIOLENCE

The majority of pediatric morbidity and mortality secondary to injury and violence affects innocent children who cannot protect themselves. While most individual parents aim to protect their children, societal policies do not reflect these individual desires. In fact, in the area of violence, the primary response is punitive. We punish those convicted of violent crimes against other individuals, rather than focusing on ways to prevent assault and homicide. Furthermore, punishment is not effective; less than 20 percent of individuals arrested for violent felonies are convicted and sentenced to at least 1 year in prison. For juveniles, the penalties are even more lenient. What is most remarkable, however, is the leniency granted to those who assault and murder children. For example, in Pennsylvania in 1986, in the 30 cases of child homicide that resulted in conviction or a plea, none of the defendants was found guilty of first degree murder. Most were convicted of the lesser charges of involuntary manslaughter and third degree murder. By contrast, for adult homicide cases (excluding those by motor vehicle accident), almost one-third of the defendants were convicted of first or second degree murder. Sentences imposed on those convicted for child homicide were also more lenient. Eighty-four percent of all Pennsylvanians convicted in 1986 to 1987 of third degree murder were sentenced to over 4 years in prison. But in the child death cases, less than one-third of those convicted of third degree murder were sentenced to more than 4 years. These statistics are consistent with the state's pattern throughout the decade and are not limited to Pennsylvania. The leniency in convictions and sentencing might be a result of the difficulty in prosecuting child abuse deaths because there is often no witness or "murder weapon." Likewise, jurists and judges may have difficulty believing that an adult can intentionally murder a child because their beliefs and values so strongly oppose those actions. There have been attempts in some states to deal with these discrepancies. In 1987, Washington state adopted a statute providing that a first degree murder charge can be found in a child death in which a pattern of abuse is demonstrated.

In the United States, the practice of using punishment for serious crimes as a deterrent to future crimes is questionable. Most state prison inmates are repeat offenders. Prevention of violence toward children would be preferable. There are a number of approaches that can be used to limit the morbidity and mortality associated with both nonviolent and violent injury in this country. First, individuals can be persuaded to voluntarily change their behaviors. This approach would be best aimed at parents and older children. For example, parents have been educated about the need for, and use of, smoke detectors. This same type of public awareness may be the first step toward preventing child abuse. Second, changes can be made in products and the environment to improve safety. Installing window guards in high-rise apartments or manufacturing shower heads and faucets with antiscald devices would help prevent unnecessary injury and death by accidental and intentional means. Finally, laws can be enacted to help prevent injury. Seat belt laws have had a significant impact on motor vehicle morbidity and mortality.

As mentioned above, no issue concerning injury prevention is argued more strongly than gun control. At the time of this writing, there is a federal bill under consideration that provides a 7-day waiting period when buying a gun, during which time a background check can be done on the buyer. This bill would be helpful, but limited in ensuring gun safety, because many firearm homicides and suicides result from sporadic acts of violence rather than patterned attacks by criminals and mentally ill individuals. Other options for improving gun control include restrictive licensing, expanded registration requirements, or bans on semiautomatic and automatic weapons. Most efforts to pass gun control laws are opposed by the National Rifle Association, a powerful, wealthy, and influential lobby. More research and study are needed to identify the epidemiology of firearm injuries and to identify preventive approaches that would be most successful in improving the safety of individuals.

Injury and violence have a major impact on the lives and health of American children. Because children cannot protect themselves and because many injuries are preventable, adults (individual parents, and local, state, and federal elected officials) must advocate methods to lessen the risks to our children.

CORPORAL PUNISHMENT

Corporal punishment, physical punishment inflicted on a child by an adult, has been used as a method of discipline throughout history. References to the use of physical punishment are found in the Bible, classic literature, and standard nursery rhymes, and its use remains widely accepted by many Americans. It is estimated that over 90 percent of American parents use physical punishment as a method of discipline, and approximately 75 percent of parents interviewed in a 1975 survey of family violence believed that spanking or slapping a 12-year-old child is necessary, normal, or good. Some parents hit their children because they believe the Bible supports this punishment; others punish physically because of frustration and loss of control. There are many who use corporal punishment because they believe that it works. While it is true that hitting a child hard enough will temporarily stop an undesirable behavior, hitting or other forms of punishment do not teach the child the expected behavior. Unfortunately, many parents who use corporal punishment are unaware of this and find themselves using spankings as their primary discipline tool. The use of corporal punishment is widespread and not considered abusive in most circumstances. However, there are many physical injuries that can result when children are spanked by a frustrated parent. These range from hematomas, ecchymoses, and fractures to muscle injury with associated myoglobinuria and renal failure, intracranial hemorrhages, and death. Although physical damage is not an end result in most spankings, the danger of corporal punishment lies in its potential for physical abuse, particularly by parents who believe themselves to be incapable of physically hurting their children.

Alternatives to Corporal Punishment

Adults do not like to be hit or embarrassed in public or to be given the message that they are worthless. It is unacceptable in American society for adults to settle their differences by hitting or beating each other. Most adults thrive on positive reinforcement and praise and can tolerate constructive criticism. Why is it that some parents therefore fail to raise their children in a loving and nurturing environment? Children who are hit may temporarily feel unloved, angry, helpless, worthless, or embarrassed. If they live in an otherwise loving and supportive household, these feelings may quickly pass. However, many children grow up believing that they are worthless and unloved. For them, physical punishment reinforces those feelings. The emotional well-being and safety of children would be improved if parents stopped relying on corporal punishment as a disciplinary measure. Children need to be disciplined, to have limits set, to learn to distinguish right from wrong, to make appropriate decisions, and to exhibit self-control. However, children can be taught a more acceptable approach or behavior by setting consistent limits, reinforcing the desirable behavior, and punishing undesirable or dangerous actions with methods that do not degrade or physically harm them. "Time out," "grounding" and suspending privileges are all methods that can successfully punish children without causing emotional or physical damage, and should be taught to parents by physicians, day-care professionals, teachers, friends, and family.

Corporal Punishment in Schools

There are laws that protect from further harm a child who has been physically injured by a parent using corporal punishment. Unfortunately, there are no written guidelines that precisely outline when corporal punishment becomes child abuse. Furthermore, the standards in this country change, depending on the child's environment. Laws are written to protect a child who is beaten and bruised with a paddle by a parent but not by a teacher. In fact, most states allow corporal punishment in schools and protect educators from child abuse charges resulting from their attempt to discipline their students.

Corporal punishment in school is defined as the infliction of pain on a student by a teacher or school official as a penalty for behavior that is deemed undesirable by the punisher. Corporal punishment is banned in schools in Europe, Japan, Israel, and communist countries but not in the United States. In a landmark case in 1977, Ingraham v Wright, the U.S. Supreme Court failed to afford students constitutional protection against physical force in school in a 5 to 4 decision. James Ingraham was then a 14-year-old student who was paddled by his principal for responding slowly to a teacher's request. The paddling caused severe bruising, and the student sued under the Eighth Amendment (beatings were cruel and unusual punishment) and the Fourteenth Amendment (corporal punishment did not allow for due process under the Constitution). Although the court did not dispute that the punishment was excessive, it held that the Eighth Amendment was designed only to protect those convicted of a crime. Furthermore, the court held that there were local and state laws that provided protection to students and felt it unnecessary for federal educational policies to impinge on state and local authorities. Despite opposition to corporal punishment by groups such as the Parent Teacher Association and the American Academy of Pediatrics, corporal punishment in schools remains legal in most states. By 1989, only 19 states, along with many large cities, had banned corporal punishment from their schools. Areas in the South and Southwest use corporal punishment more than those in the Northeast. Higher corporal punishment rates are associated with poverty, minority children, high illiteracy rates, and low per pupil expenditures on education. There are no strict guidelines or consistent patterns of behavior that result in physical punishment. In reviewing cases of corporal punishment in schools that were severe enough to attract media attention, Hyman reports that 80 percent of students were beaten for nonviolent offenses. In contrast to what many people would think, the majority of children who are hit are young children in primary or intermediate schools.

Advocates of Corporal Punishment

There are numerous arguments proposed by teachers, administrators, and even parents in defense of corporal punishment. Many believe that banning corporal punishment would render teachers powerless to control students and that it is needed for teacher protection. However, as children get older, stronger, and pose more of a physical danger to adults, the incidence of corporal punishment decreases. All states and school districts that ban corporal punishment recognize the right of teachers to protect themselves, other students, and school property against student assaults. Such exclusions are written into laws and allow the use of force for self-protection. Some supporters argue that corporal punishment is an effective disciplinary method. Students may behave, but they may also be angry, humiliated, scared, revengeful, and lose interest in school. Fear of being physically punished may quell unwanted behavior, but it does not foster a healthy environment for student enthusiasm and learning. Unfortunately, many educators have a limited repertoire for responding to misbehavior, and most are not given intensive or ongoing training in disciplinary techniques. Techniques that have proved successful in preventing disciplinary problems include encouraging low teacher-to-student ratios in the class, consistently applying rules, recognizing academic weaknesses in students and providing specialized instruction, and showing students respect. Rules for disciplining children at home should apply to schools. Students should be given positive reinforcements to excite them about learning and to increase their self-esteem. They should be given punishments that are reasonable, consistent, and physically painless.

Crime in Schools

Schools are theoretically a place where children learn without fearing for their physical safety. However, children are not only unprotected from physical assaults by their teachers, in many other ways, schools are becoming increasingly dangerous. Each year, an estimated 3 million street crimes are attempted on school grounds, 135,000 children carry guns to school daily, and hundreds of thousands more bring knives with them. Children report having missed school days because they are scared to attend. Learning cannot be accomplished easily in schools terrorized by crimes. Some urban schools use metal detectors to decrease the number of weapons students carry to school. As individuals interested in the health and success of our country's children, we can all support legislation to reduce violence in our schools. Professionals can participate in advisory committees to school boards and can support groups that oppose violence in the schools. Physicians have a responsibility to report abuse that occurs in schools and to discuss with parents effective disciplinary methods that do not cause physical and emotional harm to children. They should be familiar with and teach methods that result in learning and self-respect, not fear or a sense of worthlessness.

POVERTY AMONG AMERICAN CHILDREN

The per capita gross national product (GNP) of the United States is the second highest in the world. Yet child poverty rates in this country continue to rise, and among industrialized countries, the United States ranks eighth. It is estimated that 20 percent of American children live in poverty, the largest single poverty group in the country. Poverty is found in both urban cities and rural areas, affecting primarily minority children, young children, and children of single parents. While one of every seven white children is poor, almost one-half of black children and more than one-third of Hispanic children live below the poverty level (i.e., $12,675 a year for a family of four). The economic status of American children has declined significantly during the past decade, despite advances made in the previous 15 to 20 years. For example, between 1960 and 1979, the ratio of government spending for the elderly-to-children was approximately 3:1. During the 1980s, however, government programs supporting children were reduced, while those benefiting the elderly increased, so that the ratio by the late 1980s was approximately 10:1. During the 1970s to mid-1980s, elderly poverty decreased by approximately 50 percent, yet childhood poverty increased by 37 percent, emphasizing the vulnerability of American children.

Federal-State Assistance Programs

For American children who cannot be economically supported by their parents, aid is provided largely through the Aid to Families with Dependent Children (AFDC) program. This federal-state program subsidizes children who are deprived of financial support from one of their parents because of death, disability, absence from the home, or in some states, unemployment. The payment programs are state and local programs administered by state welfare agencies under plans developed by individual states. The past decade has seen a decline in the percentage of poor children receiving aid, from approximately 75 percent in 1979 to approximately 50 percent in the late 1980s. In addition, only two states (California and Maine) have kept AFDC benefits in line with inflation over the last 20 years. Actual family benefits for families of three range from approximately 84 percent of the poverty level to as low as 15 percent, and in 38 states, the cost of renting available housing exceeds a family's entire monthly AFDC payment. Another program that benefits poor, pregnant women and their children, the Special Supplemental Food Program for Women, Infants and Children (WIC), reaches less than 60 percent of those who are eligible, despite its cost-effectiveness and its significant impact on improving health. A similar problem exists in the area of early education. The Head Start program, a federal program that provides quality preschool for poor children, reaches less than 20 percent of eligible children, despite its success in decreasing school failure and dropout rates. Successful implementation of programs like WIC and Head Start is necessary if we are to limit the impact that poverty has on the health and development of our children.

Developmental Problems

Poverty places children at risk for a number of adverse developmental problems. This is probably because of the association of poverty with illness (including perinatal insults), family stress, and inadequate social support. For example, stress, especially chronic stress owing to unemployment, lack of material goods, and so forth, is more prevalent in poor families. Studies have shown that children who live in highly stressed environments are at increased risk for a number of developmental problems such as low IQ, impaired language development at 4 years of age, greater school problems at school age, and even poorer performance on developmental tasks at 8 months of age. Poverty is also associated with higher rates of low birth weight babies, and studies have shown that poverty places these children at greater developmental risk. The cost of poverty to children is great. Approximately two-thirds of all children who test as mentally retarded grew up in poverty. The cost to society is measured by the alarming rates of illiteracy, school dropouts, juvenile delinquency, and unemployment. While early intervention programs (e.g., Head Start) have been shown to decrease school dropout rates, adolescent pregnancies, juvenile delinquency, and unemployment for young adults, only 28 states and the District of Columbia invest their own funds in these programs.

POVERTY AND HEALTH

The detrimental impact that poverty has on the health of American children is evident by excessive morbidity and mortality rates. Children living in poverty are less likely to be well nourished, to have received immunization, and to have had preventive routine pediatric care. In the United States, neonatal mortality rates are most influenced by birth weight, that is, the lower the birth weight, the higher the mortality rate. Poverty increases the risk of having a low birth weight baby, owing to the increased risk of prematurity and intrauterine growth retardation (IUGR). The exact mechanisms by which prematurity and IUGR are affected by poverty are unclear but are probably related to maternal nutrition, increased stress, obstetric risks, and lack of adequate prenatal care. Minority children, through their increased risk of poverty, are at greater risk for inadequate prenatal care, low birth weight, and inadequate immunizations. Black children in particular are twice as likely to be born with low birth weight than nonminority children.

Health Problems

Mortality rates from infectious diseases, sudden infant death syndrome (SIDS), household fires, motor vehicle accidents, and other trauma are higher for poor children, as is the morbidity caused by a multitude of medical problems. Poor children lose more school days because of illness than do nonpoor children, and poverty is associated with higher rates of iron deficiency anemia, failure-to-thrive, lead poisoning, hearing loss, and chronic otitis media. Some of these problems are attributable to inadequate housing, poor nutrition, and other health problems. The unavailability of adequate medical care contributes to morbidity. Preventive and therapeutic medical care has been shown to reduce the occurrence and morbidity associated with many childhood health problems including asthma, appendicitis, seizure disorders, lead poisoning, and anemia. Access to quality medical care can lessen the negative effects of poverty on the health of American children.

PROVIDING HEALTH CARE TO AMERICAN CHILDREN

The United States, despite its advanced medical technology, well trained physicians, and relative wealth, does not provide adequate health care to its children. In fact, when compared with other countries, the United States ranks poorly in many important areas of child health care. It ranks 19th in infant mortality, 22nd in mortality rates for children younger than 5 years old, and has more low birth weight infants born than 28 other countries. For nonwhite babies, polio immunization ranks 49th. The United States spends a smaller percentage of its GNP on child health care than 18 other industrialized countries and is only one of two industrialized nations that does not provide universal health coverage to its children. Much of pediatric morbidity and mortality can be prevented. Multiple barriers limit the access of children to optimum health care.

Cost of Health Care

Health care has become extremely expensive and most Americans cannot afford medical insurance. For poor children, Medicaid is the single most important source of medical coverage and accounts for more than one-half of all public expenditures for child health care. Eligibility for Medicaid is determined by individual states, based largely on the AFDC program. Because of state variations in the AFDC requirements, eligibility for Medicaid varies greatly among states. Although providing health insurance to poor children improves access to medical care, by the late 1980s, the mean state eligibility for Medicaid was only 45 percent of the federal poverty level.

Owing to the failure of AFDC eligibility requirements to keep up with inflation during the 1980s, almost 500,000 families lost Medicaid benefits. The percentage of families that lived below the poverty level and received Medicaid decreased from 83 percent in 1973 to approximately 50 percent in 1985. Recent federal laws will help reverse this trend. The most recent, effective in April 1990, mandates Medicaid coverage for all children younger than 6 years old whose families live below 133 percent of the federal poverty level. Eligibility for older children remains at the discretion of individual states.

Inaccessible Health Care

Although the recent federal laws will expand health insurance coverage to more poor people, there are still an estimated 12 million children who are medically uninsured. Between 1981 and 1986 alone, there was a 14 percent increase in the number of uninsured children. Although some of these children live below the poverty level, most are from families of the "working poor," families where there is at least one full-time employed parent whose income is up to two times that of the poverty level. In fact, children of poor, working parents are less likely to have insurance than children whose parents are unemployed. Employment-based private health care insurance is the most common source of health insurance in the United States. Because of rising health care costs and a trend during the 1980s away from providing employee benefits, families have been burdened with more of the costs of health care. Many small firms, especially in retail trade, construction, and personal services, no longer offer employee health plans. Families living above the poverty level but earning relatively low wages have difficulty paying rent, feeding and clothing their children, and paying for doctor's visits. Uninsured children have 15 percent less physician care than privately insured children and 33 percent fewer doctor's visits than children who receive Medicaid benefits. Uninsured children are less likely to have a regular source of health care and receive fewer childhood immunizations. For children who have private insurance, coverage is inadequate and neglects the medical needs of most children. Children are often covered for hospitalizations and surgery, services needed more for adults, but not for preventive services, outpatient care, and immunizations.

Being poor or uninsured predisposes children to other barriers to care. These children often receive their care at health clinics, where they can wait hours before seeing a doctor. The clinics are often inconveniently located, and transportation is often unavailable or too costly. The facilities often provide services during limited hours, forcing many families to use emergency departments and multiple sources for care. Care is therefore uncoordinated and inadequate. For some families, medical care is not accessible because there are few physicians available to provide services. Medicaid reimbursement rates for providers are low, and some physicians therefore refuse to care for children with public insurance. Some areas of the country are significantly underserved. For example, the National Health Service Corps, the main federal program that places doctors in underserved areas in the country, has lost over 90 percent of its physicians in recent years.

Finally, care is inaccessible to many poor families because of ignorance. Some parents do not understand the importance of preventive care and immunization; these parents need to be educated. Others lack the skills to access needed care.

The federal government alone has over 35 health programs in 16 different agencies that serve children. Applications for Medicaid coverage are extremely lengthy in some states. Children sometimes require services from multiple agencies, which predisposes to inadequate coordination of care. Other children, while clearly needy, are often ineligible. If the foundations of adult health are laid down during childhood, today's ineffective, inequitable health care system needs significant revision to ensure access to health care for all children.

PREVENTION AND SOLUTIONS

The elimination of poverty from American society would have the single greatest effect on the well-being of our children. Infant mortality rates would decrease, the health of our children would improve, the impact of injury and violence would be lessened, and fewer children would be abused and neglected. Unfortunately, the trends are moving in the wrong direction, and those most affected, children, are a voiceless and powerless minority. Children do not vote, they do not make campaign contributions, and they do not lobby. Until recently, they have not had powerful adult organizations to lobby for them. Poverty seems to be an integral part of American society, yet improvements need to be made. All children must have access to health care; they need to live in decent housing in safe neighborhoods; and they must learn to read and write in school no matter how poor they are. Preventive services such as WIC and Head Start need to reach all eligible children, since they have proved effective and cost-effective. Ensuring the tangibles that many of us take for granted can only improve individual and family functioning and lessen the risks to our children.

The thought of "societal changes" seems overwhelming to most Americans, but these changes will only occur if individuals are willing to advocate for children at a local and even personal level. Although there are groups that have begun to advocate nationally for children, such as The Children's Defense Fund (CDF) and the American Academy of Pediatrics, there is much that each individual can contribute. Americans can become informed about poverty and its impact on the health and development of American children. They should know how their local and state government officials feel and vote about childhood issues. A good source of information is the CDF, a nonprofit private organization that is committed to child advocacy through research, education, and lobbying. With national headquarters in Washington, D.C., the CDF can provide anyone with an interest in helping children with data on how individual states handle children's issues and how individual elected government officials vote on these issues. With this information, citizens can contact their representatives and voice their opinions about these issues. Additionally, they can inform family members, friends, and colleagues about these problems and encourage them to advocate for children.

→ It is impossible to have a society that ignores the basic needs of its children, yet successfully prevents child abuse and neglect. While individual social workers continue to work with families at risk, doctors continue to report suspected abuse and neglect, and lawyers continue to prosecute perpetrators, it must be recognized that significant changes will only come when the collective society deems it important.

SELECTED READINGS

1. American Academy of Pediatrics Special Report: Barriers to care. Available from the American Academy of Pediatrics, Elk Grove Village, IL, 1990
2. American Academy of Pediatrics, Committee on Psychosocial Aspects of Family and Health: The pediatrician's role in discipline. Pediatrics 72:373, 1983
3. American Academy of Pediatrics, Committee on School Health. Corporal punishment in schools. Pediatrics 73:258, 1984
4. Blotzer J: Killers of children meet with leniency. Pittsburgh Post-Gazette. Monday, February 13, 1989
5. Children's Defense Fund: Children 1990—a report card briefing book and action primer. Children's Defense Fund, Washington, D.C., 1990
6. Children's Defense Fund Reports: Improving the health of medicaid eligible children. Children's Defense Fund 11:1, 1990
7. Christoffel K: Violent death and injury in U.S. children and adolescents. Am J Dis Child 144:697, 1990
8. Christophersen E: The pediatrician and parental discipline. Pediatrics 66:641, 1980
9. DePalma A: Ten-year-old boy is charged as adult in fatal shooting of 7-year-old-girl. New York Times National, August 26, 1989, p. 6
10. Division of Injury Control, Center for Environmental Health and Injury Control, Centers for Disease Control: Childhood injuries in the U.S. Am J Dis Child 144:627, 1990
11. Downes J: The health care crises for children in the USA (commentary). Soc Pediatr Anesth 7, 1990
12. Drabman R, Jarvie G: Counseling parents of children with behavioral problems: the use of extinction and time out techniques. Pediatrics 59:78, 1977
13. Gladstein J, Slater EJ: Inner city teenagers' exposure to violence: a prevalence study. Maryland Med J 37:951, 1988

14. Harvey B: Toward a national child health policy. JAMA 264:252, 1990

15. Helfer RE: The neglect of our children. Pediatr Clin North Am 37:923, 1990

16. Hyman I: Reading, Writing and the Hickory Stick: The Appalling Story of Physical and Psychological Abuse in American Schools. Lexington Books, Lexington, MA, 1990

17. Hyman I, Bongiovanni A, Friedman RH, McDowell E: Paddling, punishing and force: where do we go from here? Children Today 6:17, 1977

18. Johnson J, Ludtke M, Riley M: Suffer the little children. Time Magazine, October 8, 1990, p. 40

19. Kellermann A, Reay GT: Protection or peril? An analysis of fire arm-related deaths in the home. N Engl J Med 314:1557, 1986

20. Krugman RD, Krugman MK: Emotional abuse in the classroom. Am J Dis Child 138:284, 1984

21. McMillan JA: What we must do for children in the 1990s. Contemp Pediatr 7:28, 1990

22. National Association of Childrens' Hospitals and Related Institutions, 1989: Profile of Child Health in the U.S. Alexandria, VA

23. Oberg CN: Medically uninsured children in the U.S.: a challenge to public policy. Pediatrics 85:824, 1990

24. Ordog CJ, Wasserberger J, Schatz I et al: Gunshot wounds in children under 10 years of age: a new epidemic. Am J Dis Child 142:618, 1988

25. Parker S, Greer S, Zuckerman B: Double jeopardy: the impact of poverty on early child development. Pediatr Clin North Am 35:1227, 1988

26. Schaar K: The corporal punishment foes strike out. Children Today 1977, p. 16

27. Select Committee on Children Youth and Families: US children and their families: current conditions in recent trends 1989. U.S. Government Printing Office, Washington, D.C., 1989

28. Sloan JH, Kellermann AL, Reay DT et al: Handgun regulations, crime, assault, and homicide: a tale of two cities. N Engl J Med 319:1256, 1988

29. Strauss MA, Gelles RJ: Societal change and change in family violence from 1975–1985 as revealed by two national surveys. Marriage Fam 48:465, 1986

30. Strauss MA, Gelles RJ, Steinmetz SK: Behind Closed Doors—Violence in the American Family. Anchor Books, New York, 1980

31. U.S. Congress, Office of Technology Assessment: Healthy children; investing in the future. No. OTA-H-345, U.S. Government Printing Office, Washington, D.C., February, 1988

32. Wessel MA: The pediatrician and corporal punishment (commentary). Pediatrics 66:639, 1980

33. Wintemute CJ, Teret SP, Kraus JF et al: When children shoot children, 88 unintended deaths in California. JAMA 257:3107, 1987

34. Wise PH, Meyers A: Poverty and child health. Pediatr Clin North Am 35:1169, 1988

35. Wolock I, Horowitz B: Child maltreatment as a social problem: the neglect of neglect. Am J Orthopsychiatry 54:530, 1984

36. Zinsmeister K: Growing up scared. The Atlantic Monthly 265:49, 1990

4

Etiology and Prevention of Abuse: Family and Individual Factors

Cindy W. Christian

In an attempt to prevent the morbidity and mortality caused by child abuse, much has been written on its causes, recognition, and prevention. Yet child abuse is being reported in ever increasing numbers, and the systems responsible for protecting identified children are being overwhelmed by the enormity of the problem. Each week there are reports in the local news of children who are injured or murdered by adults who were responsible for their well-being. Occasionally these reports gain national attention and are met with public outrage and cries for severe punishment. Caring adults are horrified by these sensationalized stories and find it difficult to understand why parents would hurt their children. Although most abusive adults love their children, the economic, familial, and personal stresses that challenge these parents are often overwhelming and contribute greatly to the risk for abuse. The etiology of child abuse is complex, and our understanding is basic. Although the variables responsible for child abuse are never exactly the same, scholars in the field of child abuse recognize four contributory factors: a society that condones

violence in many forms; a parent who, because of past experiences and present needs, may lose control; a child who is provacative and is perceived as being abnormal in some way; and a crisis that throws the family into a dysfunctional state. The previous chapter explored the societal contributions to the problem of child maltreatment. This chapter examines the family and individual factors that promote abuse.

FAMILY FACTORS

Isolation and the Nuclear Family

The family unit has changed enormously during the 20th century; families are becoming increasingly isolated. Most children no longer live with their extended families, and single parent households now comprise approximately 25 percent of American families. In the early 1900s, children often lived with large numbers of siblings and cousins, learning child development and child care as they grew up playing together and caring for each other. The isolated, nuclear family of the late 20th century does not promote the learning of normal child development. More adults enter parenthood with minimal exposure to infants and children. The extended family also served as a support for parents who, today, often do not have relatives who are accessible for support and relief when everyday stresses become overwhelming. Routine contact with neighbors and friends can also provide support for parents and function as a monitor of parental behavior. Unfortunately, neighborhoods where children used to play in the streets while their parents gathered to socialize are now becoming war zones, fueled by drug and gang wars. It is no longer safe in many urban communities to permit this freedom of association. Parents without neighborhood ties not only lack adult support, but they may feel less accountable to other adults for their actions. Physical and social isolation also make it less likely that abuse will be discovered by individuals outside of the family. Isolation is a risk factor for abuse and is becoming more pervasive in our society. Families may respond to the presence of abuse in the household by becoming more isolated. The criminal justice system arrests parents for abusing their children, and the public often demands harsh punishment for those convicted. Although child abuse offenders need to be held accountable for their crimes, this approach often causes adults, who are having difficulty parenting, to retreat from their family and neighbors for fear of "being caught," rather than seeking the support they often desperately need. Likewise, government mandated child protection services are viewed by many families as punitive rather than helpful, and parents resist services and attempt to hide their problems instead of accepting social services as a resource.

External Stresses

The external stresses that face families contribute to the growing problem of child abuse. Poverty is one contributing factor. Although it is well recognized that child abuse occurs in all social classes, reports of abuse are disproportionately represented in low socioeconomic groups. While this may be due in part to reporting bias, stresses associated with poverty (e.g., overcrowded living arrangements, limited money for food, rent, clothing, utilities, and transportation) increase the risk for abuse. When the effects of drugs and alchohol are added to this equation, the risk for both physical and sexual abuse escalates dramatically. In Philadelphia, drugs are presently a factor in approximately two-thirds of reported abuse cases.

Family Violence

Family violence is common in our culture, and there is a strong association between types of family violence, such as spousal and child abuse. Strauss and Kantor have explored the relationship between family stress and child abuse. Their study found that child abuse rates are significantly higher in families whose parents identified their own fathers as having hit their mothers, that is, in families where there is a generational history of abuse. In addition, child abuse was found to be 30 percent more likely in families in which there was violence between the parents in the preceding year. In both spouse and child abuse, an adult with relatively greater power abuses an individual with significantly less power. Sometimes the same individual abuses multiple family members, such as a man who beats both his wife and his child. Alternatively, an abused wife may turn her frustration and anger toward the child.

Even in families that are not considered to be violent by societal standards, physical punishment is commonplace. It is estimated that between 84 and 97 percent of American families use corporal punishment as a means of discipline. Children exposed to both severe physical abuse and corporal punishment learn that people who care for each other use physical force to settle conflicts which, for some, legitimizes intrafamilial violence.

PARENTAL FACTORS

The "Abusive Parent" Profile

Our society accepts a certain degree of violence, and the families in our society are faced with many stresses. Yet ultimately, a child is abused by another individual. What causes one parent to abuse a child, while another, faced with similar circumstances, does not? The initial literature on the etiology of child abuse focused on the psychological attributes of the abusive parent. These adults were described as having severe emotional problems or as being sadomasochistic, egocentric, narcissistic, depressed, or impulsive. In essence, emotional abnormalities were viewed as the cause for child abuse. Today's view holds that significant psychopathology is found in the same proportion of child abusers as in the general population and is not a contributing factor in the majority of cases. There are societal and cultural factors that lead to abuse, dispelling the idea that there is a certain parental profile that can be identified as abusive. Many theorists contend that any parent, given the correct set of circumstances, can be an abusive parent. Child abuse is not limited to any particular race, religion, educational level, or socioeconomic group, but many agree that poor, single females of all races with young children at home are the most vulnerable. Although no two abusers are exactly alike, there are common patterns of behavior and emotional characteristics that are seen in varying degrees in abusers.

History of Abuse as a Child

Many investigators regard a history of having been abused as a child as a parental risk factor for child abuse. Although there are many clinical reports of this relationship in the literature, Kaufman and Zigler feel there is little objective evidence to support this theory and that most relevant studies rely on limited clinical reports, are retrospective in design, or lack appropriate controls. Accounting for an inability to compare different studies, it is presently believed that about 30 percent of adults who were abused as children abuse their own children. On the other hand, many parents who abuse their children were not abused themselves. It is clear that the cycle is not inevitable.

There are multiple interactive factors that help us to understand what leads to successive generations of abuse. For example, Egeland et al. examined factors that might protect women who were abused as children from becoming abusive parents. This study found that the mothers who did not go on to abuse their own children were able to identify supportive relationships as children and as adults, had an awareness of their past history of abuse, and recognized the effects that parental abuse had on their lives. Other, less fortunate individuals who have been abused enter parenthood with the belief that physical violence and sexual mistreatment are acceptable methods of family interaction. Sometimes acceptance of the use of physical beatings as an appropriate method of discipline is so in-grained into adults' belief systems that their own childhood beatings are not identified as having been abusive. Par-ents who have been sexually abused as children sometimes strongly identify with their abusers and develop a moral approval of intrafamilial sexual relations, that is, the "if this was done to me, why shouldn't I" attitude. Some go so far as to justify sexual abuse by claiming that ex-periencing sex within a loving family is the best approach to sex education. Re-gardless of whether adults recognizes their past history of abuse, all children who are abused by a parent share a poor parental model from which to draw their own parental practices. In support of this sometimes cyclical nature of abuse, Kempe and Helfer have introduced the "world of abnormal rearing" model of child abuse. In this model, children who are abused or neglected fail to learn basic skills that lead to a sense of well-being in adulthood. Rather, they learn that they are no good, and develop low self-esteem and minimal abilities for forming close peer relationships, appropriate mate se-lection, and ultimately, good parenting techniques.

Unrealistic Demands and Expectations

Parenting is a demanding, challenging, and often exhausting job that stresses even the most capable person. Yet chil-dren are born each year to young, inex-perienced individuals who are unaware of the demands of parenting. Pregnant single adolescents often perceive parent-hood unrealistically, fantasizing about a baby to love, yet being unaware of the potential for sleepless nights, colicky in-fants, and the "terrible twos." Although these inexperienced parents may not un-derstand normal child development, most are able to raise their children without abusing them. It is not simply parental ignorance that puts children at risk, but unrealistic expectations and demands that parents place on their children. Many women become pregnant hoping that a child will fulfill their own needs for love. This is especially true if the parents were raised in an environment that did not pro-vide emotional nurturing or was overtly abusive. Parents who were raised in an uncaring environment often lack self-es-teem and on becoming parents them-selves, expect that the new child will meet their emotional needs and restore lost self-esteem. Ultimately, the parent places unrealistic expectations on the child. For example, an abusive mother who is attempting to toilet train a 15-month-old child might see the child's failure as disobedience rather than an inappropriate expectation. Likewise, the seemingly constant crying of a 2-month-old infant might be misinterpreted as lack of love for the mother who was expecting unconditional love and obedience. Fon-tana and Robinson have studied interac-tions between abusive mothers and their children. Their work suggests that abu-sive mothers have difficulty tolerating normal play and exploration and are often focused on the child's performance. The abusive mother is so geared to getting the child to perform that the child's feelings and signals are not attended to. In es-sence, the child is overwhelmed by the parent and her needs. Furthermore, abu-sive mothers are often inconsistent in their interactions with their children; they have poor impulse control, yet they fear losing control over their children. When these maternal characteristics are coupled with a toddler whose develop-mental goal is independence, for exam-ple, the risk for abuse is great.

Sexual Abuse

Adults who sexually abuse children all have some degree of sexual attraction to children. In pedophilia, the offender's primary sexual orientation is to children. For others, the attraction is only intermittent, and may or may not be intense. Added to this attraction is the willingness of the perpetrator to act on these desires. There are many variables—societal, familial, and personal—that contribute to the likelihood that a given adult will sexually abuse a child. The personal characteristics seen in sexually abusive parents are in some ways similar to those seen in physically abusive parents. Sexual abuse offenders commonly lack self-esteem, and they are sometimes influenced by their own childhood sexual experiences. Most importantly, they disregard the developmental and emotional needs of the abused children while satisfying their own.

CHILDHOOD FACTORS

Finally, we need to consider the child's role in the etiology of abuse. It is not uncommon to find families where only one child is abused, while others are tolerated or protected. What makes a child vulnerable?

The "Abnormal" Child

Much work has focused on the abnormal child. Many pediatric conditions have been described in the literature that are associated with an increase risk of abuse, including prematurity, low birth weight, cerebral palsy, congenital anomalies, emotional handicaps, and chronic illness. Clearly, having a child with special needs puts enormous stress on families. Yet, when examined critically, these studies have not been able to determine which factors, if any, are responsible for the increased risk of maltreatment of these children. Furthermore, it is often unclear whether a handicap was the precipitating factor leading to abuse or a result of previous abuse. A few studies have explored this causal relationship, and the results suggest that children with disabilities are more at risk of being neglected than overtly abused. This argument may be more easily understood by considering the example of a child with a condition such as Down syndrome. When such children are first recognized, a host of medical, social, and family supports are often identified for the family. The child's abnormal behavior and delayed development are not seen as an attempt to disobey the parent or as a reflection of poor parenting skills. These children are not expected to behave as healthy children, and it is less likely that their failure to do so will result in parental aggression against the child. On the other hand, these families go through a mourning period during which the emotional needs of the child may not be adequately met. Many disabled children have extensive medical, educational, and physical needs, and coping with these is difficult for families. Without support, there is a risk that these needs will be neglected. Some children with physical or developmental disabilities are abused. These children are often very difficult to care for, and given a parent with low self-esteem, the need for a child that fits the ideal, and the daily stress of caring for an "imperfect" child, the risk for abuse is sometimes great.

The "Difficult" Child

A second group of children at high risk for abuse are those who are "normal," but are in some way "difficult." Babies with feeding difficulties or overactive toddlers fit into this category. Consider the young mother of a 2-month-old colicky infant. Thinking there may be something wrong with the child, the baby is brought to the doctor, who reassures the mother that she has a healthy, normal baby who happens to cry a lot. This mother might then interpret her baby's difficult temperament as being either a reflection of inadequate parenting skills or an indication that her baby does not like her. If this parent has a low threshold for physical violence, given the right set of external circumstances, this baby might be physically maltreated.

The "Rejected" Child

There are other child factors that increase the risk for abuse, even though the child is not in any way considered abnormal. Sometimes a child differs from a parent's fantasy of that child. The child may be the wrong sex or resemble a disliked relative or rejected mate. Some infants are the result of an unwanted pregnancy. All of these factors increase the risk of physical abuse, given the correct set of circumstances. Finally, the child may seem to invite abuse. This is not an unusual defense in child sexual abuse cases, where the perpetrator claims that the 4-year-old child was provocative and seductive. While it is clear that there are young children who exhibit hypersexual behaviors, most clinicians agree that these are almost always learned behaviors, and that it is rare for children who have not been sexually maltreated to have such a strong sexual focus. Likewise, many professionals have had experience with children who are so provocative that abuse somehow seems understandable. Although ultimately the child is never to be blamed for having been abused, these children often have a long history of

abuse and learn that the only successful way (however inappropriate) to get parental attention is to misbehave. These children are not only at risk for abuse in their own homes but with foster families as well, and may account in part for some of the abuse that occurs in foster homes.

PREVENTION

The importance of preventing child abuse seems obvious. Children die each year at the hands of caretakers, and others live with the physical and emotional scars that result from maltreatment. Some victims spend their childhood moving from one temporary foster care home to the next, without any sense of permanence in their lives. Preventing abuse would improve the quality of life for countless numbers of children and would help to break the intergenerational cycle of violence against children. The impact of abuse extends far beyond the individual family. Many adult survivors have difficulty with relationships and suffer from low self-esteem. They may end up in prisons or on the street as part of our nation's homeless population. A recent prospective study by Widom suggests that children who are abused are at increased risk of arrests for juvenile delinquency, adult criminal, and violent criminal behavior.

Unfortunately, it is premature to realistically consider the primary prevention of child abuse as an attainable goal. Our understanding of the etiologies of abuse is too basic to think we can successfully prevent future abuse. Much of what we presently call prevention is actually reactive; we identify high risk families, monitor them, and provide psychotherapy and counseling, when available. When the danger is too great, we call on the criminal justice system to assist with our attempts to modify behavior.

Education

Regardless of these limitations, we need to consider child abuse as a symptom of family dysfunction and consider ways in which we can assist families that are experiencing enormous stress. We can begin by providing families with education and assistance. Money must be made available for day-care programs and respite care, so that parents can be employed outside the home or get much needed relief from demanding children. Parental education must begin early. We need early education for both young children and adolescents about the realities of parenting. All pregnant women need access to medical care, and the teaching of basic parenting skills needs to begin prenatally. Parents with young infants should have nurses, social workers, or trained community adults who are available for support and further education. Parents who need help must have access to "hotlines" and to self-help programs that have had success in many communities. Once families are identified as being at high risk for abuse, there need to be effective systems established to evaluate and monitor these families. This requires cooperation and effective communication among physicians, social workers, and child protective service workers, and police and law enforcement professionals. Finally, there needs to be effective intervention for these families, such as intensive home visitations by skilled nurses and social workers.

An attempt to prevent sexual abuse has begun in many school systems. A wide range of programs has been developed to teach children about sexual abuse and how to respond to inappropriate sexual advances. Opponents to this approach argue that children might begin to fear family members unnecessarily and that preventive education, along with other forms of sexual education, belongs in the home. Although the beneficial and potentially dangerous effects of these programs have not been fully evaluated, many agree that they constitute a reasonable approach to educating potential victims. In fact, these programs sometimes help to identify children who have already been abused.

Education needs to be available in the home, also, and must begin before school age. Parents need to trust the adults who care for their children. This is especially relevant in our society, where many working parents entrust their children's safety to babysitters and day-care centers. As toddlers develop a sense of gender and as language skills improve, parents should help their children understand that they have control over their bodies. Children should be encouraged to resist behaviors that make them uncomfortable, such as being tickled or kissed when they do not want to be. As children become more interested in reproduction, parents should offer age-appropriate, but honest, answers to their questions. Most important, parents need to continually communicate with their children and be available to listen to their concerns.

Extended Services

As child advocates, we can play an important role in child abuse prevention. We need to consider abuse as a diagnostic possibility and acknowledge our responsibilities when suspicions are identified. Fatal abuse is often preceded by more minor manifestations of maltreatment, which are sometimes ignored by physicians, teachers, social workers, and others who are in frequent contact with children. Children should never die because of our inability to confront the possibility of abuse. Physicians need to educate the families they serve. Although office visits are often busy and time is a limiting factor, anticipatory guidance regarding normal child development and appropriate discipline must be incorporated into well-child care visits. Some physicians have developed group well-child care visits, where groups of parents with children of similar ages meet together with the doctor to discuss behavioral, developmental, and safety issues. Child care professionals need to be a good resource for families who are stressed. They need to know what services are available in the community and how parents can access these services.

Abused children need to be protected, and adults who abuse children must be held accountable for their actions. To meet these needs, we presently force social services on families who are unwilling to accept help, remove children from their natural families, place them in foster homes, and sentence some convicted child abusers to jail. Although this last response is sometimes necessary and appropriate, punishment is often unsuccessful in deterring unacceptable behavior. Until we better understand the complex factors that lead to child abuse and can focus resources on ways to promote positive parenting, our interventions will come too late, and children will continue to be hurt by those responsible for their well-being.

SUGGESTED READINGS

1. Blumberg M: Sexual abuse of children: causes, diagnosis and management. Pediatr Ann 13:753, 1984
2. Cohn A: Preventing adults from becoming sexual molesters. Child Abuse Negl 10:559, 1986
3. Connecting: Challenges in Health and Human Services in the Philadelphia Region. The Pew Charitable Trusts, Philadelphia, 1989
4. Dubowitz H: Prevention of child maltreatment: what is known. Pediatrics 83:570, 1989
5. Egeland B, Jacobovitz D, Stroufe LA: Breaking the cycle of abuse. Child Dev 59:1080, 1988
6. Faller KC: Child Sexual Abuse: An Interdisciplinary Manual for Diagnosis, Case Management, and Treatment. Columbia University Press, New York, 1988
7. Finkelhor D, Gelles RJ, Hotaling GT, Straus M: The Dark Side of Families: Current Family Violence Research. Sage Publications, Beverly Hills, 1983
8. Fonatana V, Robinson E: Observing child abuse. J Pediatr 105:655, 1984
9. Gelles R: Child abuse as psychopathology: a sociological critique and reformulation. Am J Orthopsychiatry 43:611, 1973
10. Helfer R: Epidemiology of child abuse and neglect. Pediatr Ann 13:745, 1984
11. Hunter R, Kilstrom N, Kraybill E, Loda F: Antecedents of child abuse and neglect in premature infants: a prospective study in a newborn intensive care unit. Pediatrics 61:629, 1978
12. Jenny C, Sutherland S, Sandahl B: Developmental approach to preventing the sexual abuse of children. Pediatrics 78:1034, 1986
13. Kaufman J, Zigler E: Do abused children become abusive parents? Am J Orthopsychiatry 57:186, 1987
14. Leventhal J, Egerter S, Phil M, Murphy J: Reassessment of the relationship of perinatal risk factors and child abuse. Am J Dis Child 138:1034, 1984
15. Ludwig S: Child abuse: causes and solutions. p. 61. In Luten R (ed): Problems in Pediatric Emergency Medicine. Churchill Livingstone, New York, 1988
16. Martin H: The clinical relevance of prediction and prevention. p. 175. In Starr (ed): Child Abuse Prediction—Policy Implications. Ballinger Press, Cambridge, 1982
17. Oates RK, Forrest D, Peacock A: Mothers of abused children: a comparison study. Clin Pediatr 24:9, 1985
18. Olds DL, Henderson CR, Chamberlin R, Tatelbaum R: Preventing child abuse and neglect: a randomized trial of nurse home visitation. Pediatrics 78:65, 1986

19. Steele B: Psychodynamic factors in child abuse. p. 81. In Kempe CH, Helfer RE (eds): The Battered Child. 4th Ed. University of Chicago Press, Chicago, 1987

20. Strauss MA, Gelles RJ, Steinmetz S: Behind Closed Doors: Violence in the American Family. Anchor Books, New York, 1980

21. Strauss MA, Kantor GK: Stress in child abuse. p. 43. In Kempe CH, Helfer RE (eds): The Battered Child. 4th Ed. University of Chicago Press, Chicago, 1987

22. White R, Benedict MI, Wulff L, Kelley M: Physical disabilities as risk factors for child maltreatment: a selected review. Am J Orthopsychiatry 57:93, 1987

23. Widom CS: The cycle of violence. Science 244:160, 1989

24. Wolfe CA: Child abuse prevention and intervention. Pediatr Ann 13:766, 1984

5

Child Abuse Fatalities

Katherine Kaufer Christoffel

Unfortunately, child abuse is the leading cause of injury death among American children, especially those younger than 1 year old. This is particularly dramatic when one considers that child abuse fatalities are notoriously underreported. If our children are to be safer in the future than they have been in the past, health professionals will need to join with other child advocates to improve the recognition, management, and prevention of child abuse deaths. Enough is known to begin this difficult task.

Before reviewing the available information on child abuse deaths, it is important to note that although the occurrence of death is critical in many ways, that a death occurred is not critical to preventing the sequence of events and interaction of factors that could prove fatal to a child. The reason is that there is often little more than chance to explain why one abused or neglected child dies, while another survives. One burn may become infected and cause death, while another, of equal or greater size but uninfected, does not. A blow to the head may result in a rapidly fatal epidural hematoma, while another leads to a slower subdural bleed, which is treated before it causes death, but perhaps not before it causes brain damage. One neglected child re-

ceives timely medical attention for neglect, as a result of an intercurrent viral illness; another child, who happens to avoid such illness and therefore does not receive medical attention, presents dead on arrival from starvation.

Because vital status is important, information about deceased children is often more readily available than information about children who could have died but did not. As a result, the information presented in this chapter is based largely on what is known about children who have died. In using this information, it is extremely important for all who are involved with abused children to treat the near-misses as seriously as the deaths; we cannot depend on chance to protect children.

EPIDEMIOLOGY

Definition

For the purpose of this discussion, child abuse homicide is defined as a childhood death that results from maltreatment—assault or neglect—by a responsible caretaker.

49

Sources of Data

Available information on child abuse deaths is gathered from several sources, each of which has both advantages and limitations.

Medical Sources

For most clinicians, medical records are the most familiar source of data, and clinical findings are generally clearest in medical records. However, medical records rarely include all the social and autopsy information necessary to clarify the cause of death. Retrieval of pertinent records for systematic review can be problematic (partly because of technical difficulties in applying International Classification of Diseases Manner of Death [ICDE] codes to child abuse deaths). Routine medical record department reports concerning child abuse deaths are generally not available.

Vital statistics are based on death certificates, and so are only as accurate as the diagnoses on the certificates. When the cause of death is uncertain (perhaps because an autopsy was not done), or certified by someone who failed to recognize signs of abuse, underreporting of child abuse is likely. Vital statistics data are summarized by state departments of health and also by the National Center for Health Statistics in annual reports, usually 2 years after the deaths have occurred.

For deaths that are referred for forensic investigation, medical examiner or coroner records provide analyzable data. These deaths do not include any that should have been referred but were not. Further limitations in these data can include the training of the person performing the autopsy (who may or may not be a forensic pathologist, and may or may not be someone familiar with child abuse), and the available nonmedical information (e.g., death scene and social information

may be critical, yet unavailable). The findings of medical examiner or coroner records are not routinely summarized, but often can be accessed concerning specific cases or for specific research projects.

Administrative Sources

State child abuse reporting agencies, which are required in all states by federal law, collect information on cases reported to them (under state statute). They do not include data on any cases of child abuse that are not reported to them. Rarely, a designation of a death as related to child abuse may be based on findings not directly related to the death (e.g., old fractures). Reporting requirements, investigative practices, and interagency collaboration, which may be critical to obtaining all pertinent data, vary by locale, limiting the ability to generalize from local findings. Reports summarizing child abuse deaths are sometimes available, but, in the absence of focused studies, often lack important detail.

Police reports of homicide, which include child abuse deaths, are collected by the Federal Bureau of Investigation (FBI), and the data are summarized in the annual Uniform Crime Report. These reports exclude highly suspicious yet uncertain cases. Because most homicides involve adults, FBI/police data on perpetrators have not identified categories that are important in child abuse (e.g., mother's boyfriend); planned changes in data gathering methods for the Uniform Crime Report may correct this deficiency.

The best data on child abuse deaths are obtained from interagency collaboration that leads to merging of available data from the sources mentioned above and others (e.g., public aid, mental health agencies, and drug abuse treatment programs). It requires a tremendous effort to develop and maintain these linkages, and in 1991 they exist in only a few locales.

In the absence of widespread, high quality linked data, our understanding of fatal child abuse is built on individually limited, but complementary, data sources. Information that arises consistently from a variety of sources is most likely to be valid.

Incidence

After the above discussion of data limitations, it is not surprising that estimates of child abuse homicides vary, depending on the source of the data on which the estimates are based. The most consistently generated estimate is that about 1000 children per year die as a result of abuse or neglect by caretakers.

Homicide is among the 10 leading causes of death for children in all age groups under age 20. Approximately one-fourth of all reported homicide deaths of children in the United States aged 0 to 19 years affect children under the age of 5 years; the most common injuries among these young victims of violent death are beatings (the most common), arson (smoke inhalation), burns, and neglect.

After infancy, homicide is among the five leading causes of death. Although other causes of death are more frequent in infancy, reported homicide rates are actually substantially higher in infancy than they are for any other age under 15 years.

Table 5-1 shows violent death rates for children younger than 5 years in Cook County, Illinois. Reported homicide rates in Cook County are comparable to reported U.S. rates. When suspicious deaths (i.e., deaths of undetermined causes for which foul play is suspected but cannot be proved to be homicide because of insufficient evidence) are included in estimates of violent death in infancy (as in Table 5-1), the results are virtually double the reported homicide rates for the youngest children. The overestimation error in these higher rates is probably less than the underestimation error in the official rates.

Risk Factors

Age
The young age of child abuse homicide victims presumably accounts for the reported observation that they are generally the youngest or the second to youngest child in the family. The most likely explanations for the inverse relationship between age and risk of child abuse death are greater biologic vulnerability to assault in infancy, owing to immaturity of the brain and other organs; less mobility (e.g., to forage for food, or to escape if attacked or left unattended in a building that catches fire); and more difficult behaviors (e.g., crying, tantrums, and toileting accidents). The information concerning the sequence of events leading up to child abuse fatalities, although scant, supports the notion that age-appropriate behaviors of young children often trigger fatal assault.

Sex
Homicide death rates are higher among male victims over the age of 1 year; the evidence is less convincing for males under the age of 1 year.

Community of Residence
As with all child abuse, the risk of fatal child abuse is highest in urban areas. The one exception to this may be neonaticide, the killing of newborns delivered after unwanted pregnancies, which has been reported to be higher in rural areas.

Social Status and Race
Fatal child abuse, like other child abuse and homicide, is highest among the poor, who are disproportionately black. It is

Table 5-1. Child Homicide in Cook County, 1977–1982, Pediatric Homicide Rates per 100,000 Persons in City of Chicago and Cook County, 1977–1982

	Homicide						Undetermined						Homicide and Undetermined					
	County			Chicago			County			Chicago			County			Chicago		
	B	W	All	B	W	All	B	W	All	B	W	All	B	W	All	B	W	All
Less than 1 y	12.31	2.14	6.22	23.58	3.68	13.62	17.23	5.34	10.49	32.75	11.95	23.12	29.54	7.48	16.71	56.32	15.62	36.74
1–2 y	6.65	1.64	3.51	14.17	4.72	8.87	8.09	1.34	4.35	16.86	4.19	10.90	14.74	2.19	7.86	31.03	8.91	19.77
3–4 y	3.56	0.46	1.63	6.82	0.00	3.36	2.49	0.62	1.42	4.55	1.63	2.99	6.05	1.08	3.06	11.37	1.63	6.35
1–4 y	5.10	1.06	2.58	10.48	2.40	6.13	5.28	0.99	2.89	10.67	2.94	6.97	10.38	2.05	5.47	21.15	5.34	13.10
5–9 y	1.39	0.47	0.88	2.81	1.73	2.27	0.86	0.12	0.41	1.41	0.43	0.88	2.24	0.59	1.29	4.22	2.17	3.14

Abbreviations: B, black; W, white; All, all races.

likely that the increased risk associated with poverty explains the increased risk of black children. Violent death rates vary among neighborhoods of comparable poverty, indicating that community factors other than poverty are also important; identifying those other factors remains elusive.

Perpetrators

Most child abuse homicide victims are fatally injured by their parents. Neonaticide is usually committed by the mother. Several studies indicate that mothers of fatally abused children started childbearing at an early age. Among parent perpetrators in other types of fatal child abuse, fathers (including stepfathers, alone or with the mother) are involved at least as often as mothers. As fathers generally spend less time caring for children than mothers do, these data suggest that they are more likely to kill their children than mothers are if exposure time is controlled for. Paternal drug use has been identified as a marker of fatal child abuse, as has the presence of an unrelated man in the household.

Individuals who are not parents, often young babysitters, are also occasionally involved as child abuse homicide perpetrators; they too are often male.

Mental illness, while not known to be associated with child abuse fatalities in general, does seem to play a role in certain types of deaths (e.g., dismemberment following "a message from God").

Protective Service Involvement

Protective service agencies themselves and the media have focused attention on the possibility that child abuse deaths represent a failure on the part of child protection agencies. Underfunding, staff turnover and burnout, and unmanageable caseloads are some of the problems that hamper the effectiveness of child protec-tion agencies. There are other factors that contribute to child abuse deaths, such as a lack of communication between the community and the agencies; for example, the agencies cannot protect children who are unknown to them. Health professionals can probably serve their patients and communities best by developing communications with their child protection agencies that will allow frank examination of problems and cooperative development of solutions.

RECOGNITION

Appropriate management of child abuse fatalities and near-fatalities requires proper recognition. The first step in recognition is suspicion; it is crucial to consider the possibility of abuse or neglect whenever an at-risk child dies or nearly dies. Because all children are at risk to some degree, the possibility of abuse must arise routinely, although often only fleetingly. For children who are demographically at highest risk (under 2 years of age, in urban cities, from poor families, with an unrelated man in the house), the suspicion of abuse must be investigated. Indeed, in such cases, the necessary information must be collected to rule out abuse as a cause of death. This is done most convincingly by establishing that there is a nontraumatic cause of death (e.g., respiratory syncytial virus pneumonia with deterioration occurring in the hospital) *and* that appropriate care was given.

To avoid missing cases of fatal abuse and neglect, it is necessary to be systematic in collection of information. While there is not yet a consensus on the items that constitute crucial information, several model protocols do exist. Desirable information is listed in Table 5-2. The items that should be routinely collected

Table 5-2. Information Useful for Determining if a Death is Due to Child Abuse or Neglect

---

Autopsy[a]
   Preferably by a forensic pathologist, including plotting of growth parameter and toxicology (in all cases in selected areas and in selected cases in all areas)

Social work interview[a]
   Preferably at the time of death, including family constellation as well as recent history

Review of medical records[a]
   Preferably including earlier records

Skeletal survey[a]
   Preferably interpreted by a pediatric radiologist familiar with child abuse

Previous child protection information on the family[a]
   May be informative, particularly if there has been abuse of this or another child in the past

Police information on death, if any[a]

Death scene investigation
   Always desirable, sometimes critical, often unavailable

Paramedic run sheets
   These often include some death scene information

Perinatal history
   This may identify medical and psychosocial risk factors (e.g., no prenatal care)

---

[a] Should be routinely collected.

are least controversial, often because they are the most available.

Because child abuse deaths are more often mistaken for deaths due to natural illness than due to unintentional trauma, a properly performed autopsy probably provides the most important information that must be obtained. A prompt and careful social work evaluation is also important, particularly in situations in which the autopsy cannot ascertain whether or not abuse occurred, for example, in some drownings and asphyxiation. The social work assessment should begin before the autopsy, since information may be available when a child is pronounced dead that may not be available later, when the parents are less psychologically affected. The interview should be conducted in a way that is both supportive to the bereaved family and informative to those who must decide whether abuse was the cause of death. Skilled pediatric social workers, who walk this fine line with grace, will help both surviving parents and any siblings potentially at risk. Although such evaluations are not now universally available, they should be considered optimal care, and an effort should be made to make them standard care.

If the social work interview and autopsy do not suffice to dispel suspicion that abuse or neglect may have occurred, the state child abuse reporting agency must become involved. Of course, it should be notified as soon as a suspicious history is obtained, even if this occurs before the autopsy is performed.

A multidisciplinary assessment, which will result if all the information in Table 5-2 is collected, is almost always better than an assessment by any one discipline, because complementary information and interpretive skills are brought into play. Such assessment should become the rule in the coming decades, as protocols continue to be developed and implemented in jurisdictions across the country.

SUSPICIOUS APNEA

Autopsies can generally reveal when assault has contributed to death, and can help to document the medical outcomes of severe neglect (e.g., starvation and dehydration). Unfortunately, autopsies cannot distinguish parental asphyxiation from sudden infant death syndrome (SIDS). Further, the risk factors for SIDS and homicide overlap (including young maternal age, high birth order, low social

Table 5-3. Suspicious Apnea:
Clinical Typology[a]

Medical apneas
 Medical evidence of a condition (e.g., airway obstruction) causing apnea, often recurrent

Environmental hazard apnea
 Evidence of an environmental condition (e.g., entrapment in a bed) causing apnea, seldom recurrent

Münchausen syndrome by proxy apneas
 Evidence (usually video) of parental asphyxiation, done at least in part to obtain medical attention, often recurrent

Abusive asphyxiation
 Evidence of battering or apnea at home, with resolution of apnea out of the home, can be recurrent (usually included in descriptions of Münchausen syndrome by proxy apneas)

[a] All can be either fatal or nonfatal (with or without brain damage due to anoxia).

quent medical records reviewed after death, should identify fatal cases of medical apnea. Failure to identify such cases can, however, occur when the history is unclear and death occurs before adequate testing is done. In some such cases, social work or psychiatric evaluation of the children's families can help to assess the need for worry about surviving or later siblings. (At times, medical apnea may be related to other evidence of maltreatment, e.g., abnormal ventilatory control in infants of cocaine-addicted mothers; at this time, clinical judgment must dictate how best to deal with this situation.)

Nonmedical apneas can be placed into three categories: environmental hazards, Münchausen syndrome by proxy, and abusive asphyxiation. Appropriate investigation should identify at least some of these.

class/black race). Information beyond autopsy and demography may be needed to confirm that a particular child has died of SIDS.

Similarly, it is often extremely difficult to ascertain when a child presenting with a history of repeated apneas has a medical problem, and when the child is being repeatedly smothered and so is at risk for homicide. Although there are no large prospective series of such cases to inform us, clinical experience and case reports allow construction of a logical approach to such patients, both before and after death.

It is useful to start with a conceptual framework (Table 5-3). Apnea can result from several medical problems including disorders of central ventilatory regulation, upper airway obstruction, seizures, aspiration, and medication overdose. Apnea resulting from these conditions, which can generally be documented, can be designated as medical apneas. Appropriate testing before death, and subse-

Environmental Hazard Apneas

Environmental hazard apneas occur when a child, either intentionally or unintentionally, is left in a situation that causes asphyxiation. Examples of situations in which children have suffocated include cribs with gaps between the mattress and the bed frame, adult beds near walls, water beds, stair or deck railings that are spaced wider than the chest but narrower than the head of a child, and overlaying by a sleeping adult in the same bed. Such asphyxiations usually are not recurrent. The problem in identifying environmental hazard apnea arises when a child is removed from the home and taken to the hospital with an unclear account from a distraught parent, or when those who answer an ambulance call fail to note crucial details as they urgently try to resuscitate the child. These are cases in which meticulous autopsy (e.g., looking for evidence of entrapment) and death scene investigation can be critical to a correct diagnosis.

Münchausen Syndrome by Proxy Apneas

In Münchausen syndrome by proxy apneas, disturbed parents smother their infants to obtain for themselves the medical attention that they crave. Although their goal is not to hurt the child, the child is hurt to achieve their goal. Table 5-4 summarizes the clinical features of these families, which can be extremely helpful in identifying suspicious cases. Several points bear emphasis about cases described in papers cited at the end of this chapter as Münchausen by proxy (or Polle syndrome, after the deceased infant son of Baron von Münchausen, who gave his own name to the adult syndrome of factitious illness). First, they vary across a spectrum of parental activity that ranges from tall tales of illness (without actual

Table 5-4. Münchausen Syndrome by Proxy: Common or Relatively Common Reported Features

---

Mother is perpetrator (almost always)

Children present with undiagnosable symptom complexes

Symptoms occur only when perpetrator is alone with child

Children often have histories of multiple unexplained disorders

Deceased young siblings

Mother's husband is absent (physically or emotionally)

Perpetrator

    Is medically knowledgeable

    Is a "model parent" in the hospital

    Befriends medical staff

    Has a personal history of maternal deprivation, and occasionally of physical or sexual abuse

    Has a diagnosable (but variable) psychiatric condition (e.g., personality disorder, depression, anxiety)

---

induction of symptoms), to repeated deadly actions. Second, apnea is estimated to account for just 15 percent of all such cases, but 40 percent of the fatal cases. Third, reports of recurrent SIDS in siblings of apnea patients must be viewed with great suspicion. In such cases, it is critically important to thoroughly review the circumstances surrounding any deaths of young siblings (SIDS or other), particularly, but not exclusively, when they are half or adopted siblings, and so genetically distant from the presenting patient. Fourth, the psychological origins of this syndrome are not yet clear; it is likely that there are several, which may be reflected in varying presentations. For example, two hypothesized mechanisms are (1) maternal deprivation of the mother and her own history of childhood illness lead her to seek emotional support from medical personnel and (2) resentment by the mother of the child leads to hatred that is denied, but played out through attacks on the child.

To date, videotape evidence of active asphyxiation has been needed to make the case in court that a child's symptoms are from Münchausen syndrome by proxy. Modern pediatric hospitals should all have rooms equipped to perform video surveillance of such children. Such surveillance, which is clearly warranted by the child's medical needs, has rarely, if ever, required special legal sanction. Once harm is documented, it is important to move quickly to protect the child, both in the short- and the long-term. For a variety of reasons, it will not always be possible to document asphyxiation in such cases. Even when asphyxiation is not documented, if suspicion is strong, such cases must be reported to the state child abuse reporting agency. When possible, an apnea free period of observation outside the home can clarify the source of the apneas.

Over time, the risks to children who

suffer from Münchausen syndrome by proxy and the best ways to manage them should become clearer. After death, little can be done to make this diagnosis, although medical records indicating extensive testing and doctor shopping, or repeated questionable medical apnea deaths in the same family, may suffice to obtain help for the families and surviving siblings.

Abusive Asphyxiations

I suspect that some cases of parental asphyxiation are not from Münchausen syndrome by proxy, as described above. Others, which are often included in discussions of Münchausen by proxy, but which differ in terms of the situations in which they occur and perhaps also in a higher prevalence of fathers as perpertrators, can be called child abuse asphyxiations. They are a result of attempts by an angry parent to quiet a crying child. In-hospital video surveillance may be less likely to detect these episodes. If there is other evidence of abuse, such as broken bones, child abuse asphyxiation is managed like any other kind of abuse. If there is no such evidence, extensive medical testing may be required to rule out medical causes. A prolonged apnea free hospitalization may provide sufficient medical and social information to make a convincing case for child protection. Elimination of apnea episodes in the hospital and in foster care would strongly suggest that some factor at home is causing the apnea.

MANAGEMENT

When a child dies, there are two urgent considerations: the surviving children and the adults' need for closure. To pro-

tect surviving siblings, medical personnel must report any case in which there is a suspicion of child abuse or neglect to the state child abuse reporting agency, which then becomes responsible for both investigation of the case and for any needed protection of surviving siblings. The parents' need for closure is perhaps most decisive when the likelihood of child abuse is real but low; they deserve to have the possibility ruled out.

Whenever a child dies, everything necessary should be done to clarify the cause of death. The attending physician is responsible for setting in motion the process for making that determination, as described above (see under Recognition).

The responsibilities of health professionals do not end with the autopsy. If the alleged perpetrator is tried in civil or criminal court for a child homicide, medical testimony is likely to be needed. Careful preparation is necessary to assure that a clear picture appears before the judge or jury. This must include shared identification of the critical issues and findings by the district attorney and the testifying health professional. Expert testimony by child abuse consultants can be helpful, and in some cases is crucial (e.g., if the defendant's attorney is putting forth an expert willing to testify that a death could have been "accidental," the testimony of a physician inexperienced in child abuse or with legal proceedings can greatly weaken the state's case).

PREVENTION

Preventing child abuse deaths requires preventing child abuse. Primary prevention is best. The only proven primary prevention approach involves the use of home visitors. Olds et al. have shown that 2 years of weekly home visits, occurring both before and after delivery, reduced the incidence of child abuse among the children of unmarried, impoverished primiparas under 19 years of age in a semirural area, when compared with alternative approaches such as prenatal visits only, free transport to clinic visits, and a package of postnatal screening and diagnostic testing. In replications of this approach in larger studies and a variety of settings, it will be desirable to examine mortality rates.

Secondary prevention of subsequent abuse, to a once-abused child and to siblings of an abused child, can be lifesaving if successful. Secondary prevention is probably most successful when it occurs early in the abusive pattern. This requires clinical acumen and a realistic degree of suspicion when dealing with families. When prevention approaches, even if unproven, are available and nonthreatening (e.g., provision of a drop-in center to reduce the isolation of mothers of young children) they can be offered at a lower level of suspicion than that necessary to report a child to the state child abuse reporting agency.

It is likely that a variety of successful prevention approaches can be developed. These will need to reflect the developmental interactions and vulnerabilities of young children and will need to be community based. Different approaches can reasonably address different aspects of the problem. Some will try to reduce the prevalence of certain risk factors, such as reducing the severity of poverty by increasing the amount of money paid to mothers on public aid. Others will attempt to reduce the frequency of precipitating events by providing child care assistance to high risk mothers. Still others will try to reduce the frequency of injury when stress occurs by training children to handle difficult infant behaviors in a nonviolent fashion, which will be useful when babysitting or when they have their own children.

There are many ideas; the will and the funds are needed to make these ideas viable prevention programs. Every day that we delay, three or four children will die.

SUGGESTED READINGS

1. Alexander R, Smith W, Stevenson R: Serial Münchausen by proxy. Pediatrics 86:581, 1990
2. Bass M, Kraveth R, Glass L: Death scene investigation in sudden infant death. N Engl J Med 315:100, 1986
3. Berger D: Child abuse simulating near-miss sudden infant death syndrome. J Pediatr 95:554, 1987
4. Christoffel KK: Violent death and injury in U.S. children and adolescents. Am J Dis Child 144:697, 1990
5. Christoffel KK, Anzinger NK, Merrill DA: Age-related patterns of violent death, Cook County, 1977–1982. Am J Dis Child 143:1403, 1989
6. Epstein MA, Markowitz RL, Gallo DM et al: Münchausen syndrome by proxy: considerations in diagnosis and confirmation by video surveillance. Pediatrics 80:220, 1987
7. Kaufman KL, Coury D, Pickrel E, McCleery J: Münchausen syndrome by proxy: a survey of professionals' knowledge. Child Abuse Negl 13:141, 1989
8. Kirschner RH, Christoffel KK, Kearns MNL, Rosman M, the Task Force for the Study of Non-Accidental Injuries and Child Deaths: Protocol for Child Death Autopsies. Illinois Department of Children and Family Services, Springfield, IL, 1987
9. Kleinman PK, Blackbourne BD, Marks SC et al: Radiologic contributions to the investigation and prosecution of cases of fatal infant abuse. N Engl J Med 320:507, 1989
10. Libow JA, Schreier HA: Three forms of factitious illness in children: when is it Münchausen syndrome by proxy? Am J Orthopsychiatry 56:602, 1986
11. Light MJ, Sheridan MS: Münchausen

syndrome by proxy and apnea (MBPA). Clin Pediatr 29:162, 1990

12. Makar AF, Squier PJ: Münchausen syndrome by proxy: father as perpetrator. Pediatrics 85:370, 1990

13. McGuire TL, Feldman KW: Psychological morbidity of children subjected to Münchausen syndrome by proxy. Pediatrics 83:289, 1989

14. Meadow R: Suffocation, recurrent apnea, and sudden infant death. J Pediatr 117:351, 1990

15. Olds DL, Henderson CR, Chamberlin R, Tatelbaum R: Preventing child abuse and neglect: a randomized trial of nurse home visitation. Pediatrics 78:65, 1986

16. Rosen CL, Frost JD, Bricker T et al: Two siblings with recurrent cardiorespiratory arrest: Münchausen syndrome by proxy or child abuse? Pediatrics 71:715, 1983

17. Rosenberg DA: Web of deceit: a literature review of Münchausen syndrome by proxy. Child Abuse Negl 11:547, 1987

18. Sneed RC: Breed or Meadow? Munchausen or Münchhausen? Pediatrics 83:1078, 1989

19. Southall DP, Stebbens VA, Rees SV et al: Apnoeic episodes induced by smothering: two cases identified by covert video surveillance. Br Med J 294:1637, 1987

20. Surveillance and Programs Branch, Division of Environmental Hazards and Health Effects, Center for Environmental Health and Injury Control, CDC, Death Investigation—United States, 1987. MMWR 38:1, 1989

21. Waller AE, Baker SP, Szocka A: Childhood injury deaths: national analysis and geographic variations. Am J Public Health 79:310, 1989

6

Biomechanics of Nonaccidental Trauma

Betty S. Spivack

The physician caring for a child who has suffered abusive injuries has certain responsibilities. First, the physician must be sufficiently educated to recognize the likelihood of abuse. Second, the history of the injury must be examined to see whether it matches the physical signs with respect to the nature and extent of the findings. Finally, the physician has the duty to report to the appropriate social agencies the concerns that were aroused by the injury and history provided.

To accomplish these tasks, there must be some knowledge of the physics underlying accidental and nonaccidental trauma, just as there must be recognition of the developmental milestones that must be reached before a child is capable of a given type of self-inflicted injury. To this end, the general principles underlying injury to biologic structures are discussed, followed by the etiologies of specific patterns of injury commonly seen in abused children. Those injuries most common in infants are concentrated on, since they are incapable of providing a history.

GENERAL PRINCIPLES

An understanding of the physics of injury is based on a knowledge of the laws that govern the interactions of forces and bodies and on an understanding of the resistance of body structures to various types of deformation. The definitions of terms used in description of forces, motion, and deformations are listed below, along with preliminary comments about their significance in human injury.

Inertia is the tendency of a body at rest to remain at rest. Similarly, the *mass moment of inertia* represents the resistance of a body at rest to angular displacement and acceleration.

For linear motion, *force* (measured in newtons) expended is equal to the product of the *mass* (in kilograms) of the object moved and the *acceleration* (in meters per second-squared) produced in the object. If there is no motion, the force is opposed by an equal and opposite force.

Moment or *torque* represents the twisting or rotational effect of a force. It is equal to the product of the force and the perpendicular distance (or *moment arm*)

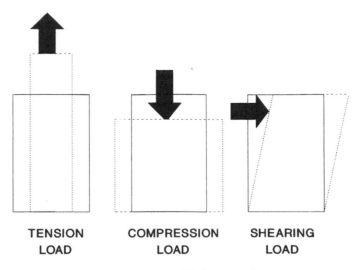

TENSION   COMPRESSION   SHEARING
LOAD   LOAD   LOAD

Fig. 6-1. Effects of deforming forces.

from the line of action of the force to the center of rotation of the object. Thus, the units of torque are newton-meters. During angular displacement, torque is also equal to the product of the mass moment of inertia and the angular acceleration, in analogy to force = mass × acceleration for linear motion. Torsion is the effect of torque on a cylinder.

Both force and torque are important in analyzing the effect of a self-generated or externally applied force on a biologic structure. In contraction, muscles generate both forces and moments. The moments determine the motion of the limb against resistance. The forces determine the load placed on the articular surface, which is essentially a fulcrum in a lever system.

In any static situation, forces and moments must be balanced. Any net force or net moment will produce either linear or angular displacement and acceleration. Based on this principle, we can calculate the forces and moments exerted on a structure from an impacting or nonimpacting injury, since at the instant of the injury there is no motion and the forces

and moments must be equal. To do this, however, we must understand the response of biologic structures to various forms of deformation.

In this context, *load* is the force exerted on the object in question. Loads (Fig. 6-1) may be *tensile* (tending to increase the length of the object), *compressive* (tending to decrease the length of the object), or *shearing* (tending to cause angular dis-

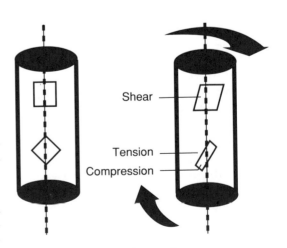

Shear

Tension
Compression

Fig. 6-2. Effects of torsion.

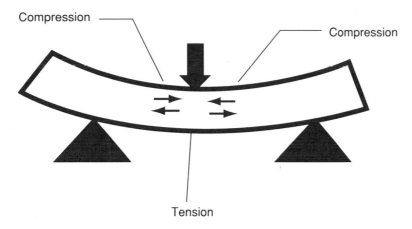

Fig. 6-3. Effects of bending.

tortion), or a combination of these effects. Most loads are complex mixtures of these simple types, causing different effects in different regions, depending on the moments or forces generated at any given site. Torsional or twisting forces produce maximal shearing effects at maximal distance from the axis of rotation, and tensile and compressive loads at 45 degree angles to the axis of rotation (Fig. 6-2). Bending produces tensile forces above the neutral axis, and compressive forces below it (Fig. 6-3), and little in the way of shearing forces, which however, are maximal at the neutral axis. Even "simple" tension or compression causes shearing along axes at 45 degrees to the direction of the applied force (Fig. 6-4).

Nature of Recipient Material

Each type of biologic material will differ in the *strain* (ratio of linear or angular deformation to the original length or angle) generated, or the *stress* (force or moment per unit area) tolerated when exposed to each type of deforming load. Materials differ as well in the manner in which the deformation is produced or resolved (Fig. 6-5).

Elastic

Elastic materials have a linear relationship of stress to strain, and when the force is released, the material returns to its original conformation. The rigidity or stiffness of the material, which reflects its resistance to the deformation produced during the application of the load, is the ratio of force applied to the amount of deformation produced. The *modulus of ri-*

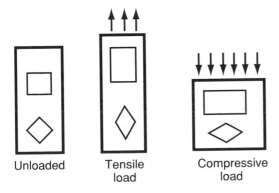

Fig. 6-4. Effects of tensile and compressive loading.

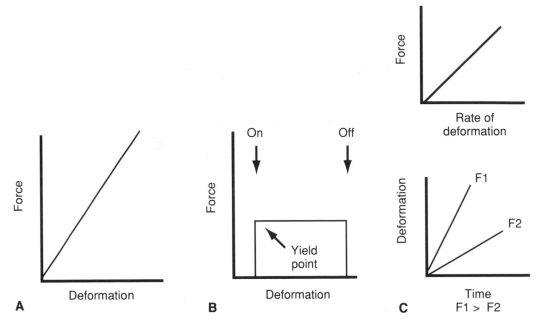

Fig. 6-5. Behavior of material types: **(A)** elastic, **(B)** plastic, and **(C)** viscous.

gidity or the *elastic modulus* is the ratio of stress to strain and increases with increasing stiffness. The energy necessary to cause the deformation is completely recoverable and is a function of the area beneath the curve.

Plastic

Plastic materials undergo permanent deformation and require no increase in deforming force to continue the amount of deformation, but they produce no deformation until the *yield point* of the material is surpassed. The total amount of deformation is dependent on the length of time force is applied after the yield point has been reached. Once again, the energy expended to cause the deformation is a function of the area under the curve, but here, some proportion of it is dissipated and is not recoverable after the deformation is ended.

Viscous

Viscous substances behave differently depending on the rate at which the load is applied, usually behaving more stiffly with quickly applied loads, than they do in response to slow, steady loading. The total amount of deformation is dependent on the degree of force, the rate at which it is applied, and the length of time it is applied.

Elastoplastic/Viscoelastic

Real materials are not purely elastic, plastic, or viscous; instead, they act as combinations of these basic sorts of materials (Fig. 6-6).

Elastoplastic materials behave elastically, with recoverable deformation, until the yield point is reached. Then they undergo permanent deformation without further increase in force. When the force is removed, the original elastic component of deformation is reversed, while the

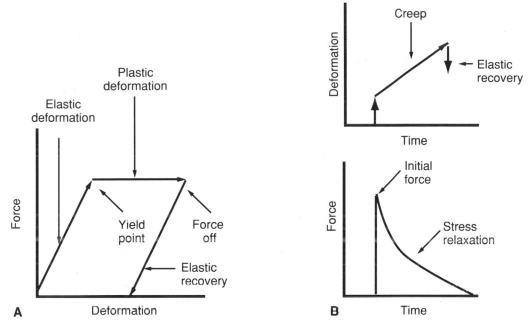

Fig. 6-6. Behavior of (**A**) elastoplastic and (**B**) viscoelastic materials.

plastic component remains. The *ultimate strength* of a material is the maximum stress that it may undergo before failure or ultimate rupture. This ultimate strength will vary, depending on the nature of the loading force. Failure may occur before this, depending on the state of the structure at the time.

In viscoelastic materials, the stress developed by application of a force is dependent on the rate of strain, and the strain is dependent on time. Creep and stress relaxation are two important consequences of this. After the instantaneous elastic deformation of a body, continued application of a force will cause a slow, steady deformation or *creep*. Conversely, a sudden deformation will induce a maximal stress in a viscoelastic substance, which will decrease over time, with recovery of the elastic elements, as the viscous elements slowly elongate. This

phenomenon of reduction in the force needed to maintain a given degree of deformation in a viscoelastic body is *stress relaxation*.

Biologic substances have aspects of both elastoplastic and viscoelastic materials. The degree to which they act as elastoplastic or viscoelastic materials differs according to the nature of the tissue itself. However, ultimate strength, creep, and stress relaxation are important features of all body tissues.

FRACTURES

Fractures, especially in infancy, represent an important segment of the range of severe physical abuse. To understand the mechanisms of such injuries, it is necessary to understand the structure and mechanical properties of bones in general, and the special characteristics of growing bones. The nature of those fractures that occur from abuse must be analyzed in the context of the implied etiologies of these injuries.

Bone Anatomy

Bone is constructed from several constituent parts. Cortical bone is a dense, usually well mineralized material. When mature, it is composed of secondary osteons or typical haversian systems. These are constructed with a central haversian canal, containing a neurovascular bundle, and surrounded by concentric lamellae of bone tissue. Between the lamellae are lacunae, connected to each other and to the haversian canal by canaliculi. However, these features are not found in fetal and infantile bone. Compact or cortical bone develops in a different way depending on whether it is membranous or endochondral in origin. However, certain features are constant. The earliest phase of true compact bone is the primary spongiosa, in which there is no lamellation, and the collagen fibers are randomly arranged. The next phase of development is the production of primary osteons or atypical haversian systems. These are roughly concentric, nonlamellar bone deposited in parallel fibers along the walls of the vascular spaces in the bone. Early in life this represents a large proportion of cortical bone. As the ossification process continues, the primary osteons and intervening interstitial bone are increasingly incorporated into mature, secondary osteons.

Trabecular or cancellous bone, by contrast, consists of a meshwork of calcified strands, within which are easily visible spaces.

Long bones generally have a thick cylinder of compact or cortical bone forming the shaft. The middle of the shaft has a few spicules of trabecular bone, but is chiefly occupied by the marrow cavity. This cavity extends in both directions outward during bone development, and in maturity, extends almost to the epiphyseal fusion line. Trabecular bone is found under synovial joints, where forces are diffused over large areas.

Long bones are formed from cartilage followed by chondrocyte death and secondary ossification. This occurs in fetal life at primary ossification centers in the diaphysis or shaft, and throughout childhood in the secondary ossification centers, usually located at each end in the epiphyses. The diaphysis and epiphysis are separated by metaphyseal regions, which represent areas of newly formed bone.

Mechanical Properties

Mechanical properties of bones differ, depending on many variables. In particular, properties of compact bone are dependent on the presence of secondary osteons, mineral content, and the nature of the loading force. The properties of trabecular bone, too, are very dependent on the mineral content of the bone. In general, as suspected, bone strength increases with degree of mineralization. It is also important to remember that bones, in general, behave in a viscoelastic manner, and therefore the rate of loading is an important consideration. Infantile bones, because of their highly cartilaginous nature, are much more plastic than bones in general, an important consideration in bone deformation.

Stiffness is an important property of bones, because it prevents collapse owing to compressive loading in upright postures. The modulus of stiffness of a bone is very dependent on its mineral content. In rabbit metatarsals, a small increase in bone mineralization can effectively triple tensile stiffness, from 60,000 to 170,000 kg(f)/cm^2. Bending and compressive strength are similarly dependent on mineral content. It is easy to see that this explains the occurrence of accidental "toddler fractures" in young, newly walking, infants. Certainly, when this is combined with the increased plasticity of infantile bones, the effects of rickets can also be easily understood.

Tensile strength is lower than compressive strength, approximately 1000 kg(f)/cm^2 as opposed to 1400 to 2000 kg(f)/cm^2. For this reason, bending loads usually cause failure in tension on the convex side. Shear strength is weaker still. Adult bones have little ability to store energy once fracture has begun; as a result, they quickly progress to a transverse or spiral fracture after tensile failure has occurred. Children's bone absorbs more energy before failure, even after a partial defect has occurred, yielding the splintered surface of the common "greenstick fracture." This occurs despite the lower bending strength of immature bone.

The maturity of the bone (i.e., the percentage of secondary osteons) is responsible for strength differences as well. In ox femora, bones that consisted of only secondary osteons were 35 percent weaker than primary bone. A significant, but lesser, difference was seen in humans. This may reflect part of the lower tendency to fracture seen in children. It must be noted, however, that the smaller cross-sectional area of a juvenile bone means that a greater stress is generated from a given load, and there may be corresponding trade-offs in tendency for bone failure.

The presence of a medullary cavity also influences the mechanical properties of long bones. Shear strain owing to torsional injury increases in proportion to the distance from the neutral axis, which is unchanged despite the central cavity. However, the strength of the bone depends on its cross-sectional area, which is diminished by the absence of bone centrally, although there is some increase in support owing to the transverse struts of midshaft trabecular bone. Why then have bones developed with this structure? By removing a central core, the weight of a bone is substantially decreased, and therefore force generated from muscle contraction generates a greater movement. Since muscle force, as part of a lever system, is related to the length of the action arm relative to the effort arm, increasing length yields increased force and velocity. This situation reaches a crisis point in racehorses, in which long, thin legs support a muscular, heavy body, and thus are very prone to fracture.

Fractures in Abused Infants

Now that we have achieved some understanding of the mechanical properties of infantile and juvenile bones, we are in a position to examine the fractures seen to occur in abused infants, and to analyze the physics of their occurrence. In particular, plastic deformation, fractures of the posterior ribs, metaphyseal-epiphyseal junctions, diaphyses, and the skull are discussed.

Plastic deformation occurs when longitudinal compression is applied to a curved bone. The tension of the convex surface, combined with compression of the concave surface, causes bending. If the elastic limit is surpassed, but not the rupture point of the bone, plastic bowing occurs without actual bone failure or fracture. The increased plasticity of juvenile bone makes this an injury restricted to the pediatric age group. In the forearm, the most frequent site, often one bone is ruptured, while the other undergoes plastic deformation; however, both may be plastically deformed. In 4 to 6 weeks, cortical thickening will occur circumferentially around the lesion, and gradual remodeling will occur. There is usually no early periosteal new bone formation. A bone scan may be helpful in the early phase to verify the injury. This lesion is usually the result of a forceful fall onto an outstretched arm. While this is usually accidental in the older child, an infant old enough to exhibit a parachute reflex (i.e., older than 9 months) will stretch out an arm for protection if flung against a wall or floor. Thus, the observed development of the child and the mechanism of injury must be carefully compared with the history provided.

Rib Fractures

Rib fractures used to be regarded as highly specific but relatively rare abusive injuries, with early series showing that such fractures accounted for only 8 percent of abusive fractures. The addition of bone scintigraphy as a technique for evaluation of bony trauma, as well as an appreciation of technical adjustments for plain film radiography, have changed this perception. In our recent series of 23 consecutive infants with abusive fractures, rib fractures accounted for 42 of the 94 bony lesions, or almost one-half. Significantly, all but one were visualized by scintigraphy, while only 76 percent were seen on chest and rib views by plain radiography. The fractures visualized on plain film had evidence of callus formation; no acute fractures were identified by plain film examination. Most abusive rib fractures occur at the posterior margin of the rib, adjacent to the vertebral body.

Recently, Kleinman et al. explained the difficulty in visualization of acute rib fractures that occur in this position, and in the process, also explained the mechanics of injury at this site. In his series of 103 abusive rib fractures in 16 infants, 64 percent were at, or medial to, the costotransverse process junction; an additional 24 percent were seen in the medial half of the posterior rib, but lateral to the articulation

site. The plain film findings were correlated with pathologic specimens of the 15 rib fractures found in the five fatal cases of abuse in the series. None of the eight acute fractures had been seen on preautopsy radiography. Histologic sections revealed nondisplaced fractures with disruption of the ventral cortex only. Similarly, autopsy examination of the healing fractures showed periosteal callus only on the ventral surface. This suggests that bending against the transverse process, which acts as a fulcrum, caused tensile failure in the side opposite to the applied force. Note that such a fracture cannot result from direct trauma, since this region of the rib is shielded by the vertebral transverse process, which is unbroken. This mechanism is compatible with other injuries that may occur when a young infant is grasped compressively around the chest, and then shaken or thrown, a common scenario in infantile abuse. The intact posterior cortex prevents displacement and decreases the visibility of an acute fracture, especially on frontal radiographs.

It is important to note that this injury does not appear to occur frequently after chest compressions are given during infant resuscitations. A recent study analyzed 41 children referred for evaluation of child abuse (all ages), 50 children who presented to the emergency department in cardiorespiratory arrest, and 22 patients with incidental discovery of rib fractures. In the 50 consecutive children examined after cardiopulmonary resuscitation (CPR) was performed, only one rib fracture was detected immediately or in follow-up, and that proved to be a healed fracture related to prior abuse. This occurred despite the fact that cardiac compressions were initiated by nonmedical providers in 40 percent of the cases. Six of the 41 children referred for an abuse work-up had rib fractures (15 percent). More significantly, seven of the children with "incidental discovery" of rib fractures proved to have other abusive lesions or a history of abuse. No other etiology (motor vehicle accident, surgery, osteoporosis, osteogenesis imperfecta) caused as many rib fractures. Thus, we may conclude that child abuse is the most common cause of childhood rib fracture, and that fresh posterior rib fractures visualized at autopsy in a child who received CPR are more likely abusive than the result of medical therapy, even if CPR was provided by untrained observers, and furthermore, that they result from sustained, intense compression directed toward the chest, rather than from a blow.

Metaphyseal-epiphyseal Fractures

Metaphyseal-epiphyseal fractures are the most highly specific lesions seen in abused children. Strangely enough, despite the extensive radiologic literature concerning these lesions, their histopathology was not studied until recently. The basic lesion is a series of planar fractures through the most immature portion of the metaphysis, in the primary spongiosa. Kleinman further indicates that the same lesion, a complete disc-like rupture of that layer, produces both the "corner-fracture" and "bucket-handle fracture" as imaging artifacts that are dependent on the spatial orientation of the x-ray beam, the limb, and the fracture planes.

The histopathology of metaphyseal-epiphyseal fractures clearly indicates the nature and mechanism of injury. First, it eliminates the long held theory that torsion or whiplash injuries caused such fractures by avulsion of bony fragments at the site of attachment of the periosteum at the metaphysis. Certainly, such a modality would not cause a discoid fracture. However, the lack of mineralization in the primary spongiosa weakens the integrity of the bone at this point, and makes it very susceptible to shearing

forces. This is certainly consonant with the torsional and whiplash effect of a child being vigorously shaken, as well as with isolated twisting above and below a joint.

Fractures that actually cross the epiphyseal growth plate are an unusual feature of abusive injury, but have been reported. Kleinman's study revealed no such fracture in his histopathologic series of four dead infants with metaphyseal fractures. Although such fractures appear rare, they are probably underdiagnosed, since the cartilage is not visualized by radiography, and, except in Kleinman's collaborative study, the metaphyseal-epiphyseal areas are not commonly examined at autopsy. The significance of such fractures cannot be overstressed, as distortion or destruction here will cause a variable degree of impairment of subsequent growth.

Bone Shaft Fractures

Shaft fractures occur in several ways. The splintering commonly seen in greenstick fractures is a reflection of the increased capacity of juvenile bone to store energy, after the initial breach of cortical integrity. It requires higher energies than does a transverse fracture, which also results from a bending or shearing stress as the result of a direct blow.

Spiral or *oblique fractures* propagate at a 45-degree angle, suggesting that a major component in their evolution is tensile failure during torsion. However, recent studies indicate that the initial failure is at the point of maximal shearing stress at the bony surface, parallel to the axis of rotation and that after the initial shearing failure, the fracture develops along the predicted lines of tensile stress. This makes sense in light of the fact that bones are generally weaker in shear than in tension. In bones that vary greatly in their diameter, a given torsional load will cause a higher degree of shear stress in the smaller regions of the bone, owing to their lower polar moment of inertia. This correlates well with the typical appearance of spiral fractures in the distal tibia rather than more proximally. This pattern increases the likelihood that shearing stresses cause the initiation of the fracture, as tensile strain should be reduced at this point, owing to the thicker cortex and smaller medullary cavity.

It should be stressed, that while spiral fractures may be a common accidental injury in ambulatory toddlers, there is no evidence that young infants can generate sufficient muscular effort to cause a self-induced spiral fracture.

Skull Fractures

Skull fractures represent the last group of common abusive fractures; they accounted for 14 of the 94 fractures in our recent series (15 percent). As was seen in the case of long-bone fractures, splintering or shattering reflects a higher energy injury than does a simple linear fracture. This accounts for the not-always-reliable set of features that "distinguish" abusive from accidental skull fractures. Thus, complexity of fracture, increased length of fracture, crossing of suture lines, and separation of the bony fragments have been suggested as characteristic of abusive fractures. To say that such fractures are always abusive is wrong and unwarranted; however, if such features are present, the proffered history should reflect the higher energies needed to sustain this sort of fracture. Such explanatory features include the velocity or acceleration of impact, as in a motor vehicle injury, the height of a fall, and whether any other forces increased the velocity or acceleration of a fall beyond the effect of gravity, or the presence of any pathology leading to decreased strength of the bone. Thus, a fall from couch or bed height would not be an adequate explanation for such an injury in an otherwise well child. The minimal height necessary for a simple fall to cause such a lesion has not been established, although falls of less than 30 in. do not appear to do so. Certainly any initial velocity of the child before the fall will increase the force of impact, and thus the likelihood of high-energy pathology.

HEAD INJURY

In 1946, Caffey's initial report of the association of multiple fractures with chronic subdural hematomas in infants, initiated the modern era of recognition of child abuse. Although Caffey did not recognize at the time that these injuries were inflicted, he did come to this conclusion shortly afterward. Since that time, inflicted intracranial injury has continued to haunt those who care for young children, since this is responsible for at least 50 percent of the deaths of children caused by nonaccidental trauma, and is also the source of the most severe sequelae of abuse. Over the succeeding years, an attempt has been made to understand the pathogenesis of inflicted head injury, an attempt that has been made more difficult by the predominant absence of reliable histories of the event.

Whiplash-Shake Injury

In the 1970s Guthkelch and Caffey independently came to the conclusion that subdural hematoma, interhemispheric subarachnoid hemorrhage, and occasional cerebral contusions seen in abused children were the result of a whiplash injury to the brain. They compared these injuries with those seen in car accidents, which were known to be caused by acceleration-deceleration phenomena rather than by direct impact. This modality was best explained by Klein, in the first edition of this text (Fig. 6-7). In this model, the shaking of the body produced differential motion between the skull and the intracranial structures, owing to rotation of the head on the neck. This differential motion further caused stretching and tearing of the bridging vessels, and also introduced the possibility of cerebral contusion or laceration. This could be caused by shearing within the brain substance itself and by laceration against the irregularities of the internal aspect of the skull, as the brain moved within the compartment. This model appeared to be consistent with the early work done in primates during studies of experimental vehicular injury. In addition, it offered a believable alternative to the frequently proferred history, that the injuries were the result of spontaneous falls from a couch or bed. Corroborating evidence that falls of less than 30 in. were inadequate to explain intracranial injuries, was generated from the clinical experience of Helfer et al. and was later substantiated by Billmire and Myers. The almost uni-

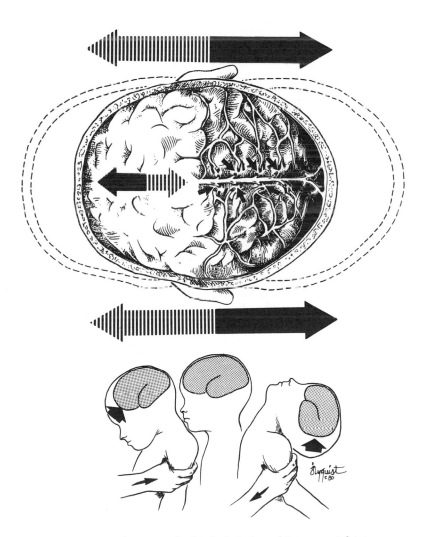

Fig. 6-7. Mechanism of whiplash-induced intracranial injury.

versal acceptance of this model led to the frequent use of the term *whiplash-shaken infant* or *shaken baby* as a description both of the intracranial injuries and the frequently associated fractures of the ribs and metaphyses.

There were some problems with the proposed model. Of the 27 infants originally described by Caffey, 6 had no intracranial injuries, and 15 were the victims of a single infant home nurse, whose explanation of shaking and vigorous burping was taken at face value. Of the remaining six children, two demonstrated impact injuries to the head: one was shaken and beaten to death with a stick, and the other had a scalp bruise, apparently incurred when her head struck the crib during a shaking episode. Over the next decade, it became increasingly clear that scalp and subgaleal hemorrhages were common associated findings in children who had died of abusive head trauma, and that skull fractures, usually linear, were not uncommon. In a study by Hahn et al. of 77 consecutive children seen over a 10-year period, who suffered abusive head injuries ranging from concussion to irreversible injury and death, only 8 percent were believed to have been caused by shaking. Forty-eight percent were caused by direct trauma to the face and head, and a further 35 percent were the result of dropping, throwing, or falling. The remaining children apparently suffered impact trauma that was not directed at the head. Fifty percent had skull fractures, mostly parietal linear fractures. The intracranial injuries noted were the ones typically described in the literature (i.e., 30 subdural hematomas [22 bilateral], 23 cerebral contusions, and 7 that were concussion only). The relatively rare incidence of shaking as an etiology in this carefully studied large group, combined with the common detection of occult impact injury in fatal cases of abuse, raised questions about the biomechanics of inflicted head injury.

The whiplash model relied on the early work of Ommaya and Gennarelli, as well as Holbourn's ground-breaking paper, for its theoretic foundation. To evaluate the extrapolations made from these data, it is necessary to review them, as well as the findings of later research.

Holbourn, a research physicist in the Department of Surgery at Oxford, published the first theoretic evaluation of the mechanics of head injuries in 1943. His conclusions were based on several principles, which are summarized below.

1. The brain has comparatively uniform density. Nerve tissue, blood, and cerebrospinal fluid all approximate the density of water.
2. The brain is incompressible to approximately the same degree as water. A reduction in volume of 50 percent would require a surrounding pressure of 10,000 tons per square inch.
3. The brain has a small modulus of rigidity, that is it changes shape easily in response to applied force.
4. The rigidity of the skull is much greater than that of the brain.
5. The shape of the skull and brain are important to the development of pathology from an injury.
6. In the case of a substance with a large modulus of incompressibility compared with the modulus of rigidity, the pulling apart of constituent particles is proportional to shear strain. A major corollary to this conclusion is that compression and tensile strains do not produce appreciable injury.

The first conclusion that can be drawn from these six principles is that brain injury is predominantly because of shearing forces, and that an analysis of shear strains generated by various sorts of injury will provide a predictive model for the resulting pathology. Holbourn further divided injuries into those resulting from skull distortion, with or without fracture, and those arising from rotational injury.

Skull Distortion Injury

Skull distortion, in injuries without fracture, causes shear strains that are mainly confined to the region close to the blow. Although waves of compression and tension are generated, these are not causes of injury. If the skull fractures, shear strains are still maximal in the immediate neighborhood of the injury. However, the larger distortion may produce extradural, subdural, and subarachnoid bleeding if the fracture line crosses the path of a relatively large vessel. This is especially true in young children, in whom the dura is relatively firmly attached to the inner aspect of the skull.

Rotational Injuries

Rotational injuries caused by blows to the head were also considered. A distinction was made between blows of long duration (>0.2 seconds) and blows of short duration (<0.002 seconds), based on a mechanical difference in the generation of shearing forces and the viscoelastic properties of the brain. In blows of long duration, the shear strain is proportional to the force alone, and hence, proportional to the acceleration of the head; it is independent of the duration of impact. In blows of short duration, the shear strain is proportional to the force multiplied by its time of action, and hence is proportional to the velocity, rather than the acceleration, of the head after the impact. Figure 6-8 demonstrates the shear strains generated by rotational injury in a gelatin model caused by blows of long duration in various planes, corresponding to different sites of impact. Holbourn also explained the appearance of subdural and subarachnoid hemorrhages from this sort of injury by the sliding of pia and arachnoid relative to the dura (which is fixed to the skull, especially in infants) secondary to the generated rotation.

While Holbourn provided the first basis for analysis of head injuries secondary to impact phenomena of the head, he did not analyze the results of pure accelerative forces. His work was extended by Ommaya who developed an experimental model for studying whiplash injuries generated in motor vehicle accidents. This early model established certain important principles. First, rotational injury without direct impact to the head could cause significant injury to the brain, and did so in the distribution suggested by Holbourn's analysis, which also mimics the regions of injury seen in abused infants; this was the principal basis of the "whiplash-shaken infant" model. Further, Ommaya found that there were no pathologic results of the injury in animals that did not sustain a concussion. Finally, he verified that the degree of acceleration necessary to cause a given injury was related to the duration of impact, when impacts lasted between 3 and 13 msec. This corroborated many of Holbourn's conclusions, including that short duration impacts (now extended to 0.013 seconds) produce effects dependent on velocity change, not accelerational change alone. Furthermore, based on accelerational and velocity requirements for concussive and pathologic change in several sizes of experimental primates, Ommaya postulated that the level of injurious rotational acceleration is inversely proportional to the two-thirds power of the mass of the brain. This provided a means of extrapolation of these results to humans, and in our specific area of interest, to infants.

Further work, principally done by Ommaya, Gennarelli, Thibeault, and their associates, established some other important features relative to Holbourn's

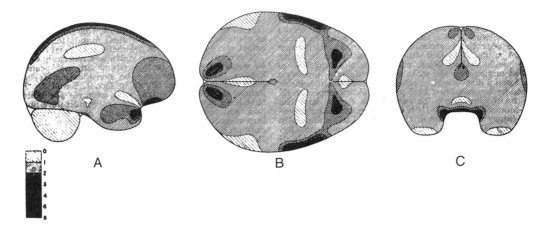

Fig. 6-8. Distribution of shear strains in a gelatinous medium with angular acceleration. (**A**) Intensity of the shear-strains resulting from a forwards rotation caused by a blow on the occiput. (**B**) Intensity of the shear-strains as a result of a rotation in the horizontal plane caused by a blow near the upper jaw or temples. (**C**) Intensity of the shear-strains resulting from a rotation in the coronal plane caused by a blow above the ear. Key—Scale of maximum shear-strain (=distortion) in arbitrary units of shear. The units differ in the three diagrams. (Adapted from Holburn,[13] with permission.)

analysis. First, these investigators confirmed that translation alone did not produce either concussion or the significant injuries seen with whiplash or rotational injury. They further confirmed the durational dependence of short duration pulses. However, they noted, in a manner unexplained by Holbourn's model, that the threshold for rotational velocity varied by a factor of two, depending on whether the injury was purely whiplash (i.e., noncontact) or generated by direct impact. In other words, higher rotational velocities were required to produce injuries when no impact had taken place.

In 1987, Duhaime, in association with Gennarelli, Thibeault, and others, published a provoking paper. In the paper, they first reviewed 48 cases of "shaken babies" seen in an 8-year span for evidence of impact injury, and then discussed their findings of the accelerations generated by shaking an appropriately weight distributed and proportioned in-

fant model, and compared these with expected accelerations and velocities necessary to produce concussion, subdural hematoma, and diffuse axonal injuries, all integral parts of the "shaken baby" syndrome.

Sixty-three percent (30 patients) had physical evidence of blunt impact to the head, as well as findings of any or all of retinal hemorrhage, subdural hematoma, subarachnoid hemorrhage, interhemispheric blood, or bilateral chronic subdural effusions. An additional six (13 percent) had evidence of blunt extracranial trauma associated with their intracranial findings. Thus, only 24 percent showed no physical evidence of a blow. The best histories obtained for 40 of these cases (no reliable history was obtained in 8), showed that only 1 was apparently caused by shaking unassociated with other trauma. Analysis of the 13 fatal cases disclosed that all had evidence of blunt cranial trauma, although this was found only on autopsy in 7 of the 13. This portion of the paper correlated well with other recent clinical and forensic studies.

In the experimental segment of the paper, models approximating the size, weight, and density of a 1-month-old infant were constructed. Three varieties of necks were devised and tested, and the models were studied with and without "skull." Accelerometers were implanted in the head and attached to the vertex in a coronal plane. Each model was tested at least 20 times, with vigorous shaking, by both male and female adults, followed by impacting of the occiput against a metal bar or padded surface. The principal finding is summarized in Figure 6-

9. Both the tangential and angular accelerations were much higher in the impacts than in the shakings. Although there was a statistically significant difference in accelerations dependent on the structure of the model's neck, this difference was not great enough to reach the levels of acceleration required to produce concussion, subdural hematoma, or diffuse axonal injury, based on estimates derived from the conversion equation proposed by Ommaya. While this conversion equation has not been verified for infants, it has been extensively verified in multiple species of nonhuman primates, and some verification for adult humans has been provided from the results of motor vehi-

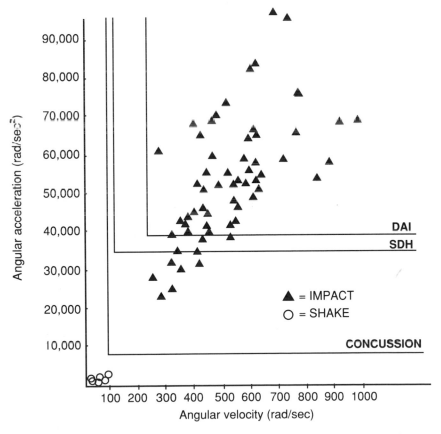

Fig. 6-9. Accelerative and velocity effects of shaking and impact in infant models. (From Duhaime et al.,[7] with permission.)

cle accidents as well. All of the impacts created angular accelerations sufficient to cause concussion, and most were severe enough to cause subdural hemorrhage and diffuse axonal injury. There were accelerational differences related to metal versus padded bar, but this did not bring the "soft" impacts out of the pathologic range. This last observation may help explain why so many abusive adults admit to severe shaking of infants, and why soft tissue injuries to the head may not be very evident. Is it reasonable to assume that a frustrated, angry adult, who has just been aggressively shaking a child will subsequently lay that child down gently in the crib? Or is it more reasonable to assume that the child will be thrown against a soft crib mattress, bed, carpeted floor or wall? Impact against a yielding surface will not alter the force delivered to the intracranial structures but will decrease the damage done to superficial soft tissues, just as a boxer may suffer a knockout from a blow delivered by a gloved hand, without any apparent facial bruise.

While it cannot be said conclusively that shaking unaccompanied by impact cannot produce any or all of the phenomena commonly described as "shaken baby syndrome," it is now beginning to appear that this modality of injury is less likely to cause abusive head injuries than was previously thought. The term *shaken baby* or *whiplash-shaken infant* should be used with caution in referring to such injuries. Certainly, no child who shows even "minor" evidence of impact injury, such as superficial or subgaleal ecchymosis, should be called a shaken baby.

BURNS

Burns represent another important segment of the spectrum of inflicted trauma in childhood; these fall into the categor-

ies of immersion, splash, contact, and flame burns. Flash burns are usually accidental.

The etiology of contact burns is usually self-evident. The burn takes the shape of the object, and usually the temperature of the object clearly exceeds the resistance of the skin to heat injury. Burns resulting from contact with hot liquids may be more problematic, however, as it is not always clear just how hot the fluid must be to cause a burn of given severity, or how long such a fluid must be in contact with the skin.

The basic science literature provides some help, although these issues cannot be completely resolved. For obvious reasons, the literature is not deluged with studies showing the effect of scalding fluids on the human body; there are no such studies in children, thankfully. Such a study was done on adult human volunteers, however, and gives us the only data from which we may draw conclusions. The nature of the inducement given to the volunteers in this study is not described, nor is the population from which they were drawn; it is likely that this research would not satisfy the informed consent requirements of modern institutional review boards, and thus, rightly, is extremely unlikely to be verified by repetition.

In this study, a technique was used that exposed the skin for a variable length of time to fluids (water or oil) that were continuously and reliably maintained at a given temperature. Temperatures ranged from 44°C to 60°C (111.2°F to 140°F). The time of exposure varied from 3 seconds to 6 hours.

The results were interesting. Third-degree burns were produced at all temperatures within the experimental range, although such burns did not occur at 44°C (111.2°F) until 6 hours of continuous exposure had been reached. At or below 47°C (116.6°F), irreversible changes ul-

Table 6-1. Critical Times for Full Thickness Water Burns

Water Temperature °C (°F)	Time for Transepidermal Burn
48.9 (120)	9 min 30 s
51.7 (125)	4 min
54.4 (130)	30 s
57.2 (135)	10 s
60.0 (140)	5 s

timately appeared without prior sensations of pain; at this temperature, first-degree burns required a minimum of 20 minutes of continual exposure, higher degrees of burn were not reached until 25 to 40 minutes. At or above 48°C (118.4°F), discomfort appeared before the onset of irreversible burns. The critical times for complete epidermal necrosis at temperatures in the typical household range of hot water are listed in Table 6-1.

The results from these experiments were compared with studies done on porcine skin by the same researchers. The results correlated closely, and closely fit a logarithmic curve relating time of exposure and fluid temperature. Assuming that the correlation persisted above 60°C (140°F), the critical exposure period for fluids of 70°C (158°F) was calculated at 1 second; however, this may be an overestimate.

It would be wrong to use these figures in a dogmatic fashion, as it is not clear that juvenile skin is as resistant as adult skin to transepidermal burning. Indeed, experience with transcutaneous monitors has taught us that extremely young infants may experience second-degree burns at lower temperatures than older children or adults. However, it does give us a guide that will, at least, provide an estimate of the range of time necessary for a given injury. The current move to set 120°F (48.9°C) as the maximum setting for

water heaters may make this discussion obsolete. Even the angriest caretaker is unlikely to restrain a kicking, screaming child for the 9 or more minutes apparently necessary to cause a significant burn at this temperature. In addition, water at the tap tends to decrease in temperature after a relatively brief interval, and surface temperature of the water also decreases relatively rapidly; this would likely extend the time needed for such an injury, even if at higher temperatures the required time of exposure for children is some fraction of the adult figure.

In immersion burns, the fluid is usually of approximately uniform temperature, but may be somewhat cooler at the surface. Burn depth is inversely related to the relative thickness of the skin, and so the plantar surfaces are usually less severely affected.

In splash or splatter burns, the depth of burn is likely to be greatest at the site closest to the origin of the fluid, as water, and water-based liquids, such as tea or coffee, cool rapidly as they move through the air. This may help distinguish accidental from inflicted splash burns. This is less of a factor when hot oil is the scalding agent, as the higher temperatures attained by oil do not permit the difference in fluid temperature to become significant in relation to susceptibility of the skin to injury.

SUGGESTED READINGS

1. Billmire ME, Myers PA: Serious head injury in infants: accident or abuse? Pediatrics 75:340, 1985
2. Caffey J: Multiple fractures in the long bones of infants suffering from chronic subdural hematoma. AJR Am J Roentgenol 56:163, 1946
3. Caffey J: On the theory and practice of shaking infants: its potential residual ef-

fects of permanent brain damage and mental retardation. Am J Dis Child 124:161, 1972

4. Cochran GVB: A Primer of Orthopaedic Biomechanics. Churchill Livingstone, New York, 1982

5. Currey JD: The mechanical properties of bone. Clin Orthop 73:210, 1970

6. Currey JD, Butler G: The mechanical properties of bone tissue in children. J Bone Joint Surg 57A:810, 1975

7. Duhaime AC, Gennarelli TK, Thibault LE et al: The shaken baby syndrome: a clinical, pathological and biomechanical study. J Neurosurg 66:409, 1987

8. Feldman KW, Brewer DK: Child abuse, cardiopulmonary resuscitation and rib fractures. Pediatrics 73:339, 1984

9. Gennarelli TK: Clinical and experimental head injury. p. 103. In Aldman B, Chapon A (eds): The Biomechanics of Impact Trauma. Elsevier Science Publishers, Amsterdam, 1984

10. Guthkelch AN: Infantile subdural haematoma and its relationship to whiplash injuries. Br Med J 2:430, 1971

11. Hahn YS, Raimondi AJ, McLone DG et al: Traumatic mechanisms of head injury in child abuse. Child Brain 10:229, 1983

12. Helfer RE, Slovis TL, Black M: Injuries resulting when small children fall out of bed. Pediatrics 60:533, 1977

13. Holbourn AHS: Mechanics of head injuries. Lancet 2:438, 1943

14. King RE: Fractures of the shafts of the radius and ulna. p. 301. In Rockwood CA, Wilkins KE, King RE (eds): Fractures in Children. JB Lippincott, Philadelphia, 1984

15. Klein DM: Central nervous system injuries. p. 73. In Ellerstein NS (ed): Child Abuse and Neglect: A Medical Reference. 1st Ed. Churchill Livingstone, New York, 1981

16. Kleinman PK, Marks SC, Adams VI et al: Factors affecting the visualization of posterior rib fractures in abused infants. AJR Am J Roentgenol 150:635, 1987

17. Kleinman PK, Marks SC, Blackbourne B: The metaphyseal lesion in abused infants: a radiologic-histopathologic study. AJR Am J Roentgenol 146:895, 1986

18. Moritz AR, Henriques FC: Studies of thermal injury: II. The relative importance of time and surface temperature in the causation of cutaneous burns. Lancet 2:695, 1947

19. Ogden JA: The uniqueness of growing bones. p. 1. In Rockwood CA, Wilkins KE, King RE (eds): Fractures in Children. JB Lippincott, Philadelphia, 1984

20. Ommaya AK: The head: kinematics and brain injury mechanisms. p. 117. In Aldman B, Chapon A (eds): The Biomechanics of Impact Trauma. Elsevier Science Publishers, Amsterdam, 1984

21. Ommaya AK, Faas F, Yarnell P: Whiplash injury and brain damage: an experimental study. JAMA 204:285, 1968

7

Multidisciplinary Approach to Child Protection

E. Peter Wilson

Individual physicians and other health care practitioners are vital to the accurate diagnosis and treatment of the physical and mental disorders resulting from child abuse and neglect. As active members of a child protection team, representing an array of professional disciplines, associations, and agencies, practitioners can profoundly influence the decision-making and subsequent actions that affect the health and welfare of children and their families.

It is estimated that there are now about 1000 teams in the United States. These include a variety of teams established by (1) state, county, and city law enforcement agencies and departments of health and human services; (2) private, nonprofit children, youth, and family service agencies; (3) private and university-affiliated hospitals; (4) military installations; and (5) community and professional child advocates.

However, in many areas of the United States, traditional approaches to funding and delivering services for the prevention and treatment of child abuse result in individuals and organizations continuing to act autonomously. These individuals include health and human services practitioners, law enforcement officers, judges,

lawyers, legislators, creative writers, and media reporters. Organizations that act independently include hospitals, schools, courts, and mental health and child welfare agencies. Although public awareness has been greatly increased by their efforts, there is little evidence that the prevalence of child abuse has been significantly reduced. In these communities, the resources for child abuse prevention, intervention, consultation, evaluation, and research remain very limited.

On the other hand, many practitioners now believe that the decisions, actions, and recommendations of effective multidisciplinary and interagency teams cannot only help the child protective agency and family court prevent the return of children to unsafe homes, but can also reduce the risk of repeated maltreatment of children remaining at home. Members of these teams can help identify barriers to service delivery, and facilitate and expedite treatment of children and their families. Teams, as well as individual members, can train new practitioners, educate the general public, and prevent or delay practitioner turnover owing to "burn-out." Finally, teams can promote new legislation and resources, and support evaluative and research activities.

HISTORY

Physician awareness of the prevalence, causes, and consequences of child maltreatment began in France with the publications of Adolphe Toulmouche, Ambroise Tardieu, and other forensic pathologists in the mid-19th century. Since then, many concerned physicians and other health care practitioners have contributed to current knowledge. As individuals, some of these practitioners have made heroic attempts to eradicate child abuse in their communities. These efforts were almost always unsuccessful, and the resulting intense frustration caused many practitioners to leave the field permanently. However, a few persistent practitioners, together with their colleagues in other disciplines, have developed and promoted a variety of collaborative approaches.

Multidisciplinary and interagency efforts to eradicate child abuse often began with the formation of child protection taskforces and ad hoc committees, most of which disbanded after completing their assigned tasks. Many child protection pilot or demonstration projects were initiated with limited-term public or private funding during the past three decades, but most have ended abruptly when the funding ceased. On the other hand, some taskforces and pilot projects became standing committees or multidisciplinary child protection teams (also known as MDTs).

Some committees and teams have developed multidisciplinary or interagency "centers," which are community-based or facility-based, or are nonprofit corporations. These centers attempt to coordinate, complement, or supplement legislatively mandated services delivered by state or county child protective service and legal agencies. Most of the centers are local or regional, with a variety of names: for example, Child Protection (San Diego, California); Children's Advocacy (Philadelphia, Pennsylvania); Parental Stress (Pittsburgh, Pennsylvania); and Supportive Child Adult Network (SCAN) (Philadelphia, Pennsylvania).

Some multidisciplinary centers are national, including the C. Henry Kempe National Center for the Prevention and Treatment of Child Abuse and Neglect (Denver, Colorado); National Children's Advocacy Center (Huntsville, Alabama); National Center for Child Abuse and Neglect (Washington, DC); and National Committee for the Prevention of Child Abuse and Neglect (Chicago, Illinois). Since 1976, the International Society for Prevention of Child Abuse and Neglect has sponsored an International Congress on Child Abuse and Neglect every 2 years, and has published a quarterly international journal (*Child Abuse and Neglect*).

Factors that have fostered the survival and expansion of multidisciplinary child protective teams, programs, centers, and corporations include: members (board, staff, and volunteer) who remain committed and contributory over many years; resources that are diversified; and services that are legislatively mandated, purchased under contractual agreements, reimbursed adequately by third parties, or sustained by community fund-raising efforts.

MULTIDISCIPLINARY CHILD PROTECTION TEAMS

The most durable multidisciplinary organizations are child protection teams, some of which have survived for decades. The earliest known facility-based teams were formed around 1958 at university-affiliated hospitals in Pittsburgh, Pennsylvania (Elizabeth Elmer, MSS, Children's Hospital); in Los Angeles, California (Helen Boardman, MSW, Children's Hospital); and in Denver, Colorado (C. Henry Kempe, Department of Pediatrics, University of Colorado Medical Center). These teams began with two or three members (generally a nurse, a pediatrician, and a medical social worker). Since then, teams have expanded to include persons representing one or more of a variety of professional disciplines or agencies.

The first child protection laws to include multidisciplinary teams were enacted by the Colorado and Pennsylvania legislatures in 1975. Colorado's Child Abuse Reporting Act mandated that in the year following the receipt by a county of 50 or more reports during the calendar year, a multidisciplinary team will be established. Pennsylvania's Child Protective Services Law (P.L. 438, Act No. 124, 11/26/75), required that each county "shall make available among its services for the prevention and treatment of child abuse multidisciplinary teams."

Since 1975, a majority of states have created, recognized, or authorized these teams. A comprehensive book, *The Child Protection Team Handbook*, describing the types, structures, functions, characteristics, and development of these teams was published in 1978 and in 1987 was followed by *The New Child Protection Handbook*.

In a recent survey of all 50 states, 27 indicated that limited federal, state, county, third-party, or private funding was available for developing and maintaining multidisciplinary child protection teams. A survey of teams indicated that 68 percent received funding support from some source. The average length of team existence was 4.3 years.

Teams may be formal (sanctioned by legislation of a governing authority) or informal (e.g., ad hoc group of child advocates). Functionally, they may be action-oriented, consultative, educational, or evaluative. In terms of structure, they may be national organizations that are facility- or community-based. A facility-based team is a group of persons, representing multiple professional disciplines or agencies, who meet periodically to assist individuals and agency representatives with planning, implementing, or reviewing services being delivered on behalf of maltreated children and their families. A community-based team is a group of persons, representing multiple community organizations and constituencies, who meet periodically to assist and monitor individuals and agencies in their efforts to improve the effectiveness and efficiency of services intended to protect children from abuse, neglect, or exploitation.

Multidisciplinary child protection teams usually operate in the context of legislated statutes and regulations. The determination of whether or not child abuse has occurred, and the protection of children from further abuse, remains the primary responsibility of state or county law enforcement or children and youth agencies. The more detailed statutes and regulations describe when teams will be established; the agency or individual that will create and host the team; and the powers, limitations, duties, and protections of the team, of team members, and of their agencies.

Teams may consist of appointees designated by statute, regulation, or governing authorities only (regulatory teams); consultants only (consultation teams); educators only (teaching teams); practitioners only (treatment teams); or any combination of appointees, practitioners, consultants, educators, case managers, paraprofessionals, and advocates for parents and children. Although most teams are generic and will accept all forms of child maltreatment, some teams specialize in child sexual abuse, institutional abuse, medicolegal issues, and so forth.

Multidisciplinary Child Protection Teams

Teams May Include as Members (In Alphabetical Order)

Administrators or executives of public or private agencies

Attorneys representing the state, county, parents, children, etc.

Educators (school teachers, counselors, etc.)

Forensic pathologists, dentists, etc.

Law enforcement officers (police, military, probation officers, etc.)

Lay therapists (parent aides, family workers, etc.)

Medical practitioners (pediatricians, radiologists, etc.)

Mental health practitioners (psychiatrists, psychologists, etc.)

Nurses (hospital, public health, school, home visiting, etc.)

Social workers (child protective, medical, psychiatric, etc.)

Some teams will include children or their alleged or adjudicated perpetrators, together with their community or legal advocates, but it is unusual for consultation and treatment teams to admit to their meetings government representatives or the media.

As a team member, a physician, nurse, or other health care practitioner can interpret medical terminology and abbreviations, explain diagnostic and thera-

peutic procedures, describe benefits and risks of alternative interventions, and discuss adverse effects of treatments. The practitioner can explain how the medical condition will affect the child and the family, and offer to facilitate or expedite needed health care services.

Together with other team members, the health care practitioner may not only contribute to the holistic diagnosis and treatment of children and families, but also help redefine problems or suggest alternative approaches or resources. Practitioners who provide support to other team members who are feeling frustrated, devastated, or overwhelmed may enable these members to continue to be effective practitioners and to persuade them to remain in the field.

As educators, practitioners may participate in the training of mandated reporters of suspected child abuse, service providers, and students, and help parents and the public understand how to prevent and remediate child abuse. As consultants, practitioners can assist the child protective service worker during the development, implementation, and review of service contracts between the parents and the court or child protective service agency. By virtue of their scientific training, health care practitioners can initiate or participate in child abuse research and evaluation activities.

Practitioners can initiate or participate in planning and implementing community action, both to remove obstacles to effective service delivery, and to increase the variety, availability, and accessibility of resources to parents and children. By invitation, practitioners can review and help oversee the implementation of state or county statutes, regulations, policies, and procedures. As respected members of their community and professional associations, they can provide leadership and advocacy for improvements in resources for parents and children by serving on governmental and voluntary task forces and committees.

TEAM EFFECTIVENESS

Teams are not a substitute for the diagnostic, treatment, educational, and research efforts of individual practitioners. The additional expenditures of compensated time and effort require that teams be productive and effective. A team is more likely to be successful when it develops and adheres to its own guidelines (see sample below).

Several factors may reduce team productivity and effectiveness, and eventually lead to progressive attrition of team members and demise of the team. A team lacking the sanction and resources provided by the parent organization (including its board, executive officers, administrators, and supervisors) will not survive indefinitely. The attendance at team meetings of persons representing agencies legally responsible for protecting the child is critical. Repeated rejection of the recommendations made by the team to the court or child protective agency will soon discourage team members.

Frequent absences or substitutions of team members do not permit a team to develop cohesiveness. A member's administrator or supervisor may prohibit attendance at a team meeting for any of a number of reasons, including the perception that the team is unproductive, fear of embarrassment or possible litigation, and nonreimbursement of the team's or member's expenses.

One or more members may be unaware of the team's purpose, goals, operations, or guidelines. Members may be unprepared, they may fear disclosure, or they may be insecure or excessively dependent and fear disapproval from peers or supervisors.

Ongoing, unresolved conflict between team members may discourage attendance or divert energy from team productivity. An ineffective team leader may allow time and effort to be wasted. A team member may be autonomous or overly confident (a "loner"); competitive with, or hostile towards, one or more team members; or manipulated by the alleged child abuse perpetrators and their supporters.

GUIDELINES FOR EFFECTIVE TEAM FUNCTIONING

Teams will (1) have a written purpose, goals, policies, procedures, and guidelines; (2) strive for consensus but acknowledge dissent; (3) be nonthreatening and supportive of its members; (4) avoid hierarchical structures (monarchy, oligarchy, etc.) and anarchy; (5) develop plans or recommendations that will include objectives (preferably measurable and attainable within a given time frame) and state who will be accountable; and (6) approve the attendance of guests and visitors.

Team members will (1) have decision-making power; (2) consider themselves peers; (3) consider all case information confidential; (4) attend meetings regularly and keep substitutes to a minimum; and (5) have the characteristics of competence, compassion, commitment, assertiveness, openness, warmth, and a sense of humor.

The team moderator will (1) prepare a written agenda, with time limits, in collaboration with team members; (2) arrange for the orientation of new team members; (3) encourage members with detailed information to share to prepare summaries and visual aids (e.g., genograms, photographs, radiographs); (4) see that agendas and summaries are distributed in advance of the meeting; (5) schedule meetings regularly, preferably weekly, early in the day, and for a maximum of 2 hours; (6) find a meeting place that is convenient and free from interruptions; (7) start and end meetings on time; (8) defer case presentation when critical information is not available; and (9) distribute team recommendations to all members.

SUMMARY

In summary, there are opportunities in most communities for health care practitioners to participate as members of multidisciplinary child protection teams, committees, and taskforces; to help create teams where none exist; and to volunteer

time or contribute donations to existing programs or centers that operate or support these teams.

SUGGESTED READINGS

1. Bureau of Child Welfare, Pennsylvania Department of Public Welfare: Child Abuse Model Standards and Guidelines for Multidisciplinary Teams, 1977
2. Hochstadt, NJ, Harwicke NJ: How effective is the multidisciplinary approach? A follow-up study. Child Abuse Negl 9:362, 1985
3. Masson JM: The Assault on Truth. Penguin Books, New York, 1985
4. Bross DC, Krugman RD, Lenherr MR et al: The New Child Protection Team Handbook. Garland Publishing, New York, 1988
5. Sgroi S: Handbook of Clinical Intervention in Child Sexual Abuse. Lexington Books, Lexington, MA, 1982

8

Child Abuse:
An Historical Perspective

Stephen Lazoritz

> And Cain talked with Abel his brother: and it came to pass, when they were in the field, that Cain rose up against his brother, and slew him.
>
> (Genesis 4:8)

From the time of this early description of brotherly discord, the thread of violence within the family has been woven into the fabric of our culture. All too often, this violence has been directed toward children. The extent of this violence, which has included murder, torture, and disfigurement, is astounding, not only in the numbers of children involved but also in that many of these brutal acts were sanctioned by the society in which they occurred.

The most frequent violent act performed against children throughout history has been infanticide (the killing of an infant). The act of infanticide has been responsible for more child deaths than any other single cause, with the possible exception of the Black Plague. The context in which infanticide occurred varied, and often met a need of the society in which it was performed.

Biblical descriptions of infanticide abound, in both the Old and New Testaments. To maintain control of the He-

brew population, the Pharoah "charged all his people, saying 'Every son that is born ye shall cast into the river, and every daughter ye shall save alive.'" (Exodus 1:22) Early in the New Testament another ruler, Herod "sent forth, and slew all the children that were in Bethlehem, and in all the coasts therof, from two years old and under . . ." (Matthew 2:16). Fearing the birth of the "King of the Jews," Herod sought to assure his death by killing all the children born in Bethlehem at the same time as Jesus.

Infanticide was an accepted feature of most ancient civilizations. In Carthage, infants were used as a sacrifice to their chief gods Baal and Tanit and several hundred infants were killed each year to appease these gods. In ancient Greece, deformed infants were killed in an effort to stem the passage of the deformity to future generations. Plato and Aristotle upheld this as a wise practice. In Sparta, defective infants were cast off Mount Taggetus at the discretion of the City officials. In Rome, the Laws of the Twelve Tables mandated the killing of defective infants.

Although countless early cultures practiced infanticide, it was not a custom limited to antiquity. The practice of killing female infants in China persisted into the 19th century, as did forms of infanticide in India and in parts of Europe. In the United States, this practice, under the guise of "baby farming," was common in the late 19th century among the impoverished inhabitants of the slums of New York City. Unwanted infants were "farmed out" to caretakers who would kill them or starve them to death.

Whether the reason is population control, appeasement of a god, weeding out defective genes, or just getting rid of an unwanted infant, infanticide demonstrated the absolute power that a parent had over the child: the power of life or death.

The belief that children were the property of the parents allowed for a gamut of brutality, exploitation, and mutilation to be perpetrated against them. Ancient Roman fathers began the practice of mutilating their children to make them more effective beggars; the practice resurfaced in the Middle Ages and again in the 17th century. Victor Hugo in his novel, *The Boy Who Laughed*, described a child whose face was mutilated surgically to appear to be continually smiling.

From ancient times through the Middle Ages, the children of the very poor were, as unwanted property, sold or abandoned. Unquestionably, the beatings that these superfluous children received were severe and regular.

The Industrial Revolution provided other avenues for the exploitation of children. The need for cheap industrial labor demanded new sources of workers, and children began their industrial careers at the age of five years. In miserable, cold, dirty surroundings, children were worked for 16 hours a day and were starved, beaten, and often chained to their machines to keep them from running away. These children often succumbed to occupational disease, malnutrition, exposure, or from the results of savage beatings.

One of the classic occupations of a young boy of the Industrial Revolution was that of chimney sweep, a world far from the joyous frolic of the sweeps in *Mary Poppins*. The young sweeps would spend hours naked in tight spaces, causing their bones to become deformed. One of the first recognized occupational malignancies, testicular cancer, resulted from exposure to coal tar, and this type of neoplasm was commonly referred to as *chimney sweep's disease*. Such exploitation occurred because of the widespread belief that the child was the property of the parents, to do with as they would.

In New York City during the 19th century, life was particularly harsh for children in poverty. Crowded into foul dwellings, farmed out, abandoned as infants, or sent to work in sweatshops, the children of the slums were abused in many ways. But out of the grimy slums of New York came the first glimmer of hope for the abused children of our country; a case of child abuse which, as Jacob Riis reported, "stirred the soul of a city, and roused the conscience of a world that had forgotten. . . ."

In December of 1873, Etta Wheeler, a missionary from St. Luke's Methodist Church who worked with the residents of the slums of New York, became aware of a child who was beaten, starved, and imprisoned by her stepparents. The child's name was Mary Ellen Wilson. Mary Ellen was abandoned as an infant and delegated to the infants' hospital on Randall's Island. While two-thirds of the infants received at that hospital died, Mary Ellen survived long enough to be released to the care of Mary and Thomas McCormack. Mr. McCormack, who claimed to be her father, died soon after, leaving Mary Ellen in the care of Mary McCormack Connolly and her new husband, Francis Connolly. No legal adoption had ever been made. It was in the Connolly home that the child was kept as a veritable prisoner and subjected to severe daily beatings with whips and other objects. The child was locked in a dark, unventilated room by day, and could only walk in the tiny yard of the tenement at night.

Mrs. Wheeler contacted the police and children's benevolent societies on behalf of Mary Ellen, but they were unable to help her. Because children were considered the property of their parents, the police and children's benevolent societies were unable to intervene. In desperation, Mrs. Wheeler approached a citizen who was renowned for aiding the helpless animals of the city, Henry Bergh. As the founder and president of the Society for the Prevention of Cruelty to Animals (SPCA), Bergh had considerable influence, and immediately verified the story of Mary Ellen and directed his attorney, Elbridge Gerry, to intervene. Bergh made it clear that he acted not as an officer of the SPCA, but by his "duty as a humane citizen." Through a loophole in the law, Gerry obtained a writ of habeas corpus to bring the child before the court.

The child's testimony in court recounted her suffering (Fig. 8-1A).

> My name is Mary Ellen. I don't know how old I am. My mother and father are both dead. I have had no shoes or stockings on this winter. I have never been allowed to go out of the rooms except in the night time . . . my bed at night is only a piece of carpet on the floor underneath a window. Mamma has been in the habit of whipping and beating me almost every day with a rawhide twisted whip. The whip always left black and blue marks on my body. The cut on my head was made by a pair of scissors in mamma's hand. I have never been kissed by mamma. Whenever she went out she locked me in the bedrooms. I do not want to go back to live with mamma because she beats me so.

Charges of assault were filed against Mrs. Connolly. She was convicted and sentenced to 1 year at hard labor, and was never to see Mary Ellen again. The fate of Mr. Connolly remains a mystery. Charges were never brought against him, and he was never heard from publicly.

Having been rescued by the court, Mary Ellen was placed briefly at the "Sheltering Arms," a home for troubled adolescents. This proved to be most unsuitable, and Etta Wheeler arranged for the child to be taken to the home of her own family in upstate New York. Eventually she was adopted by Mrs. Wheeler's sister and her husband, Elizabeth and Darius Spencer. Mary Ellen thrived in the loving environment of the Spencer home (Fig. 8-1B). At the age of 24, she married Louis Schutt and was a loving mother to two daughters, Etta, named for Etta Wheeler, and Florence.

The case of Mary Ellen received a great deal of public attention. There were daily press reports of the progress in the case, and court officials were flooded with requests to adopt the child. Increasingly, the question was asked of Henry Bergh, "could [there] now be a Society for the Prevention of Cruelty to Children?" On December 28, 1874 the first meeting of the Society for the Prevention of Cruelty to Children (SPCC) was held. As Bergh stated at that first meeting, "The slaves were first freed from their bondage; next came the emancipation of the brute creation, and next the emancipation of the little children was about to take place."

The founding of the SPCC soon led to the passage of legislation designed to protect children. One of the early efforts was in the area of child labor. Abraham Jacobi, recognized as the Father of American Pediatrics, founded the first department of Pediatrics in 1869. At that time the problems of the abused child were considered to be beyond the scope of medicine; however, Jacobi, as president of the New York

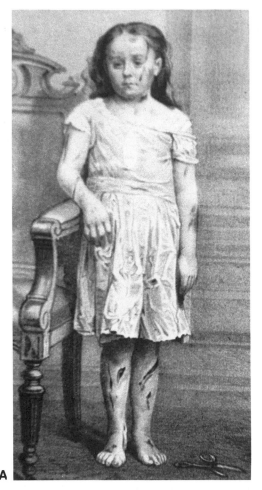 

Fig. 8-1. (**A**) Mary Ellen before her rescue, in her tattered clothing and bearing the wounds of her years of abuse. (**B**) Mary Ellen in new clothing, after being rescued and placed in a more caring environment.

Medical Society in 1882, formed a committee to work with the New York SPCC in the formulation of improved child labor laws.

Medicine's involvement with child abuse, except for the treatment of child abuse victims, was dormant until 1946. Dr. John Caffey, chief of Radiology at Babies Hospital in New York City, published a landmark article in the *American Journal of Roentgenology* entitled "Mul-

tiple fractures in the long bones of infants suffering from chronic subdural hematoma." He described six children who had a total of 23 skeletal fractures and concluded that the fractures were traumatic in origin, despite the fact that there was no history of injury. This article clearly stated that children with subdural hematomas had been traumatized, and a search for other evidence of trauma, specifically long bone fractures, should be made. However, Caffey stopped short of attributing the cause of this trauma to parental abuse.

Over the next 15 years, evidence that unexpected fractures were intentionally inflicted mounted as several other radiologists agreed with Caffey's belief that the fractures seen in these children were the result of trauma. In 1951, Dr. Frederick Silverman related these injuries to the caretakers of the injured children and stressed the importance of obtaining a precise history.

In 1955, in their article "Significance of skeletal lesions in infants resembling those of traumatic origin" in *Journal of the American Medical Association*, Drs. Paul V. Woolley Jr. and William A. Evans, asked "What is the nature of the injury-prone environment that predisposes to skeletal lesions without a history of violence . . . ?" They presented case after case of emotionally unstable parents and broken families and quite astutely pointed out that when the children who received these fractures were removed from their environments, the fractures healed and they developed no new lesions. The authors were quite clear in stating that the "undesirable vectors of force" that caused the fractures in many of these children were caused by their parents.

The undisputed landmark of medicine's involvement with child abuse came in 1962. Dr. Henry Kempe and his coworkers published the article "The battered child syndrome" in the July 7 issue of the *Journal of the American Medical Association*. This article established the groundwork for our present approach to the problem of child abuse and made clear the integral role of the physician in its management. No other single publication has had such a profound effect on the welfare of children. Our present system of mandated reporting of suspected child abuse and neglect can be directly traced to the efforts of Dr. Kempe. "The battered child" became at once a medical diagnosis and a part of America's conscience. Almost 30 years later, we continue to practice by these words of Henry Kempe: "Physicians have a duty and a responsibility to the child to require a full evaluation of the problem and to guarantee that no expected repetition of trauma will be permitted to occur."

Since Kempe's landmark article, awareness of the battered child by the medical profession has increased tremendously. All of the 50 states now have laws mandating the reporting of suspected child abuse and neglect. Medical journals and textbooks devoted to this area have been published, and organizations of medical professionals, such as the Section on Child Abuse and Neglect of the American Academy of Pediatrics, have been organized. Despite the progress we have made in our organized response to this problem, over 50,000 children have died at the hands of their parents, and more than 2.5 million more have been abused and neglected.

As staggering as these numbers are, cases of individual victims of child abuse more forcefully point out our failings. On November 2, 1987, in New York City, a six-year-old girl was found comatose, filthy, bruised, and naked in her parents' apartment, which was later described as a "cave." Her 18-month-old brother was tied around the waist to a playpen, clutching a sour bottle of milk. The girl, Lisa Steinberg, died of her head injuries 3 days later. Like the case of Mary Ellen, the "soul of the city" was stirred by press reports of a child brutally beaten by a parent.

Joel Steinberg, a lawyer, and Hedda Nussbaum, Lisa's "father" and "mother," were neither her natural nor adoptive parents. Joel Steinberg's knowledge of the loopholes of the law allowed him to obtain her at 7 days of age from a 19-year-old unwed mother. A legal adoption had never been made, as had been the case with Mary Ellen over 100 years before. Both children had fallen through the cracks of the systems designed to protect them.

Lisa's death again brought the battered child to the headlines and awakened previously unaware citizens to the horrors of the violence that is inflicted on children. Calls for reform of the child protection system and for additional resources dedicated to child protection were heard. No other single case in recent history had brought forth such an indignant response and demands for action.

Unfortunately, the history of child abuse continues to be in progress. In dealing with our own patients, our own "Lisas" and "Mary Ellens," we will become part of this history. It would serve us well not to look at the enormity of the problem before us, but rather to how far we have come. If "the past is prologue," we should look to the lessons taught to us by Etta Wheeler, Henry Bergh, John Caffey, Henry Kempe, and others who have contributed to the welfare of children. As Kempe so eloquently put it, "It is just not possible to worry about all of the children all of the time. There lies frustration and total inaction as well. For each of us there must be only one child at a time. . . ."

SUGGESTED READINGS

1. Caffey J: Multiple fractures in the long bones of infants suffering from chronic subdural hematoma. Am J Roentgenol 56:163, 1946
2. English P, Grossman H: Radiology and the history of child abuse. Pediatr Ann 12:12, 1983
3. Kempe CH, Silverman FN, Steele BF et al: The battered child syndrome. JAMA 181:17, 1962
4. Johnson J: What Lisa Knew. Putnam, New York, 1990
5. Lazoritz S: Whatever happened to Mary Ellen. Child Abuse Negl 14:143, 1990
6. Radbill SX: Children in a world of violence: a history of child abuse. p. 3. In Kempe CH, Helfer RD (eds): The Battered Child. 4th Ed. University of Chicago Press, Chicago, 1987
7. Stevens P, Eide M: The first chapter of children's rights. American Heritage 41:84, 1990
8. Williams G: Cruelty and kindness to children: documentary of a century, 1874–1974. p. 68. In Williams G, Money J (eds): Traumatic Abuse and Neglect of Children at Home. Johns Hopkins University Press, Baltimore, 1980
9. Zigler E, Hall N: Physical child abuse in America: past, present and future. p. 38. In Cicchetti D, Carlson V (eds): Child Maltreatment, Theory and Research on the Causes and Consequences of Child Abuse and Neglect. Cambridge University Press, New York, 1989

9

Skin and Soft Tissue Injuries

Allan E. Kornberg

Dermatologic manifestations of child abuse are important for several reasons. The skin is the most common site of involvement of physical abuse. It may be the first identifiable location for abuse before visceral, bony, and central nervous system injuries become apparent. Skin lesions are apparent to nonhealth professionals (e.g., day-care workers, teachers, social workers, friends, neighbors, and relatives) in a way that internal injuries are not.

Photographs of skin injuries are dramatic and easily interpreted evidence for serious trauma by judges and other court personnel. Although the judicial system can understand the importance of metaphyseal fractures, retinal hemorrhages, visceral injuries, and other abusive trauma with expert testimony guidance, medical photography of skin trauma gives immediate notice of the presence of child abuse.

As in other forms of child abuse, the history offered may not be consistent with the injuries observed. Sometimes the parent or other caretaker may state that the child caused the injury. However, the level of the child's developmental skills could not account for the type of injury seen. For example, 6-month-old babies do not climb up on surfaces, and a fall cannot be explained that way. Three-month-old infants do not crawl, as is sometimes given as an explanation for an injury from an area removed from the child's environment. Whenever a narrative given for an injury describes developmental skills too advanced for the child, a false history is furnished and nonaccidental trauma must be suspected.

A discussion of specific kinds of cutaneous manifestations of child abuse follows. Human bite marks are virtually pathognomonic of deliberate injury (see Ch. 14) and burns are frequently abusive in nature (see Ch. 10).

BRUISES

Ecchymoses, hematoma, and abrasion can be the result of accidental or intentional trauma. The aging of bruises is quite important in determining if the history offered corresponds with the injuries observed. Bruises in different stages of healing are frequently the result of repeated beatings. If a yellow-brown bruise is described as having occurred from an accident in the preceding 48 hours, the

91

Table 9-1. Dating and Description of Bruising

Age of Bruise	Findings
0–2 d	Swollen, tender
0–5 d	Red, blue, purple
5–7 d	Green
7–10 d	Yellow
10–14 d	Brown
2–4 w	Cleared

history does not conform with the physical examination, and child abuse must be considered. Table 9-1 summarizes the changes noted routinely as bruises evolve.

The location of bruises can be suggestive of intentional versus accidental trauma. Ellerstein wrote that injuries to the genitals, buttocks, cheeks, thighs, neck, and torso are more likely to be abusive than accidental (Fig. 9-1). Pascoe et al. described similar findings and also found that lacerations are more common in accidental than intentional trauma. Children tend to run into objects with the anterior surface of their bodies. Forehead, nasal, and periorbital bruises are quite common accidental injuries, especially in toddlers. Trauma to shins, knees, elbows, and hands are frequently accidental. A child old enough to stand, walk, and pivot, with injuries primarily to the back and forearms, suggests a defensive posture from an assault. Bruises to areas that are frequently accidentally traumatized may still be intentional in certain settings (Fig. 9-2).

Usually, a determination can be made as to whether or not bruises are likely to

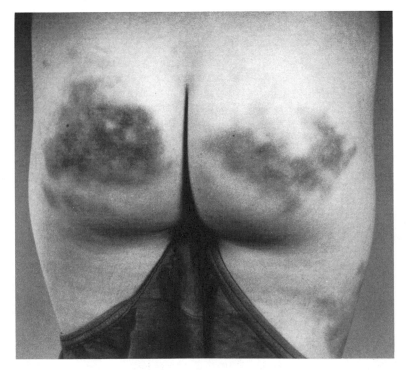

Fig. 9-1. Buttock bruising secondary to excessive corporal punishment.

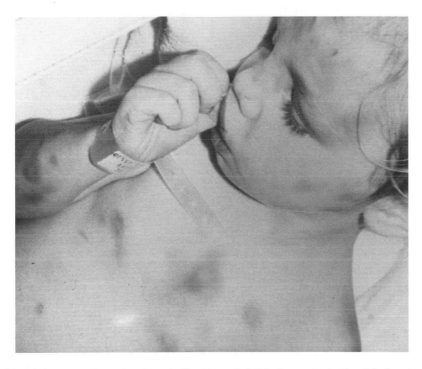

Fig. 9-2. Multiple amorphous bruises indicative of child abuse. Note the "defensive posture" bruises on the forearm.

be the result of accidental or intentional trauma, based on the history and physical examination, keeping in mind the child's developmental skills, the age of the bruises, and their location. Laboratory studies are occasionally helpful in deciding whether a bruised child has an underlying bleeding tendency, and may be useful in convincing a court of the absence of hematologic disease in a child abuse victim. With the exception of easily identifiable underlying lesions such as hemangioma, there are only four etiologies for bleeding into the skin, or other organs.

Causes of Skin Bleeding

The following are causes of skin bleeding: trauma—accidental or intentional; coagulation protein disorders; platelet disorders—quantitative and qualitative; and vasculitis.

A standard clotting screen will include platelet count, prothrombin time (PT), and partial thromboplastin time (PTT). A bleeding time may be requested to exclude platelet function disorders and von Willebrand's disease. There is no test, short of skin biopsy, to exclude vasculitis; biopsy is rarely indicated. The most common vasculitis in young children is Henoch-Schönlein purpura, which predominates in the lower extremities and buttocks, may have associated joint, abdominal, and renal findings, and can usually be diagnosed by inspection.

O'Hare and Eden evaluated 50 consecutive bruised children with suspected child abuse for bleeding disorders. Eight (16 percent) had abnormal studies. One of these children was not believed to be a victim of child abuse. She had an elevated PTT associated with a circulating inhibitor. Of the remaining seven, four had elevated PTT, two had von Willebrand's disease, and one was inappropriately given aspirin. The latter three patients were only identified because bleeding times were performed. Of great importance is that intentional trauma was proven in seven of these eight patients, demonstrating that child abuse and bleeding disorders are not mutually exclusive.

The bruises of children with clotting profile and platelet disorders predominate in those anatomic areas where normal children accidentally bruise. They simply have more and larger bruises. Bruises of abused children predominate in areas infrequently injured accidentally, such as the back. Facial petechiae occur either accidentally from severe coughing, sometimes associated with upper airway obstruction, or intentionally from attempted strangulation. A search for trauma to the neck should be conducted in this setting.

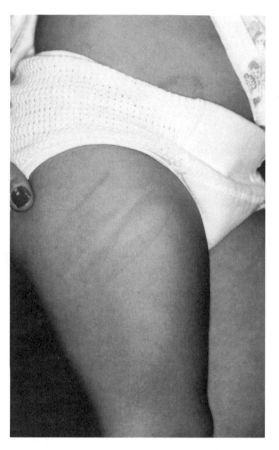

Fig. 9-3. Sharp borders and multiple lesions in the shape of a foreign object (in this case a belt) are pathognomonic for intentional trauma.

BRANDING/LOOP MARKS/ RESTRAINT MARKS

Sometimes belt buckles and other man-made objects are used as implements of abuse (Fig. 9-3). The value of obtaining well done, timely photographs cannot be overemphasized, as these can document assault with a weapon, and the injuries will fade into amorphous bruises rapidly. It is important that child protective workers or the police go to the home promptly once a bruise caused by a recognizable object is made, to secure that object as evidence. Bruises taking the shape of identifiable objects are rarely accidental.

Handprints are a particularly common recognizable bruise. Their size docu-

ments an injury caused by an adult (Fig. 9-4); they rapidly fade. When other injuries caused by restraint are noted, for example, immersion burns, handprints should be sought away from the primary injury. The force required to leave handprints is sometimes sufficient to break bone or traumatize viscera.

The most common bruise caused by a recognizable object is the loop mark (Fig. 9-5). Loop marks are caused by a pliant object such as an electric cord or rope being folded over and used to strike a

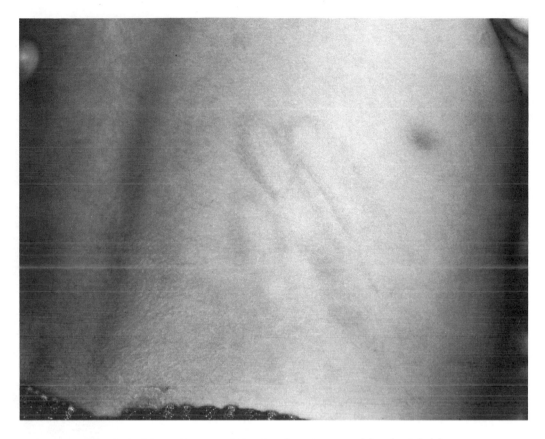

Fig. 9-4. Three fingers of this handprint are readily identifiable.

child. Loop marks are pathognomonic of child abuse. They are typically ecchymotic but may appear as lacerations, burns, or scars. These lesions are most frequent on the back, and are also commonly seen on the buttocks. Multiple linear bruises in these locations are indicative of the child being struck by a rigid object such as a stick.

Circumferential wounds about the extremities, typically ankles and wrist, are indicative of restraint (Fig. 9-6). These are caused by forcibly tying and shackling one or more of the child's limbs. Given the sharp borders of these injuries, without a transition zone between normal and damaged skin, an accidental mechanism of trauma is not plausible. Sharp borders

without transition zones are typical of many abusive bruises and burns. Restraint marks may occasionally be seen about the neck, in which case a life-threatening assault occurred (Fig. 9-7).

It is not generally necessary to obtain laboratory studies to exclude the possibility of a bleeding diathesis when evaluating a child with bruises in the configuration of a recognizable object. These lesions do not expose an underlying bleeding disorder, but demonstrate the existence of child abuse. Radiologic studies may be indicated if there is concern regarding fracture or visceral injury beneath the bruise. Skeletal survey, seeking coexisting occult fracture, is frequently appropriate in a child victimized by sub-

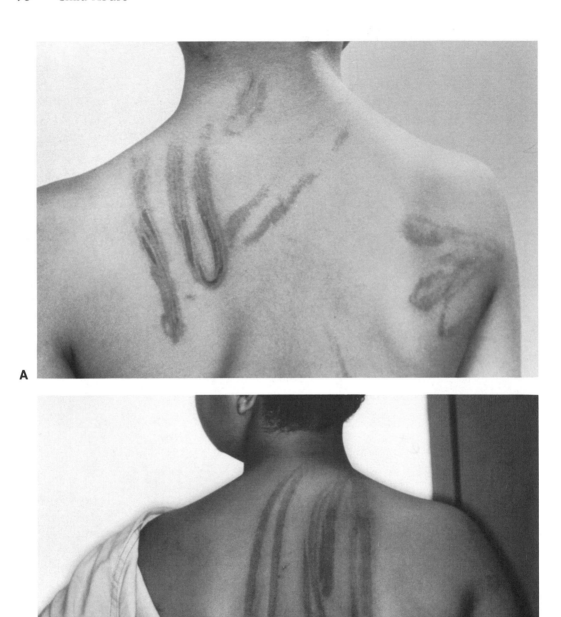

Fig. 9-5. (**A & B**) Loop marks caused by folding over a cord-like object and striking the child, causing the typical curvilinear lesions. Note the typical location on both children's backs, as the victims turn away from the assailant.

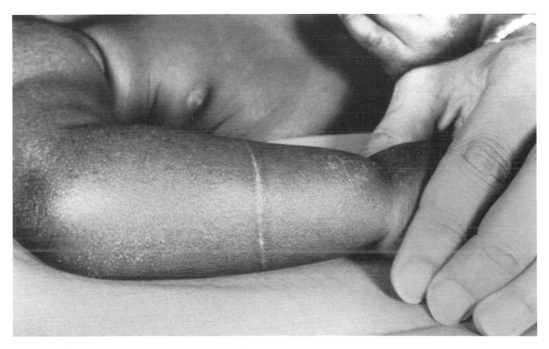

Fig. 9-6. Circumferential restraint mark about this infant's forearm.

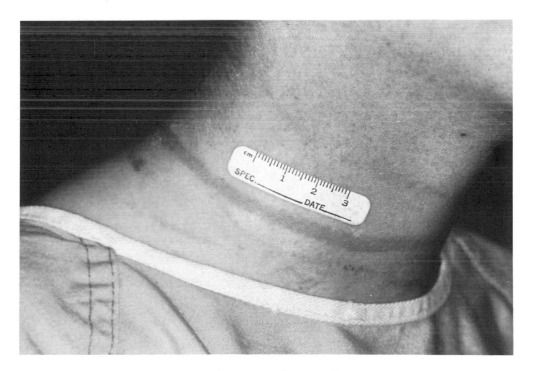

Fig. 9-7. Attempted strangulation.

stantial skin injury from intentional trauma. Skeletal survey and bone scan have a much higher incidence for uncovering asymptomatic fractures in the preschool age child than in the older child (see Ch. 13).

Clinicians and other mandated reporters sometimes evaluate a child for entirely unrelated concerns and note scars resembling recognizable objects. It is likely that child abuse occurred at some time in the past. Must one make a report to the child protective services in this setting? If an old wound in an otherwise well appearing child is explained adequately, no report is required. If there is reason to suspect that abuse is ongoing, a report is mandatory.

HAIR LOSS

Traumatic alopecia is another manifestation of child abuse. An adult forcibly rips hair out while pulling the child along by the hair (Fig. 9-8). Well demarcated borders, typical of many child abuse lesions, with patchy hair loss are frequently seen.

Several disorders associated with alopecia need to be distinguished from child abuse. In alopecia areata, the borders are usually quite sharp, and hair loss is generally complete within the affected area (Fig. 9-9). Tinea capitis, a fungal infection of the scalp, is perhaps the most frequent etiology for alopecia in childhood, particularly in blacks. Borders between normal and infected scalp are poorly defined, the alopecia is patchy, loose hairs are noted, inflammation may be present, and fungi may be cultured from the infected area (Fig. 9-10). Traction alopecia can occur unintentionally secondary to overzealous braiding. The history, distribution of hair loss, and the presence of braids make this nonabusive pattern obvious.

An uncommon disorder causing alopecia called trichotillomania is sometimes difficult to distinguish from

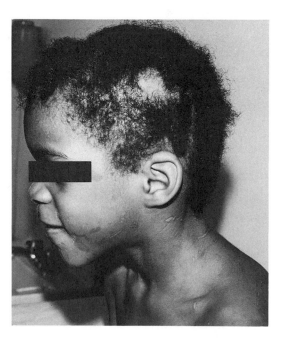

Fig. 9-8. Traumatic alopecia.

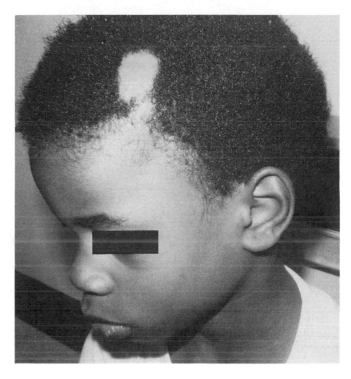

Fig. 9-9. Alopecia areata, with the typical sharp margins and total hair loss within the affected region.

child abuse. In this ailment, the child, sometimes mentally ill, will forcibly remove his own hair. The pattern of hair loss may resemble that seen in the abused child, as the child is abusing himself (Fig. 9-11). Careful history and observation distinguish trichotillomania from alopecia associated with child abuse.

BIZARRE SKIN LESIONS

Anytime dermatologic or other disorders in a child cannot be explained by known disease processes, child abuse should be considered. As in other areas of medicine, unusual presentations of common diseases such as child abuse are more common than rare diseases. For example, Kohl et al. reported a child undergoing an extensive immunologic work-up for multiple bacterial skin infections caused by unusual organisms. The mother was injecting fecal material into the child's skin. This pattern is typically seen in Münchausen syndrome by proxy, a disorder where a parent purposely makes the child ill so that the child is hospitalized. The parent receives some secondary gain from the attention given the child's "disease." This illness is discussed in Chapter 16.

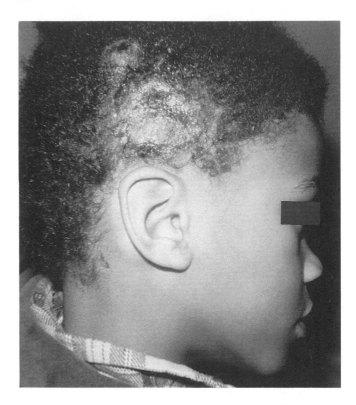

Fig. 9-10. Inflammatory scalp lesion, known as a *kerion*, one of the presentations for tinea capitis.

SKIN DISORDERS CONFUSED WITH CHILD ABUSE

Congenital Skin Lesions

The medical literature has several case reports of dermatologic conditions that were first thought to be child abuse, and subsequently were diagnosed as underlying illness or accidental trauma. Typically, these are either rare diseases or unusual presentations of more common conditions. Mongolian spots are grey-blue areas of discoloration seen in many newborns. When these are found, they have always been present since birth. However, mongolian spots sometimes become more prominent in the first few weeks of life, as they may be hidden by edema associated with delivery. Mongolian spots typically occur over the buttocks and lower back but may be noted elsewhere (Fig. 9-12). They are particularly common in dark complexioned infants and are occasionally confused with fresh bruises. They are nontender, and most fade away slowly over several months. When in doubt, the lack of rapid evolution of mongolian spots compared with the typical evolution of bruises can be used to distinguish between them.

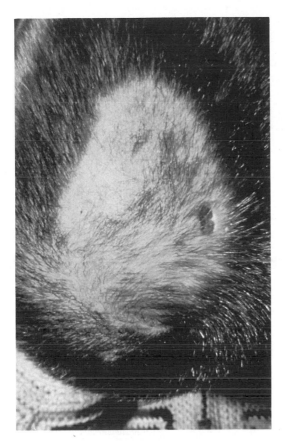

Fig. 9-11. Trichotillomania that has progressed to the point that a mental health referral is appropriate.

Coagulopathies

Coagulopathies such as hemophilia, thrombocytopenia, and platelet function disorders have all been reported as first being diagnosed as child abuse. However, as previously noted, the two conditions may coexist. It may be important to document normal clotting ability in the hematology lab when evaluating a child with multiple bruises. This is not generally necessary if the bruises conform to the shape of a recognizable object.

Brown and Melinkovich reported the case of an 8-month-old boy who initially presented with red, swollen, tender ears and face. A diagnosis of child abuse was considered. Subsequently, palpable purpura developed over much of his body. A skin biopsy was consistent with Henoch-Schönlein purpura. Since this disorder is the most common pediatric vasculitis, it is not surprising that atypical presentations may originally be seen as child abuse. When the more typical lower extremity and buttock purpura predominate, the diagnosis is obvious. The involvement of other organ systems revealing arthritis, hematuria, proteinuria, bloody stools, or intussusception occurs in about one-half of cases, also pointing to the correct diagnosis. Development of additional lesions under observation also can be used to rule out child abuse. Only rarely is skin biopsy necessary. Waskerwitz et al. first reported hypersensitivity vasculitis being confused with intentional trauma.

Connective Tissue Disorders

Ehlers-Danlos syndrome is a connective tissue disorder associated with easy bruisability, poor wound healing, and frequent scarring. Elasticity of skin, observation of poor wound healing, and a positive family history all support the diagnosis.

Photodermatitis

An interesting case of photodermatitis was described by Dannaker et al. A toddler presented with lesions of the face and anterior trunk resembling a scald burn. As no description of an accidental burn was offered by the family, the history was not consistent with the physical examination, and child abuse was suspected. The child had been sucking on a

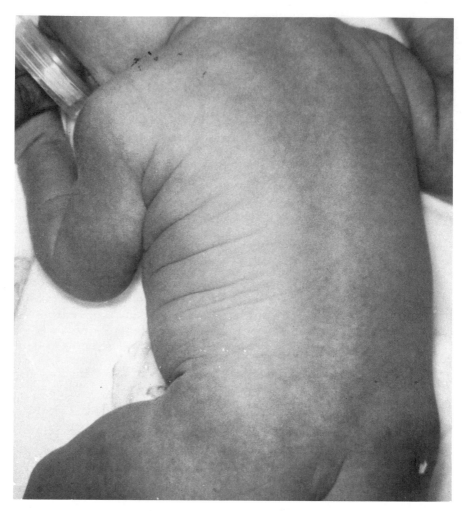

Fig. 9-12. The darker pigmented areas on the buttocks, thighs, and arms are examples of mongolian spots, which can be confused with bruising in neonates.

fresh lime while undressed from the waist up, dripped juice on his body, and a phototoxic reaction occurred between the plant furocoumarins and bright sunlight on the child's skin.

Hair-Tourniquet Syndrome

Sometimes a parent or other caretaker's hair will wrap around an infant or toddler's penis, fingers, or most commonly toes (Fig. 9-13). This can cause edema, and eventually ischemia, of the distal part, hence the term *hair-tourniquet syndrome*. Usually the hair comes from the mother, since long hair is more likely to cause this effect. Hair-tourniquet syndrome is accidental, and a report of child abuse is not indicated. Typically, the hair can be carefully removed in the office or emergency department setting, but occasionally, a trip to the operating room is necessary.

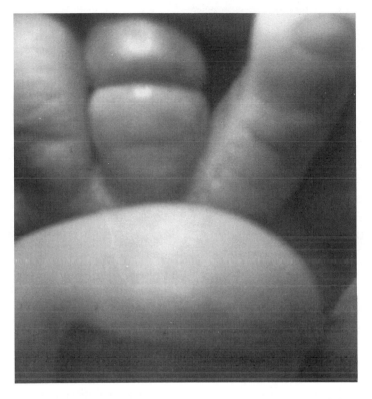

Fig. 9-13. The tourniquet effect with distal edema is noted in the toe of this infant suffering from hair-tourniquet syndrome.

Cultural Practices

Cultural practices that are unfamiliar to North Americans may at first be diagnosed as child abuse. Coin rolling was described among Vietnamese by Yeatman and Dang and among Chinese by Rosenblat and Hong. This is a custom intended to treat fever, headache, and chills. Oil is applied to the chest or back and massaged until warm. The edge of a coin is vigorously rubbed against the skin. Rubbing typically occurs from the midline laterally. Bilaterally symmetric multiple petechiae or purpura with sharp borders are noted (Fig. 9-14). Asner and Wisotsky described a Russian and Eastern European ritual called *cupping,* used to treat pain. A cup or glass is heated and placed on multiple locations on the child's skin, predominantly on the trunk. Round, well marginated erythematous areas are noted. Coin rolling and cupping cause only minimal discomfort and do not scar. Although it is reasonable for the Western-oriented health practitioner to discuss the lack of efficacy of these procedures, a report of child abuse is not indicated, since these practices are harmless and well intentioned.

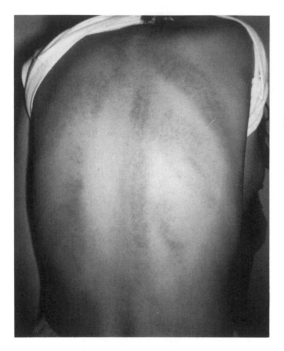

Fig. 9-14. Coin rolling on the back of this child of Southeast Asian descent.

SUGGESTED READINGS

1. Asner RS: Buttock bruises-mongolian spot. Pediatrics 74:321, 1984
2. Asner RS, Wisotsky DH: Cupping lesions simulating child abuse. J Pediatr 99:267, 1981
3. Brown J, Melinkovich P: Schonlein-Henoch purpura misdiagnosed as suspected child abuse. JAMA 256:617, 1986
4. Coffman K, Boyce WT, Hansen RC: Phytophotodermatitis simulating child abuse. Am J Dis Child 139:29, 1985
5. Dannaker CJ, Glover RA, Goltz RW: Phytophotodermatitis. A mysterious case report. Clin Pediatr 27:289, 1988
6. Dungy CI: Mongolian spots, day care centers, and child abuse. Pediatrics 69:672, 1982
7. Ellerstein NS: The cutaneous manifestations of child abuse and neglect. Am J Dis Child 133:906, 1979
8. Feldman KW: Pseudoabusive burns in Asian refugees. Am J Dis Child 138:768, 1984
9. Johnson CF: Constricting bands. Manifestations of possible child abuse. Case reports and a review. Clin Pediatr 27:439, 1988
10. Kohl S, Pickering LK, Dupree E: Child abuse presenting as immunodeficiency disease. J Pediatr 93:466, 1978
11. Narkewicz RM: Distal digital occlusion. Pediatrics 61:922, 1987
12. O'Hare AE, Eden OB: Bleeding disorders and nonaccidental injury. Arch Dis Child 59:860, 1984
13. Owen S, Durst RD: Ehlers-Danlos syndrome simulating child abuse. Arch Dermatol 120:97, 1984
14. Pascoe JM, Hildebrandy HM, Tarrier A et al: Patterns of skin injury in nonaccidental and accidental injury. Pediatrics 64:245, 1979
15. Raimer BG, Raimer SS, Hebeler JR: Cutaneous signs of child abuse. J Am Acad Dermatol 5:203, 1981
16. Reece RM, Grodin MA: Recognition of nonaccidental injury. Pediatr Clin North Am 32:41, 1985
17. Roberts DL, Pope FM, Nicholls AC et al: Ehlers-Danlos syndrome type IV mimicking nonaccidental injury in a child. Br J Dermatol 111:341, 1984
18. Robertson DM, Barbor P, Hull P: Unusual injury? Recent injury in normal children and children with suspected nonaccidental injury. Br Med J 285:1399, 1982
19. Rosenblat J, Hong P: Coin rolling misdiagnosed as child abuse. Can Med Assoc J 140:417, 1989
20. Sandler AP, Haynes V: Nonaccidental trauma and medical folk belief: a case of cupping. Pediatrics 61:921, 1978
21. Showers J, Bandman RL: Scarring for life: abuse with electric cords. Child Abuse Negl 10:25, 1986
22. Waskerwitz S, Christoffel KK, Hauger S: Hypersensitivity vasculitis presenting as suspected child abuse: case report and literature review. Pediatrics 67:283, 1981
23. Yeatman GW, Dang VV: Cao gio (coin rubbing). JAMA 244:2748, 1980

10

Burn Injuries

Gary F. Purdue
John L. Hunt

One common and often unappreciated method of child abuse is by burning, a mechanism that accounts for about 10 percent of all child abuse. Conversely, approximately 10 to 25 percent of pediatric burns are deliberately inflicted by adults. Because 30 to 70 percent of abused children are at risk for subsequent injury, this factor must be considered when dealing with burn injuries. The observer of a pediatric burn should be aware of the potential for deliberate injury, reinforcing the need for continual alertness in diagnosis and the use of a team approach to the problem. Thorough familiarity with the patterns of accidental burns permits appropriate recognition of deliberate injury. While burn injuries result from a wide variety of causes, the majority of inflicted burns are caused by hot water (82 percent in our series of 101 abused children under 10 years of age). A very large proportion (86 percent) of these scald injuries are caused by tap water, in contrast to accidental injuries, where less than 16 percent are caused by tap water ($P < 0.001$). Deliberate injury by flame and hot solids are much less frequent than scalds (8 percent of total abuse) in

abused children admitted to the hospital, although the proportions of flame and hot solid injuries are higher in outpatient series, owing to their smaller burn size. Burn size distributions are the same for abused and nonabused children, although the amount of full thickness or third-degree burn is higher in abused children.

The age distributions of both abused and nonabused burned children show significant difference in two subgroups of patients. Infants younger than 1 year of age have limited mobility and climbing skills. While accidental spill scald burns are common in this age group, immersion burns are very rare. In children aged 5 years or older, abuse by burning of any type is relatively rare and is usually associated with the presence of neurologic or developmental defects.

Occasionally, the corpse of a child abuse victim killed in another manner, or an adult homicide victim for that matter, will be burned after death by the perpetrator in an attempt to conceal evidence. It is the responsibility of the criminal justice system and medical examiner's office to thoroughly investigate circumstances of this sort.

105

INJURIES SUGGESTIVE
OF ABUSE

History

Inflicted burns often have characteristic patterns of injury that fortunately, are rarely concealed. These patterns are very well described in a classic paper by Lenoski and Hunter. The history of the injury must be carefully correlated with the observed pattern of injury, burn depth, and general wound appearance. The exact timing of the injury and its purported cause and the presence of witnesses must be ascertained, as well as the type of clothing worn by the child, if any, and whether a diaper was worn. A carefully detailed history includes previous trauma, presence of recent illnesses, immunization status, and the status of routine medical care.

Physical Examination

The physical examination of all burned children includes careful evaluation of the entire skin surface for the presence of other trauma such as healed burns, multiple simultaneous burns, bruises, slap, bite, or whip marks, and evidence of sexual abuse. Multiple burns of varying ages and types, which obviously could not have occurred from the same accident (e.g., cigarette and scald burns or different types of scald burns), are proof of child abuse. While the presence of other nonburn trauma mandates further investigation, the absence of other injuries does not rule out abuse, since the majority (up to 80 percent) of deliberately inflicted burns are not associated with other trauma. Evaluation and documentation of the burn size and pattern should be precise and include careful drawings that accurately depict the burn pattern. Burn size is expressed as a percentage of the total body surface area. Ideally, a Lund-Browder or Berkow chart (Fig. 10-1), which corrects body proportions for age, should be used to reliably determine burn size. This drawing includes notation of splash marks, uniformity of burn depth, bilateral symmetry ("stocking or glove" distributions), presence of nonburned (spared) areas within the burn, and sharpness of the junction of burned and unburned areas. The soles of the feet and palms of the hands are evaluated for the presence of more superficial burns than on surrounding areas (first degree). Photographs of the burns taken in the anatomic position (arms and legs extended, palms forward) provide excellent documentation of the injury.

First-degree burns are characterized by erythema, appearing sunburn-like, and are not included when calculating burn size. While not usually depicted on burn drawings, they should be noted in cases of suspected abuse. Second-degree or partial thickness burns often have blisters containing clear fluid and pink underlying tissue. However, bright red tissue underlying the blister usually signifies a third-degree or full thickness burn. While third-degree burns are classically dry, leathery, and translucent in appearance, clinical diagnosis of burn depth is seldom that clearcut. Some burns, often called fourth degree, are so deep that they penetrate to deep tissues (fat, muscle, and bone).

The exact extent and depth of injury is often very difficult to accurately assess immediately postburn. This is especially true for scald burns and/or dark-complexioned children. Hence, re-evaluations of the burn wound should be performed, ideally by the same examiner, at 24 and 48 hours after injury. The purported cause of injury is carefully correlated with the child's observed motor skills. Exposure to any environment hot enough to burn will cause pain and immediate with-

DALLAS COUNTY HOSPITAL DISTRICT

DALLAS, TEXAS

BURN RECORD

To be completed upon admission:

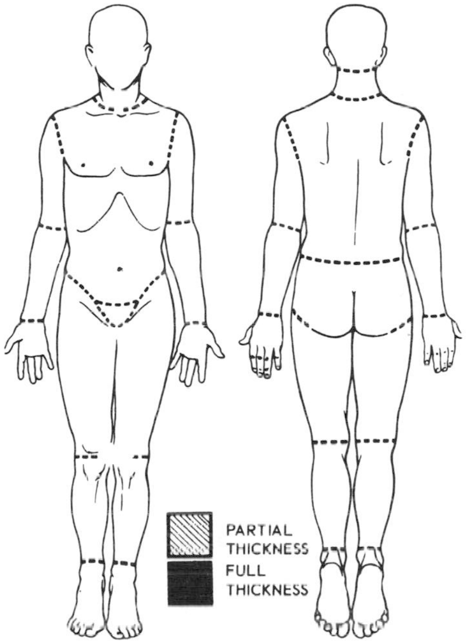

Date: _____

Height: _____ Weight: _____

2° _____ + 3° _____ = _____ %

PARTIAL
THICKNESS
FULL
THICKNESS

Percent Surface Area Burned
(Berkow Formula)

AREA	1 YR.	1–4 YRS.	5–9 YRS.	10–14 YRS.	15 YRS.	ADULT	2°	3°
Head	19	17	13	11	9	7		
Neck	2	2	2	2	2	2		
Ant. Trunk	13	13	13	13	13	13		
Post Trunk	13	13	13	13	13	13		
R. Buttock	2½	2½	2½	2½	2½	2½		
L. Buttock	2½	2½	2½	2½	2½	2½		
Genitalia	1	1	1	1	1	1		
R.U. Arm	4	4	4	4	4	4		
L.U. Arm	4	4	4	4	4	4		
R.L. Arm	3	3	3	3	3	3		
L.L. A m	3	3	3	3	3	3		
R. Hand	2½	2½	2½	2½	2½	2½		
L. Hand	2½	2½	2½	2½	2½	2½		
R. Thigh	5½	6½	8	8½	9	9½		
L. Thigh	5½	6½	8	8½	9	9½		
R. Leg	5	5	5½	6	6½	7		
L. Leg	5	5	5½	6	6½	7		
R. Foot	3½	3½	3½	3½	3½	3½		
L. Foot	3½	3½	3½	3½	3½	3½		
TOTAL								

034

PS 352

Fig. 10-1. Age-corrected burn surface area chart. (Courtesy of Dallas County Hospital District, Dallas Texas.)

drawal by the accidentally injured child. The child is also evaluated for presence of normal sensation and reflexes.

Laboratory Studies

There are no specific laboratory studies that will help distinguish deliberate from accidental injury. Microbiology tests such as culture and Gram stain may be performed to help distinguish vesicles or bullae caused by bacteria such as staphylococcus from the blistering of second-degree burns. Tsanck preparation, a Wright stain of scrapings from the base of a vesicle that has been air dried, will demonstrate multinucleated giant cells and/or intracytoplasmic inclusion bodies in the presence of herpesvirus, the other common infectious agent causing blistering. These tests can also be used to diagnose infections secondarily complicating burns.

Radiologic Studies

Long bone, chest, and skull radiographic series need to be performed on all burned children with suspected abuse.

MECHANISM OF INJURY

The characteristics of each type of burn injury are very different. Scald burns are the most common type of burn seen in all children, and may be caused by any hot liquid, including tap water, other water (often described as "boiling water"), water-like liquids (usually tea and coffee), and thicker liquids (those containing solids, soups, and grease). Deliberate burns are very rarely caused by these thicker liquids. Scald burns can be di-

vided into spill/splash and immersion types, depending on the mechanism of injury. The characteristic patterns (as described by Lenoski and Hunter) of scald burn in our series included immersion (65 percent), random splash (23 percent), and forced immersion (12 percent). The random splash category included those injuries caused by running water. No accidental full thickness tap water scald burns were noted. Burn distribution in abused children centers on the buttocks, perineum, and distal limbs, in contrast to accidental injury, which has a random distribution. Deep scald burns of the buttocks, perineum, and both feet were pathognomonic of deliberate injury, but no accidental scald injuries had this pattern.

Spill Injuries

Spill injuries occur when hot liquid falls from a height onto the victim (Fig. 10-2). The burn pattern is characterized by irregular margins and a nonuniform depth. The natural tendency of liquids to flow downward, cooling as they move, produces a deeper burn in the upmost burn area, with the depth becoming progressively more shallow as the fluid proceeds downward ("arrow-head" pattern). No abused children in our series exhibited a classic spill injury. Pediatric burns caused by deliberately throwing or pouring hot liquids on a child are rare. Rather, the injury is caused by placing the child under flowing liquid or by immersion in the liquid. Although a random spill/splash type of injury may occur deliberately, other historical or physical factors would have to be present to prove deliberate injury. This is in contrast to an adult's assault on another adult, where throwing and pouring of hot liquid are extremely common.

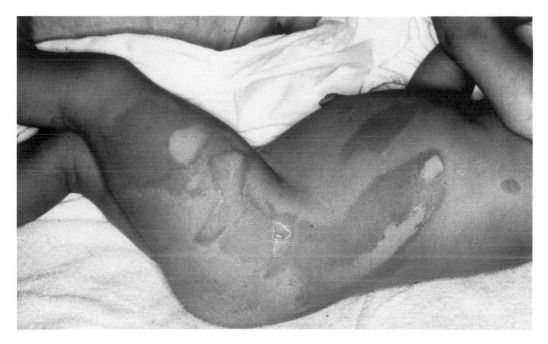

Fig. 10-2. Spill injury in a toddler, characteristic of an accidental burn.

Immersion Burns

Immersion burns result from the patient falling or being placed in a container of hot liquid. Accidental injuries display splash marks, varying depths of burn, indistinct borders between burned and unburned skin, and multiple areas of burn as the child struggles. Burn depth of the accidental injury tapers from deep to shallow as the body part is immersed, pain is felt by the child, and the limb is withdrawn. In deliberate immersion burn, depth is uniform and almost monotonous in appearance. In most instances, the child shows no evidence of motion during the immersion. Burn wound borders are very distinct, and are present as sharply defined "waterlines." These are straight lines delineating the areas of unburned skin from the burned areas in a manner analogous to the waterline of a ship. Clinically, these lines are seldom perfectly

straight because of the varying contours of the human body and angle of immersion (Fig. 10-3). Uniform burn depth occurs because the body part is held in contact with the hot liquid for a relatively long time compared with the time of motion into and out of the water. Seventy-five percent of the scald burns in our series were of the immersion type, with nearly all occurring in hot tap water. The remainder of scald burns were caused by immersion in "boiling water." Ten percent of the scald burns were forced immersion injuries. These had centrally spared areas on the buttocks caused by contact with the cool bottom of the container with exclusion of hot water in this area (Fig. 10-4).

Most children with deliberate immersion burns sustain burns of the buttocks and/or perineum. This pattern is consistent with the observation that many of these injuries involve toilet training or

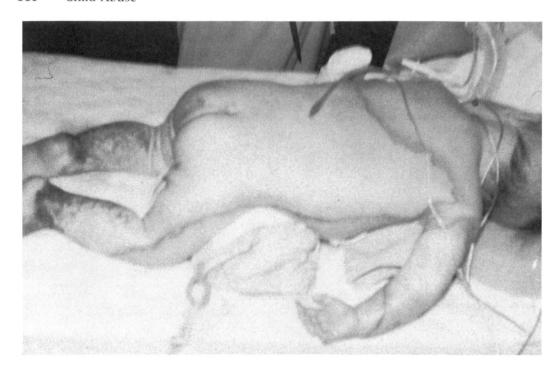

Fig. 10-3. Immersion burn, demonstrating characteristic "waterlines."

soiling of clothing. Diapers (both washable and disposable) have an outer barrier layer and inner absorbent layer and if children are wearing them provide nearly complete protection against scald burns (Fig. 10-5). Other immersion injuries involved deep, uniform, circumferential burns of the extremities in the distribution of stockings or gloves (Fig. 10-6).

Burn depth is a function of temperature, exposure time, and skin thickness. Moritz and Henriques described the relationship of time and temperature required to cause a second degree burn in an adult as shown below.

48.9°C	(120°F)	300	s
54.4°C	(130°F)	30	s
60.0°C	(140°F)	5	s
65.0°C	(150°F)	1.5	s

While water at 40.5°C (105°F) is uncomfortable on initial contact, prolonged exposure to about 43.3°C (110°F) is required to create a cutaneous injury. Despite the short times required to cause a severe burn injury, it is extremely improbable that the unrestrained child will sustain isolated full thickness buttock or extremity burns by accidental immersion in hot tap water. Adults in the United States understand the burning hazards associated with hot tap water, and these burns should not be excused by purported lack of knowledge. This is confirmed by the virtual absence of accidental tap water burns in nonimpaired adults.

Flame Burns

Flame burns are a much less common cause of burn injury. These burns are characterized by extreme depth (often

Fig. 10-4. Forced immersion burn illustrating sparing of the central buttock ("donut" pattern), as this area is protected by the heat-resistant bathtub bottom.

fourth degree) and relatively circumscribed nature when compared with accidental flame burns. In nearly all cases, the given history is not consistent with the observed injury (by both pattern and depth).

Hot solids burn by contact. While accidental injuries have a lack of apparent pattern, owing to patient movement under the hot object, deliberately inflicted burns faithfully depict the outline of the hot object, such as the sole of an iron or lattice of a grate. (Fig. 10-7). Note, however, that very brief accidental contact with a hot object can produce a superficial second-degree burn with the pattern of the object.

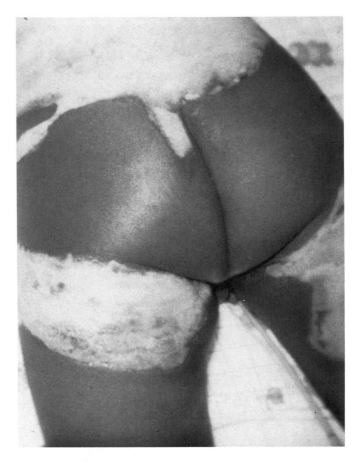

Fig. 10-5. Immersion burn with sparing of diaper-protected area.

Natural Course

Delay in seeking medical attention very rarely occurs following accidental burn injury. By contrast, nearly one-third of abused children have a significant delay in obtaining any type of medical help. Unusual circumstances surrounding the injury are frequently present. Burns resulting from child abuse tend to be deeper than for a given cause of accidental injury, and the length of hospital stay is significantly longer. This is especially apparent with small burns of less than 10 percent total body surface area.

In addition, discharge is delayed beyond that deemed medically necessary in about one-third of abused patients. Legal proceedings are the most frequent cause of discharge delay. The mortality of deliberately burned children has been reported as high as 30 percent, while death occurs in only about 2 percent of accidentally burned children. This is in part caused by large and deep burns in infants, the age group usually spared this type of accidental injury. The most common cause of death is pneumonia. Poor nutritional status often complicates care of the abused child.

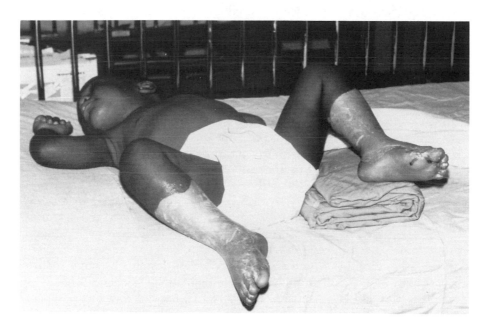

Fig. 10-6. Stocking distribution burn.

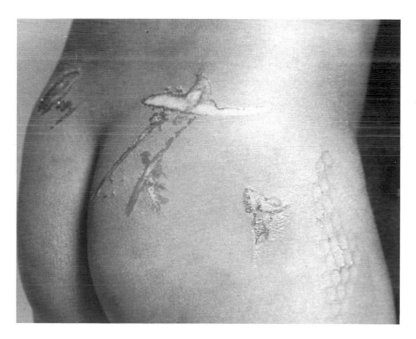

Fig. 10-7. Pattern ("branding") burn, caused by deliberate contact of hot object against child's buttock.

INJURIES THAT MAY SIMULATE ABUSE

Cutaneous infections generate patterns that may mimic deliberate injury. Impetigo, severe diaper rash, and early scalded skin syndrome (toxic epidermal necrolysis) may sometimes resemble a scald injury. A careful history, sometimes microbiologic tests, and observation of these lesions over a 2- to 3-week period usually permit separation of these causes.

Hypersensitivity reactions can sometimes be mistaken for intentional burns. For example, substances in several fruits (e.g., limes) when in contact with the skin and exposed to sunlight, can predispose to severe photodermatitis. The pattern may resemble a splash burn, and if no history of exposure to hot liquid is offered, abuse may be suspected. An allergic reaction causing severe local skin irritation may be mistaken for a burn. This has been reported with the use of dermatologic preparations such as topical antiseptics. Exposure history should allow differentiation of these reactions from burns.

Cigarette burns can be either accidental or abusive. Accidental cigarette burns may arise when sudden movement causes momentary contact with the lighted cigarette. These injuries often occur about the face and eye when a child walks or runs into a cigarette held by an adult at waist height. Cigarette burns located on parts of the body, such as the back and buttocks, which a child is unlikely to injure by walking into a lighted cigarette, are suspect for intentional trauma. Accidental cigarette burns are usually more shallow, more irregular, and less circumscribed than deliberate ones. Multiple cigarette burns are pathognomonic for child abuse (Fig. 10-8).

Moxibustion is an Asian folk remedy that entails placement of a hot substance, often burning yarn, on the skin of the abdomen or back. The resulting circular lesions are usually 0.5 to 1.0 cm in size. The practice of cupping, whereby a small amount of flammable substance is placed in a cup or glass, ignited, and then placed on the skin, may cause a burn-like circular lesion.

Deliberate burns caused by hot solids are the most difficult to distinguish from accidental injuries. While cigarette and iron burns are the most frequent injuries of this type, the surface of a car seat may have a temperature exceeding 80°C (176°F), when left in the summer sun. A child placed in such a seat may sustain second- and even third-degree burns. Full thickness burns have resulted from contact with a hot seat-belt buckle. Likewise, pavement that has been heated by the sun may also reach a temperature of 80°C (176°F). While burns occur rapidly, the unrestrained child is unlikely to receive deep burns from this latter source.

Curling irons can cause a characteristic burn pattern. Most accidental injuries occur either when a hot iron is grasped or when it falls. These injuries are usually second degree and randomly placed, as might occur when the hot iron strikes the skin in multiple places as it falls. The more superficial nature of these injuries distinguishes them from the much deeper "branding" injuries.

In nearly all of these cases, careful correlation of the history of injury with the observed pattern and depth of injury by an individual experienced in burn care differentiates accidental from nonaccidental injury.

LONG-TERM OUTCOME

Long-term outcome is determined primarily by the child's ability to receive appropriate wound care and physical therapy. The recovery period from a major

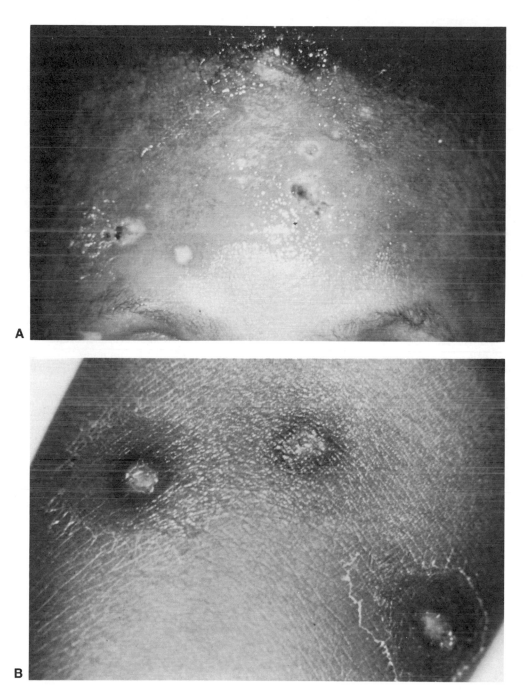

Fig. 10-8. Multiple cigarette burns are indicative of child abuse: **(A)** acute burns on the fore-head, **(B)** scarring from old injury on an extremity.

burn injury is usually prolonged. Very active outpatient therapy is required for a period of about six to eight times that of the inpatient hospitalization. After this period, the child is evaluated at least annually until growth stops. Burn scars are strong enough to sublux joints and inhibit bone growth, especially on the feet.

Suspicion and investigation of suspected burn abuse is a major responsibility for physicians caring for burned children. False accusation and suspicion affect the doctor-family relationship, and certain types of injury may be misdiagnosed. A team approach to child abuse provides the knowledge required for accurate diagnosis and appropriate follow-up. This team must have appropriate expertise and should be at least partly free of the primary care team and ideally should include a burn surgeon, social worker, pediatrician, and pediatric psychiatric consultation and therapists. A team approach permits prompt recognition, specialized consultation, continuity with legal authorities, and long-term evaluation of the deliberately burned child.

SUGGESTED READINGS

1. Caniano DA, Beaver BL, Boles ET: Child abuse: an update on surgical management in 256 cases. Ann Surg 203:219, 1986

2. Dannaker CJ, Glover RA, Goltz RW: Photodermatitis. A mysterious case report. Clin Pediatr 27:289, 1988

3. Deitch EA, Staats M: Child abuse through burning. J Burn Care Rehab 3:89, 1982

4. Fowler J: Child maltreatment by burning. Burns 5:83, 1978

5. Gil DG: Violence Against Children. Physical Child Abuse in the United States. Harvard University Press, Cambridge, MA, 1970

6. Hight DW, Bakalar HR, Lloyd JR: Inflicted burns in children. Recognition and treatment. JAMA 242:517, 1979

7. Lenoski EF, Hunter KA: Specific patterns of inflicted burn injuries. J Trauma 17:842, 1977

8. MacMillan BG, Freiberg DL: Special problems of the pediatric burn patient. In Hummel RP (ed): Clinical Burn Therapy. John Wright, PSG Inc., Boston, Bristol, London, 1982

9. Moritz AR, Henriques FC: Studies of thermal injury, II. The relative importance of time and surface temperature in the causation of cutaneous burns. Am J Path 23:695, 1947

10. Purdue GF, Hunt JL: Child abuse—an index of suspicion. J Trauma 28:221, 1988

11. Robinson MD, Seward PN: Thermal injury in children. Pediatr Emerg Care 3:266, 1987

12. Smith SM, Hanson R: 134 battered children: a medical and psychological study. Br Med J 3:666, 1974

13. Stone NH, Rinaldo L, Humphrey CR, Brown RH: Child abuse by burning. Surg Clin North Am 50:1419, 1970

Neurosurgical Aspects of Child Abuse

Derek A. Bruce

Injury to the brain and upper spinal cord accounts for 75 percent or more of child abuse (nonaccidental trauma) deaths in children. The majority of these fatalities occur in children younger than 8 years of age and predominantly in those younger than 2 years of age. Physical abuse of sufficient severity to warrant medical attention accounts for less than 10 percent of reported abuse cases. Nonaccidental trauma accounts for approximately 10 percent of injuries to children under 2 years, yet 80 percent or more of the deaths in this age group are caused by nonaccidental trauma. The distribution of nonaccidental trauma with regard to race and economic status appears to be no different from that for accidental trauma, and the suspicion of child abuse should be no less in the upper and middle class family than it is in the poor family.

Homicide is now the leading cause of death in children between 1 month and 1 year of age, accounting for 17 percent of all deaths. This figure increased by 25 percent between 1985 and 1987. Five percent of all childhood deaths are due to homicide compared with 1 percent of adult deaths and, as noted above, 17 percent of deaths in the first year of life. Prevention is clearly the only perfect solu-tion to this problem. There is good understanding, at least at an academic level, of the phases of childhood development. It is a major failure of public education that our society has failed to educate parents in the development of conscious awareness and responsiveness to an external world. Parents must understand that babies do not maliciously disturb grown-ups and that physical violence is never an acceptable response to an infant or small child. Physical violence that results in death or permanent brain damage to a child constitutes unacceptable behavior and must be prevented.

PATHOPHYSIOLOGY

The child under 2 years of age, and especially under 1 year, experiences a particular form of brain injury that is the result of the size of the head relative to the body, the relative weakness of the cervical musculature, the absence of postural control of head and neck, and the anatomy of the foramen magnum and upper cervical spine. In addition, the higher water content of the infant brain, the relatively minor degree of myelina-

117

tion, the large subarachnoid space, and open fontanelles and sutures all play a role in the production of the "shaken baby syndrome." It is possible that the way that children are abused has changed since the early description of this type of injury by Caffey such that we are seeing the use of a greater amount of force. It is also likely that, with the increase in the number of injuries, many different mechanisms are involved. What separates the "shaking impact injury" from other forms of infant trauma is the usual absence of external evidence of trauma. Also, the history given by the caretaker is often deliberately misleading, making this form of injury very easy to overlook or misdiagnose in the clinical setting. It is common that there is no other evidence of abuse and that this injury, despite its severity, is usually the result of a single episode of loss of control and is rarely premeditated. The mechanism of injury is that of deceleration for the cranial injury and possibly a combination of acceleration and deceleration for injury to the cervical spine and medulla. At autopsy, the pathology differs a little in the baby less than 6 months old from that seen in the older infant and toddler. In the former, gliding contusions or tears at the gray matter-white matter interface are found, whereas in the older infant, diffuse axonal damage with corpus callosum lesions is found. The following lesions are found in each age range: acute subdural hematomas, usually along the falx and medial occipital lobes; subarachnoid hemorrhage; and severe brain swelling, often with ischemic neuronal damage and tentorial herniation. Occasionally, damage may be confined to the cervicomedullary junction, with brain swelling as the only intracranial pathology. Death results either from prolonged apnea and hypotension as a consequence of cervicomedullary damage, or from elevated intracranial pressure (ICP). In each case, the underlying

pathophysiology is cerebral anoxia, ischemia, or a combination of both. Duhaime et al. reported that in those children who die, there is autopsy evidence of blunt trauma to the calvaria, usually in the occipitoparietal area, inferring that an impact injury has occurred. Experimental data in the same study showed that shaking a model could induce acceleration forces of only 10g, a level inadequate to produce brain injury. Impacting the model, even against a soft mattress, resulted in deceleration forces of 300+g, well within the range to produce subdural hematoma and shearing injury. Thus, at least in those children with severe injury, it is more appropriate to consider this injury as a shaking-impact injury. This differentiation is important in the courts, where the presence of an impact lesion at autopsy is used by the defense as an argument against child abuse by shaking. It is more correct to use the designation *shaking-impact* to describe the mechanism of trauma than to be restricted by using the term *shaken baby syndrome*. Deaths have been reported without evidence of impact injury to the brain. These babies showed signs of cervicomedullary injury as the cause of death. The shaking-impact form of injury rarely produces a lesion that requires surgery. However, surgical intervention may be required for an acute subdural hematoma. All children with a shaking-impact injury are at risk to develop severe brain swelling and require close observation regardless of their coma score on admission. Follow-up computed tomographic (CT) and magnetic resonance imaging (MRI) scans in the group of infants who are admitted with significant disturbance of consciousness show very rapid loss of brain tissue and calcifications in the cerebral tissue. This is believed to be the result of the ischemic damage that occurs at the time of the injury and before proper medical care.

Other types of nonaccidental trauma do occur to young children and may produce slightly different pathologic lesions or may demonstrate obvious external signs of injury. Children who are punched in the face and head seem to be more likely to develop acute subdural hematomas requiring surgery. These children will have external evidence of facial trauma. Similarly, children whose heads are impacted against hard objects, such as a wall or a table, will show signs of external trauma and both these groups of children may have other evidence of previous abuse such as rib or long-bone fractures. After 2 years of age, it is unusual to see a shaking-impact injury. The child's head, control postural reflexes, and weight all make it unlikely that this form of discipline will be used. Acute subdural hematomas and occasionally epidural hematomas, or brain contusions and intracerebral hematomas occur in older children, usually as a result of very severe impact injuries (e.g., violent beatings) frequently associated with abdominal visceral injury. The hematomas are frequently unilateral, associated with brain distortion, and often require surgery. In my experience, sexual abuse is often seen in this setting and should be looked for on the clinical examination. In the older child, it is usually clear that trauma has occurred, and misdiagnosis is less likely.

Chronic subdural hematomas and hygromas have not been clearly linked to child abuse or inappropriate disciplining techniques in infants and toddlers. When seen, there is always concern that abuse has occurred and investigations (skeletal survey and family interview) should be pursued. However, chronic subdural hematomas or hygromas are rarely seen on the follow-up CT scan after a shaking-impact injury unless extensive brain damage and cerebral atrophy have occurred. It is difficult to be adamant that abuse has occurred when a large head, chronic sub-

durals, and normal development are seen in a baby. In this setting, long-bone and chest x-rays may help by showing other evidence of chronic abuse. It is possible that chronic subdural hygromas represent the least evidence of brain injury from chronic shaking without impact.

Deliberate asphyxiation can easily be misdiagnosed as sudden infant death syndrome (SIDS) and abuse should be suspected in all unexpected deaths in children.

CLINICAL PRESENTATIONS

The first step in diagnosis is usually taking a history. In a small child who is a victim of abuse, the history is likely to be at best misleading and more often either false or not available from the child's attendant. Any infant or toddler who presents for medical attention with an altered level of consciousness and no history must be suspected of having sustained nonaccidental head trauma. Likewise, if the history is of a minor fall (e.g., rolled off the couch, fell, and hit the coffee table) nonaccidental trauma should be suspected. It is rare that infants under 1 year of age sustain serious head injury, because their exploratory skills and environment are usually quite limited and limiting. When severe head injury does occur, it is usually the result of an automobile accident, and such an event is likely to be witnessed. The minimal expression of the shaking-impact injury or other nonaccidental trauma in the small child is that of a somnolent yet irritable baby. There may be a history of "seizures" before coming to the hospital. The more severely injured children present with a more markedly altered conscious level, seizures, opisthotonic posturing, respiratory arrest, or they may be dead on arrival at the hospital. Hypotension is unusual but when present is a result of either major damage to the cervicomedullary junction or accompanying abdominal or chest trauma. A high index of suspicion of abuse is necessary if a traumatic cause for the child's state is to be sought, since the presentation, especially in the infant under 6 months, is very similar to that of meningitis, near SIDS, or metabolic diseases.

The examination is of prime importance, since the history given is often deliberately misleading if abuse has occurred. A rapid examination of the whole baby undressed will establish the presence of any signs of external trauma. This must include the vaginal and rectal areas, even in infants. Any sign of bruising or belt marks will establish a likely diagnosis of nonaccidental trauma; their absence, however, does not rule out this diagnosis. Vital signs and evaluation of respiratory function are next, since hypoventilation or Cheyne-Stokes ventilation may signify severe central nervous system injury. Hypotension requires immediate fluid therapy. Seizure activity, if present, must be carefully observed, since what is recorded as a seizure is more likely to be an episode of opisthotonic posturing, owing to high ICP or subarachnoid hemorrhage. During examination of the skin and scalp for evidence of soft tissue swelling, the fontanel is examined, and the degree of fullness or tenseness is evaluated. A tense fontanel, especially when associated with opisthotonus, suggests marked intracranial hypertension, and plans should be made for treatment at the earliest possible moment. Treatment may vary from osmotic diuretics, endotracheal intubation, subdural tap, or a combination of these. (The choice of therapy is discussed later.) The tone in the neck is checked, as for meningitis, and despite the difficulty involved, a major effort must be made to examine the optic fundi. This is easier in

the unconscious child but significant retinal hemorrhage can usually be identified quite easily without dilating the pupils. The presence of retinal hemorrhages is a mark of severe trauma, and is not seen after simple falls, even in the presence of a skull fracture. Apart from a shaking-impact injury, retinal hemorrhages may be seen after high impact automobile injuries or after rupture of an aneurysm or cerebral atriovenous malformation (AVM). There have been rare reports in which retinal hemorrhages have been noted after prolonged cardiopulmonary resuscitation in settings where nonaccidental trauma has been thought to be unlikely. If this phenomena occurs, it is very uncommon. Retinal hemorrhages in an infant without a history of severe accidental trauma is extremely suggestive for child abuse. At this point in the examination, before a CT scan is done, the pupils should not be chemically dilated because they are an important parameter of cerebral herniation.

Examination of the level of consciousness in the infant under 6 months of age is notoriously difficult. There are several infant coma scales that have been proposed. The best tested on infants is the Adelaide scale but it is not used in most hospitals. The most frequently used scale is the Glasgow Coma Score (GCS) and, while parts of it are inapplicable to the infant, this scale can be applied to children of all ages when its limitations are understood. The various speech responses can be replaced by "crying" or "no crying." Eye opening can also be misleading in infants; a form of spontaneous repetitive eye opening can occur despite severe cortical injury and is easily rated too high on the score. A GCS of less than 8 signifies a severe injury. In infants, the use of the motor examination alone may be the best indication of the severity of brain injury (Table 11-1). Even this part of the examination may be misleading in

Table 11-1. Glasgow Coma Scores: Indication of Severity of Brain Damage

Eyes	
Open	
Spontaneously	4
To verbal command	3
To pain	2
No response	1
Best motor response	
To verbal stimuli[a]	
Obeys	6
To painful stimuli	
Localizes pain	5
Flexion-withdrawal	4
Abnormal flexion	2
Flaccid	1
Best verbal response	
Oriented, converses	5
Disoriented, converses	4
Inappropriate words	3
Incomprehensible sounds	2
No response	1
Infant's response[b]	
Cries	6
Does not cry	1

[a] Not applicable in infants.
[b] Replacement for infants.
(Modified from Jennett et al.,[20] with permission.)

infants since spontaneous bicycling movements of the legs and occasionally of the arms can occur even if very severe brain damage has occurred. I have seen this movement in the presence of a flat electroencephalogram (EEG) and absence of intracranial blood flow.

The evaluation of level of consciousness in children under 6 months of age should include eye opening, tracking, head control, crying, sucking, motor activity, and developmental reflexes (e.g., Landeau posture, righting reflex, stepping reflex, and Moro's reflex). Pupil responses, oculocephalic or oculovestibular responses, gag and respiration, as in the older child, evaluate the status of the brain stem and medulla. The evaluation of the degree of disturbance of consciousness is relatively easy in the more se-verely injured child, if the potential pitfalls of eye opening and motor movement referred to above are taken into account. It is the child with more subtle disturbance of consciousness who is the greatest risk, since the misleading history and superficially unremarkable examination often lead to a false diagnosis of meningitis. It is in this setting that the examination of the fundus becomes very important, since the presence of retinal hemorrhages will alert the physician to potentially serious brain insult and result in careful monitoring of the child and appropriate radiologic tests. Not uncommonly, the examination is done superficially; trauma is not suspected; and a lumbar puncture is performed. This shows bloody cerebrospinal fluid (CSF), which then may alert the physician to the diagnosis of trauma or may again be misinterpreted as a traumatic tap. While most children under 1 year of age do not harbor a significant mass lesion, a lumbar puncture is not necessarily contraindicated but, because some children will have a unilateral mass and all are at risk for herniation syndromes, it is preferable that the diagnosis be made clinically, and a CT scan obtained. The decision to perform a lumbar puncture can then be made if it is considered necessary.

EMERGENCY THERAPY

The awake, irritable child requires an IV and, if stable, a CT scan. Oversedation to obtain the scan must be avoided. With current fast scanners, the baby can usually be held still without sedation.

In unconscious children, the usual ABCs of resuscitation are followed: establish an open airway, give oxygen, intubate using drugs, and take precautions to avoid further elevations of ICP. Rarely is intubation appropriate in an awake patient. Routine blood samples are drawn, and heart rate, blood pressure, oxygen saturation, urine output, and temperature are monitored. If the fontanel is tense and either a decerebrate or flaccid motor response is present, then tapping the fontanel may be a valuable way to acutely lower the ICP. Several milliliters of bloody CSF can be obtained with an improvement in the clinical examination. Seizures, if present, require therapy. Iorazepam is currently the drug of choice. If there is a history of seizures but none are observed, it is better not to give medication until a CT scan is obtained. The CT scan is the best initial study and should be obtained as soon as possible.

Children in shock require appropriate fluid resuscitation and diagnosis of the site of fluid loss. Typically, the site is in the abdomen as a result of blunt trauma to the liver or a hollow viscus. The scan should be delayed until the hemodynamic parameters are stable.

There is concern about cervical spine and lower medullary damage in these children. The diagnosis is best made on clinical examination. Infants who are apneic and flaccid can be assumed to have a cervicomedullary injury. However, this should not delay intubation, since the neck radiographs are usually normal (SCIWORA) and the vertebrae are usually stable. To relieve any elevated ICP, the head is positioned in the midline and elevated about 15 degrees. Moderate hyperventilation is induced (PaCO$_2$ about 25 mmHg).

RADIOLOGY

Skull radiography can be helpful in delineating the type of trauma that has occurred but is of little value in defining the degree of injury. Infants sometimes fall accidentally from a height of 4 feet or less from a parent's arms or off a table. Usually no fracture occurs, but short linear skull fractures are not rare in this setting. Less commonly, longer linear skull fractures crossing suture lines or diastatic fractures may occur in the accidental setting (Fig. 11-1). Diastasis at suture lines may be noted if coexisting elevated ICP is present, whether the trauma was accidental or abusive. Older infants who are placed in walkers and fall down a flight of stairs are very likely to suffer skull fractures. Depressed skull fractures are unusual in the first year of life from any cause. They are generally caused by hitting a corner or edge, or being struck with a blunt object. The presence of a depressed fracture when given a history of hitting a flat surface such as a floor is suspect. The presence of skull fracture does not necessarily raise the likelihood of brain injury. Indeed, babies with dramatic skull fractures may have the least evidence for brain injury as the skull absorbed potentially damaging forces to the brain. Additionally, severe brain injury can occur without external trauma in the shaken-impact syndrome by violent shaking with deceleration against a soft object such as a pillow.

A skull series is not an emergent study, and generally should not be obtained in the emergency department for a patient who may be unstable. A cross-table lateral cervical spine radiograph is standard practice in the emergency department with subsequent additional views of the cervical spine, keeping in mind the possibility of SCIWORA. A chest x-ray is obtained as part of the standard trauma evaluation. Skeletal survey should be deferred in the potentially severely injured child until the child is stable.

Computed tomography is the initial study of choice for assessing brain injury. There is rarely an initial need for contrast enhancement. If there is concern about associated abdominal injury, the CT scan should include this area as well. The most

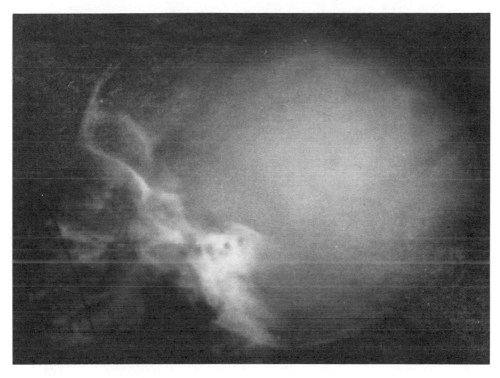

Fig. 11-1. Diastatic linear fracture sustained by a fall to a hard floor from a kitchen counter. Neurologic examination normal. No retinal hemorrhages.

common initial CT finding in the shaken-impact syndrome is a parafalcine subdural hematoma in the parietal and occipital region (Fig. 11-2). Sometimes, small acute subdural hematomas may be difficult to see on CT because of the similar high density of the adjacent cranium.

A repeat CT scan may be indicated a few days later. Patients requiring surgery will be scanned soon thereafter to ensure that the lesion has not recurred. Patients with initially low or easy to control elevations of ICP require a repeat scan if the ICP becomes harder to control to be sure that there is not a delayed hematoma, to view the state of the brain, and to be sure that there is no acute hydrocephalus.

It is remarkable how quickly brain parenchyma can disappear in children who have sustained shaking-impact injury, with high density lesions, atrophy, and frequently, communicating hydrocephalus occurring within 1 to 2 weeks of the injury (Fig. 11-3).

Magnetic resonance imaging is very useful for follow up and may give a better reflection of the degree of damage. It is able to demonstrate with exquisite anatomic detail the brain's relations to CSF spaces and the presence or absence of extracerebral collections and blood products. It is more sensitive to small subdural hematomas, contusions of the cortex, and deep white matter lesions.

Magnetic resonance imaging of child abuse victims has been particularly useful because of its ability to subacutely detect thin layers of methemoglobin within the subdural space. Subacute cortical hemorrhagic contusions are also shown well as cortical ribbons of high signal intensity methemoglobin. Methemoglobin

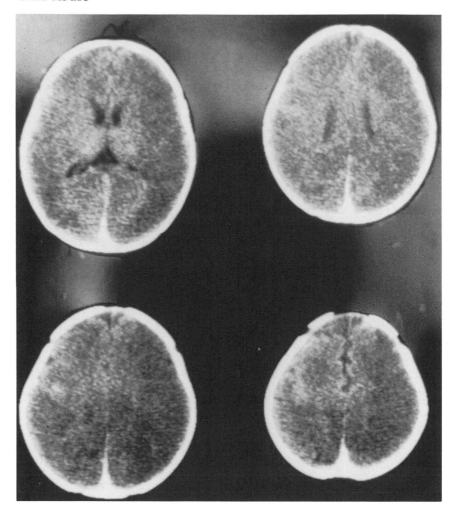

Fig. 11-2. Computed tomography scan obtained acutely of a 4-month-old infant presenting with seizures, depressed consciousness, full fontanel, and retinal hemorrhages. History given was that the infant rolled off the couch. Note interhemispheric subdural hematoma, small right intraparenchymal hematoma, diffuse low density brain.

is formed approximately 3 days after clot formation when oxidation of deoxyhemoglobin to methemoglobin occurs. When available, it may also be advantageous to obtain MRI a few days after presentation of an infant who may be a victim of shaken-impact syndrome, but where the diagnosis is not clear and the initial CT scan appears normal.

Not all victims of child abuse present to medical attention acutely. In these pa-tients the initial CT scan may show brain surrounded by enlarged fluid-filled spaces but may not clearly demonstrate blood products within these spaces. MRI is able to show chronic subdural hematomas as proteinaceous collections with variable signal density caused by differences in age, protein content, and compartmentalization.

Magnetic resonance imaging requires much longer data-acquisition times than

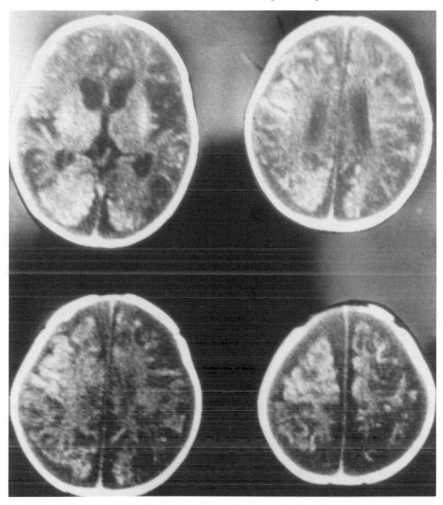

Fig. 11-3. Same patient as in Figure 11-2, obtained 2 weeks later. History of shaken-impact syndrome was obtained. Note parenchymal calcifications and severe atrophy.

does CT. If motion occurs during any of the images obtained during MRI, the image quality will degrade. Thus for MRI to be successful, motion has to be controlled by either sedation, neuromuscular paralyzing agents, general anesthesia, or taking advantage of the depressed mental status of the patient. In comparison, each CT image takes only 3 to 5 seconds to obtain. Motion during a CT slice distorts only that specific slice, which can be readily repeated if necessary. MRI is more expensive and, although becoming

more available, is still not as easy to obtain as CT in many places. Table 11-2 compares CT and MRI.

SURGERY

Surgically treatable intracranial lesions are uncommon in the shaking-impact syndrome. Other types of impact injury to the small child seem more likely to produce sizable subdural hematomas and if found

Table 11-2. Computed Tomography (CT) versus Magnetic Resonance Imaging (MRI) for Child Abuse Head Injuries

	CT	MRI
Appropriate initial study	Yes	No
Sensitivity for small subacute bleeds	Fair	Excellent
Anatomic detail	Good	Outstanding
Dating of traumatic lesions	Fair	Good
Data acquisition time	Brief	Extensive
Controlling for motion artifact	Easy	Difficult
Expense	Moderate	High
Availability	General	Limited

on CT scan, require evacuation. In the older child where the degree of trauma and the type of injury is different, subdural, epidural, and intracerebral hematomas that require surgical removal may all be found. These may be treated with medical decompression, for example mannitol or hyperventilation may be employed to prevent herniation before going to the operating room. Small hematomas associated with severe brain swelling may not require surgery and should be treated medically to control ICP.

INTENSIVE CARE

Apart from the occurrence of an operable lesion, children are treated to prevent any secondary injury that could result from hypoxia, hypercarbia, systemic hypotension, or intracranial hyperten-sion. The two primary areas of therapy are the control of seizures and intracranial hypertension.

When seizures are present, therapy should be intensive enough to stop them. This may require EEG monitoring and frequent measurements of blood levels of antiseizure medications. When no clinical seizures have been observed, there is no evidence for the use of prophylactic anticonvulsants.

The methods of controlling ICP are no different from other clinical settings in children. It is not possible to measure accurately the ICP by feeling the fontanel; it is much more accurate to measure the true ICP using a ventricular catheter, a bolt, or a solid state or fiberoptic transducer. The actual measurements are important to ascertain accurately the need for therapy, its effect when given, the timing for further therapy, and to minimize the amount of, and therefore any side effects from, the therapy. This may require appropriate head positioning, hyperventilation, osmotic diuretics, sedation with high doses of barbiturates, muscle relaxants, or a combination of the above. Most of the deaths are the result of uncontrollable elevated ICP. It is likely that much of the severe secondary damage results from the same cause. Unfortunately, in the worst cases, much of the secondary damage has occurred in the interval between the incident and the instigation of appropriate therapy. The only way to limit the amount of such damage is to ensure early medical attention through parent and doctor education.

There is a tendency among physicians and nurses caring for abused children to adopt an adversarial role towards the parent or person suspected of having harmed the child. This behavior helps neither the child nor the family and may make it even harder to obtain a history of the events that led to the injury. The role of medical personnel is to identify the cause of the injuries and to treat them. Physicians are often in the best position to sympathetically elicit the true story, if they do not assume an adversial attitude. In the majority of cases, the injury was not premeditated, and it is important to understand how a momentary loss of control can result in severe injury to a baby. It is all too easy for medical personnel to give the family clues that result in many changes of story, making it impossible to elicit the correct history. I believe it is important to point out to the child's parents that the damage is the result of a severe injury to the head and that this did not result from a simple fall, as from a sofa. It is neither necessary nor helpful to volunteer ways in which this injury could have occurred. The parents, whether they are the perpetrators or not, will be contrite, frightened, and it must not be assumed that they do not care about the child. There is always guilt and fear associated with this type of trauma, and part of the medical care is to care for the family. If the child survives the injury, there must be a safe environment to which the child can return. This can be worked on from the earliest contacts with hospital personnel.

A second dilemma that occurs in the intensive care unit is the reluctance of the physician staff to declare death when it is clear that irreversible cerebral dysfunction has occurred. There is a fear that because this is a homicide, the diagnosis of death and subsequent stoppage of ventilator support, will result in the physician being held responsible for the child's death. This is a damaging misconception that has no legal basis. Many children who die of this type of trauma can become organ donors for transplant and this is often a way to ease some of the feelings of futility and loss that such a death generates. If permission for donation of organs is to be requested from the parents, it is essential that the physician has received permission from the local

medical examiner. If the parents obtain some solace from their dead child being able to help some other parents' child, it is an additional cruelty to have to inform them, after they have already agreed to organ donation, that it is now impossible because the medical examiner is against it. Establishing a good working relationship with the medical examiner is the best way to obtain permission for donation in as many cases as possible.

OUTCOME

Of the children who present with clear alteration of consciousness, approximately one-third will die, one-third will be mentally and/or physically disabled, and the final one-third will have a good recovery. These statistics are worse than those for motor vehicle accidents and emphasize the seriousness of this type of abuse in children. Most of the children who die, enter the hospital in deep coma with abnormal motor activity present on examination. These children usually show poor differentiation between gray matter and white matter on the initial CT scan and have very high ICP on admission. As in other forms of hypoxic ischemic injury, controlling the ICP is very difficult and often results in delaying, rather than preventing, death. In the children who survive with severe or even moderate disability, there is the previously noted loss of brain tissue with intracranial calcification, which is also the result of secondary ischemic damage. In these children, intensive care may permit survival, but our current knowledge and therapies are inadequate to reverse the early secondary damage. For children who survive and recover, it is likely that the degree of injury was less and that this was the major contributing factor to outcome, rather than specific benefits of treatment. This is not to infer that early therapy is not important, rather to highlight that prevention, rather than treatment, is the only satisfactory answer to nonaccidental central nervous system trauma to children.

CONCLUSIONS

In the absence of a clearly described and witnessed severe injury to an infant or child, the findings of a disturbed level of consciousness and retinal hemorrhages are sufficient to make a diagnosis of nonaccidental trauma. Falls from tables, chairs, and beds have not been shown to produce sufficient acceleration-deceleration forces to induce subarachnoid and subdural hemorrhage or brain damage. CT scans showing subdural blood along the falx, subarachnoid hemorrhage, or diffuse low density brain are indications of child abuse.

SUGGESTED READINGS

1. Baker ME, Waller AE: Childhood injuries: state by state mortality facts. Johns Hopkins University School of Public Health, Baltimore, January 1989, p. 14
2. Bass M, Kravath RE, Glass L: Death scene investigation in sudden infant death. N Engl J Med 315:100, 1986
3. Billmire ME, Myers PA: Serious head injury in infants: accident or abuse? Pediatrics 75:340, 1985
4. Bohn D, Armstrong D, Becker L, Humphreys R: Cervical spine injuries in children. J Trauma 30:436, 1990
5. Bruce DA: Central nervous system injuries. p. 209. In Welch KS, Randolph JG, Ravitch MM et al (eds): Pediatric Surgery. Year Book Medical Publishers, Chicago, 1986
6. Bruce DA: Treatment of severe head injury. In Tinker J, Zapol WM (eds): Care of the Critically Ill Patient. 2nd Ed. Springer Verlag, New York, 1990
7. Bruce DA, Zimmerman RA: Shaken impact syndrome. Pediatr Ann 18:482, 1989
8. Caffey J: The whiplash shaken infant syndrome: manual shaking by the extremities with whiplash induced intracranial and intraocular bleedings linked with residual permanent brain damage and mental retardation. Pediatrics 54:396, 1974
9. Calder IM, Hill I, Scholtz CL: Primary brain trauma in non accidental injury. J Clin Pathol 37:1095, 1984
10. Christoffel KK: Homicide in childhood: a public health problem in need of attention. Am J Public Health 74:68, 1984
11. Cristoffel KK, Zierserl EJ, Chiarmonte J: Should child abuse and neglect be considered when a child dies unexpectedly? Am J Dis Child 139:876, 1985
12. Cooper A, et al: Major blunt abdominal trauma due to child abuse. J Trauma 28:1483, 1988
13. Daro D, Mitchel L: Child abuse fatalities remain high: the results of the 1987 annual fifty state survey. The National Committee for the Prevention of Child Abuse. 1988, p. 14
14. Duhaime AC, Gennarelli TA, Thibault LE et al: The shaken baby syndrome: a clinical pathological and biomechanical study. J Neurosurg 66:409, 1987
15. Greist KJ, Zumwalt RE: Child abuse by drowning. Pediatrics 83:41, 1989
16. Hadley MN, Sonntag VKW, Rekate HL et al: The infant whiplash-shake injury syndrome. A clinical and pathological study. Neurosurgery 24:536, 1989
17. Hahn YS, Chyung C, Barthei MJ et al: Head injuries in children under 36 months of age: demography and outcome. Child Nervous System 4:34, 1988
18. Hahn YS, Raimondi AS, McLone, DC et al: Traumatic mechanisms of head injury in child abuse. Child Brain 10:229, 1983
19. Jason J, Gilliand JC, Tyler CW: Homicide as a cause of pediatric mortality in the United States. Pediatrics 72:191, 1983
20. Jennett B, Teasdale G, Galbraith S et al: Severe head injuries in three countries. J Neurol Neurosurg Psychiatry 40:291, 1977

21. Krugman RD: Fatal child abuse: analysis of 24 cases. Pediatrician 12:68, 1985
22. Ludwig S, Warman M: Shaken baby syndrome: a review of 20 cases. Ann Emerg Med 13:104, 1990
23. Merrick J: Child abuse and the lack of care. Ugeskr Laeger 151:870, 1989
24. Pang D, Wilberger JE: Spinal chord injuries without radiographic abnormalities in children. J Neurosurg 57:114, 1982
25. Raphaely RC, Swedlow DB, Downes JJ et al: Management of severe pediatric head trauma. Pediatr Clin North Am 27:715, 1980
26. Reilly PL, Simpson DA, Sprod R et al: Assessing the conscious level in infants and young children: a pediatric version of the Glasgow Coma Score. Child Nervous System 4:30, 1988
27. Rivera FP, Kamitsuka MD, Quan L: Injuries to children younger than 1 year of age. Pediatrics 81:93, 1988
28. Waller AE, Baker SP, Syocha A: Childhood injury deaths, national analysis and geographic variations. Am J Public Health 79:310, 1989
29. Zimmerman RA, Bilaniuk LT, Bruce DA et al: Computed tomography of craniocerebral injury in the abused child. Radiology 130:687, 1979

12

Thoracoabdominal Trauma

Arthur Cooper

Much has been learned about child abuse since the first edition of this reference was published a decade ago. It is now known to be only one manifestation of the tragic and vicious cycle of family violence, learned in childhood, and transmitted across generations in affected kinships. It is also recognized to be one part of a more inclusive and insidious syndrome of child abuse and neglect. By some estimates, as many as 5 to 10 percent of all American children have been victims of inappropriately severe corporal punishment or uncontrolled violent physical abuse. Perhaps twice this number, mostly girls, are now believed to have been victims of chronic familial sexual abuse (i.e., incest). Fortunately, serious (i.e., life- or limb-threatening) physical abuse constitutes a relatively small percentage of the total number of reported cases of child abuse, approximately 2.6 percent of the more than 2.4 million annual reports that are brought to the attention of state and local authorities (i.e., 60,000 nationwide). Nevertheless, more than 1200 children die annually in the United States as a result of battering. It is now the most common cause of death in infants 6 to 12 months of age, second only to sudden infant death syndrome (SIDS) in infants 1 to 6 months of age, and there is evidence that this number is increasing.

The aim of this chapter is to familiarize the reader with the recognition and management of thoracoabdominal injuries owing to physical child abuse. However, more than one-half of all victims of major trauma caused by physical abuse are already known to the responsible child welfare agencies from previous episodes of abuse or neglect, underscoring the point that the *missed* diagnosis of abuse or neglect is probably most dangerous to the child at risk. Elsewhere in this volume is important information concerning the etiology and protean manifestations of the syndrome of child abuse and neglect that may assist the reader in identifying possible cases of abuse or neglect. Indeed, only by prevention are the potentially fatal consequences of major trauma owing to physical abuse likely to be avoided.

SPECTRUM OF THORACOABDOMINAL INJURIES

The victims of serious physical abuse in the pediatric age group are most often infants and small children between the ages of 6 months and 3 years. Boys are involved twice as often as girls, while pre-

131

mature infants and stepchildren are especially vulnerable. The former are injured at approximately three times the overall rate, and the latter, about four times the overall rate. Approximately one-third of all children who present with severe injuries caused by nonaccidental trauma are less than 6 months of age. Approximately two-thirds are less than 3 years of age. There are a number of reasons for this. (1) The smaller child is more vulnerable to injury, since the kinetic energy transmitted to the body during blunt impact(s) is dissipated over, and absorbed by, proportionately larger, yet less well protected areas of the body, thus increasing both the severity of injury, and the likelihood of multiple organ injury. (2) The diminutive size, lesser mobility, and inherent defenselessness of smaller children vis a vis larger children make them more convenient targets of abuse, as they are easier to handle, less likely to escape successfully, and virtually unable to resist. (3) Smaller children generally have younger parents who, even if they are not frankly lacking in basic parenting skills, generally will be far less able than more mature individuals to cope with the stresses of everyday living, let alone childrearing. Two-thirds of these parents are products of broken homes.

Physical maltreatment is the cause of about 2.5 percent of injuries deemed serious enough to warrant treatment in pediatric trauma centers. As is the case with most thoracoabdominal trauma in children, regardless of etiology, the mechanism of injury in slightly more than 90 percent of these cases is blunt force. By contrast, a penetrating object is the responsible agent in about 5 percent of the cases, although there is evidence that this number is increasing. The remainder of abuse related injuries are caused by choking, suffocation, and other such acts.

It is important that the treating physician recognize the spectrum of physical injuries observed in children who are victims of physical abuse. If injuries caused by burns, sexual abuse, neglect, and other trauma not a result of blunt force are excluded, about 70 percent of children will be found to have sustained soft tissue injuries only. Of the remainder, about 25 percent will have sustained either a serious head injury or a long-bone fracture, which occur with nearly equal frequency. Occasionally, both, in addition to soft tissue injuries will occur. Certainly no more than 5 percent of children will have serious intrathoracic or intra-abdominal injuries. However, in contrast to other types of injuries, associated soft tissue damage will be present in only one-half of all children with internal truncal injuries.

Intrathoracic Injury

Fortunately, serious intrathoracic injury owing to blunt trauma is a rare event in childhood, regardless of etiology (Table 12-1). This is because the chest wall is extremely compliant; the great flexibility of the cartilaginous ribs that comprise the thoracic cage allow the forces associated even with direct impacts to be absorbed without serious injury to underlying structures. Major intrathoracic injuries, such as disruption of large airways or great vessels, are especially rare in physically abused children. Blows that are forceful enough to cause rib fractures can also result in tension pneumothorax or hemothorax, owing to lacerations of the lung parenchyma or intercostal vessels. Such injuries place the child in grave danger of sudden, marked ventilatory and circulatory compromise. The exceptional mobility of the mediastinum in childhood allows significant pressure to develop within the ipsilateral hemithorax, subsequently leading to compression of both the ipsilateral and

Table 12-1. Severity of Physical Abuse-Related Injuries in Selected North American Pediatric Trauma Centers (1985–1990)

Body Region	Patients (%)	Mortality (%)	Pediatric Trauma Score ≤8[a] (%)
Head only	96 (20)	19 (20)	69 (72)
Face only	5 (1)	0	0
Thorax only	5 (1)	1 (20)	5 (100)
Thorax & other	28 (6)	3 (11)	26 (93)
Abdomen only	13 (3)	0	6 (46)
Abdomen & other	30 (6)	10 (33)	16 (53)
Thorax, abdomen, & other	7 (1)	0	6 (86)
Extremities only	88 (18)	0	43 (49)
External only	69 (14)	0	9 (13)
Other multitrauma	121 (25)	17 (12)	100 (83)
No information	12	—	—
Totals	491	50 (10)	266 (54)

[a] Indicates injuries with significant mortality risk.
(From National Pediatric Trauma Registry,[26] with permission.)

contralateral lungs, and compromise of venous return as the mediastinum shifts.

Complications such as these occur infrequently. Somewhat more common are pulmonary and myocardial contusions, which often occur without overlying bony injury, but rarely cause serious physiologic derangements. However, isolated rib fractures occur with some frequency, and, although they are rare in infants less than 6 months of age, are the most common thoracic injury associated with physical child abuse. The posterolateral aspects of the lower ribs are the most frequent sites of these fractures, as the flanks are the areas most often struck by assailants.

Intra-Abdominal Injury

Serious intra-abdominal injuries are the second most common cause of death in battered children (Table 12-1) and appear to result from one of three mechanisms: (1) crushing of solid upper abdominal viscera against the vertebral column following a heavy blow to the lower ribs or the anterior wall of the upper abdomen, resulting in laceration and hemorrhage; (2) sudden compression of hollow upper abdominal viscera against the vertebral column following blunt trauma inflicted by a direct blow, such as a direct punch or kick to the hypogastric area, resulting in gastrointestinal perforation and peritonitis; and (3) shearing of the posterior attachments or vascular supply of the upper abdominal viscera following rapid deceleration, resulting in mesenteric or cavomesenteric disruption. Massive injuries to the solid viscera of the upper abdomen (the liver, and, to a far lesser extent, the spleen) account for the overwhelming majority of these deaths. Fortunately, injuries of this type occur in only about one-half of the cases, for the exsanguination that invariably accompanies such injuries leads inexorably and inevitably to irreversible hemorrhagic shock unless treated promptly, which happens only rarely. Bursting injuries to the hollow viscera account chiefly for the few remaining deaths. These result from irreversible sepsis and multiple organ system failure that usually follow an extraordinary delay in the presentation of generalized peritonitis caused by forceful transmural disruption of the proximal jejunum, duodenum, and occasionally, the stomach or transverse colon. Such injuries normally are cured by timely recognition and prompt surgical intervention. Renal and pancreatic injuries seldom require operation, and rarely are fatal unless they are associated with extensive hepatic or cavomesenteric disruptions. The same is true for mesenteric or intramural hematoma(s) of the intestinal tract. The exception is the rare intramural duodenal hematoma that causes high intestinal obstruction, which does not resolve spontaneously and therefore requires surgical evacuation.

The inherent vulnerability of the pediatric abdomen to serious injuries is due to several factors. (1) Flexible ribs cover less of the abdomen, and thinner layers of muscle and fat provide less protection to the solid viscera of the upper abdomen. These factors, together with the proportionately larger size of these organs in the child, render them particularly liable to disruption, bleeding, and early development of shock. (2) The small size of the pediatric abdomen predisposes the child to multiple injuries during the dissipation of energy from a blunt force. (3) Marked gastric distension, as a result of the air swallowing associated with crying, bloats the stomach, making it far more susceptible to rupture. Gastric distension also contributes significantly both to ventilatory compromise, owing to limitation of diaphragmatic motion and increased risk of aspiration, as well as to circulatory

compromise, owing to vagally mediated dampening of the normal tachycardic response to hypovolemia.

The remarkable similarity in observed patterns of intra-abdominal injury (Table 12-2) suggests a number of conclusions about major blunt abdominal trauma. (1) Four distinctive patterns of injury can be recognized. (2) Mortality is specifically related both to type and severity of injury, hence the rapidity and degree of blood loss. (3) The presenting vital signs and initial hematocrit values taken together serve as reliable clues to the extent of blood loss, and may therefore be useful in guiding further therapy. Because the vital signs and hematocrit *jointly* reflect the extent of blood loss, they are good indicators of the type and severity of injury. Patients with duodenal or pancreatic hematomas present with low normal hematocrit levels but stable pulses and blood pressure levels, indicative of mild blood loss limited to a confined space with full circulatory compensation. Patients with duodenal or jejunal disruptions present with normal or high normal hemotocrit levels, with fever and tachycardia indicative of a systemic response to peritonitis. Patients with minor solid visceral injuries present with low hematocrit levels, tachycardia, and mild hypotension that respond promptly to volume resuscitation, is indicative of moderate blood loss that proves to be self-limited. Mortalities generally are rare among patients with duodenal or pancreatic hematomas, minor solid visceral injuries, and duodenal or jejunal disruptions. However, patients with major solid visceral—particularly hepatic—or retroperitoneal vessel injuries, if not dead on arrival at the hospital or in frank traumatic cardiac arrest, present with low hematocrit levels, marked tachycardia, and profound hypotension. These signs are indicative of exsanguinating hemorrhage and profound shock, which is often irreversible be-

Table 12-2. Frequency of Injury to Intrathoracic and Intra-Abdominal Organs Reportedly Due to Physical Abuse in Published Literature[a]

	Neck	Heart	Lung	Dia-phragm	Head/ Thorax	Liv-er	Kid-ney	Spleen	Pan-creas	Stom-ach	Small Intes-tine	Large Intes-tine	Mesentery	Other
Thoracic														
McCort and Vaudagna[23]	2	—	2		—									
Sivit et al.[31]	4	—	3	—	1									
National Pediatric Trauma Registry[26]	5	2	2	1	—									
Totals	11	2	7	1	1									
Abdominal														
McCort and Vaudagna[23]	8					2	—	—	—	1	7	—	1	—
Touloukian[34]	5					—	—	—	3	—	5	1	3	1[b]
Gornall et al.[13]	6					2	—	—	—	—	2	1	—	—
O'Neill et al.[28]	9					3	1	—	1	—	2	1	1	—
Cooper et al.[10]	22					9	2	1	1	—	9	—	4	—
Ledbetter et al.[21]	24					8	3	—	2	—	{6 & 2}		—	—[c]
Sivit et al.[31]	14					6	2	3	1	—	2	1	1	1
National Pediatric Trauma Registry[26]	45					16	9	3	2	1	15	9	—	1
Totals	133					46	17	7	10	2	48	15	10	2

[a] Note that the eight "bowel" cases reported by Ledbetter et al. are not further delineated with regard to anatomic site. For the purpose of constructing this table, it is assumed that the expected distribution was in fact observed.

[b] Common bile duct.

[c] Urinary bladder.

cause of the nearly universal delay in presentation observed in cases of physical maltreatment. Even so, the value of the foregoing indicators notwithstanding, it cannot be emphasized too strongly that the hematocrit level can be properly interpreted only when considered *together* with hemodynamic status and response to a fluid challenge.

RECOGNITION OF THORACOABDOMINAL INJURIES

Although the abused child may present with major, life-threatening injuries, the usual presentation includes less serious injuries resulting from the use of excessive force in physical discipline. However, as previously noted, the child who initially presents with minor injuries unrecognized as child abuse may return subsequently with lethal injuries, underscoring that accurate diagnosis is vital. Unfortunately, because parental histories are notoriously inaccurate—whether for fear of self-incrimination, or for simple lack of knowledge of what may have transpired while the child was under the supervision of another adult—the diagnosis of child abuse is rarely straightforward, and occasionally confounds the most seasoned expert. Thus, a high index of suspicion is the most important tool in the diagnostic armamentarium of the physician who assumes responsibility for victims of physical maltreatment.

Physical Examination

Because the history proffered in cases of physical abuse is most often vague or evasive, the physical examination is key to identifying and categorizing injuries, including those in the thoracoabdominal region. Fortunately, the clinical manifes-tations of child abuse caused by blunt trauma, the mechanism of injury in most cases of physical maltreatment, have by this time been well characterized and categorized. Moreover, that these injuries are known to occur in distinctive patterns will lead the knowledgeable physician to search for other lesions commonly associated with the particular mechanism of injury that is postulated. However, while the physically abused child may have injuries to many organ systems, the overwhelming majority, perhaps as many as 70 percent, have injuries that are limited to the soft tissues of the head and neck, torso, and extremities. Of the remainder, most will have sustained closed head or long bone injuries in addition to soft tissue injuries. Only a small fraction, no more than about 5 percent, will have suffered serious internal injuries of the chest or abdomen. Unfortunately, despite their rarity in the physically abused child, external signs of associated overlying soft tissue damage may be lacking in as many as one-half of these cases, particularly those involving the abdomen.

Since a large proportion of physically abused children with significant torso injuries will show no external signs of trauma, the physical examination must be especially thorough. Swelling, deformity, discoloration, and point tenderness are the main signs of underlying bony or internal injuries. Thus, in addition to an external physical examination looking for fresh and old bruises, lacerations, burn sores, and scars, careful examination of the head, neck, chest, abdomen, spine, and extremities must also be performed. The child also must be evaluated for signs of coexisting sexual abuse, which is often ignored if the attention of the treating physician is focused on the more obvious injuries.

The axiom that a high index of suspicion is required to make a diagnosis of child abuse is especially poignant insofar as thoracoabdominal injuries are concerned, for two reasons: (1) since physical child abuse most commonly involves the skin, the soft tissues, the bones, and the head, the possibility of serious thoracoabdominal injury is often overlooked and (2) the histories proffered by the child's caretakers, while they, also, follow typical patterns, are often misleading. The latter is especially true for abdominal trauma. Patients with hollow visceral injuries usually present with nonspecific dysfunctional gastrointestinal complaints. Patients with solid visceral injuries often present with lethargy or coma, depending on the degree of hemodynamic stability, either of unknown cause, or subsequent to a seemingly trivial episode of head trauma, such as a fall from a bed. The mortality rate for serious intra-abdominal injuries of this type approaches 50 percent, a statistic that has not changed appreciably since the appearance of the first detailed review of this subject nearly a generation ago. Failure of parents to seek prompt medical attention obviously contributes to this unacceptably high mortality rate. However, while it is unclear to what extent lack of early recognition at the time of the initial examination may contribute to this problem, there is little doubt that the attention of the treating physician may, on some occasions, be directed elsewhere.

Obviously, the physician's attention must be directed specifically to the chest if there is any history of chest pain, noisy or rapid breathing, respiratory insufficiency, or hemoptysis. Similarly, a history of abdominal pain, tenderness, distension, or vomiting, especially if the emesis is stained with blood or bile (the latter, incidentally, is the most common symptom in physically abused children who have sustained significant intra-abdominal injury) mandates an especially thorough abdominal examination. If abnormal findings are noted, attention should be redirected to other areas of the body in a careful search for associated conditions that may have been overlooked. The amount of force required to seriously injure the chest or abdomen of a child, and the usual mechanism by which this force is transmitted (i.e., kicking or punching), suggests that other areas of the body may also have been severely battered and perhaps injured occultly.

Chest Examination

In examining the chest, the physician's first responsibility is to rule out immediately life-threatening chest injuries, such as those that compromise the adequacy of ventilation or oxygenation. Therefore, the sufficiency of gas exchange is first assured by visualizing bilateral chest rise and auscultating breath sounds. The presence of unilaterally decreased breath sounds with hyperresonance or dullness to percussion, with or without tracheal shift, suggests the development of tension pneumothorax or hemothorax, respectively; both must be treated emergently. The presence of point tenderness, palpable bony deformity, crepitus, or subcutaneous emphysema suggests rib fracture(s); the presence of firm, nodular masses of the anterior chest wall that directly overlay the junctions between the rib and cartilage suggests costochondral disarticulations. Incidentally, these cannot be seen on radiographs and occasionally are mistaken for bone tumors.

Abdominal Examination

In examining the abdomen, the physician must first be aware of the extent to which gastric distension may confound evaluation; it can mimic or mask life-threatening, intra-abdominal hemorrhage, and may cause sufficient abdominal tenderness to simulate peritonitis. Thus, the first step in examining the abdomen, if abdominal distension is present, is to insert a nasogastric tube to empty the stomach and, simultaneously, to look for blood or bile. An abdomen that remains distended following gastric decompression, particularly if hemodynamic instability is present, strongly suggests intra-abdominal bleeding, most often from the spleen or liver. However, if fever, marked tenderness, and involuntary guarding are present together with abdominal distension, particularly if the nasogastric aspirate is stained with blood or bile and bowel sounds cannot be auscultated, acute peritonitis caused by enteric perforation, and subsequent irritation by chyme, should be suspected.

Rectal Examination

Rectal examination, often overlooked in the pediatric trauma victim, may yield valuable information that otherwise might be ignored. The presence of blood, obvious or occult, usually indicates that the rectum or sigmoid colon has been damaged; bleeding from more proximal sites is unusual. Anterior rectal tenderness may indicate parietal peritoneal irritation owing to intraperitoneal blood or feces. Obviously, loss of normal sphincter tone suggests the possibility of coexisting sexual abuse.

Laboratory Evaluation

Laboratory evaluation is an integral part of the workup of all child trauma victims. A complete blood count must be obtained in all physically abused children to exclude anemia, which suggests bleeding. However, since the initial value, by itself, will be of limited utility unless equilibration has occurred, serial hematocrit values may offer more reliable clues to the extent of bleeding, if any. Blood clotting studies, such as platelet count, bleeding time, partial thromboplastin time, and prothrombin time, must also be obtained to exclude unexpected coagulopathy, especially in patients with multiple bruises. Elevation in the serum con-

centration of amylase indicates the presence of injury to the pancreas, and possibly the spleen, because it is contiguous with the tail of the pancreas. Similarly, elevations in the serum concentrations of the hepatic transaminases suggest injury to the liver. Urine that is grossly bloody, or that is positive for blood by dipstick or microscopy showing 20 or more red blood cells per high power field, suggests renal damage, and, indirectly, damage to adjacent organs, owing to the high incidence of associated injuries in blunt renal trauma. However, it must be noted that myoglobinuria, which turns the urine brown, and is sometimes mistaken for hematuria despite the absence of confirmatory microscopic findings, also yields positive results on dipstick examination. If this should occur, and elevation of the skeletal muscle fraction of creatine phosphokinase is subsequently demonstrated, the presence of deep contusions is confirmed, even if there is no visible evidence of damage to overlying skin. Treatment for probable crush injury (i.e., rhabdomyolysis) is then undertaken. Likewise, hemoglobinuria, which turns the urine pink and typically is associated with a normal urinary sediment, also has been reported as a consequence of physical abuse. If this is detected, transfusion reaction must be excluded, and the patient treated, as in rhabdomyolysis, by means of aggressive hydration.

Radiologic Examination

Radiologic examination constitutes a vitally important part of the overall evaluation. If there is any evidence or suspicion that the injuries sustained are potentially serious, a specific trauma series of radiographs (lateral cervical spine, supine chest, and combined supine abdominal and pelvic) is ordered. This is assuming that the patient does not require emergent surgery. Arrangements should also be made at this time, before any other radiographs are ordered, to obtain computed tomographs (CT) of the head and abdomen. These must include the administration of dilute meglumine diatrizoate (Hypaque R) suspension via the nasogastric tube if CT is required (see below). Once these have been obtained, whatever other radiographs are required should be taken, as indicated by clinical findings.

A few points concerning interpretation of plain radiographs of the chest and abdomen must be emphasized insofar as the diagnosis of thoracoabdominal trauma is concerned. (1) While any child who requires resuscitation will have had a supine anteroposterior chest radiograph as part of the workup for multiple trauma, geometry and gravity both dictate that small amounts of blood or air, which "layer out" anteriorly and posteriorly, respectively, when the child lies flat, may make detection extremely difficult. Thus, as soon as possible after physiologic stability has been achieved, a posteroanterior chest radiograph should be obtained with the child in the upright position, which is better for identifying small apical pneumothoraces or hemothoraces in the costophrenic sulcus. (2) The sine qua non of radiographic detection of child abuse is the presence of multiple fractures in various stages of healing, particularly rib fractures. Thus, chest or rib radiographs must be carefully scrutinized for evidence of callus formation as well as bony discontinuity. Callus formation indicates that fractures are old or healing, and bony discontinuity indicates that fractures are recent. If the fractures noted involve the lower ribs, bony discontinuity also suggests that there may be associated injuries to the spleen or liver. It must be noted that posterolateral rib fractures, if undisplaced, may be difficult or impossible to diagnose by plain radiograph in

the acute phase. Oblique views or nuclear bone scan should therefore be obtained if these injuries are suspected. (3) The most common signs of solid visceral injury on x-rays are a ground-glass appearance of the abdominal cavity as a whole, suggesting the presence of intraperitoneal hemorrhage, and medial displacement of the lateral border of the stomach—marked by the nasogastric tube—by the spleen, suggesting splenic laceration or hematoma, particularly if bleeding from short gastric vessels gives the fundic mucosa a "saw tooth" appearance. However, signs of hollow visceral injuries are much more subtle; indeed, short of contrast studies, the only clue to duodenal or proximal jejunal hematoma, when a nasogastric tube is in place, may be the relative lack of gas in the distal small intestine, although this is rarely an early sign. Similarly, disruptions of the duodenum or proximal jejunum may be heralded only by tiny retroperitoneal (i.e., perirenal) gas shadows, which may not be seen, on the right side of the abdomen, adjacent to and slightly below the liver, and ileus, which is a nonspecific finding. As radiopaque contrast studies may or may not demonstrate the injury, the pneumoperitoneum, which would obviously confirm its presence but which is rarely identified on plain radiograph, may not be detected unless air injected via the nasogastric tube is used as a radiolucent contrast agent.

Imaging Modalities and Other Diagnostic Procedures

The introduction of sophisticated imaging modalities such as nuclear scanning, ultrasonography, and CT has revolutionized the management of all pediatric abdominal trauma, including physical abuse. In general, CT is best for evaluation of solid visceral injuries, such as those to the liver, spleen, and kidneys, and to a lesser extent for detection of hollow visceral injury, such as to the gastro-intestinal area. Ultrasonography is best for evaluation of pancreatic injuries and to rule out the presence of free intraperitoneal fluid, that is, blood, in the splenic and pelvic fossae. The use of CT, however, depends on the use of both oral and IV contrast agents. These agents usually are contraindicated in patients with histories of anaphylactoid reactions to iodinated contrast agents, unless they are known to have been successfully pretreated with corticosteroids or antihistaminics. The use of CT also depends on the patient lying still, which occasionally may require the use of sedation or neuromuscular blockade, providing that adequate ventilation, oxygenation, and perfusion can be maintained throughout the course of the study.

Fortunately, the need for studies such as these is limited. Abdominal CTs should be obtained whenever there are signs of internal bleeding, such as abdominal distension or bruising, or a history of shock that responds to volume resuscitation. However, they also should be obtained if there are injuries that suggest significant intra-abdominal trauma. Ultrasonography is reserved for suspected cases of intra-abdominal injury when CT cannot be obtained, whether owing to lack of equipment or a history of allergy to iodinated contrast agents; it is also used in screening for the presence of intraperitoneal blood. Nuclear scans, which remain the "gold standard" for detection of splenic and hepatic injuries, are now reserved for follow-up of solid visceral injuries initially detected by CT; they are also indicated when such injuries are suspected but CT cannot be obtained and ultrasonography is negative.

The radiographic diagnosis of blunt renal injuries has rapidly evolved in recent years. Ultrasonography has become the diagnostic study of choice when information is sought regarding the struc-tural integrity of the kidneys, while nuclear renal perfusion scans have become the standard test of renal function. Nonetheless, abdominal CT, if obtained, will serve to rule out major abnormalities, and will generally suffice, unless minor injuries are suspected that are beyond the resolution of the scanner. Finally, while IV urography has been largely replaced by these techniques, it is still used in situations where isolated blunt renal injury is suspected: for example, if neither clinical findings nor a mechanism of injury indicate damage to adjacent structures, if urinalysis shows significant microscopic hematuria (i.e., 20 or more red blood cells per high power field), and if no other reliable test of renal function is immediately available. Arteriography is only required for the diagnosis of renal pedicle injury if specific information regarding vascular anatomy is needed prior to emergent surgery. Although such an injury is rare, it should always be suspected since hematuria, gross or microscopic, is not always present.

Splenic and hepatic lacerations in most children will heal spontaneously without the need for surgery, rendering diagnostic peritoneal lavage moot in most instances since the need for surgery is based not on the presence or absence of intraperitoneal blood, but on the ongoing transfusion requirement. Diagnostic peritoneal lavage is therefore reserved for patients for whom the usual diagnostic modalities of serial physical and laboratory evaluation are unavailable or unreliable, for example, patients who are unconscious, or who are about to undergo general anesthesia for operative treatment of associated, usually musculoskeletal, injuries. It has no place in the management of the hemodynamically unstable patient who requires laparotomy for control of intra-abdominal bleeding, since it will add nothing to what is already known, and will serve only to delay definitive surgical therapy.

Some authorities have suggested that there may be a role for routine diagnostic peritoneal lavage in individuals who have sustained blunt or penetrating injuries, which may have violated the integrity of the bowel. However, most experts in pediatric trauma believe that frequent serial examination for signs of peritoneal irritation by a surgeon experienced in the management of childhood trauma is probably the more sensitive test. It certainly avoids the complications associated with diagnostic peritoneal lavage. It also negates the possibility that later physical or radiographic examinations will be confounded by tenderness resulting from intraperitoneal blood from the puncture site on the abdominal wall, or air introduced at the time of the procedure.

MANAGEMENT OF THORACOABDOMINAL INJURIES

An in-depth discussion of the management of the seriously injured child is beyond the scope of this chapter. The medical care of the intentionally injured child should be initiated by a physician experienced in the management of pediatric emergencies and directed by a surgeon experienced in managing childhood trauma. Initial assessment of the abused child trauma victim should proceed according to established guidelines, such as those contained in the pediatric trauma sections of the *Advanced Trauma Life Support Student Manual* and the *Advanced Pediatric Life Support Student Manual*. Resuscitation of the battered child in actual or impending cardiorespiratory arrest should follow the standards outlined in the *Textbook of Pediatric Advanced Life Support*. Manage-

ment of specific injuries will be directed by the appropriate surgical specialist.

General Considerations

The basic principles governing resuscitation of the child with thoracoabdominal injuries resulting from physical abuse, priority attention to the airway, breathing, and circulation, are no different than for the child who has sustained nonintentional injuries to these body cavities. This combined "primary assessment" and "resuscitation phase" obviously precedes the head-to-toe evaluation of the patient for signs of specific injuries, which constitutes the "secondary assessment." During the secondary assessment, definitive management of serious thoracoabdominal injuries is first undertaken, unless there is an injury to the chest that poses an immediate threat to the integrity of ventilation. Fortunately, such injuries are rare in physically abused children, except when a penetrating instrument is used. On the other hand, less than one-half of the patients who sustain serious intrathoracic or intra-abdominal injuries have external signs to suggest that blunt force was the causative agent. This means that the diagnosis of internal hemorrhage may be delayed, adding to the already considerable morbidity and mortality observed in this group of patients.

Blunt trauma may not be recognized immediately as the true cause of illness in the physically abused child, underscoring the necessity of a physiologic approach to the resuscitation of all critically ill children, regardless of diagnosis. Rapid clinical assessment of ventilation, oxygenation, and perfusion is fundamental to this process. Any child presenting with respiratory distress should immediately be given 100 percent oxygen via a nonrebreathing mask if the airway is patent and breathing is spontaneous. If the child further deteriorates or presents with frank respiratory failure, such as cyanosis or overwhelming fatigue in addition to the above symptoms and signs, the airway must be opened and 100 percent oxygen provided by artificial means (e.g., a bag-valve device or an endotracheal tube). Any child presenting with shock or major trauma is also a candidate for oxygen therapy.

In general, shock is present in a child when there is tachycardia and impairment of circulation to the extremities. Normal systolic blood pressure for any age is calculated as 80 + [2 × age (in years)], while the diastolic blood pressure is approximately two-thirds of this number. In early or compensated shock, systolic blood pressure remains normal as diastolic blood pressure increases, owing to the remarkable capacity of the child to vasoconstrict in response to hypovolemia. In late or decompensated shock, systolic blood pressure decreases below 70 + [2 × age (in years)], indicating failure of the compensatory mechanism. Thus, life-threatening hemorrhage is indicated by the presence of hypotension or hypovolemia that does not respond promptly to administration of sufficient fluid to replace 25 to 30 percent of circulating blood volume, that is, two to three 20 ml/kg boluses of lactated Ringer's solution. With few exceptions, such patients cannot survive without emergent surgery.

Volume resuscitation is best performed by means of short, fat peripheral lines placed percutaneously in the median cubital veins at the elbow or saphenous veins at the ankle, or by cutdown in the saphenous veins at the ankle or groin. Insertion of central venous lines will not be needed, except in very rare cases where venous access cannot otherwise be obtained; measurement of urine output and examination of distal pulses and dermal perfusion will usually suffice for monitoring volume status. Any child whose circulation cannot be stabilized with 40 to 60 ml/kg of lactated Ringer's solution is likely to need emergent surgery. Equally urgent at this point, however, since oxygen carrying capacity as well as intravascular volume will be jeopardized by continued hemorrhage, is the need to replace ongoing blood loss using type-specific blood if immediately available, type O negative blood if not, in rapidly infused aliquots of 10 to 20 ml/kg of packed red blood cells or 20 to 40 ml/kg of whole blood.

Any child who presents with respiratory insufficiency or shock or requires resuscitation in an emergency department should be admitted to a critical care unit for further treatment, regardless of whether trauma is present or surgery is ultimately performed. Fortunately, few children who are physically abused sustain injuries serious enough to require resuscitation; nevertheless, some means of assessing the physiologic risk of injury should be used routinely to ensure that potentially life-threatening injuries are not overlooked. Children should be considered for triage or transfer to a regional pediatric trauma center if the mechanism of injury suggests that this level of care may be required or if their Pediatric Trauma Score is eight or less (Table 12-3). Generally, it is safe to proceed with "routine" admission and workup of the potential child abuse victim if the chosen index falls within the low risk category.

With the single exception of the hypopharyngeal soft tissue upper airway obstruction that accompanies head injury severe enough to produce coma, virtually all serious respiratory problems will be caused by serious injuries to the upper airway or chest. Similarly, virtually all instances of shock observed in children who have been physically abused will be because of serious intra-abdominal injuries, since shock resulting from intrathor-

Table 12-3. Pediatric Trauma Score

	+2	+1	−1
Size (kg)	>20	10–20	<10
Airway	Normal	Maintained	Unmaintained
Systolic blood pressure (mmHg)	>90	50–90	<50
Central nervous system	Awake	Obtunded	Coma
Open wound	None	Minor	Major
Skeletal trauma	None	Closed	Open-multiple

(From Tepas et al.,[32] with permission.)

acic or isolated intracranial or skeletal injuries is extremely rare. The general diagnosis and treatment of these injuries are outlined below. Other acute problems such as head, skeletal, soft tissue, and thermal injuries are managed according to guidelines discussed elsewhere in this volume.

Thoracic Injuries

Serious chest injuries are uncommon in childhood and usually will not require major surgery. Major intrathoracic injuries caused by physical abuse are especially rare, and not usually life-threatening. Most abuse related thoracic injuries are limited to the chest wall and are managed either expectantly or by simple tube thoracostomy. Accompanying pulmonary or myocardial contusions must be carefully monitored by serial physical and radiographic examinations, oximetry, capnography, blood gas determinations, serial cardiac enzyme determinations, electrocardiography, and echocardiography. Tension pneumothorax, massive hemothorax, cardiac tamponde, and flail chest are also life-threatening conditions that, if present, require urgent attention.

Specific resuscitative measures for these are outlined elsewhere.

Abdominal Injuries

Treatment of serious intra-abdominal injuries has changed rapidly in recent years, an evolution largely driven by the extraordinary power of current imaging technologies. The definitive therapy is frequently nonoperative, especially with respect to lacerations, hematomas, and extravasations of the liver, kidneys, and spleen. However, the term *nonoperative* does not mean *nonsurgical*. As with appendicitis, for example, surgical judgment is needed to determine if and when surgical intervention is required, and the type of operation that should be performed. If at all possible, a pediatric surgeon experienced in the management of nonaccidental trauma should be consulted.

Liver
The liver is the solid organ most commonly injured by blunt trauma in physically abused children. The nonoperative management of small capsular lacera-

tions, which have ceased active bleeding, and self-contained subcapsular hematomas, is now widely accepted as safe. However, large stellate lacerations and subcapsular hematomas that have eroded through Glisson's capsule rarely stop bleeding without surgical intervention. Moreover, since most abused children with injuries of this type do not present until they are in profound shock, the mortality of these injuries is high. Given the delay in presentation that is inherent to this particular form of trauma, it is doubtful if the mortality rate will improve significantly as a result of further refinements in diagnosis and treatment.

The clinical presentation of hepatic trauma is dependent on the extent of damage to the liver and ranges from nonspecific abdominal pain to post-traumatic cardiac arrest. Most liver injuries encountered in battered children are minor and may go undetected. On the other hand, the key to effective management of severe liver injuries is timely recognition and treatment of shock. If the child presents in decompensated shock, or compensated shock that fails to stabilize or stabilizes only transiently following administration of three successive 20 ml/kg boluses of lactated Ringer's solution, it is likely that abdominal bleeding is present. Emergent laparotomy is therefore indicated, and must be preceded by the rapid administration of 10 to 20 ml/kg of packed red blood cells or 20 to 40 ml/kg of whole blood, type specific if available, O negative if not.

Patients with liver injuries who do not present in decompensated shock and respond promptly to volume resuscitation will likely not require laparotomy for control of bleeding, which usually will have ceased spontaneously. However, if the ongoing transfusion requirement exceeds 50 percent of estimated circulating blood volume (i.e., 40 ml/kg) during the 24 hours immediately following injury, lap-

arotomy should be undertaken for control of bleeding. Patients who have achieved this degree of hemodynamic stability generally will have undergone CT so the extent of injuries usually will be known before operative intervention is begun. This does not relieve the surgeon of the responsibility for making a careful, thorough search of the abdominal cavity for unanticipated injuries, if laparotomy is ultimately required.

Kidneys

After the liver, the kidneys are the solid organs most commonly injured in cases of physical child abuse. This may seem paradoxical at first, since these organs are so well protected by the paraspinous muscles and are embedded in fat pads enclosed by tough fascial envelopes. However, the flanks are the areas of the body perhaps most often struck repeatedly and forcefully, and injuries to these organs will not be infrequent. Yet, because the kidneys are so well protected, tremendous force is required to injure them; it is therefore hardly surprising that injuries to adjacent, less well protected organs occur in as many as 80 percent of the cases in which renal injury is present. For this reason, any suggestion of renal injury mandates an aggressive workup of the kidneys and associated organs.

Because the classic findings of renal injury—flank pain, tenderness, and a mass—are difficult to elicit in the child, the absence of these symptoms and signs in no way excludes the diagnosis of renal trauma. The diagnosis of significant renal injury is heralded by the presence of significant hematuria, either gross or microscopic (i.e., more than 20 red blood cells per high power field). It is confirmed by CT or other imaging techniques, initiated in response to the presence of blood in the urine, or a mechanism of injury that suggests damage to upper abdominal viscera. Unfortunately, there does not seem to be any direct correlation between the degree of hematuria and the severity of injury. Thus, any child who presents with significant hematuria must be assumed to have sustained serious injury until proved otherwise.

It is uncommon for renal injuries to require direct operative intervention in the acute stage as most renal injuries are not severe. Contusions and small capsular lacerations predominate; rarely, retroperitoneal extravasation may develop when communication exists between the renal calyx, usually at the pelvocaliceal junction, and the perinephric space, and leaks through a rent in Gerota's fascia. While this injury may ultimately require surgical repair, it is rarely necessary in the acute stage, unless there is major disruption or frank transection of a portion of the main collecting system. Most small urinary leaks, in fact, are self-sealing, particularly if they are parenchymal in origin. However, if the "urinoma" persists or becomes infected, surgery will be necessary.

Spleen

The spleen is the solid organ most commonly injured in childhood when all etiologies of trauma are considered. However, it is less frequently injured than either the liver or the kidneys in blunt trauma owing to physical abuse. The reasons for this are not entirely clear. It is probably because of the relative degree of protection afforded by the ribs, which is not available to the hollow viscera of the upper abdomen, the pancreas, and much of the liver. The symptoms and signs of this injury are identical to those observed in other types of blunt splenic trauma: left upper quadrant pain, which may radiate to the left shoulder, and left upper quadrant tenderness. The diagnosis is also suspected if there is persistent

unexplained leukocytosis, or, as previously noted, hyperamylasemia, and is confirmed by the appropriate radiographic studies.

Management of blunt splenic injury is usually nonoperative; conservative treatment is generally successful, and exploration via laparotomy is required only rarely. The same caveats that apply to blunt hepatic injury regarding presentation in decompensated shock are also true for blunt splenic injury. On the other hand, nonoperative management is somewhat more successful than similar management of hepatic injuries. In part, this is because the transverse orientation of most parenchymal lacerations, parallel to the blood vessels, and the thicker, more elastic nature of the splenic capsule in childhood, combine to increase the likelihood of spontaneous cessation of bleeding when the patient is hypotensive or placed on strict bed rest. However, that the overwhelming majority of splenic injuries, even those caused by physical abuse, will heal spontaneously on a regimen of limited activity, must not lull the responsible surgeon into a false sense of security. Children who require replacement of 50 percent or more of their circulating blood volume within 24 hours of injury are candidates for operation. Moreover, splenic lacerations that have ceased active bleeding, and previously contained subcapsular hematomas, may subsequently leak or rupture, classically on the third to fifth day following injury. Thus, the surgeon who selects a nonoperative course of management must be prepared for an extended period of careful observation, including frequent reexamination.

In the rare instance that operation does prove to be required, the spleen is found to be bleeding actively and control of hemorrhage is impossible either by direct suture repair or topical application of bovine collagen or regenerated cellulose hemostat. Splenectomy should be avoided and a splenic salvage procedure utilized if at all feasible. This is because the incidence of overwhelming postsplenectomy infections in childhood—particularly those caused by encapsulated bacterial organisms such as *Streptococcus pneumoniae*, and, to a lesser extent, *Haemophilus influenzae, Neisseria meningitidis, Staphylococcus aureus*, and *Escherichia coli*—is considerable. Fortunately, the results of splenorrhaphy, or partial splenectomy, have been as good as with nonoperative management. However, care must be taken to ensure that sufficient splenic mass is left intact so that the organ can function normally. While the data are based largely on animal studies and therefore are not directly applicable to humans, it appears that 50 percent or more of the splenic mass is required for protection. Any patient requiring a splenectomy should receive antipneumococcal vaccine as soon as possible before surgery. Even more important, splenic salvage procedures should not be undertaken if there are any untoward risks. While it is better to save the spleen than to remove it, it is better still to save the child's life.

Pancreas

The pancreas is not commonly injured in cases of physical abuse. Its location deep in the upper abdomen accounts for its relative invulnerability. However, its fixed position directly anterior to the vertebral column suggests that when the impact is of sufficient force, it will absorb the full dose of kinetic energy applied to it. Therefore, serious injuries to the pancreas tend to be central, and consist mainly of moderate to severe pancreatic hematomas and, in severe cases, transection. Disruption of the pancreatic duct is a constant feature of transection, but may also occur as a result of hematomas. In these instances, unless the injury is self-sealing or there is free communication with the lesser peritoneal sac, a pancreatic pseudocyst will begin to develop within 3 to 5 days; this is in contrast to chemical peritonitis, which results immediately from leakage of pancreatic fluid into the peritoneal sac causing pancreatic ascites.

However, while severe pancreatic injury is rare, traumatic pancreatitis is commonly observed in cases of physical abuse. As previously noted, the disease is suspected if there is deep epigastric pain radiating to the back or deep tenderness on palpation of the upper abdomen. Its presence is confirmed by elevated serum levels of amylase or lipase. Together with other activated pancreatic enzymes, amylase and lipase are responsible for the inflammation and the erosive, necrotizing pancreatic autolysis or chemical peritonitis associated, respectively, with the more localized and more generalized forms of the disease. Detection of pancreatitis in the physically abused child is vital for two reasons. (1) The amount of force required to cause injury to the pancreas makes injury to adjacent organs (e.g., the stomach, colon, duodenum, and spleen) that much more likely. (2) As trauma is by far the leading cause of pancreatitis in childhood, child abuse must be suspected in high-risk cases, unless there is reason to suspect a medical cause, such as gallstones, or the presence of certain drugs and medications, such as alcohol, corticosteroids, and antineoplastics. Moreover, while cases of isolated traumatic pancreatitis owing to physical child abuse have been reported, they are not common. Thus, any child who presents with signs of pancreatic injury without adequate explanation should be completely evaluated for other injuries associated with child abuse.

Treatment of simple traumatic pancreatitis is expectant, and consists of bed and bowel rest, nasogastric decompression as tolerated, IV fluids as necessary, and, if pain persists for more than a few days, total parenteral nutrition. Refeeding with clear liquids, followed by a low fat diet, is allowed when pain and tenderness subside, and the serum amylase level returns to normal. While serum amylase may again rise to an abnormal level after oral intake begins, reversion to bowel rest and parenteral nutrition generally is unnecessary unless the patient develops a recrudescence of symptoms, even if abnormal serum amylase levels persist for weeks to months. By contrast, patients in whom a pancreatic pseudocyst develops will require 6 to 8 weeks of complete bowel rest and total parenteral nutrition in preparation for an internal drainage procedure. Obviously, patients with evidence of severe pancreatic injury (i.e., a large, tender, epigastric mass caused by massive hematoma or abscess, or acute peritonitis owing to chemical irritation by ascitic fluid containing pancreatic enzymes, or abnormal sonographic or tomographic findings) are candidates for early surgery.

Alimentary Tract

While, as a group, solid visceral injuries are somewhat more common than hollow visceral injuries, the latter occur with considerable frequency. The central upper abdominal organs (e.g., stomach, duodenum, proximal jejunum, and transverse colon) are most commonly injured. With the exception of the duodenum, whose fixed retroperitoneal location makes it particularly susceptible to intramural hematoma, "blowout" injuries are the type most frequently encountered. As previously noted, they are best detected by means of plain radiographic studies in which air is used as a contrast agent, although there clearly is a role for water-soluble radiopaque contrast agents, particularly in CT. However, the sine qua non in diagnosis of these injuries is frequent serial physical examination, looking particularly for signs of parietal peritoneal irritation, which invariably will develop within 6 to 12 hours of injury if the integrity of the gut has been violated.

Although rare, perforations of the stomach (notorious for their rapid onset of pain, tenderness, and spasm of the abdominal musculature) and early development of shock (owing to the fluid shifts resulting from exposure of the peritoneal cavity to large amounts of gastric acid) do occasionally result from physical abuse. By contrast, intestinal ruptures, while much more common than gastric perforations, are also far more insidious in their presentation; abdominal pain, distension, and vomiting are invariably present, as well as fever, abdominal tenderness, and spasm. These symptoms and signs develop gradually, and become florid only when 6 to 12 hours have elapsed since the time of injury. However, if presentation or diagnosis is further delayed, the child may present in profound septic shock, which may ultimately prove lethal.

While the histories proffered in such cases by parents will not ordinarily be helpful, the presence of an acute surgical abdomen is an ominous finding that warrants immediate resuscitation and urgent operation, regardless of cause. Thus, failure to suspect child abuse in such cases will seldom delay appropriate therapy; the true etiology of the injuries usually will become apparent after pathologic examination. Treatment of gastric and enteric perforations, once they are recognized, is relatively straightforward and consists of primary suture repair and nasogastric decompression. Perforations of the transverse colon, however, may require diversion, that is, colostomy, if the degree of contamination and inflammation is so great that direct repair cannot safely be performed.

Intramural hematoma of the duodenum is virtually pathognomonic of child abuse, unless there is a specific history of blunt injury to the upper abdomen. Like the pancreas, its fixed retroperitoneal location and rich vascular supply make it especially susceptible to injury when impacting forces are transmitted to the retroperitoneum. The hematoma forms beneath the mucosa, which is loosely attached to the deeper layers of the intestinal wall. It usually does not completely obstruct the duodenum until several hours or days have elapsed, during which time the hematoma further expands with edema fluid. The diagnosis is suspected when a child presents with unexplained bilious vomiting in the absence of fever or parietal peritoneal irritation, although a slightly tender, "boggy" epigastric mass occasionally can be felt. It is confirmed fluoroscopically when high-grade, proximal duodenal obstruction is demonstrated on upper gastrointestinal examination with barium as a contrast agent, particularly if the duodenal mucosa has the appearance of a "coiled spring."

Immediate management of duodenal hematoma consists of IV fluid and electrolytes to repair the often severe dehydration and hypochloremic, hypokalemic metabolic alkalosis present in this condition. Nasogastric decompression also is used, primarily to alleviate the discomfort, and to prevent the concomitant worsening of mucosal edema, which accompanies repeated episodes of vomiting. Before the advent of total parenteral nutrition, surgical evacuation and drainage of the hematoma was the treatment of choice. However, this treatment has now been rendered obsolete, unless perforation also occurs, for all but a few cases in which the hematoma does not reabsorb spontaneously. The hematoma normally resolves sufficiently to allow passage of liquid foodstuffs after 7 to 10 days of bowel rest, by which time the patency of the duodenum, heralded by a marked de-crease in nasogastric drainage, may be confirmed by a second upper gastrointestinal examination.

Retroperitoneum

Injuries to the retroperitoneal structures, other than the kidneys and pancreas, are confined nearly exclusively to the great veins, and fortunately are quite rare. They are caused by the shearing effect associated with massive deceleration, and therefore chiefly affect the junctions of these veins with smaller feeding branches, such as lumbocaval anastamoses, although larger vessels may also be involved (e.g., the cavomesenteric and cavohepatic venous junctions). In the former case, hemorrhage usually proves to be confined to the true retroperitoneal space and if seen at laparotomy, will present as a small retroperitoneal hematoma that is usually best left undisturbed. However, if the great veins themselves are involved, the hematoma will be large; the overlying peritoneal membrane also may have been disrupted, resulting in massive intraperitoneal bleeding. In these instances, prompt control of bleeding is necessary if the child's life is to be saved. This may occasionally require ligation of the great veins in lieu of repair, which, while not well tolerated initially, is usually not incompatible with life, given the abundant available collateral vessels.

Penetrating Thoracoabdominal Injuries

Penetrating injuries in children, as previously noted, are being encountered in greater numbers than ever before. Since management by pediatric surgeons experienced in child abuse cases is required, all such children should be referred to a pediatric trauma center. Involvement of law enforcement and child welfare agencies is mandatory in all cases of pediatric nonaccidental penetrating trauma. The proper individuals must therefore be notified as soon as possible after admission to the hospital. Specific treatment of penetrating thoracoabdominal injuries is outlined in other texts.

SUMMARY

This chapter has focused on the medical management of pediatric nonaccidental thoracoabdominal trauma. However, while competent, compassionate medical treatment for serious chest and abdominal injuries is of great importance, it must always be remembered that the syndrome of child abuse and neglect is the primary disease, and that the child's physical injuries are only its manifestations. Thus, the physician who treats the intentionally injured child must keep in mind that, while management of the child's physical injuries may at times require priority attention, the emotional wounds are usually much deeper and far more resistant to therapy.

SUGGESTED READINGS

1. American Academy of Pediatrics and American College of Emergency Physicians Joint Task Force on Advanced Pediatric Life Support: Advanced Pediatric Life Support. American Academy of Pediatrics and American College of Emergency Physicians, Elk Grove Village and Dallas, 1989
2. American College of Surgeons Committee on Trauma: Advanced Trauma Life Support Student Manual. 3rd Ed. American College of Surgeons, Chicago, 1989
3. American Heart Association and American Academy of Pediatrics Working Group on Pediatric Resuscitation: Text-book of Pediatric Advanced Life Support. American Heart Association, Dallas, 1988
4. American Pediatric Surgical Association Committee on Trauma: Principles of Pediatric Trauma Care. American Pediatric Surgical Association, Pasadena, 1990
5. American Society for Protecting Children: Highlights of Official Child Neglect and Abuse Reporting: 1986. American Humane Association, Denver, 1988
6. American Society for Protecting Children: Highlights of Official Aggregate Child Neglect and Abuse Reporting: 1987. American Humane Association, Denver, 1989
7. Bass BL, Eichelberger MR, Schisgall R et al: Hazards of nonoperative therapy of hepatic injury in children. J Trauma 24:978, 1984
8. Cobb LM, Vinocur CD, Wagner CW et al: Intestinal perforation due to blunt trauma in children in an era of increased nonoperative management. J Trauma 26:461, 1986
9. Cooper A, Floyd T, Barlow B et al: Major blunt abdominal trauma due to child abuse. J Trauma 28:1483, 1988
10. Cosentino CM, Luck SR, Barthel MJ et al: Transfusion requirements in conservative nonoperative management of blunt splenic and hepatic injuries during childhood. J Pediatr Surg 25:950, 1989
11. Giacomantonio M, Filler RM, Rich RH et al: Blunt hepatic trauma in children: experience with operative and nonoperative management. J Pediatr Surg 19:519, 1984
12. Gornall P, Ahmed S, Jolleys A et al: Intra-abdominal injuries in the battered baby syndrome. Arch Dis Child 47:211, 1972
13. Haller JA: Injuries of the gastrointestinal tract in children: notes on recognition and management. Clin Pediatr 5:476, 1966
14. Heins M: The "battered child" revisited. JAMA 251:3295, 1984
15. Hodge D, Ludwig S: Child homicide: emergency department recognition. Pediatr Emerg Care 1:3, 1985
16. Holgersen LO, Bishop HC: Nonoperative treatment of duodenal hematomata in childhood. J Pediatr Surg 12:11, 1977
17. Jewett TC: Chest and abdominal injuries. p. 165. In Ellerstein NS (ed): Child Abuse

and Neglect: A Medical Reference. 1st Ed. Churchill Livingstone, New York, 1981

18. Kane NM, Cronan JJ, Dorfman GS et al: Pediatric abdominal trauma: evaluation by computed tomography. Pediatrics 82:11, 1988

19. Karp MP, Jewett TC, Kuhn JP et al: The impact of computed tomography scanning on the child with renal trauma. J Pediatr Surg 21:617, 1986

20. Ledbetter DJ, Hatch EI, Feldman KW et al: Diagnostic and surgical implications of child abuse. Arch Surg 123:1101, 1988

21. Lieu TA, Fleisher GR, Mahboubi S et al: Hematuria and clinical findings as indications for intravenous pyelography in pediatric blunt trauma. Pediatrics 82:216, 1988

22. McCort J, Vaudagna J: Visceral injuries in battered children. Radiology 82:424, 1964

23. Mukherji SK, Siegel MJ: Rhabdomyolysis and renal failure in child abuse. Am J Roentgenol 148:1203, 1987

24. National Center on Child Abuse Prevention Research: Current Trends in Child Abuse Reporting and Fatalities: The Results of the 1989 Annual Fifty State Survey. National Committee for Prevention of Child Abuse, Chicago, 1990

25. National Pediatric Trauma Registry: Biannual Report. Tufts University School of Medicine, Boston, 1990

26. Oldham KT, Guice KS, Ryckman F et al: Blunt liver injury in childhood: evolution of therapy and current perspective. Surgery 100:542, 1986

27. O'Neill J, Meacham W, Griffin P et al: Patterns of injury in the battered child syndrome. J Trauma 13:332, 1973

28. Pearl RH, Wesson DE, Spence LJ et al: Splenic injury: a 5-year update with improved results and changing criteria for conservative management. J Pediatr Surg 24:121, 1989

29. Rimer RL, Roy S: Child abuse and hemoglobinuria. JAMA 238:2034, 1977

30. Rosenberg N, Bottenfield G: Fractures in infants: a sign of child abuse. Ann Emerg Med 11:178, 1982

31. Sivit CJ, Taylor GA, Eichelberger MR: Visceral injury in battered children. Radiology 173:659, 1989

32. Tepas JJ, Mollitt DL, Talbert JL et al: The pediatric trauma score as a predictor of injury severity in the injured child. J Pediatr Surg 22:14, 1987

33. Thomas PS: Rib fractures in infancy. Ann Radiol (Paris) 20:115, 1977

34. Touloukian RJ: Abdominal visceral injuries in battered children. Pediatrics 42:642, 1968

35. Woolley MM, Mahour GH, Sloan T: Duodenal hematoma in infancy and childhood: changing etiology and changing treatment. Am J Surg 136:8, 1978

36. Ziegler MM, Finley EA, Schwartzburt E: Child Abuse: Results of a Five Year Survey of 1,501 Cases. The Children's Hospital of Philadelphia, Philadelphia, 1981

13

Radiographic Signs of Skeletal Trauma

Leonard E. Swischuk

Since Caffey's original description of children with subdural hematomas and unexplained fractures in 1946, the radiographic findings in the battered child syndrome have become well known. Of these, the most pathognomonic is the healing epiphyseal-metaphyseal fracture; this is especially true in young infants in whom this type of injury seldom is seen other than in the battered child syndrome. These injuries, of course, are exclusive to children and result from shearing forces across the epiphyseal-metaphyseal junction. In older children, such forces are common in everyday injuries, but in infants, they are most often encountered with the twisting or jiggling occurring in the battered child syndrome. The young infant who might fall on an outstretched extremity is more likely to sustain a metaphyseal cortical buckle (torus) fracture, for this is the weakest part of the bone. As the child grows older, the cortex becomes stronger and the epiphyseal-metaphyseal junction becomes the relatively weaker of the two regions.

However, as pathognomonic as these epiphyseal-metaphyseal fractures are, it must be added that they probably occur in only 50 percent of cases. Indeed, many battered infants show no evidence of skeletal injury at all, and those who do, often demonstrate innocuous appearing transverse or spiral fractures of the mid-shafts of the long bones. To be sure, these fractures are probably as common as the epiphyseal-metaphyseal injuries, but are not at all pathognomonic of the battered child syndrome. Because of this, knowledge as to which fractures are the most significant and how they are likely to have been sustained is important. Indeed, it is not the injury itself so much that enables diagnosis, but rather the lack of correlation between the type of injury observed, the known mechanism required for its production, and the proported mechanism of its production.

RADIOGRAPHIC AND ISOTOPE BONE SURVEYS

The primary role of radiology is to detect occult or subtle injuries and to confirm known injuries. In terms of the skeleton, a complete bone survey is required, for many of these injuries are "relatively silent" and detected only by the radiographic bone survey. This is especially true of healing fractures. Isotope bone

151

surveys also can be used to locate the fractures, but are less useful for they yield relatively nonspecific information. Fractures become positive within 24 to 48 hours and remain positive well after clear-cut radiographic healing is observed. Since the metaphyseal regions of the long bones routinely are quite "hot" on bone scans, epiphyseal-metaphyseal fractures are more difficult to evaluate, especially if they are bilateral and symmetric. In our institution we do not use the isotope bone scan for imaging suspected cases of child abuse. However, this is not to say they should not be used and indeed are useful in detecting fractures in flat bones such as the ribs, scapulae, pelvis, and so forth before they are visible radiographically. However, this is not so much the rule, as the exception. In the end, each institution must make its own decision as to exactly which course to pursue.

The radiographic bone survey ("skeletal survey") has its highest yield in children less than 2 years old. Occult fractures are diagnosed less often in abused children between 2 and 5 years old, and the yield is quite low over the age of 5. It is reasonable practice to routinely obtain a complete bone survey for all physically abused children less than 2 years of age. Less frequent ordering is sensible for older children, but each case should be individualized.

Every institution performing skeletal surveys on potentially abused children should have a protocol for which specific views are obtained. This generally involves multiple views of the child's skull, spine, chest, abdomen, pelvis and extremities (Appendix D). Some radiologists continue to obtain "babygrams," anteroposterior and lateral views on two overlapping 17 by 14 inch radiographs of the child from chest to lower extremities along with anteroposterior and lateral skull views. Suspicious areas are than focused on with repeat radiographs. Con-

siderable experience and willingness to obtain repeat views is necessary with this approach to avoid missing subtle fractures. Most pediatric radiologists and child abuse consultants recommend multiple views on the initial bone survey. Our protocol is to obtain (1) an anteroposterior view of the chest and upper extremities, (2) an anteroposterior view of the pelvis and lower extremities, (3) a lateral view of the complete spine and chest, and (4) anteroposterior and lateral views of the skull. This is just short of the approach suggested in Appendix D, but generally has been satisfactory for us in over 25 years of experience.

Isotope bone surveys also can be used to locate occult child abuse fractures. Fractures become positive within 24 to 48 hours and remain positive well after clear-cut radiographic healing is observed. They can sometimes pinpoint fractures not readily seen on radiographic bone survey, especially rib fractures. Since the metaphyseal regions of the long bones routinely are quite "hot" on bone scans, epiphyseal-metaphyseal fractures are more difficult to evaluate, especially if they are bilateral and symmetric. Isotope bone survey is not useful for skull fracture. Bone scans cannot differentiate between infection, tumor, and fracture. A positive scan in the setting of an abused child is highly suspicious for fracture, but a radiograph of the involved area needs to be subsequently obtained. Isotope bone scan requires the availability of a diagnostic nuclear medicine facility, while radiographic bone survey is more readily available.

In summary, most radiologists still rely on the radiographic bone survey. The isotope bone scan as a screening study is probably more sensitive for certain occult fractures, particularly ribs. Those radiologists who favor the bone scan as a screening study are currently in the minority. Some physicians will use the isotope bone scan as an additional study in difficult and perplexing cases.

MECHANISMS OF INJURY AND RADIOGRAPHIC APPEARANCES OF THE FRACTURES

Different mechanisms lead to different bone and joint injuries, and it is important to appreciate just which mechanisms result in which injuries. The reason for this is that the diagnosis of the battered child syndrome depends on the discrepancy between alleged mechanisms of injury and the mechanisms that are actually responsible. Basically, these mechanisms include direct blows, twisting forces, shaking, and squeezing.

Direct Blow Injuries

Direct blows to the extremities usually result in transverse or spiral diaphyseal fractures (Fig. 13-1). These fractures, although quite common, are not pathognomonic of the battered child syndrome. On the other hand, under certain circumstances, they can arouse suspicions. For example, a transverse fracture of a long bone in a 3-month-old baby is a much more suspicious injury than the same fracture in a 6 year old. The 3-month-old baby simply is not developed enough to self-initiate such an injury. This may prompt a bone survey, whereupon other fractures may be observed (Fig. 13-2). Alone, however, these fractures must be assessed with caution, even though they account for approximately 50 percent of the fractures seen in abused children.

A direct blow to the clavicle results in a midshaft fracture, and in the battered child syndrome, this fracture is quite common (Fig. 13-3A). However, because this fracture also is common in the gen-eral pediatric population, it has little diagnostic specificity. Direct blows to the scapula also can result in nonspecific linear or stellate fractures (Fig. 13-3B). Because these fractures are relatively uncommon in infants and young children, their presence should cause suspicion. The same pertains to the uncommon sternal fracture resulting from a direct blow (Fig. 13-3C).

Direct blows to the face produce a variety of facial and mandibular fractures, and direct blows to the calvaria produce linear, curvilinear, or depressed fractures (Fig. 13-2B). Often such fractures are associated with intracranial injury, and computed tomography (CT) or magnetic resonance imaging (MRI) scanning is the best modality for its demonstration. It also is important to note that these intracranial injuries can occur in the absence of skull fractures and that the calvaria may appear entirely normal in some patients. In others, spreading of the calvarial sutures because of increased intracranial pressure (ICP) can provide a clue to the presence of an underlying problem (Fig 13-1C).

Direct blows to the abdomen result in visceral injuries, while direct blows to the chest result in rib fractures, and occasionally, associated findings such as pleural effusions, hemothorax, pneumothorax, and pulmonary contusions. Most commonly, however, rib fractures alone are present and result from squeezing of the thorax. These fractures frequently occur bilaterally and are discussed later.

Twisting-Jiggling Force-Induced Injuries

Long bone spiral fractures are very specific for child abuse in the preambulatory infant, and generally result from the application of twisting force to an extremity (Fig. 13-1). Bruising should be searched for, but is frequently not found. Spiral fractures in older ambulatory children are not specific for child abuse, but com-

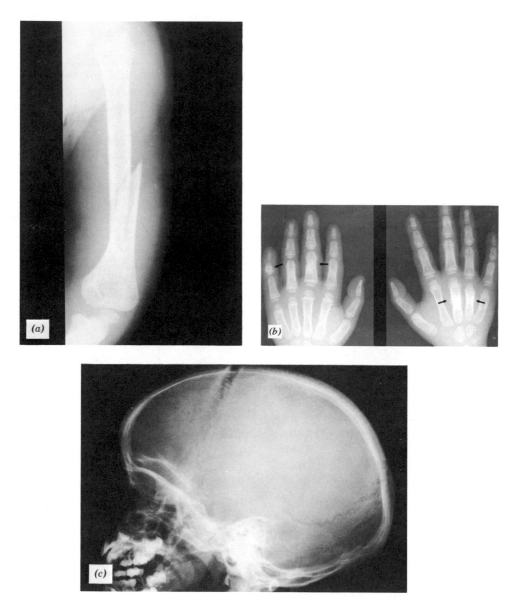

Fig. 13-1. Battered child syndrome: injuries from direct blows. **(A)** Note the spiral fracture of the humerus. **(B)** Numerous fractures, some older than others, are present in the small bones of both hands (arrows). **(C)** Note spread sutures indicating increased intracranial pressure. This was secondary to a subdural hematoma. This patient did not demonstrate any classic epiphyseal-metaphyseal fractures.

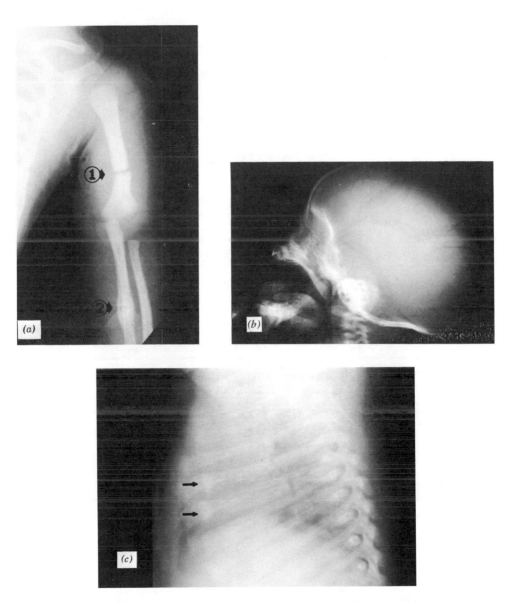

Fig. 13-2. Battered child syndrome: transverse fracture as a signal of other injury. (**A**) Note the innocuous appearing transverse fracture through the upper humerus. The mother brought this infant in because he would not move his arm. However, another older fracture was seen in the midshaft of the radius. This prompted a bone survey, and the other arm demonstrated typical epiphyseal-metaphyseal fractures. Similar fractures were seen in the left tibia and fibula. (**B**) Radiograph of the skull demonstrates a number of fractures and spread sutures. (**C**) Lateral view of the chest demonstrates exaggerated cupping of the anterior aspect of some of the ribs (arrows), characteristic of costochondral separations.

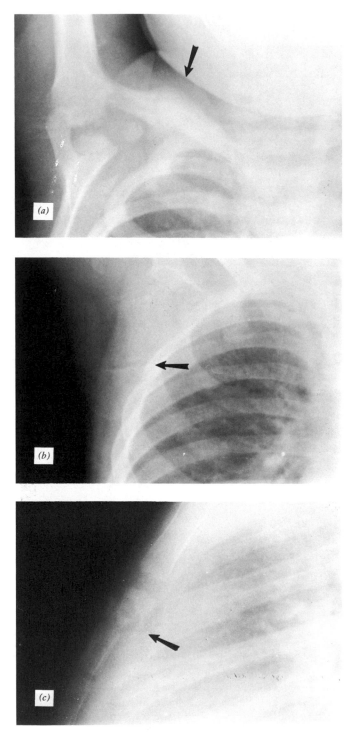

Fig. 13-3. Direct blow injuries: other than long bones. (**A**) Typical healing midclavicular fracture (arrow). (**B**) Transverse fracture through the scapula (arrow). (**C**) Displaced fracture of the sternum (arrow).

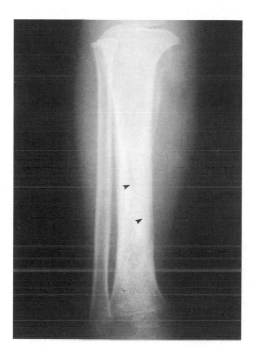

Fig. 13-4. Spiral ("toddler's") fracture of the tibia. First note early periosteal new bone deposition around the tibial shaft. Then note the spiral fracture (arrows). This type of fracture is not pathognomonic of the battered child syndrome, but it commonly occurs in the syndrome.

monly occur in the battered child syndrome. Spiral fracture of the tibia is particularly common, resulting in the so-called toddler's fracture (Fig. 13-4). These frequently occur accidentally from a modest fall with twisting of the lower extremity, although spiral tibia fractures may occur in child abuse. Most accidental toddler's fractures involve the distal third of the tibia. Spiral femur fractures may occur accidentally in toddlers, but they are frequently caused by child abuse, and should be thoroughly evaluated.

The other fracture resulting from twisting forces is the epiphyseal-metaphyseal fracture, and it is this fracture that is the most pathognomonic of the battered child syndrome. The epiphyseal-metaphyseal junction is one of the weakest parts of the

long bones, and because of this, it is easy for the shearing forces produced by twisting or jiggling to cause separation of the epiphysis from the metaphysis. Similar injuries also can result when the child is shaken violently and the extremities are allowed to dangle and lash back and forth.

In the initial stages, epiphyseal-metaphyseal injuries often manifest in nothing more than soft tissue swelling around the fracture site (Fig. 13-5). In other cases, a small avulsed metaphyseal, or occasionally, epiphyseal, fragment can provide a clue to the presence of the injury (Fig. 13-6A), but often, it is not until healing occurs that the fractures become clearly apparent. With healing, callus formation is abundant, periosteal new bone deposition often profound (Figs. 13-5B and 13-6B), and in some cases, changes are so striking that systemic diseases such as scurvy, leukemia, or congenital lues are first considered (Fig. 13-7).

Bleeding into the adjacent joint is not uncommonly associated with these epiphyseal-metaphyseal injuries, and in the hip or shoulder, widening of the joint space is the hallmark of such bleeding (Fig. 13-5). When either of these joint spaces is widened and surrounding soft tissue swelling is present, it can be assumed that an epiphyseal-metaphyseal injury has been sustained. In the remaining joints, joint space widening does not occur for the ligaments are too strong to allow distraction of the bone. Rather, there is distortion of adjacent fat pads. In the knee, accumulation of fluid in the suprapatellar bursa causes compression of the suprapatellar fat pad against the femur and posterior displacement of the popliteal fat pad. In the ankle, there is outward displacement of the anterior and posterior juxtacapsular fat pads, whereas in the wrist, generalized swelling around the joint is seen.

Twisting or jiggling forces can produce injuries similar to those seen at the epi-

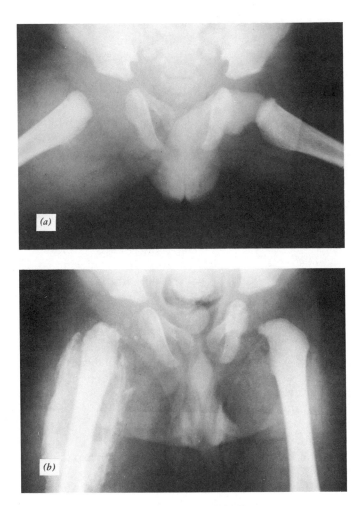

Fig. 13-5. Battered child syndrome: early soft tissue findings. (**A**) First note that the soft tissues around the right hip are thickened and whiter than those on the left. This indicates soft tissue edema. Next note that the joint space is much wider than the one on the left. This finding indicates bleeding into the joint and an underlying epiphyseal-metaphyseal fracture should be suspected. (**B**) Two weeks later, note marked periosteal new bone deposition around the right femoral shaft and proximal healing changes.

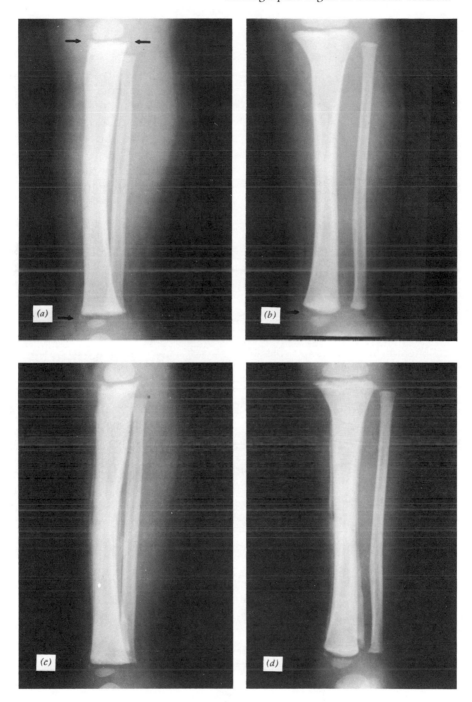

Fig. 13-6. Battered child syndrome: epiphyseal-metaphyseal fractures. (**A**) Minimal changes are seen, but small avulsion or corner fractures are present proximally and distally in the tibia (arrows). (**B**) Frontal view demonstrates the distal fragment (arrow) only. (**C**) There is clear-cut evidence of healing of these suspected fractures 2½ weeks later. Periosteal new bone deposition is seen and the corner fractures are more readily visible. (**D**) Similar findings on frontal view.

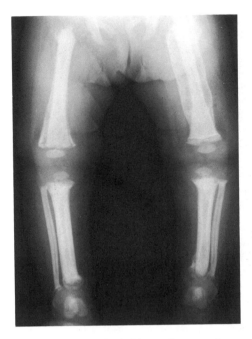

Fig. 13-7. Battered child syndrome: changes mimicking systemic bone disease. Note epiphyseal-metaphyseal fractures at the ends of all of the long bones. Periosteal new bone deposition is profound in some areas, and this together with metaphyseal fragmentation can cause a suspicion of such conditions as leukemia, scurvy, rickets, etc.

physeal-metaphyseal long bone junctions in certain other bones. Indeed, some of these are as pathognomonic as are the long bone injuries and, for the most part, include fragmentation fractures of the distal end of the clavicle, fragmentation of the acromial process of the scapula, and separation (with widening and cupping) of the costochondral junctions of the ribs. In any of these cases, the fractures are more readily apparent when healing occurs, for callus formation draws attention to their presence (Fig. 13-8).

Shaking Injuries

Shaking injuries result when the infant is grasped around the torso and shaken violently back and forth or when one extremity is violently shaken. Under such circumstances, it is readily apparent how the shaken extremity, or the dangling extremities in a shaken infant, is subject to twisting-jiggling injury (i.e., epiphyseal-metaphyseal fractures), but it is less well appreciated that the calvarial contents also can be injured. Indeed, it has been suggested that as the head bobbles back and forth, subdural hematomas can result. In addition, violent shaking can lead to retinal hemorrhages and spinal injury. In some cases, frank dislocations of the spine occur, while in others, hyperflexion of the spine leads to compression fractures and/or anterior notching (Fig. 13-9).

Squeezing Injuries

Squeezing of the infant usually involves the thorax, and rib fractures are the result. These fractures occur at points of maximal stress (i.e., posteriorly, laterally, and anteriorly at the costochondral junctions), and in addition, they often are bilateral (Fig. 13-10). Infant rib fractures are very specific for child abuse. Cardiopulmonary resuscitation rarely causes rib fractures in infants. Underlying intrathoracic visceral injury also can result from severe squeezing.

Multiplicity of Fractures

A classic feature of the battered child syndrome is "multiple fractures at different stages of healing." However, there are those infants in whom only one fracture is seen, but this point notwithstanding, multiplicity of injuries and fractures appearing in different stages of healing still are the most suggestive ra-

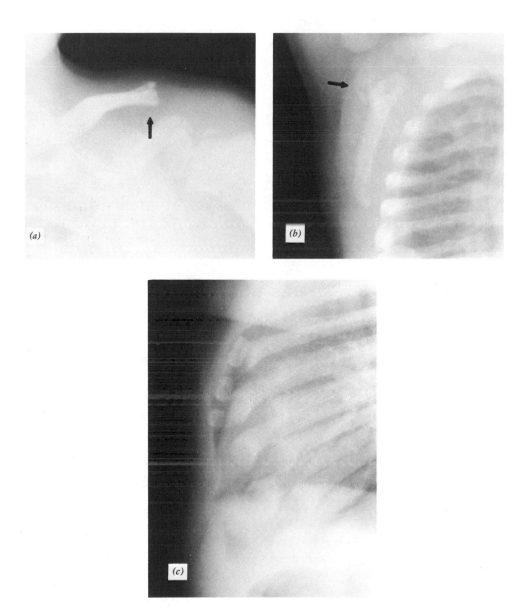

Fig. 13-8. Fragmentation fractures: other than in long bones. **(A)** Note the healing fragmentation fracture of the distal clavicle (arrow). **(B)** Note irregular fragmentation of the acromial process of the scapula (arrow). **(C)** Note extreme cupping and flaring of the rib ends. This is typical of the healing phase of a costochondral separation.

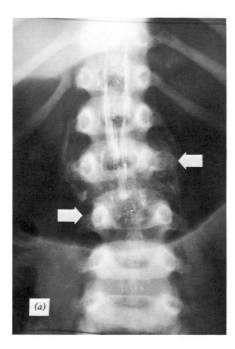
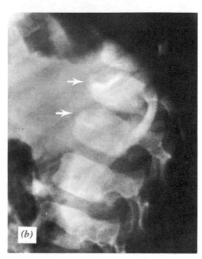

Fig. 13-9. Battered child syndrome: spine trauma. **(A)** Note abundant callus formation and calcified hematoma around the dislocated lumbar spine (arrows). **(B)** Another infant demonstrating notch defects (arrows) and associated intervertebral disc space narrowing. The notches result from hyperflexion of the spine and may or may not be associated with extrusion of the nucleus pulposus anteriorly. This latter problem results in the disc space narrowing.

diographic features of the battered child syndrome.

Miscellaneous Injuries

The foregoing mechanisms of injury and the resulting fractures are the usual ones encountered in the battered child syndrome. Occasionally, however, tendon avulsions, periosteal avulsions, and other bizarre injuries can occur (Fig. 13-11). In addition, in older children, multiple injuries to the small bones of the hands can be seen (Fig. 13-1B), and of course, ordinary cortical buckle or torus fractures of the extremities also can be seen in the battered child syndrome. Finally, any injury that can occur accidentally also may be the result of intentional trauma.

DATING THE FRACTURE

Dating a fracture is most important because important discrepancies between historical data and that yielded by the radiographic appearance of the fracture may be detected. Furthermore, fractures in different stages of healing are often seen, and multiple episodes of injury can be documented. In these cases, it is of the utmost importance to determine just when the different injuries occurred, but while it is relatively easy to date a fracture in its early stages, it is more difficult later on (Table 13-1).

In dating a fracture, look for (1) soft tissue changes, (2) visibility of a fracture line, (3) calcification of callus, and (4) ossification of newly laid periosteal bone. Soft tissue changes occur early and con-

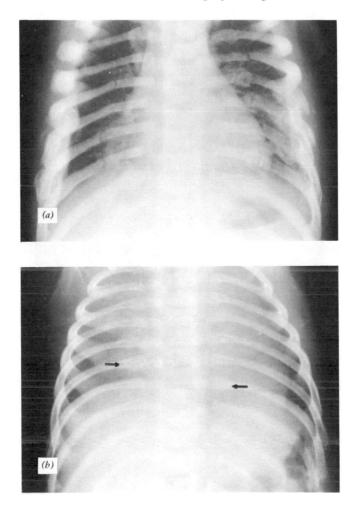

Fig. 13-10. Rib fractures. (A) An infant demonstrating numerous fresh and healing rib fractures. (B) Old healed posterior rib fractures produce bulbous expansion of the posterior ribs (arrows). This patient also has expansion of the costochondral junctions, best seen on the lower right and fresh fractures in the lower left. Also see Figure 13-2C.

sist of edema and/or fluid-blood accumulations in the joint space. Immediately after a fracture, blood and exudate pour out between the ends of the broken bone, and as this involves the soft tissues, edema and swelling result. After 4 or 5 days, granulation tissue forms at the fracture site and osteoblasts from the adjacent bone form osteoid. This osteoid forms callus, and the callus is the natural splint for the fracture. Calcification of the callus does not occur for about 10 to 14 days after injury, and consequently, in the early stages, it is invisible radiographically. At about 10 to 14 days, faint, hazy calcification occurs, but astute inspection is required for its identification. Later, calcification becomes more profound, and in some cases, is very exuberant.

In most instances, a fracture line is visible, but it should be noted that in some cases, a clear-cut fracture line is never

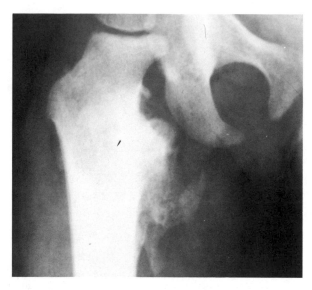

Fig. 13-11. Battered child syndrome: miscellaneous injury. Note abundant callus formation secondary to avulsion of the iliopsoas muscle from the lesser trochanter.

Table 13-1. Dating Fractures

0 to 10 Days
  Soft tissue edema
    Joint fluid
    Visible fracture fragments
    Visible fracture lines
10 Days to 8 Weeks
  Periosteal new bone (layered)
  Callus (first subtle and then heavy)
  Bone resorption along fracture line makes fracture line more visible
  Metaphyseal fragments often more visible
8 Weeks and Over
  Periosteal new bone matures, becomes thicker
  Callus formation becomes more dense and smoother
  Metaphyseal fragments are incorporated into metaphyseal callus and become smoother
  Fracture line less visible and then invisible
  Deformities and cortical bumps persist

seen. In these cases, the fracture is hairline thin, and even during healing, often remains invisible. On the other hand, in some cases, and in all instances in which a fracture line is visible initially, bone resorption along the fracture line edges occurs within a few days and enhances its visualization. With epiphyseal-metaphyseal fractures, since the fracture line occurs through the growth plate (physis), bone resorption occurs along the adjacent epiphyseal and metaphyseal edges. The resulting picture can be quite bizarre with alternating radiolucent and radiodense areas visible. Generally, a fracture line in the shaft of a long bone remains visible from 4 to 8 weeks.

The last feature of fracture healing to be evaluated is periosteal new bone deposition. With any fracture, bleeding under the periosteum causes its elevation and displacement away from the cortex. However, there is no radiographic evidence that this has occurred until 10 to 14 days has passed. It is at this point that osteoblasts from the deep layer of the per-

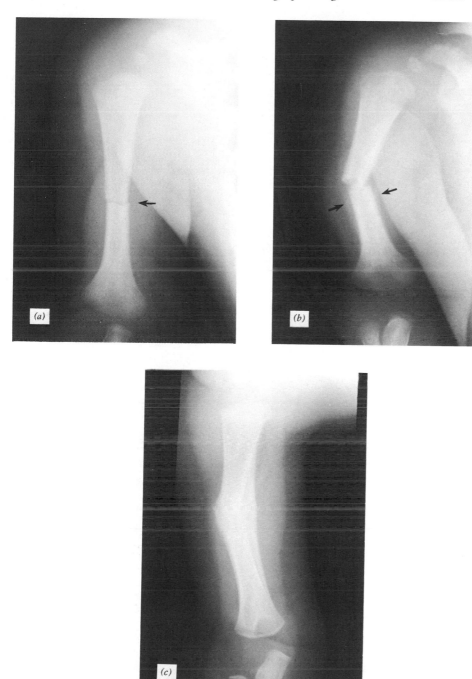

Fig. 13-12. Transverse fracture: healing stages. (**A**) *At 2 to 3 days:* note the fresh transverse humeral fracture (arrow). (**B**) *At 12 days:* early periosteal new bone deposition is seen (arrows). (**C**) *At 6 weeks:* note that periosteal new bone is extensive, callus formation is marked, and that the fracture line has almost disappeared. However, a radiolucent space between the periosteal new bone and the old cortex still exists.

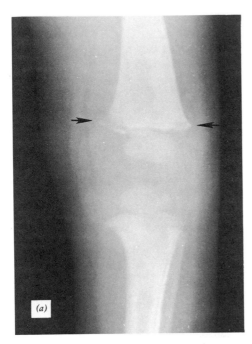

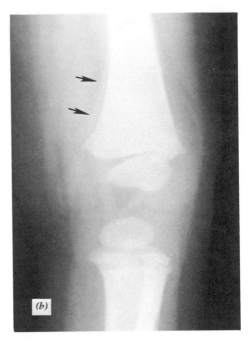

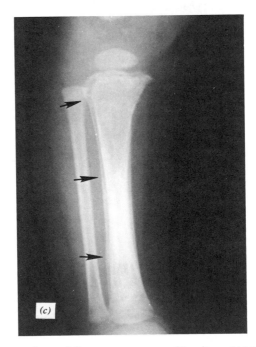

Fig. 13-13. Epiphyseal-metaphyseal fractures: stages of healing. **(A)** *Fresh fracture (under 10 days):* note rarefaction of the bone underneath the epiphyseal plate. For other early injuries, see Figures 13-5 and 13-6. **(B)** *Ten days to 2 weeks:* note early periosteal new bone deposition (arrows). **(C)** *Two to 4 weeks:* note more pronounced periosteal new bone deposition and epiphyseal-metaphyseal changes (arrows) characteristic of this stage of healing.

iosteum deposit a strip of new bone, just under the elevated periosteum, and parallel to the old cortex. Progressively, this stripe of new bone becomes thicker, and eventually fuses with the old cortex.

Zero to Ten Days

Calcified callus and periosteal new bone deposition are not seen for at least 10 to 14 days after the injury. Depending on just how recent the injury is, soft tissue edema may be extensive (Fig. 13-5). Overall, however, between 0 and 10 days after injury, radiographic signs of bone healing are absent (Figs. 13-5, 13-12, and 13-13).

Seven Days to Eight Weeks

After 10 to 14 days, periosteal new bone deposition becomes evident (Figs. 13-12 and 13-13), and resorption of bone along the fracture line or epiphyseal-metaphyseal junction occurs (Figs. 13-12 and 13-13). At the same time, callus formation can be detected as faint, hazy calcification of the callus. With epiphyseal-metaphyseal injuries, avulsed metaphyseal fragments often become more clearly visible at this stage (Figs. 13-5, 13-6, and 13-12), and toward the end of the 8-week period, the periosteal new bone stripe becomes even thicker. However, it still remains separate from the cortex of the bone. In the meantime, callus calcification pro-

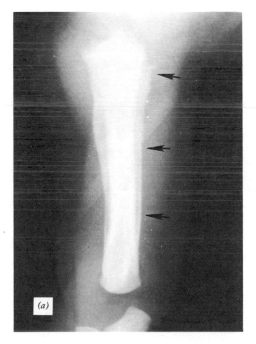 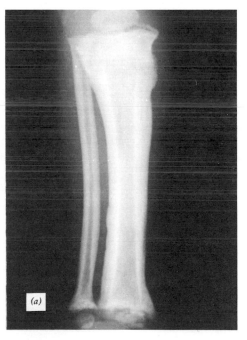

Fig. 13-14. Epiphyseal-metaphyseal fractures: later stages of healing. (**A**) *Four to 8 weeks:* note the more mature appearance of the periosteal new bone (arrows). The space between it and the cortex is disappearing slowly and changes around the epiphyseal-metaphyseal junction are maturing. (**B**) *Twelve weeks and over:* with more maturation, the periosteal new bone becomes thicker and the space between it and the old cortex is obliterated. The new cortex now appears grossly thickened and uneven. The entire bone (tibia) is involved and the overall contour is somewhat lumpy.

gresses and in some cases becomes quite exuberant and flocculent (Figs. 13-12 and 13-13).

Over 8 Weeks

The periosteal new bone stripe becomes even thicker after 8 weeks, and with time, more closely apposed to the shaft of the bone (Fig. 13-14). Eventually, it blends completely with the old cortex, and at the same time, any callus present begins to remodel and become incorporated into the shaft of the long bone. Fracture lines previously visible tend to become obliterated, and eventually, there may be nothing more than subtle bumps along the bones at the site of old callus formation, areas of thickened cortex where periosteal new bone had been deposited, or residual bending deformities and epiphyseal-metaphyseal growth disturbances (Fig. 13-15).

DIFFERENTIAL DIAGNOSIS

Often the appearance of the healing epiphyseal-metaphyseal fractures in the battered child syndrome causes consideration of some underlying hematologic, metabolic, or dysplastic bone disorder (Fig. 13-7). For the most part, however,

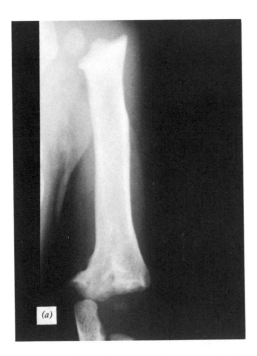 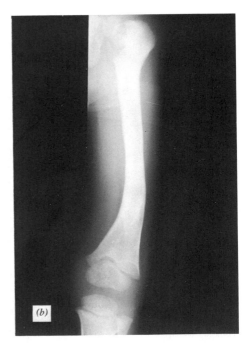

Fig. 13-15. Old deformities. **(A)** Note the lumpy, markedly deformed humerus. Both metaphyseal regions are quite irregular and reflect the aftermath of old epiphyseal-metaphyseal injuries. Irregularity of the shaft is caused by old periosteal new bone deposition. **(B)** Another patient demonstrating bowing deformities, epiphyseal-metaphyseal growth disturbances resulting in tilting of the upper tibial epiphyseal-metaphyseal junction and scalloping abnormalities of both the distal and proximal femoral metaphyses. Also note the irregular cortex of the femur.

these possibilities can be discounted when it is recalled that in most cases, the bones of a battered child are normal in contour and "healthy appearing," except for the fact that they are fractured. In other words, there is no evidence of bone destruction, dysplasia, or modeling error. If fracturing is a result of some underlying pathologic condition of the bones, such changes usually are present (Fig. 13-16). In some battered infants, however, demineralization of the bones can occur (i.e., a few of these infants also are neglected and malnourished), but usually the bones are relatively well mineralized.

Epiphyseal-metaphyseal fractures, virtually indistinguishable from those seen in the battered child syndrome, commonly occur in the newborn infant (Fig. 13-17). They are most likely to be seen with breech deliveries and to the unwary, can pose a significant problem. However, as an aid to this dilemma, it has been stated that if an infant, 11 days or older, demonstrates a fracture that shows no signs of healing, the injury should be considered one sustained after birth. The reason for this is that fractures sustained during delivery usually show periosteal new bone deposition and callus formation by 7 to 11 days.

In older children, epiphyseal-metaphyseal fractures similar to those encountered in the battered child syndrome can

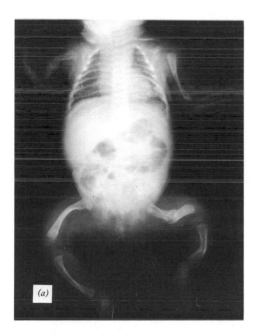
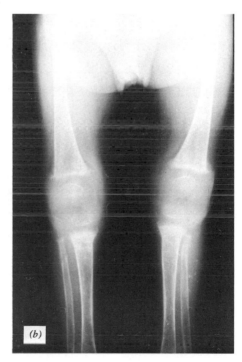

Fig. 13-16. Differential diagnosis of battered child syndrome. **(A)** Osteogenesis imperfecta. Note numerous fractures and bending deformities of the long bones. Also note the dysplastic appearing, thin ribs showing numerous fractures. Clearly the fractures are secondary to some generalized bony abnormality. **(B)** Epiphyseal-metaphyseal changes in this infant might be misinterpreted for those of a battered child. However, note that the bones are extensively demineralized, the cortices quite poorly formed, and the epiphyses very shaggy around their periphery. This patient had severe rickets.

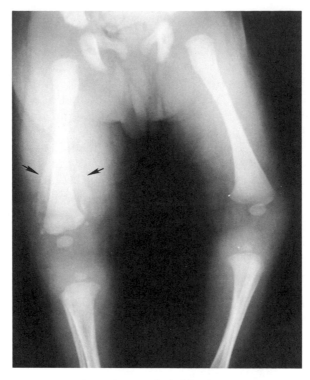

Fig. 13-17. Birth injuries mimicking battered child injuries. Note extensive periosteal new bone deposition (arrows) secondary to an epiphyseal-metaphyseal fracture. Note the bony fragments in the distal femur. This was a breech-delivered infant.

be seen in the congenital insensitivity to pain syndrome (a very rare disease), and in infants with underlying neurogenic or muscular disease. Patients with congenital insensitivity to pain may be difficult to differentiate from those truly battered, but the problem of diagnosis in children with underlying neuromuscular or neurogenic disease is not so difficult.

Osteogenesis Imperfecta

Osteogenesis imperfecta (OI) is a rare genetic disorder characterized by bone fragility and frequent fractures. Infants and occasionally toddlers presenting with unexplained fractures may have OI raised as a possible explanation for the fractures.

OI is a rare condition with an incidence estimated to be between 1 in 15,000 to 1 in 60,000 births. Child abuse is much more common.

Most OI victims have blue sclerae. Abnormal teeth (dentinogenesis imperfecta) and hearing impairment are frequently found. Osteoporosis and abnormal fracture healing are common components. Wormian bones, which are found in the skull as sutural bones of at least 4 × 6 mm, are usually associated with OI, and tend to be multiple and arranged in a mosaic pattern. Other associated findings may include joint laxity, easy bruisability, and short stature.

OI is not one disease. Four types have been identified with several subtypes. Type I is most common, involving 70 to

80 percent of all patients. Inheritance is autosomal dominant, with isolated reports of spontaneous mutations. Blue sclerae are almost always present. Bone disease is mild to moderate. Type II is profoundly severe, frequently leading to fetal death, or death in the neonatal period. Inheritance is felt to be a spontaneous mutation. Type III is rare, and is associated with severe bone disease not readily confused with child abuse. Inheritance is spontaneous mutation with possibly a few autosomal recessive cases. Type IV is rare and is inherited as an autosomal dominant gene, with occasional spontaneous mutation. Bone fragility, fractures, and healing abnormalities vary from mild to moderate. Blue sclerae and hearing impairment are uncommon. Some patients will have abnormal dentition, but when present will obviously not be apparent in young infants as the average age for first tooth eruption is 6 months. Most patients have wormian bones.

Thus it is generally uncomplicated to distinguish OI from child abuse (Table 13-2). In the unusual problematic case, a skin biopsy to obtain a cell culture for collagen analysis can be considered. The most likely situation where OI could be confused with child abuse is a mild type IV case. The likelihood of a clinician seeing a child with mild type IV OI and with white sclerae, normal hearing, normal dentition, negative family history, and no wormian bones is exceedingly rare. Taitz estimated this incidence to be between 1 in 1,000,000 and 1 in 3,000,000 births. In a city of 500,000, one case of this sort would occur every 100 to 300 years. Physicians seeing a child with unexplained fractures should consider OI when appropriate. Nonetheless, the frequency of child abuse is orders of magnitude greater than OI, especially for subtle cases of OI. Providing initial protection to likely victims of child abuse

Table 13-2. Osteogenesis Imperfecta Versus Child Abuse

Finding	Osteogenesis Imperfecta	Child Abuse
Incidence	Rare	Common
Family history	Common	Common
Blue sclerae	Common	Rare
Abnormal teeth	Common	Rare
Hearing impairment	Common	Uncommon
Osteoporosis	Common	Rare
Abnormal fracture healing	Common	Rare
Wormian bones	Common	Rare
Joint laxity	Common	Rare
Short stature	Common	Occasionally
Fracture recurrence in protected environment	Common	Rare

should not be significantly delayed by a prolonged search for a rare disease.

FAILURE-TO-THRIVE OR DEPRIVATIONAL DWARFISM

For the most part, these patients are neglected infants, and are more a problem of failure-to-thrive. In some cases, battering and deprivation occur together, but frequently they occur separately. Deprivational (psychosocial) dwarfs present with short stature, a picture not unlike that seen with hypopituitarism. Indeed, these infants may suffer a transient lack of growth hormone, but once they are removed from their deprived environment, the deficiency resolves rapidly and brisk

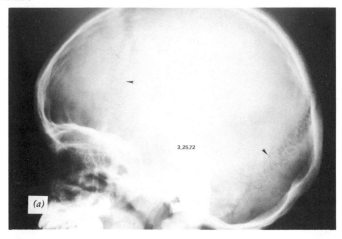

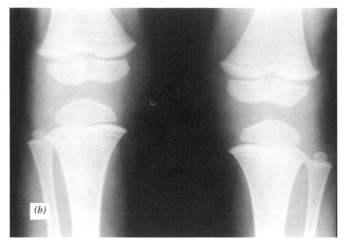

Fig. 13-18. Deprivational or psychosocial dwarfism. **(A)** Skull film demonstrating spreading of sutures. This is due to catch-up growth of the brain. Nine months later the skull was normal. **(B)** Same patient demonstrating numerous growth arrest lines in the distal femurs and proximal tibias.

growth results. The brain partakes in this vigorous catch-up phenomenon; because of this, ICP increases and a spreading of the calvarial sutures is seen. Such a spread is easier to see in the young infant, but also occurs in the older child. In the older child, it may take longer to appear. All of these patients also demonstrate a delay in bone age and multiple growth arrest lines (Fig. 13-18), a finding that serves to differentiate them from patients with true hypopituitarism.

SUGGESTED READINGS

1. Ablin DS, Greenspan A, Reinhart M, Grix A: Differentiation of child abuse from osteogenesis imperfecta. AJR 154:1035, 1990

1a. Afshani E, Osman M, Girdany BR: Widening of cranial sutures in children with deprivation dwarfism. Radiology 109:141, 1973

2. Akbarnia B, Torg JS, Kirkpatrick J et al: Manifestations of the battered child syndrome. J Bone Joint Surg 56:1159, 1974

3. Beals RK, Tufts E: Fractured femur in infancy: the role of child abuse. J Pediatr Orthop 3:583, 1983

4. Caffey J: Multiple fractures in long bones of child suffering from chronic subdural hematoma. AJR 56:163, 1946

5. Caffey J: The parent-infant traumatic stress syndrome (Caffey-Kempe syndrome) (battered baby syndrome). Am J Roentgenol Rad Ther Nucl Med 114:217, 1972

6. Caffey J: The whiplash shaken infant syndrome: manual shaking by the extremities with whiplash-induced intracranial and intraocular bleedings, linked with residual permanent brain damage and mental retardation. Pediatrics 54:396, 1974

6a. Capitanio MA, Kirkpatrick JA: Widening of the cranial sutures. A roetngen observation during periods of accelerated growth in patients treated for deprivation dwarfism. Radiology 92:53, 1969

7. Cumming WA: Neonatal skeletal fractures: birth trauma or child abuse? J Can Assoc Radiol 30:30, 1979

8. De Levie M, Nogrady MB: Rapid brain growth upon restoration of adequate nutrition causing false radiologic evidence of increased intracranial pressure. J Pediatr 76:523, 1970

9. Ellerstein NS, Norris KJ: Value of radiologic skeletal survey in assessment of abused children. Pediatrics 74:1075, 1984

10. Ellison PH, Tsai FY, Largent JA: Computed tomography in child abuse and cerebral contusion. Pediatrics 62:151, 1978

11. Gloebl HJ, Capitano MA, Kirkpatrick JA: Radiographic findings in children with psychosocial dwarfism. Pediatr Radiol 4:83, 1976

12. Haase GM, Ortiz VN, Sfakianakis GN, Morse TS: Value of radionuclide bone scanning in the early recognition of deliberate child abuse. J Trauma 20:873, 1980

13. Hayden CK Jr, Swischuk LE: Para-articular soft tissue changes in infections and trauma of the lower extremity in children. AJR 134:307, 1980

14. Hernandez RJ, Poznanski AK, Hopwood NJ et al: Incidence of growth lines in psychosocial dwarfs and idiopathic hypopituitarism. AJR 131:477, 1978

15. Javdes PK: Comparison of radiography and radionuclide bone scanning in detection of child abuse. Pediatrics 73:166, 1984

16. Kempe CH, Silverman FN, Steel J et al: Battered child syndrome. JAMA 181:17, 1962

17. King J, Diefendorf D, Apthorp J, et al: Analysis of 429 fractures in 189 battered children. J Pediatr Orthop 8:585, 1988

18. Kleinman PK, Marks SC, Blackbourne B: The metaphyseal lesion in abused infants: a radiologic-histopathologic study. AJR 146:895, 1986

19. Kleinman PK, Zito JL: Avulsion of the spinous processes caused by infant abuse. Radiology 151:389, 1984

20. Kogutt MS, Swischuk LE, Fagan CJ: Patterns of injury and significance of incommon fractures in the battered child syndrome. AJR 121:143, 1974

21. Lauer B, Ten Broeck E, Grossman M: Battered child syndrome: review of 130 patients with controls. Pediatrics 54:67, 1974

22. Merten DF, Osborne DRS, Radkowski MA, Leonidas JC: Craniocerebral trauma in the child abuse syndrome: radiological observations. Pediatr Radiol 14:272, 1984

23. Merten DF, Radkowski MA, Leonidas JC: The abused child: a radiological reappraisal. Radiology 146:377, 1983

24. Money J: The syndrome of abuse dwarfism (psychosocial dwarfism or reversible hyposomatotropism). Am J Dis Child 131:508, 1977

25. Mushin AS: Ocular damage in the battered baby syndrome. Br Med J 3:403, 1971

26. O'Neill JA Jr, Meacham W, Griffin P et al: Patterns of injury in the battered child syndrome. J Trauma 13:332, 1973

27. Powell GF, Brasel JA, Blizzard RM: Emotional deprivation and growth retardation simulating idiopathic hypopituitarism. I. Clinical evaluation of the syndrome. N Engl J Med 276:1271, 1967

28. Radkowski MA, Merten DF, Leonidas JC: The abused child: criteria for radiologic diagnosis. Radiographics 3:262, 1983

29. Silver HK, Finkelstein M: Deprivation dwarfism. J Pediatr 70:317, 1967

30. Silverman FN: Unrecognized trauma in infants, the battered child syndrome, and the syndrome of ambroise tardieu. Rigler lecture. Radiology 104:337, 1972
31. Smith FW, Gilday DL, Ash JM, Green MD: Unsuspected costo-vertebral fractures demonstrated by bone scanning in the child abuse syndrome. Pediatr Radiol 10:103, 1980
32. Sty JR, Starshak RJ: The role of bone scintigraphy in the evaluation of the suspected abused child. Radiology 146:369, 1983
33. Swischuk LE: Spine and spinal cord trauma in the battered child syndrome. Radiology 92:733, 1969
34. Taitz LS: Child abuse and osteogenesis imperfeta. Br Med J 295:1082, 1987
35. Tomasi LG, Rosman NP: Purtscher's retinopathy in the battered child syndrome. Am J Dis Child 129:1335, 1975
36. Zimmerman RA, Bilaniuk LT, Bruce D et al: Computed tomography of craniocerebral injury in the abused child. Radiology 130:687, 1979

14

Dental Trauma and Bite Mark Evaluation

Joseph E. Bernat

Oral lacerations, jaw and teeth injuries, dental neglect, and epidermal bite marks are among the general manifestations of child maltreatment. Fractured, luxated, or avulsed teeth, contusions and lacerations on the lips and tongue, and acute jaw fractures are all specific examples of injuries seen in maltreatment cases. In addition, the torn labial frenum in the preambulatory infant is thought by some authorities to be highly suggestive of child abuse, and abuse should be considered in the toddler with a frenum tear. Sequelae of oral trauma can be seen in the older child; these include the presence of discolored and devitalized teeth, old root and jaw fractures, and scarring in and around the mouth. Many of them, individually, would not necessarily arouse the suspicion of the examiner as to the true cause of the injury.

Neglect of a child's dentition is another aspect of the maltreatment of children. Dental caries is human's most prevalent disease, with epidemiologic studies showing that 50 percent of 2-year-old children have at least one carious lesion. By the time a child has reached school age, this number has increased to eight lesions. Clearly, dentition can be an area of severe neglect; this is especially true considering the high sucrose diet of today's children. Every physician should be familiar with the many clinical signs and symptoms of dental caries. They include discolored, fractured, and grossly carious teeth. If the examining physician has any doubts about the condition of the teeth, a dental consultation is in order. Not having teeth repaired, whether they are permanent or deciduous, can be very painful and debilitating for the child.

Reports by numerous authors have demonstrated that the head is a common area of injury. Studies have shown that approximately 50 percent of examined physical abuse patients have head or facial injuries. The incidence of intraoral injuries has been reported to be as low as 1 percent. However, all of these studies have been retrospective in nature. The authors reviewed hospital records from the initial examination of the physically abused child with no "on the spot examination" by a dentist. One recent study examined all physically and sexually abused children presenting to a pediatric emergency department over a 4-month period. Detailed dental examinations were performed on 170 children at the same time as all other evaluations. It was found that approximately 25 percent of physically abused children and 15 percent of sexually abused children demonstrated injuries in and around the mouth. Interestingly, only one patient had a frenum injury, and there were significant injury pattern differences between physically and sexually abused children.

A bite mark has been defined by MacDonald as "a mark made by the teeth either alone or in combination with other mouth parts." As incriminating evidence, bite marks have been found in foodstuff, human flesh, and other objects. Like fingerprints, teeth marks can be used for identification, and their use historically predates that of fingerprints. This section of the chapter is devoted to the recognition of oral injuries in suspected child maltreatment cases.

NORMAL DENTITION

As mentioned earlier, there are several injuries in and around the mouth that are suggestive of abuse. In order to recognize abnormal manifestations, the normal should be understood.

The first teeth appear in the mouth at approximately 6 months of age, and from this point until around 3 years of age the normal child will be completing deciduous dentition. From 3 to 6 years, the dentition remains relatively stable with only minor growth changes being evident. At approximately 6 years of age, the permanent dentition begins to appear and is complete around age 12 except for the third molars. For the sake of simplicity, only the normal complete deciduous dentition will be discussed. Except for tooth size and configuration, the normal deciduous and permanent dentitions will look the same.

Figure 14-1 shows the normal complete deciduous dentition and surrounding oral structures. First, note that the lips are symmetric and of normal size. The vermilion border is intact and without scars. On opening, the commissures (corners of the mouth) are symmetric. If the lips are reflected, they reveal the maxillary and mandibular labial frena. In their normal state they are V-shaped and attach the lips to the alveolar ridges. The apex of the V attaches from 1 to 5 mm above or below the midline between the two central incisors. The mucosa of the lips, cheeks, and alveolar processes is smooth, pink, keratinized to varying degrees, and intact. The tongue basically fills in the space between the lower teeth. It should be mobile enough to protrude from the mouth, touch the posterior portion of the palate, and have enough lateral movement to protrude from each cheek. When the tongue is lifted, it reveals the lingual frenum. Like its counterparts the labial frena, the lingual frenum is a V-shaped muscle attachment in the midline of the mouth.

There are 20 teeth. Both arches should be parabolic in shape without any displaced teeth. The plane of occlusion demonstrates a gentle curve from anterior to posterior. A space or diastema between the teeth is either at the midline or bilateral in nature. As the child approaches the age of 6, the upper and lower anterior teeth will begin to show some mobility. Before this age, the teeth should be firm. All teeth should have a uniform white color, show no fractures, and should not be carious. When the mandible is closed, all parts should meet simultaneously, painlessly, and without noise.

When examining the normal dentition, the practitioner must keep in mind that the mouth, like other parts of the body, is subject to a wide range of normal variability.

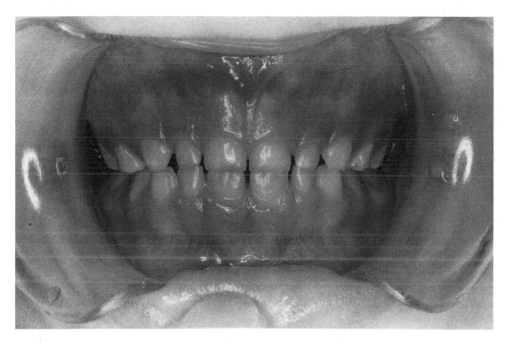

Fig. 14-1. The normal dentition of a 5-year-old child. Note that there are no broken or carious teeth; all teeth meet evenly and at the same time. There are bilateral spaces (diastema) between the teeth. The maxillary labial frenum is intact.

ORAL INJURIES

As mentioned previously, many different injuries can be seen in the abused and neglected child. Although many of these injuries are best treated by a dentist, a discussion of recognition and initial management is appropriate for the physician.

Frenum Tears

The frequency of frenum tears in child abuse has probably been overestimated in many studies but is an important injury, nonetheless. Recognition is fairly easy; reflect the lip and look for separation of the frenum. The tear may be linear or three corner in nature. Usually, a history of falling will be given. The tear can occur through two mechanisms. One is a direct blow to the mouth, possibly to silence a screaming or crying child. Besides the split frenum, there may be associated contusions, broken teeth, and fractures of the facial bones. A second mode of injury occurs at feeding time. An angry parent, frustrated at a slow eater, may force a spoon or bottle into the baby's mouth, ripping the frenum. There are usually no other injuries associated with this injury (Fig. 14-2). However, the circumstances surrounding the tear will arouse suspicion. The age of the child is significant. A frenum tear can happen accidentally to the toddler who falls on a coffee table while learning to walk. Generally, children less than 6 months of age do not have the opportunity to traumatize themselves; and 2- to 5-year-old children are usually more stable. Therefore, the

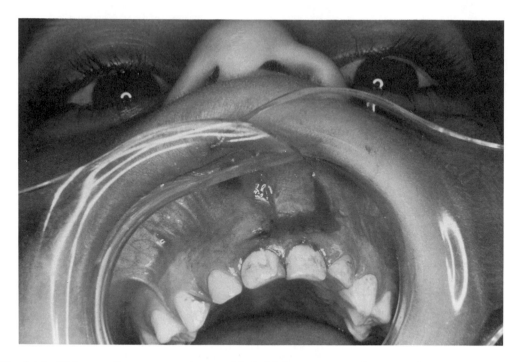

Fig. 14-2. This torn frenum in a 4-year-old child demonstrates the typical three corner tear. The lip has been retracted upward and, since there is no separation of the wound, no sutures are needed.

frenum tear in a nonambulatory infant must evoke a careful history on the part of the examining physician, since it is unlikely to have been caused accidentally.

The treatment of frenum tears is similar to that of any laceration with one exception: the healing time in a healthy child's mouth is very short. Thus, in small and medium tears, suturing may not be necessary. In some instances the sutures may even retard healing. When determining the treatment of these lacerations, several factors must be considered. These include the patient's age, medical history, need for other medical treatment, size of the tear, and lip mobility.

As is true with all intraoral injuries, a history of rheumatic fever or cardiac defects must elicit special consideration. It has long been recognized that an event that may cause bacteremia from oral or-

ganisms can be the primary factor in subacute bacterial endocarditis. With this in mind, the child with a cardiac problem must be treated with the appropriate antibiotic.

Lip Injuries

The lip may be injured at the same time that the frenum is torn, but in most cases, they appear as separate injuries. Lip injuries are the most frequently seen oral injuries and appear as contusions, lacerations, and abrasions (Fig. 14-3). Occasionally they may present as burns. Most of the injuries to the lips that result from child abuse are not very serious. In most cases they look much worse than they actually are, and the treatment is conservative. Treatment consists mostly of ob-

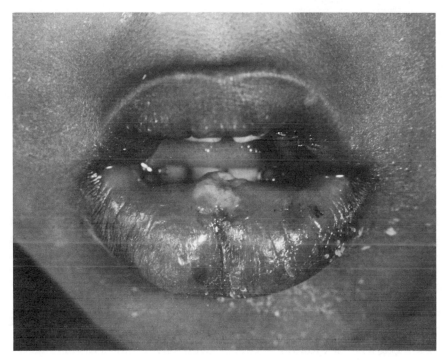

Fig. 14-3. Abraded mucosal surface of the lower lip caused by a slap. This can be painful, but no treatment is necessary. The teeth must be checked for fractures and mobility.

servation; this is especially true of contusions. The mechanism of lip wounds is that of a blunt force trapping the lip between it and the teeth. This produces a wound where the skin or mucosa is not broken. Contamination and infection of the wound are seldom seen, but the wound may be extremely painful owing to the abraded epithelial tissue.

If the lip is lacerated as well, this wound should be treated first. As with all lacerations, superficial and deep closure may be necessary. Suturing the lip requires that close attention be paid to the alignment of the vermilion border. This is the red margin of the upper and lower lip that begins at the exterior edge of the intraoral mucosa and extends outward to the extraoral labial cutaneous junction. If this is not properly aligned, a cosmetic

defect will result. If there is any question about the proper positioning of the flaps of the wound, an oral or plastic surgeon should be consulted. If a tooth is also broken, be sure that the piece is not embedded in the lip; a radiograph may be the best method of detection.

Lip burns can be seen in child abuse cases and are caused by hot utensils or cigarettes. The management of these wounds is the same as that for other burns, unless the angle, or commissure, is involved. If the commissure is involved it is possible that the opposing lips may adhere to one another during healing. This will cause scarring and contractions of one side of the mouth, with the result being an asymmetric mouth. A plastic or oral surgeon should be involved in the treatment and follow-up of these injuries.

Tooth and Alveolar Injuries

Traumatic injuries to the deciduous teeth of preschool children are very common. Some authorities report the incidence to be as high as 50 percent; that is, one-half of all children younger than 5 years old will exhibit evidence of oral trauma. Obviously, only some of these injuries can be attributed to abuse. However, child abuse cannot be ruled out in any of the injuries unless the examiner is sure that the reported history is true. Certainly, if the injury is accompanied by other physical injuries consistent with abuse, suspicions must be aroused. Teeth injuries can fall into the following categories: luxation, intrusion, avulsion, and fractures.

Luxation

Luxated teeth are those that are loosened in the mouth but have not left the socket. Both deciduous and permanent teeth are easily luxated by a blow to the mouth. With luxation, the tooth may be displaced in any direction. The severity of the blow need not be intense, as a well directed hit may loosen the teeth. It is very difficult to hit only one tooth, so although only one is apparently luxated, all teeth must be examined to assess their degree of mobility. A tooth is considered to be mobile if it moves more than 1 mm in any direction when force is placed on it. Notations as to which teeth are mobile and their specific degree of mobility should be made in the chart.

Treatment of luxations will depend on the age of the patient, the degree of mobility, the occlusion of the patient, and other injuries to the surrounding tissue. A child who is 5 or 6 years old usually has some loose teeth, owing to normal exfoliation and eruption patterns. Therefore, any severe luxations in the deciduous dentition of this group should be considered for removal. Those that occur in the younger age group should be retained for functional, esthetic, and orthodontic considerations. They can be left alone without any treatment if there is no danger of the teeth being aspirated, they do not interfere with the occlusion, and there are no other intraoral injuries. Luxated permanent teeth need immediate dental treatment. The patient should be referred to a dentist as soon as possible.

Intrusions

Intruded teeth are those that have been forced into the alveolar bone. Clinically, they will appear to be shorter than the rest of the teeth in the arch. Intrusions are caused by a severe blow to the incisal edge of the tooth. Deciduous teeth are more prone to being intruded than permanent teeth, owing to their short crown/root ratio. Many times, the teeth will be hit hard enough to drive them completely out of sight and give the clinical appearance of avulsed teeth. A complete dental examination including radiographs will reveal the true extent of the injury.

Avulsions

Avulsions are those injuries in which the teeth are totally removed from the socket. A sharp blow to the facial side of a tooth can cause the tooth to be removed from the socket. This injury happens more commonly with permanent teeth. The examiner must make an attempt to locate the missing tooth, as it may have been swallowed or aspirated. A dental radiograph is also necessary to determine the location of the tooth, since many times it will have been intruded. It may be necessary to take chest and abdominal radiographs to rule out aspiration. Once the tooth has been located, determine whether it is deciduous or permanent, evaluate the wound for the need of a tetanus booster, and begin immediate treatment.

The treatment of an avulsed tooth is immediate replantation. Studies by Andreasen have shown that the most important factor in successful replantation is the amount of time the tooth remains outside the mouth. Deciduous teeth cannot be replanted; those that are avulsed should be treated as if the tooth had been extracted, if there are no other injuries. For permanent teeth, the tooth must be put back into the socket. If replaced within the first 15 minutes after avulsion, the success rate approaches 90 percent. However, after 1 hour, the success rate decreases to less than 15 percent. To replant the tooth, hold it by the crown only (touching the root may cause later rejection) and gently remove any foreign bodies and debris. This is best done with sterile water and a syringe. Next, gently return the tooth root first to the socket and carefully push it in as far as it will go. Have the patient hold his finger on the tooth so that it will not come out again, and obtain immediate dental treatment. Do not wait for the dentist to replant the tooth. Replant the tooth even if it has been out longer than 1 hour, since it is more desirable to have a tooth in place for even a short period of time than to have a prosthetic device. If it is impossible to put the tooth back into its socket, clean it off, keep it moist, and obtain dental treatment as soon as possible. It appears that the best intermediate storage media include sterile Ringer solution, sterile saline, milk, saliva (in the patient's mouth) and water. Evaluate the need for a tetanus booster and begin antibiotic coverage.

Teeth Fractures

Fractured anterior teeth in children are a common finding. Only a small percentage of these are the result of intentional trauma. Most fractures are the result of a severe blow to the teeth with a fairly hard object. These most likely occur during falling or other accidents but can also be

the result of being struck. A fracture can occur along any part of the tooth from the incisal edge to the tooth apex. All fractures should be examined with a dental radiograph. As with avulsion, time is the most important factor in the treatment of fractures. Injuries first seen in an emergency department and dismissed by the examiner as "only a chip" have resulted in the loss of the tooth because of the long time lapse between the accident and treatment. Treatment of these injuries can be done only by a dentist, and patients should be referred immediately.

Facial Fractures

Jaw fractures occur most commonly following automobile accidents and in assault cases. Maxillary fractures are relatively rare in children; when they do occur, they are usually the result of severe trauma and are accompanied by extensive and complicated damage to soft tissue and bones. The mandible, on the other hand, is very susceptible to fracture. Structurally, the mandible is a hoop of bone suspended at either end by ligamentous joints. The strongest part of the structure is the middle of the hoop or the chin, and the weakest parts are the two ends or the condyles. The severity of a jaw fracture coupled with other body injuries of a suspicious nature should certainly arouse timely questions on the part of the examiner.

A complete radiographic survey is essential in all suspected fracture cases. This survey includes a minimum of right and left lateral oblique views, posteroanterior views, and a panoramic radiograph of the midface.

Bilateral fractures of the mandible occur with such frequency that it is assumed that all fractures are bilateral until proved otherwise. A condylar fracture on one side is often accompanied by a body or ramus fracture on the other side; bilateral condylar fractures happen as a result of a blow to the chin. If these fractures are suspected, a lateral oblique jaw film on the side of the suspected fracture will show the injury best. In addition, the improvements made in the techniques involved in taking the panoramic dental radiograph make this ideal for showing fractures of the mandible. Many of the machines can be adjusted to take special views of the condyles and ramus.

Diagnosing maxillary fractures on routine radiographs can be very difficult. If a fractured maxilla is suspected, the radiograph of choice is a Waters view. Other special views are available for the various fractures of the face. These would include films of the zygomatic arches, the orbits, and the maxillary sinuses. Some authorities believe that if standard radiographs fail to demonstrate a fracture that is still suspected clinically, a lateral skull radiograph should be taken. If on this radiograph the frontonasal suture line is open, a fracture of the maxilla is very likely. If the suture line is not open, the maxilla still may be fractured, and the clinician must rely on the facial and intraoral examinations for further information. In cases in which jaw fractures have been demonstrated and in those in which extraoral radiographs are unable to demonstrate the break, a series of intraoral radiographs of the suspected area should be taken. These radiographs (called periapical x-rays) will show not only routine jaw fractures, but also alveolar fractures, breaks through tooth buds, and symphyseal fractures.

Examination

The first step in diagnosing facial fractures is the extraoral examination. It should begin with noting any contusions around the jaws. Many fractures will result in a contusion directly above the fracture site. Next, judge the symmetry of the face. Then palpate the mandibular condyles and the temporomandibular joint. This is done while standing directly in front of the patient, with both forefingers placed in the external auditory meatuses with the balls of the fingers turned forward, and the other fingers resting along the posterior border of the mandible. When the mandible opens, the unfractured condyle will move out of the glenoid fossa. A condylar fracture is suspected if the condyle does not move out of the fossa or if the mandible deviates to one side on opening. The shift of the midline (as determined by the teeth) will be toward the affected side. Using the remaining fingers, palpate the posterior border of the ramus for any discontinuities. This entire examination should be done with extreme care, as the patient with a fractured jaw will experience pain and difficulty on opening.

The next area of examination is the zygomatic arch. Fractures of the posterior portion are common even when there are no other facial fractures. A dimple over the arch area is considered pathognomonic of a fracture. Palpate the entire length of the arch and continue to the infraorbital ridge and lateral rim of the orbit. A notch or moving fragment will indicate a fracture site. If both the posterior segment of the zygoma and the lateral rim of the orbit are fractured, the zygoma will be completely separated from the maxilla. If bilateral zygomatic arch fractures are found, a transverse facial fracture must be suspected. Pay close attention to any bleeding from the ears, cerebrospinal rhinitis, and general neurologic abnormalities. Any of these signs can indicate serious fractures involving the base of the skull and require immediate consultation with the neurosurgery department.

Begin the intraoral examination by determining whether the arch form is intact. An abrupt change in the occlusal plane of the teeth, diastemata, and gingival tears should all arouse suspicion. When the mouth is closed, all of the patient's teeth should meet at the same time. The maxillary arch overlaps the entire mandibular arch in the normal occlusion, and deviations from this will suggest a fracture. If there are no obvious teeth displacements, the jaws should be examined manually.

Examine the jaws by first placing the forefingers of each hand on the occlusal surfaces of the teeth and the thumbs along the lower border of the mandible. The left forefinger is placed as far distal as possible on the right side of the mandible, and the right forefinger is placed approximately 3 to 4 cm mesial. An up-and-down motion is made while moving the fingers around the arch. If there is a fracture present, the pieces should move apart with pain and crepitus. The maxilla is examined by placing the forefinger on the palatal surface of the teeth and the thumb on the facial surface. The segments are rocked back and forth to test for mobility. The normal child will not exhibit any mobility. The examination is first done in the posterior segments and then in the anterior segments. Any fracture will demonstrate movement of the segments or of the entire maxilla. The anterior border of the mandibular ramus is palpated bilaterally by running a forefinger up and down its length. The coronoid process can best be palpated intraorally at this time.

Treatment

As with most fractures, facial fractures should be treated as soon as possible. The type of treatment necessary will depend on the age of the child, the location of the fracture, and the severity of the fracture. It must be remembered that bone heals rapidly in children; therefore, treatment must begin immediately. It is best to consult with an oral surgeon for treatment of these injuries, since the skills required for reduction and especially fixation are often complicated and are best handled by these specialists.

Tongue Injuries

A tongue can be injured during a blow to the mandible forcing the teeth shut and trapping it between them. Most injuries occur on the lateral border. These suggest trauma to the chin, and it is essential that the examination include the mandible and the surrounding structures. Injuries caused by the teeth will have jagged edges and will exhibit a crushed appearance. When examining the tongue, it is best to ask the patient to extend it as far as possible while holding gauze just outside the mouth. As the tip of the tongue enters the gauze, grasp the tongue with the gauze and retract it as far as possible. This will allow you to see all parts of the tongue.

Treatment of tongue lacerations can be difficult because of the problem of holding the tongue still. This problem can be overcome with adequate local anesthesia and rapid suturing techniques. The best way to obtain profound anesthesia of the tongue is through a lingual block rather than through infiltration around the wound.

Neglect

As mentioned earlier, neglect of dental needs can certainly cause a child pain and discomfort. However, there are certain problems in determining whether a child's poor dentition is a result of malicious neglect or of the normal neglect caused by ignorance, fear, or lack of money. It is virtually impossible for an examining physician or dentist to tell by physical examination alone whether or not the oral conditions seen are a result of unjustifiable neglect. Only through an adequate history and repeated attempts to secure treatment for the child can neglect be proved. Even then, the degree of severity certainly does not compare with that of withholding care from truly ill children. Keeping this in mind, neglected dental care can be used as an additional piece of evidence in the context of other medical neglect.

On seeing a mouth full of carious lesions, an examining physician must refer this child to a dentist for treatment. If neglect is suspected, a follow-up call to the dentist is recommended. If the parents have been adequately counseled about the importance of the treatment and can afford it, repeated attempts to secure treatment must be made. If the parents still do not conscientiously seek treatment, neglect must be assumed and the proper authorities notified.

BITE MARKS

Bite marks are important in child abuse cases because they can aid in identifying the perpetrator. They are rarely accidental and are good indicators of genuine child abuse. They are frequent findings in abuse cases, and the literature contains numerous reports. All bites should be considered intentional until proved otherwise. However, care must be taken in the evaluation of the marks, without immediately making the assumption that they were inflicted by an attacker. Marks found on infants tend to be in different locations than on older children or adolescents and reflect punitive measures often in response to crying or soiling. Punishment for soiling is usually centered around the genitalia or buttocks. Often, there is evidence of other injuries as well. Older children, as opposed to infants, tend to exhibit bite marks that fall into two categories: assault, in which

bites are inflicted in a rapid, random, enraged manner; and sexual abuse, in which a well defined bite mark is evident and frequently associated with a suck mark. There have also been reports of self-inflicted marks, made by the victim to stifle cries during an attack.

Sims et al. reported three cases of bite marks in child abuse. In each of these cases, the marks were used to identify the perpetrator. Trube-Becker demonstrated 11 of 48 child abuse cases showing bite marks. Each case resulted in death (not from the bites), and the most common areas where bites were found were the limbs, abdomen, and cheeks. To be certain, dental evidence, and in particular bite mark dental evidence, has been recognized as an important tool in solving many types of assault and murder cases. Bite mark evidence must not be overlooked in abuse cases as a means of identifying the attacker. In this section, the recognition of bite marks, their differentiation from animal wounds, the basic differences between an adult and a child bite, the procedures that must be followed to properly record the mark, and how to identify the suspected attacker are presented.

Bite Mark Recognition

Human bite marks are identified by their shape and size. To best understand the scientific basis of the recognition of human bite marks, it is essential to have a knowledge of the mechanisms of the mark. These mechanisms have been studied extensively and are widely reported in the literature. A bite mark is the mark or registration of the tooth's cutting edges on a substance, either alone or in combination with other mouth parts. In many instances, two other marks are inflicted at the same time—a suck mark and a thrust mark. The suck mark ("hickey") is caused

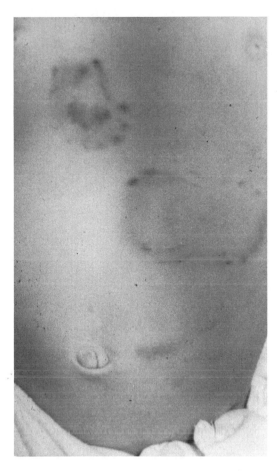

Fig. 14-4. Bite marks show an extremely varied clinical picture, both with and without a central hematoma. Photographs should identify the anatomic location as well as include a scale for future reference.

by a pulling of the skin into the mouth by negative pressure or suction. The thrust mark is caused by the tongue pushing against the skin trapped behind and between the maxillary and mandibular teeth. This action results in a mark similar to the one shown in Figure 14-4. All marks resemble this mark in that they are ovoid to circular areas with tooth imprints. The inner aspect of the mark will either be clear or contain the hickey or thrust mark. These two marks are similar

in appearance in that each resembles a contusion in the central portion of the mark. Their difference, if any, is that a thrust mark occasionally will demonstrate the impression of the rugae or anatomic landmarks of the lingual portion of the teeth on the victim's skin. Although it seems that this may be a relatively simple act, bite marks are frequently complex and need to be studied closely.

To recognize a bite mark, the individual components must be recognized. The marks caused by tooth pressure alone are from the incisal edges of the anterior teeth or the occlusal surfaces of the posterior teeth. The exact nature of the marks made will depend on the force applied, the duration of the application, the degree of movement of the tissues between the teeth during the force, and the position of the tissues between the teeth during the bite. The most clearly defined bites are caused by slow, deliberate, and forceful pressure by the anterior teeth, whereas the poorly defined marks are those caused by rapid, ripping, slight pressure acts by either the anterior or posterior teeth. In the well defined marks, the incisal edges leave pale areas that represent these edges. Immediately adjacent are areas of bruising caused by damage to the vessels at the area of maximum stretching next to the relatively fixed tissue in contact with the incisal edges. It is the action of the teeth that gives the bite mark its identification. Bite marks rarely contain more features than those exhibited by the anterior teeth, which leave a unique "tool mark." The mark will have the parabolic shape of the human dental arch, no one tooth will be prominent (as the canines are in animal bites), and most importantly, the marks can give a clear indication of irregularities of size, shape, or position of individual teeth.

The appearance of the mark will also be modified by the mechanical properties of the skin at the site of the bite. For example, skin and subcutaneous tissue on the back are firmer than that on a breast. The binding between the skin and subcutaneous tissue varies from site to site. For example, directional variations, those governed by the movements and extensibility of an area, will produce distortions of bite marks that are dependent on the position of the subject during biting. Distortions and changes can also occur after the bite, with movements and changes of body position. These changes are affected by the elapsed time following the bite. Soon after being inflicted, the area will be highly edematous and stiff and will not change as much with movement. However, as the edema subsides, movement of the body, resolution of the ecchymosis, and fading of the bite will cause extensive changes. Finally, whether biting took place first and sucking second or vice versa will produce quite different marks.

Knowing the mechanisms of the mark, the examiner must now determine whether the lesion can be positively identified as a bite mark. Bite mark identification entails several steps: recognition of the wound, documentation, and interpretation. Early recognition is critical if valuable information is to be preserved.

Bite marks frequently go undetected by police officers, physicians, and pathologists. If a mark is seen that has any possibility of being a bite mark, a forensic dentist should be notified immediately. The collection of data should begin immediately since artifacts can be introduced quickly, complicating or negating existing evidence. Do not wash the body or begin an autopsy before the marks have at least been photographed. Even disturbing the tissues may distort the mark to the point where it will be impossible to be used for suspect identification. The collection of the data is discussed in a later section.

Distinguishing Bite Marks

Human bite mark characteristics include an elliptical or ovoid pattern containing tooth and arch marks. The tooth marks, usually inflicted by the upper and lower incisors, are thin rectangles or portions of rectangles. The marks left by the canines, however, are triangular in shape, and the marks made by premolars are circular. The arch mark is identified when four or five marks of adjacent teeth are present. The maxillary arch mark is usually diffuse, but the mark caused by the mandibular teeth is generally more distinct.

Animal versus Human Bites

There are three areas where human bites will differ from those of an animal. They are the size of the mark, the form of the dental arch, and the mechanisms of the bite. Most domestic animal bite marks are smaller than those of a human's. The common animal bites are those of dogs, cats, and rodents. In general, the incisal edges of an animal are smaller and sharper than those of a human; therefore, animal bite marks are deeper and narrower. Animal bites tend to be ripping in nature, whereas human ones are crushing. In addition, the longer, sharper canines of an animal will cause deep wounds at the corners. Very often, severe animal bites will resemble surgical wounds and are common in death investigations. They are frequently seen where the body is in a confined space accessible to pets.

Adult versus Child Bites

The obvious difference between a child's bite and an adult's is one of size, which can be measured in two places; the size of the arch width and the width of the individual teeth. Studies done by Moorees found that the difference between a 5-year-old child's arch width and an adult's is approximately 4.4 mm in the maxilla and 2.5 mm for the mandible. The differences in the widths of individual teeth are even more striking. This same study showed that cumulative widths of the six upper deciduous teeth were 10-mm smaller than those in the permanent dentition. In the lower arch, the differences were approximately 7 mm. Using these basic measurements as a guideline, it is usually possible to distinguish a child's bite from that of an adult.

Collecting Bite Mark Data

Once a mark has been assumed to be caused by a bite, identification procedures must begin immediately. Even the slightest delay may cause the loss of valuable data. Teeth marks that do not break the skin last from several minutes to 24 hours. In those cases where the skin is broken, the marks will last several days, depending on the thickness of the tissue. In all suspected bite marks, photographs, saliva washings, impressions, and a detailed description of the wound must be collected to ensure successful suspect identification.

The first step is to take photographs of the wound, both in color and in black and white. Numerous photos that include anatomic landmarks should be taken to illustrate the mark; others can be close-ups. Each should be taken with a millimeter rule in the visual field alongside, and an identification number. "Instant" photographs are not acceptable but are better than nothing. The ruler must be in the same focal plane as the mark, and the wound must be photographed parallel to the film plane or else the mark will be distorted. If the marks are on a curved surface, separate photos of the upper and lower arches may have to be taken. The photos should be taken immediately and then repeated at 24-hour intervals for at least 7 days. This is very important, owing to the histologic changes that take place in the skin (thereby changing the definition of the bite) of both the living and the dead. One of these pictures will show the best definition of the mark.

The second step in collecting the data is to take saliva washings of the area. The amount of saliva deposited at a bite mark is approximately 0.3 ml and is distributed over about 6.5 cm^2. ABO blood groupings can be determined from saliva washings. It is very difficult to obtain enough saliva from many of the bites seen, but an attempt should always be made. The most common technique used is swabbing the area with cotton moistened in saline, bottled, labeled, and refrigerated for processing by a forensic serologist. The washing should be started at the periphery of the bite and directed centrally in a circular motion. The most information can be obtained by comparing these washings with specimens of blood and saliva from the victim and all suspects.

Obtaining bite mark impressions is relatively easy and inexpensive. Several dental impression materials are available to make an accurate and detailed mold of the bite and at least a 0.5-in. margin. This mold is then used to make a plaster model of the wound, which provides additional information including the relative depth of penetration. Any dentist should be able to make an acceptable impression.

Description of the bite mark should include the anatomic location including surface, contour, and tissue characteristics. Also, the shape, size, color, and injury type are documented. The injury types include hemorrhage, abrasions, lacerations, incisions, avulsions, and artifacts.

Evidence gathered from both the victims and suspects must be obtained in accordance with accepted procedures and proper authorization must be received from the appropriate authorities. Both victims and suspects may object to having photographs, impressions, and examinations but Supreme Court decisions have ruled that identification procedures such as these do not infringe on the rights of the individual. In all instances where an individual objects, a court order is obtained before proceeding.

The final step is to obtain dental casts of all possible suspects. A limited number of people have the opportunity to bite the child. These are typically limited to the parents, siblings, or baby-sitters who have close access to the victim.

Suspect Identification

It can be possible to include or exclude suspects by noting whether the bites are consistent with their dentition. This is not as difficult as it seems, since only a limited number of people have access to a child. On the basis of the size of the arch, all adults or all children can be excluded. Individual characteristics like wear, missing teeth, rotations, arch form, diastemata, dental restorations, fractured teeth, carious teeth, and malposed teeth are seen with enough frequency and certainty to either include or exclude all but the perpetrator of the assault in most cases. However, many authors feel that a person's dentition, like fingerprints, is unique to that person. Therefore, not only the dentition, but the configuration of each mouth is unique, as is the bite it creates. Keeping this in mind, even poorly defined marks may give a clue as to the identity of the assailant.

SUGGESTED READINGS

1. Anderson WR, Hudson RP: Self-inflicted bite marks in battered child syndrome. Forensic Sci Int 7:71, 1976
2. Andreasen JO: Treatment of fractured and avulsed teeth. J Dent Child 38:29, 1971
3. Andreasen JO: Proceedings of the annual meeting of the American Academy of Pedodontics. American Academy of Pedodontics, Chicago, IL, 1977
4. Baker MD: Human bites in children. A six-year experience. Am J Dis Child 141:1285, 1987
5. Barbanel JC, Evans JH: Bite marks in skin-mechanical factors. J Forensic Sci Soc 14:235, 1974
6. Beckstead JW, Rawson RD, Giles WS: Review of bite mark evidence. J Am Dent Assoc 99:69, 1979
7. Brook I: Microbiology of human and animal bite wounds in children. Pediatr Infect Dis J 6:29, 1987
8. Cameron JM, Johnson HP, Camps FE: The battered child syndrome. Med Sci Law 6:2, 1966
9. Cameron JM, Sims BG: Forensic Dentistry. Churchill Livingstone, Edinburgh, 1974
10. Cleft A, Lamont CM: Saliva in forensic odontology. J Forensic Sci Soc 14:241, 1974
11. Cowlin W: Current legal status of bite marks. Evidence transactions of the Annual American Academy of Forensic Science meeting, Atlanta, 1979
12. Dailey JC, Shernoff AF, Gelles JH: An improved technique for bite mark impressions. J Prosthet Dent 61:153, 1989
13. Drinnan AJ, Melton MJ: Court presentation of bite mark evidence. Int Dent J 35:316, 1985
14. Ellis RG, Davey KW: The Classification and Treatment of Injuries to the Teeth of Children. 5th Ed. Year Book Medical Publishers, Chicago, 1970
15. Furness J: Bite marks in non-accidental injuries of children. Police Surg 6:75, 1974
16. Gold MH, Roenigk HH, Smith ES, Pierce LJ: Evaluation and treatment of patients with human bite marks. Am J Forensic Med Pathol 10:140, 1989
17. Gold MH, Roenigk HH, Smith ES, Pierce LJ: Human bite marks. Differential diagnosis. Clin Pediatr 28:329, 1989
18. Goldstein EJ, Citron DM, Finegold SM: Role of anaerobic bacteria in bite-wound

infections. Rev Infect Dis, suppl. 1:S177, 1984

19. Guidelines for bite mark analysis. American Board of Forensic Odontology. J Am Dent Assoc 112:383, 1986

20. Gustafson G: Forensic Odontology. American Elsevier Publishing, New York, 1966

21. Harvey W: Dental Identification and Forensic Odontology. Henry Kimpton Publishers, London, 1976

22. Havel DA: The role of photography in the presentation of bitemark evidence. J Biol Photogr 53:59, 1985

23. Hennon DK, Stookey GK, Muhler JC: A survey of the prevalence and distribution of dental caries in preschool children. J Am Dent Assoc 79:1405, 1969

24. Infante PF, Owen GM: Dental caries and levels of treatment for school children by geographical region, socioeconomic status, race, and size of community. J Public Health Dent 35:19, 1975

25. Jonason C, Frykholm KO, Frykholm A: Three dimensional measurement of tooth impression of criminological investigation. Int J Forensic Dent 2:70, 1974

26. Korns RD: The incidence of accidental injury to primary teeth. J Dent Child 27:29, 1971

27. Krauss TC, Warlen SC: Photographic techniques of concern in metric bite mark analysis. J Forensic Sci 29:633, 1985

28. Kruger GO: Textbook of Oral Surgery. CV Mosby, Saint Louis, 1974

29. Levine LJ: The solution of a battered child homicide by dental evidence: report of a case. J Am Dent Assoc 87:1234, 1973

30. Lindsey D, Christopher M, Hollenbach J et al: Natural course of the human bite wound: incidence of infection and complications in 434 bites and 803 lacerations in the same group of patients. J Trauma 27:45, 1987

31. Luntz LL, Luntz P: Handbook for Dental Identification. JB Lippincott, Philadelphia, 1973

32. MacDonald DG: Bite mark recognition and interpretation. J Forensic Sci Soc 14:229, 1974

33. MacDonald DG, Laird WRE: Bitemarks in a murder case. Int J Forensic Dent 3:26, 1976

34. MacFarlane TW, MacDonald DG, Sutherland DA: Statistical problems in dental identification. J Forensic Sci Soc 14:247, 1974

35. Martin LT: Human bites. Guidelines for prompt evaluation and treatment. Postgrad Med 81:221, 1987

36. McDonald RE, Avery DR: Dentistry for the Child and Adolescent. CV Mosby, Saint Louis, 1978

37. Moorees CFA: The Dentition of the Growing Child. Harvard University Press, Boston, 1959

38. O'Neill JA, Meachum WF, Griffen PP et al: Patterns of injury in the battered child syndrome. J Trauma 14:332, 1973

39. Rao VJ, Souviron RR: Dusting and lifting the bite print: a new technique. J Forensic Sci 29:326, 1984

40. Rawson RD, Koot A, Martin C et al: Incidence of bite marks in a selected juvenile population: a preliminary report. J Forensic Sci 29:254, 1984

41. Rawson RD, Ommen RK, Kinard G et al: Statistical evidence for the individuality of the human dentition. J Forensic Sci 29:245, 1984

42. Rowe NL: Fractures of the facial skeleton in children. J Oral Surg 26:505, 1968

43. Sims BG, Grant JH, Cameron JM: Bitemarks in the "battered baby syndrome." Med Sci Law 13:207, 1973

44. Skinner AE, Castle RL: A retrospective study. National Society for the Prevention of Cruelty to Children, London, 1969

45. Skrzeckas J: Supararbitrium, betr. die Verletzung zweier Finger usw. Vjschr Gerichtl Med Ban 21:118, 1974

46. Sognnaes RD: Forensic stomatology. Part III. N Engl J Med 296:197, 1977

47. Sognnaes RD: Forensic bite-mark measurements. Dent Surv 17:27, 1979

48. Solheim T, Leidal TI: Scanning electron microscopy in the investigation of bite marks in foodstuffs. Forensic Sci 6:205, 1975

49. Stafne EC: Oral Roentgenographic Diagnosis. 3rd Ed. WB Saunders, Philadelphia, 1969

50. Tate RJ: Facial injuries associated with the battered child syndrome. Br J Oral Surg 9:41, 1971

51. Trube-Becker E: Bite marks on battered children. Z Rechsmedizin 79:73, 1977
52. Waite DE: Pediatric fractures of jaw and facial bones. Pediatrics 51:551, 1973
53. Whittaker DK: Some laboratory studies on the accuracy of bite mark comparison. Int Dent J 25:166, 1975
54. Yano M: Experimental studies on bite marks. Int J Forensic Dent 1:13, 1973

15

Ophthalmologic Manifestations

Alex V. Levin

Ocular injury as a result of child abuse has been known for centuries. Children were blinded either as a form of punishment or as a means of increasing their value as beggars. Perhaps the first medical report was Aikman's 1928 description of an abused infant with retinal hemorrhages and abnormal eye movements. Caffey's early description of the association between subdural hematoma with skeletal fractures included ocular signs in five of his six patients. However, it is Kiffney who is commonly credited with first stating clearly that ocular injury could be a result of child abuse.

Virtually any injury to the eye may be a result of child abuse (Table 15-1). The face is a site of injury in 11 to 45 percent of child abuse cases. Ophthalmologic manifestations may be seen in 5 to 61 percent of cases. The eye may be affected as a result of physical abuse, sexual abuse, or neglect. For this reason, it is important that ocular assessment be considered in the evaluation of abused children, especially those under the age of 3 years who may be unable to communicate clearly about a possible visual defect without obvious associated external signs of trauma. Slit lamp examination and dilated fundus examination with an indirect ophthal-

moscope by an ophthalmologist are essential parts of the evaluation of ocular injury. Even with the use of a direct ophthalmoscope in a dilated pupil, the non-ophthalmologist may fail to detect ocular abnormalities that could prove invaluable to the child's evaluation and care. The ophthalmologist is also particularly skilled in assessing the visual acuity and eye movements in children, which may reflect central nervous system (CNS) injury. In fact, the ophthalmologist may be the physician who makes the initial diagnosis of child abuse in 4 to 6 percent of cases. Ophthalmic investigation may also be helpful from the forensic standpoint by providing information regarding the mechanism or time of injury. Eye injuries may occur with or without injury to other parts of the body. A complete physical examination is essential in all cases of suspected nonaccidental trauma to the eyes.

PHYSICAL ABUSE

Periorbital Injuries

Child abuse may result in ecchymosis, laceration, or abrasion to periorbital soft tissues or fracture of the bony orbit. Such

Table 15-1. Reported and Observed Ophthalmologic Manifestations
of Child Abuse

Structure	Category	Manifestations[a]
Periorbita	Physical	Ecchymosis, hematoma, laceration, scratches, abrasion, edema, ptosis, burn
	MBP	Periorbital cellulitis
Conjunctiva	Physical	Subconjunctival hemorrhage, glue
	Sexual	Subconjunctival hemorrhage, ?gonorrhea conjunctivitis
	MBP	Chemical conjunctivitis and scarring
Anterior segment		
Cornea	Physical	Scarring, edema, microcornea, enlarged cornea, blood staining, Descemet layer breaks, abrasion
Anterior chamber and iridocorneal angle		Hyphema, glaucoma (neovascular, open angle, or closed angle), fibrovascular membranes
Iris		Mydriasis, sphincter tears, anisocoria, atrophy, neovascularization, abnormal pupil shape, iridodialysis, ectropion uvea
	Neglect	Exposure keratitis
	MBP	Chemical keratitis with corneal scarring, mydriasis
Lens	Physical	Cataract (total, anterior or posterior subcapsular), subluxation, dislocation
Vitreous	Physical	Vitreous hemorrhage, subhyaloid hemorrhage, fibroglial organization, postmortem vitreous electrolyte abnormalities
Retina		Exudates (including snowbanking), hemorrhages (sub-, intra-, and preretinal, nerve fiber layer), traumatic retinoschisis with hemorrhage, commotio, RD, (exudative, rhegmatogenous, [holes, tears, dialysis, or avulsion] or traction), chronic RD with fixed folds and cysts, chorioretinal scars, preretinal gliosis with/without wrinkling, macular hole/cyst/ridges, pigmentary changes, ?CR vein obstruction, CR artery obstruction, choroidal atrophy
	Sexual	Hemorrhage
Optic nerve and cortical pathways	Physical	Marcus Gunn pupil, anisocoria, papilledema, optic atrophy, optic nerve sheath hemorrhage, cortical contusion/edema/infarction/atrophy/laceration, blindness, hemianopsia, cavernous sinus thrombosis, ?internuclear ophthalmoplegia, amblyopia, functional visual loss/micropsia
	Neglect	Amblyopia
Eye movements	Physical	Nystagmus, gaze preference, strabismus (esotropia, exotropia, and hypertropia), ophthalmoplegia, 6th cranial nerve palsy
Orbit	Physical	Proptosis, ?optic nerve canal fracture, posterior orbital hemorrhage

Abbreviations: MBP, Münchausen syndrome by proxy; RD, retinal detachment; CR, central retinal.

[a] Manifestations not listed in order of frequency.

injuries can lead to cellulitis or amblyogenic obstruction of the visual axis by edematous tissues or ptosis. Periorbital ecchymosis is a common ocular manifestation of physical abuse, occurring in 14 to 20 percent of victims. Rao et al. report periorbital injuries in 57 percent of victims at autopsy. Facial burns occur more frequently in nonaccidental injury than in accidental injury.

Differential Diagnosis

It is important to rule out the presence of coagulopathies or other blood dyscrasias that may lead to periorbital ecchymosis. Of course, the presence of a coagulopathy does not exclude nonaccidental injury as a possible cause of the ecchymosis. Metastatic neuroblastoma with orbital involvement may present as bilateral periorbital ecchymosis, as may basilar skull fractures secondary to true accidents. Injuries to the forehead, including minor blunt accidental trauma, may lead to significant bilateral periorbital ecchymosis. However, any bruising in a child less than 6 months old should be considered suspicious until proved otherwise.

Lacerations in the area of the orbital rims need not be caused by sharp implements. Blunt trauma can cause compression of the soft tissues against the bony orbital rim, resulting in laceration.

Owing to the strong blink reflex, accidental burns characteristically leave a spared strip of skin just proximal to the lid margin and lashes, even though the lashes may be burned (Fig. 15-1). This strip was buried in the folds of the strongly closed lids. The cornea is often spared when the normal blink reflex is allowed to occur. Some authors believe

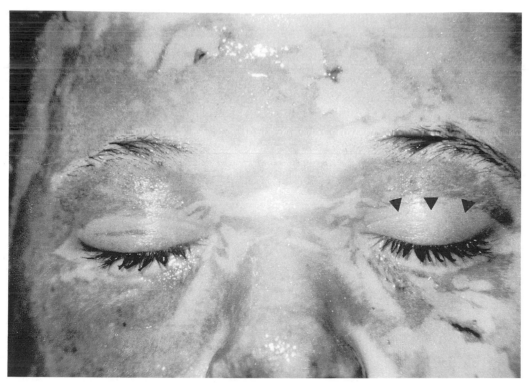

Fig. 15-1. Accidental facial burn demonstrating spared strips of skin just proximal to lid margins.

that the absence of burns in the submental and axillary regions betrays a history of the child's pulling a hot liquid off a counter or stove.

As with other skin injuries, the physician should search for pattern-type lesions such as slap marks or belt marks. Perhaps owing to the potential tissue space volume of the periorbita, blood accumulation can be significant and lead to marked ecchymotic eyelid swelling. Accumulation of blood often makes ecchymosis look relatively darker than bruises at other sites. Therefore, periorbital ecchymoses will appear to be at least 1 to 2 days older than they truly are, as compared with the usual progression of bruising at other sites. In addition, the increased volume of blood leads to a slower resolution.

Management

Lid injuries can result in chronic abnormalities of lid position and function or other deformities. Lacerations that cross the eyelid margin, are associated with ptosis, or penetrate into deep tissues should be referred to an ophthalmologist for repair. Even small lacerations of the upper lid may represent full thickness penetration and potential entry into the intracranial space via the orbital roof. Computed tomography (CT) scanning of the head may be indicated. Any periorbital injury should lead the examining physician to rule out trauma to the underlying globe. Even in situations where massive eyelid swelling appears to make examination impossible, ophthalmology consultation may be helpful in obtaining this necessary information.

Conjunctival Injuries

Although the conjunctiva may be lacerated or burned, only subconjunctival hemorrhage (SCH) and chemical injuries

have been described as a result of child abuse. Subconjunctival hemorrhage may occur in 2 to 4 percent of abused children with ocular manifestations. Direct trauma, or perhaps increases in thoracic pressure by chest compression, may be a cause. Subconjunctival hemorrhage has also been reported in sexually abused children, perhaps as a result of strong Valsalva maneuvers. The hemorrhaging may be small and focal, or it may be a large dark diffuse collection possibly extending for 360 degrees around the cornea (Fig. 15-2) and associated with marked conjunctival swelling (chemosis). In these latter cases, there is a higher likelihood that the eyeball itself has sustained serious injury, if not rupture.

Chemical instillation may be a feature of Münchausen syndrome by proxy (see below). There is one reported case of nonaccidental application of cyanoacrylate glue into the palpebral fissure.

Differential Diagnosis

Subconjunctival hemorrhage may occur in the presence of hypertension, blood dyscrasias and coagulopathies, or infectious conjunctivitis. It may also be seen in 0.5 to 13 percent of normal births, and is correlated with multiparity of the mother, rapidity of second stage of labor, traumatic facial cyanosis at birth, greater birthweight, greater head circumference, later gestational age, and being black. Following birth, SCH tends to be focal and small, most frequently located at the nasal or temporal corneal rim. Data have not been generated regarding time for disappearance of SCH associated with birth. In non-neonates, large SCH may take as long as 2 to 3 weeks to resorb completely. Dating cannot be accomplished accurately as with ecchymosis of the skin. In an abused newborn, it may be difficult to distinguish whether SCH is secondary to birth or trauma.

The nonaccidental instillation of chem-

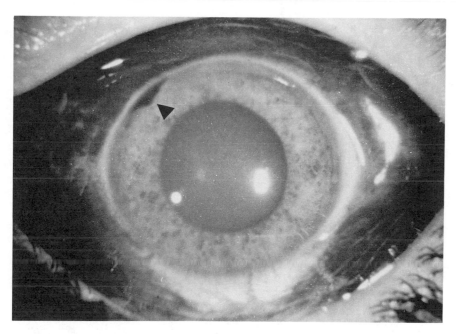

Fig. 15-2. Marked subconjunctival hemorrhage with mild chemosis. Note small hyphema (arrow) in anterior chamber.

icals into the palpebral fissure may have a characteristic appearance. There is a disproportionate involvement of the lower palpebral conjunctiva. This may be a result of the forced pulling down of the child's lower lid by the perpetrator, and the reflex turning up of the eye (Bell's phenomena) in response to the noxious forced opening of the palpebral fissure (Fig. 15-3).

Management
Subconjunctival hemorrhage usually has no visual sequelae unless there is enough conjunctival elevation to interefere with proper corneal wetting by the tear film. Artificial tear products may be helpful in such cases. Although cyanoacrylate is usually nontoxic to the eye, injection, chemosis, and corneal abrasion may occur. Gentle traction may be enough to achieve lid separation and glue removal, but surgical intervention may be required. Instillation of other chemicals

into the palpebral fissure, in particular alkaline substances, can be quite harmful, with resultant permanent visual loss from corneal damage. Copius irrigation, with pH monitoring, is the cornerstone of managing such injuries. Ophthalmology consultation may be helpful, but irrigation is the management priority.

Anterior Segment Injuries

The anterior chamber includes the cornea, anterior chamber (aqueous humor), trabecular meshwork and iridocorneal angle (outflow system for anterior chamber), iris, and pupil, all of which may be subject to the effects of nonaccidental injury. Large series of abused children with eye injuries have shown anterior segment trauma in 0 to 5.5 percent. Hyphema appears to be a marker for severe ocular injury. Belt beatings in which the eye is struck either during the use of the belt on

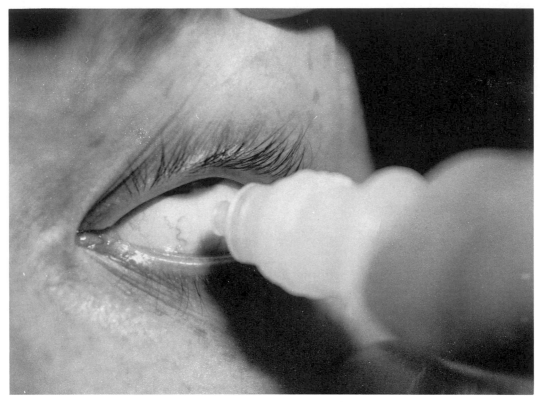

Fig. 15-3. Bell's phenomena during forced instillation of eyedrops. Inferior palpebral and bulbar conjunctiva will be most affected by adverse effect of instilled chemical. If involved, lower portions of cornea will be more affected.

the face or when the child moves to avoid being hit at another site may be a frequent mode of injury. Other reported injuries or sequelae of abuse include corneal scarring, corneal edema or haziness, microcornea, enlarged corneas, corneal blood staining following hyphema, glaucoma, asymmetry of pupil size, traumatic mydriasis, iridodialysis (disinsertion of the iris from its peripheral base), pupillary sphincter tears, and iris atrophy. Anterior segment injuries are usually caused by direct blunt trauma and are not often seen in the shaken baby syndrome (SBS). Disorders of pupillary reactivity in SBS usually occur as a result of interruption of neuronal pathways and are discussed below.

Differential Diagnosis

Each of these reported eye injuries can result from accidental trauma. However, with the exception of anisocoria, in almost every case these nonaccidental injuries occur in the setting of severe multistructural ocular damage. Of course, the differential recognition of nonaccidental versus accidental trauma also depends on the presence of nonocular signs of injury and characteristic psychosocial features. Bilateral trauma is also more characteristic of nonaccidental trauma.

Congenital malformations may mimic the sequelae of trauma. Anterior segment dysgenesis may lead to abnormalities of pupil shape and size, as well as iris atrophy. These conditions are usually bilateral and readily apparent with slit lamp examination. Congenital glaucoma, which may be unilateral or bilateral, is not characterized by either neovascularization or hyphema, which appear to be the leading causes of glaucoma in abused children. Congenital abnormalities of corneal size do occur and are apparent at birth, whereas the microcornea and enlarged corneas in abused children are acquired phenomena secondary to injury. Corneal scars can occur from previous ulceration or herpetic keratitis. Historical information of severe conjunctival injection and ocular pain should be available. Such inflammatory disorders are almost invariably unilateral. Corneal clouding, scarring, and hyphema have been reported to occur as a result of forceps-assisted vaginal deliveries; however, these injuries are usually discovered in the newborn nursery or shortly thereafter. In addition, forceps injuries result in characteristic markings on the inner corneal surface which can be seen by slit lamp examination. Spontaneous hyphema may rarely occur in juvenile xanthogranulomatosis. Characteristic iris masses and skin lesions are usually present.

Management
It is beyond the scope of this chapter to detail the management of all anterior segment injuries. However, it should be clear that an ophthalmology consultation is essential for both diagnosis and management. Subtle grades of hyphema with only suspended red blood cells or tiny clots in the iridocorneal angle could otherwise go unnoticed (Fig. 15-2). In addition, serious injury to the anterior segment may be associated with posterior segment trauma. The anterior segment injuries reported in cases of child abuse have all been associated with poor visual outcome. To the contrary, I have cared for two cases of relatively small hyphema secondary to belt beatings which, with prompt intervention, resulted in normal vision.

Lens Injuries

The lens of the eye, supported by the zonular ligaments (zonules), which extend from the lens equator to the region of the ciliary body, may become partially dislocated (subluxed) or completely dislocated into the posterior or anterior portion of the eye. Subluxation may occur with or without associated cataract and may be unilateral or bilateral, with lens decentration in any direction. Only one case of complete lens dislocation has been reported in an abused child. Although several studies did not find cataracts in abused children, one study cited a 5.5 percent incidence reporting two patients with bilateral dense cataracts. Posterior subcapsular and anterior subcapsular cataracts have also been reported.

Differential Diagnosis
There are many causes of cataracts in children, including metabolic, congenital, inflammatory, syndromic, chromosomal, and steroid induced. Likewise, subluxation of the lens can be caused by such disorders as Marfan syndrome, homocystinuria, syphilis, and Weill-Marchesani syndrome. Trauma is the most common cause of lens subluxation. Reported cases of traumatic cataract or lens subluxation in abused children have always occurred in association with other evidence of nonocular or ocular trauma. In addition, nonaccidental injury may cause unilateral cataracts or subluxation, whereas many of the nontraumatic causes of both entities (e.g., chromosomal, syndromic, metabolic) are usually bilateral. Another clue to possible covert trauma as the cause of a lens injury is the presence of a pigmented ring on the anterior lens surface (Vossius ring) that is caused by the

impact of the pupillary rim against the lens as a result of blunt trauma.

Nontraumatic idiopathic cataracts and subluxation do occur. However, when the clinician is faced with either unilateral or bilateral cataracts or lens subluxation, in the absence of disease, risk factors, or a family history (family members should be examined by an ophthalmologist in these circumstances), trauma must always be considered in the differential diagnosis.

Management

Dense cataracts may be easily detected with the unaided eye as a white opacity in the pupillary space. The diagnosis of lens opacities may also be made by using the direct ophthalmoscope at a distance of about 20 cm set on +5.00 (black number 5) to look for dark areas in the red reflex. This technique will also allow for diagnosis of significant degrees of lens subluxation. However, diagnosis of small cataracts may be difficult, abnormalities of the red reflex may be equivocal, and subluxation may be very slight. Therefore, ophthalmology consultation is important whenever a lens abnormality is suspected.

When cataracts have been reported in abused children, they have been associated with poor visual outcome, usually owing to other aspects of severe ocular trauma. However, if there is no significant associated ocular injury, if surgical intervention is prompt, and if vigorous postoperative visual rehabilitation is undertaken, the visual outcome for childhood traumatic cataracts is generally good.

Vitreoretinal Injury: Retinal and Vitreous Hemorrhages

Although retinal hemorrhages (RH) may result from abuse at all ages, they are one of the cardinal manifestations of SBS

with 50 to 80 percent of infant victims affected. They have been reported in up to 100 percent of children who have serious neurologic complications or death as a result of SBS. The presence of RH is associated with a worse acute neurologic presentation but does not predict outcome. However, it is important to note that SBS may occur without RH.

The hemorrhages most often affect the macula and the area around the disc and vascular arcades (posterior pole) but may extend to the anterior edges of the retina at the ora serrata. They may be severe or small and few in number (Fig. 15-4). Retinal hemorrhages may occur within the superficial retinal nerve fiber layer (flame-shaped hemorrhages), within the deeper layers of the retina (dot and blot hemorrhages), or on the surface of the retina where they obscure the examiner's visualization of the retinal blood vessels (preretinal or subhyaloid hemorrhages) (Figs. 15-4 and 15-5). Subretinal hemorrhage, wherein the observer would see the retinal blood vessels coursing unimpeded over the hemorrhage, has only been reported in three cases. Flame hemorrhages are the most common type of RH in SBS.

The pathophysiology of RH in SBS is not well understood. They may be a result of one or more of the following mechanisms. As the head is being shaken, the vitreous gel is also moving. The vitreous is attached to the retina at several points, most importantly at the macula and around retinal blood vessels. The shaking vitreous can therefore cause traction on the retina such that the retinal layers are split from one another, with blood filling the resultant cystic cavity. This has been labeled traumatic retinoschisis and has been confirmed both clinically and pathologically. These elevated retinal cavities may be quite large, even involving the entire macula, and may have a horizontal demarcation line that delineates the

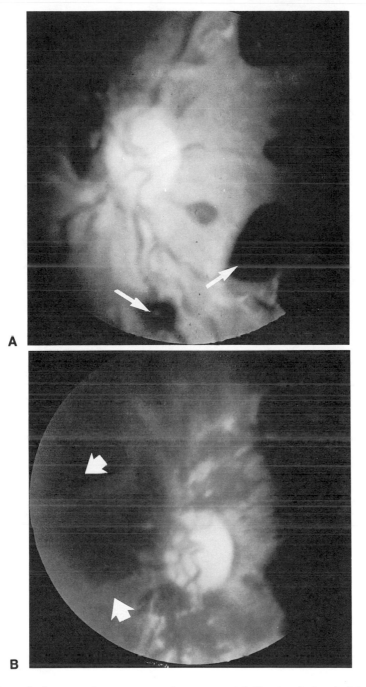

Fig. 15-4. Clinical photographs or retinas showing variability in shaken babies. (**A**) Scattered intrarctinal and preretinal hemorrhages involving the posterior pole around the optic nerve. Some have white centers. Note the association of many of the preretinal hemorrhages (small arrows) with underlying retinal blood vessels. This may be caused by vitreous traction at these sites of vitreous adhesion during shaking. (**B**) Severe intraretinal, preretinal, and vitreous hemorrhage (large arrows) surrounding optic nerve. Note that papilledema may be absent. Compare these clinical photographs with Figure 15-5.

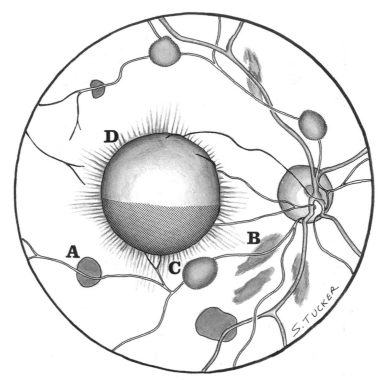

Fig. 15-5. (**A**) Intraretinal (dot or blot) hemorrhage. Note blood vessels can be followed through area of hemorrhage. (**B**) Superficial nerve fiber layer hemorrhage. Note flame shape. (**C**) Preretinal hemorrhage. Note that blood vessels are obscured by overlying hemorrhage. (**D**) Traumatic retinoschisis of macula. Elevated cavity contains blood with horizontal level.

upper blood fluid level or perhaps the settling of red blood cells below serum (Fig. 15-5). Other authors have theorized that there is a transmitted venous pressure from the increased intrathoracic pressure that is created as the victim's chest is compressed by the perpetrator's hands, thus causing venous stasis and blood vessel rupture in the retina (Purtscher's retinopathy). Hemorrhage found within the dura or in the subdural and subarachnoid spaces of the optic nerve or in the soft tissues of the posterior orbit around the nerve at autopsy may be related to the pathophysiology of RH and may be pathognomonic for abuse. It is not known if this represents direct extension of intracranial hemorrhage, rupture of bridging dural vessels in the optic nerve sheath from transmitted increased intracranial pressure, or direct injury to the optic nerve owing to shaking. Blunt trauma to the eyeball can also result in retinal hemorrhage.

Vitreous hemorrhage (VH) may occur from extension of retinal, or more often, preretinal hemorrhage. Evidence in the literature suggests that VH is not an acute event that occurs at the time of the shaking injury. Rather, the onset of VH is usually delayed for 2 to 47 days following the onset of retinal and preretinal hemorrhage. Therefore, the presence of VH may have significance in determining the time of occurrence of the injury. The same cannot be said for RH, which may resolve in a few days if they are small and superficial, or take weeks to months in the cases of large, preretinal hemorrhages. Macular hemorrhages are the slowest to resorb.

Differential Diagnosis

Although some authors have suggested that the presence of RH in children under the age of 3 years is pathognomonic for child abuse, other causes of RH in infants include meningitis, severe hypertension, endocarditis, sepsis, vasculitis, blood dyscrasias, and coagulopathies. Traumatic retinoschisis with hemorrhage has only been reported in SBS. Retinal hemorrhages in infants do not occur as a result of hemoglobinopathies or diabetes mellitus. The chest compressions of cardiopulmonary resuscitation have been labeled as a possible cause of RH. Only one study has addressed this issue systematically, finding that 6 (12 percent) of 51 patients who received chest compressions had RH. Four were under 2 years old and victims of child abuse; a 1 year old had severe hypertension after a cyanotic seizure of unknown etiology; and a 6 year old was a pedestrian when struck by an automobile. This data suggest that the chest compressions of cardiopulmonary resuscitation (CPR) are not an isolated cause of RH. Retinal hemorrhages have also been reported in the presence of intracerebral hemorrhage secondary to a ruptured arterial aneurysm in an infant. Of course, aneurysms are much less common than SBS, have a distinct CT scan appearance, and occur without other evidence of trauma.

Retinal hemorrhages can also be a result of normal birth either by spontaneous vaginal delivery, assisted vaginal delivery, or cesarean section (although much less common). Any perinatal situation can result in RH. In the first 24 hours of life, the incidence may be as high as 19 to 32 percent but by 1 week this figure drops to 2 to 15 percent. Flame hemorrhages are most common and resolve by day 5. Only large dense hemorrhages last longer than 3 weeks, with only one report of a large macular hemorrhage lasting to 6 weeks of age. Retinal hemorrhages secondary to birth have never been associated with anatomic or functional sequelae. After birth they can be very similar to those found in SBS. However, child abuse should be strongly suspected in the absence of other medical risk factors when RH are seen in a baby after 6 weeks of age, when flame hemorrhages are seen after 5 days, when there is a secondary anatomic or visual deficit, or when there is retinal detachment (see below).

Retinal hemorrhages caused by SBS can be present in spite of a normal CT scan of the brain or a CT scan that shows only cerebral edema. However, RH are so commonly associated with SBS as opposed to other clinical entities, that a magnetic resonance imaging (MRI) scan must be ordered to rule out definitively the presence of subdural or parenchymal hemorrhage as a result of SBS.

Management

Although RH may be easily visible with a direct ophthalmoscope in many cases of SBS, dilated examination using an indirect ophthalmoscope must be performed in all cases, even in the presence of severe neurologic injury. If there is concern about interfering with the interpretation of pupillary responses (although it is extremely unusual that pupillary responses would be the only critical factor in determining if neurologic decompensation is occurring), the ophthalmologist should be asked to use short-acting weaker mydriatics such as phenylephrine 1 percent and tropicamide ½ percent. It is important that the pupils be examined for abnormalities in size, shape, and reactivity before the instillation of mydriatics. Although nonophthalmologists will certainly enhance their ability to view RH using the direct ophthalmoscope by dilating the pupil, an indirect fundoscopic examination is greatly superior to the direct ophthalmoscope. The ophthalmologist may also be able to document subtle abnormalities in pupillary reactivity or iris anatomy that would otherwise be obscured if mydriatics were given.

Vitreoretinal Injury Other Than Retinal or Vitreous Hemorrhage

Ever since Kiffney's early description of bilateral retinal detachments (RD) in an abused child, it has been evident that both acute and chronic vitreoretinal changes can lead to serious visual sequelae in abused children. The retina may become detached as a result of tears or holes that allow vitreous fluid to track underneath the retina, disinsertion of the retina from its insertion at the ora serrata (retinal dialysis), subretinal hemorrhage or exudate, traction from scarring (gliosis), or traction from vitreous organization following VH. Other reported retinal abnormalities include retinal exudates or dramatic collections on the inferior retina called snowbanks, areas of retinal edema owing to blunt trauma (also known as retinal contusion, Berlin's edema, or commotio retinae), and hypopigmented or hyperpigmented areas of retinal scarring in the peripheral retina. This latter finding may be particularly characteristic of long-term survivors of child abuse, with scars found particularly in the temporal peripheral retina (most often bilaterally) in the presence of a normal macula and good visual acuity. Similar findings can be found as early as the first year of life in survivors of SBS. Gliotic elevated concentric rings and ridges around the macula have been described in SBS. Central retinal artery obstruction, which causes irreversible severe loss of retinal function, may also occur in abused children, although the

pathophysiology is not well understood. In addition to the macular sequela of SBS, macular changes such as cysts, scarring, wrinkling, and holes can be a result of blunt injury to the globe or from RH.

Differential Diagnosis

Blunt trauma is the leading cause of RD in children and adolescents. The differential diagnosis of RD in children includes retinoblastoma, congenital retinal abnormalities, infectious retinitis, and retinopathy of prematurity (ROP). Macular scarring can also result from many causes. Many of these entities have characteristic appearances that facilitate differentiation. Retinopathy of prematurity, almost by definition, occurs in babies under 32 weeks' gestation and weighing less than 1500 g. Retinal detachment secondary to congenital dialysis may occur, but the tears are almost always nasal and often associated with a congenital defect in the edges of the lens. In addition, it is important to remember that retinal tears and holes almost never occur spontaneously in young children, perhaps with the exception of the longer "stretched" retinas of highly myopic (nearsighted) eyes. In fact, bilateral RD or bilateral VH/organization should be considered pathognomonic of trauma until clearly proved to the contrary. Avulsion of the vitreous from its peripheral base, which appears as an opaque floating garland in the peripheral vitreous, especially when it occurs in the superionasal quadrant, is pathognomonic of ocular trauma, although it has not been specifically reported in an abused child.

Gliosis, pigmented retinal demarcation lines, intraretinal cysts in a detached retina, or fixed nonmoving folds in the detached retina are signs of chronicity. Because traumatic RD may be asymptomatic, especially when they occur inferiorly without involvement of the macula, several months or even years may elapse before diagnosis. However, in abused children, patients with this degree of ocular trauma tend to have repeated bouts of ocular and nonocular injury that would, it is hoped, bring them to diagnosis within such a time period.

Management

The diagnosis and management of vitreoretinal injuries require ophthalmology consultation. The visual prognosis for vitreoretinal trauma is largely dependent on the status of the macula. If left untreated, RD can lead to a blind, painful, or shrunken (phthisical) eye that may even require enucleation. The reader is referred to other texts for a better understanding of vitreoretinal trauma and surgical treatments.

Optic Nerve and Cortical Injury

The visual pathways from the retina to the occipital cortex may be injured as a result of child abuse. Such injuries are most often seen in the setting of SBS and are largely responsible for the poor visual outcome seen in many cases. Papilledema has been described both clinically and pathologically in abused children. This optic nerve head swelling is most often caused by raised intracranial pressure, although direct injury to the nerve or orbital hemorrhage can be a cause. Further evidence for optic nerve damage is seen in reports of abnormal pupillary responses to light or afferent pupillary defects (Marcus Gunn pupil), which are largely optic nerve functions, and followup examinations that reveal optic atrophy. Unlike papilledema, which is almost exclusively bilateral, optic atrophy may be unilateral or bilateral. Optic atrophy may also be a result of central retinal artery obstruction as discussed above. Damage to the intraparenchymal visual

pathways is a major manifestation of SBS. Occipital infarcts, contusion, laceration, or edema may be seen in up to 28 percent of SBS victims resulting in visual field deficits or reduced visual acuity. The cerebral injuries of SBS are discussed further in Chapter 11.

Differential Diagnosis

Papilledema and resultant optic atrophy may be the result of any condition that raises intracranial pressure or causes inflammation of the optic nerve. Acute leukemia, meningitis, and cyanotic congenital heart disease can cause papilledema with RH. The papilledema of leukemia may be unilateral and is often whiter, owing to neoplastic infiltration of the nerve head. Pseudopapilledema may occur, owing to hyperopia (farsightedness) or other anomalies of the optic nerve. The physician must look for the constellation of features that are common in SBS and abused children when faced with otherwise unexplainable visual pathway damage. The onset of papilledema may be hyperacute (less than 24 hours) or delayed (2 to 3 days after injury), thus making forensic evaluation difficult with regard to time of injury. The timing of papilledema in SBS specifically has not been studied.

Management

Cortical and optic nerve injuries are perhaps the most irreparable and visually damaging of all the ocular manifestations of child abuse. In addition to RD they represent a major cause of blindness in these children. Unilateral or bilateral blindness or other major visual disabilities from neurologic injury may occur in up to one-half of the victims in SBS. Atrophic changes in brain parenchyma are visible on follow-up CT scans. Other than prompt recognition and intervention for cerebral injury with elevated intracranial pressure, there are no known treatments to prevent visual loss. Surgical decompression of the optic nerve sheath has been used in other causes of papilledema in children and adults. There may be some future role for this procedure in selected cases of abused children. Close follow-up of infant victims of SBS is important to look for signs of visual disability so that early intervention programs may begin.

Traumatic Disorders of Ocular Movement

A number of abnormalities of eye movement and gaze without consistent patterns have been described in abused children. These manifestations appear to be caused by an efferent neurologic or afferent sensory visual etiology, rather than being secondary to direct orbital or muscular trauma. In fact, only two cases of proptosis, indicating retrobulbar pathology, have been reported. Cavernous sinus thrombosis as a secondary result of trauma has been a proposed mechanism for this proptosis, and this may cause palsies of cranial nerves III, IV, or VI that run through the cavernous sinus, as well as abnormalities of pupillary constriction (III). At least one of the two patients reported by Jensen et al. appears to have had a 6th cranial nerve palsy as a result of raised intracranial pressure.

Strabismus may be a presenting symptom or a long-term sequela in 3 to 30 percent of abused children. Nystagmus ophthalmoplegia and chronic gaze preferences have also been reported. One of the patients of Greenwald et al. had bilaterally poor adduction of the eyes, suggesting brain stem injury (internuclear ophthalmoplegia). All of these disorders of eye movement are markedly more common in victims of SBS than in other forms of physical abuse. Ludwig and Warman

reported that 50 percent of their babies with SBS had a gaze disturbance.

Differential Diagnosis and Management

The discussion of these abnormalities is beyond the scope of this chapter. Suffice it to say that an ophthalmologist should be involved in the care of all children affected with disorders of ocular movement. The presence of these abnormalities should lead to a thorough investigation of the CNS.

SEXUAL ABUSE

Gonorrhea

Neisseria gonorrhoeae can cause an acute purulent conjunctivitis with a potential for secondary cellulitis and corneal damage or perforation. With the exception of outbreaks caused by the use of urine as an ocular remedy in folklore, gonorrheal conjunctivitis is rarely seen in non-neonatal prepubertal children. In children of this age group with known gonorrhea at another anatomic site, the incidence of gonorrheal conjunctivitis varies from 0 to 20 percent. There is a predilection for children under the age of 5 years. The importance of gonorrhea at nonocular sites in child sexual abuse is discussed in Chapter 19. Yet, reports of gonorrheal conjunctivis beyond the neonatal period have always assumed that autoinoculation or nonsexual transmission via fomites has been the route of transmission. In fact, gonorrheal conjunctivitis in a sexually abused child has not been reported. However, many of these studies are flawed by inadequate or unexplained sociomedical evaluations for sexual abuse and therefore may have erroneously assumed nonsexual transmission. We have conducted in-depth sociomedical evaluations of three cases and found no evidence of sexual abuse. Folland et al. have reported similar findings. Sleeping in the same bed with an infected adult without sexual contact was a common risk factor in two of our cases.

Since it appears that nonsexual transmission to the conjunctiva is possible, and since conjunctival gonorrhea is associated with infection at other sites that are indicative of sexual abuse, all non-neonatal prepubertal children with gonorrheal conjunctivitis should be considered victims of sexual abuse until proved otherwise. Complete social and medical work-ups should be performed according to the guidelines discussed in this book. When possible, family members should be cultured for gonorrhea to identify potential sources of either sexual or nonsexual transmission. With proper understanding and sensitivity, these procedures can be explained to the parents to lessen any adverse effect of investigations that fail to uncover sexual abuse. Only after such exhaustive investigation is negative for sexual abuse and in the presence of identifiable risk factors for nonsexual transmission, should this latter mode of transmission be accepted. The treatment of gonorrheal conjunctivitis has been reviewed in the literature.

Other Sexually Transmitted Diseases

Infections with *Chlamydia trachomatis* (serotypes D–K), lymphogranuloma venereum (LGV, *C. trachomatis* scrotypes L1–3), *Treponema pallidum*, human immunodeficiency virus (HIV), human papilloma virus (HPV), herpes simplex viruses 1 and 2 (HSV), and molluscum contagiosum have been reported to occur in adults as a result of sexual contact. Each of these entities may have ocular manifestations (Table 15-2). With the

exception of molluscum and LGV, these infections have also been reported to occur in children as a result of sexual abuse. However, when isolated ocular manifestations have been reported in non-neonatal prepubertal children, the issues of possible sexual abuse have not been discussed. In fact, no case of either isolated ocular manifestations or of ocular manifestations in conjunction with findings at another site, has been reported in sexually abused children.

Herpes simplex virus infections involving the eyelids, periorbital skin, conjunctiva, and cornea are not infrequent in children. As with isolated herpes stomatitis, nonsexual inoculation is the presumed route of transmission. However, viral serotyping, cultures from nonocular sites, and medicosocial evaluations for possible sexual abuse have not been performed. Likewise, although uncommon, HPV infection of the conjunctiva in pediatric patients has not been attributed to sexual contact. Chlamydia conjunctivitis is extremely rare in non-neonatal prepubertal children. Infection has only been attributed to prolonged carriage of the organism following perinatal infection from the birth canal. Ocular manifestations of HIV, although reported in children with documented nonsexual acquisition of the infection, have not been seen in prepubertal children with sexual contact as the mode of transmission. However, each of these ocular infections, when seen in adults, has been reported to occur as a result of sexual contact or as a result of autoinoculation with secretions from another site that was infected as a result of sexual contact.

Therefore, when ocular manifestations of these sexually transmitted diseases are seen in non-neonatal prepubertal children, sexual abuse should always be considered. In particular, nonsexual transmission of syphilis and LGV has not been reported in children in this age group, so

Table 15-2.   Ophthalmologic Manifestations of Sexually Transmitted Diseases

Infectious Agent	Disease	Ophthalmologic Manifestation[a]
Neisseria gonorrhoeae	Gonorrhea	Purulent conjunctivitis, corneal erosion/ulcer/perforation, uveitis, periorbital/orbital cellulitis
Chlamydia trachomatis		
Serotypes D–K	Chlamydia	Chronic follicular conjunctivitis, corneal infiltrates, corneal scarring/pannus
Serotypes L1–L3	Lymphogranuloma venereum	Conjunctivitis, Parinaud oculoglandular syndrome, corneal infiltrates/pannus, uveitis, papilledema, retinal venous tortuosity/dilation
Treponema pallidum	Syphilis	Keratitis, uveitis, papillitis, optic neuropathy/atrophy, vasculitis, Argyll Robertson pupils, anisocoria, neuro-ophthalmologic abnormalities
Human papilloma virus	Condyloma	Papilloma of conjunctiva
Human immunodeficiency virus	AIDS	Kaposi sarcoma, AIDS retinopathy, vasculitis, cytomegalovirus, retinitis, toxoplasma retinitis, herpes simplex/zoster, opportunistic infections, neuro-ophthalmologic abnormalities
Herpes simplex virus 1 or 2		Periorbital skin infection, conjunctivitis, keratitis, corneal vascularization and scar, uveitis, ?retinitis
Molluscum contagiosum		Periorbital skin lesions, conjunctivitis, keratitis

[a] Manifestations not listed in order of frequency.

they should be considered diagnostic of sexual contact. As discussed in the section on sexual abuse and by other authors, infections with HSV-2, chlamydia (serotypes D–K), HPV, and HIV, although not pathognomonic of sexual abuse, should arouse suspicion. At the very least, their presence in a child of this age should lead to medicosocial evaluations for sexual abuse. Unfortunately, viral typing of ocular lesions caused by HPV or HSV may be difficult or unavailable, so that routine use may be impractical, making it difficult to determine if the specific organism involved is a sexually or nonsexually transmitted type. Molloscum contagiosum is such a commonly nonsexually transmitted infection that care must be taken to avoid the overzealous pursuit of the possibility of sexual abuse.

Neglect

Although ocular complications of failure to thrive have not been reported, parental neglect of organic ocular conditions can lead to irreversible visual damage or deformity. In particular, the neglect of such problems as strabismus, high refractive errors, and amblyopia or the failure to obtain appropriate postsurgical follow-up care after ocular procedures can lead to the development of irreversible visual loss. Amblyopia in these settings is caused by a CNS retardation of visual development in a medically "disadvantaged" eye, so that disparate input from the two eyes is eliminated. For example, the brain must suppress the visual input from a crossed eye to avoid double vision. By doing so, one eye is favored for vision (and the child will function entirely normally with that one normal eye), while vision is suppressed in the other eye. Amblyopia is treatable and usually reversible if attended to before the age of 8 or 9 years. Beyond that time, it is irreversible. Therefore, compliance with medical treatments (e.g., patching, glasses) and regular follow-up are essential.

It is often difficult to delineate noncompliance that is abusively neglectful from that which may be attributed to other confounding variables. Transportation for physician visits may be expensive, time consuming, or unavailable. Alternate caretakers may not be available for siblings. Children may have behavioral objections to patching or glasses. Family and individual support systems may be deficient. Caretakers may not adequately understand the medical implications of their child's problem. After exploration of the situation with the parent to address real complicating variables as well as issues of neglectful medical care, a trial period may be attempted to allow for improvement in parental compliance. There is no acute need to intervene in situations of strabismus, amblyopia, or refractive errors. However, should the problem of medical neglect remain chronic after the issue has been discussed or if an acute ocular problem is not receiving appropriate urgent medical attention (e.g., glaucoma, trauma, and infantile cataracts), then reporting may be indicated. After attempts to overcome socioeconomic barriers and address issues of neglect, a clear statement may be written into the chart indicating the minimum requirements of parental compliance that will avoid a report being made. This statement should be signed by the parent, physician, and a witness. If noncompliance with the requirements ensues, prompt reporting should be initiated. Badger has suggested guidelines for reporting cases of neglect based on a strict protocol of parental and school nurse notification.

OTHER OPHTHALMOLOGIC MANIFESTATIONS OF CHILD ABUSE

Functional and Hysterical Visual Loss

Functional and hysterical visual loss are well recognized childhood disorders. Other functional symptoms may include excessive blinking, photophobia, diplopia, or visual obscurations. Functional symptoms may be associated with increased stress in the child's life, owing to a variety of causes (e.g., school difficulties, death of a family member, or new siblings in the home). Catalano et al. reported functional visual loss in both sexually and physically abused girls. Rada et al. have also suggested that functional or hysterical visual symptoms may be related to sexual conflicts or stresses. Therefore, when ophthalmologic evaluation rules out an organic cause for visual symptoms, it is appropriate to search for evidence of stresses in the child's life that are particularly related to the onset and occurrence of the visual symptom. The physician must be alert to the possibility of undiagnosed physical or sexual abuse.

Münchausen Syndrome by Proxy

Münchausen syndrome by proxy (MBP) is a form of child abuse in which a parent, almost always the mother, creates factitious illness in the child by falsifying history and altering laboratory findings (e.g., placing menstrual blood in a child's urine specimen), or creating factitious physical findings (e.g., covert suffocation to induce apnea and seizures). The classic features of MBP include a disease process with no medical explanation, chronicity, multiple affected siblings, onset of symptoms witnessed only by the parent, parental history of psychosocial problems or psychiatric disease, perpetrator with history of paramedical training, abnormal bonding between parents and children, and a prompt disappearance of symptoms when the child is separated from the perpetrator (see Ch. 16). Three cases of MBP have been reported with ocular manifestations: anisocoria induced by atropine from ocular instillation of home nebulizer treatments, periorbital cellulitis secondary to an injection of a metallic substance into the subcutaneous periorbital tissues of a 1-year-old girl by her grandmother, and chronic progressive corneal scarring associated with bouts of recurrent acute conjunctivitis and eye pain suggestive of covert instillation of chemicals into the conjunctiva. As the vast number of clinical manifestations of MBP seem to be limited only by the imagination of the MBP perpetrator, it is reasonable to suspect that there will be other reported ocular manifestations.

Postmortem Vitreous Toxicology

Postmortem analysis of the chemical composition of vitreous samples may be helpful in determining the cause of death. Zumwalt et al. have reported the diagnosis of forced salt ingestion, dehydration, and forced fluid ingestion by postmortem analysis of vitreous electrolytes. Measurements of vitreous levels of creatinine or electrolytes may be helpful in establishing the time of death, although normative values are not available in children. Potassium levels in the vitreous have received wide usage by adults for this purpose, as they show a linear rise after death. However, 95 percent confidence intervals may be as long as 26 hours, and values may be affected by sampling and analysis techniques or body temperature at the time of death. Vitreous creatinine levels may be useful for determining the cause of sudden unexplained deaths in outpatients where the time between death and vitreous sampling is greater than 2 to 3 days. Again, 95 percent confidence levels may be up to 2 days. Values of vitreous urea, sodium, and chloride may be helpful in diagnosing dehydration, although sodium and chloride alone, as well as vitreous glucose, show poor correlations with time of death. Vitreous sampling may also identify ingested drugs, although this application has not been reported in child homicide victims.

Vitreous sampling is particularly useful in cases where death occurred before medical intervention and when antemortem blood sampling is not possible. The procedure does not disfigure the corpse and is relatively easy to perform. Vitreous can be aspirated from the globe via an anterior or posterior approach, using a large-bore sharp needle and then removing the sticky vitreous with a sponge or forceps. It is best to use the needle technique through an anterior approach just posterior (3 mm) to the limbus (corneal rim) and aspirate slowly. This will avoid incorporation of retinal cells into the sample, which may affect levels of potassium or creatinine in particular. It is also important to get as much vitreous as possible, since electrolytes may not be evenly dispersed throughout the vitreous. Perhaps this procedure should be included in all cases of unexplained death in children. Removal of the eyes and optic nerves for gross and microscopic examination in such cases is not a problem if vitreous sampling is desired. It is only important to sample the vitreous before chemical (i.e., formalin) fixation of the globe. However, traction of vitreous removal could possibly induce artifactitious RD or RH. Hemorrhage could potentially alter chemical values. Limited and gentle vitreous sampling may help to avoid these complications.

Postmortem gross and microscopic examination of the eyes and optic nerves can be extremely valuable forensically, especially when antemortem ocular examination was not performed (Fig. 15-6).

The eye can be removed without significant alteration in the appearance of the corpse. At autopsy, the eyes should be removed for examination in all cases of unexplained death in children, particularly in children under 3 years of age. There may also be value in postmortem removal of the entire soft tissue contents of the orbit through a combined intracranial and anterior approach following brain removal. We have demonstrated possible characteristic patterns of posterior orbital hemorrhage and intraorbital optic nerve injury, which may help to differentiate between accidental head trauma and shaking injury.

SUGGESTED READINGS

1. Aikman J: Cerebral hemorrhage in infant, aged eight months: recovery. Arch Pediatr 45:56, 1928

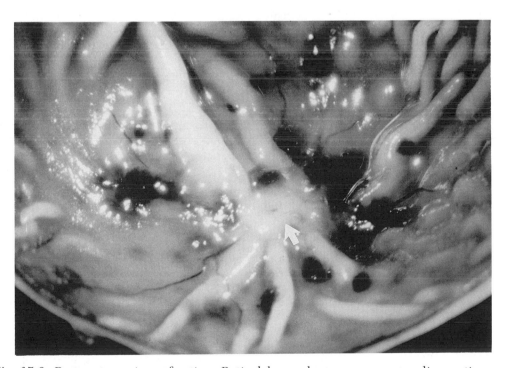

Fig. 15-6. Postmortem view of retina. Retinal hemorrhages seen surrounding optic nerve (arrow). Retinal folds are fixation artifacts.

2. Alfonso E, Friedland B, Hupp S et al: *Neisseria gonorrhoeae* conjunctivitis: an outbreak during an epidemic of acute hemorrhagic conjunctivitis. JAMA 250:794, 1983

3. Allue X, Rubio T, Riley HD: Gonoccocal infections in infants and children: lessons from fifteen cases. Clin Pediatr 12:584, 1973

4. Aron JJ, Marx P, Blanck MF et al: Signes oculaires observes dans le syndrome de Silverman. Ann Oculist 203:533, 1970

5. Bacon CJ, Sayer GC, Howe JW: Extensive retinal haemorrhages in infancy—an innocent cause. Br Med J 1:281, 1978

6. Badger GR: Dental neglect: a solution. J Dent Children 49:285, 1982

7. Baum JD, Bulpitt CJ: Retinal and conjunctival haemorrhage in newborn. Arch Dis Child 45:344, 1970

8. Bennett HS, French JH: Elevated intracranial pressure in a whiplash-shaken infant syndrome detected with normal computerized tomography. Clin Pediatr 19:633, 1980

9. Benson WE: Retinal Detachment: Diagnosis and Management. JB Lippincott, Philadelphia, 1988

10. Blinder KJ, Scott W, Lange MP: Abuse of cyanoacrylate in child abuse. Arch Ophthalmol 105:1632, 1987

11. Branch G, Paxton R: A study of gonococcal infections among infants and children. Public Health Rep 80:347, 1965

12. Cameron JM, Johnson HR, Camps FE: The battered child syndrome. Med Sci Law 6:2, 1966

13. Catalano RA, Simon JW, Krohel GB, Rosenberg PN: Functional visual loss in children. Ophthalmology 93:385, 1986

14. Coe JI: Vitreous potassium as a measure of the postmortem interval: an historical review and critical evaluation. Forensic Sci Int 42:201, 1989

15. Cooperman MB: Gonococcus arthritis in infancy: a clinical study of forty-four cases. Am J Dis Child 33:932, 1927

16. Cox MS, Schepens CL, Freeman HM: Retinal detachment due to ocular contusion. Arch Ophthalmol 76:678, 1966

17. DeJong AR: Sexually transmitted diseases in sexually abused children. Sex Transm Dis 13:123, 1986

18. Devgun MS, Dunbar JA: Biochemical investigation of vitreus [sic]: applications in forensic medicine, especially in relation to alcohol. Forensic Sci Int 31:27, 1986

19. Doyle JO: Accidental gonoccocal infection in the eyes of children. Br Med J 1:88, 1972

20. Eisenbrey AB: Retinal hemorrhage in the battered child. Child Brain 5:40, 1979

21. Feenstra J, Merth IT, Traffers PD: A case of Münchausen syndrome by proxy. Tijdschr Kindergeneeskd 56:148, 1988

22. Fekete JF, Brunsdon FV: The use of routine laboratory teats in postmortem examinations, J Can Soc Forensic Med 7:238, 1974

23. Folland DS, Burke RE, Hinman AR, Schaffner W: Gonorrhea in preadolescent children: an inquiry into source of infection and mode of transmission. Pediatrics 60:153, 1977

24. Frank Y, Zimmerman R, Leeds NM: Neurologic manifestation in abused children who have been shaken. Dev Med Child Neurol 27:312, 1985

25. Friendly DS: Ocular manifestations of physical child abuse. Trans Am Acad Ophthalmol Otolaryngol 75:318, 1971

26. Gaynon MW, Koh K, Marmor MF, Frankel LR: Retinal folds in the shaken baby syndrome. Am J Ophthalmol 106:423, 1988

27. Giangiacomo J, Barkett KJ: Ophthalmoscopic findings in occult child abuse. J Pediatr Ophthalmol Strabismus 22:234, 1985

28. Gilkes MJ, Mann TP: Fundi of battered babies. Lancet 2:468, 1967

29. Greenwald MJ, Weiss A, Oesterle CS, Friendly DS: Traumatic retinoschisis in battered babies. Ophthalmology 93:618, 1986

30. Griest KJ, Zumwalt RE: Child abuse by drowning. Pediatrics 83:41, 1989

31. Harcourt B, Hopkins D: Ophthalmic manifestations of the battered-baby syndrome. Br Med J 3:398, 1971

32. Harley RD: Ocular manifestations of child abuse. J Pediatr Ophthalmol Strabismus 17:5, 1980

33. Hovland KR, Schepens CL, Freeman HM: Development giant retinal tears associated with lens colobomas. Arch Ophthalmol 80:325, 1968

34. Jain IS, Singh YP, Grupta SL, Gupta A: Ocular hazards during birth. J Pediatr Ophthalmol Strabismus 171:14, 1980

35. Jensen AD, Smith RE, Olson MI: Ocular clues to child abuse. J Pediatr Ophthalmol 8:270, 1971

36. Johnson CF, Showers J: Injury variables in child abuse. Child Abuse Negl 9:207, 1985

37. Kanter RK: Retinal hemorrhage after cardipulmonary resuscitation or child abuse. J Pediatr 180:430, 1986

38. Kiffney GT: The eye of the "Battered Child." Arch Ophthalmol 72:231, 1964

39. Lambert SR, Johnson TE, Hoyt CS: Optic nerve sheath hemorrhages associated with the shaken baby syndrome. Arch Ophthalmol 104:1509, 1986

40. Levin AV: Ocular manifestations of child abuse. Ophthalmol Clin North Am 3:249, 1990

41. Levin AV, Magnusson MR, Rafto SE, Zimmerman RA: Shaken baby syndrome diagnosed by magnetic resonance imaging. Pediatr Emerg Care 5:181, 1989

42. Low RC, Cho CT, Dudding BA: Gonoccocal infections in young children. Clin Pediatr 16:626, 1977

43. Ludwig S, Warman M: Shaken baby syndrome: a review of 20 cases. Ann Emerg Med 13:104, 1984

44. Markham RH, Richmond SJ, Walshaw NW, Easty DL: Severe persistent inclusion conjunctivitis in a young child. Am J Ophthalmol 83:414, 1977

45. McLellan NJ, Prasad R, Punt J: Spontaneous subhyaloid and retinal haemorrhages in an infant. Arch Dis Child 61:1130, 1986

46. Mushin AS: Ocular damage in the battered-baby syndrome. Br Med J 3:402, 1971

47. Neinstein LS, Goldenring J, Carpenter S: Nonsexual transmission of sexually transmitted diseases: an infrequent occurrence. Pediatrics 74:67, 1984

48. Ober RR: Hemorrhagic retinopathy in infancy: a clinicopathologic report. J Pediatr Ophthalmol Strabismus 17:17, 1980

49. Piette M: The effect of post-mortem interval on the level of creatine in vitreous humour. Med Sci Law 29:47, 1989

50. Planten JT, Schaaf PC: Retinal haemorrhage in the newborn. Ophthalmologica 162:213, 1971

51. Rada RT, Meyer GG, Kellner R: Visual conversion reaction in children and adults. J Nerv Ment Dis 166:580, 1978

52. Rao N, Smith RE, Choi JH et al: Autopsy findings in the eyes of fourteen fatally abused children. Forensic Sci Int 39:293, 1988

53. Roussey M, Betremieux P, Journel II et al: L'ophtalmologiste et les victimes de sévices. J Fr Ophtalmol 10:201, 1987

54. Ruttum NS, Nelson DB, Wamser MJ, Balliss M: Detection of congenital cataracts and other ocular media opacities. Pediatrics 79:814, 1987

55. Sezen F: Retinal haemorrhage in newborn infants. Br J Ophthalmol 55:248, 1970

55a. Shore WB, Winkelstein JA: Nonvenereal transmission of gonoccocal infections to children. J Pediatr 79:661, 1971

56. Smith SM, Hanson R: 134 battered children: a medical and psychological study. Br Med J 3:666, 1974

57. Taylor D, Bentovim A: Recurrent nonaccidentally inflicted chemical eye injuries to siblings. J Pediatr Ophthalmol 13:238, 1976

58. Tomasi LG, Rosman P: Purtscher retinopathy in the battered child syndrome. Am J Dis Child 93:1435, 1986

59. Tseng SS, Keys MP: Battered child syndrome simulating congenital glaucoma. Arch Ophthalmol 94:839, 1976

60. Ullman S, Rousell TJ, Forster R: Gonococcal keratoconjunctivitis. Surv Ophthalmol 32:199, 1987

61. Valenton MJ, Abendanio R: Gonorrheal conjunctivitis: complication after contamination with urine. Can J Ophthalmol 8:421, 1973

62. Vanderlinden RG, Chisolm LD: Vitreous hemorrhages and sudden increased intracranial pressure. J Neurosurg 41:167, 1974

63. Vrabec TR, Levin AV, Nelson LB: Functional blinking in childhood. Pediatrics 83:967, 1989

64. Weidenthal DT, Levin DB: Retinal detachment in a battered infant. Am J Ophthalmol 81:725, 1976

65. Wilkinson WS, Han DP, Rappley MD, Owings CL: Retinal hemorrhage predicts neurologic injury in the shaken baby syndrome. Arch Ophthalmol 107:1472, 1989

66. Wolter JR: Coup-contrecoup mechanism of ocular injuries. Am J Ophthalmol 56:785, 1975

67. Wood PR, Fowlkes J, Holden P, Casto D: Fever of unknown origin for six years: Münchausen syndrome by proxy. J Fam Pract 28:391, 1989

68. Zimmerman RA, Bilaniuk LT, Bruce D et al: Computed tomography of craniocerebral injury in the abused child. Radiology 130:687, 1979

16

Unusual Injuries

Josephine Ross Welliver

Even the health professional well seasoned in dealing with child abuse suffers disbelief and incredulousness with each new case. This occurs with pathognomonic cases, and is particularly evoked with those involving more obscure methods of inflicting injury to children. Review of the medical literature shows that the methods used to abuse a child are limited only by the perpetrator's creativity and medical knowledge. In the 1980s, one can find case reports of continued ritualistic practices such as female circumcision (the removal of some or all of the clitoris, labia majora and minora, and suturing of the remaining two sides of the vulva) or intentional banding (placing a tight occlusive band around a distal extremity or appendage). Neurosurgical literature still comments on the attempted infanticide written of in Persian novels in which sewing needles are inserted into the brain. With the advance of science, reports of more modern forms of abuse have surfaced, including intentional microwave burns in which the entire child was placed in the oven; instilling glue (cyanoacrylate adhesive) into the eye; and the forced aspiration of objects ranging from pepper to tacks and screws. This chapter reviews unusual injuries of child abuse including Münchausen syndrome by proxy, poisoning, and rhabdomyolysis

in an effort to prepare the trusting health professional for dealing with the modern perpetrator.

MÜNCHAUSEN SYNDROME BY PROXY

In 1977, Meadow admonished physicians that "at times doctors must accept the parent's history and indeed the laboratory findings with more than the usual skepticism." By his description of two cases, Meadow elucidated the pediatric counterpart of a syndrome previously described in adults by Asher in 1951. This *Münchausen syndrome by proxy* (also referred to as Meadow's or Polle's syndrome) has become recognized as a form of child abuse in which the child is victimized by an illness induced or fabricated by the parent. This illness may then result in numerous unnecessary hospitalizations for invasive diagnostic or surgical procedures, leading to a life-threatening situation or the ultimate death of the child.

There are no definitive data as to the actual incidence of Münchausen syndrome by proxy. Approximately 200 cases of this syndrome have been cataloged in the medical literature since Meadow's first notation in 1977. Review of these

213

cases does establish the age most susceptible to this form of abuse. Most children are younger than 5 years of age by the time the diagnosis of Münchausen syndrome by proxy is made. However, the past medical history of each of these children is significant for recurrent, unexplained illnesses dating back to the child's infancy or second year of life. This age group is most likely to suffer a sudden catastrophic death at the hands of the parent. Children who are diagnosed with this syndrome in the later years of childhood or as an early adolescent have a tendency to participate in fabrication of this illness along with the parent.

The characterization of the family dynamics described by Meadow in his original writing has been confirmed by other authors. Characterization of the parent includes the following. (1) In almost all cases, the mother is the perpetrator. Occasionally, the father is the primary abuser but more often his participation is peripheral. Both Meadow and Zitelli et al. have described the father's disbelief in the diagnosis and his strong support of his wife when confronted with the proof of her involvement. (2) Even though the parents are married, the father is noticeably absent, that is, the father is frequently away from the home because of employment or marital discord. (3) The parent has some medical knowledge, whether by training or through reading medical literature. (4) In at least 20 percent of cases, the parent has Münchausen syndrome or a past medical history of numerous unexplained medical symptoms. (5) The parent's devotion to this child is in striking contrast to relationships with other family members. These other family members are often described in ambivalent terms. (6) When the child is hospitalized, the parent remains constantly at the child's bedside, actively participating in all levels of the child's care including nursing responsibilities such as

the collection of samples. (7) The parent is very friendly with the hospital staff and may become involved in their private lives. (8) The parent often seems remarkably unconcerned by the apparent severity of the child's illness. (9) The child and parent develop a mutual dependence so that the child may actively participate in the parent's deception.

Health professionals may inadvertently become participants in the ongoing abuse of the child. Failure to recognize the diagnosis of Münchausen syndrome by proxy leads to further futile diagnostic attempts, including dangerous invasive tests. In other cases, such as those in which the parent intermittently suffocates the child, failure of the physician to recognize the parent's pathology may provoke more severe action by the parent, with fatal results. Eventually, the judicial system may become actively involved in the protection of a child with Münchausen syndrome by proxy. The court must be convinced that these seemingly loving parents are capable of malicious acts toward their child. Unless separation of the child from the family and competent rehabilitation are prescribed, the abuse will continue.

Recognition

The most common presentation of Münchausen syndrome by proxy is a supposed neurologic abnormality. Fifty percent of the cases are presented as daytime sleepiness, apnea, seizures, or an acute life-threatening event. Less common fabrications include fever of unknown origin, hematuria, gastrointestinal bleeding, diarrhea, bacteremia, hyper- or hyponatremia, hypoglycemia, and rashes. Unique cases of immunodeficiency, cystic fibrosis, and food allergies have also been noted. Physician awareness of the common features or "warning signals" repeated in each of these cases is important if the diagnosis of Münchausen syndrome by proxy is to be established.

History

Meadow provided physicians with a list of "warning signals" in an effort to expedite a "certain and speedy" diagnosis.

These include the following:

1. An unexplained illness, prolonged over months or years, which has caused experienced physicians to comment on the uniqueness of the cases.
2. A description of symptoms and signs that are inappropriate or incompatible.
3. A history of previous therapies for this same illness that have been ineffective.
4. The listing of numerous foods and drugs to which the child is allegedly allergic.
5. A history in the family of previous, unexplained infant deaths.
6. A history of many family members also alleged to have serious but vague illnesses.
7. A lack of parental concern while providing this dramatic, concerning history.

Once alerted to the possibility of Münchausen syndrome by proxy, the physician must investigate every detail of the history. Any event described by the parent that has taken place in the presence of another person must be investigated. The witnesses should be personally called and the exact details surrounding the incident reviewed. In many cases, the child may have a genuine illness that can be distorted or manipulated by the parent. For example, a child with a central venous catheter for bowel disease may present with repeated polymicrobial bac-

teremia, or a patient with a known seizure disorder may present with 10 times the number of seizures at school reported by the mother than by the teacher. As Meadow noted, however, "the fact that one episode of genuine illness is established does not rule out the possibility that many fabricated events are happening also."

Physical Examination

The physical examination is not especially helpful in establishing the diagnosis of this syndrome. The child may appear remarkably healthy with normal growth parameters. Some children, however, may have actual findings of a disease process. For example, the patient with simulated cystic fibrosis was poorly nourished, had a mild increase in anteroposterior diameter of the chest, and moderate digital clubbing; the children recorded as having the allergic form of this syndrome did have some mild degree of atopy or allergic rhinitis. Given an abnormal physical finding, the physician must be cognizant that Münchausen syndrome by proxy can (1) still exist in the presence of a genuine illness and (2) the finding may have been directly induced by the parent, that is, scraping the skin to produce rashes, poor growth as a result of a severely restricted diet, or chronic-induced emesis.

Laboratory Findings

Deciphering laboratory results in a patient with Münchausen syndrome by proxy is a challenge. Often, the laboratory results are repeatedly normal despite the patient's continued reported illness. For example, a child with recurrent apnea secondary to parentally-induced asphyxia may have a normal electroencephalogram

(EEG), electrocardiogram (EKG), scinti-scan, polysomnographic recordings, and toxicology screenings on several occasions. Alternately, laboratory results may vary from normal to grossly abnormal in the same child from day to day. This phenomenon is related to parental tampering with specimens. The parent's cunning use of medical knowledge has led to the use of animal blood or parental blood to simulate hematuria, hematemesis, or other bleeding. Salt has been added to breast milk to explain a child's hypernatremia, while fat has been added to stool to produce an abnormal amount of fecal fat to suggest cystic fibrosis. In one case, a sputum sample was produced by a parent after she had masqueraded as a "pharmacist student" who needed sputum samples from teenage cystic fibrosis patients for a research project. Finally, the patient may have abnormal results on presentation that normalize once the child is hospitalized and supervised. For example, a child with documented hypernatremia as an outpatient did not have any problem with sodium homeostasis when fed a normal diet in the hospital.

Radiologic Studies

It is difficult for a parent to tamper with the results of radiologic evaluation, so these studies are reliable in a suspected case of Münchausen syndrome by proxy. In most cases, the results of these studies will be normal, even on repeated testing. This frequently leads to more extensive investigation, such as chest computed tomography (CT) scan or magnetic resonance imaging (MRI) if the chest radiograph is normal. A positive result does not preclude the possibility of Münchausen syndrome by proxy as a genuine disease can coexist with a fabricated illness.

Table 16-1. Common Presentations of Münchausen Syndrome by Proxy and Mechanism of Induced Injury

Presentation	Mechanism
Apnea, lethargy, acute life-threatening event	Drugs, poisoning, induced asphyxiation
Electrolyte abnormalities	Excessive water or salt ingestion via feeding or nasogastric tube
Hematuria, hematemesis, other bleeding	Animal or parental blood added to sample
Recurrent fever, polymicrobial bacteremia	Injection of feces or contaminated water directly into bloodstream or IV line
Recurrent emesis	Ipecac poisoning, feeding stool or blood to the child
Seizures	Drugs, poisonings, suffocation

Mechanism of Injury

As with all other forms of child abuse, Münchausen syndrome by proxy is suspected when the injury, or in this case, the disease process, is not substantiated by the history or objective findings. The mechanism of injury may be more difficult to determine and constant supervision of the parent, particularly with a hidden camera and video recorder, is helpful. Some of the more common presentations and their known mechanisms are listed in Table 16-1.

Natural Course

Unless the diagnosis of Münchausen syndrome by proxy is made in a timely fashion, the child will suffer at the hands of the parent. "Doctor shopping" may be employed by the parent to continue the deception. Meanwhile, the child may experience significant morbidity, including (1) permanent organic damage, for example, severe anoxia from asphyxiation or hypoglycemia, and delayed development from prolonged failure-to-thrive; (2) disfigurement and scarring from surgical procedures including gastrostomies, colectomy with colostomy, or suturing of the fundus of the stomach around the esophagus (Nissen fundoplication); (3) repeated anesthetic procedures; and (4) repeated blood sample collection. Young children (younger than 5 years of age) are at a greater risk of death from continued life-threatening abuse. Older children may acquiesce and adopt the parent's perception so that the child actively participates in the entire process. Even when removed from the natural home and perpetrating adult, the child may still have a self perception of being "abnormal" and feel incapable of normal childhood activities and future adult patterns of living such as employment and marriage. Finally, the child may learn to perpetuate the abuse on himself and become an adult with Münchausen syndrome.

Long-Term Outcome

Medical literature provides scant data as to the long-term outcome of these children and their families. In a review of 117 patients by Rosenberg, 10 patients (9 percent) died and 8 percent of the remaining 107 children developed long-term morbidity such as permanent disfigurement or impairment of function. Even Rosenberg concluded that the long-term morbidity rate was most likely an underestimate. Siblings of the victims of Münchausen syndrome by proxy have also been found to be at risk. Again, as noted by Rosenberg, there were 10

deaths occurring in unusual circumstances in the siblings of the 117 original victims of Münchausen syndrome by proxy. The psychological prognosis for the child and parent is also obscure. Many children develop secondary behavioral patterns in response to the parental abuse. For example, the infant may begin to ruminate as a result of prolonged, thwarted feeding experiences; the toddler may become hyperactive and antagonistic when subjected to complete control of his environment. Psychotherapy for the perpetrator is frequently unrewarding.

INTENTIONAL POISONING

Child abuse inflicted by means of poisoning refers to the deliberate, willful administration of a drug, toxin, or other injurious substance to a child. Historically, this form of abuse has been separated from Münchausen syndrome by proxy. It differs from accidental poisoning (even repeated episodes) because of intent. This becomes evident in the history provided by the parent when the child presents for medical care. The parent of the child with accidental injury will give a truthful explanation, while the parent who has inflicted the intentional injury will provide a poor or distorted history. The actual incident of poisoning will be omitted, evaded, denied, or falsified.

Children of all ages are susceptible to this form of abuse, as cases ranging in age from newborn to adolescence have been reported. However, 50 percent of cases occur in children younger than 2 years of age. The poisoning may be a single episode or may be chronic and continue in up to 30 percent of cases, even while the child is hospitalized. In 20 percent of poisonings, the child may also present with evidence of physical abuse. The most common etiologic agents include excessive salt ingestion with water restrictions, excessive water ingestion, and barbiturate and tranquilizer poisoning.

The incidence of intentional poisoning is unknown, although well over 50 cases have been reported in the literature, excluding those involving obvious Münchausen syndrome by proxy. This form of abuse, with its incredible range of presentations, remains a challenge for any physician or health professional providing care to the child.

History

The key to this diagnosis is the parental/caretaker explanation for the child's presentation, as well as a high index of suspicion on the part of the physician. In an intentional injury, the possibility of poisoning is *not* mentioned by the parent, and when suggested, is falsified or denied to the extreme. The presenting complaints are numerous, including coma, apnea or apparent life-threatening event, drowsiness, ataxia, lethargy, vomiting, diarrhea, dehydration, stridor, or even red diapers.

Physical Examination

The findings on physical examination will depend on the toxin and the time interval since ingestion. Presentation in extremis is common, and the examination is usually abnormal. As any physical finding is possible, the best approach for the health professional is a complete physical examination, with particular attention to facial and nasal mucosa for odor, burns, or presence of powder; neurologic status and the possibility of drug ingestion; skin and extremities for signs of concurrent physical abuse, restraint, or IV injection.

Laboratory Studies

Although the screening of urine and blood for toxins may be helpful in the diagnosis of intentional poisoning, it will usually be normal. The typical poisoning agents include common household products, especially salt and water, but also include pepper, hot peppers, Tabasco sauce, vitamin A, epsom salts, pine oil or lye, or drugs not routinely part of the toxicologic screen, such as ipecac or insulin. The most common pharmacologic agents used in this form of child abuse would, however, become evident on the routine screen, including benzodiazepines, cocaine, and narcotics. Therefore, a toxicologic screen should be performed on any patient in whom intentional poisoning is suspected. When interpreting the result, however, one must be mindful that a negative result does not rule out the possibility of poisoning.

Mechanism of Injury

The poison is most often administered orally, with some degree of force required in all but the youngest infants. Other routes that have also been used include inhalation (cocaine or pepper aspiration) and ophthalmologic instillation (cyanoacrylate adhesive).

Natural Course

Most intentional poisonings are chronic in nature, with continuing morbidity for the child even after hospitalization. There is also associated physical abuse in 20 percent of cases. The perpetrator in this form of abuse frequently suffers from some degree of character disorder and requires prolonged psychiatric intervention. Therefore, the abuse will continue in most cases until it is discovered by an observant health professional or until the child dies.

Long-Term Outcome

Overall, most children fully recover physically when removed from the abusive environment. However, there is always a risk of significant morbidity and mortality. In one study, which cataloged 48 cases of intentional poisoning, eight children (17 percent) died. In the same series, one child became mentally retarded as a result of a pine oil poisoning. Review of the literature as to psychological recovery reveals a paucity of data.

RHABDOMYOLYSIS AND MYOGLOBINURIA

In the pediatric population, rhabdomyolysis with myoglobinuria is rare and is frequently associated with massive crush injuries, viral infections, or toxins and poisonings. Since 1975, when Kempe heightened awareness of the unusual manifestations of this syndrome, 13 children have been documented to have suffered from this type of child abuse.

No pediatric age group is exempt from this form of abuse, and there does not appear to be a gender preference. The child exhibits widespread muscle injury, evidenced by ecchymoses, edema, or lacerations of the overlying skin. Most often, beating is the mechanism of injury. None of these children exhibited direct renal trauma, even after intravenous pyelogram or renal ultrasound examinations were performed on 9 of the 13 patients. Remarkably, other injuries commonly associated with such soft tissue injury were noticeably absent, including fractures, intracranial injury, and abdominal organ

trauma. Only one child sustained a small upper gastrointestinal bleed.

The diagnosis of rhabdomyolysis with myoglobinuria redefines the child's condition to a more serious, potentially life-threatening one. Medically, the child is at risk for developing hyperkalemia or renal failure; death may also be a consequence. Most courts would appreciate the difference in intent to cause bodily harm when comparing soft tissue bruises versus rhabdomyolysis; some may then assign the case to a criminal system instead of a civil one.

History

In reviewing the documented cases, the mechanism of injury was determined to be a beating. The initial complaints were quite varied and included swelling and discoloration of the distal extremities; difficulty in walking; lethargy and vomiting; lightheadedness and tachycardia; and unresponsiveness. Occasionally, the child was able to admit that a beating had been inflicted. As always, the most important indicator was the discrepancy between observed injuries and the history proferred.

Physical Examination

Rhabdomyolysis occurs after approximately 1 to 5 percent of the total body muscle mass has been destroyed. It presents with muscle pain, bruising of the overlying skin, and muscle weakness if the injury is severe. In each of the documented cases, the patients presented with bruises of varying size and degree of healing. All areas of the body were involved, with some predilection for the face and head as well as the buttocks, thigh, and lower back areas. Scratches, lacerations, or older healing scars were also common. In some children, even the light touching of the skin overlying a muscle group caused exquisite pain. Edema of involved areas, joint effusion without fracture, and muscle cramps were noted. Muscle weakness was also evident on physical examination. Infants and young children were often irritable, with few spontaneous movements and some degree of paradoxic irritability. Although not present in these cases, rhabdomyolysis may also cause neuromuscular irritability as a result of hypocalcemia, a compartment syndrome with neurovascular compromise, and signs of established renal failure such as dependent edema.

Laboratory Studies

A complete urinalysis is the first step in the diagnosis of this disease process. Myoglobinuria, hemoglobinuria, and hematuria produce discolored urine that tests positive for heme on dipstick examination. On microscopic examination, however, red blood cells will be seen in hematuria but will be absent in myoglobinuria and hemoglobinuria. A serum haptoglobin level further distinguishes myoglobinuria (normal serum haptoglobin level) from hemolytic states producing hemoglobinuria (decreased serum haptoglobin). Actual measurement of urine or serum myoglobin levels can be performed by radioimmunologic means, but it is difficult. Problems include limited number of laboratories equipped to perform the assay; short half-life of myoglobin, requiring serum testing early in the presentation, since serum levels normalize within approximately 34 hours; urinary excretion, depending on a minimum serum myoglobin level of 1.5 mg/dl with normal serum levels of 0 to 0.003 mg/dl.

Creatinine phosphokinase is also released as a result of muscle damage and is therefore a useful marker in rhabdomyolysis. Creatinine phosphokinase (CPK) levels 20 to 200 times normal were documented in the 13 children previously mentioned. Care must be taken when analyzing a CPK serum level, since this enzyme has a serum half-life of approximately 48 hours.

With a suspicion of rhabdomyolysis, the patient must be initially evaluated and then followed-up for the possibility of renal failure. Routine serial measurements to assess a rise in blood urea nitrogen (BUN) and creatinine, hyponatremia, hyperkalemia, hypocalcemia, and decreasing urine output are crucial in management.

Radiographic Studies

In any patient with renal compromise, there is a risk of inducing acute renal failure by the injection of contrast dye for further specialized radiographic studies. Each case of child abuse presenting with rhabdomyolysis must be individually assessed for the possibility of direct renal trauma and subsequent diagnostic evaluation. The purpose of renal radiographic studies in this setting should be to diagnose renal trauma, not rhabdomyolysis. In one adult study, 50 patients with acute renal failure successfully tolerated intravenous pyelogram studies after surgery to correct prerenal factors. Of the 13 documented cases of child abuse-induced rhabdomyolysis, 9 patients completed further renal evaluation without the initiation of therapy for rhabdomyolysis (i.e., aggressive hydration, serum alkalinization to maintain urine pH greater than 6.5, and forced diuresis).

Other radiographic studies should be performed as indicated to diagnose associated injuries, such as x-rays for possible fractures, or a noncontrast head CT scan to diagnose intracranial bleeding.

Mechanism of Injury

The 13 children recorded in the medical literature developed rhabdomyolysis after sustaining a beating, the bruises of which were evident on physical examination. Primary massive muscle injury causes rhabdomyolysis in the same manner as the other etiologies for this disease process (i.e., cell membrane injury with alteration of sodium and calcium flux, subsequent cell death, and lysis). Therefore, although the etiologies for rhabdomyolysis differ, the presentations are similar.

Natural Course

All patients with rhabdomyolysis will present with myoglobinuria and increased CPK enzyme levels. The degree of renal involvement will vary. Approximately one-third of patients will develop acute renal failure. The remaining two-thirds may have transient oliguria or no renal compromise.

Injuries Suggestive of Abuse

The differential diagnosis for myoglobinuria and rhabdomyolysis includes primary muscle injury as with crush injuries, beating, toxin- or drug-related injury, hypoxic muscular compromise, infectious agent damage, or abnormality of muscle energy production. Therefore, child abuse-induced rhabdomyolysis may occur after an intentional poisoning, strangulation, or drowning attempt, beating, or other intentional massive physical trauma.

Long-Term Outcome

All of the children with documented child abuse-induced rhabdomyolysis recovered without incident, but this is a small sample. Further review of the pediatric literature does not provide additional information. Adults with rhabdomyolysis usually have full recovery of their renal function but may sustain permanent muscle wasting as a result of crush injuries.

SUGGESTED READINGS

1. Dine MS, McGovern ME: Intentional poisoning of children—an overlooked category of child abuse: report of seven cases and review of the literature. Pediatrics 70:32, 1982
2. Epstein MA, Markowitz RL, Gallo DM et al: Münchausen syndrome by proxy: considerations in diagnosis and confirmation by video surveillance. Pediatrics 80:220, 1987
3. Griffith JL, Slovik LS: Münchausen syndrome by proxy and sleep disorders medicine. Sleep 12:178, 1989
4. Hickson GB, Altemeier WA, Martine ED et al: Parental administration of chemical agents: a cause of apparent life threatening events. Pediatrics 83:772, 1989
5. Kempe CH: Uncommon manifestations of the battered child syndrome. Am J Dis Child 129:1265, 1975
6. Kohl S, Pickering LK, Dupress E: Child abuse presenting as immunodeficiency disease. J Pediatr 93:466, 1978
7. McGuire TL, Feldman KW: Psychologic morbidity of children subjected to Münchausen syndrome by proxy. Pediatrics 83:289, 1989
8. Meadow R: Management of Münchausen syndrome by proxy. Arch Dis Child 60:385, 1950
9. Meadow R. Münchausen syndrome by proxy: the hinterland of abuse. Lancet 2:343, 1977
10. Nicol AR, Eccles M: Psychotherapy for Münchausen syndrome by proxy. Arch Dis Child 60:344, 1985
11. Orenstein DM, Wasserman AL: Münchausen syndrome by proxy simulating cystic fibrosis. Pediatric 78:641, 1986

12. Robotham JL, Haddow JE: Rhabdomyolysis and myoglobinuria in childhood. Ped Clin North Am 23:279, 1976
13. Ron D, Taitelman U, Michaelson M et al: Prevention of acute renal failure in traumatic rhabdomyolysis. Arch Intern Med 144:277, 1984
14. Rosen CL, Frost JD, Bricker T et al: Two siblings with recurrent cardiorespiratory arrest: Münchausen syndrome by proxy or child abuse? Pediatrics 71:715, 1983
15. Rosenberg DA: Web of deceit: a literature review of Münchausen syndrome by proxy. Child Abuse Negl 2:547, 1987
16. Schwengel D, Ludwig S: Rhabdomyolysis and myoglobinuria as manifestations of child abuse. Pediatr Emerg Care 1:194, 1985
17. Sutphen JL, Saulsbury FT: Intentional ipecac poisoning: Münchausen syndrome by proxy. Pediatrics 82:453, 1989
18. Waller DA: Obstacles to the treatment of Münchausen by proxy syndrome. J Am Acad Child Psychiatr 22:80, 1983
19. Warner JO, Hathaway MJ: Allergic form of Meadow's syndrome. Arch Dis Child 59:151, 1984
20. Zitelli B, Seltman MF, Shannon RM: Münchausen's syndrome by proxy and its professional participants. Am J Dis Child 141:1099, 1987

17

Special Problems in Caring for the Sexually Abused Child

Stephen Ludwig

Child sexual abuse reports have increased dramatically over the past decade. The number of sexual abuse reports in many states now matches or exceeds the number of physical abuse reports (Fig. 17-1). The U.S. Department of Health and Human Services Incidence Study shows child sexual abuse to be present in 2.5 per 1000 children (Table 17-1). Other surveys conclude that sexual abuse may be experienced by 1 in 4 females and 1 in 10 males. The American Academy of Pediatrics has suggested that approximately 1 percent of children will experience some form of abuse each year. Whichever specific statistics are believed to be accurate, it is certain that sexual abuse is a common societal phenomenon.

The problems of child sexual abuse are as complex and multifaceted as other forms of abuse. The cases have wide variability depending on the age of the child, whether the abuse is intrafamilial or extrafamilial, and the extent and chronicity of abuse. The variability extends from initial signs and symptoms, to extent of findings, to methods of case management and treatment. Cases of child sexual abuse are filled with a distinct set of challenges for

the clinician. Among these are challenges imposed by the nature of the victim, those imposed by the strength of the perpetrator, those contributed by parents, and issues pertaining to the current state of our knowledge and investigative techniques. Despite these challenges the clinician must be sensitive to the widespread incidence of sexual abuse and the need to report suspected cases of sexual abuse. Understanding the challenges will be helpful to the health care provider who must struggle to overcome them.

CHALLENGES POSED BY THE VICTIM

Age and Developmental Level

In reviewing the case experience at the Children's Hospital of Philadelphia, it was noteworthy to find 52 percent of the child sexual abuse victims were younger than 5 years old. The age and concomitant developmental level of these children present a distinct management challenge.

Table 17-1. National Incidence Study (1988) Rates Per 1000 Children

	Abuse (43%)	Neglect (63%)
Physical	5.7	9.1
Emotional	3.4	4.6
Sexual	2.5	3.5

Many children in this preschool group do not have fully formed language skills. Their words for their own sexual anatomy may be rudimentary and imprecise. For example, some children at this age are unable to distinguish between their genitals and their anus. Others use terms such as "peepee" or "hinie" without distinct meaning. Children younger than five years old may also have difficulty with two other developmental skills: (1) sense of time and (2) sequencing ability. Some children may be unable to differentiate last week or last month from yesterday. Others will be unable to sequence a story as to what happened first, second, third, and so forth. Both of these developmental deficiencies may result in difficult-to-understand histories and what seem to be changing or impossible stories.

Children at older developmental levels may be reluctant to reveal and describe their abuse for fear of negative peer or parental reaction or because of a feeling that they will be seen as being a contributor to the abuse. They may be old enough to realize the embarrassment and shame that come with being a victim, even an innocent victim. A clever perpetrator will know how to gauge a child's developmental level and use the child's developmental stage to the perpetrator's own benefit.

Positive Relationships With the Perpetrator

Beyond the aforementioned developmental stages there are other barriers that affect the child sexual abuse victim. For

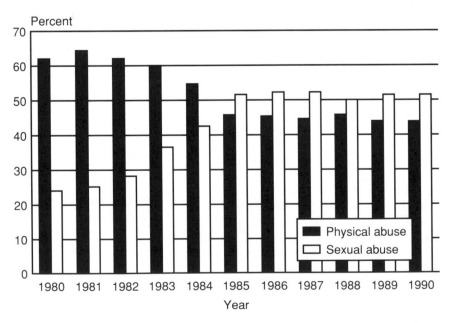

Fig. 17-1. Percent of physical abuse and sexual abuse. (Data from Official Child Abuse Reports from the Commonwealth of Pennsylvania, 1980–1990.[24])

example, child sexual abuse is usually perpetrated by someone who has an existing and often positive relationship with the child. The perpetrator uses this positive relationship to gain control and power. However, in the course of becoming a victim, the child may experience many positive aspects of the relationship with the abuser. Some children report liking the perpetrators because they are giving of their time, attention, and at times, material goods. The positive relationship between the victim and perpetrator may pose a challenge to the health care team, especially if the team members act on the common sense assumption that all victims dislike their perpetrators. In child sexual abuse the clinician/health care worker may need to overcome a positive victim–perpetrator relationship.

Fear of the Victim

In some situations the victim has been terrorized with fear. The perpetrator may do and say things that render the victim so fearful that positive outreach by the health care provider cannot overcome the negative fear tactics that the perpetrator has employed. In some sexual abuse encounters the perpetrator may tell the victim, "If you tell I will kill your mother" or "Our family will be destroyed" or "They will take you away and put you into a foster home." Children report these and any other statements that generate high levels of fear and anxiety. Some perpetrators have not only imparted their threats verbally but have demonstrated them by killing young animals, showing frightening photographs, or producing other documentation of their potential power.

Other Dynamics

Family functioning, cultural beliefs, and socioeconomic forces are other dynamics that will present a challenge to the clinician. Some children may be more abuse prone because of their own dysfunctional family dynamics. Children who feel unwanted, alone, rejected, or overlooked by their parents may be more prone to cultivation by an abusive adult. Certainly, sexual abuse has the potential to occur in any family, weak or strong. However, in some families the dynamics are such that abuse will happen more readily. Cultural beliefs may also make some children more prone. Different cultural groups have varying mores and sanctions for sexual contact across generational boundaries, and some may hold mistaken folk medical beliefs. For example, in a Caribbean island group, it was believed that the only cure for male urethritis was to have sexual intercourse with a young, "clean" virgin female. This type of belief obviously promoted child sexual abuse. Socioeconomic factors are important because for some children the promise of money and material things is a strong force that lures them into sexual abuse involvement and prevents disclosure. Some young adolescents are capable of doubling their parents' income through their participation with a pedophile (see Ch. 22). With this amount of financial gain, questions may not be asked of the child and parents may rationalize or overlook the source of the victim's income.

Accommodation Syndrome

Summitt has elegantly written about the child sexual abuse accommodation syndrome. Traumatized children may dissociate themselves from their abusive experience as a defense mechanism. This in turn may lead to a lack of memory for the event or uncertainty on the part of the child. In some children initially clear reports of abuse may be followed by recan-

Table 17-2.   Child Sexual Abuse
Accommodation Syndrome

Secrecy (precondition)

Helplessness (precondition)

Entrapment and accommodation

Delayed, conflicted, and unconvincing
   disclosure

Retraction

(From Summitt,[21] with permission.)

tations. Elements of the accommodation
syndrome are shown in Table 17-2.

CHALLENGES POSED BY THE PERPETRATOR

Strength of Sexual Abuse Drive

Many adults who engage in child sexual abuse do so because of their own altered or abnormal childhood experiences. Regardless of the psychodynamics, these perpetrators have a very strong drive to act out their sexual desires with children. It is impressive to see how resistant these drives are to traditional psychotherapeutic or penal interventions. Sexual abuse perpetrators are often quite bright, clever, and very determined. The strength of this abnormal drive represents a distinct challenge to the child advocate. Nicholas Groth has noted that adults who sexually abuse children can be classified into two groups: those who are fixated into a persistent pattern and those who regress into the behavior. He states, "A fixated child offender is a person who has, from adolescence, been sexually attracted primarily or exclusively to significantly younger people and this attraction has persisted throughout life, regardless of what other sexual experiences he has had."

Fear Tactics

The child sexual abuse perpetrator may use many different means to gain access to the child victim. The use of fear has already been noted as the primary means for keeping sexual abuse a secret. Additionally, positive reinforcement may be used effectively. Abusers may be excellent and well respected teachers, clergy, scout leaders, or physicians. Such positive functioning is not inconsistent with deviant behavior in the isolated realm of their sexual lives. Perpetrators are uncanny and powerful in their ability to find and keep a likely victim under their control. At times they are quite brazen and seemingly unconcerned about detection.

CHALLENGES POSED BY THE PARENTS

Complicity

Some parents of abused children will be virtually compliant with the abusing adult. In a large number of cases, children may have told or tried to inform their parents that they were being abused only to be rebuffed. In cases of father-daughter incest, the psychodynamics may include a tacit approval by the mother to avoid her own sexual involvement with the father. Abusive acts are often written off to alcohol abuse, temporary loss of control, or some other excuse. Some parents do not wish to pursue a sexual abuse allegation on behalf of their child, for fear it would bring a bad reputation to the family. Whatever the reason, the parent may work unwittingly on behalf of the perpetrator.

Disbelief

Some parents simply do not believe that sexual abuse has occurred. They deny it because the thought is too repugnant to be believed. Denial is not a function of education or intelligence but is more likely a psychological defense. Parental denial leads to major challenges for the health care provider. Without the cooperation and compliance of the parent the child's needs cannot be attended to.

CHALLENGES POSED BY THE STATE OF THE ART

Reliance of Historical Findings

The diagnosis of child sexual abuse is based primarily on the history provided by the patient interview. Often there are no physical signs. The child's developmental stage and lack of specific interview skills make obtaining a child sexual abuse history difficult (see Ch. 21). The health care provider must rely on a history that at times does not seem reliable. Any weakness in the history may reflect factors other than the truth of the child's allegation.

Questions About Signs and Symptoms

The signs and symptoms of abuse are nonspecific. For example, following an episode of sexual abuse, a little girl may become enuretic. There are multiple causes of enuresis and that resulting from sexual abuse is no more specific than any other cause. A child may refuse to go to nursery school because of sexual abuse contacts from a teacher. However, the child may also be refusing for other reasons such as fear of separating from the parent or avoidance of a class bully. Even physical signs may be nonspecific. Vaginal erythema without a history of injury or positive culture does not specifically indicate child sexual abuse.

What are Normal Findings?

Medical information gathering about normal genital growth and developmental changes is just beginning. Particularly with the use of the colposcope, clinicians have been seeing and documenting findings more clearly. However, in some cases, it is still unclear as to what is normal and what is abnormal. These concepts are developing as a result of the work of McCann et al., Emans et al., and others. Even in the matter of sexually transmitted diseases, the body of knowledge is incomplete. Although some infections are virtually always transmitted through sexual contact, others may be transmitted through multiple routes and with varying attack rates and incubation periods.

Paradise has emphasized the need for interpreting findings based on statistical methods that look at predictive value, positive and negative, rather than through the statistical differences between groups of children. According to decision analysis theory this type of analysis is critically important to the scientific foundations of clinical decision-making (Fig. 17-2).

False Allegations

False allegations are an additional challenge to the clinician. There are two forms: (1) parental misinterpretations and (2) intentional. In the first form, parents may misinterpret findings usually because of their own fears and suspicions. Often these parents have experienced sexual abuse in their own backgrounds, and thus, are prone to imagining abuse in their children. In the second form, one

Disorder

		Yes	No	Total
Diagnostic test	Abnormal	True positives (a)	False positives (b)	All positives
	Normal	False negatives (c)	True negatives (d)	All negatives
	Total	Disorder present	Disorder absent	Grand total

Fig. 17-2. Calculation of positive predictive value for decision analysis. The positive predictive value is the proportion of patients with a positive test who will have the disorder in question [positive predictive value equals a/(a + b)]. (From Paradise,[18] with permission.)

parent consciously evokes a sexual abuse mechanism as a means to harm the estranged parent. Intentional false allegations seem to occur less frequently when compared with misinterpretation. Couples separate for many reasons and usually in the course of a separation and divorce, sexual conflicts occur. It is neither surprising that these conflicts are reflected on the child nor that a parent has sexual contact with the child in the midst of the turmoil. In either case, the clinician has the challenge of sorting through these allegations. Faller has looked at three factors that may be helpful in differentiating false from true allegations. These include (1) the child will provide significant detail about the encounter; (2) the child will describe sexual behavior; and (3) the child will have emotional reaction to the maltreatment or to its recounting. Faller is careful to point out possible reasons for exception to each of these points. Thus,

there is no surefire way to easily determine false allegations.

Unilateral Investigation

Another factor that makes the investigation of a sexual abuse complaint difficult is that health care providers are privy to only one side of the story, the victim's. Rarely do they have the opportunity to hear and evaluate the history of the alleged perpetrator. By hearing both sides of the history, the investigation may be made easier in some cases. Certainly, some perpetrators would give histories that would be incriminating, others may be skilled enough to deflect suspicion. Certainly, in cases in which there are allegations of sexual abuse in the context of custody disputes it would be helpful to evaluate both parents.

Reliance on Simple Solutions

One of the greatest challenges for health care professionals who work with sexually abused children is the temptation to look for simple solutions to a complex problem. Thus, colposcopy and vaginal diameter measurement are attractive simple solution "fads" that may provide an accurate and reliable means for identifying the sexually abused child. Working with sexually abused children will never be simple or easy. Thoughts of simple solutions need to be eliminated or else too much time and energy will be wasted traveling down dead end highways.

SUMMARY

Health care professionals who care for sexually abused children face many challenges. Some challenges are posed by the children and their families, others by the perpetrator, and still others by a lack of professional knowledge and skill. Despite these challenges children who have been abused must be identified and protected. Child sexual abuse must be prevented from occurring in the first place and the fight to tear down the barriers and accomplish these goals must continue. The chapters that follow in this section will provide health care providers with the most up-to-date information.

SUGGESTED READINGS

1. Bresee P, Stearns GB, Bess BH et al: Allegations of child sexual abuse in child custody disputes. Am J Orthopsychiatry 56:560, 1986
2. Brayden RM, Altemeier WA, Yeager T: Interpretations of colposcopic photographs: evidence for competence in assessing sexual abuse? Child Abuse Negl 15:69, 1991
3. Burgess AW, Groth AN, Holmstrom LL, Sgroi SM: Sexual Assault of Children and Adolescents. Lexington Books, Lexington, 1978
4. Corwin DL, Beriner L, Goodman G et al: Child sexual abuse in custody disputes: no easy answers. J Interpers Violence 2:91, 1987
5. Criville A: Child physical and sexual abuse: the roles of sadism and sexuality. Child Abuse Negl 14:121, 1990
6. DeJong AR, Hervada AR, Emmett GA: Epidemiological variations in childhood sexual abuse. Child Abuse Negl 7:155, 1983
7. Demb JM: Reported hyperphagia in foster children. Child Abuse Negl 15:77, 1991
8. Emans JE, Woods ER, Flagg NT et al: Genital findings in sexually abused, symptomatic and asymptomatic girls. Pediatrics 79:778, 1985
9. Faller CK: Criteria for judging the credibility of children's statements about their sexual abuse. Child Welfare 72:389, 1988
10. Finkelhor D: Sexually Victimized Children. Free Press, New York, 1979
11. Greenwood CL, Tangalos EG, Maruta T: Prevalence of sexual abuse, physical abuse, and concurrent traumatic life events in a general medical population. Mayo Clin Proc 65:1067, 1990
12. Hunter RS, Kilstrom N, Loda F: Sexually abused children: identifying masked presentation in a medical setting. Child Abuse Negl 9:17, 1985
13. Jason J, Williams SL, Burton A et al: Epidemiology differences between sexual and physical child abuse. JAMA 247:3344, 1982
14. Lindblad F: Child sexual abuse evaluation of allegations—a hermeneutical approach. Acta Pediatr Scand, supp 358:1, 1989
15. Mannarino AP, Cohen JA: A clinical-demographic study of sexually abused children. Child Abuse Negl 10:17, 1986

16. McCann J, Voris J, Simon M, Voris J: Comparison of genital examination techniques in prepubertal girls. Pediatrics 85:182, 1990

17. McCann J, Wells R, Simon MD, Voris J: Genital findings in prepubertal girls selected for nonabuse. Pediatrics 86:428, 1990

18. Paradise JE: Predictive accuracy and the diagnosis of sexual abuse. Child Abuse Negl 13:169, 1989

19. Paradise JE, Rostain AC, Nathanson M: Substantiation of sexual abuse changes when parents dispute custody or visitation. Pediatrics 81:835, 1988

20. Pokorry SE: Configuration of the prepubertal hymen. Am J Obstet Gynecol 157:950, 1987

21. Summitt RC: The child sexual abuse accommodation syndrome. Child Abuse Negl 7:177, 1983

22. U.S. Department of Health and Human Services: Study of national incidence and prevalence of child abuse and neglect, 1988. National Center for Child Abuse Neglect, Washington D.C., 1988

23. U.S. Department of Justice: National Center for Missing and Exploited Children, Child Pornography and Prostitution. Background and Legal Analysis, Washington D.C., 1987

24. Woodling BA, Heger A: The use of the colposcope in the diagnosis of sexual abuse in the pediatric age group. Child Abuse Negl 10:111, 1986

25. Wyatt GE, Peters SD: Issues in the definition of child sexual abuse in prevalence research. Child Abuse Negl 10:231, 1986

18

Genital and Anal Trauma

Allan R. De Jong

Genital and anal injuries are generally described in the context of child sexual abuse. However, physical child abuse may also be associated with injuries of the genital and perineal sites. The purpose of this chapter is to summarize the currently evolving approach to the evaluation of genital and anal injuries in children. The focus shifts from the physical examination and normal anatomic variation, to specific patterns of inflicted genital injuries and anal trauma in boys and girls, and to patterns of residual findings of sexual trauma.

PHYSICAL EXAMINATION

The physical examination is an essential component of the assessment of the child alleged to have been sexually abused, regardless of the interval between the last episode and disclosure or the absence of symptoms. The physical examination serves two major purposes. First, it can both identify physical and forensic abnormalities resulting from the alleged activities. Second, it can begin therapeutic intervention by supporting the child's sense of normality. For child victims who experience an "altered body image" and "feelings of damaged goods"

following sexual assault, a normal examination can help improve their self-image. The nonabusing parent(s) of the child may also be relieved to find that the child has not suffered any permanent physical damage.

The examining physician should be thoroughly familiar with the genital and anal anatomy, and the appropriate descriptive terminology. Although routine examination of boys' genitalia during well child visits is not uncommon, girls rarely undergo routine genital examination. Only 77 percent of 129 pediatricians and family practitioners surveyed about their knowledge of sexual abuse indicated that they routinely examine the genitalia of prepubertal females 50 percent of the time and 17.2 percent examined the genitalia less than 10 percent of the time. Failure to incorporate the genital examination as a routine part of health maintenance assessment of the prepubertal child limits the pediatrician's ability to recognize subtle normal anatomic variations and provide a knowledgeable opinion as to whether a specific finding might have resulted from trauma.

Sexually abused children have been deceived, betrayed, and coerced into inappropriate sexual activities and frequently will have difficulty in developing trusting relationships. The examiner should explain to these children in age-appropriate terms, the procedures and purpose of the examination. Observations concerning acute injuries and the collection of appropriate forensic specimens should be done within 72 hours of the alleged event. Although some residua to genital trauma may exist beyond 72 hours, the potential to collect seminal products and other body fluids is minimal. Emergency evaluation is indicated in cases with acute abuse or recent contact (less than 72 hours ago), or in children with physical symptoms (i.e., bleeding, dysuria, discharge) at the time of presentation. However, in cases of chronic abuse when the abuse is disclosed more than 72 hours following the last episode, the evaluation may be scheduled more appropriately in a setting outside of the emergency department. If the presenting signs and symptoms warrant an immediate examination and the child is uncooperative, an examination under anesthesia should be considered. This will most likely occur following serious acute genital and anal trauma. Other circumstances rarely warrant this approach.

Examination of the genitalia should always be done in the context of an overall physical examination. Primarily, the general examination helps remove the focus on the child's genital area and helps emphasize the child's physical normality. Likewise, a complete review of systems is also important, although particular attention should be focused on the genitourinary and gastrointestinal systems.

A complete physical also allows recognition of extragenital signs of trauma. Since few patients will experience an assault that follows the rape model, extragenital signs of trauma reflective of force and restraint will generally not be present. When present, they usually are manifested as grasp marks to the thigh, buttocks, breasts, and neck.

The child victim can be examined in a variety of positions. The ideal examination position is one in which the child feels most comfortable and is most cooperative. The most comfortable and least threatening position for the small child is often the supine frog leg position on the examination table or while being held in the accompanying adult's lap. While in the supine frog leg position, placing the examiner's second and third fingers on the buttocks at the 5 and 7 o'clock position and exerting downward and lateral traction will spread the labia and allow visualization of the hymenal membrane and perihymenal tissues. When the tissues are redundant, grasping the labia between the thumb and index finger and exerting gentle traction in the posterior lateral direction may improve visualization of the tissues. Some examiners prefer to use the prone knee-chest position as described initially by Emans and Goldstein for evaluating the child for vulvovaginitis. The effect of gravity in the prone knee-chest position may improve visualization of the membrane orifice, particularly when redundant tissue is present. This position allows better relaxation of the pubococcygeus muscle and will sometimes permit visualization of the cervix. With the child in this position, the thumbs of the examiner or assistant are placed on the buttocks at the 10 and 2 o'clock position and gentle lateral and superior traction is applied. The anus is easily visualized in the knee-chest position. In boys, examining the anus in the prone knee-chest position can be threatening, and the left lateral decubitus or supine frog leg position with the knees flexed onto the abdomen (supine knee-chest position) is better tolerated. The prepubertal child's examination is principally a careful external visualization. Instrumentation of the prepubertal child with a vaginal or nasal speculum is generally not necessary. The pubertal child is best examined in the lithotomy position.

Optimal visualization of the genital and anal tissues can be accomplished through the use of supplemental lighting, filters, and magnification. A good light source may be as simple as a flashlight or gooseneck lamp or as sophisticated as a colposcope. A magnified view is most helpful in prepubertal children for the identification of subtle acute and chronic residua to trauma. Magnification can be accomplished by a hand-held magnifying glass, an illuminated magnifying lamp, or a colposcope. Only the colposcope provides a variety of magnifications. Colposcopes are binocular visualizing instruments developed primarily for evaluation of diseases of the uterine cervix. However, colposcopic examination has been reported to increase the yield of positive findings by 4 to 12 percent among sexually abused victims. The use of a red-free filter (green filter) of an ophthalmoscope or colposcope enhances visualization of vascular patterns, abrasions, and scar tissue. The use of toluidine blue dye in identifying acute superficially abraded mucosal injuries has been proposed. Although denuded areas will have increased dye uptake, the procedure is unnecessarily messy and the same observations can be made with a red-free filter.

Colposcopes are equipped with a variety of capabilities and can differ significantly from one manufacturer to another. Good optics, multiple magnification, and photographic capabilities are the most important features. The most useful magnification range is between × 4 and × 15. Greater than × 15 magnification provides an extremely limited field and depth of view. A permanent photographic record can serve as objective documentation of the appearance of the genitalia, which can be referred to in the future. Polaroid and videotape cameras can be used, but the most practical and least expensive photographic attachment is the 35 mm camera. Slides are recommended because they are inexpensive, can readily be duplicated, and prints can be obtained from them, if necessary. A less expensive alternative to colpophotographic documentation is a hand-held 35 mm camera equipped with a macrofocusing lens and ring flash. The limitation of this system is that it will generally not provide greater than 1:1 magnification.

FEMALE GENITAL ANATOMY

Terms such as perineum, vulva, vaginal vestibule, and introitis are commonly used clinically, but are not specific enough for localizing inflicted injuries (Fig. 18-1). The child's genital and anal anatomy should be characterized in descriptive terminology. When strict definitions of anatomic structures are contrasted with the clinical nomenclature, the confusion that exists in the clinical literature becomes apparent.

The terms *perineum* and *vulva* are of little descriptive value. The vulva includes all the components of the external genitalia, encompassing the mons pubis, labia majora, labia minora, clitoris, vestibule of the vagina, Skene's and Bartholin's glands, and the opening of the urethra and vagina. The term perineum is used to describe the perianal tissues in addition to the vulva. The specific structures that need to be described are the appearance of the labia majora and minora, the vaginal vestibule and all of its component structures, the hymenal membrane, the posterior fourchette, anus, and perianal tissues.

The term *vaginal vestibule* is also confusing. The vaginal vestibule refers to the area bordered by the labia minora laterally, the clitoris superiorly, and the fourchette posteriorly. Within the vesti-

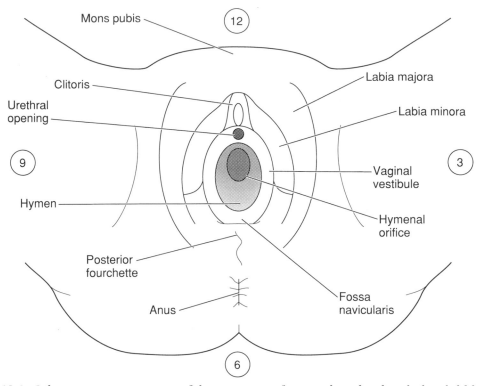

Fig. 18-1. Schematic representation of the perineum of a prepubertal girl with the child lying on her back, in the supine frog leg position. The labia majora are retracted to allow visualization of the hymen. The numbers (3, 6, 9, 12) have been superimposed to show the orientation of the perineal structures with the face of a clock.

bule is the hymenal membrane. The outside surface of the hymenal membrane is referred to as the vestibular surface and is perforated by the urethra, paraurethral ducts (Skene's gland), hymenal orifice, and greater vestibular glands and ducts (Bartholin's gland). The area between the attachment of the hymenal membrane to the posterior vaginal wall and where the labia minora join posteriorly (fourchette) is called the fossa navicularis. The fossa exists because the hymen is recessed within the vaginal canal. This recessed position of the hymenal membrane helps protect it from trauma. Therefore bicycling, gymnastics, or horseback riding are extremely unlikely to contribute to specific injuries of the membrane itself. Scientific data do not support the common

misperception that activities other than sexual contact cause injury to the hymen.

The term *introitus* or *introital opening* also causes confusion. An introitus is generally defined as the entrance to a canal or space. The confusion exists because there is little certainty without further description that the introital diameter is a measurement anterior to the hymenal membrane or of the membrane orifice itself. Any reference to the opening into the vaginal canal should be specific to the hymenal membrane orifice and include its configuration along with its measurements.

The tissues of the labia, the vaginal vestibule, and the vaginal mucosa in the prepubertal child have a somewhat glazed appearance and a reddish color owing to the thinness of the tissues in the absence of estrogen stimulation. This normal appearance should not be misinterpreted as erythema. The labia minora in the prepubertal child have thin edges. With the onset of puberty, there is a gradual increase in fat deposition that thickens the mons pubis and increases the size and fullness of the labia majora. The surfaces of the labia begin to show fine wrinkles, which become more marked as menarche approaches. The labia minora are also affected, they lose their sharp edges and become more rounded.

The Hymenal Membrane

In evaluating a child for the possibility of sexual abuse, more attention is given to the hymen than to any other structure. Unfortunately, there is an exceptional amount of misunderstanding concerning the hymen. A common misconception is that there is a clinical entity known as congenital absence of the hymen. This condition cannot exist on an embryologic basis as an isolated congenital anomaly, with otherwise anatomically normal genitalia. Hymenal tissue was present in 1131 consecutive female newborns examined by Jenny et al., supporting the implausibility that any female infant could be born without a hymen. Based on this data, the highest possible frequency of congenital absence of the hymen would be less than 0.3 percent. Porkorny found that only 6 of 124 prepubertal girls had either absent hymens or hymenal remnants present. Five of these six children had substantive evidence of sexual abuse, and the sixth was lost to follow-up before adequate evaluation of suspected abuse by her grandfather.

The prepubertal child's unestrogenized hymenal membrane tends to be thinner and is easier to examine than the more thickened redundant tissue of the pubertal child. The prepubertal membrane will vary considerably in thickness and presumably in its degree of elasticity. Some membranes appear thin, translucent, and taut while others may be thickened and redundant. There are no published reports in the literature that describe an objective way to judge the elasticity or distensibility of the hymenal membrane. Therefore, comments on hymenal elasticity are purely subjective.

The hymenal membrane and orifice may be quite variable in configuration. The orifice may have the following basic shapes: crescentic (posterior rim hymen), annular (circumferential), septate, cribriform (containing more than one opening), fimbriated (consisting of redundant tissue that appears as overlying flaps), microperforated, or imperforate. About 3 to 18 percent of hymens have minor anatomic variants such as hymenal tags and transverse hymenal bands. Additional descriptive terminology concerning the appearance of the basic shapes exists in the literature. Examining physicians should avoid nondescriptive terminology such as intact, broken, virginal, or marital to characterize the hymen. The edge of the hymenal orifice may be thin and translucent or it may appear rounded. Frequently (20 to 65 percent), the margins of the orifice have rounded areas (bumps or mounds), angular projections, or clefts. At times, redundancy and infolding of the membrane may result in a dramatically different appearance of the orifice, depending on the position in which the child is examined and the child's state of relaxation. Interpretation of rounding or irregularity of the edge of the membrane as residual to repeated introduction of a foreign body remains subjective, unless this is found as an objective change from a previous examination or other confirmatory stigmata of trauma. No experimental model exists which has looked at how repeated frictional trauma alters the genital tissues.

The orifice may be anteriorly, centrally, or posteriorly placed and vary considerably in its transverse diameter. Changes in the transverse diameter can be quite dramatic, depending on the child's position and the state of relaxation during examination. Because the membrane is attached laterally to the vaginal wall, the degree of relaxation of the bulbocavernous and ischiocavernous muscles may produce variation in the size of the orifice. Recent clinical studies have demonstrated differences in the transverse diameter by up to 50 percent and variability in the configuration and contour of the hymenal membrane within a given child, depending on the child's position and the amount of traction used during the examination.

The prepubertal, unestrogenized mucosa of the vestibular surface of the hymenal membrane, fossa navicularis, and medial aspects of the vaginal wall anterior to the hymenal membrane will have a diffusely reddened appearance. Caution is advisable when details of the history are provided, which suggest that a child's genitalia were abnormally reddened by a caretaker, as this observation is subjective and nonspecific. The normal vascular pattern of the vestibular surface is commonly described as reticular, fine lacey, symmetric, and without interruption. Interruptions in the vascular pattern of the mucosa are frequently interpreted as the residua to trauma and reflective of scar tissue. Congenital midline interruptions or fusion defects can inadvertently be interpreted as scar tissue. When scar tissue is suspected, a history suggestive of sufficient trauma to result in this form of residua should be obtained. Traction on the tissues may result in blanching of the vascular pattern in the midline and should not be interpreted as a vascular interruption. The membrane itself is also rich in nerve fibers and can be exquisitely tender in the prepubertal child in the absence of trauma.

Hymenal Orifice Diameter

Unfortunately, there is limited normative data concerning the transverse hymenal orifice diameter of prepubertal and pubertal nonabused children. Cantwell observed that 74 percent of girls examined with a history of sexual abuse had a transverse orifice diameter greater than 4 mm. Emans et al. reported that the average hymenal opening measured 2.8 ± 1.5 mm in a control group of girls ranging in age from 1 to 14 years without a history of sexual abuse. White et al. reported that the hymenal opening diameter was less than 4 mm in all but 4 of 98 children in a control group without a history of abuse. Goff et al. recently studied 273 prepubertal girls from 1 through 7 years of age. They found that the mean hymenal opening size increased with age, but the maximum measurement across the age range was 4 mm in the supine frog leg position and 5 mm in the supine knee-chest position. No attempt was made to separate redundant hymenal folds, and the mean measurement was 1 mm or less in both positions up to 4 years of age. The mean measurement remained 1 mm or less in the supine frog leg position, but ranged from 1.24 to 2.50 mm in the supine knee-chest position between ages 4 and 7 years. McCann et al. reported generally larger average diameters and variability of both vertical and horizontal (transverse) measurements of the hymenal orifice in their study of nonabused prepubertal girls. Measurements were greater if traction was applied to the labia majora with the child in the supine position or if the child was in the prone knee-chest position, compared with the child examined in the supine frog leg position without labial traction. The average and range of transverse (horizontal) diameter measurements was found to increase with increasing age of the child. Depending on the position and method of measurement used, the mean transverse orifice diameter was 3.9 to 5.2 mm (maximum 8.0 mm) in 2- to 4-year-old children, 4.2 to 5.6 mm (maximum 9.0 mm) in 5- to 7-year-old children, and 5.7 to 7.3 mm (maximum 11.0 mm) in prepubertal children older than 7 years of age. Despite the desire of clinicians for a number that might simplify decision making, no such number currently exists. Paradise's analysis of predictive accuracy of the transverse orifice diameter puts into perspective the difficulties that arise when assigning too much weight to a given finding. Considerable variability in the orifice diameter can exist from moment to moment depending on the child's state of relaxation, the use of traction, the examination position, and the method of measurement. The most accurate way of obtaining measurements is through the use of the intraocular scale of a colposcope. Measurements should be obtained in all examinations. A maximum and minimum transverse and vertical measurement will document the variability of the diameter. It is the maximum diameter that may help assess the probability that an object was placed through the orifice.

In determining the probability that an object was placed through a hymenal orifice, it is helpful to know the diameter of objects that might be placed through the orifice. The average transverse diameter of an erect adult penis is cited by Paul as being 35 mm. Therefore, if an object the size of a penis is introduced through a prepubertal child's hymenal orifice, then obvious residua should be apparent. Objects of smaller diameter, such as a digit or foreign body, will be less likely to result in residual damage. However, a scarred hymen may appear grossly abnormal, even though the orifice has a normal diameter. Since no studies exist that detail the degree of distensibility of the hymenal tissue, judging whether a particular orifice could dilate to accommo-

date an object of a particular diameter is subjective. It does make sense that an orifice must be greater than 4 mm for an object such as a digit or penis to have penetrated through it. However, an examiner, for example, should not conclude that a 7 mm opening without other stigmata of injury means that a child has been sexually abused. This emphasizes the need for corroborating details of the history.

GENITAL INJURY IN GIRLS

Muram studied 31 sexually abused girls in whose cases there was a 100 percent confession by the perpetrators of sexual abuse; 18 of 31 specifically confessed to vaginal penetration. In that study, 45 percent of the children had specific abnormal findings suggestive of abuse. Twenty-six percent of the children had nonspecific findings, and 29 percent did not have any findings of trauma. Inflammation, bruising, and irritation were seen in all girls evaluated within 1 week of the confessed abuse, while none of the girls evaluated more than 1 week later had positive findings of inflammation. A normal examination was present in 54 percent of cases where penetration was denied, but only 11 percent of cases with admitted penetration had normal examinations. Sixty-one percent of those children who had penetration through the orifice by a penis or digit had hymenal tears extending to the vaginal wall. In the general population referred for an evaluation of sexual abuse, it is unlikely that the percentage of abnormal findings will be this high, since this was a select population with perpetrators who had confessed to the activities.

In a study of 242 children evaluated for sexual abuse by White et al., 47 percent of the children who provided a convincing history of sexual contact or who had gonorrhea had a transverse diameter greater than 4 mm. However, 53 percent of the same children, including 27 percent of this population who provided a history of sexual contact with digital or penile penetration, had an orifice diameter of less than 4 mm. Children reporting repeated abuse were twice as likely, and those reporting penetration were three times as likely, to have hymenal orifice diameters greater than 4 mm as children reporting a single episode or nonpenetrating abuse, respectively. Emans et al., in a prospective study of symptomatic and asymptomatic sexually abused children, found that sexually abused girls were more likely than asymptomatic controls to have increased friability of the posterior fourchette, attenuation of the hymen, scars, and synechia of the hymen to the vagina. Emans et al. noted that the group of sexually abused girls had larger transverse hymenal orifice diameters than the group of nonabused girls, but the average difference in diameter between the two groups was only 1.6 mm. Despite this small difference, Emans et al. advocated that a transverse measurement of more than 7 mm and an anterior posterior diameter of more than 6 mm in 3- to 6-year-old girls may support the diagnosis of suspected abuse. All children with hymenal tears gave a history of pain associated with vaginal penetration. The incidence of hymenal orifice clefts and bumps did not appear to be statistically different among the sexually abused, control, or nonabused symptomatic groups. Rounding of the hymenal orifice border and the absence of attenuation was not significantly different between the groups in the study by Emans et al. Interestingly, there was no statistical difference between the sexually abused group and the symptomatic genital complaint group in respect to the occurrence of friability,

scars, attenuation of the hymen, rounding of the hymen, bumps, clefts, or synechia of the hymen to the vagina. It would be difficult to explain how scars developed in the genital complaint group in the absence of a history of genital trauma. This points out that before concluding that an avascular area is scar tissue, a history supportive of injury should be present. An avascular area can be used to corroborate a history of sexual abuse. However, the presence of an avascular lesion does not absolutely prove that abuse occurred, regardless of the history.

There are both legal and medical definitions of penetration. From a legal perspective, penetration may be defined as between the labia, whereas medically it is most widely considered to be through the hymenal orifice. Children experience a subjective sensation of penetration when an object such as the convex side of the shaft of the penis is placed between the labia within the context of vulvar coitus. A digit placed between the labia may also be perceived as inside without findings of penetration through the orifice. Nonpenetrating injuries to the genitalia and anus will most likely result in only superficial injuries that are observed as abrasions, contusions, erythema, edema, and superficial lacerations.

The pattern of trauma and residua from specific penetrating and nonpenetrating activities may vary, depending on the position in which the activity occurred, the frequency of the contact, the depth of penetration, and the degree of force. If residua from fondling the female genitalia are to be apparent, they will generally be observed as erythema, edema, superficial abrasions, and possibly contusions of the medial aspects of the labia and perihymenal tissues. If an object such as a digit is placed through the hymenal orifice, it is possible, depending on the size differential between the orifice and the digit, that no residua will exist, or that a tear might be present. Some examiners refer to rounding of the edge of the membrane, which is believed to occur when an object is repeatedly introduced through the orifice. Interpretation of rounding of the membrane edge is subjective unless accompanied by other stigmata of trauma. Clinically, injuries between the 9 and 3 o'clock position occur more frequently in fondling/digital penetration as the finger enters over the mons pubis and urethra. The pelvis is used as a fulcrum, and the injuries are produced by the upward directed forces. Vulvar coitus can result in trauma to the medial aspects of the labia. The residua can include erythema, edema, superficial abrasions, and contusions. Because of the direction of force applied by the convex side of the shaft of the penis, trauma to the fossa navicularis and the posterior fourchette are likely, and residua may be observed as a frank tear or friability of the tissues. The convex side of the penis may also rub over the vestibular surface of the hymenal membrane without penetrating through the orifice. Acute signs of trauma to the surface of the membrane or healed residua in the form of changes in vascular pattern and synechiae distorting the orifice may be seen.

With penile penetration, all the findings present in vulvar coitus will generally be present, along with a more specific trauma suggestive of penetration through the hymenal orifice, as manifested by tears to the edge of the hymenal orifice extending to the posterior vaginal wall. Penile pressure during vaginal intercourse is directed towards the posterior fourchette and posterior vaginal wall because forward movement is prevented by the symphysis pubis. Although circumferential mucosal tears may be present, most lacerations of the membrane will occur between the 3 and 9 o'clock position with the victim supine, with most found between the 5 and 7 o'clock posi-

tion. The hymenal injuries typically involve not only the membrane itself but extend to the fossa navicularis, posterior fourchette, or the vaginal mucosa. Anatomic variants producing notching or folds of the hymen can be distinguished from the majority of scars because the variants involve only the hymenal tissue itself.

Accidental straddle injuries typically occur between the 9 and 3 o'clock positions as the labia, clitoris, and mons pubis are crushed between the pubic bones, thigh, and object. Swelling, bruising, abrasion, and occasionally laceration of these external structures are found in straddle injury, but usually the hymen and posterior fourchette area are not involved. It is unlikely that self-stimulatory behavior results in any injury other than superficial erythema and possibly abrasions that heal without residua. Children generally masturbate clitorally and therefore do not introduce objects through the hymenal orifice and into the vagina. Therefore, findings of trauma to the membrane itself should not be presumed to be self-inflicted.

MALE GENITAL INJURIES

Male external genital anatomy is very straightforward and requires the examiner to observe and document the presence or absence of circumcision, the appearance of the glans and its frenulum, shaft of the penis and scrotum, presence or absence of hernias, inguinal adenopathy, and Tanner staging. Accidental penile trauma is typically associated with either a toilet seat falling on the penis of a young boy while he is standing to void or to entrapment of the foreskin or penile skin in a zipper. Toilet seat injuries may produce bruising or edema, and infrequently may produce transverse, superficial laceration of the penile shaft. Rarely are these accidents accompanied by deep injuries to the corpora cavernosa or to the urethra. Less commonly, a constricting ring of hair may encircle the penis, leading to circulatory compromise, pain, and swelling. The foreskin may also become inflamed, owing to poor hygiene, and the glans penis may become secondarily involved. Acute signs will include pain, erythema, and swelling, and chronic signs of phimosis and adhesions of the foreskin to the glans may result.

The male external genitalia are an infrequent site of injuries in reports of physical abuse. Injury to the external genitalia or to the perineum in general constitutes from 2 to 7 percent of physical abuse injuries. Little detail is provided about the injuries found in these studies, but many of these injuries were probably caused by hot water immersion in children younger than 4 years of age. Pinch mark bruises of the glans penis have been described infrequently, and inflicted ligature or banding injuries of the penis have been reported. Many of these injuries are inflicted as punishment for bedwetting or lack of cooperation with toilet training.

Male genital injury is also infrequently reported among sexually abused boys. Some case series specifically report no genital injuries, and others do not mention male genital injuries. Other studies of sexually abused boys report frequencies of injury ranging from 1.5 to 7 percent including penile and "perineal" bruises, bite marks, "rashes," penile discharge, scrotal burns, and erythema. Orogenital contact and masturbation may result in superficial abrasions, erythema, edema, petechiae, and contusions. Forceful fellation of a male victim may also produce tears of the frenulum of the glans and bite marks of the glans, shaft of the penis, or scrotum. Under most circumstances force is not used during fellatio, and no injuries are apparent. Because the genitalia are external, the documentation of these injuries does not generally pose a problem. Findings with a history of masturbation or orogenital contact should be corroborated. A careful search for genital trauma is indicated, although injuries of the boys' genitalia are infrequently found and may be nonspecific.

Anal and Perianal Findings

The anal anatomy is less complicated than the female genital anatomy, but it is equally important to understand the appropriate descriptive terminology (Fig. 18-2). The tissue overlying the subcutaneous external and sphincter is called the anal verge, which begins at the most distal portion of the anoderm and extends exteriorly to the margin of the anal skin. Within this loose connective tissue surrounding the external anal orifice is the external hemorrhoidal plexus of the perianal space. The anoderm extends from the anal verge to the pectanate or dentate line. At the point where the anoderm meets the rectal ampula, the alternating rectal sinuses and columns create a scalloped appearance. The external anal tissue generally has regularly aligned circumferential radiating rugal folds formed by the corrugator cutis ani muscle. The flexibility of the anal opening is such that a small object such as a digit could be introduced into the anus repeatedly without discomfort, force, or anticipated residua. A child may occasionally state that an object was placed inside the anus when pressure over the anal verge was perceived as inside rather than over.

McCann et al. observed that smooth, fan-shaped areas in the midline of the verge, either with or without depressions, appear to be a congenital anomaly of the superficial division of the external sphincter muscle fibers; this observation is important, since it emphasizes the need

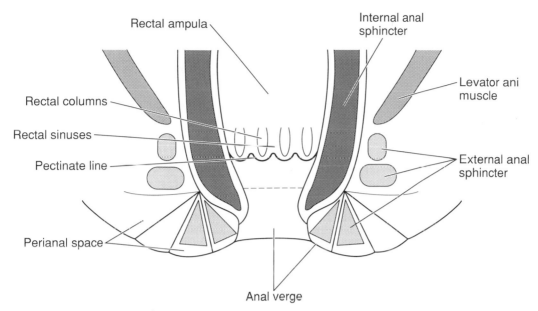

Fig. 18-2. Schematic representation of the cross-section of the anus.

to exert caution when interpreting midline findings of the anal verge tissues. Most serious penetrating injuries of the anus also will occur in the midline position. Therefore, it can be difficult for even the experienced examiner to differentiate the congenital variants from the residua of trauma. Anal skin tags also require differentiation of congenital versus post-traumatic etiology. An anal tag can form if sufficient trauma was exerted to result in formation of a hematoma of the verge tissues in effect stretching and prolapsing the tissues. Interpreting the cause of a tag without characteristics of acute injury is difficult.

A variety of perianal findings have been considered to be the residua of anal trauma. These findings include perianal erythema, swelling of the perianal tissues, laxity and reduced tone of the anal sphincter, shorting or eversion of the anal canal, reflex anal dilatation, fissures, venous congestion, reversible and permanent skin changes, twitchy anus (alter- nate contraction and relaxation of the external sphincter), funneling (a deep-dished anal appearance), and bruising or hematomas. Forty-two percent of the 337 children who were determined by Hobbs and Wynne to have been sexually abused had anal findings. Muran reported that 34 percent of 310 prepubertal sexual abuse victims had abnormal anal and perianal examinations. Only 16 percent of those describing anal assault had normal examinations, but 85 percent of those denying anal assault had normal examinations.

Paul has proposed a "triad" of signs that would be confirmatory of frequent anal intercourse. This triad includes (1) thickening of anal verge skins with reduction or obliteration of anal verge skin folds, (2) increased elasticity of the anal sphincter muscle allowing the introduction of three or more examining fingers with ease, and (3) reduction of the power of the anal sphincter muscle to contract with reduction of the power of that "anal grip." Paul cautions that the absence of any one of the "triad" should lead to doubt concerning the diagnosis of frequent and long-standing anal intercourse. Paul also considers a healed anal fissure to be further corroborative physical evidence. This triad represents very subjective observations and must be corroborated by history. There is no experimental model that documents the residua of the repeated introduction of a foreign body into the mammalian anus with the use of mild, moderate, and excessive force. Paul also suggests that following acute penetration there is a laxity of the anal sphincter, which persists from a few hours to a few days and will be followed by marked spasm that will occur in the absence of complete transection of the sphincter. In addition, he suggests that 12 or more acts within a period of 6 months may be sufficient to cause laxity of the anal sphincter and is often associated with a "positive lateral traction test in which the anus is seen to gap slightly when the buttocks are gently separated." However, many variables are likely to modify the effects of penetration, including the time interval since the last penetration or between acts of recurrent penetration, the number of episodes, the degree of force used with each episode, the size of the object introduced, the use of lubricants, and the relative degree of cooperation by the child. It is too simplistic to quantitate the number of events with particular findings unless all of the variables are quantified.

McCann et al. observed that a variety of perianal soft tissue changes seen in abused children can also be observed frequently in nonabused children. This study involved the examination of 267 prepubertal children (161 girls and 106 boys), ranging in age from 2 months to 11 years. Forty-one percent of nonabused children had perianal erythema, 30 percent had increased perianal pigmenta-tion, 73 percent had venous congestion at sometime during the examination, 49 percent had anal dilatation, 62 percent had intermittent anal dilatation, 26 percent had congenital smooth areas, 11 percent had skin tags, and 2 percent had scars. Of the children with anal dilatation, 98.8 percent had dilatation of less than 20 mm. All of the skin tags were anterior in location, and all scars except one were midline. No abrasions, hematomas, fissures, or hemorrhoids were discovered. This study should not be interpreted to imply that these findings cannot be caused by sexual abuse but emphasizes the need for corroboration of the history provided and consideration of other explanations. Perianal skin tags or scars outside the midline, anal dilatation of 20 mm or greater without the presence of stool in the rectal ampulla, marked irregularity of the anal orifice during dilatation, and a prominent anal verge were all unusual findings.

In a study of 171 children referred for pediatric gastroenterology evaluations, less than 5 percent had perianal or anal findings. All these children did not admit to sexual abuse, and were examined specifically for inflammation, redness, swelling, perianal rash, ulceration, skin tags, and fissures. No child had dilatation of the anal opening or distortion of the shape of the anus. Lazar and Muram suggest that when perianal or anal findings are present, sexual abuse should be considered. However, this population is skewed, and when its findings are contrasted to the observation of frequent perianal findings in nonabused children, the question is posed: what is the incidence of perianal or anal findings in the sexually abused child? Spencer and Dunklee, in both a retrospective and prospective review of 140 sexually abused boys, found that 68 percent had physical evidence of actual or attempted penile anal penetration. This is a composite statistic and includes a variety of perianal and anal findings that occurred following either single or multiple episodes of contact. Most cases involved penile anal penetration, but nearly one-fourth involved either digital or foreign body penetration. Erythema (37 percent) and abrasions (30 percent) were the most common acute lesions, and anal dilatation (50 percent) was the most common chronic lesion noted. A retrospective study of 311 children, of which 25 boys and 20 girls had a history of attempted and/or completed sodomy, had evidence of penetration in 44 percent of the cases as reported by Rimza and Niggeman. In another retrospective study of 145 children, of which 16 were boys, Ellerstein and Canavan found that seven (44 percent) had anal or perianal findings. Reinhart found anal abnormalities in 54 (29 percent) of 189 boys evaluated for sexual abuse, with one half of all the boys describing anal penetration or attempted anal penetration. Erythema (10 percent) and anal laxity (13 percent) were the most common acute and chronic signs noted, respectively. Comparison of these studies is clouded by the inability to contrast operational definitions, details of the history of alleged activities, and categories of findings. Published studies reflect a limited number of cases, and larger collaborative studies are needed.

Reflex anal dilatation was present in 49 percent of the children in a study of a nonabused population conducted by McCann et al. Only 1.2 percent of these children's anal dilatation was greater than 20 mm when the buttocks separation test was applied. These findings are contrasted with Hobbs and Wynne who found dilatation present in 86 percent of the 38 boys and 49 girls who had anal signs consistent with sexual abuse. Again, these studies illustrate the need for standardized definitions, observations, and data analysis to optimize the usefulness of the clinical observations. Individual physical findings can be given greater weight when corroborated by history or an association with other physical findings.

RESIDUA TO TRAUMA

Genital or perianal erythema is often considered a sign of trauma. However, erythema is a nonspecific finding, since it can be found commonly among both abused and nonabused children. McCann et al. reported that one-half of nonabused prepubertal girls they studied had erythema of the vaginal vestibule. Therefore, erythema can be consistent with superficial injury from sexual contact, but it may also be consistent with no abuse. Acute injuries to the genitalia and anus most commonly involve erythema, edema, abrasions, bruises, and lacerations. Emans et al. reported that sexually abused children were more likely than asymptomatic controls to have increased friability of the posterior fourchette, attenuation of the hymen, scars, and synechiae from the hymen to the vagina. Abrasions, hymenal tears, intravaginal synechiae, and condyloma acuminata were found exclusively among the abused children in this study.

Observations concerning the healing chronology of acute anal and genital trauma emphasize the need to apply basic pathology principles of healing to the interpretation of sequelae. Superficial injuries will heal by the pathologic process of regeneration of labile cells. Regeneration proceeds at a rather rapid and somewhat predictable rate. Denuded mucosa regenerates at the rate of approximately 1 mm/24 h and a new emergency epithelium can be formed within 24 to 48 hours. By the fifth day following injuries, differentiation of cells is advanced and may be complete. Most superficial injuries will not be evident to the naked eye by 96 hours post-trauma. Consequently, most children with a history of superficial trauma will not have residual physical findings at the time of their disclosure.

Repeated frictional trauma appears to heal with little or no residua unless a chronic inflammatory process is present. Chronic inflammation may be contributory to the development of labial agglutination, since it has not been described in newborns. Agglutination is a clinical presentation of adhesions that bind the opposing inner surfaces of the labia. Labial agglutination has also been called labial fusion, vulvar fusion, vulvar synechiae, and labial coalescence. Some controversy exists as to the factors contributing to this acquired phenomenon. Berkowitz questions whether labial agglutination is a marker of sexual abuse. Theoretically, genital fondling, masturbation, and vulvar coitus can all result in mucosal irritation or inflammation, which then heal by forming adhesions. McCann et al. reported six sisters in one family with labial agglutination, all of whom were sexually abused. More recently however, the same researchers identified labial adhesions in 40 percent of a group of nonabused prepubertal girls. Emans et al. found a high incidence of labial agglutination among sexually abused girls (18 percent), but this was not significantly different from the rate in symptomatic and asymptomatic girls who served as controls (7 percent). A corroborating history should be obtained when considering agglutination as residual to sexual abuse. Vulvovaginitis, seborrheic dermatitis, poor hygiene, pinworms, and the prepubertal hypoestrogenic state may be contributory to development of agglutination in the nonabused child. Typical labial agglutination involves very smooth, superficial, semitransparent membranes. Traumatic adhesions may be thicker, more irregular, opaque, and associated with other scars. When labial agglutination is present, the physician should inquire as to the cause but should not necessarily assume that abuse has occurred.

Serious genital or anal trauma as the residua to penetrating injuries is easily recognized when presenting acutely. Deep lacerating wounds heal by repair, a pathologic process. Repair results in scar formation. In contrast to the healing of superficial injuries, the formation of scar tissue may take 60 days or longer. Initially, granulation tissue fills the defect and has a neovascular appearance, but the color and volume of the scar tissue change as it matures. The contraction of the wound throughout healing can eventually result in scar tissue only a fraction of the size of the initial wound. In addition, scar tissue can distort the genital tissues in ways that might be unanticipated, based on observations of the acute trauma and its healed residua. Injuries can heal with one of three possible results: no scar, a scar that is smaller than the original injury, or scarring with distortion of the tissues in an unexpected manner. Therefore, a retrospective interpretation of residua to anal and genital trauma can be difficult.

SUMMARY

Our understanding of genital and anal injuries in abused children is starting to take shape as we begin to define the variations of normal anal and genital anatomy. Positive genital and anal findings may represent acute or chronic signs of abuse. Some findings may be almost diagnostic of abuse.

Specific findings[a]

Hymenal bruising or tears

Recent or healed lacerations of hymen extending to the vaginal mucosa (including intravaginal synechiae) or fossa navicularis

Posterior fourchette scarring

Genital bite marks

Sexually transmitted diseases (see Ch. 19)

Thickening of anal verge tissues with alteration of normal rugal pattern

Marked irregularity of the anal orifice

Perianal scars or tags outside of midline location

Anal dilatation of >20 mm

Nonspecific findings[b]

Normal genital, anal, and perianal examination

Generalized or localized erythema or increased vascularity of genital or perianal areas

Posterior fourchette or fossa navicularis midline avascular areas

Labial agglutination

Hyperpigmentation or hypopigmentation of genital or perianal areas

Hymenal irregularities, notches or bumps not extending to the vaginal mucosa or fossa navicularis or not associated with vascular pattern alterations

Significantly enlarged hymenal orifice

Small skin fissures in posterior fourchette and perianal areas

(Continued)

Purulent vaginal discharge

Perianal venous congestion

Perianal smooth areas or anal tags in midline location

Anal dilatation of <15 mm

---

[a] These findings appear to be physical indicators of sexual contact and are not typically found among nonabused children.

[b] These findings may be seen among sexually abused children, but also may occur in nonabused children.

Although the history of the abuse is always important, these findings should arouse suspicion of abuse even when an initial history does not confirm abuse. Further invesigation into these cases may result in corroborative histories, since children are not always ready to disclose their abuse at a particular time to a specific individual. Other physical "abnormalities" may be found among either abused or nonabused children. These nonspecific findings are supportive of the diagnosis of sexual abuse, although not pathognomonic. In these cases, the corroborating history of abuse is essential. Finally, a normal physical examination with no acute or chronic signs of injury can be consistent with sexual abuse, since injuries will not always occur initially and some injuries may heal without residual scarring. Most pediatric sexual abuse involves fondling or other sexual stimulation, which is neither violent nor deeply penetrating. Therefore, many contacts would be likely to produce no acute physical signs, or very minor acute injuries that would heal without scarring.

SUGGESTED READINGS

1. Berkowitz CD: Sexual abuse of children and adolescents. Adv Pediatr 34:275, 1987

2. Berkowitz CD, Elvik SL, Logan MK: Labial fusion in prepubescent girls: a marker for sexual abuse? Am J Obstet Gynecol 156:16, 1987

3. Burgess AW, Holmstrom LL: Sexual trauma of children and adolescents: pressure, sex, secrecy. Nursing Clin North Am 10:551, 1975

4. Cantwell H: Vaginal inspection as it relates to child sexual abuse in girls under thirteen. Child Abuse Negl 7:171, 1981

5. Chadwick DL, Berkowitz CD, Kerns D et al: Color Atlas of Child Sexual Abuse. Year Book Medical Publishers, Chicago, 1989

6. Clemente CD (ed): Gray's Anatomy. 30th Ed. Lea & Febiger, Philadelphia, 1985

7. De Jong AR, Emans SJ, Goldfarb A: Sexual abuse: what you must know. Patient Care 23:145, 1989

8. De Jong AR, Emmett GA, Hervada AR: Epidemiologic factors in the sexual abuse of boys. Am J Dis Child 136:990, 1982

9. Ellerstein NS, Canavan JW: Sexual abuse of boys. Am J Dis Child 134:255, 1980

10. Emans SJ, Goldstein DP: The gynecologic examination of the prepubertal child with vulvovaginitis; use of the knee-chest position. Pediatrics 65:758, 1980

11. Emans SJ, Woods E, Flagg N et al: Genital findings in sexually abused, symptomatic, and asymptomatic girls. Pediatrics 79:778, 1987

12. Enos WF, Conrath TB, Beyer JC: Forensic evaluation of the sexually abused child. Pediatrics 78:385, 1986

13. Finkel MA: Anogenital trauma in sexually abused children. Pediatrics 84:317, 1989

14. Goff CW, Burke KR, Rickenback C, Buebendorf DP: Vaginal opening measurement in prepubertal girls. Am J Dis Child 143:1366, 1989

15. Herman-Giddens ME, Frothingham TE: Prepubertal female genitalia: examination for evidence of sexual abuse. Pediatrics 80:203, 1987

16. Hobbs CJ, Wynne JM: Buggery in childhood: a common syndrome or child abuse. Lancet 2:792, 1986

17. Hobbs CJ, Wynne JM: Child sexual abuse—an increasing rate of diagnosis. Lancet 2:837, 1987

18. Hobbs CJ, Wynne JM: Sexual abuse of English boys and girls: the importance of anal examination. Child Abuse Negl 13:195, 1989

19. Huffman JW, Dewhurst CJ, Capraro VJ (eds): The Gynecology of Childhood and Adolescence. 2nd Ed. WB Saunders, Philadelphia, 1981

20. Jenny C, Kuhns MLD, Arakawa F: Hymens in newborn female children. Pediatrics 80:399, 1987

21. Johnson CF, Showers J: Injury variables in child abuse. Child Abuse Negl 9:207, 1985

22. Ladson S, Johnson CF, Doty RE: Do physicians recognize sexual abuse? Am J Dis Child 141:411, 1987

23. Lauber AA, Souma ML: Use of toluidine blue for documentation of traumatic intercourse. Obstet Gynecol 60:644, 1982

24. Lazar CF, Muram D: The prevalence of perianal and anal abnormalities in a pediatric population referred for gastrointestinal complaints. Adolesc Pediatr Gynecol 2:37, 1989

25. McCann J, Voris J, Simon M: Labial adhesions and posterior fourchette injuries in child sexual abuse. Am J Dis Child 142:659, 1988

26. McCann J, Voris J, Simon M et al: Perianal findings in prepubertal children selected for non abuse: a descriptive study. Child Abuse Negl 13:211, 1989

27. McCann J, Voris J, Simon M, Wells R: Comparison of genital examination techniques in prepubertal females. Pediatrics 85:182, 1990

28. McCann J, Wells R, Simon M, Voris J: Genital findings in prepubertal girls selected for non abuse: a descriptive study. Pediatrics 886:428, 1990

29. McCauley J, Gorman R, Gutzinski G: Toluidine blue in the detection of perineal lacerations in pediatric and adolescent sexual abuse victims. Pediatrics 78:1039, 1986

30. Muram D: Anal and perianal abnormali-

ties in prepubertal victims of sexual abuse. Am J Obstet Gynecol 161:278, 1989

31. Muram D: Child sexual abuse—genital findings in prepubertal girls I. The unaided medical examination. Am J Obstet Gynecol 160:328, 1989

32. Muram D: Child sexual abuse: relationship between sexual acts and genital findings. Child Abuse Negl 13:211, 1989

33. Muram D, Elias S: Child sexual abuse—genital findings in prepubertal girls II. Comparison of colposcopic and unaided examinations. Am J Obstet Gynecol 160:333, 1989

34. Paradise JE: Predictive accuracy and the diagnosis of sexual abuse. Child Abuse Negl 13:169, 1989

35. Pascoe JM, Hildebrandt HM, Tarrier A, Murphey M: Patterns of skin injury in nonaccidental and accidental injury. Pediatrics 64:245, 1979

36. Paul DM: The medical examination in sexual offenses. Med Sci Law 15:154, 1975

37. Paul DM: The Medical examination in sexual offenses against children. Med Sci Law 17:251, 1977

38. Paul DM: What really happened to baby Jane? The medical aspects of the investigation of alleged sexual abuse of children. Med Sci Law 26:85, 1986

39. Pokorny SF: Configurations of the prepubertal hymen. Am J Obstet Gynecol 157:950, 1987

40. Purdue GF, Hunt JC, Prescott PR: Child abuse by burning—an index of suspicion. J Trauma 28:221, 1988

41. Reinhart MA: Sexually abused boys. Child Abuse Negl 11:229, 1987

42. Ricci LR: Medical forensic photography of the sexually abused child. Child Abuse Negl 12:305, 1988

43. Rimza ME, Niggeman MS: Medical evaluation of sexually abused children; a review of 311 cases. Pediatrics 69:8, 1982

44. Schmitt BD: The battered child syndrome. p. 177. In Touloukian RJ (ed): Pediatric Trauma. John Wiley & Sons, New York, 1978

45. Seidel JS, Elvik SL, Berkowitz CD et al: Presentation and evaluation of sexual misuse in the emergency department. Pediatr Emerg Care 2:157, 1986

46. Slosberg E, Ludwig S, Duckett J, Mauro AE: Penile trauma as a sign of child abuse. Am J Dis Child 132:719, 1978

47. Spencer MJ, Dunklee P: Sexual abuse of boys. Pediatrics 78:133, 1986

48. Sproles ET: National Center for Prevention and Control of Rape. The evaluation and management of rape and sexual abuse: a physicians' guide. U.S. Department of Health and Human Services, Public Health Services, NIMH, Rockville, MD, 1985

49. Summit R: The child abuse accommodation syndrome. Child Abuse Negl 7:177, 1983

50. Teixeira WR: Hymenal colposcopic examination in sexual offenses. Am J Forensic Med 2:209, 1981

51. Tilleli JA, Turek D, Jaffee AC: Sexual abuse in children. N Engl J Med 302:319, 1980

52. Tipton AC: Child sexual abuse: physical examination techniques and interpretation of findings. Adolesc Pediatr Gynecol 2:10, 1989

53. White ST, Ingram DL, Lyna PR: Vaginal introital diameter in the evaluation of sexual abuse. Child Abuse Negl 13:217, 1989

54. Woodling BA, Heger A: The use of the colposcope in the diagnosis of sexual abuse in the pediatric age group. Child Abuse Negl 10:111, 1986

55. Woodling BA, Kossoris PD: Sexual misuse: rape, molestation, and incest. Pediatr Clin North Am 28:481, 1981

19

Sexually Transmitted Diseases

Margaret R. Hammerschlag
Sarah A. Rawstron

Sexual abuse of children has become a topic of increasing concern. Children who are victims of sexual abuse are at risk for acquiring a sexually transmitted disease (STD). Until recently, attention has been mostly directed at infections caused by *Neisseria gonorrhoeae*. However, these children may be at risk for acquiring other infections prevalent in the adult population, including *Chlamydia trachomatis*, bacterial vaginosis, genital warts, trichomoniasis, and genital herpes. The identification of an STD in a child has both medical and legal implications. Increasingly, some infections are being used legally as indicators of abuse. This chapter examines the infectious complications of sexual abuse in children and discusses further studies that are necessary to provide adequate diagnosis, prophylaxis, and treatment of these complications, as well as the accuracy of these infections as markers of sexual abuse.

RISK OF INFECTION

An accurate determination of the risk of sexually transmitted conditions in victims of sexual abuse has been hindered by a variety of factors. The prevalence of sexually transmitted conditions may vary regionally and among different populations within the same region. Few studies have attempted to differentiate between infections existing prior to the assault and those acquired during the assault. This differentiation may be accomplished by examining the victim immediately after the assault to detect preexisting infection and performing a follow-up examination beyond the incubation period of any putative acquired pathogens. The presence of preexisting infection in adults is usually related to prior sexual activity. In children, preexisting infection may be related to prolonged colonization after perinatal acquisition, inadvertant nonsexual spread, prior peer sexual activity, or prior sexual abuse. The incubation periods for STDs range from a few days for *N. gonorrhoeae* to several months for human papilloma virus. The incubation period and timing of an examination after an episode of abuse are critically important in detecting infections. Multiple episodes of abuse have been found to increase the risk of infection, probably by increasing the number of contacts with an infected individual. Delayed reporting of the abuse for weeks or months afterwards can allow for incubation and prolonged carriage, especially if the infection is asymptomatic.

In most cases, the site of infection is consistent with the child's history of assault. Rates of infection will also vary with respect to the type of assault initially described. Vaginal or rectal penetration is more likely than fondling to lead to detectable infection. However, most children who are abused will have no physical complaints related either to trauma or infection.

GONORRHEA

Neisseria gonorrhoeae is the most common STD found in sexually abused children. A positive culture for *N. gonorrhoeae* from any site in a child without prior peer sexual activity is strongly suggestive of sexual abuse, although *N. gonorrhoeae* may rarely be spread by sexual play among children, or nonsexual contact. Branch and Paxton found a history of sexual abuse in 18 of 20 1 to 4-year-old children and 24 of 25 5- to 9-year-old children with positive cultures for *N. gonorrhoeae*. There is also a high rate of detection of gonococcal infection in contacts of infected children, which further supports the concept that *N. gonorrhoeae* infection in nonsexually active children is almost entirely due to sexual abuse. Even when sexual play among peers has occurred, the index case has frequently acquired the infection from abuse.

Neisseria gonorrhoeae has been found in approximately 5 percent of children suspected of having been sexually abused. As many as 20 to 25 percent of children with genital cultures containing *N. gonorrhoeae* may be asymptomatic, and an even higher number of rectal and pharyngeal infections are asymptomatic. Groothius et al. reported asymptomatic gonococcal pharyngeal infection, often without genital infection, in 7 of 16 (44 percent) children, and Rawstron et al. found that seven of eight children with rectal infections had no symptoms. The importance of obtaining cultures from multiple sites (pharynx, urethra/vagina, and rectum) in children suspected of having been sexually abused is illustrated by a survey of pharyngeal gonorrhea in Connecticut. The survey found a significant increase in the number of pharyngeal gonococcal isolates from one particular city hospital over a 1-year period. Subsequent investigation showed that a new pediatrician who was trained in detecting sexual abuse had joined the staff and was emphasizing the need to take cultures from pharyngeal and rectal sites when sexual abuse was suspected. DeJong reported that only 56 percent of abused children with gonorrhea in his series were symptomatic, emphasizing the need to culture all three sites in children suspected of having been sexually abused.

Recently, there has been a significant increase in the number of isolates of penicillinase-producing *N. gonorrhoeae* (PPNG) in the United States. Since children usually acquire their infection from adults, it is not surprising that there have been increasing numbers of children with these PPNG strains. Rawstron et al. reported on 33 children with gonorrhea, 9 (26.5%) of whom had PPNG strains. The importance of this increase is that therapy can no longer include penicillin or amoxacillin. The Centers for Disease Control (CDC) recently recommended ceftriaxone as the drug of choice for all pediatric gonococcal infections, with spectinomycin as an alternative regimen. One of the advantages of ceftriaxone is that it is effective in treating pharyngeal gonorrhea, in contrast to most other drugs.

Gram stain of the vaginal discharge in

a child with suspected gonorrhea may reveal gram-negative intracellular diplococci, but may be misleading since normal flora may also be gram-negative diplococci. Gram stain of a urethral discharge in a male is more helpful, since there are rarely false-positive results from this site.

Cultures of the pharynx, rectum, and vagina/urethra should be taken and immediately plated onto media appropriate for isolation of *N. gonorrhoeae*. The media that may be used include chocolate blood agar and Thayer-Martin media. The plates should then be placed in an atmosphere enriched with CO_2, the easiest method being an extinction candle jar. *Neisseria gonorrhoeae* are gram-negative, oxidase-positive diplococci, and their presence should be confirmed with additional tests, including rapid carbohydrate tests, enzyme-substrate tests, and rapid serologic tests. Failure to perform appropriate confirmatory tests may lead to misidentification of other organisms as *N. gonorrhoeae*. Whittington et al. found that 14 of 40 presumptive gonococcal isolates from children sent to the CDC for confirmation had been misidentified as *N. gonorrhoeae*. They included other *Neisseria* species, *Moraxella catarrhalis*, and *Kingella dentrificans*. The finding of *N. gonorrhoeae* in any culture from a child has very important implications. Therefore, it is recommended by the CDC that confirmation of an organism as *N. gonorrhoeae* should include at least two procedures that use different principles (e.g., biochemical and enzyme-substrate or serologic.)

SYPHILIS

Syphilis is not commonly found among sexually abused children, although it has been reported in a few instances. White et al. detected six cases among 108 of 409 prepubertal children on whom serologic tests were performed. Only one of the six was symptomatic with chancres, and five of the six had additional STDs. DeJong found 1 of 532 abused children had a positive serologic test for syphilis, and Hammerschlag et al. found no positive serologic tests for syphilis among 50 abused children.

Children with syphilis acquired through sexual abuse present in the same way as adults, with primary chancres, secondary syphilis, or merely with positive serologic tests for syphilis and no symptoms. Ginsberg described three patients with acquired syphilis, one of whom presented with a primary chancre and two with rashes of secondary syphilis. Similar findings have been described by Ackerman et al., who reported on three abused children presenting with rashes or condylomalata of secondary syphilis. Primary and secondary syphilis among heterosexual adults in large cities in the United States has increased dramatically in the last few years, as has congenital syphilis. It is therefore likely that we will encounter more abused children with syphilis. In our hospital in the last few months, we have seen a 2-year-old girl who had been sexually abused and presented with a typical rash of secondary syphilis. Physicians and health care workers who see patients with suspected sexual abuse should be aware of the signs and symptoms of syphilis, and every patient who is suspected of having been abused should have a serologic test for syphilis performed.

CHLAMYDIA TRACHOMATIS

Infections caused by *C. trachomatis* are probably the most prevalent STDs in the United States today. It has been suggested that the isolation of *C. trachomatis* from a rectal or genital site in children without prior sexual activity may act as a marker of sexual abuse. Although evidence for other modes of spread, such as through fomites, is lacking for this organism, perinatal maternal-infant transmission resulting in vaginal or rectal infection has been documented with prolonged infection for periods up to 2 years. Pharyngeal infection for up to 3 years has also been observed. Schachter has detected subclinical rectal and vaginal infection in 14 percent of infants born to women with active chlamydial infection. Several children were culture positive at 18 months of age.

Reports of vaginal infection caused by *C. trachomatis* in prepubertal children were uncommon before 1980. The possibility of sexual contact was frequently not discussed. In 1981, Rettig et al. reported concurrent or subsequent chlamydial infection in 9 of 33 (27 percent) episodes of gonorrhea in a group of prepubertal children. This compares with rates of concurrent infection in men and women of 11 to 62 percent, depending on the study. *C. trachomatis* was not found in any of 31 children presenting with urethritis or vaginitis that was not gonococcal. No information was given about possible sexual activity. Recent studies have identified rectogenital chlamydial infection in 2 to 17 percent of sexually abused children when routinely cultured for the organism. The majority of those with chlamydial infection were asymptomatic. In two studies that had control groups, similar percentages of control patients were also infected. The control group in one study consisted of children who were also referred for evaluation of possible sexual abuse, but were found to have no history of sexual contact, and siblings of abused children. The mean age of this group was 4.5 years, as compared with 7.5 years for the group with a history of sexual contact, suggesting a bias related to the inability to elicit a history of sexual contact from younger children. In the second study, the control group was selected from a well-child clinic. Three girls in this group were found to have positive chlamydial cultures; two who had positive vaginal cultures were sisters who had been sexually abused 3 years previously and had not received interim treatment with antibiotics. The implication of this observation was that these children were infected for at least 3 years and were totally asymptomatic. The remaining control child had *C. trachomatis* isolated from her throat and rectum; no history of sexual contact could be elicited.

The possibility of prolonged vaginal or rectal carriage in the sexually abused group was minimized in the study of Hammerschlag et al., since the chlamydial cultures obtained at the initial examination were negative and the infection was only detected at follow-up examination 2 to 4 weeks later. However, the two abused girls who developed chlamydial infection were victims of a single assault by a stranger. In the setting of repeated abuse by a family member, over long periods of time, development of infection would be difficult to demonstrate.

Recently, several culture-independent tests have been introduced for the diagnosis of chlamydial infection: enzyme immunoassays (EIA) (Chlamydiazyme [Abbott Diagnostics], Pathfinder [Kallestad Diagnostics], MicroTrak EIA [Syva]), direct fluorescent antibody tests (DFA) (MicroTrak [Syva], Pathfinder [Kallestad]), and a DNA probe (Pace II [GenProbe]). The DFA uses a fluorescein-conjugated monoclonal antibody to detect the organism directly in smears of clinical specimens. EIA and DFA are roughly equivalent in terms of sensitivity (70 to over 90 percent) and specificity (about 95 percent), compared with chlamydial culture in genital specimens from adults. The ranges of sensitivity are because of variations in specimen collection and culture methods in the studies that have compared these methods with chlamydial culture. (Data on the performance of DNA probes are preliminary.) These tests also have different advantages and disadvantages. The EIA takes 2 to 4 hours to perform, requires special equipment, and the adequacy of the specimen cannot be evaluated. However, it is objective and suitable for processing large numbers of specimens. The DFA may be faster, only 15 minutes to read a smear, but requires a very experienced and well trained reader and a fluorescent microscope. It is not an "office" test. There is a significant subjective component; individual elementary bodies have to be identified as whole inclusions are rarely seen. As of this writing, these tests are only approved for urethral or cervical specimens from adults, and for ocular and respiratory specimens from infants. The bulk of the data on test performance is from these types of specimens. There are few data available about the use of these tests in rectogenital specimens from prepubertal children, and the data that are available suggest that they are neither sensitive nor specific.

Two studies have compared DFA (MicroTrak) results with culture in vaginal and rectal specimens from over 100 sexually abused children. *C. trachomatis* was isolated from 5 of 271 tissue culture specimens, whereas the DFA was negative in all these specimens. The DFA was positive in two specimens that were culture negative. The overall prevalence of chlamydial infection (by culture) in this group of children was low, 2 percent. False positive results that may occur with the use of the DFA occur when artifactual fluorescence and bacteria are misidentified as *C. trachomatis* elementary bodies. This may even happen with experienced technicians.

Similar problems occur with the use of

EIA, specifically Chlamydiazyme, at genital sites. We recently compared the results of Chlamydiazyme with culture in vaginal specimens from 65 girls being evaluated for suspected sexual abuse. Five girls (7.7 percent) had EIAs that were initially positive; all were culture negative. On repeat testing before treatment, four had negative EIAs. The remaining girl with the persistent positive EIA test result also had group A streptococcal vaginitis. We were able to demonstrate that some strains of group A streptococcus can cause a positive reaction with the EIA. Cross-reactions also have been reported with other bacterial species commonly present in the anogenital area, including *Acinetobacter*, *Escherichia coli*, *Gardnerella vaginalis*, *N. gonorrhoeae*, and group B streptococcus.

Even the best nonculture methods have a low rate of false-positive results. If a new test has a specificity of 97 percent, by definition it yields approximately 3 percent false-positive reactions. In a low prevalence setting, this false-positive rate will create problems in interpreting the results. For example, in a population with a 3 percent prevalence of infection (seen with sexually abused children), a positive result in a test with 97 percent specificity could have a predictive value of only 50 percent. Considering the potential legal implications of a positive genital or rectal chlamydial specimen in a prepubertal child, one should only obtain cultures. The CDC in the 1989 Sexually Transmitted Diseases Treatment Guidelines strongly recommends that direct specimen antigen detection tests or DNA probe tests *not* be used on specimens from *any* victim of sexual abuse. Isolation of *C. trachomatis* by culture is standard. Isolates should be stored at $-70°C$ for possible future studies, and the use of a reference laboratory should be considered.

In summary, chlamydial infection may

be acquired by children through sexual abuse but may also be the result of perinatal exposure. Unfortunately, the probability of the latter is not known, nor do we know how long these infections will persist. In addition, these rectovaginal infections usually are totally asymptomatic. Even with a positive culture, it is difficult to define exactly how the infection was acquired.

BACTERIAL VAGINOSIS

Bacterial vaginosis (nonspecific vaginitis) is a polymicrobial infection that is apparently due to the interaction of G. vaginalis and several anaerobic bacteria. The diagnosis of bacterial vaginosis is made by examination of the vaginal secretions for clue cells (e.g., vaginal epithelial cells heavily covered with bacteria) (Fig. 19-1), the development of a fishy odor after the addition of 10 percent KOH to vaginal secretions, ("whiff test"), and a vaginal pH of more than 4.5.

Although bacterial vaginosis has been noted to be very common among adult women, it has been diagnosed infrequently in children. One possible reason is that prior studies of pediatric populations have concentrated on the isolation of G. vaginalis and have not routinely examined vaginal secretions for clue cells or odor. The CDC has stated that cultures for G. vaginalis are not useful and are not recommended for the diagnosis of this syndrome. Studies in children have suggested that G. vaginalis may be part of the normal vaginal flora, occurring in 4.2 to 13.5 percent of children.

One study examined a group of sexually abused children and a control group of children. Although G. vaginalis was isolated from the vaginal cultures of 14.6 percent of the abused girls, it was also found in 4.2 percent of the control pa-

tients. Presence of G. vaginalis was not associated with vaginal discharge in these children. Another study reported finding G. vaginalis in vaginal specimens from 37 percent of nonsexually active postmenarcheal girls (median age 15.9 years, range 13 to 21 years). Although some practitioners have suggested that the presence of G. vaginalis is an indicator of sexual abuse, the preceding data suggest otherwise.

There are data suggesting that acquisition of bacterial vaginosis is related to sexual activity. In a major study, Amsel, who diagnosed nonspecific vaginitis in 69 of 397 females consecutively presenting to a student health center gynecology clinic, failed to demonstrate the disease among 18 patients who had no history of previous sexual intercourse. Four of these sexually inexperienced patients had positive vaginal cultures for G. vaginalis, which suggests that other organisms or factors are involved in the sexual transmission of bacterial vaginosis. Other investigators have found that male partners of women with bacterial vaginosis have a high prevalence of urethral colonization with G. vaginalis.

No data exist on transmission of bacterial vaginosis between infected mothers and their infants. In addition, minimal data exist on the prevalance of bacterial vaginosis in sexually inexperienced female children. Hammerschlag et al. obtained paired vaginal wash specimens from 31 girls within 1 week and 2 or more weeks after sexual assault. None had bacterial vaginosis as defined by the presence of both clue cells and a positive whiff test at the initial examination. Vaginal pH was not used as a diagnostic criterion because the normal pH range in prepubertal girls is not well defined. At follow-up examination, four of the 31 (13 percent) girls had bacterial vaginosis. Two girls were asymptomatic. Treatment with metronidazole was followed by clin-

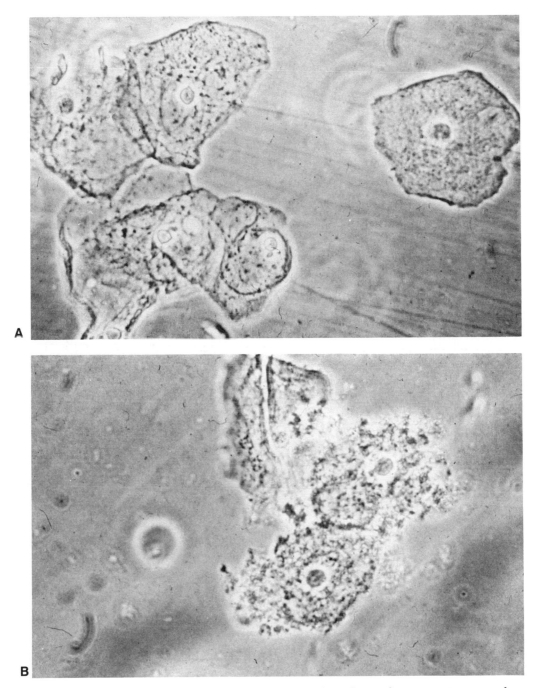

Fig. 19-1. **(A)** Photomicrograph of wet mount of vaginal washings demonstrating normal vaginal epithelial cells. **(B)** Photomicrograph of wet mount containing clue cells that are epithelial cells studded with bacteria.

ical improvement. None of the 23 control patients (nonabused children) had bacterial vaginosis.

Although bacterial vaginosis can be acquired after sexual activity, it also appears to be a common cause of vaginal discharge in children without sexual contact. We have examined vaginal washes from 29 girls, 3 months to 1 year of age, with symptomatic vulvovaginitis. Bacterial vaginosis was diagnosed in 9 (31 percent) of these 29 children. All complained of discharge that was uniformly found to be thin and ranged from gray-white to yellow in color; only three (33 percent) of these girls had a history of sexual abuse. One child also had *N. gonorrhoeae* isolated from a pharyngeal culture. Treatment with metronidazole resulted in reversion of the vaginal secretions to normal on follow-up examination. The relatively common occurrence of bacterial vaginosis in children may be partially a result of the frequent colonization of the prepubertal vagina with anaerobes, especially *Bacteroides* species.

TRICHOMONIASIS

Although nonsexual transmission of *Trichomonas vaginalis* has been reported between infected mothers and their infants, the exact risk to the infant is unknown. However, the presence of this organism in prepubertal girls strongly suggests sexual abuse. As with other STDs, perinatally acquired infection can be an important confounding variable. The length of perinatally acquired trichomoniasis has been assumed to be very short, 2 to 3 months after birth. We have recently seen two female infants with well documented neonatal trichomonal infection that persisted for 6 and 9 months, respectively, before the infants were finally treated. In most reports of infection with *T. vaginalis* in prepubertal children published before 1978, the possibility of sexual activity or abuse is not discussed. In one study of unselected girls presenting to a well-child clinic, *T. vaginalis* was identified in two girls. Both were postmenarcheal and one was sexually active. Both were symptomatic.

In most reported studies, wet mounts were infrequently performed in asymptomatic sexually abused children and often were not performed in abused girls who had a vaginal discharge. Patients with trichomoniasis may be asymptomatic and have negative wet preparations. In one study in which both wet mounts and cultures were used, trichomoniasis was found in 2 of 31 abused children at a follow-up examination, but not at an initial examination. *T. vaginalis* was not identified in the children who served as control subjects. Trichomonads are not infrequently seen in urine collected for other purposes. If they are bagged specimens from young children, especially girls, they may have their source in the vagina, or may represent fecal contamination. There is one commensal species, *Trichomonas hominis*, which can inhabit the colon and is thought to be nonpathogenic. The only way the two species can be differentiated is by the presence of an undulating membrane that extends most of the length of the organism in *T. hominis* but only one-half the length of the organism in *T. vaginalis*. In addition, old urine specimens may also be contaminated with *Bodo* species or other free-living flagellates, especially if the urine collection vessel is open to the air and is not sterile. The presence of a trichomonad in a vaginal specimen has greater significance. Although some workers feel that wet mount examinations are as efficient as culture for the diagnosis of *T. vaginalis* infection, current evidence suggests that cultivation methods are superior. There are several commercially available culture media. Recently, a conjugated monoclonal antibody stain that appears to be both sensitive and specific has been described, but available clinical data are limited. It has not been evaluated as yet for the diagnosis of trichomoniasis in children.

Although it has been suggested that infection with *T. vaginalis* may be accidentally transmitted via fomites, no cases have been reported in the literature. In conclusion, the presence of *T. vaginalis* beyond the first year of life is suggestive of sexual abuse or contact in a prepubertal girl.

CONDYLOMA ACUMINATA (GENITAL WARTS)

Genital papillomas in adults are transmitted by sexual intercourse. The majority of these are caused by human papilloma virus type 6 (HPV-6) or HPV-11, and smaller numbers are caused by HPV-16 and HPV-18. The etiology of genital papillomas in children is less well studied but sexual abuse by an infected adult, or less likely, contact with warts at other body sites has been suggested. Human papilloma viruses can also be transmitted to infants at birth, causing laryngeal papilloma. The condyloma may affect the vulva, perineum, vaginal introitus, and periurethral areas. Girls seem to be affected twice as frequently as boys, although this may reflect a difference in patterns of reporting rather than a true epidemiologic observation.

The risk of developing genital warts in sexually abused children has not been adequately assessed because no studies included data on long-term follow-up. However, one-half of the cases of genital warts in children reported since 1976 were related to sexual abuse. A recent report examined genital tract papillomas in five children for the presence of HPV DNA by molecular hybridization. Papilloma virus DNA was detected in each sample. The samples were found to contain HPV-6, HPV-11, or HPV-16. These types are the same as those responsible for genital warts in adults. Sexual abuse was thought likely to have occurred in three of these children. Although there was no history of maternal condylomata at the time of birth in the remaining two children, many genital infections in women are subclinical, and flat warts of the vulva and vagina may go unnoticed by the affected individual and the physician.

It is very unlikely that hand or common warts are transmitted from caretakers to children, with resultant genital warts. Modern HPV typing has not revealed HPV-1 and HPV-2, which are the types associated with common warts in the anogenital area. Studies have found no correlation between the frequency of hand warts and genital warts.

The major confounding variable in linking the presence of genital warts with sexual abuse is ruling out perinatal acquisition. Maternal HPV infection may be more common than previously thought. One study has found evidence of HPV as defined by DNA probes in 4 percent of male infants undergoing routine circumcision. The prolonged incubation period, or period of latency before clinical condyloma are evident, further complicates this issue. It is impossible to define the longest latency period between virus infection at delivery and the presence of clinical disease. The average latency period appears to be approximately 3 months but may range up to 2 years. A child who is first found to have perianal condylomata at 20 months of age may have had visible disease that could have been detected on close inspection (with colposcopy) 6 months earlier.

Most cases of childhood condyloma occurring beyond the plausible incubation period (2 years) after acquisition at delivery are probably due to child abuse. Other means of transmission are unlikely. It is theoretically possible for anogenital condylomata to be inadvertently transferred from caretakers during activities such as shared bathing, but this has never been proved conclusively. The prolonged incubation period would also make it difficult to determine when abuse occurred.

INFECTIONS WITH GENITAL MYCOPLASMAS

The genital mycoplasmas include *Ureaplasma urealyticum* and *Mycoplasma hominis*. *U. urealyticum* causes an unknown proportion of cases of nongonococcal urethritis in men and has been associated with chorioamnionitis, spontaneous abortion, and low birth weight. *Mycoplasma hominis* can cause pyelonephritis, pelvic inflammatory disease, postpartum and postabortal fever, and rarely, scalp abscesses and central nervous system infection in infants.

Colonization with the genital mycoplasmas in adults is strongly correlated with sexual experience. Both *M. hominis* and *U. urealyticum* may be isolated from vaginal or urethral cultures of 10 to 20 percent and 30 to 75 percent of sexually active adults, respectively. There is one controlled study of colonization of abused and normal children with genital mycoplasmas. Pharyngeal, anorectal, and genital cultures from 47 girls who had been sexually abused and from 36 healthy girls who served as controls were examined for *M. hominis* and *U. urealyticum*. *M. hominis* was isolated from the anorectal and vaginal cultures of 11 (23 percent) and 16

(34 percent) of 47 abused girls as compared with 3 (8 percent) and 6 (17 percent), respectively, of 36 control patients. *U. urealyticum* was isolated from the anorectal and vaginal cultures of 9 (19 percent) and 14 (30 percent) of the abused girls as compared with 1 (3 percent) and 3 (8 percent) of 36 control patients. An association of colonization with genital mycoplasmas with the presence of an abnormal discharge was also found in these children.

Although both *M. hominis* and *U. urealyticum* were isolated more frequently from the vaginal and anorectal cultures of abused compared with control children, the organisms were still found in a sizeable percentage (3 to 17 percent) of the control patients. Colonization was also not associated with any symptoms. In conclusion, the presence or absence of genital mycoplasmas may not be useful as an indicator of sexual abuse, since they occurred frequently in the control children.

HERPES SIMPLEX VIRUS INFECTION

Primary genital herpes infections occur most frequently in adolescents and young adults. There have been less than 20 cases of genital herpes infection reported in prepubertal children. As with many of the other STDs discussed here, the possibility of sexual abuse was not even mentioned in all the cases reported before 1968. In the cases reported later, sexual abuse was documented in the majority of the children. Although most genital herpes simplex virus (HSV) infections in adults are type 2, as many as 10 percent may be caused by type 1. It has been suggested that HSV-1 infections in children are probably primarily nonsexually transmitted. A study reviewed charts of children younger than 13 years for culture-proven HSV infection. Six children were identified; five had HSV-1 and one had HSV-2. Sexual abuse was documented in four of these children, including three of the five with HSV-1. The other two children were thought to have autoinoculated themselves in the genital area from an oral infection. This latter mode of acquisition of HSV infection is not uncommon, but the appearance of the genital lesions can usually be documented as shortly following the appearance of oral lesions.

Since usually only those children with a clinical presentation suggestive of herpes are cultured, we do not know if there is a genital reservoir of HSV in normal children. The risk of acquiring herpes after sexual abuse has not been quantified accurately. It should be possible to match isolates from a child and possible perpetrator by restriction endonuclease analysis (DNA fingerprinting).

HUMAN IMMUNODEFICIENCY VIRUS

Consideration should also be given to screening for human immunodeficiency virus (HIV) infection in victims of sexual assault, including children. Although there are no studies available documenting the risks of transmission in this situation, there have been individual reports where acquisition through sexual assault seemed likely. HIV, like hepatitis B virus (HBV), can be transmitted through homosexual or heterosexual activity, and screening for infection may be indicated in each instance. There is one reported case of HIV infection in a 10-year-old girl, ostensibly acquired through prior sexual abuse. Unfortunately, like several other STDs, a major confounding variable in the association of HIV and sexual abuse is the possibility of perinatally acquired infection. In the previously mentioned case, the child's mother's sexual partner was an IV drug abuser, HIV status unknown. The mother subsequently died of AIDS. There were no data given on the status of the father. It is possible in this case that the child acquired her HIV infection from the mother. In many of the cases of pediatric HIV infection thought to be acquired through sexual abuse that we have reviewed, the mother has been HIV positive.

Investigators in Newark, New Jersey have reported some children with probable perinatally acquired HIV, first presenting with infection at 8 to 9 years of age. Although the usual incubation period appears to be 18 months, it is possible that it may extend for years in some individuals. The group in Newark now screen all sexually abused children for HIV, not for forensic purposes, but because they feel that sexual abuse is an epidemiologic risk factor for HIV infection in their population.

HIV can be tested for in several ways. The most widely available methods are serologic. Serologic testing uses enzyme-linked immunosorbent assay (ELISA) kits to detect antibodies to HIV. The kits have been rated as highly sensitive and specific, but the sensitivity and specificity may vary among kits, laboratories, and populations. There are false-positive and false-negative results, and predictive value of a positive test will be dependent on the prevalence of HIV infection in the population tested. In a population where the prevalence of HIV infection is rare, the predictive value of a positive ELISA test will be low. To rule out false-positive results, all positive ELISAs are usually repeated. Then if still positive, a more specific test, usually Western blot (immunoblotting) or less commonly, radio-immunoassay or indirect fluorescence assay, is done. In the Western blot test, the patient's serum reacts with electrophoretically separated viral antigens, which results in a banding pattern of antibody to specific viral proteins. Although the Western blot is considered to be a specific confirmatory test, technical difficulties and varying criteria for interpretation may lead to invalid results. Sometimes, the band pattern will not meet the criteria for being positive, but bands are present, indicating an immunoreaction to some viral proteins. These results are usually reported as indeterminate, and the patient will need to be retested later.

Serodiagnosis in infants and children can be more difficult than adults. Passively acquired maternal HIV antibodies may persist for more than 1 year after birth. Unfortunately, there are no consistently useful methods for detecting anti-HIV IgM.

The other types of methods that can be used for diagnosing HIV infection are those that detect the virus directly. Unfortunately, culture of HIV is expensive, and insensitive as well as not generally available. Recently, several assays have been made available that can screen blood or other body fluids for HIV antigens, specifically the P24 core antigen. These assays have not yet been fully evaluated. Preliminary studies have shown, however, that many HIV infected children do not have detectable antigen in serum.

The newest method for directly detecting HIV is the polymerase chain reaction (PCR), which can be used to detect HIV DNA in peripheral blood leukocytes. In this test, small quantities of HIV DNA can be detected. The HIV DNA is enzymatically amplified and then detected by means of a system of HIV specific nucleotide primers and probes. PCR is still an investigational technique.

OTHER INFECTIONS

There are several other STDs of either relatively low frequency in the adult population or that have not yet been described in children who have been sexually abused. Lymphogranuloma venereum (LGV), which is caused by the LGV biovar of *C. trachomatis*, is a systemic infection of relatively low frequency, but it appears to be increasing. In the classic presentation, the infected individual initially develops a painless papule on the genitalia, which is usually asymptomatic. The patient (usually male) presents later with painful inguinal adenopathy with fever, headache, and malaise. The buboes may rupture, leading to formation of fistulae. Women frequently do not present with buboes, since the lymphatic drainage of the labia and vagina are to the retrovaginal fistulae. Rectal infection with the LGV biovar can result in a proctocolitis that can mimic ulcerative colitis. There have been 20 possible cases of LGV in children reported in the English literature since 1935. The most recent case was reported in 1973.

Chancroid is caused by *Haemophilus ducreyi*, a small, nonmotil, gram-negative, nonspore-forming rod. Clinically, chancroid usually presents initially with a small inflammatory papule on the preputial orifice or frenulum in men, and on the labia, forchette, or perianal region in women. The lesion becomes pustular and ulcerative within 2 to 3 days. There is also an associated painful, tender, inguinal adenopathy in over 50 percent of cases. Unlike LGV, the characteristic ulcer of chancroid is concurrent with lymphadenopathy. Recently, there has been a dramatic increase in reported cases of chancroid in the United States, especially in urban areas such as Los Angeles, New York, and Miami. Although no reports of chancroid in children have been found in the literature, we may see it with increasing incidence in the adult population.

Infection with HBV may also be a complication of sexual abuse. It has been recommended that male victims of homosexual rape be screened for HBV infection. While homosexual behavior is a well recognized risk factor for acquiring IIBV infection, there is also a similar increased risk among heterosexuals with multiple sex partners. Screening for HBV probably should also be included in the medical evaluation of the child victim of sexual assault.

PROPHYLAXIS AND TREATMENT

The laboratory procedures that are indicated for the evaluation of a sexually abused child are listed in Table 19-1. The CDC recommends that children receive prophylaxis only if there is evidence that the assailant is infected. Follow-up cultures and serology testing are required in cases of acute assault or molestation. Treatment guidelines are given in detail in Appendix E. For therapy of gonorrhea, the CDC now recommends the use of ceftriaxone, 125 to 250 mg IM because of the increasing prevalence of PPNG. In cases of penicillin allergy, spectinomycin, 40 mg/kg as a single IM injection may be used. Spectinomycin may fail to eradicate N. gonorrhoeae from the pharynx. Five days of oral trimethroprim/sulfamethoxazole can be effective in this situation. Therapy with ceftriaxone will also treat incubating syphilis.

The recommended regimen for early, primary, secondary, or latent syphilis of less than 1 year duration, is benzathine penicillin G, in a total dose of 50,000 U/kg IM to a maximum of 2.4 million U. The

Table 19-1. Laboratory Studies That are Indicated as Part of the Evaluation of Sexually Assaulted Children at Initial and Follow-Up Examinations[a]

Gram stain of any genital or anal discharge	+
Cultures for *Neisseria gonorrhoeae* and *Chlaymydia trachomatis*, if available	+[b]
Serologic tests for syphilis	+
Wet preparation for trichomonads and clue cells	+(girls)
Whiff test	+(girls)
Vaginal culture for *Trichomonas vaginalis*, if available	+(girls)
Frozen serum sample	+
Cultures of lesions for herpes simplex virus	+
Hepatitis B surface antigen	+[c]
Human immunodeficiency virus antibody	+[c]

[a] All studies should be repeated 7 days later, except for syphilis and hepatitis B serologies, which should be obtained 12 weeks later.
[b] Systematic genital and extragenital cultures should be obtained from all children.
[c] Obtain if there is supportive epidemiologic evidence.

patient with syphilis should be followed up with repeat nontreponemal titers at 3, 6, and 12 months after treatment. If nontreponemal antibody titers have not decreased fourfold by 3 months with primary or secondary syphilis, or by 6 months in early latent syphilis, or if signs or symptoms persist and reinfection has been ruled out, patients should have a cerebrospinal fluid examination and be retreated appropriately.

Chlamydial infections may be treated with oral erythromycin, 50 mg/kg/d to a maximum of 2 g/d in adolescents, for 7 to 14 days. Children older than 8 years of age may be treated with tetracycline, 25 to 50 mg/kg/d for 7 days.

There is little clinical information on

the treatment of bacterial vaginosis in children. Metronidazole 15 mg/kg/d, q8h for 7 days appears to be effective. Ampicillin and amoxicillin have been recommended as alternative regimens, when the use of metronidazole is contraindicated, but they are less effective. The combination of amoxicillin and clavulonic acid (Augmentin, Beecham) may be effective, since it offers better coverage for anaerobic bacteria, especially *Bacteroides* species.

Although there are no published studies in children, trichomoniasis in adult women can be successfully treated with a single oral 2.0 g dose of metronidazole or 250 mg by mouth three times daily for 7 days. The few cases of trichomoniasis in prepubertal girls reported in the literature were treated with 7-day courses of metronidazole.

None of the currently available therapies is completely satisfactory for the treatment of genital warts in adults, and less information is available for children. Children have been treated with local application of podophyllin, cryosurgery, electrosurgery, ablation with carbon dioxide laser, and 75 percent trichloroacetic acid. Treatment of genital warts in children can be complicated and should be performed in consultation with an expert.

Genital herpes infection is a viral disease that may be chronic and recurring, and for which no known cure exists. Antiviral agents may shorten the duration of symptoms and promote faster healing, but they do not eliminate the virus from the body. For the first clinical episode in adults, oral acyclovir, 200 mg by mouth five times daily for 7 to 10 days, when initiated within 6 days of onset of lesions will shorten the median duration of first episode eruptions by between 3 and 5 days and may reduce systemic symptoms. However, therapy with acyclovir will not affect the subsequent risk, rate, or severity of recurrence. More than one-half of

the cases of genital HSV infection in abused children reported in the literature have had recurrences. Some of these children received topical acyclovir, but oral therapy is now preferred. Unfortunately, treatment with oral acyclovir has only minimal benefits in patients with recurrent episodes.

SUGGESTED READINGS

1. Ackerman AB, Goldfaden G, Cosmides JC: Acquired syphilis in early childhood. Arch Dermatol 106:92, 1972
2. Branch G, Paxton R: A study of gonococcal infection among infants and children. Public Health Rep 80:347, 1965
3. Centers for Disease Control: 1989 Sexually transmitted diseases treatment guidelines. MMWR 38:No.S-8, 1989
4. Davis AJ, Emans SJ: Human papilloma virus infection in the pediatric and adolescent patient. J Pediatr 115:1, 1989
5. DeJong AR: Sexually transmitted diseases in sexually abused children. Sex Transm Dis 13:123, 1986
6. Ginsburg CM: Acquired syphilis in prepubertal children. Pediatr Infect Dis 2:232, 1983
7. Glaser JB, Hammerschlag MR, McCormack WM: Epidemiology of sexually transmitted diseases in rape victims. Rev Infect Dis 11:246, 1989
8. Groothius J, Bischoff MC, Javregui LE: Pharyngeal gonorrhea in young children. Pediatr Infect Dis 2:99, 1983
9. Hammerschlag MR, Cummings M, Doraiswamy B et al: Nonspecific vaginitis following sexual abuse in children. Pediatrics 75:1028, 1985
10. Hammerschlag MR, Doraiswamy B, Alexander ER et al: Are rectogenital chlamydial infections a marker of sexual abuse in children? Pediatr Infect Dis 3:100, 1984
11. Hammerschlag MR, Rettig PJ, Shields ME: False positive results with the use of chlamydial detection tests in the evaluation of suspected sexual abuse in children. Pediatr Infect Dis J 7:11, 1988
12. Ingram DL, White ST, Durfee MR et al:

Sexual contact in children with gonorrhea. Am J Dis Child 136:994, 1982

13. Neinstein LS, Goldenring J, Carpenter S: Nonsexual transmission of sexually transmitted diseases: an infrequent occurrence. Pediatrics 74:67, 1984

14. Rawstron SA, Hammerschlag MR, Gullans C et al: Ceftriaxone treatment of penicillinase-producing *Neisseria gonorrhoeae* infections in children. Pediatr Infect Dis J 8:445, 1989

15. White ST, Coda FA, Ingram DA et al: Sexually transmitted diseases in sexually abused children. Pediatrics 72:16, 1983

16. Whittington WL, Rice RJ, Biddle JW, Knapp JS: Incorrect identification of *Neisseria gonorrhoeae* from infants and children. Pediatr Infect Dis J 7:3, 1988

20

Specimen Collection in Sexual Abuse

Mireille B. Kanda
Lavdena A. Orr

Modern society has viewed the sexual victimization of children with incredulity and great ambivalence. For many, childhood is romanticized as a protected time of blissful innocence that should not be marred by expressions of sexuality, let alone the horrors of sexual exploitation. At the same time, the media bombard us almost daily with detailed accounts of child sexual abuse usually perpetrated not by strangers but by trusted adults.

To reconcile these conflicting paradigms, professionals and others look for explanations beyond the obvious. The credibility of children is questioned as well as the motivation of the adults who bring forth allegations of abuse. Sometimes the rights of the child are denied in an effort to protect the adult.

In cases of alleged sexual abuse, circumstances unique to the victimization of children make the assessment process particularly challenging. The pediatric patient may be too young or may be too developmentally delayed to offer a clearly articulated history of sexual contact. The older child may be subjected to bribery, intimidation, or even threats and so may be more likely to recant previous allegations or refuse to provide information. The parent who accompanies the child, usually the mother, may find herself defending the child's credibility, particularly if her own relationship with the alleged offender is so antagonistic that she could be falsely accusing him.

Sexual contact may have occurred a long time before disclosure of the abuse and may have been of such a nature that the activity did not produce permanent physical injuries. Even in cases of recent abuse, it is not unusual for the results of the physical examination to lack enough specificity to attribute the findings exclusively to sexual abuse.

The medical evaluation becomes a complex and delicate task fraught with many subtleties and the potentiality for conclusions that can evoke catastrophic consequences for either the victim or the alleged perpetrator. Forensic tests may produce the only objective evidence that sexual contact has occurred, and an entire criminal prosecution may rest on this evidence. It is thus essential that specimen collection of forensic evidence take place in an organized, consistent, efficient, and reliable manner.

FORENSIC EVIDENCE

Forensic evidence may serve four major purposes:

1. It may support and validate historical and physical findings.
2. It may determine that sexual contact has occurred by proving the presence of sperm or semen and/or documentation that the victim has a sexually transmitted disease.
3. It may specifically identify an offender or it may exonerate a given suspect.
4. It may provide a reasonably accurate time frame for the occurrence of certain events, particularly in fatal cases.

GENERAL GUIDELINES

Procedural guidelines are essential for optimal specimen collection. The examiners should have a definite idea about what should be collected; should go about the process in an organized sequence that can be later defended in court if necessary; and finally, should clearly document their activities.

Patient Communication

It is very useful to explain to the child or adolescent what is going to take place. This both builds trust in the examining physician and helps to demystify the process. The quality of the specimens collected will depend greatly on the ability of the examiner to elicit cooperation from the patient. An uncooperative patient may render the process meaningless and, even worse, negative results from poorly performed tests may create a false sense of security particularly where sexually transmitted diseases (STDs) are concerned.

Even the older adolescents who do not want to press charges against an offender may be encouraged to have the abuse documented, because this information may have future value if they change their mind or in jurisdictions where rape victims are required to report an assault if they are to access victim assistance resources or publicly funded abortion services.

Protocols

Institutional, departmental, or professional protocols are quite useful as outlines of a prescribed sequence of activities. Protocols prevent oversight of certain procedures or the conduct of unnecessarily "creative" approaches or shortcuts, which in the final outcome may detract from the validity of the tests. Each institution should have a clearly written protocol, which delineates the types of tests to be done and the manner in which they are to be performed. The protocol should also specify responsibility for transport and processing of collected specimens. The protocols will vary in length and complexity, depending on the size of the institution and the number of individuals who will become involved in collecting and handling specimens.

Protocols also present the advantage of serving as useful quality assurance tools; however, it should be noted that once guidelines are established, failure to follow them may result in institutional and personal liability. For these reasons, protocols should be carefully and clearly constructed and in-service training provided to those who will use them.

Chain of Possession Procedures

These procedures are a good adjunct to protocols, documenting the passage of specimens through the hands of various professionals and technicians. Chain of possession forms track the evidence from initial collection to final results, and their use prevents challenges in court about the possibility of mixed patient identity and inaccurate laboratory results. These forms can be easily developed internally by institutions. Figure 20-1 provides an illustration of the form used at Children's National Medical Center, Washington, D.C.

CHILDREN'S HOSPITAL
NATIONAL MEDICAL CENTER
DEPARTMENT OF LABORATORY MEDICINE

ALLEGED SEXUAL ASSAULT
SPECIMEN CHAIN OF POSSESSION FORM
Slip #552

ADDRESSOGRAPH

SPECIMENS SUBMITTED
(Physician: Please check appropriate boxes; do not write in space for Acc. No.)

CLINICAL MICROBIOLOGY
CLINICAL VIROLOGY
SMEARS AND WET MOUNTS

Neisseria gonorrhoeae   Acc. No.

1. ☐ Urethral Gram Stain   _____

Trichomonas vaginalis   Acc. No.

2. ☐ Wet Mount   _____

Chlamydia trachomatis
Direct Fluorescent Antibody   Acc. No.

3. ☐ Cervix   _____
4. ☐ Urethra   _____
5. ☐ Rectum   _____

CULTURES

Neisseria gonorrhoeae Acc. No.	Chlamydia trachomatis Acc. No.	Herpes simplex virus Acc. No
6. ☐ Cervix _____	11. ☐ Cervix _____	16. ☐ Cervix _____
7. ☐ Vagina _____	12. ☐ Vagina _____	17. ☐ Vagina _____
8. ☐ Urethra _____	13. ☐ Urethra _____	18. ☐ Urethra _____
9. ☐ Rectum _____	14. ☐ Rectum _____	19. ☐ Rectum _____
10. ☐ Throat _____	15. ☐ Throat _____	20. ☐ Throat _____

MISCELLANEOUS

Treponema pallidum   Acc. No.   Acc. No.

21. ☐ Rapid Plasma Reagin   _____   22. ☐ Sperm Motility   _____

CLINICAL CHEMISTRY
                            Acc. No.   Acc. No.

23. ☐ Urine Pregnancy Test (βHCG)   _____   24. ☐ Acid Phosphatase   _____

OTHER *(Please specify)*
                            Acc. No.   Acc. No.

25. ☐ ....   _____   26. ☐ ....   _____

IMPORTANT

Submitting physician must sign at right to document that specimen chain of possession was properly initiated.

Laboratory director(s) must sign at right to verify that specimen chain of possession was properly maintained.

Submitted by _____
              Physician   Date

Verified by _____
              Director, Clin. Micro.   Date

            _____
              Director, Clin. Virol.   Date

            _____
              Director, Clin. Chem.   Date

CHNMC FORM 201 (FRONT) (Rev 7/87) Not on Disk

A

Fig. 20-1. (A & B) Chain of possession form. (*Figure continues.*)

FORENSIC (MEDICOLEGAL) SPECIMENS
CHAIN OF POSSESSION

Any case in which sexual abuse is suspected has potential medicolegal significance. In all such cases, it is essential that the continuity of possession be unbroken from the time the sample is obtained until the laboratory analyses are completed. If you suspect that a specimen will develop forensic importance, each hand through which it passes must be documented by the donor and the recipient. Complete and accurate identifying information must be affixed to all specimen containers and forms. The form below will assist in documenting all such transactions. Please call the laboratory for instructions if you are uncertain as to how to handle the specimen.

REMEMBER, the results of the test may have no judicial value if the chain of possession is not completed.

Received From: _____
By: _____
Date: _____ Time: _____
Location: _____ Specimen Nos.: _____

Received From: _____
By: _____
Date: _____ Time: _____
Location: _____ Specimen Nos.: _____

Received From: _____
By: _____
Date: _____ Time: _____
Location: _____ Specimen Nos.: _____

Received From: _____
By: _____
Date: _____ Time: _____
Location: _____ Specimen Nos.: _____

Received From: _____
By: _____
Date: _____ Time: _____
Location: _____ Specimen Nos.: _____

Received From: _____
By: _____
Date: _____ Time: _____
Location: _____ Specimen Nos.: _____

B

Fig. 20-1 *(Continued)*. **(B)**

Sex Offense Kits

Sex offense kits ("rape kits") augment the value of protocols. By providing all the necessary collection receptacles and instruments in one compact package, the kit allows the examiner to follow a step-by-step approach and to be sure that all appropriate procedures are completed. Sex offense kits tend to be designed for adult rape victims and may require some modifications in technique to accommodate children and young adolescents. Figures 20-2 and 20-3 provide an example of a commercially produced sex offense kit.

Sex offense kits are relatively expensive, but the convenience that they offer is well worth the cost. They are often purchased by the police and provided to hospitals and practitioners at the time of the medical evaluation.

If a commercially manufactured kit is not available, one may be created to sat-isfy the needs of a particular institution. Consultation with the forensic laboratory that will process the specimens is advisable. In developing a kit, the type and shelf life of any required preservative solutions should be considered. The contents of the kit should include a chain of possession form and a checklist to ensure that no specimen is missed or misplaced. Finally, the kit should have a permanent closure with a seal to prevent evidence tampering after collection.

METROPOLITAN POLICE DEPARTMENT Criminal Investigations Division Sex Offense Branch Cat. No. MDC-100 **SEX OFFENSE KIT**	SEX CASE NUMBER COMPLAINT NUMBER CSES NUMBER

This kit contains materials for collecting evidence in alleged Sex Crimes. Directions for each step are printed on the appropriate envelope or card. Each specimen or sample must be clearly identified.

PROTOCOL

Step No. 1 — Debris Collection	Step No. 5 — Head Hair Pulled
Step No. 2 — Pubic Combings	Step No. 6 — Swab Specimens
Step No. 3 — Pubic Hair Pulled	Step No. 7 — Saliva Sample
Step No. 4 — Head Hair Combed	Step No. 8 — Whole Blood Sample

☐ MALE

☐ FEMALE

NAME OF PATIENT

MEDICAL RECORD NO.

NAME OF EXAMINING PHYSICIAN

NAME OF HOSPITAL/CLINIC

LAW ENFORCEMENT USE ONLY

DATE OF OFFENSE

TIME OF OFFENSE

LOCATION OF OFFENSE

SEX INVESTIGATOR

CSES TECHNICIAN

DATE

TIME

LAB USE ONLY

LAB NUMBER

DATE RECEIVED

EXAMINED BY

Fig. 20-2. Sex offense kit (front view).

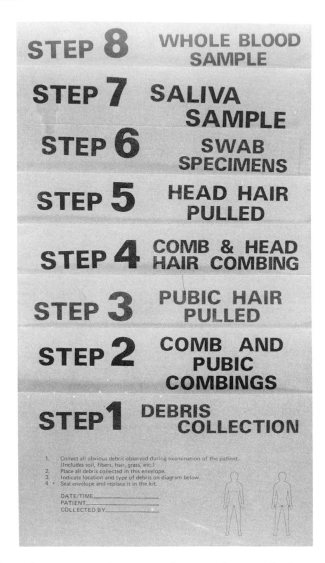

Fig. 20-3. Sex offense kit: steps are documented on envelopes to facilitate collection process. (Manufactured by Sirchie Finger Print Laboratories, Raleigh, North Carolina.)

The evidence collected with sex offense kits is usually only recoverable during the first 72 hours following the last sexual contact. Consequently, these kits have little value if the events occurred more than 3 days before the examination. Unless there is a suspicion or a disclosure suggesting that the abuse is of recent origin (72 hours or less), the use of the sex offense kit is not mandatory or cost-effective.

Kits generally do not include collection materials for tests for sexually transmitted diseases. These tests are usually handled according to a separate protocol. However, the presence of an STD obviously has the forensic value of suggesting sexual victimization in a child who is too young to give informed consent to voluntary sexual activity.

Documentation

Documenting the collection of forensic evidence supplements the other components of the medical evaluation (history and physical examination). This documentation must be accurate, complete, and legible. It should be part of the medical record and not included solely in the police report via medicolegal forms. It must be retrievable long after the examination has taken place, because there is often a considerable delay in the criminal prosecution of sexual abuse cases.

As long as a protocol prescribes in detail the procedures to be followed in cases of alleged sexual abuse, the medical record does not have to list every test performed, it may instead state "sex offense kit completed." The examiner should be prepared to explain the tests that were conducted. Any deviation from the protocol should be explained and documented.

Medicolegal forms vary in length from one jurisdiction to another depending on their content and the level of detail that each one requires. They may be as brief as a one page document or they may cover several pages. In many jurisdictions they are used as the initial statement by the examining physician and they may be supplemented by the more elaborate report contained in the patient's medical record. Both documents should be completed fairly concurrently to avoid discrepancies or inconsistencies that would later create court challenges. The least amount of information required on some of these forms refers to the size of the introitus (vaginal opening), the condition of the hymen, and the anal sphincter tone. Many other observations may be made in the course of the examination and the description of additional findings (e.g., scars, skin tags, fissures, etc.) adds to the corroborative value of other evidence.

METHODS OF COLLECTION

The methods of collection described below are applicable to the assessment of children and adolescents when the examiner suspects that sexual contact has occurred within the last 72 hours. A more limited collection takes place when the abuse is less recent.

Photography

Photography brings a new dimension to the forensic evaluation of child sexual abuse. It allows a permanent visual documentation of injuries and evidence with much greater clarity than the written word can usually provide. It is not universally available but can be of great benefit.

Current techniques vary from photography of gross injuries to the painstaking interpretation of colposcopy findings. Investigators will sometime bring their own equipment to the emergency department or the office and take photographs themselves. By virtue of their role, they can do so without permission from the patient.

By contrast, if a physician includes photography as a part of the forensic examination, it is advisable to obtain written consent from the patient or the parent accompanying the minor. The consent form should clearly state the purpose and intended use of the photographs (i.e., forensic documentation, teaching, and diagnosis). The patient should also be told of the circumstances in which the photographs will be released and the parties who would be entitled to request them.

Videotaping the entire medical evaluation for forensic documentation may become more of an accepted practice in the future. A decision to employ such a technology in cases of child sexual abuse should be made after careful consideration of advantages and drawbacks.

Clothing

If the patient is wearing the same clothing that was worn during the assault, the garments should be scanned with a Wood's lamp for evidence of seminal fluid, which may present as fluorescent stains. If stains are observed, the item of clothing should be placed in a plastic bag and given to the investigator. If the infant or toddler is wearing a diaper, it should be collected and added to the evidence. The same applies to any tampon or sanitary pad worn by the postpubertal victim after the assault.

Debris and Foreign Material

Any debris or foreign material found on the patient should be placed in an envelope and also added to the collected evidence. Any area of fluorescence on the patient's body should be gently swabbed with a cotton-tipped applicator that has been moistened in normal saline. The swab should be labeled and saved for analysis. Fingernail scrapings should be obtained if there is any history or evidence of struggle during the assault.

Hair

Hair sampling is obtained for the comparison of specimens belonging to the victim with any yet unidentified samples (collected at the scene or during the examination), which may belong to an alleged offender. Hair samples, which consist of both loose hair obtained from combings and hair plucked from the scalp or pubic area, are used as control specimens definitely known to belong to the patient.

Although plucked hairs are preferable because they provide the hair bulb, it may be more practical and less painful to cut the hair close to the skin when children have already been traumatized by an assault. Prepubertal children obviously cannot provide pubic hair samples.

Hair and fiber analysis, although involving microscopic study specimens, does not provide the same level of specificity that other tests offer. Neutron activation analysis is much more precise but is costly and its use limited to a few forensic facilities.

Saliva

Saliva may be obtained by swabbing the oral cavity or by asking the patient to expectorate on a piece of filter paper or gauze. Saliva collection is best done early in the sequence of tests to allow the specimen to air-dry while the other samples are being collected.

Blood

In cases of recent assault, a blood specimen is required for typing. A single venipuncture may provide enough blood for typing and other serologic tests for syphilis, herpes, hepatitis B, and human immunodeficiency virus (HIV) if these are deemed to be necessary based on history and physical findings. Like the bacteriologic tests for STDs, the serologic tests are usually processed separately from the other forensic tests.

Orogenital Specimens

Although the initial history may only suggest genital contact, it is not unusual to find out later that sexual victimization has involved other sites of the body. Consequently, the oropharynx, the rectum, and the vagina or penile urethra are sampled in the course of evidence collection.

These specimens are obtained to detect specific markers of sperm or seminal fluid. Additional inference of the occurrence of sexual contact is drawn from the presence of STDs. In acute cases of STDs, the presumption is that any such disease predates the assault, although in some instances it is possible to recover an organism such as the gonococcus within 72 hours of contact. Usually, however, initial sampling for venereal pathogens is part of a baseline evaluation, documenting that the acquisition of the organisms took place at the time of the assault and became manifest days to weeks later. Presence of an STD in the preadolescent strongly suggests molestation. As many pediatric victims are repeatedly sexually assaulted over long periods of time, the documentation of an STD at the "baseline" examination supports the history of molestation.

The specimens are obtained with sterile swabs, moistened with nonbacteriostatic, sterile saline solution to avoid uncomfortable scraping of tender mucosal surfaces, particularly in the urethral and vaginal areas. Specific collection techniques are discussed in Chapter 19.

Table 20-1 lists the tests that are required in acute situations, and Table 20-2 lists the sites to be sampled when the assault occurred more than 72 hours before the examination.

All swabs except the ones collected for

Table 20-1. Sexual Abuse Forensic Testing: Lapse Less Than 72 Hours

Site/Specimen	Test
Vagina/cervix	Gram stain[a] (sperm identification)
	Swabs for seminal fluid (acid phosphatase, semen glycoprotein (P30), mouse anti-human sperm-5 (MHS-5) monoclonal antibody, DNA fingerprinting[a]
	Gonorrhea culture[b]
	Chlamydia culture[b]
	Routine vaginal culture[b]
	Wet mount[b] (Sexually transmitted disease and motile sperm)
Rectum	Wet mount (sexually transmitted disease and motile sperm)
	Swabs for seminal fluid[a] (as above)
	Gonorrhea culture[b]
	Chlamydia culture[b]
Penile urethra	Gonorrhea culture[b]
	Chlamydia culture[b]
	Wet mount[b] (sexually transmitted disease)
Oropharynx	Gonorrhea culture[b]
	Wet mount or Gram stain[b] (sperm)
	Saliva[a]
	Swabs for seminal fluid[a] (as above)
Blood	Serology test[b] for herpes,[c] syphilis, human immunodeficiency virus antibody,[c] hepatitis[c]
	Typing[a]
Urine	Urinalysis[b]
	Urine culture[b]
	Pregnancy in postpubertal girls[b] (repeat in 2 weeks)
Other	Clothing and debris collection[a]
	Fingernail scrapings[a]
	Hair samples[a]

[a] Part of sex offense kit. Give to investigators.
[b] Deliver to hospital laboratory.
[c] As indicated.

Table 20-2. Sexual Abuse Forensic
Testing: Lapse More Than 72 Hours

Specimen	Test
Urine	Urinalysis[a] Urine culture[a] Pregnancy in postpubertal girls (repeat in 2 weeks)
Blood	Serology tests for herpes,[a] syphilis, human immunodeficiency virus antibody,[a] hepatitis[a]
Vaginal/cervical swabs	Gonorrhea culture Chlamydia culture Routine vaginal culture Wet mount (for sexually transmitted disease)
Pharyngeal swab	Gonorrhea culture
Penile urethral swab	Gonorrhea culture Chlamydia culture Wet mount (for sexually transmitted disease)
Rectal swabs	Gonorrhea culture Chlamydia culture

[a] As indicated.

cultures and wet mounts should be thoroughly air-dried before storage. Avoid lengthy storage in plastic bags, which do not allow for air circulation and thus promote the overgrowth of molds. All specimens should be labeled and promptly delivered to the investigator for transportation to the forensic laboratory, where the samples will be frozen until processing can take place. Cultures should reach the bacteriology laboratory expeditiously to avoid drying and loss of organisms.

Along with the collected specimens, a couple of dry, unused and untouched swabs from the same batch should be sent to the forensic laboratory; they can be used as controls, if necessary.

LABORATORY TESTS

Documentation of Sexual Contact

Sperm Detection and Motility

The presence of sperm in the body orifices of a victim provides reliable evidence that sexual contact has occurred. However, the circumstances usually surrounding the sexual victimization of children make this discovery less likely than in adolescent and adult rape cases: the assessment of child victims often takes place days to months after the last sexual contact has occurred and the sexual activity tends to include fondling and vulvar coitus more than full vaginal or rectal penetration. The prepubertal child does not produce cervical mucus favorable to spermatozoa so that sperm deposited intravaginally has a decreased survival time.

Spermatozoa are identified microscopically from a Gram stain preparation or a Papanicolaou smear. Additional information may be gained by examining a fresh wet mount specimen from the vagina or cervix of a rape victim. Motility usually ceases within a few hours of ejaculation although it has been reported up to 72 hours after coitus. In live victims, spermatozoa are rarely recovered from the vagina after 72 hours although in homicide cases this interval may be expanded to months.

Acid Phosphatase

Difficulty in identifying spermatozoa in vaginal samples has led to the search for other components of the ejaculate. Prostatic acid phosphatase, which is produced independently from sperm, has been used as a sensitive marker of recent coitus. The respective merits of these two tests have been debated at length by a number of investigators. It would appear at this time that both tests are extremely valuable and complementary. Because there is no correlation between the survival time of sperm and that of acid phosphatase, they should be used concurrently. One of their common limitations is the short period of time (less than 72 hours after coitus) during which either or both of them can be identified. In addition, the age of the victim, the nature of the sexual encounter, and other factors specific to the perpetrator may further decrease the efficiency of sperm or acid phosphatase detection. These factors include sexual dysfunctions, alcoholism, and other pathologic or surgical conditions that produce oligospermia or aspermia.

Other Tests

P30, a semen glycoprotein of prostatic origin, was first isolated in 1978 and has been described variously as γ seminoprotein, semen E1 antigen, and prostate specific antigen. It is detected by an enzyme-linked immunoabsorbent assay (ELISA) and it is male specific so that its presence in any amount in vaginal specimens indicates sexual contact. P30 can be recovered up to 48 hours after intercourse and is very stable on dried specimens. It offers levels of sensitivity and specificity superior to the acid phosphatase test and is now used extensively in forensic laboratories.

Mouse anti-human sperm-5 (MHS-5), a monoclonal antibody, binds to a sperm coating peptide secreted by human seminal vesicles and allows the identification of seminal fluid in forensic specimens. It is part of a new technology and is currently available in a kit for laboratory use. It is very recent and appears promising in confirming sexual contact.

Pregnancy Tests

These tests document indisputably that sexual contact has occurred. They may be supplemented by ultrasonography to ascertain the age of the pregnancy and determine whether the time of conception matches the time of the alleged assault.

Sexually Transmitted Diseases

The prevalence of STDs in sexually abused children is relatively low. However, it varies among studies, with a high number of 12 percent for gonorrhea and 17 percent for chlamydia. Thus, the presence of an STD in a child too young to provide informed consent to sexual activity is strongly suggestive of sexual abuse. The weight of this evidence varies depending on the STD under consideration. For example, gonorrhea has been convincingly shown to be most often associated with sexual abuse in prepubertal children beyond the newborn period. Chlamydia infections, although very suggestive of abuse, may represent a persistent infection acquired at birth in very young children.

The forensic assessment of suspected cases of sexual abuse is strengthened by testing for the most common STDs, which include gonorrhea, syphilis, chlamydial infections, and trichomoniasis. Depending on history and physical findings, it might be advisable to test for herpes genitalis, hepatitis B, and HIV antibody. The association of HIV infection with sexual abuse is currently under study by several researchers and definitive guidelines for testing will have to await the conclusion of these studies. Unless seroconversion is clearly documented after an assault, the lengthy interval between infection and the development of symptoms renders any causal association between acquired immunodeficiency syndrome (AIDS) and a specific incident of child sexual abuse rather tenuous. In cases in which the abuse occurred less than 72 hours before the medical evaluation, the patient should be retested at a later date (1 month for other STDs and 3 months for syphilis and HIV infection), to ensure that no incipient or asymptomatic infection was missed.

Perpetrator Identification

The tests described so far serve to establish that sexual contact has taken place by corroborating the history given by the victim. Another group of tests is directed toward the identification of specific offenders.

Blood Typing

It has been demonstrated that 75 to 80 percent of individuals in the general population secrete water-soluble blood group substances such as semen, vaginal secretions, and saliva into their body fluids. If the alleged offender is a secretor and if blood typing shows that the markers recovered from the victim or at the crime scene are identical to those secreted by him, a strong inference may be drawn from the test results. Further clarification can be attained by using other blood grouping systems such as ABH, Lewis, and MN systems. If further specificity is desired, human phosphoglucomutase typing may be used.

Paternity Tests

In cases in which a pregnancy resulting from sexual abuse culminates in the delivery of a live birth or a fetus, HLA typing or DNA fingerprinting may be used to establish the paternity of the suspect.

DNA Fingerprinting. In the early 1980s, Jeffreys developed a technique that allows the identification of a specific individual through the analysis of blood, semen, and other body fluids. This process, based on the unique genetic makeup of each individual, matches DNA fragments from a specimen under study with known radioactive fragments known as "DNA probes." Hybridization of complementary strands occurs and when the preparation is placed in contact with x-ray film, an image of bands with a specific pattern appears on the film. This unique banding pattern may then be compared with other specimens and a conclusion can be drawn regarding the similarity or dissimilarity of the samples. This test has been used in paternity suits and in other legal proceedings when questions arise regarding the genetic relationship of two or more individuals. To date, the most dramatic application of this technique has been linkage of a potential suspect with an unknown sample collected from the vagina of a rape victim or at the scene of a crime. Because of its recent development, the test has been accepted in certain courts but challenged in others. As its use spreads to more forensic laboratories, its acceptability will become more widely established. The specificity provided by DNA fingerprinting surpasses by far that of other tests such as ABO typing or hair analysis. According to researchers in the field, the chances that two unrelated individuals will have the same DNA fingerprint are 1 in 1 quadrillion. Even in siblings (except identical twins) the chances of identical DNA fingerprints are 1 in 10 trillion. Figures 20-4 and 20-5 illustrate the DNA fingerprinting process.

In summary, careful collection of forensic evidence is an indispensable part of the medical evaluation in cases of suspected child sexual abuse. Although this process may not produce a great yield when the abuse occurred more than 72 hours before the examination, the identification of specific markers or the presence of a sexually transmitted disease contributes immensely to the corroboration of historical or physical findings that may lack specificity. This evidence may make the difference between cessation of the abusive activity or its continuation with potentially severe and permanent sequelae for the child victim.

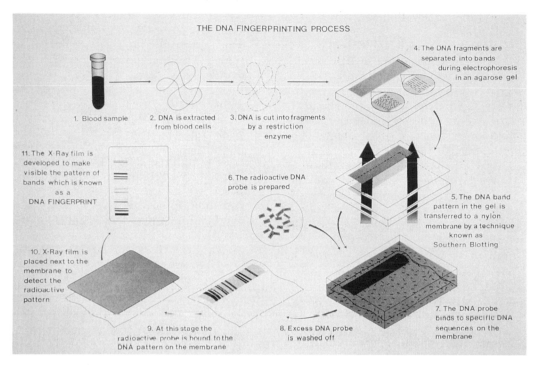

Fig. 20 1. The DNA fingerprinting process. (From Cellmark Diagnostics Manual,[2] with permission.)

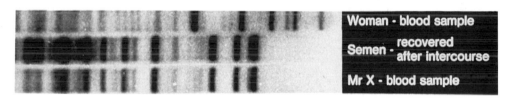

Fig. 20-5. DNA fingerprinting banding pattern allows for comparison of different specimens. (From Cellmark Diagnostics Manual,[2] with permission.)

SUGGESTED READINGS

1. Academy of Pediatrics: Guidelines for the evaluation of sexual abuse of children. Pediatrics 87:254, 1991
2. Cellmark Diagnostics Manual: DNA Fingerprinting. Cellmark Diagnostics, Germantown, Maryland, 1988
3. DeJong AR, Finkel MA: Sexual abuse of children. Curr Probl Pediatr 20:535, 1990
4. DeJong AR, Finkel MA: Sexual abuse of children. Curr Probl Pediatr 20:539, 1990
5. DeJong AR, Rose M: Frequency and significance of physical evidence in legally proven cases of child sexual abuse. Pediatrics 84:1022, 1989
6. Dodd BE: DNA fingerprinting in matters of family and crime. Nature 318:506, 1985
7. Enos WF, Conrath TB, Byer JC: Forensic evaluation of the sexually abused child. Pediatrics 78:385, 1986

8. Forensic Science: Don't Miss a Hair. FBI Law Enforcement Bulletin, Washington, D.C., 1976

9. Graves HCB, Sensabaugh GF, Blake ET: Post coital detection of a male-specific semen protein. N Engl J Med 312:338, 1985

10. Herman-Giddens ME, Frothingham TE: Prepubertal female genitalia: examination for evidence of sexual abuse. Pediatrics 80:203, 1987

11. Herr JC, Summers TA, McGee RS et al: Characterization of a monoclonal antibody to conserved epitope on human seminal vesicle—specific peptides: a novel probe/marker system for semen identification. Biol Reprod 35:773, 1986

12. Jeffreys AJ, Wilson V, Thein SL: Individual-specific "fingerprints" of human DNA. Nature 316:76, 1985

13. Kanda MB, Thomas J, Lloyd D: The role of forensic evidence in child abuse and neglect. Am J Forensic Med Pathol 6:7, 1985

14. McCann J: Use of the colposcope in childhood sexual abuse examinations. Pediatr Clin North Am 37:863, 1990

15. Neinstein LA, Goldenring J, Carpenter S: Nonsexual transmission of sexually transmitted diseases: an infrequent occurrence. Pediatrics 74:67, 1984

16. Paradise J: The medical evaluation of the sexually abused child. Pediatr Clin North Am 37:839, 1990

17. Price CJ, Davies A, Wraxall BGD et al: The typing of phosphoglucomutase in vaginal material and semen. J Forensic Sci Soc 16:29, 1976

18. Ricci LR: Medical forensic photography of the sexually abused child. Child Abuse Negl 12:305, 1988

19. Ricci LR, Hoffman SA: Prostatic acid phosphatase and sperm in the post coital vagina. Am Emerg Med 11:530, 1982

20. Schwarcz SK, Whittington WL: Sexual assault and sexually transmitted disease: detection and management in adults and children. Rev Infect Dis, suppl. 12:S682, 1990

21. Silverman EM, Silverman AG: Persistence of spermatozoa in lower genital tract of women. JAMA 240:1875, 1978

22. Soules MR, Pollard AA, Brown KM et al: The forensic laboratory evaluation of evidence in alleged rape. Am J Obstet Gynecol 130:142, 1978

23. The Bureau of National Affairs, Inc: HLA testing for paternity. Family Law Reporter 13:1557, 1987

24. The Bureau of National Affairs, Inc: DNA Fingerprinting ID method may streamline investigations. BNA Criminal Practice Manual 1:425, 1987

25. Wintrobe M: Clinical Hematology. 8th Ed. Lea & Febiger, Philadelphia, 1981

21

Special Interviewing Techniques

Toni Seidl

> Grown-ups never understand anything by themselves, and it is tiresome for children to be always explaining things to them.
>
> *The Little Prince*
> by Antoine De Saint-Exupéry

Fortunately, we practice at a time when the sexual abuse of children is, for the most part, no longer denied and no longer tolerated by our society. The children that come to us for care are the first generation of children who have permission, in a sense, to disclose their abusive encounters to a generation of professionals who are able to hear them. Yet the diagnosis of the problem and the accurate and thorough assessment of child victims is far from being accepted as an exact science. Controversy exists about how complaints of sexual abuse of children should best be managed by each of the many complex systems involved, about the role of the criminal justice system, about the efficacy of various treatment modalities, and, of primary importance for our purposes, the process and adequacy of interviews with child victims.

The assessments and interventions by those who care for children and who are therefore mandated by law in all jurisdictions to report the suspicion of child sexual abuse to the child welfare system, and, in some communities, to the criminal system as well, have come under increased scrutiny. This scrutiny is continually fueled by the backlash movement. The movement to doubt children's reports of abuse and to criticize and undermine those who serve as advocates on their behalf evolved in the 1980s when parents and community members were forced by the increasing number of persistent complaints to acknowledge that children were indeed being sexually abused by trusted adults. This was not an easy acknowledgment for a society that views children as primarily asexual, for a society that views itself as child centered, and for a society that views adults as being in control of their darker impulses. In addition, the public sector's mandated response to the problem was evaluated as threatening to the pervasive concept of children as property. For many individuals and groups, any questioning of boundaries within the family unit was considered to be intrusive. Unfortunately, the result may very well be decreased reporting of child sexual abuse owing to fear and anxiety on the part of health care practitioners. We hope that this will not occur. Rather, the necessary

279

response by practitioners needs to be thoughtful and responsible assessment with reporting as obliged and full cooperation with the mandated agents. No one is in a better position to advocate for children than pediatric health care practitioners who have made children their professional priority.

PREPARING FOR CHILD ADVOCACY

Two mind sets are imperative when practitioners are called on to integrate child sexual abuse interviewing into their professional repertoire of skills. First, a good interview will be therapeutic for the child, and second, health care practitioners need not and should not see themselves as investigators or validators of complaints. As practitioners, our role is to diagnose whether a suspicion of child sexual abuse exists. Through this definition of role comes clarity of purpose: we are assessors of risk and mandated reporters if we suspect child sexual abuse. Our purpose is to enable the child to be heard and understood by the individual systems responsible for investigation and validation of child sexual abuse. Indeed, our work may ultimately be used by the child welfare system, with the goal of protecting children, and by the criminal justice system as part of an adversarial process. However, that is not our primary purpose, which is an honest and valid assessment of children and their needs.

The question arises: which profession is best suited to evaluate children suspected of being sexually abused? Because health care practitioners are perceived by children and their families as being unconditionally child oriented, being fluent in child development, and acting as neutral forces in the community, they are often called on by parents, care-

takers, and professionals of all disciplines to offer an impression as to whether child sexual abuse has occurred. However, health care professionals must also possess other qualities that are helpful when interviewing and assessing child sexual abuse, such as awareness of sexuality issues and a high comfort level for discussing sexual material with children. Additionally, they must be in control of their own feelings regarding the sexual abuse of children and those who perpetrate it. This is no easy task, as we know how outrageous an act it is and how damaging sexual abuse is to a child. Certainly, those who are nonplussed by the abuse of children should not be doing this work. On the other hand, those who believe that each and every abuser should be executed cannot be effective either. Practitioners need to be in control of their feelings to be effective. Those feelings often include frustration with systems that do not adequately protect children, rage at persons who abuse children, and the need to rescue children from less than adequate parents or caretakers. What is most difficult to tolerate and mask is the pain experienced when a child describes sexual activity that is beyond belief, and that violates every tenet of adult-child behavior.

THE INTERVIEW

It is safe to say that the interview with the child is the keystone on which the assessment of child sexual abuse rests. Without it, we have only a set of behavioral, and possibly physical symptoms. A prompt complaint or concern of a parent or caretaker is often absent. The exception being the rare instance where the abuse is observed and reported by a credible third person in a timely fashion and accepted by the child welfare and criminal justice systems at face value.

Many preconceived notions exist regarding the interview with the child. One that can impinge not only on the interviewer, but on the parent/caretaker as well, is the belief that the interview is inherently traumatic. On the contrary, we have found that when the interview is well orchestrated, thoughtful, and sensitive, the child is not traumatized, but psychologically freed. Children who have walked into an emergency department or a physician's or social worker's office, burdened and anxious, can literally skip out after a supportive disclosure. Conversely, the poorly conducted interview by an ill prepared or insensitive practitioner who is unaware of the child's needs will, at the very least, increase the child's anxiety and decrease the child's ability to report a history of sexual abuse. Poorly conducted interviews are counterproductive for the child's safety in that potentially protective information may very well be lost. Care must be taken not to turn a nonrevealing interview into a negative one where the child is badgered or cajoled.

The Setting For the Interview

The site of the interview is frequently but not necessarily the emergency department. This route to help is often made by parents or caretakers in response to their "sense of crisis" rather than the need for acute medical care or the collection of forensic evidence. Whenever possible, the visit, or at least the interview portion of the visit, should be rerouted to an alternate site that offers privacy, quiet, and the absence of interruption.

The presence of two practitioners is the ideal for evaluating and interviewing the child. Most children can establish a rapport with more than one person with relative ease provided that the interviewers have mutual goals and complementary styles. One individual will need to assume primary responsibility for the interview with the other assuming the role of recorder and supplementary interviewer if necessary. Most children are tolerant of the interviewer who states, "Let's see if Dr. Steve understands what we are talking about" or "Let's see if Dr. Steve has any questions for you."

Without a doubt, being subjected to many interviews and possibly many interviewers over a period of days or even weeks, is disruptive for any one of us, including children who have experienced sexual abuse. Expanding the number of individuals who interview a child to more than two needs to be accomplished in a thoughtful and purposeful manner and only under extraordinary circumstances. The child, no matter how young, needs to be told who the individuals are and why they are in the room. One then needs to establish with the child that it is "OK" for each person to participate. Young children need to be asked for permission for another interview whenever possible. This is an issue that arises frequently in academic settings where the tension always exists between advocating for the individual child and advocating for children in general by encouraging others to pursue this work.

Process of the Interview

To proceed in the most fluid way possible, the interview can be divided into four discrete components: (1) parents/caretaker and child together; (2) parents/caretaker alone; (3) child alone; and (4) closure with parents and child together. This fourth step may need to be divided into two if the parent(s) previously had minimal awareness of the nature and extent of abuse as revealed by the child. Practitioners also want to avoid the parents' intemperate expression of emotion in front of the child, who may feel responsible for their upset.

Parents and Child Together

The purpose of meeting with the parents or caretaker and child together is primarily to establish, for all involved, the reasons why the visit was requested and to determine what can be achieved. This effort creates a context in which the practitioner can join with the family and establish trust and credibility. The stage is then set for the practitioner to request that parents give their children permission to engage with the practitioner alone, out of the parents' presence. Positive interaction between parents and practitioner serves to enhance the concepts of permission and trust.

As health care providers we must be aware that we are indirect players in the process of child protection and the elaborate community systems of accountability. We must be realistic with parents about what we cannot do for them and for their child, as well as what we can do. We can inform, but cannot direct the civil and criminal systems. We can attempt to facilitate a statement from a child that confirms or denies child sexual abuse as part of the physical assessment. Every parent or caretaker we serve needs to know from the outset that interviewing children is a skill and an art, dependent on many variables, for example, the setting, establishing a relationship, the child's internal and fluctuating sense of relevancy of the conversation, timing, distractibility, and sometimes luck. In other words, just as the physical examination alone is not the acid test for child sexual abuse, the one-time interview does not usually offer the answer to the question, "Has this child experienced sexual abuse?" On the positive side, the interview may in fact be diagnostic. However, it may only serve to suggest the direction for clinical investigation in search of the truth. In the end it is this truth that will provide protection for the child.

The practitioner must also determine the parents' motivation and the steps they have taken prior to coming for help. Has the child been assessed prior to the visit? Have the civil and criminal systems already been involved? Are the parents solely in pursuit of the response they want, or are they open to the possibility that sexual abuse may not have occurred? Are they realistic about what the practitioner can offer? What is the history of their concern? Is the concern child or adult generated? Do they support the practitioner interviewing the child alone? And if not, why not? Parents also need to be informed of the process and possible outcomes of intervention by the mandated systems that may, of necessity, be involved. They need to be apprised of the practitioner's mandate to share records and offer opinions, regardless of whether these are the opinions the parents desire. All of the above are areas and issues that differentiate between interviewing by health care practitioners and interviewing by mandated investigative persons. The process is always directed toward establishing a trust with parent and child. This can only be created through clearly elucidated ground rules and parental awareness and acceptance of our mission as child advocates to do our best with and for the child. This is essential, not only because it imposes a tacit contract, but also because it affords protection for the professionals who must accomplish their tasks objectively and in good faith. To function any other way, we risk not championing the independent cause of the child, and we make ourselves unnecessarily vulnerable as professionals in what we know is an overly litigious environment.

Parent Alone

When meeting separately with parents or caretakers the practitioner's goal is to gather information about the child. What is the child's routine, and where and with whom does the child spend time? Do conflicts exist about parenting? Are the parents concerned about a specific person or a particular setting? Where is the child in school, in relation to cognitive development and language skills? Is this a family with open doors, or are the boundaries rigid and the doors always closed? Are sexually active adolescents in the picture? What are the sleeping arrangements? What are the child care arrangements? What are the parents' perceptions of the child's awareness regarding sex and sexuality before this presentation? Is child custody an issue? Are drugs and alcohol involved? And, finally, with which words does the child describe genitals and toileting practices? At this point, practitioners should note and clarify the language but they should not make any assumptions about meaning. We have heard specific words mean anything and everything. "Butt" can be the buttocks or the vagina and "private parts" can mean the nipples.

We frequently use the time alone with parents to reiterate our approach and our mandates. We hope that they will begin to form a trusting relationship with us on behalf of their children.

Child Alone

Having established, in the parent's presence, that the practitioner is a person who "talks to children when parents are worried that something may have happened that shouldn't have," the child will usually be able to allow the parent to leave the interview room or office and wait outside. All but the most traumatized and needy children will permit this, the exception being young preschoolers who are demonstrating an appropriate and

predictable developmental stage. Ways of encouraging children to stay in the room include asking the parent to leave a coat, briefcase, or pocketbook in the room, and/or allowing the child to move out a chair "for daddy or mommy to wait on." Sometimes, the ambivalent child can be helped to establish distance and to separate by leaving the door open a bit. This enables young children to "touch base" and view a parent if they need to.

Practitioners may need to go to terrific lengths to interview children out of the presence, and therefore the influence, of their parents, whenever possible. This is a goal, simply because it is the best way, given the constraints of time, to establish a relationship with the child and get the most reliable, detailed information. Even highly motivated, well informed, and emotionally stable parents are hard put not to react emotionally when they hear sexually explicit material come from their child's lips or see demonstrations or drawings of sexual acts. Parents who are greatly in need of righting a wrong, expiating guilt, and establishing control have a hard time refraining from directing the interviewer and coaching the child.

Establishing Rapport. For individuals who are experienced in working with children, rapport can be established rather quickly and with relative ease with comments about the office setting and its contents, family, school, pets, and peers. This not only serves to get adult and child in synchrony but adds to the data base of information and helps to assess developmental and psychological status. It is important for children to be told at the appropriate cognitive level why a practitioner is speaking with them. By asking children to relate why they think that they were brought to the office is not only a good jumping-off point, it also serves to alert the interviewer to any misinformation the child may have and creates the opportunity to inform. Most children find sufficient reassurance when they are told that the practitioner is the person at the hospital whose job it is to talk to kids "about worries and feelings and to make sure that they are safe." Practitioners also add that they do this because they choose to and because they really like being with children.

Developmental Sensitivity. Obviously, these concepts are presented in a developmentally appropriate way, with care not to be condescending to the latency age children who are often struggling to be mature beyond their years. These 9- to 11-year-old children have special issues that are important to acknowledge. Latency age children are notoriously adept at appearing as if they know much more than they do about adult material, including sex and sexuality. They often know the sexual words and stylized behaviors, but not the true meaning of the words and behaviors. Unfortunately, this only serves to mislead practitioners into believing that children have mastery over more than they really do. To complicate matters further, latency age children are known to be hesitant about their emerging sexuality, leaving them at great psychological risk. This is in contrast to children who are too young to understand the implications of the perpetrator's aberrant behavior, and in contrast to some adolescents who may have age appropriate peer reference points for sex and sexuality. It is hoped that adolescents who have had one-time abusive encounters can begin to respond to our support with an intellectual understanding regarding the alleged perpetrator's misuse of power. A painful exception to this is the adolescent who finally discloses years of sexual abuse and is therefore at exquisite psychological risk. Unfortunately, this is the more prevalent presentation for adolescents. This is not to say that sexual abuse at any age is benign, because it never is.

Engendering Child Comfort. A few additional conditions for the interview are very important. An anxious or upset child will need to be interviewed in the presence of the uninvolved parent. Children do best when they are allowed reasonable choices about where they wish to sit or which toy they would like to explore. The presence of another professional to observe and record the interview frees the practitioner to fully attend to the child and the task at hand, unencumbered by the need to maintain an accurate recording. This process also proves to be much less distracting to the child. Additionally, interviewers need to be comfortable with their own bodies, to allow children to point to and touch the interviewer's body, if necessary.

Specifics of Sexual Abuse. As the child is guided from the general areas of school friends and home life to the specific purpose of the visit, interview tools such as markers and paper, a doll house, and anatomically correct dolls and drawings may be helpful. For all but the very youngest children, markers and paper have been found to be the most productive, and least leading, interview tools. In the end, however, it cannot be emphasized enough that the most useful tool is the practitioner's skill in understanding and establishing relationships with children.

The act of drawing while talking with the children is a helpful activity with several purposes. It is the best way to engage a child effectively; it is a demonstration of caring and valuing; it establishes that practitioners are approachable adults; and it serves to help the child to feel in control. After all, drawing is perceived as "kid stuff." The content of the drawing provides grist for discussion because it represents the child's world, for example, family, household members, pets, peers, and the house. As each character is drawn, or as the rooms of the house are plotted, directed conversation follows, and relationships and feelings are explored. With the child's permission, the drawing may be dated and labeled and, if the child allows, the conversational exchanges may be written in as they are described. Children overwhelmingly find this to be great fun, and the professional has an on-the-spot, mutually created, recording.

The details of sexual contact unfold with the use of nonleading and open-ended questions such as, "Have you ever been touched where you didn't want to be?" If the response is affirmative, the next question is, "Who was it that touched you?" and then if indicated, "What did the person touch you with?" Child health care practitioners are required to keep in check the natural impulse to provide the child with directed answers. Although directed answers temporarily rescue the child, in the end they undermine the validity of the complaint. Exceptions to this process must, however, be made when the likelihood of sexual abuse is high and the child is unable to respond to indirect questioning. Examples of this would be the child with a sexually transmitted disease or an injury to the genitalia. To protect those children, direct questioning may need to be employed. The child will benefit from hearing, at the appropriate times, comments directed toward avoiding guilty feelings. Such a comment might be, "It's not your fault that this happened." As interviewers do this, they must be sensitive to the quality and character of the relationship between the child and the alleged perpetrator. Hearing from the interviewer that the person is "bad" and "should be punished" is not necessarily beneficial to the child; this may indeed exacerbate the child's vulnerable state, since children frequently have ambivalent feelings about the perpetrator, and the dynamics of sexually abusive interactions almost always result in the child feeling somewhat responsible for the abuse and the abuser.

At The Children's Hospital of Philadelphia, we find the anatomically correct dolls to be helpful specifically with the very young or verbally limited child. We do not use these dolls as a first line diagnostic tool, but rather to help clarify what a child has said, drawn, or acted out. We have found that using the dolls initially only results in demonstrations without a context for understanding and can lead to inaccurate interpretations of behaviors. Additionally, we find doll play distracting, and we are almost always hard pressed to redirect the very young child with functional attention and separation spans of 20 minutes or less.

Filling in Detail. If and when the child is able to describe an abusive contact, it is best to establish when and where the abuse occurred and who was present, and to obtain as much detail as possible about the actual contact. Here, the practitioner must be concrete and very specific in choosing the words and language used in questioning the child. A child with gonorrhea vaginitis may respond "on" in answer to the question, "Were your panties on or off when Uncle Joe touched your private parts?" However, we need to look at the question and rephrase it from the child's point of view, that is, "Tell me where your panties were." Here the answer may very well be, "Around my feet, silly!" Then we can ask, "How did they get there?" or "Who put them there?" Most ambiguous and confusing statements from children are due to clumsy questioning, rather than incompetent children. As interviewers, we do our best when questions and statements are most direct. We prefer statements such as,

"Tell me his words," when inquiring about the perpetrator's statements to the child, rather than, "What did he say," which is a vague question, at best, for a young child.

Determining the timing of the abusive event(s) may prove to be more difficult than establishing a history of sexual contact. Child-relevant markers such as routines, holidays, and events should be used, rather than real time, which logically has no relevance for young children. Questions such as, "Was it a night Mommy went to bingo?" or "Was it when Dad was at work?" or "Before or after your birthday?" are the most productive. In reality, establishing the time of the event the child describes may only be helpful to a point, because most children are abused over a period of time, and the reporting typically and predictably telescopes multiple events. Because of this, practitioners should not ask children to ascribe a number to the abusive events. It is enough to ascertain whether it happened once or "lots of times." We doubt that adults could accurately cite the number of times a comparable occurrence took place in their lives.

Assessing Safety. A crucial factor in diagnostic interviewing is the assessment of the safety of the child. This translates into knowing the means of disclosure, if it occurred before the interview. Was it accidental, observed by a third party, or solely through the diagnosis of an injury or a sexually transmitted disease? Was it purposeful disclosure on the part of the child? To be thorough, the practitioner should explore the possibility that an adult other than the alleged perpetrator colluded in the maintenance of secrecy. The question to the child can simply be, "Did anyone else see or know that Uncle Joe was touching your private parts?" If this is the first disclosure, the clinician will need to explore why the child did not report the abuse before. Were bribes or special privileges involved? Was the child coerced or threatened, or was actual physical injury inflicted? Always, it must be asked whether other children were involved. None of us can afford to underestimate the lengths that those who exploit children will go to in terms of access to children and manipulation of them for selfish purpose.

Finally, if children are old enough, the following questions should be asked, "What do you think is going to happen now that you told?" "What do you want to happen?" Here, the clinician has the opportunity to reassure them, possibly to correct misperceptions, and, occasionally, to mold the system's response to their needs and wishes, thereby offering effective control to children who have been deprived of control of their body.

Resistant Patients. Special mention is due the resistant child, that is, the child who is unable to disclose abuse but who has profound behavioral or physical indicators, a sexually transmitted disease, or a related injury. It is counterproductive and countertherapeutic to "push" the resistant child. An indirect approach is much preferred, involving the exploration of the child's anxieties and fears about the hypothetical "child who told." Our children are asked, "What do you think might happen?" One must be ever aware that realistically or not, children who have experienced sexual abuse over time are preoccupied with concerns about separation and loss and the integrity of their bodies. Furthermore, they do not in any sense control their often unpredictable worlds. Consequently, reporting something as untoward as sexual abuse is, from the child's point of view, a complex and frightening task.

Terminating the Interview. Our mission, when terminating the interview alone with a child, is that the child should leave feeling safe, cared for, and with a sense of having done a good job, whether or not the interview is productive from our view. This is a relatively easy task for the child who discloses but one that must be handled well. The children should be told simply and warmly that they did "a good job," that "telling the truth is always the best thing to do," that we are "proud of them," and are "sure that their parents are too." It is our opinion that stickers, treats, and disproportionate rewards can be counterproductive, especially with the needy and deprived population that many of us frequently are called on to assess. We want to avoid the disclosure process taking on a life and purpose of its own that may serve more complex needs and create child historians who are excessively invested in telling. This is rare, but worth a word of caution, especially if criminal proceedings are to follow.

The inconclusive interview raises other issues for the clinician and child alike. Neither party should consider it a failure. We suggest leaving the door open for reinterview with yourself or someone else, and setting the stage for a later interview with the comment that you are "sure that you will be able to tell soon!"

Closure for Parents and Child

In the presence of the parents, children need to learn that the practitioner/clinician is available to them for the disclosure of more detail, if there is any, and for help. The child needs to know that the clinician will need to share information gathered, but that this does not mean it is "everyone's business." If the children are old enough, they must be asked what they hope will happen to the alleged perpetrator. Some children are extraordinarily protective of the person, and others will

bluntly state, "I want him to go to jail." Try to keep your feelings neutral. Remember that the child and family may feel ambivalent about the alleged perpetrator. Do feel comfortable in telling the child that this is not the way grownups are supposed to show children they care about them. Parents need to be helped to return the child's world to normal. They benefit from some very specific anticipatory guidance as it relates to talking about the subject when the child brings it up, but not quizzing the child or being obsessive about how the child is coping. If the child is in day-care or in school, the child's immediate return is prescribed and parents are encouraged to request that the civil and criminal child abuse response system not interfere with the child's lifestyle any more than absolutely necessary. Clinicians should offer themselves as a resource.

In an attempt to assure the parents that the child did well and that they are good and effective parents, the child's disclosure should be affirmed directly to them, they should be complimented on their child, and on the good job they have done. Finally, the system's response and the clinician's role both in and out of the system should be reviewed.

Of course the needs of parents, as well as their ability to protect their child, are essential to any thorough assessment of child sexual abuse. Most parents are realistically filled with rage at the alleged perpetrator and consumed by a sense of violation and grief. These feelings are both legitimate and predictable. The innocence treasured as a part of childhood has been lost, and the child has been exposed to sex and sexuality prematurely and in a distorted form. Parents of boys who have been abused by a male need to be helped to understand that this does not mean their son is homosexual and that there are no predisposing characteristics about their son that encouraged the event. They also need to understand that, to the best of our knowledge, an abusive contact with a male is not a predictor of future sexual preference. Parents of girls most often focus on concepts like "intactness" and virginal status. They need to hear from the practitioner, if at all possible, that their daughter is "undamaged." Most studies reveal that sexually abused children overwhelmingly have normal physical examinations; the small percentage who are diagnosed with sexually transmitted diseases respond well to treatment.

Some parents respond to the abuse with such high emotion and loss of control as to put their son or daughter at psychological risk. The clinician will then need to locate the source of the emotion and help the parents share their pain and rage.

Another reason for extreme emotion and a projection of vulnerability in a parent, even with support and mobilization of the extended family, is the parent's own history of sexual victimization. To our knowledge, no accurate statistics are available on this phenomenon, but more and more providers are coming in contact with families where sexual abuse is part of the family history. For some parents, the victimization of a child may be the first time they have either felt psychologically able to acknowledge their own victimization and seek help, or the first time they have disclosed the abuse and had it acknowledged by a professional. This response is an alert to the clinician that there are now two patients in need of crisis intervention, each with extraordinarily pressing issues. Expectations of the parents need to be treated carefully, and support will need to be abundant from both the clinician and the family system.

In general, what parents need most when their son or daughter has suffered a sexual assault is validation of feelings, support, and a relationship with a provider. They need an intelligent and sensitive listener to use as a sounding board for their feelings. In addition to anticipatory guidance, they may need concrete direction and professional advice.

ANATOMICALLY DETAILED DOLLS

Considerable controversy surrounds the use of anatomically correct or anatomically detailed dolls. Initially, criticism was leveled almost exclusively by officers of the court and defense attorneys, with the result that information facilitated through the dolls was seen as tainted and unreliable. Assessments that relied on the use of dolls during the interview were sometimes characterized as "play," and the use of the anatomically correct dolls was considered to be the equivalent of the application of leading questions. Since the mid-1970s, when attention was directed to the sexual abuse of young children, anatomically correct dolls were used in most centers without protocols, research, or the evaluation of presumably normal populations of young children. Those interviewing with dolls were largely self-taught and for the most part without specific training. But as clinicians began to see an increasing number of children with a variety of presentations and family compositions, the need for research to analyze data regarding the use and potential misuse of anatomically detailed dolls became clear. The first protocols were established in the mid-1980s.

At this juncture in the field of child sexual abuse, we have at our disposal the beginnings of a body of research to guide our work with young children. Interestingly, that research supports the empirically based practice tenets that evolved for many conscientious and self-critical clinicians who have been called on to evaluate young children. For the most part, those clinicians find the anatomically correct dolls to be most effective when they are used to supplement information gleaned from the interview with the child. Demonstrations by young children of sexual activity without the benefit of an historical context suggestive of sexual contact are not on their own diagnostic for sexual abuse.

On the other hand, it is important to note that the dolls in and of themselves are not provocative and dangerous for children. Recently, Cohn analyzed the interactions with anatomically detailed dolls of young children. The doll play of 35 two- to six-year-old children referred to a hospital child abuse clinic was then matched with that of 35 control children from the ambulatory care clinic. All of the children were assessed developmentally and observed in unstructured play with anatomically correct dolls. An interviewer was present for only part of the session. Coders who were blind to the children's group status coded the child's interaction with the dolls. Cohn concluded from her data that the dolls did not overstimulate children into sexual demonstrations or cause the children undue anxiety. She also found that sexual abuse could not be concluded from doll play alone and that there were more similarities than differences between the study group and the control group.

A second relevant study was recently completed by Levanthal et al. This analysis of the charts of 83 children supported the dilemma faced by clinicians every day (i.e., the problem of getting conclusive diagnostic information). Levanthal et al. isolated the information gleaned from doll play and assessed its value in determining the likelihood of the child having experienced sexual abuse. They concluded that the dolls were indeed a valuable supplement with all children, particularly for those younger than 3 years of age. Levanthal et al. also stressed what cannot be emphasized too much, that those who assess children must be fluent with child development, and well trained and experienced in evaluating children in general.

RECORDING THE INTERVIEW

Fastidious recording of all professional encounters is a measure of good work. Unfortunately, good work cannot stand on its own, and the creator of the reporting document is often called on to either substantiate or supplement it in both the criminal and civil court systems where sexual abuse complaints may, of necessity, be addressed. Both systems, the civil and the criminal, have different procedures but good recording is essential for both. Legible, timely, and accurate recordings not only serve to protect the child's interest, but also protect the interviewers by refreshing their memory. Adequate recording includes (1) the facts of the case, (2) the time taken for interviewing, (3) the site of the interview, (4) who was present, (5) the specifics of the allegations, (6) the emotional tenor or "texture" of the contact, and (7) the child's affect during and after the disclosure. It is also important to record and explain any special steps taken outside of usual practice. For example, if a parent was in the interview room, owing to the child's difficulty in dealing with separation, that fact should be stated and explained. Brief, pointed explanations will suffice. In our center and jurisdiction, we find it adequate to document our general inquiry of the child rather than specific questions. We do, however, take great care to record with specificity and accuracy the child's responses that are germane to the sexual contact, prior disclosures, and sense of safety from future abuse, since those issues are the domain of the court and possibly the content of our subsequent testimony. As a practice, we find it counterproductive when recording the interview to become obsessive about projecting what could happen in court regarding our testimony. A far better position is to simply create an accurate and unbiased, yet descriptive, record that one is comfortable with standing by in the future.

In this age of technology it is indeed tempting to audiotape or videotape the evaluations of young children since it appears as if the public ascribes a higher degree of authenticity to what is viewed or heard on tape than what is testified to, or documented. This appeals to us as child advocates with the theory being that we might very well save the child from multiple interviews. Compelled as we may be as advocates for children, it is worth noting that the use of videotaping is limited to children complaining of sexual abuse, rather than crime victims in general. This practice appears to be but one more indicator of society's reluctance to believe children's statements. In our experience, videotaping does not protect the child from multiple interviews and each system responding has had a need to collect its information in its own way for its particular investigative purpose. Another confounding factor is that the creation of an audiotape or videotape forces an inordinate amount of attention on the interviewer, with dissection of the technique used rather than placing the emphasis where it should be, on the child's complaint. It seems that the best approach may well be the more conventional one since the criminal justice system has yet to formulate a consistent response to the handling of taped interviews and their use in the prosecutorial process.

SPECIAL PROBLEMS: FALSE ALLEGATIONS, CUSTODY DISPUTES, AND RECANTATION

No event has created more controversy among otherwise like-thinking professionals than sexual abuse of children. This issue taps into our sense of the political, our concepts of power and vulnerability, our own personal intrapsychic material, and professional and institutional conflicts. Once we acknowledge the depth and breadth of sexual abuse, we become, of necessity, adversarial with societal belief systems. We are then called on to at least think about the socialization of our children, female as well as male, the inadequacy of our expenditure of public funds, and the ordering of national priorities. Only after thinking through the above issues can we be truly informed about the special problems commensurate with this work.

Much controversy exists regarding false allegations of child sexual abuse; in fact, child generated false allegations are infrequent, and therefore references to the issue overshadow the true measure of the problem. The whispering down the lane of false allegations is disproportionate from their actual documentation in children, not only in the literature but in practice. One type of false allegation occurs when an adult consciously imposes a history of sexual assault on a child and insists that the child repeat that history to investigative persons. In our experience, that fact pattern is very rare. One reason for this is that it is quite difficult to impose direction on a young child and assure success in the repetition of that story.

Young children almost never fabricate sexual abuse histories on their own. The reasons for this are that (1) sexual abuse content should not be within the realm of the child's world and (2) that children are not complex enough thinkers to conjure up a history of sexual abuse for the purpose of achieving their own ends. Over the years, we have seen one memorable case involving a child who initially presented with a self-generated sexual abuse complaint. This 6-year-old girl was brought to our hospital emergency department after reportedly telling her mother that her male psychotherapist had touched her genitals during a therapy session. The patient was due to testify in court the next week about another sexual abuse complaint. The child proceeded to give the social worker a detailed and clinically sound history of the sexual abuse contact. Questions were asked in several directions, and the history made sense. What was worrisome, but certainly not diagnostic, was this child's lack of congruent affect. In the end, this very bright, articulate, but vulnerable child was able to disclose to the very same police officer who was involved in her first complaint that her mother had pressured her to make the statement and that she complied to get her mother to leave her alone. What became patently clear to all involved was that although the first complaint was valid, this child's sexual abuse had fractured her mother's coping skills and that the mother was projecting her own sexual abuse history onto her child. Clearly, this was a mother-daughter dyad in need of immediate intervention.

What we see far more commonly are parents and caretakers who misperceive and make assumptions about the child's behaviors and statements. This is unfortunately fueled by the issue of child custody. The motivator is commonly child protection rather than malice. Typical examples are the 4-year-old child who returns from a visit with her mother and tells her father that "mom stuck a stick up my butt." A fastidious history and the request that the father call the mother to talk about the weekend reveals that the stick was in fact a rectal thermometer, and the father uses an oral one. Excessive masturbatory behaviors and sex play are other misunderstood behaviors which, although not necessarily related to sexual abuse, reveal either a stressed child and family system, a child who has been exposed to the sexual activities of adults or adolescents in the household, or inappropriate visual input. Certainly, these are children at risk whose families may very well require psychosocial intervention. However, they are not sexually victimized children. Here again, at the assessment level, the importance of the clinician's knowledge of child and family development cannot be stressed enough. Each scenario requires the exploration of possible content in terms of touching, hurting, the imposition of secrecy, the use of pressure and threats, and the requisite exploration of relevant details. While pediatric health care clinicians must be aware that false allegations do exist, to become obsessive about unearthing them to the point where the veracity of a child's statement is always in question is an inappropriate position.

Custody disputes are certainly difficult for all concerned, including the clinician, but they are most difficult for the child, since they are the ultimate manipulation by people who usually care very much. The extreme emotion, hurt, and hypervigilance that predictably surround separation and divorce are more responsible for sexual abuse complaints being generated at that time than the premeditated and organized false reporting. Our caution to practitioners is that they should proceed with great care in separating independent concerns gleaned from the child, from the parents' or caretakers' perception of the problem. Essential to the thorough and unbiased assessment is the awareness by the clinician that custody disputes and child sexual abuse can co-exist and that separation from the abuser may very well give rise to disclosure.

Recantation as a predictable behavioral response to the disclosure of child sexual abuse is eloquently described by Summit in his delineation of the components of the process by which children accommodate to sexual abuse. Summit aptly explains that the recantation or retraction by a child of a history of sexual abuse occurs when the reality imposed by the disclosure is worse than the abuse itself and that the wished-for relief is virtually nonexistent, at least from the child's point of view. The stress on the child may be disruption of living patterns, rage, and rejection by a loved one. Multiple interviews, loss of relationship, responsibility for the event, and other side effects of the disclosure take precedence over the relief. Since recantation is not only frequent, but predictable, it needs to be considered as part and parcel of the disclosure process, rather than as an unusual event that can lead to its being interpreted as evidence that the child's report does not possess the veracity it should.

Nonetheless, the question for practitioners then becomes, how can recantation be managed effectively without sabotaging the safety of the child? How can recantation of a true report be prevented? We find it very helpful to tell the child in the presence of the family, if age appropriate, that "sometimes things happen after you tell that makes you wish you hadn't told." Specific examples are then given to the child and family. Anticipatory guidance should be given to supportive family members about how to return the child's world to normal, how to manage the possible changes in the child's eating and sleeping patterns, play, relationships, and school work. Recommendations will also need to be directed as to whom and whom not to inform about the sexual abuse and how to, although in crisis, maintain family stability on behalf of the child. The physical and psychological safety of the child should be the priority when making these decisions. What we find to be most effective is the establishment of a supportive relationship with the caretaker. A separate relationship with the child should also be established if the child is at least of school age. This partnership throughout the disclosure and intervention process does a great deal to circumvent recantation in that it serves to reduce the anxiety on the part of the victim. These are the emotions that ultimately fuel denial and repression that is manifested as a recantation.

LOOKING TOWARD THE FUTURE: WHAT ARE OUR GOALS FOR INTERVIEWING?

On first consideration, every professional who deals with assessing children for sexual abuse has at least momentarily been eager for the creation of standards and validation tests for the evaluation of young children. What a relief it would be to have questionnaires and checklists that lead to the conclusion of "yes" or "no" to the possibility of a sexually abusive event being perpetrated on a child. Diagnostic dilemmas would be curtailed, as would stressful hours on the witness stand, the arduous creation of reports, and the stress frequently sustained. However, this position is a fleeting one for the thoughtful practitioner who understands children, child development, and the dynamics and mechanics of the sexual abuse process. Because children have varying developmental levels, cognitive and social skills, and language acquisition skills, their evaluation of such a serious incident with overwhelming medical and psychosocial implications can never be reduced to the application of tests and standards. This is not to say that our field should not generate well thought out guidelines for assessment and educational programs for clinicians. It should. But the first imperative needs to be the encouragement and support of research in the areas of child sexual abuse intervention and normal child sexual development, and the use of supplementary tools such as dolls and drawings. We are barely in our adolescence as a pediatric specialty area and as a community of child advocates. To date we possess only minimal data in these critical areas of inquiry. If we are to increase the identification of vulnerable children, we need to make real and appropriate services available to families. Finally, but most crucially in our estimation, is the integration of child sexual abuse course content into the curriculum of all professional training programs and multidisciplinary response systems in all settings that deal with children.

SUGGESTED READINGS

1. Boat BW, Everson MD: Use of anatomically correct dolls among professionals in sexual abuse evaluation. Child Abuse Negl 12:171, 1988
2. Boat BW, Everson MD: Using Anatomic Dolls: Guidelines for Interviewing Young Children in Sexual Abuse Investigations. University of North Carolina, Department of Psychiatry, Chapel Hill, 1986
3. Child Guidance Center: Young Sexual Abuse Victims: An Interview Protocol (video). Child Guidance Center, Cleveland, Ohio, 1986
4. Cohn DS: Anatomic dolls: do they accurately diagnose sexual abuse? Research presented at National Child Abuse Conference: Preparing for the Next Decade. Philadelphia, March 1989
5. Faller KC: Child Sexual Abuse: An Interdisciplinary Manual for Diagnosis, Case Management and Treatment. Columbia University Press, New York, 1988
6. Garbarino J, Stott FM, and Faculty of the Erickson Institute: What children can tell us. Josey-Bass, San Francisco, 1988
7. Jampole L, Weber M: An assessment of the behavior of sexually abused and non-abused children with anatomically correct dolls. Child Abuse Negl 11:187, 1987
8. Levanthal J, Hamilton J, Rekedal S et al: Anatomically correct dolls used in interviews of young children suspected of having been sexually abused. Pediatrics 84:900, 1989
9. MacFarlane K, Waterman J, Conerly S et al: Sexual Abuse of Young Children: Education and Treatment. Guilford Press, New York, 1986
10. Position Statement of the American Academy of Child and Adolescent Psychiatry: Guidelines for the clinical evaluation of child and adolescent sexual abuse. Child Adolescent Psychiat 27:655, 1988
11. Sgroi SM: Handbook of Clinical Intervention in Child Sexual Abuse. Lexington Books, DC Health, Lexington MA, 1983
12. Summit RC: Child sexual abuse accommodation syndrome. Child Abuse Negl 7:177, 1983
13. White S, Strom G, Santilli G, Halpin B: Interviewing young sexual abuse victims with anatomically correct dolls. Child Abuse Negl 10:519, 1986

22

Sex Rings, Pornography, and Prostitution

Ann Wolbert Burgess
Carol R. Hartman

Sexual abuse of children has traditionally focused on incest or family member (intrafamilial) abuse of girls. However, various reports indicate that a growing number of abusers are from outside the family (extrafamilial) and they abuse both boys and girls. Furthermore, reports from both the United States and the United Kingdom emphasize the need for health professionals and law enforcement personnel to increase their efforts to protect children from sex ring crimes, which involve multiple victims of the same offender.

This chapter describes sex ring crimes, child pornography, types of collectors, and youth prostitution within the context of the impact on the victim, as well as medical and psychological interventions.

SEX RING CRIMES AGAINST CHILDREN

The term sex ring crime is used to describe sexual victimization of several children by one or more adult offenders. There are three different types of child sex rings: solo, transitional, and syndicated.

Solo Sex Rings

In solo sex rings, the offender occupies a position of authority and familiarity with the children. Additionally, the children know each other and are aware of each other's participation in sexual acts with the offender. The adult recruits the children by offering them psychological, social, monetary, and other rewards in exchange for sexual services. Solo sex rings are primarily organized by age: toddlers (age 2 to 5 years), prepubescent (6 to 12 years), or pubescent (13 to 16 years). The adult meets the children through a job, occupation, or official association, through another child, or they may live in the adult's neighborhood.

Transition Rings

Although pedophilia is a sex offense in all states, there is a strong need among pedophiles to communicate with each

295

other in the spirit of camaraderie. In transition rings, the offender exchanges photographs and/or children with other pedophiles. There may be several other reasons for this type of ring. As the child in a solo ring grows older, the adult loses interest sexually and leads the child to adolescent type rings, which include prostitution.

Syndicated Rings

Syndicated rings are well structured organizations that recruit children for direct sexual services and pornography for an extensive network of customers. Many adults operate the rings, and access to children is often through an adult association.

A common feature to all the rings is that the adult uses pornography (child and adult) as a technique to normalize adult-child sex, or to demonstrate to the child how and what to model, either for pictures or for sexual activity.

CHILD PORNOGRAPHY AND COLLECTORS

There has always been a preoccupation with sexual behavior as have been recorded by paintings, graphics, pottery, and engravings. Are these works regarded as erotic art or as pornography? How is the distinction made? Similarly, it is important to distinguish between child pornography and child erotica. Child pornography is defined as any visual or print medium depicting sexually explicit conduct involving a child. Child erotica is defined as any material relating to children that is sexually arousing to an individual. Both are used for sexual arousal and gratification, but child por-

nography has the added dimension of the *effect* on the child portrayed.

What motivates the collection of child pornography? First, the collection is a way to validate the activity, and second, child pornography is a graphic acknowledgment of the activity. For the child molester, there are various uses for child pornography, including sexual gratification, lowering sexual inhibition, blackmail, a medium of exchange, and economic profit.

There are several types of collectors. (Collectors are persons who collect, maintain, and prize child pornography materials.) Indepth interviews conducted with collectors indicated that they were leaders of sex rings and were discovered because of their involvement with children in the production and use of pornographic materials. Collectors may be categorized as closet collectors, pedophile collectors, amateur or cottage collectors with a group of children, or commercial collectors with multiple groups of children.

The Closet Collector

The closet collector keeps secret his interest in pornographic pictures of nude children engaged in a range of behaviors and denies involvement with children. There is no acknowledged communication with other collectors. Materials are usually purchased discretely through commercial channels. The closet collector consciously acknowledges that children should not be used sexually by adults.

The Pedophile Collector

The pedophile collector chooses to engage in sexual activity with one child at a time, usually an immediate family member, children of neighbors, nephews, nieces, friends' children, or children in his care. This type of collector may also seek children by traveling to another community.

The pedophile collector's organization and use of pornographic materials varies from casual to meticulous. A predominant feature is their belief that they are not harming the child. They deny that fear, force, or overpowering strategies demand the child's participation, a denial they maintain even when confronted with evidence that the children were frightened, trapped, and forced.

Collectors usually deny their involvement with children. Often they say that the child encouraged their behavior and that they were kind to the child. The sexual activities and the photography sessions, no matter how degrading, are not viewed as harmful to the child.

The Cottage Collector

The cottage collector is a pedophile who sexually exploits children in a group setting. The financial component of the pornography is noncommercial; that is, large amounts of money are not involved. The intent of the pornography is for the relationships it creates with other pedophile collectors and is a method of communication.

Children keep silent because they are persuaded that they are totally responsible for, and have much to lose by disclosing, the activities. Collectors also have much to lose because they are respected on the outside for their interest in and relationships with children.

The networking of cottage collectors is more pronounced than that of the preceding two categories of collectors. In fact, they often team up to lead a group of children. Although each collector uses

the pornography for self-interests, each is active in its production.

When confronted, it is not unusual for cottage collectors to represent themselves as being concerned about the children involved; they believe that it is the judicial system that threatens the well-being of the children. These collectors also suggest that they have done more for the child than the child's parents, and hold the parents responsible for the child's participation, in part, because the parents allowed their child to be with the collectors.

The Commercial Collector

The commercial collector is a pedophile who has his own group of children, he also has a wide access to other collectors with their own groups. These pedophiles, who tend to be syndicated, represent a highly organized, commercial level among collectors. Information on this group is limited.

CHILD PROSTITUTION

Prostitution is an exchange of sexual activity for money, drugs, shelter, or protection. It is closely aligned with children who run away or try to escape from intolerable family situations. There are some cases of prostitution that are an integral part of the initial sexual exploitation of a child, as in sex ring cases. Both boys and girls are vulnerable to the activity.

Once a prostitute, it is difficult to stop the pattern because of the reward item itself and its significance to the survival of the child, and the psychological reaction of the child to the abuse and the excessive sexual activity. Children feel ashamed, desperate, humiliated, and guilty.

These children are at high risk for attempting suicide, abusing drugs, or of being murdered. Sexually transmitted diseases, malnutrition, and aftermath of trauma are also severe problems. A thorough physical, complete blood screening, and psychological evaluation are therefore necessary to assess the child's physical and psychological state. Hospitalization, both voluntary and involuntary, may be necessary.

IMPACT ON CHILDREN

There are medical, psychological, cognitive, social, and behavioral effects on children who are used in sex rings, pornography, and prostitution.

A study of 66 children and adolescents exploited by adults through sex rings and pornography shows that three-fourths of the victims demonstrated patterns of negative psychological and social adjustment after the rings were exposed. More than 61 percent of the victims had been ring members for more than 1 year, and slightly more than one-half of the victims had been used in pornographic photographs. Victims who had recovered and integrated the exploitation were those who had spent the least amount of time in the ring and who were least likely to have been involved in pornography and prostitution. Boys were the sexual preference of many adult male ringleaders. The following are important descriptive findings uncovered by Burgess et al.

A sex ring introduces children to an elaborate socialization process that not only binds them but locks them into patterns of learned behaviors. This partially explains why children do not reveal their involvement to parents and other authority figures and why it is so difficult to

leave. They see the leader using a peer network to force a pattern of adaptation that perpetuates aggressive and sadistic behaviors. The longer the child remains in the ring, the more the group deviant behavior is locked into a normative, accepted value pattern for the child. Children who were in rings for less than 1 year had no identification with the exploiter; those who were in rings for more than 1 year and who participated in pornography and/or prostitution identified with the exploiter.

The sexual abuse of the children by the adult is compounded by the adult support of the sexual abuse of smaller, weaker children by older and stronger children. The adult acts as the benevolent one and uses group members against each other, encouraging abuse of the more vulnerable members of the group, while vicariously enjoying the peer sadism.

A child's involvement represents much more than a sexual triumph for the adult. Money and heightened emotional arousal are obtained through the unchallenged power position easily held and sustained by the adult at the expense of the child.

The introduction of pornography further links the child to the group; its lucrativeness is a powerful reinforcement for the group, as well as an important dimension in underscoring the consequences of betrayal. Pornography also adds a peculiar dimension by providing special attention to the children involved. The dimensions of modeling for the pictures are especially important. The posing, teaching, and mentor activities of the adult further reinforce attachment to the group by appealing to the child's need for attention, approval, and affection. Use of alcohol and drugs, plus promises of extra money for the pictures themselves, entice the child. The child is bound by seemingly good, as well as fearful and negative, forces.

The "business" enterprise locks the

child in the group. This not only increases the demand for secrecy but increases the price for any member who dares betray the group. The children continue to feed on each other. Extortion is increased now that each has resources. Pressure is reduced when a member can bring in a new child. It is not unusual for siblings to bring their younger siblings into the ring.

The study also focused on the cognitive development of the children in response to the sex ring events. This revealed patterns of belief, which when adopted by the children, integrate the exploitation through distorted processes of justification. These value patterns are the result of an active inculcation of group behavior and beliefs by the perpetrator, maintained for social and psychological survival by the children 2 years after disclosure. After disclosure these cognitive patterns continue the presuppositions that the victim is to blame and that deviant behavior is justified. Dimensions of the total experience in a sex ring that cannot be consciously mediated in the children by these cognitions are handled by dissociation, repression, and denial.

For those children who remain in the ring, but on disclosure manifest internalizing processes marked by anxiety, depression, guilt, and social withdrawal, the struggle for recovery requires a tremendous amount of working through of experiences beyond the pale of the issues of early sexual arousal and abuse. The adaptive stress patterns are less clearly predictive. There is some indication that this group continues to be victimized and abused, particularly through prostitution activities.

For those youths who externalize their reactions, serious acting out behaviors often occur. It is not only the sexual experiences in the rings but also the introduction of pornography modeling and prostitution, coupled with drugs and alcohol and compounded by psychological

and/or financial payment, that locks the child into deviant patterns.

PRINCIPLES AND LEVELS OF INTERVENTION

Intervening with the child or adolescent who has been abused in a sex ring presents many challenges. Children may resist the efforts of concerned individuals because of untreated past abuse. Professionals need to appreciate the clinical differences between abused and nonabused children to develop an effective treatment plan and to overcome the child's resistance to participation. Medical intervention and examination of the sexually abused child has been outlined in Chapter 17. This section discusses psychological intervention by level of untreated sexual trauma.

The first general intervention principle is to provide safety. The experience of sexual abuse shatters the child's sense of safety and protection. It is essential to ensure that the child feels safe in all environments, including the home, school, and institution. The clinician's professional background should be explained, as should the reasons why the child is being seen, others who will be present during the session, and any legal concerns. The child needs to know that the basis of this contact is to provide immediate care and help. Because of the legal mandate to report all cases of child abuse, medical personnel need to refer to agency protocol regarding reporting procedures.

The second general intervention effort is to build on the resources of the child. This principle requires assessment of the child's strengths or coping skills, paying particular attention to relaxation exercises. Because talking about the abuse will generate anxiety, the clinician needs to know prior to such discussion how the child handles tension and anxiety. Depending on the developmental level of the child and preferred mode of expression, this principle may include drawing, play, and verbal communication.

The third principle is trauma-specific and includes discussion of the abuse. The clinician, after fostering the child's sense of safety and coping skills, attempts an orderly discussion of the abuse. The use of a tri-level assessment approach based on how long the trauma remained untreated is outlined.

Level 1

This approach is aimed at early disclosure of sexual abuse (e.g., less than 1 month) and includes rape (forced sexual penetration without consent). It is necessary to find out the history of the child's disclosure and family reaction.

In the acute phase of rape trauma syndrome, there is a great deal of disorganization in the child's life, and the following acute somatic manifestations may be evident: physical trauma, skeletal muscle tension, gastrointestinal irritability, and genitourinary disturbances. Fear of physical violence and/or death is usually the primary affect experienced during the rape.

The long-term process of reorganization is the second phase of the rape trauma syndrome. Although the time of onset varies among victims, this phase often begins several weeks after the assault or identification of the rape. Various factors will affect the coping behavior of victims regarding the trauma, for example, age, cultural views of rape, injuries, and family support. Intrusive thoughts of the rape break into the child's conscious mind (daymares) as well as through sleep (nightmares). Traumatophobia, in which fears and phobias develop, serves as a defensive reaction to the circumstances of the rape. A diagnosis of post-traumatic stress disorder may be made. Medical, social, and psychological treatment is essential.

Level 2

This level of assessment is for the child who has been in a sexually abusive situation for up to 1 year, including incest and sex rings. In addition to level 1 assessment, these children need to be evaluated for general physical and sexual health, sexually transmitted diseases and human immunodeficiency syndrome (HIV) infection, and drug and alcohol use.

If chronic post-traumatic stress disorder is diagnosed, the next step is to evaluate the child's dominant character organization and to appreciate its cognitive defensive structure. The clinician, by working within the context of that defensive structure, can confront the behaviors that block thoughts and reasoning that inhibit the youth's capacity to express vulnerability. This vulnerability is rooted in the abuse experience and is psychologically experienced through humiliation, betrayal, and powerlessness. In addition, the abuse is embedded with social responses of being blamed and being told that the activities were encouraged or wanted.

Once the trauma has surfaced, the working phase of therapy includes processing the trauma, beginning when the child is able to talk directly about the abuse. The therapist's task is to reconstruct a description of the abuse from the child's symptoms and begin to link the child's behavior to other symptoms of the experiences. The trauma experience is separated from its fear-induced symptoms. The therapy then focuses on altering the negative behaviors that resulted from the abusive situation. The processed trauma is then moved to past memory, and the child is introduced to strategies for filing the experience as memory, for example, therapeutic forgetting. This enables the child to selectively control memories of the abuse.

Level 3

This level of assessment is aimed at the child who has had a long history of ongoing sexual abuse and has continued aggressive and sexual behavior. These children are generally older and exhibit externalizing behaviors; they are usually adolescents, "tough kids," who carry weapons and survive on the streets by criminal means, they may be under the influence of another person such as a pimp or a drug boss, and may require special protection from them. In addition to level 2 assessment, these youths need to be stabilized in a safe environment; encouraged to use existing skills for work; helped to decrease their tension and anxiety; detoxified for drug and alcohol abuse; and assessed for potential aggression toward themselves as well as toward others.

For all youths in treatment with unresolved sexual abuse, sexual abuse of others must be evaluated. Youths who have been repeatedly abused sexually have adopted both passive and aggressive behaviors regarding sex. Treatment will require resolution of the unresolved trauma and integration of aggressive and avoidant sexual behavior.

Treatment of internalizing victims is complicated by their unconscious identification with aggression and denial of vulnerability. In addition, there is conflict in terms of right and wrong, assertiveness and aggressiveness, and sexuality and deviance.

Treatment of externalizing victims is complicated by their aggressive manifestations of their experiences. Another concern is the disclosure aspect of the abuse. Disclosure confronts males with issues of bisexuality. Gender identity, sexual preference, and sexual performance are key clinical issues. The offender may have told male victims that they would be able to function sexually with girls, but with disclosure they are confronted with their homosexual activities. Suicidal attempts and drug use may be seen as a way to suppress their confusion.

A treatment protocol for children abused in sex rings includes measures for assessment of cognitive, psychological, and social functioning; the determination of impact of abuse on the child and the child's social network; strategies for confronting avoidant and acting out responses and for addressing the sexualization of relationships and the acting out of the deviant patterns; and techniques for establishing a strong alliance with the family or social network through varied and often lengthy treatment.

SUGGESTED READINGS

1. Burgess AW, Grant CA: Children traumatized in sex rings. National Center for Missing and Exploited Children, Arlington, VA, 1988
2. Burgess AW, Hartman CR, McCausland MP, Powers P: Response patterns in children and adolescents exploited through sex rings and pornography. Am J Psychiatry 141:656, 1984
3. Hartman CR, Burgess AW, Lanning KV: A typology of collectors. p. 93. In Burgess AW (ed): Child Pornography and Sex Rings. Lexington Books, Lexington, MA, 1984
4. Janus MD, McCormack A, Burgess AW, Hartman CR: Adolescent Runaways. Lexington Books, Lexington, MA, 1987
5. Wild NJ, Wynne JM: Child sex rings. Br Med J 293, 1986

23

Failure-to-Thrive/Starvation

Stephen Ludwig

Failure-to-thrive (FTT) is a clinical diagnostic term used to describe children who are not growing according to expected norms. The term has been defined variously by different authors and investigators, and its lack of precision often noted. Despite a lack of a rigid or universally accepted definition, the term continues to be operationally useful as it identifies a child who, at a given point in time, is unhealthy as far as physical growth is concerned. The use of the term *failure-to-thrive* communicates from one health care provider to another the working diagnosis of a child who is not growing when the underlying cause for growth failure has not yet been defined or identified. What constitutes failing to grow according to norms? This may be an absolute deficiency that is, less than 2 standard deviations (SD) below the mean weight or height for age. In other cases it is a relative deficiency or a shifting in the growth pattern (i.e., a child who was growing at the 75 percentile who has now shifted to the 10 percentile curve). Both of these types of growth inadequacy are considered FTT. Starvation is the term of extreme FTT when a child dies of lack of food intake.

This chapter explores the types of FTT and a number of causes for this phenomenon. It further concentrates on recognizing and treating those children who are failing-to-thrive on a nonorganic or environmental basis.

TYPES OF FAILURE-TO-THRIVE

Until the later half of the 20th century, it was presumed that FTT was always the result of an organic disorder. The child in question was not growing because of an underlying physiologic dysfunction in one or more body systems. Only recently have we come to understand that a child's environment may be the cause of growth failure. Such concepts resulted from the specific study of children in orphanages in the post-World War II period and from a general acceptance of the psychological basis of organic disease. Thus, the term FTT was subdivided into two types, organic FTT, indicating that once investigated a physical impairment could be found to explain the growth failure, and nonorganic FTT, indicating that this physically intact child needed a change in environment to resume normal growth. A number of different investigators have reported on varying proportions of the two types of FTT.

In the early 1980s, Homer and Ludwig

published a review of FTT cases and attempted to categorize the cases in one of the two types. This proved impossible as a significant proportion of the children had a combination of physical and environmental problems. Thus, a third type of FTT was determined, mixed FTT. In the mixed FTT category were children who had a combination of problems: a minor organic problem and a family constellation unable to cope with that deficit. Correcting the physical problem would not be possible nor would changing the family. Both aspects of the problem had to be therapeutically attacked with equal vigor to improve the child's state of health. Gordon and Vasquez have further categorized the mixed FTT into three subgroups: (1) an abnormal environment that has lead to an affected child being poorly cared for; (2) an affected environment and an affected child occurring simultaneously; (3) an affected child whose care requirements disrupted the family and caused environmental breakdown. The possible variations of FTT are shown in Figure 23-1.

Table 23-1 shows the body systems that were affected in a series of organic FTT cases. Table 23-2 lists possible nonorganic FTT causes. It is important to de-

Table 23-1. Causes of Failure-to-Thrive With an Organic Basis[a]

Affected Body System	Number of Patients
Neurologic	52
Cardiac	38
Gastrointestinal	26
Congenital anomalies	22
Cystic fibrosis	
Respiratory	17
Urinary tract	16
Endocrine	14
	12

[a] N = 287.
(From Shaheen and Barbaro,[45] with permission.)

lineate the types of FTT as they point to the root causes of FTT, which in turn indicate directions for evaluation and management of individual cases. It is also important that more precise terminology be developed and used so that future research efforts will be more standardized and replicable.

By understanding the types of FTT it becomes clear that not all FTT is subsumed in the term *child abuse*. There are many cases of organic FTT and perhaps

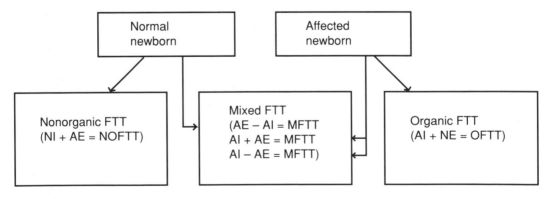

Fig. 23-1. Classification scheme for failure-to-thrive (FTT). AI, organically affected infant; NI, normal infant; AE, affected environment; NE, normal environment; MFTT, mixed FTT; OFTT, organic FTT; NOFTT, nonorganic FTT. (From Gordon and Vasquez,[25] with permission.)

Table 23-2. Classification of Causes of Nonorganic Failure-to-Thrive

Lack of education/preparation for parenting
    Missing information
    Lack of experience

Lack of family resources
    Food
    Money
    Housing
    Health care
    Alternate caretakers

Parental dysfunction
    Postpartum depression
    Parental substance abuse
    Parental psychosis
    "Apathy futility" syndrome (Polansky)

Difficult infant
    Temperamental differences
    Feeding difficulties
    Minor organic disorder

Parent-child interaction problems
    Bonding failure
    Vulnerable child[a]
    Unwanted child/pregnancy
    Overinvolvement—enmeshment

Family system dysfunction
    Isolated family
    Marital stress
    Chaotic home

[a] Green M, Solnit AJ: Reactions to the threatened loss of a child: a vulnerable child syndrome. Pediatrics 34:58, 1964.

Fig. 23-2. Relationship between failure-to-thrive (FTT) (organic, nonorganic, and mixed FTT) and child abuse (physical abuse, sexual abuse, emotional abuse, and physical neglect).

significant numbers of nonorganic and mixed FTT cases in which parental neglect is not the issue. The relationship between FTT and child abuse is shown in Figure 23-2. The remainder of this chapter focuses on recognizing and treating that group of children with nonorganic or mixed FTT in which parental neglect/abuse is an important component.

IDENTIFYING NONORGANIC FAILURE-TO-THRIVE

There are a number of telltale historical points, signs, and symptoms that can be useful in identifying nonorganic FTT as a part of the child abuse/neglect syndrome. Table 23-3 lists some of the historical points to be considered when evaluating a child with growth failure.

In identifying children with nonorganic FTT, the history often has a magical

Table 23-3. Historical Factors Suggesting Nonorganic Failure-to-Thrive

Is there a history of adequate intake? (e.g., difficult feeder)

Is there a history of abnormal loss? (e.g., vomiting, diarrhea)

Does the parent recognize a weight problem?

What is an average day like for the family?

Is the child's growth delay timed to other life events?

How are parents meeting other needs of the child and needs of other children?

Are there any other signs or symptoms of illness?

What is the child's diet?

What are the child's developmental milestones?

What has been the child's eating/feeding development?

quality, not unlike some of the "magical" physical abuse conditions for which the caretaker has no possible explanation for the obvious injury. In nonorganic FTT, the child will be described as eating an ideal diet while having no abnormal loss either through diarrhea or vomiting. In addition, the history of growth failure may not be recognized by the parent. Often the visit will be prompted by a complaint other than weight loss or growth failure. In some cases, it is possible to time the growth failure historically to other untoward life events. For example, a mother may report that she and the baby's father separated at a specific time. That time will correlate with a growth decline on the child's growth chart. Nonorganic FTT may be part of an overall pattern of neglect in which case the history will show a lack of prenatal and postnatal care for the mother, a lack of immunizations and other health maintenance for the child, and a disorganized or chaotic family life-style. Asking the parent what an average day is like may be responded to in a way that indicates that there is no pattern or schedule to this family's life.

After taking a specific history for non-organic FTT, there are specific markers that should be identified on the physical examination. Table 23-4 lists some of the specific signs of malnutrition. Figures 23-3 to 23-6 illustrate some of these findings. Beyond looking for these signs it is most useful to construct a detailed growth assessment, including careful measurement of the child's height, weight, and head circumference. A skin fold thickness measurement is also helpful as an indicator of fat stores. In addition to measurement at one point in time it is most instructive to get a series of measurements over time. Having these will show the pattern of growth. A child's growth measurements should be evaluated against the child's own specific pattern of growth and the idealized pattern of

Table 23-4. Physical Examination Findings in Nonorganic Failure-to-Thrive

Signs of malnutrition
    Decreased pulse, temperature, blood pressure
    Decreased adiposity
    Prominent ribs and bone structure
    Sparse fragile hair
    Pallor, "pastel children"
    Excessive perspiration
    "Old" skin, hyperpigmented nevi
    Heart murmur secondary to anemia
    Protuberant abdomen
    Hepatomegaly
    Decreased activity, apathy, hypotonia
Growth assessment
    Basic measures include weight, length, head circumference, triceps, skin fold thickness
    Serial measurements are important
    Plot measurements on proper growth curves
    Patterns of growth assessment may be suggestive of specific diagnoses

growth as indicated on standardized growth charts (see Appendix H). In using any growth chart one must be aware of the population used to construct the standard and whether a specific patient is suitably evaluated by using that standard. For example, if a growth chart was constructed by using a cross section of full-term babies born in the United States, should it be used to evaluate the growth of a premature baby born in South East Asia?

In any assessment of the child's growth genetic potential is an important factor. A detailed cataloging of the parents' size, growth pattern, timing of puberty, and similar assessment of other family members may be helpful.

Abnormal growth curves will have recognizable patterns of abnormality. For example, when a child with nonorganic FTT fails to receive adequate nutrition, the growth failure is reflected first and

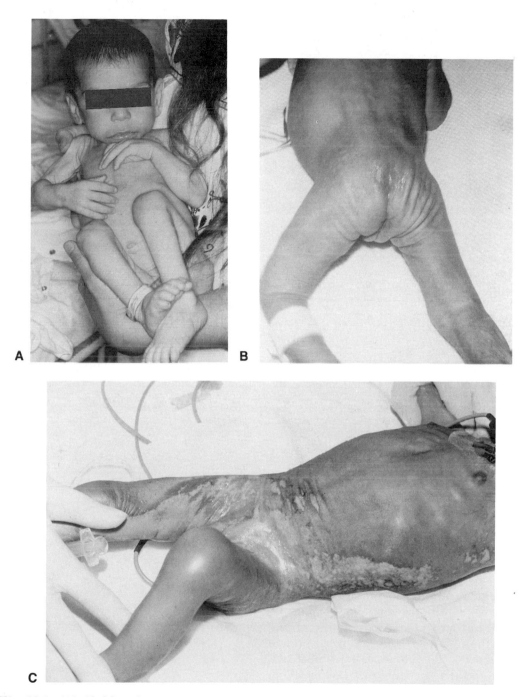

Fig. 23-3. (**A**) Child with nonorganic FTT showing wasted extremities and protuberant abdomen. (**B**) Wasted buttocks with loose skin. (**C**) Signs of gross neglect, hyperpigmented diaper rash.

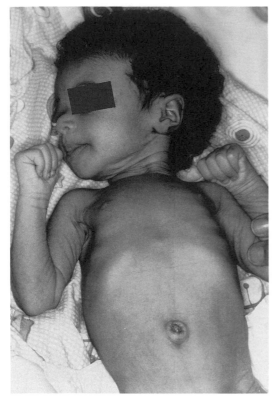

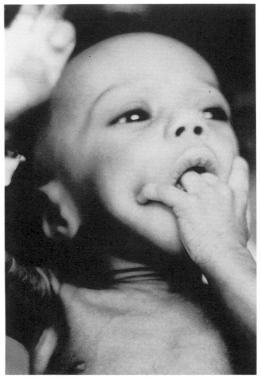

Fig. 23-4. Child with FTT and acute dehydration.

Fig. 23-5. A child with FTT and self-stimulating oral contact.

most severely in the measure of body weight, secondly in height, and finally in a delay in head circumference (Fig. 23-7). Other conditions will be reflected in other patterns.

Perhaps one of the most difficult aspects of identifying cases of nonorganic FTT is the distinction between children with nonorganic FTT and those who have sustained intrauterine growth retardation (IUGR). Children with IUGR may be small but have normal weight/height ratios; they may not regain normal growth percentiles despite excellent postnatal care; and may be from families in whom some of the same social, economic, and stress factors for nonorganic FTT can be identified. For example, the child who is identified as failing-to-thrive who was

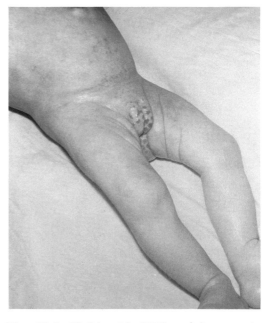

Fig. 23-6. Child with FTT and hypertonic body posture.

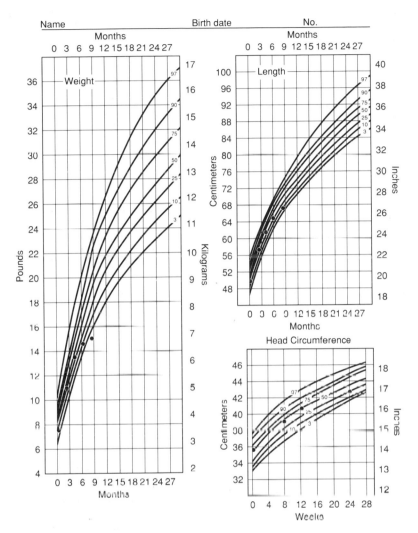

Fig. 23-7. Typical growth curve (indicated by black dots) of an 8-month-old boy with nonorganic FTT.

born to an alcoholic mother. Is the growth failure caused by intrauterine effects of fetal alcohol syndrome or to the postnatal neglect of a chronically intoxicated mother? Some of the indicators of IUGR and other subtle organic causes of FTT are listed in Table 23-5. In total, these causes account for less than 5 to 10 percent in most series. Because fetal alcohol syndrome is a common element in this differential diagnosis, the specific signs and symptoms of fetal alcohol syndrome are listed in Table 23-6.

The third element in the evaluation of nonorganic FTT beyond the history and physical examination is the observation of the parent, the child, and their interaction. In Table 23-7 some of the key observations are noted. In observing the parent look for signs of attachment be-

Table 23-5. Findings of Intrauterine Growth Delay and Other Subtle Causes of Growth Delay

Evidence of intrauterine growth retardation
    Nutrition of mother
    Placental size
    Chromosomal abnormality
    Intrauterine infections
    Drug and alcohol use
    Smoking
Signs of birth asphyxia
Evidence of endocrine abnormality (5%)
    Hypothyroidism
    Hypopituitarism
    Psychosocial dwarfism
Findings of neurologic abnormality
Signs of gastrointestinal disease
    Sucking or swallowing problems
    Vomiting
    Malabsorption (e.g., cystic fibrosis)

Table 23-6. Findings in Fetal Alcohol Syndrome

Features necessary to characteristic face
    Eyes
        Short palpebral fissures
    Nose
        Short and upturned in early childhood; hypoplastic philtrum
    Maxilla
        Flattened
    Mouth
        Thinned upper vermillion
Associated facial features
    Nose
        Flat nasal bridge, epicanthal folds
    Mouth
        Prominent lateral palatine ridges, cleft lip with or without cleft palate, small teeth
    Mandible
        Retrognathia in infancy, micrognathia or relative prognathia in adolescents
    Ears
        Posterior rotation, abnormal concha

Continued

Table 23-6. (*continued*)

Other associated malformations
    Cardiac
        Atrial septal defects
        Ventricular septal defects
        Aberrant great vessels
        Tetralogy of Fallot
    Central nervous system
        Malformations of neuronal and glial migration
        Microcephaly
        Hydrocephaly
        Anencephaly
        Porencephaly
        Meningomyelocele
        Lumbosacral lipoma
    Cutaneous
        Hemangiomas
        Hirsuitism in infancy
    Embryonal tumor
        Neuroblastoma
        Adrenal carcinoma
        Hepatoblastoma
        Ganglioneuroblastoma
        Sacrococcygeal teratoma
    Genitalia
        Hypospadia
        Labial hypoplasic
    Hepatic
        Extrahepatic biliary atresia
    Muscular
        Hernias of diaphragm, umbilicus, or groin
        Diastasis recti
    Skeletal
        Hypoplastic nails
        Shortened fifth digits
        Radioulnar synostosis
        Flexion contractures
        Camptodactyly
        Clinodactyly
        Pectus excavatum and carinatum
        Klippel-Feil syndrome
        Hemivertebrae
        Scoliosis
    Renal
        Aplastic, dysplastic, or hypoplastic kidneys
        Horseshoe kidneys
        Ureteral duplications
        Megaloureter
        Hydronephrosis
        Cystic diverticula
        Vesicovaginal fistula

(From Clarren,[12] with permission.)

Table 23-7. Observation Points in Children with Nonorganic Failure-to-Thrive and Their Parents

---

Observations of the parent(s)
　　Physical contact, cuddling
　　Response to separation from child
　　Signs of depression, apathy
　　Loss of self-esteem
　　Lack of perception of child's needs
　　Observe feeding
Observations of the child
　　Developmental level, in particular, delays in verbal and social adaptive
　　"Radar eyes" (watchful)
　　Body tone either rigid or floppy
　　Autoerotic or rumination behavior
　　Sad, apprehensive face
　　Decreased stranger anxiety
　　Indiscriminate affection
　　Frog leg, deprivation posture
　　Observe feeding

---

tween parent and child. Also look for signs of apathy, depression, or other parental deficiencies. The child may be observed to have abnormal body tone in response to handling. The child's eyes are often revealing in their dull, apathetic, and noninteractive qualities as shown in Figure 23-8. Many children with nonorganic FTT will demonstrate autoerotic or oral self-stimulating behavior. In a smaller number, this will evolve to actual ruminating behavior during which children cause their own regurgitation and reingestion of gastric contents.

The best way to observe the behaviors of the child and parent is to observe an actual feeding. This is a highly diagnostic procedure that yields important information about the child, the parent, and most importantly, their relationship. In most cases of nonorganic FTT, it is the relationship that is the core of the problem. Thus, there is no substitute for direct and careful observations. When observing the feeding, determine if the problem is caused by the child, the choice of foods,

or the dynamics around feeding. Satler has listed feeding behaviors that support homeostasis and attachment (Table 23-8) and those that support separation and individuation (Table 23-9). As with other aspects of development there are times to attach and times to individuate.

Laboratory studies are the fourth way of evaluating the child for FTT. Studies by Sills, Berwick, and others have found that laboratory tests are generally nondiscriminatory, if the other elements of evaluation (i.e., history, physical examination, and observed interaction) have been carefully done. Particularly if the investigator is not "tracking down" a specific symptom or physical finding, the yield of positive laboratory tests is less than 2 percent. Nonetheless, most physicians have a bias for testing, for fear that an organic cause of FTT might be missed. Table 23-10 lists a reasonable testing battery. A complete blood count (CBC) and free erythrocyte protoporphyrin (FEP) are useful for identifying children with

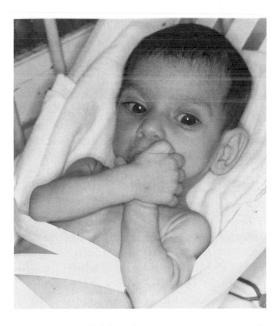

Fig. 23-8. A child with nonorganic FTT, with dull eyes and averting gaze.

Table 23-8. Parent Behaviors That Support Homeostasis and Attachment

Follow the baby's signals about what time to feed

Feed promptly when the baby is hungry, before the baby becomes aroused from heavy crying

Hold the baby securely but not restrictively

When using a bottle, hold it still at an appropriate angle; do not jiggle the bottle or the baby

Be sure the nipple flows at an appropriate speed

Stimulate the rooting reflex by touching the baby's cheek

Touch the nipple to the baby's lips and let the baby open the mouth before feeding

Let the baby decide how much to have, and at what tempo

Let the baby pause, rest, socialize, and go back to eating

Talk and smile, but do not overwhelm the baby with attention

Burp only if the baby seems to need it; do not disrupt feeding with unnecessary burping and wiping

Stop the feeding when the baby refuses the nipple or indicates satiety and lack of interest in eating by turning away, refusing to open the mouth, or arching the back

(From Satler,[43] with permission.)

Table 23-9. Behaviors That Support Separation and Individuation

Feed when the child wants to eat, but gradually evolve a time structure that is appropriate for everyone in the family

Seat the child straight up and facing forward

Sit directly in front of the child

Hold the spoon so the child can see it

Be engaging but not overwhelming; take care not to overload the child with talking or behavior

Talk in a quiet and encouraging manner

Wait for the child to open up and pay attention before feeding

Let the child touch the food and eat with fingers

Let the child self-feed when ready

When the child is self-feeding, remain present in the situation, but do not take over

Let the child decide how fast to eat

Let the child decide how much to eat

Respect the child's food preferences

Respect the child's caution about new foods

Remember, all children learn to eat eventually

(From Satler,[43] with permission.)

iron deficiency anemia and anorexia secondary to iron deficiency. The CBC along with the sedimentation rate may identify children with occult malignancies. The urinalysis and urine culture, blood urea nitrogen (BUN), and serum creatinine seek to identify children with renal disease or urinary tract infection, a difficult group to otherwise identify. Serum electrolytes along with the urinalysis are indicators of renal tubular acidosis or other metabolic derangements. A tine test or PPD may identify the rare child with tuberculosis as the cause of growth failure. In some centers, a skeletal survey for trauma is routinely performed on all chil-

Table 23-10. Laboratory Tests in Children With Suspected Nonorganic Failure-to-Thrive

Complete blood count, free erythrocyte protoporphyrin, sedimentation rate

Urinanalysis and culture

Electrolytes, blood urea nitrogen, creatinine

Skeletal survey

Tuberculosis skin test

Calorie count

Testing for human immunodeficiency virus infections

Testing for syphilis

dren with suspected nonorganic FTT to rule out other manifestations of abuse. Kleinman has suggested that a radiograph of the bones may also be useful in detecting skeletal growth arrest lines, maturational delay, rickets, or other manifestations of poor nutrition. Depending on where a physician is practicing there may be need for routine human immunodeficiency virus (HIV) and syphilis testing in children with FTT. The dramatic increase in both of these diagnoses may make such testing more widespread in the future.

Perhaps the best diagnostic test is a count of the child's caloric intake. If the parent can keep a diary of 2 weekdays and 1 weekend day (as these may be very different depictions of the family's lifestyle), an accurate caloric count can be constructed. This tells a great deal about why the child has not grown.

INDICATION FOR HOSPITALIZATION

Once the child with nonorganic FTT has been identified, the next issue to be addressed is whether the child needs to be hospitalized. Table 23-11 lists some of the indications for hospitalizations of a child with FTT. The indications are based on assessment of the child's risk. Risk, in turn, relates both to the child's vulnerability (i.e., age and extent of growth failure) and to the estimated capacity for caring/hostility of the environment. If the child has signs of physical abuse along with FTT, this is a clear mandate for hospitalization. As with other forms of abuse the issue is "Is the home safe?" If the home is unsafe or if there is any question about safety, the child should be hospitalized and protected. If the child does not require hospitalization, then close follow-up is not only indicated

Table 23-11. Indications for Hospitalizing Children With Failure-to-Thrive

Infant less than 6 months old
Below birth weight at 6 weeks
Head circumference falling off curve <6 months
Signs of abuse
Signs of gross physical neglect
Failure at outpatient therapy
Organic diagnosis being pursued
Home unsafe
Caretaker deemed inadequate

but required. If an aggressive follow-up system is not in place then reconsideration of hospitalization is warranted. If the child is less than 6 months old, and in a period of potential rapid growth, weekly follow-up is required. For older children, follow-up care needs to be close but change cannot be expected too rapidly or the parents and care providers may become too frustrated.

TREATMENT

The treatment of nonorganic FTT includes several steps as indicated in Table 23-12, the first of which is assessment of the child and family. Family assessment must include not only risk assessment but an evaluation of family strengths as well. It is the strength of the family that must be built on in the treatment phase. Thus, it is important to identify family strengths, successful family accomplishment, and family resources. These issues apply to families of all socioeconomic circumstances. In addition to assessing family strengths and weaknesses, it is also important to evaluate the child's nutritional and developmental status. Some children

Table 23-12. Steps in Management of Children With Failure-to-Thrive

Assessment
    Family
        Strengths and weaknesses
    Child
        Physical, nutritional development
Stabilize acute medical problems
    Hospitalization is needed
Determine feeding regimen
    Type of foods
    Quantity of food
    Developmental level
Organize family support systems
Institute treatment plan based on family needs
Close, dedicated follow-up

may be delayed as a result of their malnutrition and this needs to be documented. For other children, the same factors that lead to neglect and nonorganic FTT also lead to developmental delay particularly in the areas of language and social development. Severely neglected children may also be delayed in gross motor and fine motor skills (see Appendix G for developmental milestones).

Simultaneous with the goal of family assessment is the goal of stabilizing the child's medical problem. Once malnutrition has existed for a time, it takes time to reestablish a positive nitrogen balance and to heal any secondary problems such as infections or anemia. The third aspect of treatment is achieving an acceptable diet. The child's diet needs to be acceptable to the child both from a nutritional and developmental point of view. Feeding a 1-year-old child a balanced caloric-rich diet through a bottle is not appropriate. One-year-old children generally have a developmental need to be participatory in their own feeding. The feeding regimen and technique must also be acceptable to the parent. For example, some parents may have difficulty seeing

their children's growth and development and thus may infantilize them. Other parents cannot tolerate the normal "mess" of infants trying to feed themselves. All these issues must be addressed as a workable nutritional plan evolves.

Developing an adequate family support system is the next step in treatment. Caring for a child who has FTT is a tiring, frustrating, and at times, unrewarding job. All parents need support. This is especially true in cases of FTT for which there are often fewer available support systems. Once the treatment plan progresses it needs to move in a direction based on the family's perception of its own needs. FTT, as with other aspects of child abuse, is a symptom of family dys-

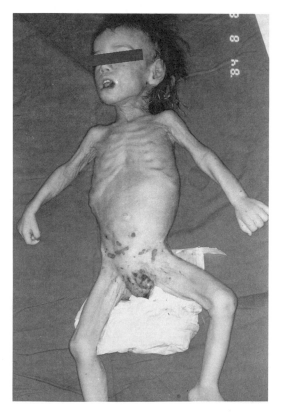

Fig. 23-9. Postmortem photograph of 24-month-old child. Death secondary to starvation.

function; therefore, treatment involves helping the family to become more functional in many areas. Often, in trying to assist the family, home-based services are helpful. Medical, social, and nursing services all have been successfully used. In some centers, paraprofessional "family workers" have been effective in role modeling for the family and in helping families negotiate the "dangerous" waters of the health care and child welfare systems.

The final step in any treatment plan is close and consistent follow-up. In reviewing the records of children with FTT, the chart notations of "lost to follow-up" is all too often seen. In many cases it seems that once the physician has established that FTT is nonorganic, the intellectual challenge and curiosity is satiated. It is at the point of making this diagnosis that the true challenge begins.

STARVATION

When proper identification of FTT does not occur or treatment measures fail, the result may be starvation. Figure 23-9 is an example of starvation. This child lived among a seemingly close-knit community, but neighbors were unaware of the child's birth. Food could have been purchased by the family and the parents had registered for a free food program but never picked up any of the food.

Starving children undergo a steady progression of body system failures (Fig. 23-10). In some severely malnourished children, immunity is weakened by the alteration of a number of normal host defenses, rendering them susceptible to fatal infections. In others, severe malnutrition leads to altered gastrointestinal absorption including mucosal abnormali-

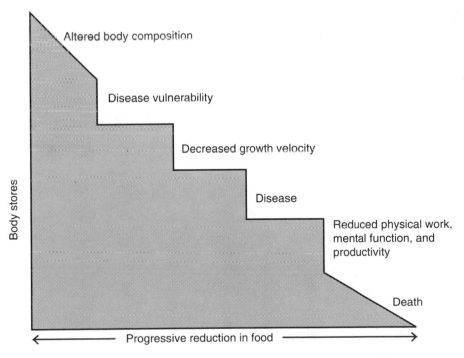

Fig. 23-10. Relationship between vulnerability and reduction in food. (From Puri and Chandra,[42] with permission.)

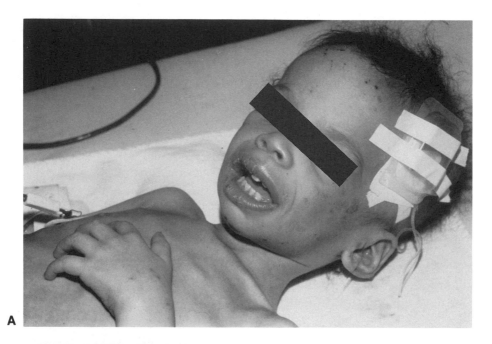

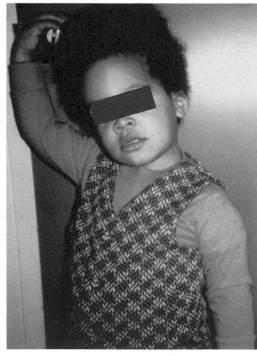

Fig. 23-11. (A) A 23-month-old boy with marked FTT and (B) recovery phase 16 months later.

ties, altered bowel flora, decreased pancreatic function, and lactate deficiency. This prompts a negative fatal spiral: the little nutrition that the child may receive cannot be absorbed and used. In yet a third group of children, it is the interaction of malnutrition and hypothermia that causes death.

The autopsy is an important source of data in the postmortem legal management of the child who has starved to death. Gross findings may include other signs of neglect, for example, hygiene, loss of fat tissue in various locations, muscle wasting, and absence of significant gastric or caloric contents. Caloric deficit may be quantified by computing expected weight and subtracting actual weight and percent of dehydration. Meade and Brissle have used this method; by knowing basic caloric requirements for a specific age, they can estimate the total number of days of malnutrition leading to death. Other aspects of the proper forensic techniques may be found in Chapter 29 and Appendix C.

OUTCOME

What happens to children who have failed to thrive? There have been relatively few follow-up studies of this subpopulation of children. Some studies have conflicting results about future growth. Others report that identified children do reach normal height and weight (Fig. 23-11); still others suggest that there may be certain critical periods of growth that once missed can never be regained. These latter studies report ongoing growth impairment.

All follow-up studies report ongoing developmental, behavioral, and educational impairment of children diagnosed with nonorganic FTT. This is because nonorganic FTT is symptomatic of deeper family dysfunction and although the child's nutritional status may be corrected, such dysfunctions may impact other important areas of childhood functioning. These findings demand a broad multidisciplinary family approach to treatment.

There are conflicting reports also on the physical impact of malnutrition on later cognitive development. This is a difficult problem to study as malnutrition is associated with many other cofactors that affect cognitive development and our ability to measure it. In one report by Hufton and Oates of a small group of children (N = 21) followed for an average of 6 years 4 months, two children died of suspicious causes.

SUMMARY

Nonorganic FTT is a clinical diagnosis that often overlaps with the definition and reporting laws governing suspected child abuse and neglect. The identification of nonorganic FTT is based on a consistent history, physical examination, and absence of positive laboratory results. Some children with nonorganic FTT are at risk and must be hospitalized. For all hospitalized and nonhospitalized patients, a broadly based, multidisciplinary, family-need-directed treatment plan needs to be instituted and monitored closely. Only such intensive services can have a positive impact on this complex form of family dysfunction.

SUGGESTED READINGS

1. Accardo PJ (ed): Failure-to-Thrive in Infancy and Early Childhood. University Park Press, Baltimore, 1982
2. Adelson L: Homicide by starvation: the

nutritional variant of the "battered child." JAMA 186:104, 1963

3. Altemeier WA, O'Connor SM, Sherrod KB et al: Prospective study of antecedents for nonorganic failure-to-thrive. J Pediatr 106:360, 1985

4. Ayoub CC, Milner JS: Failure-to-thrive: parental indicators, types, and outcomes. Child Abuse Negl 9:491, 1985

5. Barbero GJ, Shaheen E: Environmental failure-to-thrive: a clinical review. J Pediatr 71:639, 1967

6. Berwick D: Nonorganic failure-to-thrive. Pediatr Rev 1:265, 1980

7. Berwick D, Levy J, Kleinerman R: Failure-to-thrive: diagnostic yield of hospitalization. Arch Dis Child 57:347, 1982

8. Bithoney WG, Newberger E: Non-organic FTT: developmental and familial characteristics. Pediatr Res 16:84A, 1982

9. Bithoney WG, Rathburn JM: Failure-to-thrive. p. 557. In Levine MD, Carey WB, Crocker AC, Gross RT (eds): Developmental Behavioral Pediatrics. WB Saunders, Philadelphia, 1983

10. Castiglia P: Failure-to-thrive. J Pediatr Health Care 2:50, 1988

11. Chatoor I, Egan J: Nonorganic failure to thrive and dwarfism due to food refusal: a separation disorder. J Am Acad Child Adolesc Psychiatry 22:294, 1983

12. Clarren SK, Smith DW: Fetal alcohol syndrome. N Engl J Med 298:1063, 1978

13. Davis JH, Ra VJ, Valdes-Dapena H: A forensic approach to a starved child. J Forensic Sci 29:663, 1984

14. Dietrich KN, Starr RH, Weisfeld GE: Infant maltreatment, caretaker-infant interactions in infantile anorexia nervosa. J Am Acad Child Adolesc Psychiatry 72:532, 1983

15. Drotar D, Eckerle D: Family environment in nonorganic failure to thrive: a controlled study. J Pediatr Psychol 14:245, 1989

16. Drotar D, Malone C, Devost C: Early psychological outcome in failure-to-thrive: predictions from an interactional model. J Clin Child Psychol 15:105, 1988

17. Egan J, Chatoor F, Rosen G: Non-organic failure-to-thrive, pathogenic and classification. Clin Procedures Children's Hospital Natl Med Center 36:4, 173, 1980

18. Elmer E, Gregg GS, Ellison P: Late results of the "failure-to-thrive" syndrome. Clin Pediatr 8:584, 1969

19. Evans S, Reinhart J, Succop R: Failure-to-thrive: a study of 45 children and their families. J Am Acad Child Adolesc Psychiatry 11:440, 1972

20. Field M: Follow-up developmental status of infants hospitalized for nonorganic failure-to-thrive. J Pediatr Psychol 9:241, 1984

21. Fosson A, Wilson J: Family interactions surrounding feedings of infants with nonorganic failure-to-thrive. Clin Pediatr 26:10, 518, 1987

22. Fryer GE: The efficacy of hospitalization of nonorganic failure-to-thrive children: a meta-analysis. Child Abuse Negl 12:375, 1988

23. Goldbloom RB: Failure-to-thrive. Pediatr Clin North Am 29:151, 1982

24. Gordon AH, Jameson JC: Infant-mother attachment in patients with nonorganic failure-to-thrive syndrome. J Am Child Psychiatry 18:251, 1979

25. Gordon EF, Vasquez DM: Failure to thrive: an expanded conceptual method. p. 69. In Drotar D (ed): New Directions in Failure to Thrive. Plenum Press, New York, 1986

26. Grantham-McGregor S, Schofield W, Powell C: Development of severely malnourished children who received psychologic stimulation: six year follow-up. Pediatrics 79:247, 1987

27. Hannaway P: Failure-to-thrive: a study of 100 infants and children. Clin Pediatr 9:96, 1970

28. Haynes CF, Cutler C, Gray J, Kempe RS: Hospitalized cases of nonorganic failure-to-thrive: the scope of the problem and short-term lay health visitor intervention. Child Abuse Negl 8:229, 1984

29. Homer C, Ludwig S: Categorization of etiology of failure-to-thrive. Am J Dis Child 135:848, 1981

30. Hufton I, Oates R: Nonorganic failure-to-thrive: a long term follow-up. Pediatrics 59:73, 1977

31. Kleinman PK: Diagnostic Imaging of Child Abuse. Williams & Wilkins, Baltimore, 1987, p. 21

32. Koel BS: Failure-to-thrive and fatal injury as a continuum. Am J Dis Child 118:565, 1969

33. Krieger I, Sargent DA: A postural sign in the sensory deprivation syndrome in infants. J Pediatr 70:332, 1967

34. Meade JL, Brissie RM: Infanticide by starvation calculation of caloric deficit to determine degree of deprivation. J Forensic Sci 30:1263, 1985

35. Mitchell W, Gorrell R, Greenberg R: Failure-to-thrive: a study in a primary care setting. Pediatrics 65:971, 1980

36. Oates RD, Oates RK, Peacock A, Forres D: Development in children following abuse and nonorganic failure-to-thrive. Am J Dis Child 138:764, 1984

37. Oates RK, Peacock A, Forres D: Long-term effects of nonorganic failure-to-thrive. Pediatrics 75:36, 1985

38. Polansky NA, Chalmers MA, Butterweiser E et al: Damaged Parents: An Anatomy of Child Neglect. University of Chicago Press, Chicago, 1981

39. Pollitt E: Failure-to-thrive: socioeconomic, dietary intake, and mother-child interaction data. Fed Proc 34:1593, 1975

40. Pollitt E, Eichler AW, Chan C: Psychosocial development and behavior of mothers of failure-to-thrive children. Am J Orthopsychiatry 45:525, 1975

41. Pulgiese M, Weyman-Daum M, Moses N, Lifshitz F: Parental health beliefs as a cause of nonorganic failure-to-thrive. Pediatrics 80:175, 1987

42. Puri S, Chandra RK: Nutritional regulation of host resistance and predictive value of immunologic tests in assessment of outcomes. Pediatr Clin North Am 32:499, 1985

43. Satler E: Childhood feeding problems. p. 1. In Feelings and Their Medical Significance, Ross Laboratories, Columbus OH, 1990

44. Saudek CD, Felig P: The metabolic events of starvation. Am J Med 60:117, 1976

45. Shaheen E, Barbaro J: Failure-to-thrive. Clin Pediatr 7:255, 1968

46. Sherrod KB, O'Connor S, Vietze PM: Child health and maltreatment. Child Dev 55:1174, 1984

47. Sills RH: Failure-to-thrive: the role of clinical and laboratory evaluation. Am J Dis Child 132:967, 1978

48. Skuse D: Nonorganic failure-to-thrive: a reappraisal. Arch Dis Child 60:170, 1985

49. Sturm L, Drotar D: Prediction of weight for height following intervention in three-year-old children with early histories of nonorganic failure-to-thrive. Child Abuse Negl 13:19, 1989

50. Suskind RM: Gastrointestinal changes in the malnourished child. Pediatr Clin North Am 22:873, 1975

51. Trube-Becker E: The death of children following negligence. Forensic Sci 9:111, 1977

52. Winick M: Starvation in children. Trans Stud Coll Physicians Phila 6:9, 1984

24

Child Neglect: General Concepts and Medical Neglect

Charles F. Johnson
Daniel L. Coury

Neglect is defined in the law but is difficult to define in medical practice. Parents are expected to provide the basic necessities for their children, including adequate food, housing, clothing, education, medical care, and emotional care. Health professionals are directed, by law, to recognize and report neglect as well as sexual and physical abuse. Studies have indicated that physicians have varying definitions of appropriate child discipline, and their propensity to report inappropriate discipline also varies. It is likely that similar disagreements and lack of knowledge about the definition of medical neglect also exists among physicians. Guidelines for recognizing and reporting neglect are uncommon in the medical literature. More often they are found in the pages of the laws or codes specific to each state, but these may not provide clarity to the physician seeking assistance. The Ohio revised code 2151.03 defines a neglected child as one who has been abandoned, illegally placed for adoption, or lacks proper parental care because of the faults or habits of parents, guardians, or custodians (PGC). Improper parental care includes a filthy or unsanitary home, permitting a child to become dependent, neglected, abused or delinquent, or failure to impose appropriate discipline. A PGC who neglects or refuses to provide a child with proper or necessary subsistence, education, medical or surgical care or other care necessary for health, morals or well being, including special care necessitated by the child's mental condition, is neglectful. The most easily defined and recognized type of neglect, physical abandonment, is considered, by the legal system, to be "the ultimate form of neglect." By contrast, many other forms of acute or chronic neglect or emotional abuse may go unrecognized.

NATIONAL INCIDENCE

As with physical and sexual abuse, the true incidence of neglect is unknown. National surveys of reports, or cases known to professionals, indicate that neglect is the most common form of child maltreatment. In 1986 an estimated 25.2 children per thousand, or 1.5 million children, were abused or neglected. The majority of these cases involved neglect (63 percent). The most common form of neglect was physical, followed by educational and emotional with rates per 1000 children of 9.1, 4.6, and 3.5, respectively. The most significant predictor of neglect was family income. The association of poverty with neglect was dramatic; poor children were 12 times as likely to be identified as neglected than children from families whose income was above the poverty level. There were no differences found that were a result of race.

MEDICAL NEGLECT

Just as physical and sexual abuse are forms of child maltreatment that are often underreported by physicians, medical neglect may be recognized more than it is reported. Statistics from Franklin County Children Services (FCCS), in Ohio, indicate that 1 percent of neglect referrals to the local protective services originated from physicians (150 of 14,529 during 1986 to 1988). By contrast, over one-half of all physical and sexual abuse cases were reported by physicians during that same time period (Fig. 24-1). Children's Hospital (CH) of Columbus made 150 reports to FCCS during that 3 year period indicating that all reports for neglect made by physicians in Franklin County came from or through the hospital. Of the 52 cases reported to FCCS in 1987 by CH, 33.3 percent were for medical neglect (Fig. 24-2).

The incidence of medical neglect is also difficult to determine because of the generic term *neglect* being used in most

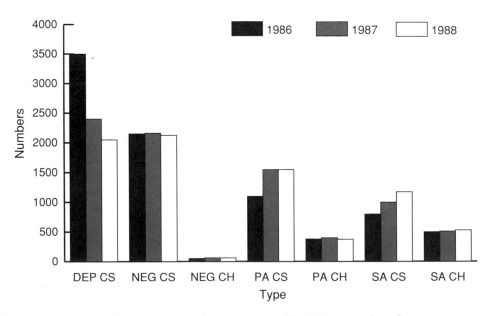

Fig. 24-1. Comparison of abuse and neglect reporting. Child abuse and neglect cases reported to Franklin County Children Services (FCCS) (CS in figure) by various sources, including Children's Hospital (CH) of Columbus, are contrasted with child abuse and neglect reports to FCCS by Children's Hospital only. Neglect (NEG) and dependency (DEP) are the most common referrals received by FCCS from all sources whereas physical abuse (PA) and sexual abuse (SA) are the most common referrals made to that agency.

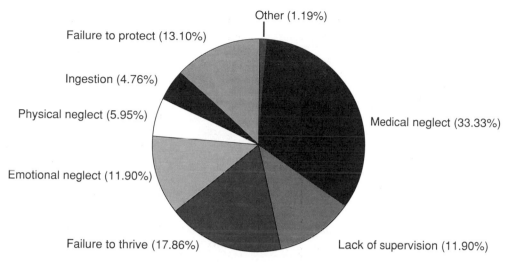

Fig. 24-2. Types of neglect reports from Children's Hospital. Of the 52 cases of neglect filed by Children's Hospital of Columbus in 1987, medical neglect was the most common.

official statistics at county and state levels. As a result, medical neglect is usually combined with physical, educational, and other forms of neglect. Medical neglect can be narrowly defined as the failure of the PGC to provide for the medical needs of the child. This would include failing to seek timely and appropriate medical care for illness or injury, and lack of compliance with prescribed treatments. Failure to seek or provide appropriate medical care, which results in impairment of the child's health or places the child at risk of serious consequences, would warrant reporting the case to protective services. Medical neglect contributing to adverse outcomes for chronic conditions has been described. Table 24-1 describes some common consequences of various forms of neglect. More specific criteria for diagnosing medical neglect would depend on the medical condition and the nature of the neglectful action or omission. Table 24-2 provides examples of common medical conditions, compli-

cations of medical neglect pertinent to them, and suggested methods of documenting medical neglect for each condition.

Parental neglect has the potential to ad versely affect the child prenatally. Parental behaviors such as drug use during pregnancy and maternal health neglect can have adverse effects on the fetus (Table 24-3).

Documentation of medical neglect may be simplified by the presence of laboratory tests confirming, for example, a failure to dispense medication. This alone may not justify a neglect report. A parent may have missed one or two doses because they ran out of medicine and lacked money or transportation necessary to obtain more. Additional important information should address the seriousness of the omission or act in terms of impending health impairment, and any recurrent pattern of omissions or acts. Failure to give a cardiac medication such as digoxin may have clear effects within 1 day. Failure to

Table 24-1. Possible Medical Consequences of Neglect

Type of Neglect	Possible Consequence(s)
Emotional	Failure-to-thrive, delayed development, depression, poor school performance, attachment disorders, withdrawal, attention seeking behavior
Hygiene	Diaper dermatitis, lice, malodorous, peer rejection, scabies, unkempt, dirty
Physical	Recurrent respiratory infections, frost bite, death
Safety	Recurrent injuries, death
Medical	Repeated avoidable urgent visits for health care, delayed diagnosis, wide vacillations in response to treatment, no response to treatment, complications, avoidable school absences, transient tissue or organ damage, permanent incapacity, shortened life span

dispense the last 2 days of a 10 day course of antibiotics for a skin infection may have no discernible effect on the outcome of the disease. When reporting medical neglect, the physician must be certain that no

environmental barriers to care exist, and that the parents clearly understand the risks, to the child, of incomplete treatment. Attempts to persuade the noncompliant family to provide appropriate care must be made, and the parents should be informed of the physician's obligation to report neglect if better compliance is not achieved. The physician must take a supportive approach to PGC rather than an adversarial stance. The neglectful parent may lack self-esteem; too much control or blame by the physician may enhance that perception. Simple failure to properly immunize a child does not imply neglect. However, when viewed as part of a recurrent pattern of missed appointments, unrefilled prescriptions, and emergency room visits for preventable illness, lapsed immunizations may represent one of several neglectful parental behaviors. Since most states require the immunizations recommended by the American Academy of Pediatrics for entrance to school, failure to immunize by age 6 may be considered neglectful. Because monitoring of nutrition and growth and development is crucial during the first year of life, failure to consult a physician for health supervision during that time period could be considered neglectful. The presence of a healthy child, despite missed appoint-

Table 24-2. Examples of Documentation of Neglect for Specific Conditions

Medical Condition	Possible Complications of Neglect	Blood or Serum Monitors of Compliance
Heart disease	Congestive heart failure	Digoxin levels
Diabetes mellitus	Diabetic ketoacidosis, general poor control of condition	Glycosylated hemoglobin levels
Epilepsy	Recurrent seizures	Anticonvulsant levels
Asthma	Wheezing episodes, avoidable emergency room visits or hospital admissions	Theophylline levels
Hypothyroidism	Poor growth, mental retardation (in infancy) or slow mentation (older child)	Triiodothyronine, thyroxine, thyroid stimulating hormone

Table 24-3.   Medical Neglect and Fetal Child Development

Time	Example	Possible Consequence to Fetus/Child
Natal	Poor nutrition, missed appointments, substance abuse	Malformed infant, small for gestational age baby
Delivery	Home delivery when ill advised or against medical advice	Hypoxia, brain damage
Neonatal	Refusal to consent to procedure for infant (Baby Doe issues)	Death

ments and access to guidance and immunizations, tends to negate the significance of omitting specific aspects of care. Documentation of a consistent pattern of neglectful behaviors or adverse outcomes should help clarify the existence of neglect.

NEGLECT AND RELIGION

A religious exception exists in the definition of medical neglect in Ohio, as "a child who, in lieu of medical or surgical care or treatment for a wound, injury, disability, or physical or mental condition, is under spiritual treatment through prayer in accordance with the tenets and practices of a well-recognized religion, is not a neglected child for this reason alone." Most cases involving cults or religious fringe groups will fail to meet the "well-recognized" requirement, while others may display a pattern of neglect that is not always consistent with their reported religious beliefs. Confusion regarding this aspect of the law should not prevent a physician from reporting suspected neglect in a child, requesting temporary custody, and providing necessary medical care. Abuse and neglect reporting laws protect the health professional, who reports in good faith, from legal retribution. Even if the court should decide that the child is not neglected, either by religious exemption or other cause, the physician has complied with reporting laws and attempted to provide necessary care to the child. Many courts have supported the position that religious preference is an adult choice, and that a minor child cannot be fully cognizant of the implications of declaring to be a member of a certain religion. As a result, a minor child cannot be denied medical care on religious grounds, and the parents may not be held neglectful.

NEGLECT AND CULTURE

Complicating efforts to provide medical care to children is a lack of agreement regarding the influence of cultural norms on neglect. This is most apparent in situations in which families immigrate to this country with inadequate knowledge about the Western health care system, and practice various types of folk medicine accepted or prescribed in their former culture. An example is Cao Gio, a practice of immigrants from southeast Asia in which the parent rubs coins on the back of a febrile child in an attempt to draw out the fever. The practice may result in skin abrasions or purpura and serve as a substitute for recommended

"Western medical" treatments. Professionals may be aware that the parent's intent is to serve their child's needs; however, this intellectual awareness and compassion for cultural differences should not replace appropriate medical care for the child. The cultural variables should be considered before reporting neglect. Practices that endanger a child or put them at medical risk may require a report to protective services. Parents who are new to our culture should be afforded the opportunity for education. Cooperative parents may not require a report; in other cases it may be necessary to file a dependency action to help assure compliance. Sponsors or special community organizations can help professionals understand immigrant behaviors, serve as translators, convey medical information to immigrants, and develop educational programs.

NEGLECT VERSUS DEPENDENCY

Poverty and parental disability are two other exemptions to the definition of neglect. Only the parent who is able to provide for a child's needs can be held culpable of neglect. State laws imply that there be a motive of negligence or intent—that the lack of care be due to "faults or habits" of the PGC. If the element of culpability cannot be proved, the child can be found to be dependent rather than neglected. Dependency is commonly seen in situations of extreme poverty or homelessness, when failure to meet the child's needs is beyond the parents' capabilities. A filing of dependency does not require proof of blame. In a dependency situation, one expects that the availability of adequate resources will result in resolution of the dependent situation.

If parents have been intentionally neglectful, the child may be at greater risk. Some parents may be more resistant to change in areas that may involve personal value systems and attitudes toward the child. It may then be necessary to remove the child until satisfactory changes in the behavior of the parents can be exhibited.

The decision of whether dependency or neglect exists is legally determined in the courtroom, primarily family or juvenile court. Perpetrators may plea bargain more serious offenses of abuse and neglect to dependency to avoid more serious punishment from the court. The determination of intent, which differentiates neglect from dependency, may be difficult. The physician, familiar with the family and its economic and emotional resources, may be a valuable asset to the court when called on to provide data. The physician should concentrate on providing specific facts regarding compliance with medical advice, and the results of efforts to improve parental behaviors impacting on the child's medical or emotional condition. Common family court recommendations are for mandatory scheduled visits for the child's medical care, enrollment in parenting classes, and even medical or psychological care for the parent if appropriate. Removal of the child from the home on a temporary or permanent basis may be done in severe cases but is by no means the major judicial response.

Physicians are unlikely to be confronted with nonmedical types of neglect unless, in the process of evaluating and reporting medical neglect, they inquire about other aspects of the child's welfare. The medically neglected child may also be experiencing educational, hygiene, clothing, food, or housing neglect. A filing for medical neglect may uncover other forms of neglect when the investigation includes home and school visits by the child welfare agency. If called to testify in court, the physician will usually be limited to responding to questions regarding medical neglect while other professionals report on their findings.

In high risk populations, such as American Indian children in the Southwest, neglect and abuse are likely to occur in the same child. Neglect may be undetected when the child presents with physical or sexual abuse. This may partially be a result of the difficulty in establishing the existence of neglect, especially emotional neglect, as compared with other forms of maltreatment.

DOCUMENTATION AND REPORTING

Because no national standards exist for determining what constitutes medical neglect for specific acute and chronic conditions, physicians must consider each situation as unique. Reporting may be facilitated through standardized forms listing all essential information required by protective services, the police, and the court. Documentation may include blood or urine levels of body metabolites, such as blood sugar levels in diabetes mellitus, and blood levels of prescribed medications such as anticonvulsants in epilepsy. Figure 24-3 illustrates the medical sections of a model form for reporting neglect, which includes the following essentials:

1. Demographic data about the child and family
2. The type of neglect being reported
3. Quotes from the child and others involved in the child's care
4. The physician's statement regarding why neglect is being filed
5. The consequences to the child of the neglect or failure to comply
6. A detailed charting of dates, problems,

objective findings, instructions, and services offered
7. The results of these instructions and services
8. The PGC's reason(s) for noncompliance

In addition the following statements should be included.

1. The PGC has been informed about the possible outcome of lack of compliance.
2. The PGC understands what is expected and the possible outcome, to the child, of a lack of compliance.
3. The PGC is able (intellectually, physically, economically) to carry out what is expected.
4. The PGC is not restrained by the precepts of an organized religion from complying.

The rest of the medical section of the report should include the following details:

1. Past medical history
2. Physical examination; laboratory tests conducted with results and interpretation
3. Medical diagnoses
4. Treatment plan, including consultations
5. Plans for follow-up

A detailed psychosocial assessment may be part of a neglect report; however, this information should be obtained by the children services worker as part of the case's assessment. The hospital-based physician has the opportunity to work with a hospital social worker who should be experienced and trained in abuse and neglect assessment and referring procedures. The psychosocial assessment should include the following details:

1. Family dynamics, including parent's education, history of abuse, disclosure process, parent/child interactions, par-

Children's Hospital, Inc.
700 Children's Drive
Columbus, Ohio 43205

CHILD ABUSE PROGRAM
REPORT OF SUSPECTED NEGLECT

PATIENT IDENTIFICATION

DEMOGRAPHIC DATA

CONFIDENTIAL
For Professional
Use Only
Complete In
Black Ink

ASSESSED IN:
☐ Emergency Department
☐ Family Development Clinic
☐ Teen Age Clinic
☐ Inpatient Unit (specify) _____
☐ Other_____

Date of Exam: _____

Time of Exam:_____ a.m. p.m.

Patient's Birthdate: _____

Patient's Name_____
    FIRST   MI   LAST

Address _____
    STREET   APT #

_____
    CITY   COUNTY

Medical Record # _____

Phone # (_____)_____

_____
STATE   ZIP

Race (circle): White, Black, Oriental, Hispanic, Combination, Other _____ Sex: M F

Regular Health Care Provided By: _____ Copy to Private Physician? Y _____ N _____

PRESENTING PROBLEM

Type of Neglect* _____
(Include quotes where significant)
Stated by: ☐ mother ☐ father ☐ stepmother ☐ stepfather ☐ social service worker ☐ other (specify) _____

☐ Continued on page 5

RATIONALE

Professional's statement why neglect being filed. Consequences of failure to comply are: **

☐ Continued on page 5

*Types of neglect may include:
    Medical: Inadequate care (missed appointments, immunizations incomplete, lack of or delay in obtaining medical/dental care)
        Failure to follow medical advice: treatment, medication, therapy
    Emotional neglect: Lack of nurturing, lack of supervision, lack of discipline
    Education   Failure to obtain schooling, excessive absences, lack of stimulation
    Physical: Heat, hygiene, clothing, food, housing
    Failure to Protect: Ingestion(s), accident(s)
    Social: Reluctance to take home, signed out AMA, inadequate visitation(s), limited access to parents (inaccessibility), parents' behavior inappropriate due
        to alcohol, drugs, emotional or intellectual problems.

** May be life threatening, worsen the course of an existing illness, or cause an illness. Lack of immunizations may increase the risk for life-threatening illness.

RSN 6/91 1/10

Fig. 24-3. (A & B) Medical section of neglect reporting forms. (Courtesy of Children's Hospital, Inc., Columbus Ohio.) (*Figure continues.*)

NEGLECT DOCUMENTATION

Date(s)	Problem(s)	Objective findings, (measurements, observations)	Instruction/Services offered (Use names of professionals/ agencies and titles)	Results	Guardian's reason(s) for non-compliance

A. Guardian has been told what is expected and possible outcome (risks to child) of a lack of compliance*   ❑ Yes ❑ No
Comments: _____
_____

B. Guardian understands what is expected and possible outcome (risks to child) of a lack of compliance*   ❑ Yes ❑ No
Comments: _____
_____

C. Guardian able (intellectually, physically, economically) to carry out what is expected*   ❑ Yes ❑ No
Comments: _____
_____

D. Guardian's organized religion does not prevent compliance.   ❑ Yes ❑ No
If it does, it may not be reported as neglect according to Ohio Law.
Comments: _____
_____

*It may be necessary to document what has been said/advised in writing with guardian's signature indicating understanding.

RSN 6/91 2/10

Fig. 24-3. (*Continued.*)

ent's affect, stress factors, and support systems

2. Significant others who are exposed to the child
3. The responsible PGC
4. Parent's marital status
5. Guardianship of the child
6. Available school information
7. Discharge planning, which should include information about recommended community referrals

Other professionals may have an important role to play in completion of a neglect report. Important observations of parent-child interactions should be documented by office or hospital nursing staff. Psychological or psychiatric consultation for the child may be necessary to document behavior, learning, or cognitive problems that can frustrate the intentions of the best parent. These professionals can also provide important information about the intellectual and emotional resources of the parents when issues of dependency versus neglect must be decided.

NEGLECT IN THE FUTURE

Articles on abuse are found more than twice as frequently as those on neglect in the popular media. The relative lack of attention to neglect is also seen in the technical literature. This "neglect of neglect" is theorized as being a result of low priority. In terms of the link between neglect and poverty, it reflects in essence the low priority afforded to the alleviation of poverty. This relative lack of professional attention to neglect belies the high mortality and morbidity associated with neglect. More than one-half of the deaths caused by maltreatment (53 percent cited in one national report), were a result of neglect and deprivation of necessities. Other studies have supported the serious

consequences of neglect. There is a need to train all health professionals in the recognition of various forms of child abuse including neglect.

To facilitate training and possibly decrease physician hesitancy to report suspicions of neglect, existing standards and recording instruments (Fig. 24-3) should be reviewed, or new standards and forms developed to assure universal acceptance and utility. The reviewers should include physicians, children's services workers, psychologists, nurses, attorneys, and judges.

Resources to serve the families of neglected children should be improved along with the quality and technical skills of foster parents. This is especially important as children with complicated problems, such as acquired immunodeficiency syndrome (AIDS), fetal cocaine and alcohol syndromes, bronchopulmonary dysplasia, or short bowel syndrome, can become neglected. Many questions exist about the short- and long-term consequences of neglect that researchers must answer in the future. Neglected children may be at higher risk for subsequent violent behavior than abused children; yet, not all children appear to suffer the adverse effects of neglect. The type of abuse; age and other factors in the child, family and environment; and variables introduced by the criminal justice and social welfare systems that may influence the consequences of neglect, must be understood if therapy and prevention are to be improved. Finally, physicians should support and participate in professional and political efforts to solve social and economic factors that may underlie neglect.

SUGGESTED READINGS

1. 1986–1987 Annual Report, Child Abuse Program, Children's Hospital, Columbus, Ohio

2. American Humane Association Annual Report, 1981: Highlights of Official Child Abuse and Neglect Reporting. American Humane Association, Denver, 1983

3. Boxer GH, Carson J, Miller BD: Neglect contributing to tertiary hospitalization in child asthma. Child Abuse Negl 12:491, 1988

4. Cantwell HB: Standards of child neglect. Denver Department of Social Services, Denver, Colorado, 1978

5. Dubowitz H: Child abuse programs and pediatric residency training. Pediatrics 82:477, 1988

6. Dubowitz H: Letters to the Editor (in reply). Pediatrics 83:806, 1989

7. Franklin County Children Services, Columbus, Ohio, Office of Public Information, 1990

8. Jaudes PK, Diamond LJ: Neglect of chronically ill children. Am J Dis Child 140:655, 1986

9. Johnson CJ: Letters to the Editor: Residency training and child abuse. Pediatrics 83:805, 1989

10. Kamine DM, Swisher TR: Child abuse, neglect and dependency in Ohio. Ohio State Bar Foundation, Columbus, Ohio 1982

11. Lujan C, DeBruyn LM, May PA et al: Profile of abused and neglected American Indian children in the southwest. Child Abuse Negl 13:449, 1989

12. Mayor's Task Force on Child Abuse and Neglect Report on the Preliminary Study of Child Fatalities in New York City, 1983

13. Morris JL, Johnson CF, Clasen M: To report or not to report: physicians' attitudes toward discipline and child abuse. Am J Dis Child 139:194, 1985

14. Morrow G III: Letters to the Editor (in reply). Pediatrics 83:807, 1989

15. National Center on Child Abuse and Neglect, 1981. Study Findings: National Study of the Incidence and Severity of Child Abuse and Neglect. National Center on Child Abuse and Neglect, Children's Bureau ACYF, Office of Human Development Services, U.S. Department of Health and Human Services. DHHS Publication No. (OHDS) 81-30325, Washington, DC

16. NCPCA Memorandum, National Committee for the Prevention of Child Abuse. Chicago, Illinois, August, 1988

17. Polansky N, Hally C: Profile of neglect: a survey of the state of knowledge of child neglect. Public Services Administration, Social and Rehabilitative Services, U.S. Department of Health Education and Welfare, Washington, DC, 1975

18. Saboe BJ, Alexander RC: Noncompliance with PKU treatment recommendations may be medical neglect in some states. Pediatr Nurs 13:202, 1987

19. Skuse DH: Emotional abuse and neglect. Br Med J 298:1692, 1989

20. Study findings: Study of National Incidence and Prevalence of Child Abuse and Neglect: U.S. Department of Health and Human Services, Office of Human Development Services, Children's Bureau, National Clearing House on Child Abuse and Neglect, Washington, DC, 1988

21. White K, Kilman ML, Wexler P et al: Unstable diabetes and unstable families: a psychosocial evaluation of diabetic children with recurrent ketoacidosis. Pediatrics 73:749, 1984

22. Widome CS: Child abuse, neglect, and adult behavior: research design and findings on criminality, violence and child abuse. Am J Orthopsychiat 59:355, 1989

23. Wolock I, Horowitz B: Child maltreatment as a social problem: the neglect of neglect. Amer J Orthopsychiatry 54:530, 1984

24. Yeatman GW: Pseudobattering in Vietnamese children. Pediatrics 58:617, 1976

25

Perinatal Abuse

Francis C. Mezzadri

Chemical dependence among women of childbearing age is increasing. Although the number of maternal and perinatal complications secondary to drug abuse is increasing, the actual number of women who use legal drugs, illegal drugs, and alcohol during their pregnancy is not known on a national scale. Surveys, as well as drug screening in neonates, have given us representation of this widespread problem. The pregnant, substance-abusing patient may be difficult to identify unless a good patient-doctor relationship exists. Unfortunately, the patient-doctor rapport is established after embryogenesis has occurred. Theoretically, substance abuse should be recognized before the patient becomes pregnant, thus eliminating this most frequent misdiagnosis in pregnancy.

The availability of substances that may alter the maternal-fetal unit and fetal well-being varies and depends on social acceptance and physical or recreational need. People ingest drugs for many reasons, owing to lifestyle, social or recreational activity, or as mood-modifying agents. In general, drugs of abuse include any compound that is taken legally, such as coffee, tobacco, or alcohol; or illegally, such as lysergic acid diethylamide (LSD) and marijuana; or substances that have recognized medical uses, such as cocaine, narcotics, barbiturates, and amphetamines. Effect on the maternal-fetal unit can be devastating, and the sequelae may be long-standing to the mother and the child (Table 25-1). These effects may be maternal or fetal or both, may be direct or indirect, and may be subtle in their representation. Some pertinent indirect effects of substance abuse are listed in Table 25-2.

This section reviews the specific substances of abuse, their effects on the fetus, and the legal ramifications.

PSYCHOLOGY OF PREGNANCY AND PREDISPOSITION TO FETAL NEGLECT

The psychology of pregnancy is relevant to fetal abuse, since patients at risk may reveal a more primitive, primary process of thinking. Although not all patients may experience this, those who have an increase in lability of affect may result in borderline functioning. Stress, primitive psychic functioning, emotional lability, and increased impulsivity may predispose to fetal neglect, as do low maternal attachment to the fetus, poor impulse control, and primitive defenses. Marital dys-

Table 25-1.   Pregnancy and Drugs of Abuse

| Agent | How Used | Abstinence Syndrome | | Teratogenic | Impaired Fetal Growth | Developmental Delay |
		Maternal	Fetal/ Neonatal			
Alcohol	Oral	Yes	Yes	Yes	Yes	Yes
Sedatives	Oral	Yes	Yes	Not proven	Yes	Not proven
Cocaine	Inhalation, IV	Yes	Yes	Probably	Yes	Yes
Narcotics	IV, inhalation	Yes	Yes	Not proven	Yes	Yes
Tobacco	Inhalation	Yes	Yes	Not proven	Yes	Not proven
Marijuana	Inhalation	Yes	Yes	Not proven	Yes	Yes
Amphetamines	Inhalation, oral, IV	Yes	Yes	Not proven	Yes	Yes
Hallucinogens (PCP, LSD, etc.)	Oral	No	No	Probably	Yes	Not proven

(Modified from Rodgers and Lee,[46] with permission.)

function, a spouse who perceives the fetus as a threat, or a family history of child abuse in previous siblings are all high-risk situations and should alert caretakers to the potential for maternal neglect.

The prevalence of depression is relatively high during the gravid state. Fatigue, change of appetite, sleeplessness, and loss of energy are symptoms of both pregnancy and depression, thus making clinical depression difficult to distinguish from pregnancy-related depression. Clinical depression during pregnancy has been reported in up to 16 percent of all pregnant patients, but symptoms and signs are much more common. Depression and poor health behaviors have been documented in the past. Depressive symptoms during pregnancy have been strongly associated with increased life stresses, decreased social support, poor weight gain, and use of cigarettes, tobacco, and cocaine. These behaviors have important clinical implications for maternal health, and increase the risk for poor pregnancy outcome. Recent documentation has demonstrated an association between depressive symptoms during pregnancy and adverse health behaviors. Although the data were skewed because

Table 25-2.   Indirect Maternal Effects of Substance Abuse

Infections
  HIV: human immunodeficiency virus (and opportunistic correlates)
  TB: tuberculosis
  Hepatitis (A, B, non-A, non-B, delta)
  Syphilis
  Endocarditis
  Pulmonary infections (bronchitis, bronchopneumonia, aspiration, pneumonitis)
Toxin-induced
  Nutritional deficiency (alcohol)
  Cardiotoxins (cocaine, alcohol, amphetamines)
  Direct pulmonary effects (marijuana, tobacco)
  Hepatotoxic (cirrhosis, solvent)
  Nephropathy (heroin)

the socioeconomic status of the patients involved was not varied and the symptoms of patients were a cause or a consequence of their poor health behaviors, the data are suggestive of a link. As with all classes of abuse and neglect, it is more desirable to prevent abuse within the high-risk group than to identify and treat existing abuse. At this time attempts to protect the fetus may impinge on the mother's rights, which is discussed later.

FETAL EFFECTS

Some of the potential fetal effects that occur when substance abuse is present are difficult to prove secondary to the prolonged neurodevelopmental follow-up that is required. There are many variables of fetal exposure that the maternal unit could endure to induce such fetal effects, including the following:

1. Rate of intake (dose) and dosage interval
2. Route of administration (IV, PO, subQ, inhalation)
3. Rate of absorption
4. Elimination rate constant (KE)
5. Lipid solubility
6. Protein binding
7. Concomitant maternal pathology (renal, hepatic, etc.)
8. Placental well-being
9. Gestational age

The gestational age of the fetus is important in determining the extent and the organ system involved when changes are expected. Most malformations result from interaction between genetic and environmental factors. Rapidly growing tissues often succumb to the effects of tissue-altering substances. The underlying principle of teratogenicity is that substances that produce the most severe malforma-

tions will affect that tissue at the maximal growth rate. Most severe malformations occur during the first 6 weeks of gestation. However, malformations of the abdominal wall, gastrointestinal tract, reproductive system, and urinary tract may occur at up to 12 weeks of gestation. The second and third trimesters may be affected globally, revealing intrauterine growth retardation and vascular disruption syndromes, with other minor deviations from normal physiology.

EPIDEMIOLOGY OF SUBSTANCE ABUSE

Complications associated with substance abuse may have devastating consequences on the maternal-fetal unit. The effect of alcohol, opiates, and other substances on maternal and neonatal health has been studied. During the past decade, cocaine has been used with increasing frequency in the United States, owing to its availability in relatively purified forms. Because cocaine is readily available and easily administered, patterns of abuse have changed. Perinatal drug abuse is prevalent in all populations and is highly underreported. There are limited data on the number of women in the United States who abuse substances during pregnancy and on the number of babies born with substance-associated defects. The National Institute on Drug Abuse (NIDA) estimates that of 56 million women between the ages of 15 and 44, 15 percent (or about 8 million) are currently substance abusers. These findings were organized for a New York Academy of Science conference and are extracted from a 1985 national household survey on drug abuse. Among illicit drugs, experimentation occurs mostly with marijuana. Among those women surveyed between the ages of 22 and 25, married and without children, 13.4 percent were marijuana users at the time of the study, while 14.9 percent were users of any drugs, including marijuana. In this same age group, 9 percent of married women with children used marijuana, while 18.2 percent used any drugs.

The NIDA investigators state that an estimated 1,960,000 women aged 18 years and older used cocaine in 1985, an increase of 59.3 percent from the 1982 figure of 1,230,000. Figures are still sparse regarding other drugs such as heroin.

The National Association for Perinatal Addiction Research and Education (NAPARE) in Chicago estimates that 375,000 infants may be affected each year by their mothers' drug use during pregnancy. In 36 hospitals across the country, NAPARE examined statistics of heroin, methadone, cocaine, amphetamines, PCP, and marijuana use. The prevalence of maternal drug use in the hospital study was 11 percent with a range of 0.4 to 27 percent. Thus, from indirect information gathering techniques, substance use is increasing, although exact numbers and reportability are still difficult to obtain. In 1983, of 1711 women registered for prenatal care at Boston City Hospital, 9 percent reported heavy alcohol intake, 37 percent reported moderate drinking, and 54 percent drank rarely or not at all. Alcohol consumption has been highly underreported, owing to its social acceptance and the lack of a proper screening test. Indirect evidence of alcohol use such as pancreatitis, anemias, and nutritional deficiencies makes the diagnosis less difficult. Tobacco consumption is common and also underreported. However, the effects of smoking are well known, and the effects on the maternal-fetal unit can be extensive and also linked to polydrug abuse and stress, which may adversely affect the pregnancy.

IDENTIFICATION

Prenatal visits can alert physicians and other medical personnel to potential problems. Unfortunately, identification occurs after the patient has already become pregnant, and the fetus has already been adversely exposed to substance abuse. Thus, prepregnancy visits are the ideal time for identification of potential problems. Unfortunately, much general care is performed in the emergency department, which is not an ideal setting for effectively addressing the effects of substance abuse on the maternal-fetal unit. Pregnancy-related medical problems could be the first clue to identifying those pregnancies at highest risk for substance abuse. All levels of health care should be involved in the identification of substance-abusing pregnant patients. Medical history significant for cirrhosis, hepatitis, gastrointestinal hemorrhage, endocarditis, pneumonia, pancreatitis, nutritional deficiencies, obvious IV "track" marks, as well as edema of the extremities, should be highly suspect for substance abuse. Usually, a history is not positive for abuse, since voluntary admission of substance abuse is not very common. Association with criminal behavior such as prostitution may also be a significant positive pertinent historical finding. A history of complications during pregnancy may be a clue to future pregnancies in which the woman uses substances that may harm the maternal-fetal unit. History of intrauterine growth retardation, protracted intensive care nursery stays, abruptio placentae, meconium-stained amniotic fluid, premature rupture of membranes, and fetal deaths have all been positive correlates of substance abuse. Vertebral, neurologic, cardiac, urogenital, and skeletal fetal abnormalities are also clues to substance abuse. Recurrent fetal loss, sudden infant death syndrome (SIDS), and premature labor can also be associated with substances that may have adverse effects on the health of the maternal-fetal unit.

SPECIFIC SUBSTANCES OF ABUSE

Tobacco Inhalation

It is well known that cigarette smoke produces mortality and morbidity in the form of respiratory disease. Malignancy, chronic obstructive pulmonary disease, exacerbation of predisposing respiratory disease, as well as the effects of second-hand smoking, are some of the problems commonly associated with tobacco smoke inhalation. Less publicized is the effect on the maternal-fetal unit.

The 1970s brought about multiple issues dealing with the effects of cigarette smoke on perinatal mortality. When no cigarette smoking, less than one pack a day, and greater than one pack a day tobacco ingestion were compared, with race, socioeconomic status, increased age, parity, and anemia cofactored, light smoking was found to increase risk of fetal death by approximately 20 percent and heavy smoking increased the risk by 35 percent. This Ontario Perinatal Mortality Study revealed that certain specific placental problems were associated with dose-response relationship.

Prematurity is also associated with increased mortality and morbidity, according to epidemiologic data, and it has been shown to be a dose-response effect. In 1980, the U.S. Department of Health, Education, and Welfare published a report of the Surgeon General that listed the effects of smoking on infant health. Birth weights of babies who are born to smoking mothers are approximately 0.5 lb lighter than babies born to comparable

nonsmoking women. This has been documented to be a dose-response relationship. This relationship can be reversed if the mother stops smoking by the fourth month of gestation. There is an increase in placental weight in relation to birth weight when the fetus is exposed to cigarette smoke, which may be reflective of fetal hypoxemia. Other data suggest that not only fetal birth weight but also long-term growth and development and behavioral characteristics may be also affected. Cigarette smokers have an excess of spontaneous abortions as compared with nonsmokers. Obstetric complications such as abruptio placentae, placenta previa, bleeding early or late in pregnancy, premature or prolonged rupture of membranes, and preterm delivery are seen with increased risk with maternal smoking. Sudden infant death syndrome has also been shown to be increased in infants whose mothers smoke. These effects may be directly or indirectly mediated by placental dysfunction. Nicotine's pharmacologic effect and the effect of carboxyhemoglobin, with the complicating maternal pulmonary effects of tobacco consumption, may cause placental dysfunction. Fetal carboxyhemoglobin concentrations are approximately twice maternal levels. Nicotine does affect placental function with subsequent aberrancy in placental well-being, fetal blood flow, and oxygen delivery to the fetus. Decreased maternal and fetal oxygen-carrying capacities may ultimately affect fetal growth and development as well as mortality.

Postpartum effects of nicotine on infants extend past the placenta. Nicotine can exert influence through breast milk as well as through the environment. Dose-related concentrations of nicotine in breast milk have been shown to effect the newborn. Case reports have shown irritability, restlessness, diarrhea, and tachycardia in exposed infants. Respiratory illnesses increase in frequency in those infants exposed to ambient cigarette smoke when compared with infants of nonsmoking mothers. Hospital admission rates, decreased level of pulmonary function, and increased respiratory symptoms are all documented sequelae of tobacco smoke exposure. Earlier studies are unclear about the relationship of prenatal exposure to these aforementioned effects.

It is clear that maternal cigarette smoking during pregnancy is associated with increased mortality and morbidity. This morbidity may be significant in the postpartum period as well. The availability and social acceptance of cigarette smoking compounds the difficulty in providing adequate preventive pre- and postnatal care.

Alcohol

Since the time of Aristotle, the adverse effects of maternal alcohol consumption on the fetus have been noted to be significant. In 18th century England, awareness stimulated requests from the Royal College of Physicians to reinstate heavy taxes on alcohol. At that time, higher rates of stillbirth and childhood death in the offspring of alcoholic women as well as the birth of normal children in women whose previously alcoholic abusive pregnancies had produced abnormal children, were documented. The renowned publication in 1973 by Jones and Smith described a unique set of abnormalities in the offspring of chronic alcoholic mothers, subsequently labeled fetal alcohol syndrome. Since that time clinical, epidemiologic, and animal studies have provided evidence of serious embryotoxic and teratogenic risks associated with excessive maternal alcohol consumption. These issues have also stimulated social concerns that have resulted in warning labels on bottles of alcohol. These labeling

requirements reflect social and medical concern for development of congenital anomalies in seriously affected infants and children. Owing to the deficits in reporting fetal alcohol syndrome in 1980, the Fetal Alcohol Study Group for the Research Society of Alcoholism agreed on minimal criteria for the diagnosis of fetal alcohol syndrome (Table 25-3). It is estimated that approximately 5 percent of all congenital anomalies may be associated with prenatal maternal alcohol consumption, making this the most common teratogen.

Several factors, including dose, chronicity of alcohol use, gestational age, and duration of exposure have significant impact on the extent of the effects on the maternal-fetal unit. Alcohol as well as its metabolite acetaldehyde are embryotoxic and may also impair transfer of blood and nutrients from mother to fetus by decreasing umbilical blood flow. Embryotoxicity

Table 25-3.   Fetal Alcohol Syndrome

Minimal criteria by the Research Society on Alcoholism
  Growth
      Pre- or postnatal growth retardation or both; weight, length, of head circumference or any combination less than the 10th percentile for gestational age
  Central nervous system function
      Signs of neurologic abnormality, developmental delay, or intellectual impairment
  Craniofacial appearance (characteristic abnormalities [at least 2])
      Microcephaly: head circumference less than the 3rd percentile
      Microphthalmia or short palpebral fissures or both
      Poorly developed philtrum, thin upper lip, and flattening of the maxillary area

(From Rosett HL: A clinical perspective on the fetal alcohol syndrome. Alcoholism 4:119, 1980, with permission.)

can also result from ethanol-induced inhibition of cell division, RNA synthesis, and protein synthesis and may interfere with critical mediators and neural cell division, migration, and differentiation. Mild to moderate mental retardation is reported frequently. Delayed motor and language development are recognized early in infancy, without improvement as the child matures. Hyperactivity, hyperacusis, hypotonia, and tremulousness are commonly described in infants affected by fetal alcohol syndrome. Evaluation by the Brazelton Neonatal Assessment Scale reveals that infants who are born to alcoholic mothers have lower levels of arousal, poor habituation, and are more restless and irritable than control infants. Nutritional factors may also play a role, although they have not been found to be independent risk factors in the past. Women who consume more than 1 oz of absolute alcohol per day are at greatest risk, but there is no clear-cut threshold at which a certain quantity will produce the syndrome. Variations in alcohol's effects on the fetus make this assessment very difficult. The smallest amount of alcohol consumption associated with fetal alcohol syndrome was reported to be six bottles of beer or 2.5 oz of alcohol daily, throughout the pregnancy. The shortest reported duration of drinking with resultant fetal alcohol syndrome was the first 8 weeks of pregnancy. Maternal blood alcohol levels correlate very well with fetal levels. Maternal intervention may be warranted if a suspicion of maternal alcohol abuse is seen. Manifestations of alcohol abuse include tremor, cirrhosis, and poor nutritional status. Concomitant use of other medications such as tobacco or other drugs of abuse should raise suspicion, and warrant intervention. If one intervenes in chronic maternal alcohol use, there are multiple studies suggesting that intervention may be helpful in avoiding some of the complications associated with maternal alcohol consumption.

Two studies that evaluated the effects of abstinence reveal improvement in both neurobehavioral and intrauterine growth in the infants of those patients who are successful in abstaining from alcohol. Both Atlanta and Seattle have had intervention programs for women who drank heavily. It is suggested that the earlier in pregnancy the intake of alcohol is curtailed, the greater the potential for improved outcome. Identification of those women at risk, and subsequently trying to avoid fetal complications, requires a multisystem approach. The potential for improving fetal outcome and maternal health is great and should be pursued.

Marijuana

Consumption of marijuana has been popular since the 1960s and has become an accepted social activity for adolescents and young women of reproductive age. Various studies have shown that the prevalence of marijuana use is significant among pregnant women, revealing an incidence of 5 to 14 percent. As with alcohol consumption, these figures are probably underreported. δ-9 Tetrahydrocannabinol (THC) is the predominant psychoactive component in marijuana. THC and cotinine, an inactive metabolite, will cross the placental barrier. The effects of marijuana ingestion are controversial and may be related to concomitant use of tobacco, alcohol, and illicit drugs. The studies available, however, do show that increased carbon monoxide levels, which causes constriction of the uterine blood vessels, may impair fetal growth; this effect results in decreased nutrients. When the fetus is exposed to maternal tobacco inhalation similar effects are seen. THC has a high affinity for lipids and is found in large concentrations in fatty tissues, including the brain. Concomitant use with cigarettes, cocaine, other drugs, and alcohol has been clearly shown by Zuck-erman et al. There are only four human studies of sufficient size that take other potential drugs into consideration. Regular use has been associated with small for gestational age infants and low-birth-weight babies. Two Boston studies that included almost 15,000 patients revealed facies similar to alcohol fetal syndrome, low birth weight, and some major malformations. Two studies that included almost 8000 patients, of whom 5 to 10 percent were marijuana users, yielded those patients at risk for shorter gestations. Studies to evaluate neurodevelopmental aptitudes have not been done.

Cocaine

In the 19th century, Freud produced the first major report on the effects of cocaine. The earliest known use of cocaine was around A.D. 600 or earlier, as suggested by the finding of coca leaves in the tombs of the Indian mummies. For centuries, Peruvian Indians have used coca for its anorectic as well as its stimulating effect, and it is more of a cultural and life-style necessity. Currently, cocaine use constitutes one of the largest epidemics of drug abuse in the history of humans. It is estimated that 30 million Americans have used cocaine. Five million use it regularly, and each day another 5000 use it for the first time. Recently, lower prices and higher quality cocaine, as well as different routes of administration, have made it more accessible. Fetal exposure is increasing, and one study showed that approximately 17 percent of women use cocaine during pregnancy. Other disturbing findings reveal that the age at which adolescents first use cocaine is decreasing, and reports of accidental exposure of infants and toddlers to cocaine are increasing.

Pharmacology

The pharmacology of cocaine is fairly complex, with different forms and salts to be used for different indications and routes of administration. Cocaine is an alkaloid prepared from the leaves of the Erythroxylon coca plant. Its hydrochloride salt, made by dissolution in hydrochloric acid, is available for medicinal use. The alkaloid form of cocaine (freebase) is soluble in alcohol, acetone, oils, and ether and is not destroyed by heating. This property allows it to be inhaled by smoking. The base form of cocaine is absorbed from mucous membranes and the gastrointestinal tract. Cocaine is detoxified by cholinesterase in plasma and liver, through the water-soluble metabolites of benzoyl-ecgonine and ecgonine methylester that are excreted in the urine. Pregnant women, infants, fetuses, and patients with liver disease may have decreased plasma cholinesterase activity, making these patient populations particularly sensitive to the effects of cocaine. The action of cocaine is to block presynaptic uptake of neurotransmitters, norepinephrine and dopamine. This produces an exacerbated response of these neurotransmitters at the postsynaptic site. This effect results in an exaggerated sympathomimetic response, producing vasoconstriction, a rise in arterial blood pressure, tachycardia, mydriasis, hyperglycemia, hyperthermia, and a predisposition to ventricular arrhythmias and seizures.

Complications

Medical complications of cocaine as they apply to the maternal-fetal unit should be viewed from the fetal as well as the maternal perspectives. The maternal aspects of the complications of cocaine use can be categorized into neurologic, cardiovascular, respiratory, and other end organs that suffer from intense vasoconstriction.

Neurologic Complications. The central nervous system complications after acute exposures most frequently tend to be seizures, focal neurologic deficits, headaches, and transient loss of consciousness. There is a strong temporal association of the use of alkaloidal cocaine with both ischemic and hemorrhagic cerebrovascular events. Recent studies may warrant toxicologic screening of urine and serum of young patients with cerebrovascular disease. Hyperpyrexia and its clinical sequelae, such as rhabdomyolysis with subsequent renal insufficiency, are also frequently reported in association with cocaine intoxication. The temperature may rise as high as 45°C. There is some suggestion that this may be the leading cause of death and should be aggressively treated. Some have suggested that hyperthermia may be a variant of neuroleptic malignant syndrome, because both conditions include muscular hypertonicity with varying degrees of altered consciousness. Antipyretic agents are generally not recommended because of their lack of efficacy; dantrolene sodium may be useful but has not been adequately evaluated for this use. In a review of deaths associated with cocaine toxicity, approximately 25 percent of users suffered a neurologic event before death. Seizures frequently respond to IV administration of diazepam, as well as neuromuscular blocking agents. Hyperpyrexia also should be treated aggressively, since this may be a common cause of death. Several reports have revealed subarachnoid hemorrhages and cerebral infarctions.

Respiratory Complications. The use of freebase or crack cocaine has been associated with reports of respiratory complications. Pulmonary edema, bronchospasm, and transient pulmonary infiltrates are seen relatively frequently and can be the initial impetus for requesting medical care. Freebasing has also been associated

with pneumothorax, pneumomediastinum, pneumopericardium, and subcutaneous emphysema. Bronchiolitis obliterans and alveoli hemorrhage are also respiratory complications of maternal use that can potentially interfere with placental well-being, as well as fetal viability. Clearly, either of these potential complications can cause changes in oxygenation as well as adverse effects on the acid base balance.

Cardiac Complications. Cardiac complications of cocaine abuse include myocardial ischemia, arrhythmias, and cardiomyopathies. These are caused by the intense changes in blood pressure in relation to oxygen supply and demand inconsistencies, as well as the result of tachycardia and intense catecholamine effects during the initial phase. Coronary artery spasm with angiographically proven normal blood vessels can cause thrombosis of the coronary arteries, leading to myocardial ischemia and infarction. However, those with anatomic defects are at increased risk. Arrhythmias can present as the fatal outcome of acute cocaine intoxication. Dilated cardiomyopathy has been reported in nonpregnant cocaine abusers. Sudden death from aortic rupture after cocaine intoxication has been seen. In these cases, postmortem examination revealed an enlarged heart consistent with chronic hypertension.

Other Complications. Intestinal complications of cocaine intoxication reflect intense vasoconstriction in the form of intestinal ischemia and perforation. Hepatic periportal inflammation, and periportal and midzone necrosis have been reported in animals subjected to chronic cocaine administration. Perinatal complications as well as the effect on future neurobehavioral development are becoming evident and well documented in the literature. Most of the retrospective studies involving neonatal outcome when the fetus has been exposed to cocaine in utero demonstrate that approximately three times as many children born to mothers who abuse cocaine are small for gestational age as compared with infants with no prenatal cocaine exposure. Infants with microcephaly, as well as some with significant depression of organization response to environmental stimuli, were also seen. Hyperirritability and transient abnormal electroencephalographic changes have also been noted. Abnormal sleep patterns, poor feeding, tremors, and hypertonia are seen at a much higher rate than normal.

Teratogenicity.   Teratogenicity is thought to be prevalent during pregnancies complicated by cocaine use. Potential teratogenicity of cocaine has been questioned, and at this time it is thought that prenatal cocaine exposure induces fetal vascular disruption. The spectrum of anomalies associated with embryonic and fetal vascular disruption could result from vascular compromise that could follow hemorrhage or embryonic or fetal vasoconstriction. Such compromise may lead to disruption of the existing structures and incomplete and altered morphogenesis of developing structures. This includes nonduodenal intestinal atresia or infarction and terminal limb defects. Congenital urogenital anomalies also have been shown to be somewhat increased in both human and animal studies. An increased rate of prematurity, intrauterine growth retardation, and perinatal complications is seen in the larger studies. This is consistent with the pharmacologic properties of cocaine. There have been some reports of cerebral infarction in infants exposed to cocaine. Other central nervous system malformations include hydroencephaly, porencephaly, hypoplastic corpus colosum with unilateral parietal lobe cleft and heterotropias, intraparenchymal hemorrhage, unilateral three vessel hemispheric infarction, and encephalomalacia. Other

transient effects such as decreased cardiac output in infants of cocaine exposed mothers have also been seen.

Perinatal Complications.   Complications during labor and delivery have also been noted in cocaine exposed patients. There is a significant increase of abruptio placentae, as well as premature onset of labor immediately following the use of cocaine, regardless of the route of administration. Stillbirths have also been reported at an increased rate. Reductions of plasma cholinesterase levels slow the clearance of cocaine, increasing complications in both fetus and mother.

Postnatal cocaine exposure often leads to postnatal complications. Reports of potential exposures through breast milk, as well as passive inhalation with subsequent seizures from cocaine toxicity, have been published. Recently, a 20-month-old infant who was exposed to cocaine in the alkaloid form developed esophagitis/epiglottitis, and it was thought that both cocaine and the chemicals used to make the alkaloid form, that is, alkaline solutions, were involved. A recent study failed to demonstrate an association between prenatal cocaine exposure and an increased incidence of SIDS.

Identifying cocaine-intoxicated patients is important for therapeutic intervention. Such intervention deals with neurologic, cardiovascular, and supportive therapy for the intense vasoconstriction, which will help to improve the viability of the maternal-fetal unit. Other stimulants such as amphetamines and phenylpropanolamine can potentially have the same medical complications, owing to their vasoconstrictive response. Methamphetamine in a new form called "ice" has similar properties when inhaled with a prolonged response when dealing with the psychological aspects of these effects. Intense paranoia and a prolonged period of stimulation are seen with this medication, and the potential for maternal-fetal effects is similar to that of cocaine.

Opioids

Heroin and methadone are the two most commonly used opioids. Methadone is often prescribed for those who are addicted to other narcotics. Heroin, which is injected, is also fairly common. These drugs are often used in combination with other illicit substances such as cocaine (speedball). It is estimated that 3 to 5 percent of newborns in New York City municipal hospitals have been exposed to either heroin or methadone.

The effects of heroin or methadone on the fetus are significant. Lower birth weight, shorter length, and smaller head circumference have all been seen. The adverse effects on growth may be hypothalamic related, but decreased cell numbers have been seen in these patients. Apgar scores have also been affected in those babies who are born to heroin addicted mothers. There is an increased incidence of prematurity as well as a decreased incidence of respiratory distress syndrome (RDS). Hyperbilirubinemia is decreased compared with control babies, and SIDS is increased by 5- to 10-fold.

Neonatal behavior as evaluated by the Brazelton Neonatal Behavioral Assessment Scale shows significant impairment of interaction, motor maturity, and organizational response. Neonatal withdrawal syndrome has been seen. Complications associated with opioid abuse can be reduced if the addicted pregnant woman is treated with adequate doses of methadone in the range of 20 mg or less per day. Teratogenicity is thought to be at increased levels in some studies but still within the normal range of the general population, and most studies fail to show

an increased risk for malformations. Maternal treatment of addicted mothers should not include abrupt withdrawal. Abrupt maternal withdrawal is associated with acute fetal withdrawal, resulting in hyperactivity, hypoxemia, merconium staining, and fetal demise.

Neonatal withdrawal syndrome can be seen not only with heroin and methadone but also with other similar agents. Methadone exposed infants experience more frequent and severe signs than infants of heroin addicted mothers, and the severity is related to the dose of methadone ingested by the mother. Most signs and symptoms occur in babies within the first 48 hours, although the duration may be a few days to a few weeks. Central nervous system excitation, gastrointestinal tract problems, RDS, and autonomic symptoms may appear in the withdrawing neonate. Irritability, tremors, hypertonicity, and seizures may also be evident (Table 25-4). Methadone exposed neonates appear to have a higher risk of seizures. Treatment of the withdrawing neonate is symptomatic and regimens include paregoric, morphine, methadone, diazepam, phenobarbital, and clonidine. It is evi-

Table 25-4. Neonatal Withdrawal Syndrome

Neurologic
  Tremors, hypertonicity, high-pitched cry, hyperactivity, seizures, exaggerated neuro and deep tendon reflexes, abnormal sleeping pattern, sleeplessness
Gastrointestinal
  Vomiting, diarrhea, poor feeding, hiccoughs, salivation, marked sucking of the hand
Respiratory
  Respiratory distress, tachypnea, respiratory alkalosis, sneezing, nasal stuffiness, apnea
Other
  Diaphoresis, low grade fever

dent that adequate maternal care, improved nutritional status, minimizing infections, and proper identification of women at risk may decrease the frequency with which infants suffer the consequences of their mothers' addiction. Pregnancy outcome as well as neonatal effects of intervention with methadone maintenance are difficult to assess. The incidence of alcohol, polydrug, and tobacco use in drug-using pregnant women is high. Those in methadone maintenance programs often continue to use other substances, such as heroin, cocaine, barbiturates, and tranquilizers. These circumstances confuse the issue of whether methadone maintenance has a positive impact on neonatal outcome. A future drug-free period for these women is optimal, and much of our input should be directed toward producing a drug-free life, making future pregnancies unaffected by narcotic influences.

Barbiturates

Barbiturates are commonly used in medical practice. Most commonly, phenobarbital is used in combination with other seizure medications. It is thought that the fetal effects are minimal. The maternal effects, however, can be devastating. Maternal and fetal withdrawal have been seen. Seizures may result as a consequence of aspiration and, unlike narcotics, withdrawal may be fatal. Phenobarbital, which is often the drug of choice on a tapering schedule for pregnant women ingesting more than 400 mg of barbiturates a day, should be administered in a hospital. There is little evidence for teratogenicity, and the neonate should be observed for withdrawal syndrome.

Tranquilizers and Sedatives

Benzodiazepines are widely used, and isolated abuse with benzodiazepines may be rare. Some early studies suggested that cleft palate and cleft lip were associated with early exposure to benzodiazepines, but other studies have not confirmed these observations. Current epidemiologic and statistical evaluations of the teratogenic effects of benzodiazepines are inconclusive. Withdrawal abstinence syndrome has been seen but is less severe than with both narcotics and barbiturates. The risk of fetal abstinence syndrome has not been seen, but since polydrug abuse is common, the effects are superimposed. Narcotics, alcohol, and cocaine influences can be seen.

Hallucinogens, Phencyclidine, and Solvents

Prenatal lysergic acid diethylamide has been shown to increase the incidence of limb defects, central nervous system effects, and ocular abnormalities. The evidence of teratogenicity is not conclusive, since previous epidemics of widespread use have not shown a significant number of malformations. Phencyclidine has been associated with behavioral abnormalities but not congenital abnormalities.

Toluene-based solvents have been abused in the past. The effects are similar to those of alcohol, without a significant withdrawal syndrome. It has been shown that both the user and the exposed fetus suffer adverse effects. Some studies with small patient numbers reveal microcephaly, central nervous system effects, developmental delay, growth retardation, and some facial dysmorphology. However, complicating issues such as polysubstance abuse may influence these potential effects. The lack of controlled studies makes the significance of these effects less conclusive; however, these case studies may indicate potential adversity.

ETHICAL IMPLICATIONS OF PERINATAL ABUSE

The decision-making process for dealing with substance abuse in pregnancy is complex both in obtaining the goal and the route through which those goals are attained. The goal may be stated as a diminution in the number of affected neonates. Laws to protect these neonates have been devised to either punish the pregnant woman or offer a public health approach. The American College of Obstetricians and Gynecologists opposes criminal sanctions on women who abuse substances during pregnancy and supports the public health-oriented approach of providing improved perinatal care, treatment for drug dependencies, and rehabilitation. In states such as Florida, Hawaii, Illinois, Indiana, Massachusetts, Minnesota, and Oklahoma, drug exposed or addicted newborns are considered to be abused and neglected under the law. California, Connecticut, Illinois, and Pennsylvania have approved proposals to provide services, education, and treatment to substance abusing pregnant women. In the state of Minnesota, obstetrician-gynecologists are obliged to test pregnant patients when there is a medical indication of possible drug use, and all positive tests must be reported to the health department. The state of Iowa offers protection against prosecution for pregnant substance abusers. Positive toxicologies are used to obtain appropriate medical and social intervention. It is clear that newborns need protection. However, in different states, the lawmakers themselves have not yet found a common stance to achieve this goal.

In July 1989, a Florida woman was convicted of child abuse for using cocaine while pregnant. Since then, at least six similar cases have been brought in Massachusetts, Florida, South Carolina, Virginia, and Washington, D.C. How far should states go in protecting unborn children from maternal influences?

The case of the *State of Florida v Johnson* is widely viewed as the nation's first criminal conviction of a woman for health endangering behavior during pregnancy. After a urine toxicology test in the newborn was positive, Jennifer Johnson faced criminal charges in Florida for child abuse in delivering illegal substances to a minor under age 18. Not only was Ms. Johnson sentenced to 1 year of community control in a drug treatment program, but she also received 14 years of probation and 200 hours of community service. The ruling also included that if Ms. Johnson should ever conceive again, she must advise her probation officer of the pregnancy and enter a prenatal care program approved by the court.

Criminal prosecution raises unresolved issues of fetal rights and legal intervention in the lives of pregnant women. Some argue that attempts to dictate how a woman should treat her fetus could lay the groundwork for overturning *Roe v Wade*, the Supreme Court decision that legalized abortion.

Mandatory testing would only give short-term solutions to a long-term problem. A positive screen reveals little about the new mother's ability to care for her child if these tests are used routinely to place newborns in foster care. Those who administer testing programs and are responsible for the direction of such programs should evaluate the program's effectiveness and fairness, the purpose of the testing, voluntary versus involuntary testing, the specificity and sensitivity of the assay, confidentiality of results, and measures to be taken if the test is positive.

To force a pregnant woman to abstain from certain deleterious behavior is unlawful under *Roe v Wade* as an infringement on the woman's constitutionally protected right to autonomy and bodily integrity during her pregnancy. The American College of Obstetricians and Gynecologists recently concluded that the use of judicial authority to implement treatment regimens to protect the fetus violates the pregnant woman's autonomy. Can we monitor all women who are pregnant and deal with them effectively? Can we ascertain if they are acting in accordance with their physician's orders, compliant with their medications, and providing appropriate prenatal care, nutrition as well as abstinence from deleterious chemicals? The best way to assure that prenatal care is not obtained is by threatening this group of patients, who already receive few services.

Treatment facilities for pregnant women are vastly underdeveloped. A recent survey of 78 drug treatment programs in New York City showed that 54 percent categorically exclude pregnant women, 57 percent refuse to treat pregnant Medicaid patients, and 87 percent specifically excluded crack abusing women receiving Medicaid. Logistically it would seem that programs would be developed combining counseling, gynecologic, prenatal, and pediatric care including parental training and job readiness, and identifying those women at risk before pregnancy. The substance abusing patient is easily identified if proper patient-physician rapport can be developed. A decision needs to be made whether to make tests like urine toxicology screening part of a comprehensive health care delivery system or whether they should be used selectively for those patients who would sometimes be excluded from the health care system if the tests were to be used for punitive reasons. We stand the greatest chance of improving prenatal care and fetal health by encouraging a patient-physician relationship as opposed to adversely using these examinations to incarcerate patients. Clearly, our current health care and penal systems cannot cope with the onslaught of patients who are at potential risk, and we must deal with this on a higher plane. The natural impulse to help a baby will continue to tempt courts into interventionist policies. Opponents of these policies will declare an impingement on constitutional rights. Our only chance for proper care for these patients is to improve the supporting systems and discard the potential barrier between the mother and child and within the judicial system.

SUGGESTED READINGS

1. American College of Obstetricians and Gynecologists: Committee Opinion No. 55. October, 1987
2. Bingol N, Fuchs M, Diaz V et al: Teratogenicity of cocaine in humans. J Pediatr 110:93, 1987
3. Blinick G, Jerez E, Wallach RC: Methadone maintenance, pregnancy and progeny. JAMA 225:477, 1973
4. Carin I, Glass L, Parekh A et al: Neonatal methadone withdrawal: effect of two treatment regimens. Am J Dis Child 137:1166, 1983
5. Chasnoff IJ, Burns KA, Burns WJ: Cocaine use in pregnancy: perinatal morbidity and mortality. Neurotoxicol Teratol 9:291, 1987
6. Chasnoff IJ, Burns WJ, Schnell SH, Burns KA: Cocaine use in pregnancy. N Engl J Med 313:666, 1985
7. Chasnoff IJ, Bussey M, Savich R, Stack CA: Perinatal cerebral infarction and maternal cocaine use. J Pediatr 108:456, 1986
8. Chasnoff IJ, Chisum GM, Kaplan WE: Maternal cocaine use and genitourinary tract malformations. Teratology 37:201, 1988

9. Chasnoff IJ, Griffith DR, MacGregor S et al: Temporal patterns of cocaine use in pregnancy: perinatal outcome. JAMA 261:1741, 1989

10. Chasnoff IJ, Lewis DE, Squires L: Cocaine intoxication in a breast fed infant. Pediatrics 80:836, 1987

11. Cindon J: The spectrum of fetal abuse in pregnant women. J Nervous Mental Dis 174:509, 1980

12. Clarren SK, Smith DW: The fetal alcohol syndrome. N Engl J Med 298:1063, 1978

13. Connaughton JF, Reeser D, Schut J et al: Perinatal addiction: outcome and management. Am J Obstet Gynecol 129:679, 1977

14. Cregler LL, Mark H: Medical complications of cocaine abuse. N Engl J Med 315:1495, 1986

15. Doberczak TM, Shanzer S, Senie RT, Kandall SR: Neonatal neurologic and electroencephalographic effects of intrauterine cocaine exposure. J Pediatr 113:354, 1988

16. Driver C, Chavkin W, Higginson G: Survey of infants awaiting placement in voluntary hospitals, 1986–1987. Report to the New York City Health Department, New York, NY, 1987

17. Finnegan LP (ed): Drug Dependence in Pregnancy: Clinical Management of Mother and Child. NIDA Services Research Monograph Series, Rockville, MD, U.S. Government Printing Office, 1978, p. 33

18. Finnegan LP: The effect of narcotics and alcohol on pregnancy and the newborn. Ann NY Acad Sci 362:136, 1981

19. Fleisher LD: Wrongful births: when is there liability for prenatal injury? Am J Dis Child 141:1260, 1987

20. Fried PA, Buckingham M, Von Kulmitz P: Marijuana use during pregnancy and perinatal risk factor. Am J Obstet Gynecol 144:922, 1983

21. Fried PA, Watkinson B, Willan A: Marijuana use during pregnancy and decreased length of gestation. Am J Obstet Gynecol 150:23, 1984

22. Greenland S, Staisch K, Brown N et al: The effects of marijuana use during pregnancy: I. A preliminary epidemiologic study. Am J Obstet Gynecol 143:408, 1982

23. Harlap S, Davis AM: Infant admissions to hospital and maternal smoking. Lancet 1:527, 1974

24. Harlap S, Shions PH: Alcohol, smoking and incidence of spontaneous abortion in the first and second trimester. Lancet 1:173, 1980

25. Herzlich BC, Arsura EL, Pagala M, Grob D: Rhabdomyolysis related to cocaine abuse. Ann Intern Med 108:335, 1988

26. Hingson R, Alpert JJ, Day N et al: Effects of maternal drinking and marijuana use on fetal growth and development. Pediatrics 70:539, 1989

27. Hoyme H, Jones K, Dixon S, et al: Prenatal cocaine exposure and fetal vascular disruption. Pediatrics 85:743, 1990

28. Interim Hearings on Parental Substance Abuse and Its Effects on the Fetus and Children. California Legislature, Senate Select Committee on Substance Abuse (1988) (testimony of Dr. Xylina Bean)

29. Interim Hearings on Parental Substance Abuse and Its Effects on the Fetus and Children. California Legislature, Senate Select Committee on Substance Abuse (1988) (testimony of Senator John Seymour)

30. Isner JM, Choksi SK: Cocaine and vasospasm. N Engl J Med 321:1604, 1989

31. Itkonen J, Schnoll S, Glassworth J: Pulmonary dysfunction in "freebase" cocaine users. Arch Intern Med 144:2195, 1984

32. Jones KL, Smith DW: Recognition of the fetal alcohol syndrome in early infancy. Lancet 2:999, 1973

33. Kaltenbach K, Finnegan LP. Neonatal abstinence syndrome: pharmacotherapy and developmental outcome. Neurotoxicol Teratol 8:353, 1986

34. Koren G: Nonmedical drug and chemical use in pregnancy. p. 143. In Koren G (ed): Maternal Fetal Toxicology, 1989

35. Lange RA, Ciggarroa RG, Yancy CW et al: Cocaine-induced coronary artery vasoconstriction. N Engl J Med 321:1557, 1989

36. Lathers CM, Tyan LS, Spino MM, Agarwal I: Cocaine-induced seizures, arrhythmias and sudden death. J Clin Pharmacol 28:584, 1988

37. Lichentfeld PJ, Rubin DB, Feldman RS:

Subarachnoid hemorrhage precipitated by cocaine smoking. Arch Neurol 41:223, 1984

38. Linn S, Schoenbaum SC, Monson RR et al: The association of marijuana use with outcome of pregnancy. Am J Public Health 73:1161, 1983

39. Luque MA, Cavallaro DL, Torres M et al: Pneumomediastinum, pneumothorax, and subcutaneous emphysema after alternate cocaine inhalation and marijuana smoking. Pediatr Emerg Care 3:107, 1987

40. MacGregor S, Louis K, Chasmoff I, et al: Cocaine use during pregnancy: adverse perinatal outcome. Am J Obstet Gynecol 157:686, 1987

41. Maden JD, Payne TF, Miller S: Maternal cocaine abuse and effect on the newborn. Pediatrics 77:209, 1986

42. Naeye RL, Blane W, Le Blanc W, Khatamee MA: Fetal complications of maternal heroin addiction: abnormal growth, infection, and episodes of stress. J Pediatr 83:1055, 1973

43. Oro AS, Dixon SD: Perinatal cocaine and methamphetamine exposure: maternal and neonatal correlates. J Pediatr 111:571, 1987

44. Roberts JR, Quattrocchi E, Howland MA: Severe hyperthermia secondary to intravenous drug abuse. Am J Emerg Med 2:273, 1984

45. Rodgers BD: Substance abuse in pregnancy. Med North Am 38:6865, 1989

46. Rodgers BD, Lee RV: Drug abuse. p. 570. In Burrow GN, Ferris TF (eds): Medical Complications During Pregnancy. WB Saunders, Philadelphia, 1988

47. *Roe v Wade*, 410 U.S. 113, 93 State Court 705

48. Rosett HL, Weiner L: Alcohol and the Fetus: A Clinical Perspective. Oxford University Press, New York, 1984

49. Roth D, Alarcon JJ, Fernandez JA et al: Acute rhabdomyolysis associated with cocaine intoxication. N Engl J Med 319:673, 1988

50. Schachne JS, Roberts BH, Thompson PD: Coronary artery spasm and myocardial infarction associated with cocaine abuse. N Engl J Med 310:1665, 1984

51. Schnoll SH, Karan LD: Substance abuse. JAMA 261:2890, 1989

52. Weiner RS, Lockhart JT, Schwartz RG: Dilated cardiomyopathy and cocaine abuse. Am J Med 81:699, 1986

53. Whatever Happened to the Boarder Babies. New York, Office of Policy Management, Office of the Comptroller, New York, 1989

54. Woods JR, Plessinger MA, Clark KE: Effect of cocaine on uterine blood flow and fetal oxygenation. JAMA 257:957, 1987

55. Zuckerman B, Frank DA, Hingson R et al: Effects of maternal marijuana and cocaine use on fetal growth. N Engl J Med 320:762, 1989

26

Other Forms of Neglect

Mary Owen
Pierre Coant

Parents have responsibilities to their children. They must provide food, clothing, shelter, health care, education, a safe environment, and emotional support. Child neglect refers to inadequate provision of these fundamental needs. It is a problem with a wide spectrum and vague diagnostic criteria, ranging in severity from suboptimal parental skills to intentional withholding of vital provisions.

Child neglect has been closely linked to child abuse. Often discussed together in studies and reviews, the problems are seen as a continuum of the same disease process. Indeed, within the same household, neglect and abuse often coexist, and the child who is neglected may be actively abused as well. Fifteen percent of maltreatment reports involve both abuse and neglect. However, the disease process, psychodynamics, and outcome are probably distinct. While both the abusive and neglectful parent may share qualities of immaturity and abnormal emotional dependency, abuse is an act of aggression and the result of active maltreatment by the parent. Neglect, by contrast, is a passive process, and in most cases there is no active intent to harm the child. Rather, acts of neglect are more often the result of lack of motivation, poor judgment, or poor understanding of the child's needs and developmental stages.

Child neglect is not specific to any one racial, religious, or socioeconomic group. Clearly, however, there are factors that predispose certain parents to child neglect. Children born to single mothers or parents who are poor, very young, and isolated with limited family and community support are at increased risk of being neglected. Also, households with more than four children per family are more likely to foster neglect. Many reports of neglect are from hospitals that serve the lower socioeconomic groups. The stresses of inadequate finances, lack of social and familial support, poor education, and unpreparedness for the responsibilities of parenthood probably predispose these groups to increased incidence of child maltreatment. By contrast, in upper socioeconomic groups some of these stresses have been removed, and child-rearing is more often postponed until full adulthood. A 1988 study on the national incidence of child neglect revealed that, compared with children from families with yearly incomes greater than $15,000, those from families with incomes of less than $15,000 were 10 times more likely to be physically neglected, 8 times more likely to be educationally neglected, and

5 times more likely to be emotionally neglected. There is no question, however, that child neglect occurs at all social and economic levels. Indeed, in one of the earliest case studies of emotional neglect, Coleman describes two children with feeding disorders, failure-to-thrive, and progressive developmental delay secondary to poor nurturing and emotional deprivation; both children had been raised in middle-class homes by successful college educated parents. Some investigators also believe that the apparent prevalence of neglect in lower socioeconomic groups is partly a reflection of underreporting among the more affluent.

It is difficult to ascertain the true incidence of child neglect as reporting patterns have changed with society's increased awareness of this problem. In 1986, the national annual incidence of child abuse and neglect was estimated at 1.5 million, and about 65 percent of these were reports of neglect. Others have estimated the yearly incidence of neglect alone to range from 500,000 to 2 million. Physical neglect is the most common form of neglect, occurring in almost one child per hundred. Emotional and educational neglect are estimated to occur in four and five children per thousand, respectively. However, these figures may not reflect the true incidence of neglect. Child neglect is difficult to diagnose because the symptoms are usually vague, physical findings are often absent, and laboratory data generally are not helpful. To compound the diagnostic difficulties, there are changing social standards, cultural differences, and constant technologic advancements that alter the standards of child care. Acceptable practice in one era may be considered frank neglect in another. For example, driving a car with unrestrained children was once commonly accepted; it is now considered neglectful, and in most states a violation of the law, to allow children to ride in cars without age-appropriate restraints.

Child neglect is manifested in many ways and takes several forms. In this chapter, we discuss physical, safety, educational, and emotional neglect. Medical and nutritional neglect are discussed in Chapter 24.

PHYSICAL NEGLECT

A child's most basic and immediate needs are food, clothing, and shelter. It is the parent's responsibility to provide a home with adequate heating and hygienic conditions, adequate clothing, and age-appropriate diet. Failure of the parent to meet these needs defines physical neglect.

Health care providers and school and day-care personnel may suspect physical neglect when an unkempt child has been inadequately bathed, smells of stool or urine, is inordinately hungry, or is inadequately clothed. Although a single demonstration of poor hygiene does not indicate neglectful parenting, consistent failure in maintaining minimal standards of a child's hygiene may reflect unsanitary conditions in the home, and attempts to improve parents' caretaking should be made. If the problem is believed to be severe, or is associated with other symptoms of neglect, a referral should be made to investigate the home and evaluate the extent of neglect.

Substandard home conditions are often brought to the attention of child protection agencies by neighbors, extended family members, or social service workers who may be involved with the family. In evaluating the home, particular attention should be paid to the presence of proper heating and ventilation, cooking facilities and whether food is present, toilets and sinks should be functional, general cleanliness and condition of garbage accumulation and disposal should be noted, and evidence of rodents and insects should also be noted. The general condition of other household members should also be appraised. If the home is believed to be suboptimal but presents no immediate risk to the child, the parents should be instructed in proper housekeeping, given specific guidelines for modifications, and follow-up should be arranged. If the home poses immediate health hazards, such as no heat in cold weather, rodent infestation, or unhealthy sanitary conditions, the family should be placed in a more suitable environment. Occasionally, physical neglect is secondary to parental drug or alcohol abuse or psychological disturbance. In such cases, children should be placed in foster care until the problem is corrected. Generally, instruction with close monitoring will aid in improving the home situation. Frequently, families will benefit from financial assistance and social service programs in the community.

Caution must be used to avoid overreporting physical neglect, and personal standards should not be used to judge the appropriateness of a situation. A child who appears unkempt but is happy, well fed, and interacts well with others should not be reported. The most important consideration is whether neglect has harmed or caused problems for the child.

SAFETY NEGLECT

Beyond simply providing physical shelter, parents are responsible for providing a safe environment with appropriate supervision. For example, medicines, poisons, and firearms in the home should be locked away; car restraints should be used when travelling; working smoke detectors should be installed; safe, age-appropriate toys should be provided; and continuous, appropriate adult supervi-

sion should be available. Although no situation can be made thoroughly childproof, injuries that occur because of inadequate safety precautions are preventable and can be considered a consequence of safety neglect.

Preventable injuries occur for several reasons. Most commonly, parents lack a good understanding of their child's developmental stages, capabilities, and risks, and they cannot anticipate potential "accidents." For example, an unsupervised young infant may fall off a bed or dresser because the parents did not understand that the baby could roll over. Injuries can occur as a result of poor parental judgment. For example, a 2-year-old child who is left by the swimming pool under the supervision of a 5-year-old sibling, is inadequately supervised and at risk of drowning. Other preventable injuries occur because parents are distracted or poorly motivated. Physicians and other health care providers and educators have the opportunity to discuss age-associated risks and preventive measures before injuries occur. Injury prevention discussions need to be a part of well-child care, and educating parents should be seen as the first step toward preventing safety neglect.

Physicians often see the outcome of inadequate safety precautions when injured children present for medical care. Inquiries need to be made regarding the mechanism of the injury, first to evaluate the possibility of abuse and then to consider how the injury might have been prevented. Parents may then be counseled on preventive measures for the future. The distraught parent who arrives in the emergency department with an injured child rarely benefits from patronizing lectures on general safety. On the other hand, if gross neglect is apparent or the parent seems inappropriately unconcerned, further investigation regarding details of the present injury and previous injuries in the patient and other siblings should be pursued.

Occasionally, a physician or other health care provider is presented with a child who has had repeated episodes of preventable injuries. Once termed "the accident-prone child," the child may actually be the victim of safety neglect. If the injuries have been serious and the child is at significant risk for further harm, if the parents cannot be educated, or if the injuries are associated with other forms of neglect or abuse, child protective services need to be involved and the child placed in a more suitable environment.

EDUCATIONAL NEGLECT

Parents' inability or unwillingness to ensure a child's school attendance is considered educational neglect. This includes permitting chronic truancy, for example, allowing a child to miss school for trivial reasons; keeping a child at home for inappropriate purposes such as to work or to babysit; or failing to obtain recommended special education services. After physical neglect, educational neglect is the second most common form of child neglect, with the majority of affected children having missed more than 25 percent of school days. Parents who have been informed of the school's concern regarding their child's absence need to take appropriate measures, such as seeking counseling or medical care and providing adequate transportation. If the parents do not respond appropriately, child protective services need to be involved. School phobia may pose a special problem to a child's attendance and education and may require specific psychological therapy.

EMOTIONAL NEGLECT

Emotional neglect is defined as a lack of nurturing and psychological support for the child by the parent or primary caretaker. Although emotional neglect reflects a passive attitude on the part of the parent, the child is hurt because of inadequate provision for the emotional needs necessary for human growth and development. According to the Study of National Incidence and Prevalence of Child Abuse and Neglect: 1988, it occurs in three to four children per thousand, and it may affect as many as 4 percent of children with chronic illnesses such as asthma. The true incidence of emotional neglect is difficult to measure because it leaves no clear traces and occurs within the secluded environment of the home.

Human development from infancy through childhood, adolescence, and adulthood depends on interactions with other human beings. An early aspect of child development is the bonding between infant and parent. This initial bonding provides a foundation for future interactions and is an active process. Emotional neglect occurs when the parent ignores the infant's attempts at bonding. Lack of stimulation leads to emotional deprivation, and the failure in meeting the child's emotional needs can have serious consequences in emotional development, just as the failure in fulfilling nutritional needs can hinder a child's physical growth. Bawkin described how emotional deprivation in young children could lead to failure-to-thrive and even death. He noted that in the early 1900s homeless infants who remained in foster care institutions frequently had very little emotional stimulation and human contact because caretakers were afraid of contagious infection. Consequently, these children had depressed affects, they were not interested in feeding, rarely smiled, and did not explore their environment. The mortality rate approached a staggering 100 percent in infants admitted to institutions for long-term care, and in one institution no child admitted under 1 year of age for chronic care lived to his second birthday. The term "hospitalism" came to describe these infants who lacked nurturing and love, and exhibited the features of emotional neglect. Later in the century, the same signs and symptoms were described in children raised in their natural homes, and the problem was referred to as emotional neglect.

All children need to be nurtured as they develop toward adulthood. Parents who love their children spend time with them in different activities, are available to answer questions, demonstrate affection, and try to develop their physical, educational, and emotional growth. In some times and cultures, providing this nurturing has been considered spoiling the child. Indeed, if the novel is any reflection of reality in pre-Victorian England, many children were raised in a most austere emotional environment, and what is now considered emotional neglect was the accepted childrearing practice then. Parents need to understand that spending time and playing with their child and displaying affection is not "spoiling" but an essential part of developing emotional security in their child.

Emotional neglect is a passive lack of nurturing and differs from the active behavior in emotional abuse, where a child's psyche is attacked by verbal abuse and instillation of fears. The relationship of emotional neglect within the larger context of psychological abuse has been discussed by Gabarino, who describes five levels of this process: (1) *rejecting*—not acknowledging a child's worth and importance; (2) *isolating*—separating a child from friends to prevent the child from learning through social relationships; (3) *terrorizing*—using verbal abuse to frighten the child and create fears that are not well founded; (4) *ignoring*—depriving the child of stimulation; (5) *corrupting*—forcing a child to engage in antisocial behavior. Of these five types, ignoring is the most passive and is, in essence, emotional neglect.

Emotional neglect is difficult to diagnose, since it leaves emotional scars, not physical markings. The diagnosis, therefore, requires an assessment of the child's developmental and emotional progress. These infants are often withdrawn and listless. Lacking external stimulation, they have turned their attentions inward, or they may demonstrate an abnormal interest in other adults by seeking emotional gratification from outside caregivers to fulfill their psychological needs. Other children may present with language and motor delay or with failure-to-thrive. Because much of parent-infant interaction occurs during feeding, problems may develop in this area, including poor feeding, self-induced vomiting, and rumination. Older children and adolescents present in more varied patterns after enduring emotional neglect. These children may be depressed or extremely aggressive. Lack of interaction with a primary caregiver hinders them as they try to develop skills for interacting with others, and school problems often occur.

The management of emotional neglect begins by suspecting the diagnosis. A history of maternal depression or parental stresses, a physical examination that reveals a poorly interactive child, or poor growth and development without any organic etiology, all suggest the diagnosis of emotional neglect. If a child with these findings is placed in the hospital or different environment and rapidly becomes more interactive with increased weight gain and developmental improvement, then the diagnosis of emotional neglect is further supported. Once the diagnosis is made, the parents should be counseled regarding nurturing skills, or the child should be placed in a more stimulating environment. Older children frequently benefit from psychological treatment. Early diagnosis is important because the longer the neglect continues, the more difficult it becomes to reverse the psychological scars. When left untreated, emotional neglect produces adults who find it difficult to love others and to interact with children and adults in society.

CONCLUSION

The recognition and management of child neglect are important issues in pediatrics. Besides the immediate problems related directly to the risks of inadequate physical and emotional support, education, and safety precautions that can be remedied by altering the child's environment, there are other longer-reaching consequences of child neglect. More so even than abused children, neglect victims manifest aggressive behavior and difficulties relating to peers that persist long after correction of the home situation is made. There is also evidence suggesting that these children may develop delinquent behavior and may become neglectful and abusive parents themselves. For these reasons, it is important to develop methods to prevent child neglect from occurring, and to diagnose and treat as early as possible neglect that is already present. Preventive measures, including strengthening maternal-infant bonding with early intervention in the perinatal period and providing home nursing and social programs to high-risk groups, are being investigated and show some promise. Nurturing nursery school and day-care programs may offer some of the love and concern that is absent in the home. Treatment of children who are already victims of neglect is best managed by a team effort. Physicians, public health nurses, counselors, social workers, and judicial personnel need to work together to diagnose and carefully document the extent of neglect. The immediate situation can be improved by providing education and appropriate social and financial support, long-term care and follow-up, and, when necessary because of poor parental response, by placing the child in foster care. As was once said by Thomas Hardy, "the little ones of our time are collectively the children of us adults of the time, and entitled to our general care." It is our responsibility to work with the parents to provide the best possible care for the child.

SUGGESTED READINGS

1. Bawkin H: Emotional deprivation in infants. J Pediatr 35:512, 1949
2. Coleman RW: Environmental retardation in infants living in families. Pediatrics 19:285, 1957
3. Gabarino J: The psychologically battered child. Pediatr Ann 18:502, 1989
4. Kempe CH, Helfer RE: The Battered Child. University of Chicago Press, Chicago, 1980
5. Kempe CH: Child abuse—the pediatrician's role in child advocacy and preventive pediatrics. Am J Dis Child 132:255, 1978
6. Morse CW: A three year followup study of abused and neglected children. Am J Childhood Dis 120:439, 1970
7. Newberger EH, Reed RB, Daniel JH et al: Pediatric social illness: toward an etiologic classification. J Pediatr 60:2, 1977
8. Newberger EH: Child Abuse. Little Brown, Boston, 1982

9. Williams GJ: Traumatic Abuse and Neglect of Children at Home. Johns Hopkins University Press, Baltimore, 1980

10. Study of National Incidence and Prevalence of Child Abuse and Neglect, 1988: U.S. Department of Health and Human Services publication. National Center on Child Abuse and Neglect, 1988

11. Widom CS: The cycle of violence. Science 144:160, 1989

27

Acute Psychiatric Manifestations

Anthony L. Rostain
Wendy E. Shumway

Child abuse in whatever form inevitably produces psychological distress in the child victim. This chapter reviews the immediate psychiatric manifestations of child abuse to enable practitioners to (1) recognize common signs of post-traumatic stress disorder and related psychological disturbances in victims of abuse, (2) understand how the child victim experiences the trauma of abuse and how the child's family and support systems function to help or hinder the child's coping process, and (3) identify treatment approaches available to the child and family.

Before the identification of child abuse, practitioners and other helping professionals will encounter children who demonstrate symptoms of distress without any clear etiology. These symptoms may take the form of behavioral, emotional, cognitive, and/or interpersonal disturbances that are quite variable in their quality and severity. Table 27-1 lists the patterns of child psychiatric disturbance that may arise from abuse. They span the entire spectrum of childhood psychopathology reflecting that child abuse is both a specific and nonspecific etiologic factor in

childhood behavior and emotional disorders. Among the symptoms reported in studies of abused children are excessive fears, startle reactions, hypervigilance, sleep disturbances, avoidance behavior, withdrawal, constriction of emotions, reexperience or reenactment of the trauma, depression, low self-esteem, guilt, psychosomatic and behavior problems, explosive rage and maladaptive expressions of anger, and sexual disorders.

Numerous factors mediate the acute psychiatric manifestations of child abuse: the type of abuse (whether physical, sexual, or psychological); the relationship of the child to the perpetrator; the intensity, severity and frequency of abuse; the circumstances of abuse (e.g., whether repeated or episodic, predictable or unpredictable, secretive versus witnessed, etc.); and the interaction of the abuse with other important variables such as the child's developmental profile (cognitive, emotional, physical), temperament and personality, typical behavior patterns, gender, attachments to important caregivers and social supports; and the family's characteristics (e.g., resources,

357

Table 27-1. Acute Psychiatric
Manifestations of Child Abuse

Behavioral
  Acting out
    Aggressive
    Hyperactive
    Delinquent
    Hypersexual
    Self-defeating
  Acting in
    Avoidant
    Regressive
    Psychosomatic
Emotional
  Depressive
  Anxious
  "Shut down"
  Self-deprecating
  Hypomanic
Cognitive
  Distractibility
  Inattention
  Memory dysfunction
  Academic difficulties
Interpersonal
  Family dysfunction
  Peer conflicts
  Challenging authority

stresses, supports, interrelationships, stability).

It is difficult for clinicians to imagine the intense emotional reactions experienced by children as they are beaten, burned, shaken, thrown down, sexually molested, or psychologically abused. The threat of physical harm or annihilation can overwhelm the senses, creating a feeling of panic or terror, and destroying the child's fundamental sense of security. In its most extreme form, abuse leads to a loss of ego functioning, including impaired reality testing, psychotic disorganization, and regression to an infantile level of mental functioning. This period of ego decompensation persists for variable lengths of time. When the clinician finally encounters a child who has been abused, the child may have already rein-

tegrated and have started to use psychological coping and defense mechanisms (described below) to handle the overpowering and intense feelings generated by the abuse.

In many ways, the distinctions between the acute and chronic manifestations of child abuse are difficult if not impossible to specify. If the abuse is quickly noticed and disclosed, clinicians may be able to observe the immediate psychological reactions of children. If the abuse is repeated chronically over a long period of time, both acute and chronic psychiatric symptoms may be present at the time of disclosure. The process of disclosure also produces a great deal of stress and potential trauma for the child and family, and the reactions of other people important to the child in the revelations of abuse profoundly influence the child's mental status.

PSYCHOLOGICAL DEFENSE MECHANISMS OF ABUSED CHILDREN

In view of these general principles, it is important to review several concepts that have been developed to explain how children handle the feelings they experience when they have been abused. The psychological defense mechanisms observed in abused children can be interpreted as attempts to protect themselves (and those they love) from the emotional pain of the abuse. *Denial* involves the refusal to acknowledge an aspect of reality. Many children simply deny that they have been abused and will not be able to recall the episodes of abuse. Others respond by escaping into fantasy and *regressing* to a younger developmental stage. Some will withdraw into themselves so as to avoid contact with other people (*avoidance*), while others will become infantile and will demand a great deal of attention from adults. In extreme situations, the child will become completely helpless and overwhelmed with feelings of rage, hatred, hopelessness, and terror (*ego disorganization and disintegration*). Children may attempt to master their feelings by acting very aggressively or seductively toward others in a replay of the abusive situation (*repetition compulsion*) or they may attempt to get others to act in an abusive fashion toward them (*reenactment*). When the child's abuser is someone on whom the child is dependent, the child may begin to imitate this person's behavior in relationships with others (*identification with the aggressor*). The child might behave in an "over-responsible" fashion with an exaggerated sense of concern for others and a pseudomature approach and attitude toward life (*reaction formation*).

Through the mechanism of *displacement*, the child channels unacceptable feelings onto people, objects, or situations that are less likely to retaliate or hurt. Commonly, the child inflicts pain on younger siblings, pets, or weaker schoolmates. Using *projection*, the child begins to view others as angry and hostile, interprets their behavior as menacing, and approaches them with the expectation of being harmed. *Splitting* is a psychological mechanism through which self and others are viewed as either exclusively "good" or "bad." When children have been abused by their parents, they may resort to splitting to preserve the fantasy that their parent is "good." They may perceive others or themselves as "bad," and will react accordingly, either rejecting the "bad" person or viewing themselves as deserving of punishment. *Dissociation* occurs when certain mental processes become fragmented and disconnected from consciousness. This may take the form of *derealization*, in which the sense of reality of certain events is disturbed; *deper-*

sonalization, in which the child experiences disturbed perceptions of self or body; or *doubling*, in which the child experiences self as being outside the body, watching as if it were someone else. Dissociation can also lead to the appearance of physical or psychological symptoms that are not directly or consciously linked to the trauma of the abuse. With the mechanism of *repression*, children automatically "forget" that they have been abused (often to the point of being completely amnesic about the event). By contrast, through the use of *suppression*, they voluntarily and actively exclude from awareness any thoughts and feelings about the abuse.

Beyond these specific defenses, abused children often suffer disturbances of social, emotional, and ego functioning. The abused child's basic trust in other human beings is undermined or destroyed. Without this trust, the child can neither develop healthy social relationships nor meet the challenges of later developmental tasks. Abuse also challenges the child's sense of self. The loss of self-esteem may be characterized by self-blame, self-doubt, self-hatred, shame, humiliation, overwhelming guilt, and a sense of being damaged and undeserving of love. The net result of these psychological injuries is an impaired ability to adapt to the constantly changing demands of life, a concept that Wolfe refers to as "adaptational failure." In other words, the specific acute and chronic psychiatric problems that abused children experience can all be understood as stemming from the developmental disruptions and unhealthy interpersonal relationship patterns that are occasioned by the abuse.

Scientific research into the psychiatric manifestations of child abuse (physical and sexual) has described a broad spectrum of childhood reactions. While a handful of studies suggests that there are no prolonged negative consequences for the child victim, the majority of studies point to multiple behavioral, emotional, and interpersonal sequelae of abuse. Given the multiplicity of outcomes from child abuse, we present several illustrative cases that highlight the most common patterns in which abuse manifests itself acutely. We focus on three types of disturbances: acting out, acting in, and posttraumatic stress disorder. It should be kept in mind that children may manifest *all* of these disturbances at some point in time, and that these cases are presented to highlight the spectrum of clinical symptomatology seen with child abuse.

Acting Out

Danny, the only child of a single mother, first came to psychiatric attention at age 7 due to his aggressive behaviors at home and in school. His mother reported that he had always been impulsive but now he was constantly hitting peers or provoking fights. He had recently attempted to stab his mother with a kitchen knife during one of his temper outbursts. Mother also was concerned that Danny, who had been toilet trained by age 3, had recently begun wetting the bed and soiling his pants. His teacher reported that Danny was masturbating during school on a daily basis. Danny's mother and teacher both reported a preoccupation with guns, weapons, policemen, and badges, which consumed Danny's play. During the first month of treatment, Danny revealed that he had been sodomized and fondled by his grandfather on several occasions from ages 5 to 7.

As illustrated above and as reported by Green, Morse et al., and Conte and Scheurman, it may often be the acting out behaviors such as fighting and arguing that first bring a child to professional attention. These behaviors reflect the child's intense anger at the perpetrator as well as a defensive posture of identification with the aggressor. By identifying with the violent and aggressive adult, children attempt to gain control of their overwhelming fear and helplessness. Danny demonstrated his identification with the aggressor both through his excessive physical aggression toward others and through his escape into violent fantasies. His preoccupation with being a policeman also demonstrated underlying wishes to be protected from abuse and to punish his abuser.

Danny's case also exemplifies age-inappropriate sexual behavior that is another type of acting out behavior frequently seen with children who have been sexually abused. James and Meyerding's study of prostitutes revealed that over one-half of them were sexually abused as children. In another study, promiscuous behavior among hospitalized adolescents was most commonly seen in girls who had been sexually abused. Hypersexual behaviors such as kissing peers, exhibiting oneself, lacking appropriate boundaries with peers and adults, masturbating excessively in public, and being preoccupied with sexual material can be understood as the child's attempt to master the traumatic event through repetition. These behaviors should be viewed as red flags for the clinician, signaling that the child may have been sexually abused. As Green mentions, these children are at risk for subsequent victimization because of their poor ego boundaries and their provocative behaviors. Other predisposing risk factors such as impulsivity and poor social skills increase the likelihood of a child being sexually victimized. Similarly, impulsivity, hyperactivity, neurologic impairment, developmental delay, and "difficult" temperament in children have been identified as risk factors for physical abuse. Occasionally, elimination disorders (encopresis and enuresis) create conflicts between parents and children that can culminate in physical abuse of the child by an overly frustrated parent.

Acting In

In contrast to disruptive behaviors that result from negative affects (anger, fear, sadness, guilt) being turned outward against others, acting in behaviors can be conceptualized as disturbances in which these affects are turned inward against the self.

> Eleven-year-old Tanya was living in a foster home for 6 months. Conflicts with her mother had resulted in several serious beatings, and Tanya's mother feared that one day she would lose control of herself and kill her daughter. Tanya came to medical attention at age 10 for "seizures." An extensive medical workup revealed no organic etiology for her seizure activity. It was noted that Tanya's seizures always stopped at the moment a needle or IV catheter was about to be placed. She was diagnosed by the neurologists who evaluated her as having pseudoseizures. Tanya's pseudoseizure episodes increased in frequency and intensity. The foster mother to whom Tanya had become rapidly attached, brought her to the mental health center because the school had refused to allow Tanya to return until her "seizures" were controlled. Tanya had been a straight "A" student and was described as a sensitive, eager-to-please child who required constant reassurance and who was extremely self-critical. Following many months of treatment, Tanya revealed that she had been raped by her mother's paramour on multiple occasions. She had told her mother of the abuse, and her mother then beat her and called her a liar.

Krystal in citing Freud and Breuer, wrote, " 'any experience which calls up distressing affects—such as those of fright, anxiety, shame or physical pain— may operate as a trauma of this kind (psychic trauma)'." These authors link psychic trauma to the development of hysterical symptoms or somatization. As seen with Tanya, these complaints may be as dramatic as pseudoseizures or may manifest as headaches, insomnia, or abdominal pain. Interestingly, as early as second century Greece, physicians such as Galen linked seizures with inappropriate childhood sexual experiences, and the connection between seizures and incest has been longstanding in Navajo culture. Goodwin et al. and Gross both report that the pseudoseizures remitted as the patients in psychotherapy addressed the incest; Gross further speculates that the seizures were a dissociative phenomenon that evolved in response to the extraordinary fear caused by the abuse. The most extreme dissociation seen, which has been linked to sexual abuse, is the development of multiple personality disorder. Less extreme forms of dissociation such as "emotional numbing and maladaptive passivity," which Peterson and Seligman suggest lead to learned helplessness, may also be seen. In children, this can result in pervasive apathy, impaired coping skills, damaged self-perceptions, poor self-esteem, generalized anxiety, and excessive fears. Some children even learn to hypnotize themselves so as to minimize the physical pain of the abuse. Both the pattern in which the abuse occurs and how the child makes sense of the betrayal by the adult influence the child's response.

In the above case, Tanya internalized the blame for the abuse and subsequently became self-critical and extremely insecure. Her rapid emotional attachment to her foster mother and her continual seeking of approval from teachers reflected her fear of repeated betrayal and abandonment. These were her attempts to minimize the likelihood of recurrent abuse. This pattern contrasts with Danny's identification with the aggressor as a means of gaining control and quelling anxiety. The need to please others, which Tanya demonstrated, is a reaction formation to the intense anger engendered by the abuse. Because this anger is too threatening for the child to experience directly, a pattern of self-effacing and dependent behavior is substituted. For children whose primary attachments are betrayed, the need to be connected to someone is overwhelming, resulting in extreme dependency and the formation of indiscriminate attachments.

Post-Traumatic Stress Disorder

Four-year-old Maria lived in a third story room in a shelter with her mother, 18-year-old sister, and 2-year-old brother. Her other four siblings lived with relatives. The entire family was known to the local child welfare agency due to concerns of neglect and abuse. Following a fist fight between her mother and father, Maria was locked in their room with her younger brother while the mother left the apartment. Wanting to be with her mother, Maria became extremely upset, ran to the window, and saw her mother driving away. Maria then opened the window, jumped out, and landed on the concrete three floors below. She was hospitalized with a pneumothorax and fractured pelvis. Upon admission, she was noted to be significantly underweight for her height. During the hospitalization, Maria developed nightmares, talked to strangers about her accident, was afraid to be left alone in her room, and cried constantly for her mother. She would lay for hours on the stretcher and in her bed, sucking and biting her fingers. Initially, she was completely withdrawn. As she began to recognize particular staff members, she would cling to them in a desperate fashion. Her doll play consisted of taking all the dolls and furniture out of the dollhouse and throwing them into a box. Maria's emotional state vacillated between anger and dullness.

Throughout the literature, there are descriptions of abused children that meet the current diagnostic criteria for post-traumatic stress disorder (PTSD). Until fairly recently, this diagnosis was not used in child abuse cases. As Benedek contends, this is a reflection of the professional's denial of the profound impact of trauma inflicted on children by adults. Even though they were not called such, the descriptions of PTSD are plentiful. Galdston described children who had been physically abused as "resembling cases of 'shell-shocked' adults. They display a profound blunting of all external manifestations of inner life." He commented further on anxiety as manifested in an indiscriminate clinging to others as Maria's case illustrated. Green, Conte and Schuerman, Eth and Pynoos, McLeer et al., and Terr describe symptoms presented by physically and sexually abused children that meet the DSM-III-R criteria for PTSD (Table 27-2).

The hallmarks of PTSD include (1) *reexperiencing phenomena* such as visualizing the traumatic event, disturbing dreams and nightmares, reenactments, or repetitive play involving the trauma; (2) *avoidance phenomena* that are marked by attempts to deny the feelings generated by the trauma including denial, psychic numbing, constricted emotional expression, detachment, dissociation, self-hypnosis, loss of interest in usual activities, and a diminished sense of the future; and (3) *autonomic hyperarousal* including sleep disturbance, poor concentration, hypervigilance, exaggerated startle reactions, irritability, and anger outbursts. Unlike adults, children rarely suffer "flashbacks" of the traumatic events, and they are more likely to display evidence

Table 27-2. Diagnostic Criteria for Post-Traumatic Stress Disorder

A. The person has experienced an event that is outside the range of usual human experience and that would be markedly distressing to almost anyone (e.g., serious threat to one's life or physical integrity; serious threat or harm to one's children, spouse, or other close relatives and friends; sudden destruction of one's home or community; or seeing another person who has recently been, or is being seriously injured or killed as the result of an accident or physical violence).

B. The traumatic event is persistently reexperienced in at least one of the following ways:
1. Recurrent and intrusive distressing recollections of the event (in young children, repetitive play in which themes or aspects of the trauma are expressed)
2. Recurrent distressing dreams of the event
3. Sudden acting or feeling as if the traumatic event were recurring (includes a sense of reliving the experience, illusions, hallucinations, and dissociative [flashback] episodes, even those that occur on awakening or when intoxicated)
4. Intense psychological distress at exposure to events that symbolize or resemble an aspect of the traumatic event, including anniversaries of the trauma

C. Persistent avoidance of stimuli associated with the trauma or numbing of general responsiveness (not present before the trauma), as indicated by at least three of the following:
1. Efforts to avoid thoughts or feelings associated with the trauma
2. Efforts to avoid activities or situations that arouse recollections of the trauma
3. Inability to recall an important aspect of the trauma (psychogenic amnesia)
4. Markedly diminished interest in significant activities (in young children, loss of recently acquired developmental skills such as toilet training or language skills)
5. Feeling of detachment or estrangement from others
6. Restricted range of affect (e.g., unable to have loving feelings)
7. Sense of a foreshortened future (e.g., does not expect to have a career, marriage, or children, or a long life)

D. Persistent symptoms of increased arousal (not present before the trauma) as indicated by at least two of the following:
1. Difficulty falling or staying asleep
2. Irritability or outbursts of anger
3. Difficulty concentrating
4. Hypervigilance
5. Exaggerated startle response
6. Physiologic reactivity on exposure to events that symbolize or resemble an aspect of the traumatic event (e.g., a woman who was raped in an elevator breaks out in a sweat when entering any elevator)

E. Duration of the disturbance (symptoms in B, C, and D) of at least 1 month.

Note: Specify *delayed onset* if the onset of symptoms was at least 6 months after the trauma.

of deep-seated rage toward others, particularly if they were abused by a trusted older person. For the most part, however, the symptoms of PTSD in children are quite similar to those experienced by adults.

The case of Maria exemplifies many symptoms of PTSD. She repeatedly talked about her fall out of the window. Her play involved throwing dolls out of the dollhouse. She became obsessed with sucking her fingers, an activity she called "eating fingers." Initially, she was emotionally withdrawn and apathetic. Over time, her range of affect improved but still remained constricted. Her sleep was disturbed, she startled easily, and she occasionally had angry outbursts. Maria's overwhelming neediness and insecure attachment to her mother are typical of children who have been abused or neglected. In this instance, however, the fear of abandonment was so extreme that it resulted in a life-threatening behavior that left her acutely traumatized. Her acute trauma was thus superimposed on a more chronic sense of loss.

From a developmental perspective, Maria's resources and coping strategies were severely impaired before her injuries, leaving her less able to handle the acute stressors that precipitated her fall. Maria was caught in a dilemma similar to that of so many other abused children. She hungered emotionally and physically but did not have a caretaker who could nurture her. She could not express her anger for fear that it would destroy her only hope for a mother. Consequently, the abusive or neglectful parent became idealized, and the cycle of disappointment and retraumatization recurred.

These cases also illustrate how child abuse always occurs in a context. Poverty, insufficient family support, social isolation, unstable relationships, and previous abusive patterns of interaction are *all* associated with an increased risk for abuse. The systemic circumstances in which children find themselves at the time of the abuse may magnify or ameliorate the impact of the abuse. Moreover, the physical and social environment within which the child is developing will have contributed to and interacted with the internal resources available to the child at the time of the trauma. An emotionally deprived child will have fewer resources than a child who has had the benefits of many positive and caring relationships. Qualities *within* the child that support coping (i.e., "resiliency") are also important mediators. Tanya, despite her inconsistent attachments, was bright, personable, and more adaptable and engaging than Danny or Maria. These traits tend to minimize the downward, negative cycle many children experience following

abuse. Despite individual differences in coping, it should always be kept in mind that the psychiatric manifestations of child abuse are *directly* the result of harmful environmental influences. While the acute symptoms are reflections of the child's reactions to trauma, the child's environment needs to change for the child to recover from the abuse.

Summary

To summarize, children's responses to abuse are variable and complex. Risk factors associated with severe reactions include high frequency and intensity of physical pain inflicted on the child, abuse inflicted by a trusted older person (particularly a parent), associated threats on the child's life by the abuser, young age and "vulnerable" personality of the child, and manifestations of family dysfunction (e.g., parental absence or abandonment, family violence, and alcohol or substance abuse). Protective factors include infrequent occurrence of abuse inflicted by someone with whom the child is *not* psychologically dependent, a strong relationship with a reliable and caring adult who empathizes with the child, older age and "resilient" personality of the child, and relatively sound family functioning. Less is known about contextual variables that mediate the manifestations of abuse. Previous interactions of the child and family with the social service, health, mental health, legal, and educational systems inevitably influence the process of discovery, treatment, and recovery. If the family is able to develop a working alliance with the helping professionals charged with caring for them, the child will feel less frightened about the investigation. If systems are able to coordinate their work, the child and family will be spared repeated interrogations and unnecessary intrusions into their lives.

THE PROCESS OF DISCLOSURE AND THE EVALUATION OF ABUSE

The process of disclosure produces tremendous stress and anxiety for everyone concerned. The child may reexperience the immediate psychological reactions of the abuse when first discussing it with professionals. Children also worry about hurting other family members and fear their retaliation for disclosing the abuse. Typical reactions of young children during the disclosure include heightened anxiety, emotional sensitivity, withdrawal, regression, and acting out behavior. If they feel threatened, children may refuse to cooperate with the evaluation, or they may deny previous statements about the abuse. Professionals must take care to respect the child's needs for safety and security, and should proceed accordingly.

Family members may respond with anger, outrage, and disbelief to the child's disclosures of abuse. These defensive reactions should not be interpreted as implying their responsibility for or involvement in the abuse. Whatever their previous knowledge or involvement, family members need to be respected and involved in every phase of the evaluation process.

Professionals involved in the evaluation of abuse often experience intense emotional reactions when encountering children who have been physically or sexually abused. These responses range from disapproval, disdain, or disgust with the alleged abuser to pity, sadness, and feelings of protectiveness toward the abused child. Often these feelings may be hidden from awareness and may be conveyed indirectly toward the child and the family. Alleged abusers might be greeted with a hostile tone of voice or might be given the message that the listener does not believe their story. The child might be treated as if a "poor little baby" or a "pathetic creature," reactions that may further embarrass the child. It is vital that professionals be aware of their emotional reactions to children and families so as to minimize the chances that these feelings will interfere with the evaluation.

A helpful approach is to view the disclosure and evaluation of abuse as the first steps in treatment and recovery. If handled well, it prepares the child and family to come to terms with the issues surrounding the abuse. If handled poorly, it exacerbates the child's distress and alienates the family from the treatment process.

The goals of the evaluation phase include supporting and protecting the child who has disclosed the abuse, preventing scapegoating of family members, respecting the family's integrity, offering immediate "psychological first aid" to symptomatic individuals, and referring the family for appropriate services and ongoing treatment. Key ingredients include (1) a multiprofessional team with an identified case manager who will follow through with the family and will serve as a liaison to the evaluation team, other professionals, and agencies; (2) strong interagency collaboration to minimize delays, duplication, and barriers to communication; and (3) ongoing family involvement.

While a general approach to the evaluation of child abuse is discussed in other chapters, several techniques that will promote child and family coping should be kept in mind.

1. Spend time joining with the child and the family. Try to enlist everyone's participation. Identify and invite any

important family members or trusted support people to join the process.

2. Address the child's shame, fear, anger, guilt, and depression with calm, direct, and supportive statements. Give the child ample time to express feelings about the abuse. Do not pressure the child into saying anything if not ready to discuss the abuse.

3. Acknowledge the family's emotional reactions in similar fashion.

4. Ensure protection from harm *and* from unnecessary separation (within family and between family service providers).

5. Listen, listen, and listen to what the child and family are saying and not saying.

6. Help family members communicate with each other. Support the child within the family and enlist others to do the same to protect the child from recriminations and further hostility. Specifically address the breaking of the code of silence and the need to prevent further splits and secrets.

7. Maintain respect for people's ability to change in the face of crisis and offer realistic hope for recovery through therapy.

8. Look for other signs of psychiatric problems including substance/alcohol abuse, depression and suicidal behavior, anxiety disorders, other forms of domestic violence, and psychosis. Evidence of these should be addressed by making a prompt referral for mental health treatment. Referrals should be made without unnecessary obstacles (e.g., delays, confusing policies, and procedures).

9. Offer crisis intervention services to all members of the family. Crisis intervention involves engaging family members in an exploration of the family's functioning and of the antecedents and responses to the abuse. It focuses on the feelings engendered by the crisis to mobilize family members to change their patterns of interaction, and to make a commitment to pursuing further treatment, as indicated.

TREATMENT FOR THE ACUTE PSYCHIATRIC MANIFESTATIONS OF CHILD ABUSE

Children who have been physically or sexually abused need some form of therapy. Treatment modalities include crisis intervention and individual, family, group, and expressive arts therapy. Typically, a combination of approaches is recommended to address the many issues involved in abuse cases. Treatment often takes several months or longer, particularly in cases in which there is severe family dysfunction and the patterns of abuse have been endemic to the family system over many generations. Major obstacles to treatment include denial of the abuse, scapegoating of the abused child, hostility toward helping professionals, and financial considerations. In many cases, only the threat (or the actuality) of losing custody of their children motivates parents to cooperate.

Individual treatment involves working with the child on a one-to-one basis to help the child feel safe and secure. Initial stages in treatment are directed toward building trust and encouraging the child to ventilate feelings (e.g., fear, guilt, shame, anger, sadness, and depression). Dreams and fantasies are explored through play, drawings, and spontaneous conversations. The primary purpose of individual therapy is to provide the child with a stable relationship with a sensitive, caring, kind, and nurturing adult. The strength of this relationship offers the child an opportunity to express and "work through" deeply troubling emotions that are too threatening to express directly to family members.

When the child abuse is intrafamilial, family therapy aims at identifying and changing the patterns of abuse. The therapist strives to engage the entire family in a process of exploring the immediate and historical (intergenerational) aspects of the abuse, focusing initially on patterns of communication, conflict resolution, and emotional support. By shifting away from a blaming stance, the therapist looks for strengths within the family and helps the family identify changes they would like to make in their lives. The family is both supported and challenged to make fundamental changes in their relationships so as to minimize the chances for the abusive behaviors to recur.

Social skills deficits and problems with self-esteem can be addressed in group therapy. The child is able to experience support from other children who have been through similar experiences. The group becomes a safe place where the abused child can feel accepted and can develop new social skills.

SUGGESTED READINGS

1. Benedek EP: Children and psychic trauma: a brief review of contemporary thinking. In Eth S, Pynoos R (eds): Post-Traumatic Stress Disorder in Children. American Psychiatric Press, Inc., Washington D.C., 1985
2. Conte JR, Schuerman JR: The effects of sexual abuse on children. In Wyatt GE, Powell GJ (eds): Lasting Effects of Child Sexual Abuse. Sage Publications, New York, 1988
3. Eth S, Pynoos R: Interaction of trauma and grief in childhood. p. 171. In Eth S, Pynoos R (eds): Post-Traumatic Stress Disorder in Children. American Psychiatric Press, Inc., Washington, D.C., 1985
4. Finkelhor D: The trauma of child sexual abuse. p. 61. In Wyatt G, Powell GJ (eds): Lasting Effects of Child Abuse. Sage Publications, New York, 1988
5. Finklehor D, Browne A: The traumatic impact of child sexual abuse: a conceptualization. Am J Orthopsychiatry 55:530, 1985
6. Fredrich WN, Reams RA: The course of psychological symptoms in sexually abused young children. Psychother Theory Res Practice 24:160, 1987
7. Galdston R: Observations on children who have been physically abused and their parents. Am J Psychiatry 122:440, 1965
8. Goodwin J, Simms M, Bergman R: Hysterical seizures: a sequel to incest. Am J Orthopsychiatry 49:698, 1979
9. Green A: Children traumatized by physical abuse. p. 135. In Eth S, Pynoos R (eds): Post-Traumatic Stress Disorder in Children. American Psychiatric Press, Inc., Washington, D.C., 1985
10. Green A: Child maltreatment and its victims: a comparison of physical and sexual abuse. Psychiatr Clin North Am 11:591, 1988
11. Gross M: Incestuous rape: a cause for hysterical seizures in four adolescent girls. Am J Orthopsychiatry 49:704, 1979
12. James J, Meyerding J: Early sexual experience and prostitution. Am J Psychiatry 134:1381, 1977
13. Krystal H: Trauma and Affect. Psychoanal Study Child 33:8, 1978
14. Ludwig S, Rostain A: Family function and dysfunction. In Levine M, Carey W, Crocker A (eds): Developmental Behavioral Pediatrics. WB Saunders, Philadelphia, 1991
15. McLeer SV, Deblinger E, Atkins MS et al: Post-traumatic stress disorder in sexually abused children. J Am Acad Child Adolesc Psychiatry 27:650, 1988
16. Morse CW, Sahler OJZ, Friedman SB: A three year follow-up study of abused and neglected children. Am J Dis Child 120:439, 1970
17. Peterson C, Seligman M: Learned helplessness and victimization. J Soc Issues 39:103, 1983
18. Rizma M, Berg R, Locke C: Sexual abuse:

somatic and emotional reactions. Child Abuse Negl 12:201, 1988

19. Sansonnet-Hayden H, Haley G, Marriage K, Fine S: Sexual abuse and psychopathology in hospitalized adolescents. J Am Acad Child Adolesc Psychiatry 26:753, 1987

20. Terr L: Childhood traumas: an outline and overview. Am J Psychiatry 148:10, 1991

21. Wolfe DA: Child Abuse: Implications for Child Development and Psychopathology. Sage Publications, Newbury Park, CA, 1987

28

Chronic Psychological Manifestations

Karen Blount

The physical sequelae of child abuse are well documented, whereas the effects on the child's psyche are not. There are a number of reasons for this, including the original definition of the *battered child syndrome*, which focused on physical signs and symptoms, objectively defined by examination, radiographs, and laboratory values, but failed to address the psychological impact. In addition, psychological symptoms are often delayed for years. Some of these children have suffered neurologic damage as the result of a head injury, making unclear the origin of symptoms manifested, whether they stem from physical injury or psychological damage.

Numerous studies have examined the relationship between childhood experiences of physical or sexual abuse and the development in later months or years of maladaptive behavior. Child abuse and neglect affects a child on a number of different levels including physical, cognitive, and emotional. These effects depend on the child's age and developmental level at the time of the event and the frequency and nature of the experience.

Many long-term effects are subtle and the observer may not be aware of the abuse history. Many caregivers do not volunteer this information and history takers may not ask. This may be a result of inexperience, a discomfort with the topic, or a lack of understanding of the importance this information will play in evaluation and treatment. If the child is in foster care, the caretaker is usually not aware of the details of the abuse, length and type of abuse, and the psychosocial climate of the home. The traits exhibited as a result of child abuse such as low self-esteem, cognitive disturbances, depression, self-destructive behavior, violence, and poor social relationships are often displayed in dysfunctional families in which children are not abused, making it difficult to discern the exact cause and effect relationship.

There is a paucity of research regarding long-term follow-up and longitudinal data, with many reports based on retrospective review and clinical observations. The importance of this gap is that generalizability is limited. It would be helpful for long-term follow-up studies to include nonabused siblings or a control group of children in dysfunctional families who were not abused. This, however, may be difficult as resistance to being enrolled in long-term studies, frequent changes of address, and separation of siblings are common hindrances.

This chapter provides a discussion of the effect of child abuse on early developmental tasks, intellectual and school functioning, mental health, peer relationships, adolescent behavior, and adult life. Child abuse may also be manifested in development of psychiatric syndromes, affective disorders, or more destructive behaviors aimed at self or society including domestic violence, juvenile delinquency, adult criminality, substance abuse, and suicide. The need for intervention strategies and further research are also explored.

EARLY DEVELOPMENTAL EFFECTS

Developmental delay and cognitive deficits may occur as a result of child abuse. These are dependent on the type of abuse (physical, sexual, or neglect), the duration of the abuse, and the environment in which the child lives.

Effects on early developmental tasks may present in a number of different ways. There may be regression to an earlier developmental stage, such as a child who was previously toilet trained may no longer be, or a toddler or preschooler who was speaking may revert to crying and infantile behavior as a way of communicating.

The child may not attain appropriate developmental milestones. In 1985 Allen and Wasserman found that infants with a history of physical abuse failed to develop appropriate language skills. Language delay may interfere with successful adjustment to interactional situations. The aggression and social withdrawal observed in abused toddlers may be par-

tially a result of very early problems in language comprehension and expression.

These children may become precocious. Many children exhibit role reversal with the parent, taking on the duties and responsibilities of the caretaker. Precociousness is exhibited in sexual abuse, but in a different manner, that of adult-like sexual behavior and attention getting, not caretaking. A case history of a physically abused child is presented below as an example of delay and regression to a previous developmental stage.

Case Report

Joseph, a 7-year-old black boy, came to attention as he was being prepared for hospital discharge after being an inpatient for 3 months because of second- and third-degree burns of the back and buttocks caused by being placed on a space heater by his mother. Before the hospitalization Joseph was in foster care from age 3 years to 6 years as a result of neglect by his mother, and was recently returned to her care. He was in kindergarten for the third time and his developmental level was at that of a 5-year-old child, with delays in language and writing skills. When nearing discharge Joseph began bed-wetting and acting out behavior and became a discipline problem for the staff where previously he was compliant and affectionate. The evaluation and treatment issues targeted his language delay, and Joseph's anger and fear at leaving a situation where he felt "safe" and returning to foster care. Referral to a specialized school program was made. This treatment was begun with limit setting and positive reinforcement involving nursing staff and a new foster mother as well as referral to an outpatient mental health center specializing in children and families.

A prospective longitudinal study investigating the developmental sequelae of physical abuse was initiated by Egeland et al. in 1983. They observed 267 mother-child pairs in a study following first born children of mothers identified as being at risk for caretaking problems caused by poverty, youth, low education, lack of support, and generally unstable life circumstances. Four maltreatment groups were identified among children who were maltreated in the first 2 years of life. Since some children experienced more than one form of abuse, there is overlap among these groups. Table 28-1 summarizes these findings.

EFFECTS ON SCHOOL FUNCTIONING

Many children who have suffered physical, sexual, or emotional abuse may not present with symptomatology until school age, or the abuse may first occur at this age. Erikson et al. examined the same children referred to in Table 28-1 at ages 4 to 6 years. They were compared with a control group and again the maltreated children presented far more problems than other children from similar backgrounds who were not abused (Table 28-2).

Psychological maltreatment has been identified as the core component, the major destructive factor, in all forms of child maltreatment. The strength of this position rests on the widely supported assumption that psychological maltreatment is inherent in all forms of child maltreatment. The major negative impact factors of child maltreatment are generally psychological in nature, effecting a broad range of strategies for living; this concept clarifies and unifies the dynamic that underlies the destructive power of all forms of child abuse and neglect.

The effects of child maltreatment on the development of interpersonal relationships in infancy and preschool years have received attention. This has resulted in recognition that maltreatment is related to maladaptive social and behavioral development in children. There is little empirical evidence on the topic, despite an awareness that these characteristics may have consequences for school performance.

Controlled studies on the relationship between school performance/readiness and maltreatment are suggestive but not conclusive. Three studies of preschool/elementary school-aged children have assessed the academic achievement of maltreated children. Friedrich et al. in a comparison of physically abused and nonabused 4- and 5-year-old children on the Wide Range Achievement Test, reported no significant differences. Gregory and Beveridge reported a significant difference in academic performance on word reading skills in favor of the nonabused group, but not on measures of word definition, comprehension, and vocabulary. McNeill and Brassard, who compared victims of father-daughter incest with matched controls on approximated intelligence quotient (IQ) scores, found significant differences in favor of the control group on standardized achievement tests, indicating that victims were underachieving relative to their ability.

The findings of research examining intellectual ability and teacher ratings of maltreated children have been more consistent. Studies of preschool and elementary school-age children have reported significant differences in favor of control subjects, ranging from 10 to 31 IQ points starting as early as 18 months. Teachers have consistently rated maltreated children as significantly less competent academically and socially, lacking adequate work habits, and engaging in a variety of

Table 28-1. Summary of Behavior of Children Who Were Maltreated During the First 2 Years of Life

Major Assessments	Physically Abused	Verbally Abused	Neglected	Emotionally Neglected[a]
3 and 6 Month feeding and play: baby's responsiveness, social behavior, activity level, coordination, etc.	Did not differ significantly from nonmaltreated infants on these measures		Less socially responsive	More robust and responsive at 3 months, but no difference by 6 months
9-Month Bayley scales of infant development	No differences between maltreated and nonmaltreated			
12-Month attachment classification	Not significant	Not significant	Two-thirds were anxiously attached (significantly more than among nonmaltreated)	43% anxiously attached
18-Month attachment classification	Significantly more of children in these groups were anxiously attached than among nonmaltreated children			Nearly all were anxiously attached
24-Month Bayley scales of infant development	Lower	Lower scores	Lower	Scores declined dramatically from 9 months and were significantly lower than mean for nonmaltreated

24-Month tool-using tasks (with mother)	More angry, frustrated, noncompliant, less enthusiastic; expressed less positive affect	More angry, frustrated, noncompliant; less positive affect, more negative affect	More angry, frustrated noncompliant; less positive affect, less enthusiastic, more negative affect; poorer coping strategies	More angry, frustrated, noncompliant, whiny; less positive affect and less enthusiastic; poorer coping strategies
42-Month barrier box (alone)	Low on self-esteem, self-control, creativity, assertiveness; highly distractable	Low self-esteem, low self-control	Similar to physically abused, but also lacked flexibility; apathetic	Differed significantly from nonmaltreated on creativity only
42-Month teaching tasks (with mother)	All maltreatment groups lacked persistence and enthusiasm for the tasks, were negativistic, noncompliant, avoidant, and showed little affection toward their mothers			
Preschool observations & teachers checklists	Noncompliant, poor self-control; expressed much negative emotion (anger and/or sadness or whininess); many behavior problems	To few children in this group attended preschool to allow analysis	Highly dependent, poor self-control, behavior problems	Noncompliant, poor self-control, highly dependent; expressed much negative emotion; presented varied & extensive behavior problems, including nervous signs & self-abusive behavior

a Psychologically unavailable caregivers.
(From Egeland et al.,[10] with permission.)

373

Table 28-2.   Summary of Behavior of Children Who Were Maltreated Between 4 and 6 Years of Age

Major Assessments	Physically Abused	Sexually Abused	Neglected	Emotionally Neglected[a]
54-Month curiosity box	Dependent, impulsive, negative affect	Dependent, impulsive	Dependent	Uninvolved
64-Month WPPSI[b] (four subtests)	Lower	Lower on block design only	Much lower	Lower on block design only
Kindergarten adjustment (based on teacher interview and behavior ratings)	Aggressive, uncooperative, disturbing in classroom, inattentive, impatient, little positive affect, dependent, unpopular; poor comprehension of classroom activities; varied emotional problems including nervousness, compulsive behavior, competence; almost one-half were recommended for retention or referred for special education	Strong need for approval, closeness, & help; anxious, withdrawn, disturbing in classroom, unpopular; poor comprehension of classroom activities; varied emotional problems	Same as physically abused, plus anxious, withdrawn; lacking initiative; strong need for approval & encouragement; lacking sense of humor; lowest of all groups on academic skills, work habits, & sociability; 65% recommended for retention or referred for special education	Aggressive, disrespectful, disturbing behavior in classroom, unpopular; poor academic skills (similar to nonmaltreated children, however, on majority of measures)

[a] Psychologically unavailable caregivers.
[b] WPPSI, Wechster Preschool and Primary Scale of Intelligence.
(From Erickson et al.,[11] with permission.)

problematic behaviors such as social withdrawal, immaturity, impulsivity, and aggression.

Given the strong relationship between successful adult adjustment and school success in our culture, and the number of maltreated children who may be at risk for school failure, systematic research on school performance and service provision to school-age maltreated children is needed.

EFFECTS ON MENTAL HEALTH/PERSONALITY

Oates studied personality development among a group of abused 5-year-old children compared with age-matched nonabused children. In contrast to the control group, the abused children had fewer friends, lower ambitions, and lower self-esteem. They were more serious, shy, and subdued on a personality assessment scale and, according to teachers, were more likely to have behavior disturbances. It has also been found that abused children were more aggressive in play and in psychological testing.

Long-Term Effects on Personality Development

There are certain hallmarks of abuse that are recognized as being a result of childhood physical violence. Child abuse has long-term effects on the personality development of children. Oates studied 5-year-old abused children after they were admitted to the hospital for treatment. This group had less friends and lower self-concept scores than control subjects. Personality questionnaire scores showed that these children were more shy and inhibited in interpersonal contacts than was the control group. The children showed apathetic withdrawn behavior at the time of initial presentation and still exhibited this inability to develop "basic trust" at the time of study. This study highlights the point that immediate and long-term effects are similar and that physically abused children need psychological evaluation and treatment as well as physical care. In an age in which a follow-up computed tomography (CT) scan is routine after severe head injury, so should follow-up of emotional development be standard. The damage to the child's psyche is no less important. Certain personality traits are also common in abused children, although not all are found in every child. Children are often aggressive and oppositional. George and Main found that the greater the severity of injury, the greater the aggressive behavior.

Some children may exhibit impulsive, exploitive, or manipulative behavior. This may be a defense mechanism to cope with feelings of helplessness after abuse. Compulsivity is also noted, perhaps as a way of avoiding further abuse, and exerting control over one's life.

Many of these children have low self-esteem and a negative self-image. These feelings may be exhibited in adulthood as a continuation of victim seeking behavior. Women may become victims of domestic violence, and become further isolated from other adults.

Personality Disorders

Some children may exhibit personality disorders. Coons et al. examined the treatment progress of 20 patients with DSM-III-R multiple personality disorder. The study included a detailed history, neurologic examination, and psychological testing of each patient. Six patients had a history of child abuse. They were found not only to have developed a personality disorder possibly as a result of abuse, but also were more difficult to treat than the other patients. The progress of therapy was hindered primarily by the defense mechanisms of regression and denial, the continued use of secrecy, which began during child abuse, and the production of numerous crises.

Herman et al. studied the correlation between childhood trauma and borderline personality disorders (defined by the DSM-III-R as "a pervasive pattern of instability of mood, interpersonal relationships and self-image, beginning by early childhood and present in a variety of contexts") in subjects who gave histories of major childhood trauma. Seventy-one percent of patients had a history of physical abuse. Abuse histories were less common (62 percent) in those with borderline traits and least common in subjects with no borderline diagnosis.

Anxiety

Some argue that abused children who do not develop a specific psychiatric disorder may develop anxiety related to depression. This anxiety may be manageable or may lead to an inability to interact with others, and may affect performance in school or on the job. The anxiety may be immediate and short-lived or may be manifested later in life. The immediate anxiety may be heightened by the observation that after suffering serious physical injury, many children who are separated from their parents feel guilty. Again, a routine part of medical care for these children has not been psychological evaluation, but should be, not only because of previous trauma, but because of the anxiety caused by separation.

Victims of child sexual abuse suffer

Table 28-3. Long-Term Manifestations of Sexual Abuse

Emotional
    Depression
    Guilt/shame
    Low self-esteem
    Panic disorders
    Social withdrawal
    Phobias
    Somatization
    Hysteria
Interpersonal
    Pseudomaturity/regressive immaturity
    Overcompliance/aggressiveness
    Poor peer relations
    Clinging/hypervigilance to touch
    Cognitive/perceptual
    Hallucinations
    Recurrent illusions
    Nightmares
    Detailed knowledge about sex
    Inability to concentrate at school
    Learning disabilities
    Language disabilities
    Language delays

(From American Psychiatry Association,[3] with permission.)

many of the same long-term effects on mental health and personality as do victims of physical abuse and neglect, although some differences may be noted (Table 28-3).

EFFECTS MANIFESTED IN ADOLESCENCE/ ADULTHOOD

Child abuse may have far reaching effects into adolescence and adulthood. Some children may turn their feelings of helplessness, low self-worth, and frustration inward. These effects may be manifested in a variety of ways, including suicide attempts and substance abuse.

The effects on development and personality formation discussed earlier, such as low self-esteem, poor social interaction, and lack of trust, frequently lead to deviant behavior. These behaviors may be an attempt to escape feelings of anxiety, or to be accepted and "fit in" with a peer group because they believe they are not worthy of a better life.

Runaway Behavior

Although running away from home is not an extraordinary occurrence in adolescence, when abuse has occurred it is extremely common. Hartman et al. examined the cycle of runaway behavior. Based on information provided by 149 runaways in a Canadian shelter, there was a significant correlation between repetitive runaway behavior and a history of physical abuse.

Substance Abuse

Substance abuse is positively correlated with child abuse. Dembo et al. found that there was a positive relation between childhood physical abuse and use of illicit drugs. This information was obtained after interviewing a randomly selected population of youths entering a juvenile detention center.

Physical assault may only be one of the etiologies of these disorders. Many of these children come from dysfunctional families, lack support systems, and parents may have a history of substance abuse themselves. Parental alcoholism may affect the child in a similar way to parental violence. Numerous studies have demonstrated the detrimental psychological and social effects of parental alcoholism on children. Chafetz et al. studied clients in a child guidance clinic and found that children of alcoholics had more school problems, delinquency, and involvement with the criminal justice system than other children. They experienced role reversal with their parents, suffered from low self-esteem, and were often socially isolated. These characteristics are also descriptive of abused children.

Some children may be so severely depressed or have such low-self esteem that they may attempt suicide. This may be related to drug or alcohol use or being in a dysfunctional family. The correlation between suicide and physical abuse, although suggested, has not been proven.

The next case illustrates the dramatic effects of abuse on mental health and personality and also briefly describes an effective treatment modality.

Case Report

Mary experienced severe physical, emotional, and sexual abuse as a child beginning in infancy and lasting until the time she was placed in a group home at age 13. She was raised by her maternal grandparents, and had daily contact with her mother. Both her mother and grand-mother were physically and emotionally abusive. She was sexually abused by an uncle from the age of 7 until the age of 13, when she left home. She had never disclosed the abuse to anyone as she had been threatened repeatedly not to tell "outsiders" family secrets. Mary attempted suicide at ages 11 and 12 by overdose and at age 13 by jumping from a fifth story window. After being hospitalized for 3 months for internal injuries, Mary was finally removed from her home and placed in a group home. She received no therapeutic intervention and lived in a total of six different homes during the following 5 years.

Mary met her future husband at age 15 and moved in with him at age 18 when she became pregnant with their first child. Her husband is an alcoholic and has been physically and emotionally abusive to her throughout their marriage. Mary sought professional help approximately 3 years ago when she attempted to kill herself and her three children by turning on their gas stove. Her attempt was stopped by her mother-in-law knocking on her door, which "snapped her out of her fog-like state." She realized that in addition to her feelings of hopelessness, worthlessness, and sadness, she was losing periods of time when she could not remember where she was and felt disconnected from herself.

She saw a total of five therapists over 3 years. Her reasons for leaving therapy included recommendations for antidepressants, family counseling, and feeling too depressed to continue with therapy. Mary continues to suffer from periodic dissociative episodes, low self-esteem, and depression. Mary fits the DSM-III-R criteria for dysthymia and dissociative disorder. (Dysthymia refers to a depressed mood characterized by chronic, nonpsychotic symptoms of depression that do not meet the criteria for a major depressive disorder. It implies an inborn tendency to experience a depressed mood. Dissociative disorder refers to a disturbance or alteration in the normally integrated functions of identity, memory, or consciousness.)

She is currently receiving therapy in an outpatient clinic and has been with the same therapist for the past year. While it is believed that Mary would benefit from antidepressants in addition to her individual supportive psychotherapy, her decision to not be on medication is being respected. In addition, family counseling is not indicated as her husband is not compliant with his alcoholism treatment and continues to be emotionally abusive. Her children are receiving therapy as well. Mary has benefited from this supportive environment in conjunction with learning strategies to cope with daily stress. This case illustrates the long lasting effects of childhood abuse and the likelihood of subsequent revictimization.

Aggressor-Victim Interaction

Betrayal by a primary caretaker leads to mistrust of others and difficulties with object relationships. Perhaps the most striking similarity between physical and sexual abuse of children is the tendency of the children to reenact and recreate their victimization with others, leading to a transmission of violence to the next generation. Like their parents who were frequently victimized during childhood, they repeat and perpetuate an "aggressor-victim" interaction in their subsequent relationships. The physically abused child has difficulty in experiencing and modulating aggressive impulses, often impacting on the society around them. These behaviors may be contained within the nuclear family in the form of child abuse or wife battering, or to the

community as juvenile delinquency or adult criminality.

LONG-TERM EFFECTS OF CHILD SEXUAL ABUSE

Sexual Relationships

The major focus of research into the long-term effects of childhood sexual victimization has been on the relationship between variables associated with the victimization situation and the victim's adult functioning. In a controlled study by Gold, it was found that victimized and nonvictimized women show significant differences on measures of attributional style (how people perceive the motivation of others related to their attempt to gain control over their environment), social supports, and coping effectiveness. Two aspects of social support were found to be related to victims' adult functioning, specifically their sexual functioning. Women who reported good quality adult social relationships (helpful and reciprocal) also tended to report satisfactory sexual relationships. The quality of support reported by these women may reflect their ability to have close relationships with others including sexual relationships. Interview data suggested that many sexually victimized women felt they had difficulty developing trusting relationships.

Deviant Behaviors

Dysfunctional life styles and family environment are significant factors that foster juvenile delinquency and adult criminality. Child abuse has been correlated with these deviant behaviors. There is considerable debate regarding etiologies for adolescent and adult prostitution, violence, and criminality. This debate involves lack of control subjects, differences between effects of abuse versus neglect, and the nature of most research as retrospective in which investigators typically ask delinquents about their early backgrounds. Furthermore, since existing studies focus primarily on violence among delinquents and adolescents, whether these childhood experiences have direct and lasting consequences for the commission of violent crimes into adulthood is unknown.

INTERVENTION STRATEGIES

In order for intervention to be effective, ideally the entire family should be involved. Treatment should be early, planned, and assessed for effectiveness. A thorough evaluation of potential deficits in development, cognition, and neurologic status should occur early to determine the type and length of treatment that are necessary.

Removing the child from the home is an intervention strategy that has been evaluated. Environmental improvements can lead to increases in developmental skills and IQ. However, removal is not always the most appropriate way to help the child. Other interventions not only need to be a standard part of the treatment, but must also be scientifically evaluated to judge effectiveness.

Research that evaluates intervention for child victims of sexual abuse has generally focused on procedures for validation and for providing short-term interventions to protect the child from future abuse. Little attention has been paid to long-term clinical intervention approaches.

Effective Mental Health Services

Three key factors impact on delivery of mental health services to child victims of abuse and must be addressed before treatment can be implemented effectively. These are protection, caretaker availability, and caretaker effectiveness. Long-term treatment can proceed only after protection for the child has been obtained. The availability of a supportive involved individual or caretaker is also critical. For example, teachers and parents can often be trained to administer and support interventions at home or at school. The caretakers can also reiterate information provided by the therapist, and can model appropriate behavior for children with limited skills. The effectiveness of the caretaker as a support system or change agent may be limited by inappropriate attitudes, affects, behaviors, and/or skill deficits. Therefore, the educational needs vis-a-vis coping with the impact of the abuse and the overall functioning of the support person may need to be assessed. This should be done before designing interventions for child victims so that caretakers may receive training or education to improve their effectiveness as parental figures and change agents for home-based treatment.

Breaking the Cycle of Abuse

Egeland et al. attempted to study the variables that distinguish mothers who broke the cycle of abuse from mothers who also abused their own children. Based on maternal interviews and questionnaires completed over a 64-month period, measures of mothers' past and current relationship experiences, stressful life events, and personality characteristics were obtained. Abused mothers who were able to break the cycle were significantly more likely to have received emotional support from a nonabusive adult during childhood, participated in therapy during any period of their lives, and had a nonabusive and more stable, emotionally supportive, and satisfying relationship with a mate. Abused mothers who reenacted their maltreatment with their own children experienced significantly more life stress and were more anxious, dependent, immature, and depressed.

Family Therapy

Treatment needs to be aimed at the family and the child. Nicol et al. compared two contrasting therapies for the treatment of child abuse: a focused casework approach for the whole family versus a structured play therapy approach for the child. There was a high dropout rate from both therapies, but of those who completed the treatment, there was a greater improvement in the focused casework regime on some of the comparisons made. Although outcome was measured and favored the casework approach, it did not discount the importance of working with the child individually. It would be helpful to evaluate the effect of the use of both modalities simultaneously.

Individual Therapy

Saucier found that play therapy can have a positive effect on the developmental achievement levels of abused children. Play therapy may also allow a child to act out feelings of anxiety and aggression and assist therapists in treatment plans.

The physically abused child has difficulty in experiencing and modulating aggressive impulses, whereas the victim of incest is often impaired in experiencing and integrating sexual feelings. The physically abused child is also at greater risk for cognitive and neurologic impairment. Intervention with the abusing parents is the first step in protecting the child from further damage. Treatment of the

child victim is necessary not only to diminish psychopathology and emotional distress, but to prevent the cycle of violence in the next generation.

CONCLUSION

A priority must be to evaluate efficacy of modalities used in treatment or prevention. These must be evaluated in a scientific manner, using control groups. Further research must also determine which effects are direct causes of abuse or are simply associated with dysfunctional families in general. These results will be important in determining treatment needs and placement issues.

Protocols for follow-up and evaluation must be determined, standardized, and tested. Standardized evaluation will ensure that all victims will receive consistent care, just as certain laboratory and radiologic studies are routinely used to diagnose underlying physical injuries and to indicate direct treatment. Standardization will also lead to improved evaluation of treatments, instead of case study or retrospective review. Also, research in the 1990s must focus on prevention strategies and evaluation of these strategies. The psychological effects of abuse, whether short- or long-term, are as important as the physical effects, once the child has been stabilized. The psychological scars are frequently more difficult to uncover and treat. Every abused child is entitled to psychological evaluation and treatment and must receive it, if the cycle of abuse is to be stopped.

SUGGESTED READINGS

1. Alexander PC, Lupfer SL: Family characteristics and long term consequences associated with sexual abuse. Arch Sex Behav 16:235, 1987

2. Allen R, Wasserman GA: Origin of language development in abused infants. Child Abuse Negl 9:335, 1985

3. American Psychiatry Association: Diagnostic and Statistical Manual of Mental Disorders. 3rd Ed. American Psychiatry Association, Cambridge, MA, 1980

4. Berliner L, Wheeler JR: Treating the effects of sexual abuse on children. J Interpersonal Violence 2:415, 1987

5. Cavaiola A, Schiff M: Behavioral sequelae of physical and/or sexual abuse in adolescents. Child Abuse Negl 12:181, 1988

6. Chafetz ME, Blane HT, Hill JJ: Children of alcoholics: observations in a child guidance clinic. Q J Studies Alcohol 32:687, 1971

7. Coons P, Bowman E, Milstein V: Multiple personality disorder. A clinical investigation of 50 cases. J Nerv Ment Dis 12:519, 1988

8. Dembo R, Williams L, Berry E, et al: The relationship between physical and sexual abuse and illicit drug use: a replication among a new sample of youths entering a juvenile detention center. Int J Addict 11:1101, 1988

9. Egeland B, Jacobvitz D, Sroufel: Breaking the cycle of abuse. Child Dev 4:1080, 1988

10. Egeland B, Sroufe LA, Erickson M: The developmental consequences of different patterns of maltreatment. Child Abuse Negl 1:459, 1983

11. Erickson M, Egeland B, Pianta R: The effects of maltreatment on the development of young children. p. 647. In Cicchetti D, Carlson V (eds): Child Maltreatment: Theory and Research on the Causes and Consequences of Child Abuse and Neglect. Cambridge University Press, Cambridge, MA, 1989

12. Finkelhor D, Browne A: The traumatic impact of child sexual abuse: a conceptualization. Am J Orthopsychiatry 55:530, 1985

13. Friedrich W, Einbernder A, Lueke W: Cognitive and behavioral characteristics of physically abused children. J Consult Clin Psychol 51:313, 1983

14. George C, Main M: Social interactions of young abused children: approach, avoidance and aggression. Child Dev 50:306, 1979

15. Gold ER: Long-term effects of sexual victimization in childhood: an attributional approach. J Consul Clin Psychol 54:471, 1986

16. Gregory H, Beveridge M: The social and educational adjustment of abused children. Child Abuse Negl 8:525, 1984

17. Hart S, Brassard M: Psychological maltreatment: integration and summary. p. 254. In Brassard M, Germain R, Hart S (eds): Psychological Maltreatment of Children and Youth. Pergamon Press, New York, 1987

18. Hartman C, Burgess A, McCormack A: Pathways and cycles of runaways: a model for understanding repetitive runaway behavior. Hosp Community Psychiatry 3:292, 1987

19. Herman J, Perry J, Vanderkolk B: Childhood trauma in borderline personality disorder. Am J Psychiatry 4:490, 1989

20. Hoier T: Child sexual abuse: clinical interventions and new directions. J Child Adolesc Psychotherapy 4:179, 1987

21. McCord J: A forty year perspective on effects of child abuse and maltreatment. Child Abuse Negl 7:265, 1983

22. McNeil L, Brassard M: The behavioral correlates of father-daughter incest with elementary school-aged girls and matched peers. Paper presented at the International Society for the Prevention of Child Abuse and Neglect. Montreal, Canada, 1984

23. Nicol A, Smith J, Kay B et al: A focused casework approach to the treatment of child abuse: a controlled comparison. J Child Psychol Psychiatry 5:703, 1988

24. Oates: Self-esteem of abused children. Child Abuse Negl 9:159, 1984

25. Oates RK: Personality development after physical abuse. Arch Dis Child 59:147, 1985

26. Saucier B: The effects of play therapy on developmental achievement levels of abused children. Pediatr Nurse 1:27, 1989

27. Stovall G, Craig R: Mental representations of physically and sexually abused latency-aged females. Child Abuse Negl 14:233, 1990

28. Widom C: The cycle of violence. Science 244:160, 1989

29

Forensic Investigation of Pediatric Deaths

Robert Goode

COMPONENTS OF INVESTIGATION

In addition to the hundreds of natural disease processes that cause fetal, infant, and childhood death, there are also numerous human and environmental factors that cause unnatural death. In most of the civilized world the evaluation of these unnatural pediatric deaths is the responsibility of one or more governmental agencies as a matter of public policy. These death investigators have the task of identifying the element—be it person, product, or policy—that has failed to provide the necessary support to the child. Such a task requires a systematic, organized approach so that the maximum amount of pertinent information can be obtained without overlooking significant issues. Because the death of a child is so poorly accepted by society and because a significant number of childhood deaths are so difficult to prove or to explain (e.g., sudden infant death syndrome, child abuse, and neglect) the investigator, the pathologist, and the regulatory agencies must go to greater lengths than those required in adult death investigations. Not only must an acceptable cause of death

be reached, but other potentially competing causes of death must be clearly identified and discarded. Pediatric death investigators must do more than their peers investigating adult deaths. The investigation seems naturally to arrange itself into the following components: history, scene, the body, tests, documentation, and correlation of findings.

The history includes all information communicated to the investigator, whether personally by witnesses, family and friends, caretakers and neighbors, or through established records, such as medical records, police and social service records, or by other investigative agencies that have a role in the investigation. In this regard, the medicolegal history may be much more extensive than the usual and customary history as obtained in the hospital record.

The importance of having information about the scene of the incident or death is not widely understood by most hospital-based physicians or by those in clinical practice where home visits are not a part of the service. Evaluation of the medical facts in the context of the scene environment may be the sole and exclusive means of establishing the cause of death in some instances.

The examination of the body is most often performed at autopsy. The medicolegal autopsy, particularly in cases of suspected child abuse or neglect, must be done with meticulous attention to detail in a highly systematized fashion, with liberal use of ancillary tests. The tests include postmortem radiographs, microbiologic studies, histopathologic preparations, toxicologic analysis, serologic evaluation, and other supportive clinical and forensic procedures. The documentation phase of the investigation must be exceedingly well recorded by photography, diagrams, clear and concise objective reporting, and consultation, where necessary.

HISTORY

When eliciting a history, the investigator must be constantly aware of two major factors: how does the informant know the information that he is relating, and how credible is the person who is giving the information. Obtaining detailed and reliable history is more of an art than a science. It requires a patient listener who can critically evaluate the information that is being related. Simply completing a questionnaire may provide consistent minimum essential information but cannot supply the richness of detail that can be achieved by the interactive process of taking a history. The telltale minutiae that make the difference between truth and lie do not often emerge in checklist histories.

The information provided by hospital personnel when reporting a death to a medicolegal jurisdiction is frequently inaccurate in some detail, which could sometimes alter an investigation significantly. This is readily understood, considering that the hospital's medical activity is to preserve life and function regardless of the cause of the disease or injury process. The initial history available to hospital personnel frequently comes from police or emergency medical personnel and is at least secondhand in its derivation. If the child survives in the hospital for any period of time, there is an opportunity to gather first-hand information from the parents or others who were responsible for the child at the time the incident occurred. Conflicting histories from multiple sources and explanations that are out of scale for the event may eventually unfold. It is necessary for the investigator to obtain histories from direct witnesses or participants and to seek independent verification from other sources. The features of the history that are important vary with the age of the child.

Abortuses and Stillbirths

It is highly desirable that there be communication among the parents, clinicians, and pathologists before, as well as after, the perinatal autopsy. This process may be applicable in the hospital clinical setting, but may not be when a death investigator becomes involved. The discarded dead fetus, the surprise delivery, and the unwanted pregnancy may all yield a history that is either useless or misleading, with no constructive value in the interpretation of the cause of death. In medicolegal situations, a dead baby that gives the appearance of having just been born must be evaluated for the specific forensic issue of live- versus stillbirth, as well as for the general forensic issues common to all medicolegal cases: identity, time of injury (birth), contributing factors, dynamic forces of the event, time of death, cause and manner of death, and medical and physical evidence.

In the case of a birth at home when the mother is still available, the customary maternal history can be taken, including the mother's health, obstetric, family, and social history, and the search for the placenta can begin so that it may be medically evaluated. A statement about the signs of life can be sought at this time. In the case of mothers who claim they did not know that they were pregnant, inquiry can be made of the mother's close friends and family, even though it is probable that they will have assumed a stance of hostile protector. The mother may have some means of keeping track of her menstrual cycle, and it may be appropriate to ask to see it to verify her position that she did not know she was pregnant.

When a newborn is abandoned, as with any found body, the history of the location may be pertinent. Knowing the people who have access to the location, its pattern of pedestrian and vehicular activity, and its usual occupants, inhabitants, or visitors may be a source of information. The investigator might then identify a witness who could describe the person who abandoned the fetus. Once the identity of the dead newborn is found, if ever, then the maternal history, history of labor and delivery, and the mother's statements about signs of life can be evaluated. The mother's attitude toward the pregnancy should be part of every perinatal death investigation.

Neonatal Period

Babies who are born at the hospital or are brought there shortly after birth and who die within the first month of life usually have a substantial amount of historical information available to be evaluated. There is usually a maternal history on file, as well as an infant medical history. These records should be reviewed and supplemented by a personal interview of the mother, the obstetrician, the anesthetist or anesthesiologist, and the pediatrician, if one has already attended the infant. It may be pertinent to interview the nursery personnel and others who may have attended or cared for the child. The details of the labor and delivery and the reactions of the fetus during and after the labor are important in an early neonatal death and may provide the critical information that determines the final diagnosis. Although it is not a part of the history per se, the placenta is a key factor in the evaluation of early neonatal death. Its importance should be recognized at the onset of an investigation and, if the placenta is not available, information about its evaluation by the obstetrician or hospital pathologist may be required.

In the later neonatal period, after the child leaves the hospital, a history of feeding, sleep patterns, voiding, activities, and the baby's reactions should be elicited from the people who were taking care of the child (Fig. 29-1). If necessary, this can be done on an hour-by-hour and day-by-day basis to establish continuity and sequences.

Infants and Children

After the neonatal period, the maternal obstetric history, the placenta, and the history of labor and delivery become less significant than the evaluation of the infant's history. The environment in which the infant resided, the mother's medical and social history, and the interviews of the people who actually took care of the infant become the key points of comparison for the other components of the investigation. History that relates to signs, symptoms, and exposure to infectious disease assume importance. The usual milestones that signify growth and development serve as an indicator of overall infant health, occult illness, malformation or other defect. The history of environ-

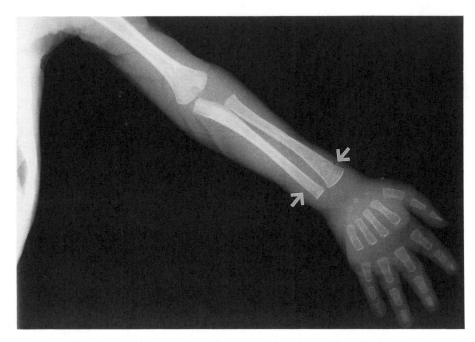

Fig. 29-1. This 3-month-old boy was born at term to a 19-year-old IV drug abuser. He became progressively more difficult to feed, requiring hospitalization on several occasions. He died of malnutrition which was thought to have been the end result of chemical brain damage in utero. Radiographs show growth arrest lines in several long bones, and soft tissue deficit.

mental factors, including food, clothing, shelter, warmth, and personal care become the elements that may raise an index of suspicion for an unnatural cause of death.

The presence of any external sign of violence on the body of a neonate, infant, or child demands a detailed accounting in the history. This is true whether the trauma be of resuscitative, therapeutic, accidental, or nonaccidental origin. A common explanation given for trauma is a fall. Background history and circumstances must first be investigated before this explanation can be accepted. Who was present? Who saw the incident? What was seen? What did the observer do? When did it happen? Where did it happen? What is the relationship of the observer to the deceased? Applicable questions also include an evaluation of

the physical factors. What were the distances involved? How was the child clothed? What were the size, dimension, firmness, and padding of the surface on which the child fell? Was the child in the appropriate developmental stage for the explanation given? Is there any physical evidence present at the site of the supposed impact? This type of information should be sought, and the body should be thoroughly examined before the history is accepted.

Sources of History

First-hand or primary witnesses should be found at every stage of the evolution of an investigation. The person who witnessed the incident, found the body, or was present when the child became ill will be the best person to describe the events as they occurred. In the case of child abuse, the investigator can be certain that the primary witness to the event will be telling only part of the truth, under the best of circumstances, or will be telling predominantly untruth under usual circumstances. The primary witness should be interviewed closely and in detail for factors that can be tested against the autopsy findings, the scene findings, and other historic information from other witnesses. It is imperative to get as close to a firsthand account of the events as possible. In some instances, the primary witness statement is the sole means of interpreting the autopsy findings. This is particularly true when the posture or position of the decedent is involved. Primary witnesses to the event include the assailant(s), parents, babysitters, guardians, siblings, friends and neighbors, passersby, and others. In some instances, immediately following the event, persons may arrive at the scene to render assistance. These people are also primary witnesses but not to the event itself. Their observations may include the condition of the premises, the amount of blood at the scene, the position of the victim on their arrival, the identification or description of those present at the scene, and environmental conditions. They may be emergency medical personnel or their equivalent, people from the neighborhood, police or fire agencies, and other family members. When any of these later primary witnesses are shift workers, the information should be obtained as soon as possible from them before they go off shift and their observations become unavailable before the autopsy. In every resuscitated child, when traumatic injuries are found at the time of autopsy, a full description of the resuscitative process should be obtained. Still later, firsthand witnesses include hospital-based personnel who in some way have rendered assistance in diagnosis and treatment. This includes emergency physicians, practitioners of all treating specialties, nurses, aides, laboratorians, and, on occasion, even visitors. Firsthand witnesses may also include those people who have handled or transported the body after the time of death and until delivery to the death investigator.

Background history can frequently be obtained from family service bureaus, prior police reports and records, past medical records, treating physician interviews and records, and other family members, relatives, friends, and neighbors. It is important to cross-check information routinely. Historical touchpoints are listed in Table 29-1.

SCENE

The purposes of a scene examination are best served when the body still lies at the place of the incident that is also the place of death. In some instances, history indicates that the incident occurred in one location and, after a variable period of survival, death occurred at another site. Both locations and any intervening form of transportation may harbor pertinent physical evidence that should be sought and evaluated. Owing to advances in life-support procedures, the victim is frequently moved from the scene of the incident or death to a medical treatment facility, and the relationship between the decedent and the place of injury or illness becomes disturbed. The practice of moving bodies from the scene of death to give the appearance of treatment and hope to visibly distraught family members is understandable, but should be discouraged.

The sole evidence for the cause of death itself may be present at the scene, as in cases of environmental hyperthermia or hypothermia, poisonings, and cer-

Table 29-1.   Important Historical Elements

Mother
  Medical: state of health, illness
  Social: habits, parenting skills, substance abuse
  Obstetric: previous pregnancies, prenatal care, labor, delivery, postpartum
Child
  Birth: weight, Apgar scores, nursery examination
  Well visits: dates, examinations, immunizations
  Medical: growth, milestones, weight, height, reaction to environment
  Daily living: eating, sleeping, cleanliness, activity, schedule
Background
  Family: caregivers, siblings, relatives, fosters, in-laws, others
  Agencies: child welfare, police, social services
  Deaths: other children, recent deaths in family
Event
  Found dead: last alive, time then, condition then, time found, by whom, why then, exact position found
  Injury: what happened, what preceded, followed, when, where, who was present
  Illness: time of onset, signs and symptoms, diagnosis, treatment
  Aid rendered: body moved, home remedy, lay/trained resuscitation, transport, medical or surgical treatment, specimens from hospital
  Witnesses: event, responders, treatment, transport

tain types of electrical injury, as well as in postural or positional asphyxias. Examination of the scene permits the documentation of environmental factors, allows for collection of physical evidence related to the death investigation, and builds a set of facts on which an opinion concerning cause of death may be based when autopsy findings are negative. Examination of the scene while the body is still there is most productive, but retrospective scene investigations may also be helpful and should not be overlooked simply because the body has been transported elsewhere. Personal observation of the scene of the incident will give a better idea of the amount of available mechanical, chemical, thermal, or electrical energy than will the evaluation of photographs or the word of a third-party witness or investigator.

Perinate

In the case of an abandoned fetus or newborn, the evaluation of the scene should concentrate on factors that would help identify the decedent, establish the time that the decedent was deposited at the location where it was found, and point to the place of birth. In the case of delivery out of hospital, the scene investigation may help to establish the sequence of rupture of membranes, time of delivery, amount of blood shed and by whom, and may provide a physical frame of reference to corroborate the history. Seldom is there a need for scene investigation at the hospital unless medical device failure, product safety, therapeutic error, or environmental factors are a consideration. A visit to the body at the hospital, however, permits early evaluation of charts and records at a stage before rationalization and self-interest can be expressed in the official documents, and may be especially helpful if change of shifts is about to take place.

Neonate and Child

Evaluation of the scene of incident and death in the case of older infants and children has almost the same import as in adults. The number and magnitude of hazards that may befall a child, however, vastly exceed those in adulthood. Household structures are more likely to be hazardous to children than to adults. Crib design, soft sleeping furniture, spatial traps, sleeping arrangements, and so forth, assume greater importance in younger children. Almost any object may be wielded by a child or adult to inflict serious injury on a young child. In those deaths where the pediatric victim shows external signs of violence, whether it be from mechanical, electrical, chemical, or thermal energy, the purpose of the scene investigation is to see if there are unsuspected or concealed causes of external trauma that were not indicated by the history, and to evaluate the type and magnitude of forces that were alleged to have been the cause of the trauma. The scene should be correlated not only with the history, but with information that may have been excluded from the history, and will provide a counterpoint to the autopsy findings. The most useful aspects of scene evaluation are listed in Table 29-2.

EXAMINATION OF THE BODY

In a medicolegal setting, the examination of the body should not be limited to only autopsy procedures and observations. The observation of the perinate, infant, or child at the scene of death may, on occasion, be more important than the autopsy observations themselves. The technical procedures will vary with the development and maturity of the pediatric decedent. The major pediatric forensic issues to be addressed at autopsy include livebirth, birth trauma, infanticide, congenital disease, infections, and accidental and nonaccidental trauma.

The autopsy should be started only after all available history has been reviewed, the pertinent issues have been identified, and the need for additional

Table 29-2.   Elements of Scene Investigation

Time and place of death
  Livor: color, distribution, degree
  Rigor: location, amount
  Clothing: arrangement, evidence
  Temperature: of body, of environment, control
  Decomposition: location, degree, insects, vegetation
Environment
  Indoors: address, type of dwelling, type of neighborhood
  Premises: rooms, furnishings, degree of shelter, food stores, heat, water and sanitation, cooking facilities, cleanliness, essentials and comforts, structural and procedural hazards
  Outdoors: location, accessibility, neighborhood or environment, weather, microclimate, traceable objects
Findings
  Investigation: date(s), time(s), person(s)
  Wounds: general preliminary characteristics, possible wounding objects, blood distribution and amount
  Evidence: food, containers, baby bottles, medicines, cribs, furniture, electrical devices, stains, fibers, etc.

history or scene information has been transmitted. In instances where the charts or records are not immediately available before the beginning of the autopsy, the pathologist should make every attempt to obtain the most pertinent, clinical, and circumstantial information from the best available sources before the dissection begins. Direct communication is the most productive. In the absence of pertinent history, discrepancy between the findings and the proposed explanation may not be discovered while there still is an opportunity to re-examine the body. Once the autopsy is complete, the opportunity to make accurate and specific correlation between history and observation may be lost forever. The techniques of the perinatal autopsy are not particularly difficult to master but require attention to detail and sequences (see Appendix C).

Perinatal

The perinatal autopsy is a special procedure in itself. The details of dissection differ from the autopsy of an older child and of an adult, particularly in the search for congenital deformities, the dissection of the heart and lungs in situ, and the method of examining the brain and spinal cord for the presence of birth trauma.

The use of a standardized autopsy checklist protocol for the pediatric autopsy has been urged, especially in the perinatal and neonatal period, regardless of whether the pathologist performing the autopsy has subspecialized in pediatric, forensic, or other anatomic specialty. The examination of the body should include a specific evaluation of clothing and other garments for signs of identity, general care, recent structural damage, blood and secretions, and trace physical evidence. Every forensic examination should have a section devoted to the clothing, even if only to register a pertinent negative.

Placenta

Examination of the placenta is indicated in perinatal and early neonatal deaths. The investigator must request it immediately as soon as the death is reported. If the birth is known to have taken place outside the hospital recently, the scene of birth should be searched for the placenta. If the infant has been born in the hospital and has died shortly thereafter, the hospital may be in a position to provide the placenta to the investigator. Many hospitals discard or pool placentas. The investigating jurisdiction may find it worthwhile to assist the hospitals in developing a hospital policy to preserve placentas identified and separated for a few days in the case of low risk, high apgar babies and to have the placenta examined routinely in the case of low apgar, high risk, and premature babies. Any placenta still not physically connected to the child can be verified through immunoserology or, if warranted, by DNA analysis.

External Examination

A detailed description of the external findings is the hallmark of a competent forensic examination. It marks the difference between a forensic and a medical autopsy because, most often, the significant forensic findings in a death investigation are visible or detectable before the internal dissection. In cases of child abuse and other forms of external trauma, the external examination alone may be decisive. In addition to the systematic visual observations made, any postmortem incisions that are above and beyond the customary autopsy incisions should be specifically identified, including the purposes and findings of those dissections. The liberal use of pertinent negative statements will remove any doubt about the extent of the examination. As Kerling observed, frequently, the most useful contribution that the death investigator may make is clearly and unambiguously to report negative findings gleaned from a carefully executed autopsy. A systematic examination by regions should be undertaken with particular attention in perinates (12 weeks gestation to day 28 of life) and neonates (first 4 weeks of life) to facies, proportions, signs of common malformations, and indicators of gestational maturity, as well as identifying features and marks of treatment and injury.

The external examination begins with the description of clothing, coverings, personal effects, and surface physical evidence. Radiographs should preferably precede dissection. It will be convenient for the person who reads the autopsy report to have all autopsy weights and measurements cross-referenced within the report to a standard value for the age, sex, and race of the decedent. The height and weight and their respective percentiles including crown-heel, crown-rump, foot length, head and chest circumference, and biparietal diameter should be recorded both in standard scientific units as well as in units appropriate for the anticipated lay audience who will be expected to read the report. The head size, shape, contour, proportions, fontanels, and palpable or visible injury are standard items of examination as are observations of the scalp pertaining to swelling, wounds, hair development and distribution, and trace evidence. Subsequent reflection of the scalp at the time of internal examination of the brain is a part of the full examination of all of the layers of the scalp and complements the external description. The position of facial features, their proportion and relationship, and presence of structural defects should be noted. The ears may indicate degree of maturity by the rotation and shape of the pinna. The position may suggest genetic abnormality, and the ear canal may reflect an infectious process. The nose should be checked for patency, septal structure, and contents, including blood, pus, vomitus, and foreign objects. The labial and lingual frenula should be examined and described specifically for wounds. The lips, gums, teeth, if any, buccal mucosa, floor of the mouth, oral contents, palate, and uvula should be fully examined and described. It may be necessary to swab the mouth and the nasal passages for bacteria and foreign residues.

Eyes

The eye examination includes the external visualization of all conjunctival surfaces, eyelids, and periorbital skin, as a minimum. Sampling of the vitreous fluid for chemical or toxicologic analysis may be performed in cases in which there is no need to remove the eye. However, because postmortem fundoscopic examination is either impossible or unreliable in most instances, enucleation of the eyeballs should be undertaken in instances of suspected child abuse, overt well documented corporeal trauma, and head and facial trauma, and whenever documentation of retinal hemorrhage or intraocular changes is required (Fig. 29-2). The globes themselves may be critical to the evaluation of the overall pattern of injury and disease. Retinal hemorrhage has a variety of etiologies, which include birth stress, chest compression, cardiopulmonary resuscitation, intracranial hemorrhage, increased intracranial pressure, clotting disorders, infant shaking, head trauma, and child abuse. In the absence of a clear explanation, retinal hemorrhage is a significant marker for nonaccidental injury. Investigation for child abuse is essential unless an obvious accidental cause of trauma is known. The "whiplash-shaken infant" syndrome involves vigorous, manual shaking of infants by the extremities or shoulders with whiplash-induced intracranial and intraocular bleeding but with no external signs of head trauma. Since the original review, the clinical and postmortem examinations of the eyes in detecting whiplash-shaken infant syndrome has become a standard practice. In a review of 48 cases of infants and young children with the diagnosis of shaken baby syndrome, it was found that all patients had a presenting history thought to be suspicious for child abuse and either retinal and subdural or subarachnoid hemorrhage, or a computed tomography (CT) scan showing subdural or subarachnoid hemorrhage with interhemispheric blood. All fatal cases had signs of blunt impact to the head, although in more than one-half of the fatal

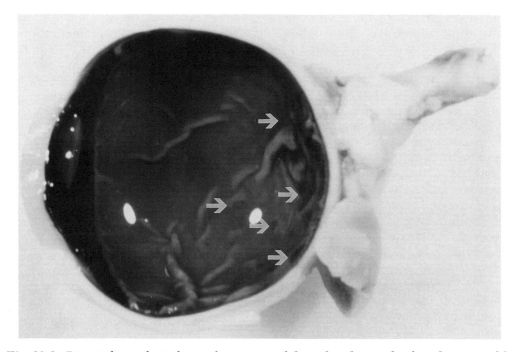

Fig. 29-2. Bisected enucleated eye shows several foci of surface and subsurface retinal hemorrhage in a 4-month-old girl who was dead on arrival at the emergency department. Her father eventually admitted to violently slapping and shaking the decedent because of stress from overwork.

cases, these findings were noted only at autopsy. Based on experimental models, it was suggested that severe head injuries, commonly diagnosed as being caused by shaking, require impact to occur and that shaking alone, in an otherwise normal baby, is unlikely to cause the shaken baby syndrome. In addition to the retina, the optic nerve sheath itself may show traumatic hemorrhage at autopsy.

Neck, Chest, and Abdomen

The neck, chest, and abdomen should be examined for wounds and evidence, and these should be clearly distinguished from postmortem artifact. Crepitus of the neck, web-like structure and hump shape should be described, if present. The contour and proportion of the chest can be mentioned in relation to maturity. The shape of the abdomen can be noted, with particular reference to abdominal distention. The umbilicus should be examined for healing reaction, type of severance, and residue. The breasts, genitalia, and anus should be examined for signs of endocrine activity and possible indications of sexual assault, including bite marks, extraneous hair, and signs of injury. Groin, axilla, and perineum can be checked for hygiene, lymph nodes, and general structure. Back and buttocks can be examined for signs of wounds, spinal malformation, and soft tissue reserves.

Extremities

The arms may show signs of grasp marks or deformity. The hands may show abnormal creases, digits, or ridge pattern, and may contain trace evidence or wounds. Legs and feet can be examined for shape and proportion, number of digits, cleanliness, wounds, and scars.

Internal Examination

If applicable, a test for pneumothorax can be performed before the internal dissection and after radiographic review, if any. The evaluation of the pleural and peritoneal cavities and the relationships of the organs should be established in situ before the organs are removed. The path of wounds, such as gunshot, shotgun, stab, and other penetrating trauma, should be clearly identified and traced before organs are removed.

Cardiovascular System
Systematic examination of the pericardium, heart, aorta, and major branches, pulmonary arteries and veins, systemic veins, and the blood should be undertaken, noting positions, measurements, characteristics, abnormalities, and pertinent negatives. Heart weight, size, shape, position, rotation, epicardium, myocardium, endocardium, valve size, structure, septa, and coronary ostia should be routinely examined.

Respiratory System
Trace the airways and the vasculature in situ before resection to evaluate congenital defects. Systematically examine the nasal passages, nasopharynx, hypopharynx, larynx, trachea, bronchi, lungs, pleurae, diaphragm, arteries, veins, and contiguous esophagus.

The alimentary tract should be examined for continuity, duplications, absences, malpositions, general structure and contents, and specific gross abnormalities. The stomach contents may be critical to the evaluation of forensic issues, particularly time of death, and may

serve as a means of cross-checking the history.

The liver size, shape, contour, edges, cut surface, as well as the gallbladder and biliary duct system should be evaluated routinely. In the presence of wounds to the liver, accurate measurement of their size and description of their location with respect to the spinal column adjacent structures, and re-examination of the overlying abdominal wall should be recorded. The position of the intestines, mesentery, continuity, contents, and diameters should be noted. Spleen, thymus, and lymph nodes should be evaluated for lymphoreticular status. The position of the kidneys, their rotation, contour, parenchymal architecture, pelvic shape, ureters, bladder, urethra, uterus, vagina, and adnexa should not be overlooked. Endocrine organs should be fully evaluated.

Musculoskeletal System
In instances of child abuse, suspected child abuse, and in the young pediatric age range, the musculoskeletal examination should routinely be accompanied by high quality radiographs. These are more efficient than is dissection in recognizing and documenting skeletal abnormality. Positive radiographic findings may lead to skeletal dissection for photography, description, chemical, and histologic evaluation. In instances of multiple fractures, extensive specimen radiography, and histologic sampling may be required. Minimum dissection in the young decedent should include full exposure of each rib.

Central Nervous System
In addition to the complete examination of the scalp, fontanels, calvaria, intracranial spaces, meninges, brain, base of skull, and dural sinuses, the middle and inner ear and spinal cord should be examined routinely. Spinal cord injury is often overlooked by the pathologist be-

cause examination of the cervical vertebral column and spinal cord is not a routine part of necropsy examination.
Damage to the cervical spinal cord may
be a manifestation of birth trauma and examination for this should be mandatory
in death following a complicated delivery. The injuries result from traction and
may complicate vaginal delivery with
either cephalic or breech presentation.
Removal of the occipital bone and the
posterior cervical spinal arches in continuity may be required to expose the
lower portion of the medulla and the
upper portion of the cervical spine in situ
rather than the customary means of separating the brain from the upper cervical
cord at the foramen magnum. Block resection of the cervical spine permits examination of the spinal cord as well as of
the vertebral artery system.

TESTS

Before and during the course of an autopsy, several tests may be performed as
required by the circumstances of the investigation. Commonly used ancillary
tests and procedures include radiographic examination, toxicology, histopathology, and microbiology studies, cytogenetics, clinical chemistry,
immunoserology and DNA analysis,
odontology, and anthropology. The application of each of these testing groups
varies among cases and laboratories.
Some pediatric pathologists recommend
routine testing in one area but not in another. There is no uniform agreement on
the minimum acceptable procedures in
pediatric autopsies because the medical
and forensic issues vary with the maturity
of the decedent.

Among stillborn infants, commonly
recommended procedures are routine
radiographs for congenital defects and

identification, microbiology for bacterial
infection, cytogenetics or cell culture for
chromosomal abnormalities and for possible subsequent DNA analysis, and photography. Blood group antibodies may be
evaluated in an edematous stillborn.
After evaluating a protocol for postmortem examination of stillbirths, the single
most useful examination was found to be
the gross autopsy. However, 44 of 124
perinates had structural physical abnormality identified at autopsy; in 35 of
these, the abnormalities were caused by
chromosomal, single gene, or polygenic
disorders. As a result, when resources are
limited, gross autopsy, photography, radiography, and bacterial cultures should
be performed in all cases of stillbirth and
early neonatal death, and karyotyping
and histopathology may be used selectively.

Radiographs

Progress in the recognition and understanding of child abuse began, for all
practical purposes, with Caffey's 1946
ground-breaking article. Since that time,
the value of clinical and postmortem radiology in cases of possible, suspected, or
probable child abuse has become axi-
omatic. High quality postmortem radiography with histologic confirmation and
correlation has recently been proposed as
an extension of a basic radiographic technique, and is eminently suitable for postmortem investigation.

Body Radiographs
A full series of skeletal radiographs
should be taken before the autopsy begins. This will avoid the superimposition
of autopsy dissection artifact into the
basic screening radiographs and will permit the pathologist to develop an index of
suspicion and to orient the dissection to
issues that are identified by the x-ray pro-

cedure. In some instances, preautopsy radiographs may provide the only clue to healing bone wounds, especially in those parts of the body where dissection is not performed routinely. However, if unanticipated trauma is found during the course of an autopsy, postmortem radiographs can still be performed quite adequately and should be undertaken.

Specimen Radiographs

Any area of bone that is suspected to have wound or disease should be excised, radiographed again using modified specimen technique, and sampled for histologic evaluation. Timing of injury and classification of disease can achieve a high degree of accuracy when correlated with specimen radiographs. All x-ray film should be clearly and specifically identified with the case if their evidentiary value is to be preserved.

Chemistry

Postmortem specimens of blood, urine, vitreous fluid, and cerebrospinal fluid may be used to evaluate dehydration, renal function, and some metabolic functions including lipids and hormones. In instances in which clinical symptoms of hypoglycemia, acidosis, respiratory failure, central nervous system signs, vomiting, hepatomegaly, or jaundice are not explained by clinical evaluation during life or by autopsy findings, a study for inborn errors of metabolism may be undertaken using postmortem specimens. The eyeball should not be pierced for its vitreous fluid if an anatomic evaluation of the globe will be undertaken for signs of trauma.

Histology

Various investigators have considered histologic evaluation worthwhile. There is an approximately 20 percent or greater success rate in performing routine microscopy of perinates, neonates, and infants. Recommended samples in perinates vary, but usually include ventricular myocardium, each lobe of the lung and liver, thymus, kidney, pancreas, adrenals, diaphragm, costochondral junction, placenta, amniotic membranes, and umbilical cord. In neonates, additionally, larynx, trachea, pituitary, thyroid, intestine, gonad, and brain should be evaluated. The sudden infant death syndrome (SIDS) protocol may also be employed.

All structurally abnormal organs and a representative sampling of wounds should be examined. It is critical in the evaluation of a child for suspected abuse that each and every vital organ, including the endocrine glands, be sampled for histology, and that wounds that do not have a similar gross appearance be liberally sampled and accurately labeled as to their origin. The timing of injuries and their attendant host response using microscopy is one of the more effective means of providing quality control for the gross evaluation of the age of wounds. If done in sufficient detail, as is justified by the importance of the issues, histopathology may provide crucial information in the administration of justice. There is no justification for failure to submit microscopic sections in the evaluation of a child abuse case. Even in the presence of decomposition, scar tissue might be demonstrable, since it is resistant to the effects of autolysis and putrefaction. A single microscopic section may also serve to demonstrate the futility of the procedure in the presence of decomposition.

Toxicology

The investigative and diagnostic value of postmortem toxicology testing cannot be overstated. During this time of rampant drug abuse, children become active and passive victims of the drug abuse of their caretakers. When the feasibility of toxicology testing was studied in cases of SIDS, it was concluded, in part, that it is practical to obtain satisfactory specimens for toxicologic analysis at the time of infant autopsies and that an anticipated 12 percent rate of positive results made for a favorable cost of benefit ratio. A study of cocaine exposure in 1120 pediatric patients indicated that cocaine or a metabolite was found in 52 patients. Four of those were neonates and three were infants from 1 to 7 months of age. In 19 cases, cocaine exposure was unsuspected until the results of routine screening tests became available. One neonate died. The passive ingestion and inhalation of cocaine by infants and toddlers have been reported in the urine of four hospitalized children who had been exposed to the smoke of freebase cocaine used by their adult caretakers. No blood quantitation was reported, however. Two of the children had transient neurologic symptoms including drowsiness and unsteady gait, and two had seizures, the cause of which could not be determined by laboratory investigation. Currently, 25 percent of pediatric toxicology submissions below 11 years of age are positive for some chemical substance, exclusive of fire-related carbon monoxide. Toxicologic testing of stillbirths, abortuses, and newborns may provide the cause of death and may give information about the condition of the mother. A small number of these cases represent an unanticipated cause of death.

Case 1

A 9-year-old boy with a history of seizure disorder, treated with carbamazepine, was administered chloral hydrate after encephalogram and was sent home with his parents. He developed drowsiness at home over the next few hours and became progressively more obtunded, requiring emergency department resuscitation 5 hours after leaving the clinic. Autopsy showed visceral congestion, cerebral edema, and mild fatty liver. Toxicologic analysis showed a postmortem blood level of methadone of 0.5 mg/L. Investigation showed that liquid methadone had been administered by the clinic instead of liquid chloral hydrate. Both medications were pink and were being held for administration in open, unlabeled medication cups on adjacent medicine trays. (Case courtesy of Sunandan Singh, M.D.)

Case 2

A 21-month-old daughter of an unmarried couple who are IV drug abusers was fed at 10 A.M. and put to sleep in her usual state of health. Three and one-half hours later, the child was found unresponsive in her crib, and resuscitation was unsuccessful. There were no external signs of trauma. The child had had measles and rubella immunizations 5 days previously and was being treated with penicillin for a cold. Autopsy revealed no gross anatomic cause of death, mild visceral congestion, and sterile blood cultures. There was no sign of bony trauma on radiographic examination. Toxicology showed a postmortem blood methadone level of 0.50 mg/L, and the liver contained 4.77 mg/kg. Investigation revealed that the mother had three 60-mg units of "take home" methadone hidden in a sofa at home. Its consumption has not been satisfactorily documented. (Case courtesy of Phito Pierre-Louis, M.D.)

Case 3

A newborn girl was eventually found in a garbage dumpster after her mother presented to the emergency department because of vaginal bleeding. The baby was full-term, weighing 3060 g. The placenta was still attached and was normal. Four stab wounds to the neck were identified as the cause of death. Lungs, stomach, and intestine contained air. Postmortem toxicology showed a brain cocaine level of 0.14 mg/kg and a brain benzoylecgonine level of 0.05 mg/kg. (Case courtesy of Rudolf Platt, M.D.)

Case 4

A 3-month-old baby girl was found unresponsive, face down in her crib in a pool of vomitus, approximately one-half hour after having been fed. The child was found to be limp, with no spontaneous respirations or pulse. Pediatric ACLS was begun, and the child was transferred to a pediatric intensive care unit where she remained in coma for 3.5 days. On the second hospital day, there was an inconclusive report of ethchlorvynol in an admission urine specimen. Autopsy showed anoxic cerebral changes and bronchopneumonia with *Candida albicans* cultured. Postmortem toxicology results consisted of the prescribed medications diazepam and temazepam but was negative for ethchlorvynol. Postmortem toxicology of a blood specimen sequestered at the hospital showed premortem blood levels of ethchlorvynol of 5.1 mg/L. Investigation revealed that the decedent's father had ground up 250 mg of a 500-mg ethchlorvynol tablet and put it into the baby's formula to quiet the child. The initial history given by the hospital that the mother had fed the child was incorrect. (Case courtesy of Phito Pierre-Louis, M.D.)

Alcoholic beverages are commonly administered to infants as part of folk remedies, occasionally resulting in acute alcoholic intoxication or poisoning. Many carelessly kept or inadvertently administered prescribed medications find their way into the pediatric population resulting in death. The passive administration of cocaine is endemic in some parts of the country. There seems to be little justification for a death investigator to omit the submission of specimens for toxicologic analysis in any death that occurs outside the hospital. It may be imprudent to forego toxicologic analysis in some deaths in the hospital setting as well. A complete list of all drugs that may have been recently administered to the decedent should routinely accompany a request for toxicology testing.

Microbiology

The usefulness of postmortem microbiologic studies varies with the circumstances of death. In fetal death without medical attendance, when the birth is reported or discovered promptly, microbiologic cultures may not only be useful but may be definitive. In an abandoned stillborn, however, depending on postmortem interval, the degree of maceration and the contaminating factors of the environment negate the value of postmortem cultures, unless pus is identified. In instances of pediatric sudden death where there is insufficient history to conclude a presumptive clinical cause of death before autopsy, and no anatomic cause of death is found at autopsy, then the use of bacterial cultures is indicated. Cultures should be taken as early in the internal dissection as possible. Pus should always be smeared and cultured (Fig. 29-3).

In many medicolegal jurisdictions, deaths from causes that might constitute a threat to public health are reportable to the medical examiner for full investigation. Thus, depending on the nature of the circumstances, when clinical infections go undiagnosed or in unusual varia-

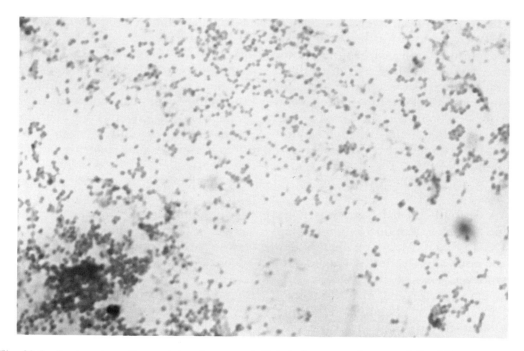

Fig. 29-3. Postmortem Gram stained smear of slightly hazy, cerebrospinal fluid from cysterna magna at autopsy. Abundant neutrophils and rare intracellular gram-negative cocci were found. Culture grew *Neisseria meningitidis*. The family was treated prophylactically.

tions of diagnosed infectious disease, it may be necessary to perform a public health-oriented medicolegal autopsy, including microbiologic cultures, immunoserology for antibodies to infectious agents, tissue sections, smears, and a histologic search for inclusion bodies. A study of the stillborn and neonatal autopsy procedures for cost-effectiveness determined that between 10 and 15 percent of autopsies provide significant postmortem bacteriologic information that could not have been obtained by the gross autopsy alone. Critical reviews of the subject have concluded that even though the procedure is disdained by many, postmortem bacteriology can provide interpretable results, especially if used regularly by the investigator. The use of antibody testing may be employed even in the absence of postmortem cultures, as has been demonstrated in the case of a postmortem study of meningococcal capsular polysaccharides. Postmortem microbiology may provide significant information in the investigation of neglect and failure-to-thrive, if only as a pertinent negative factor.

Cytogenetics

A number of authors have embraced the value of cytogenetics in selected cases. The highest yield is among malformed fetuses and perinates, macerated but normally formed stillbirths, and normally formed unmacerated stillbirths. Heart blood, lung, gonad, and skin are suitable specimens in the absence of gross degeneration of tissues. In the case of abandoned stillbirths and in perinates, cytogenetic studies may provide an explanation for intrauterine death or premature labor, and may provide adjunctive information to some gross malformations observed at autopsy. Cytogenetic studies have been recommended in all stillbirths and infants dying at less than 28 days of age, except in cases of isolated central nervous system malformation, in SIDS, trauma, or known single gene defect. Cell culture in preparation for cytogenetic studies in the case of an abandoned fetus may also provide a specimen suitable for DNA analysis as a means of identification, as well as a motive for unauthorized abortion and abandonment.

DOCUMENTATION

Documentation of a death investigation begins with the history and should include the sources of all information, as well as the time that each piece of information was obtained. An investigation is acknowledged to be an ongoing process and should not be expected to have a complete set of facts at the outset. Since several facets of an investigation continue simultaneously, the documentation of the sequence of availability of information may be helpful in reconstructing reasons why conclusions were reached. In addition to the scientific reasons for detailed documentation of the medical facts, the issue of public accountability of the investigative process also requires that documentation be an essential component of the investigation. When a consultant, agency, or other interested person reviews the case file of any death investigation, there should be sufficient factual information present, both positive and negative, so that the reviewer may understand the essential facts on which the investigator's conclusions are based and, it is hoped, arrive at the same or similar conclusion. Numerous contested conclusions have arisen simply because essential documentation did not exist. It is easy to create doubt when information is incomplete; however, clear documentation prevents any doubt as to the accuracy of conclusions reached. A practical rule of thumb is that if it was not written down, it did not happen.

Photography

Photographs are absolutely necessary in the documentation of abnormalities or the lack thereof. Amateurish photographs are to be avoided at all costs, since they create confusion. A 35-mm camera format or larger is satisfactory. The ability to take close-up photographs for detail of wounds is highly desirable, and this may include the use of a 100-mm macro lens in addition to the normal lens for overall photographs. A balanced electronic flash and suitably matching color film are the most suitable and practical means of documentation. Black and white film is not adequate to the task.

Overall photographs set the perspective. Closer range orienting photographs, including the wound and the anatomic region, set the stage for further close-up photography that will demonstrate wound detail. Taking pictures at right angles to the body or to the item of interest, provides proper perspective and reduces distortion. In the case of wounds on the back of the body, positioning the body face down and taking overhead photographs of the back is the most demonstrative technique. Initial photographs should be taken before cleaning off the body and the wounds. Using a scale in the field of vision when taking pictures provides a uniform reference, but a photograph without a scale may be particularly helpful to demonstrate wound detail without distraction. Evidence should be photographed in place before removal, then secured, labeled, and identified for suitable storage. After cleaning a wound, ensure that all blood and extraneous fluids have been removed and the surfaces are blotted dry. Either color transparency film or color negative film is suitable. A color reference may be helpful with print film.

Diagrams

A diagram of wounds should be prepared in every case of external violence that is not solely a result of therapeutic trauma. Each wound should be positioned and identified in suitably dark ink or pencil that will photocopy clearly.

Reports

The autopsy report should include a minimum description of each organ and its major anatomic components. For example, the heart description should include the overall description of the heart, including weight, size, shape, pericardium, epicardium, myocardium, endocardium, valves, and chambers. The description of an organ as unremarkable is not descriptive. The use of pertinent negatives is imperative and represents the fullest professional expression of an objective description. Pertinent negatives indicate that the pathologist knew what to look for, looked for it, and saw that it was not present. Absence of pertinent negatives creates doubt and uncertainty, and may lead to improper conclusions on the part of the reader. The general outline of an autopsy report is presented in Table 29-3.

Reports from other investigative agencies or health care facilities should be incorporated into the record, either whole or by abstraction. The autopsy report should have associated with it a statement of historical circumstances that will form a frame of reference for interpretation of

Table 29-3.   Outline of Atopsy Report

Case identifiers
 Name, case number, date, etc.
External examination
 Clothing, valuables, personal effects, evidence
 Radiographs, if any
 Identifying features
 General observations
 Marks of treatment
 Marks of injury (integrated with subsequent internal examination)
 External dissections, if any
Internal examination
 General observations
 Systems evaluation
  Cardiovascular
  Respiratory
  Digestive
  Lymphoreticular
  Endocrine
  Urogenital
  Central nervous system
  Musculoskeletal
Specimens
Gross findings
History and circumstances
Opinion of cause and manner of death
Photo list
 List of photos taken (optional)
Wish list
 Items outstanding (for office use only)

the autopsy findings. The police report, fire officer's report, report of evidence analysis, hospital chart, doctor's office record, consultant laboratory report, consulting physician's report, consulting engineer's report, and so forth may become part of the official record depending on either local custom, formal policy, regulation, or laws relating to records and archives.

CORRELATION

Consultation may be desirable with the obstetrician, pediatrician, radiologist, pediatric pathologist, neuropathologist, and others. Reports or a summary of consult should be correlated with the remainder of the investigation.

At the conclusion of the initial phase of the examination, a work list or plan of operations should be developed and written down to outline the items of information or documents that will be required to finalize the case. When all of this information is received, a conclusion may be reached. However, each piece of information should be reviewed as soon as it becomes available, since it may affect the continuing necessity for other testing or the redirection of resources toward a more pertinent objective.

The conclusion of the medical examiner should incorporate all the objective findings, all the documented historical information, and all the opinions of consultant experts. The pathologist medical examiner is under no obligation to accept any piece of information as the determining factor in the conclusion reached. Work and pretrial conferences, and staff review of difficult cases should be held regularly.

A family conference is frequently of some help in finalizing cases. Although this may not necessarily be part of the investigative function of medical examiners, in cases where it is not contraindicated by a suspicion of homicide or an investigation for known homicide, it is a useful ancillary service to the public.

SUGGESTED READINGS

1. Bateman DA, Heagarty MC: Passive free-base cocaine ('crack') inhalation by infants and toddlers. Am J Dis Child 143:25, 1989
2. Benson PF, Fensom AH: Genetic biochemical disorders. p. 4. In Benson PF, Fenson AH (eds): Oxford Monographs on Medical Genetics. No. 12. Oxford University Press, Oxford, 1985
3. Caffey J: Multiple fractures in the long bones of infants suffering from chronic subdural hematoma. Am J Roentgenol 56:163, 1946
4. Caffey J: The whiplash shaken infant syndrome: manual shaking by the extremities with whiplash-induced intracranial and intraocular bleeding, linked with residual permanent brain damage and mental retardation. Pediatrics 54:396, 1974
5. Challener RC, Morrissey AM, Jacobs MR: Postmortem diagnosis of meningococcemia by detection of capsular polysaccharides. J Forensic Sci 33:336, 1988
6. Clark EGI, Zumwalt RE, Schanfield MS: The identification of maternity in an unusual pregnancy-related homicide. J Forensic Sci 35:80, 1990
7. Coe JI: Post-mortem biochemistry of blood and vitreous humour in paediatric practice. p. 191. In Mason JK (ed): Paediatric Forensic Medicine and Pathology. Chapman and Hall Medical, London, 1989
8. Duhaime AC, Gennarelli TA, Thibault LE et al: The shaken baby syndrome. A clinical pathological and biomechanical study. J Neurosurg 66:409, 1987
9. du Moulin CC, Paterson DG: Clinical relevance of postmortem microbiologic examination: a review. Hum Pathol 16:539, 1985
10. Dykes LJ: The whiplash shaken infant syndrome: what has been learned? Child Abuse Negl 10:211, 1986
11. Egge K, Lying G, Maltau JM: Effect of instrumental delivery on the frequency and severity of retinal hemorrhages in the newborn. Acta Obstet Gynecol Scand 60:153, 1981
12. Finkle BS, McCloskey KL, Kopjak L, Carroll JM: Toxicological analysis in cases of sudden infant death: a national feasibility study. J Forensic Sci 24.775, 1979
13. Friendly DS: Ocular manifestations of physical child abuse. Trans Am Acad Ophthalmol Otolaryngol 75:318, 1971
14. Froede R, Goode R: Medicolegal investigation and forensic procedures: a problem oriented approach. p. 2. In Froede R (ed): Handbook of Forensic Pathology. College of American Pathologists, Northfield, IL, 1990

15. Gilchrist KW, Gilbert EF, Esterly JR: Pediatric necropsies by general pathologists. Arch Pathol Lab Med 102:223, 1978

16. Gillebo K, Bostad R, Oftedal G et al: Perinatal retinal hemorrhages and development. Acta Pediatr Scand 76:745, 1987

17. Ito Y, Tsuda R, Kimuna H: Diagnostic value of the placenta in medicolegal practice. Forensic Sci Int 40:79, 1989

18. Jones AM, Weston JT: The examination of the sudden infant death syndrome infant: investigative and autopsy protocols. J Forensic Sci 21:833, 1976

19. Kanter RK: Retinal hemorrhage after cardiopulmonary resuscitation or child abuse. J Pediatr 108:430, 1986

20. Keeling JW: The perinatal autopsy. p. 1. In Keeling JW (ed): Fetal and Neonatal Pathology. Springer-Verlag, Berlin, 1987

21. Keeling JW: Intrapartum asphyxia and birth trauma. p. 209. In Keeling JW (ed): Fetal and Neonatal Pathology. Springer-Verlag, Berlin, 1987

22. Khan SG, Frenkel M: Intravitreal hemorrhage associated with rapid increase in intracranial pressure (Terson's Syndrome). Am J Ophthalmol 80:37, 1975

23. Kiffney GT: The eye of the "battered child." Arch Ophthalmol 72:231, 1964

24. Kleinman P, Blackbourne BD, Marx SC et al: Radiologic contributions to the investigation and prosecution of cases of fatal infant abuse. N Engl J Med 320:507, 1989

25. Kleinman PK, Marx SC, Blackbourne B: The metaphyseal lesion in abused infants: a radiologic-histopathologic study. Am J Roentgenol 146:895, 1986

25a. Koneman WE: Postmortem bacteriology. CRC Crit Rev Clin Lab Sci 1:5, 1970

26. Lambert SR, Johnson TE, Hoyt CS: Optic nerve sheath and retinal hemorrhages associated with the shaken baby syndrome. Arch Ophthamol 104:1509, 1986

27. Langley FA: The perinatal postmortem examination. J Clin Pathol 24:159, 1971

28. McLellan NJ, Prasad R, Punt J: Spontaneous subhyaloid and retinal hemorrhages in an infant. Arch Dis Child 61:1130, 1986

29. Manchester DK, Shikes RH: The perinatal autopsy: special considerations. Clin Obstet Gynecol 23:1125, 1980

30. Mueller RF, Sybert VP, Johnson J et al: Evaluation of a protocol for postmortem examination of stillbirths. N Engl J Med 309:586, 1983

31. Naeye RL: The investigation of perinatal deaths. N Engl J Med 309:611, 1983

32. Pryse-Davies J, Hurley R: Infections and perinatal mortality. J Antimicrob Chemother 5:59, 1971

33. Turtscher O: Noch ubekannte Befunde nach Schadeltrauma. Ber Zusammenkunft Dtsch Ophtlalmol Ges 36:294, 1910

34. Rao N, Smith RE, Choi JH et al: Autopsy findings in the eyes of fourteen fatally abused children. Forensic Sci Int 39:293, 1988

35. Shannon M, Lacouture PG, Roa J, Woolf A: Cocaine exposure among children seen in pediatric hospital. Pediatrics 83:337, 1989

36. Sutherland GR, Carter RF: Cytogenetic studies: an essential part of the pediatric necropsy. J Clin Pathol 36:140, 1983

37. Valdes-Dapena M, Huff D: Perinatal Autopsy Manual. Armed Forces Institute of Pathology, Washington D.C., 1983

38. Weedn VW, Mansour AM, Nichols M: Retinal hemorrhage in an infant after cardiopulmonary resuscitation. Am J Forensic Med Pathol 11:79, 1990

39. Yates PO: Birth trauma to the vertebral arteries. Arch Dis Child 34:436, 1959

30

Neuropathology

Lucy Balian Rorke

Significant nervous system damage leading to death or permanent neurologic dysfunction is a common feature of child abuse. It may be obvious on gross examination or detectable only if the index of suspicion is high and the examiner focuses attention on specific areas of the brain and spinal cord on both gross and microscopic study. This section provides a general guide to those professionals who must determine whether observed lesions resulted from natural disease, accidental trauma, or abuse. If such lesions are a consequence of abuse, the questions of how and when must be answered to establish the identity of the perpetrator of the crime.

GENERAL APPROACH TO CASE EVALUATION

The forensic pathologist is ordinarily presented with a body and sketchy information concerning circumstances surrounding the death. It is only after completion of the postmortem examination that a decision can be as to whether the reported events leading to unnatural death of the infant or child are consistent with the observed lesions. In many cases, they are not. The story related by the caretaker often implies that death was sudden and unexpected, especially if the victim had not been hospitalized. Determination of cause (primary disease) and manner (mechanism, i.e., natural consequence of primary disease or unnatural causes such as accident, suicide, homicide) requires meticulous attention to three major areas of investigation: (1) clinical history and events surrounding the death; (2) examination of the entire body including skin, hair, bones, internal organs, brain, spinal cord, and eyes; and (3) microscopic evaluation of visceral tissues, including bruises, fracture sites, eyes, brain, and spinal cord. Information derived from these studies allows the pathologist to determine when the injury occurred, which, in turn, often allows law enforcement officials to prosecute the perpetrator of the crime if the death has been ruled a homicide. There is considerable published literature on these subjects, but several points require emphasis before proceeding to discussion of specific types of nervous system lesions.

THE BODY

The body may show no external abnormality, or lesions may be minimal, subtle, or obvious. There are many ways

403

to injure or kill an infant or child, including beating, biting, burning, shaking, drowning, poisoning, smothering, neglect or starving, tying with ropes or chains, incarcerating in a confined space, throwing against a hard object, out of windows, down stairs, or into the air without catching. Penetrating injuries, that is, inflicted with knives or bullets, are uncommon. This list is by no means complete, as human beings seem to have a limitless capacity to express aggression in novel ways. While external lesions are often found, they tend to be absent when smothering or shaking alone has occurred. An assessment of the age of the lesions must be made, and a full body radiograph should be taken in all cases of suspected abuse. Evaluation of the nature and distribution of bruises is made within the context of the clinical history. For example, if there is a bruise on the head accompanying the story that the child fell down a flight of stairs, the pathologist should ask whether the location and character of the injury are consistent with such an event. Infants or children with injuries of various ages in odd places (trunk, head) are more than likely to be victims of abuse.

It has been suggested that infants do not sustain lethal brain damage following shaking alone, that is, in the absence of blunt trauma. While the majority of infants who have been shaken also have evidence of blunt trauma, a small proportion do not. These infants do indeed die of the effects of the whiplash-shaking injury (see below for description of lesions). Of importance in this context is the imprecise use of the term *shaken baby syndrome* by individuals who are really dealing with battered children in whom one aspect of the battering may have been shaking; these infants/children have evidence of other injuries as well.

The Story

The story provided by the caretaker of an abused infant/child is rarely a true account of the actual events. This is generally established later, when the medical evidence clearly contradicts the history. In some instances, the perpetrator will confess, but more often a judge or jury may be required to reach a verdict based on the defendant's testimony and the medical evidence provided. A brief case summary will illustrate this problem.

A seven-week-old infant was found dead in the crib by her mother on return from shopping. The infant's father was asleep in his bed. Emergency assistance was obtained, and the infant was taken to the local hospital where sudden infant death syndrome and Potter's syndrome were diagnosed because the infant's ears appeared to be low set. Necropsy disclosed massive, acute, bilaterally symmetric galeal and periosteal hemorrhages over the temporoparietal regions (the cause of the ear displacement), acute fracture of the occipital bone, brain swelling, and minor contusion injury of the olfactory bulbs and tracts.

When questioned, the father gave, in order, the following stories: (1) the baby rolled from the sofa to the carpeted floor (a height of about 18 to 20 in.); (2) the baby was in his arms, and her head was bumped against the wall as he walked from the kitchen to the bedroom; (3) the baby's head became stuck between two open slats in the crib; (4) the baby's crying interfered with his enjoyment of a baseball game on television so he squeezed the head between his hands.

The final story is most likely the correct one, as this would explain the massive, symmetric, laterally placed scalp and periosteal hemorrhages and could explain the occipital fracture, although it was not clear whether the back of the head was also struck against a hard object during this episode of anger.

The father was convicted.

THE GROSS AND MICROSCOPIC EVALUATION

Gross and microscopic evaluation of the nervous system must include careful attention to lesions of the scalp (hair should be shaved, if necessary), skull, soft tissues surrounding the vertebral column, dural coverings of the brain and cord, eyes, and the brain and cord themselves. The size and tension of the fontanels and the width of sutures are important in the assessment of significant brain swelling. It is especially important to examine the corpus callosum while the brain is in situ, as it may fracture on handling, especially in young infants. The callosum is most easily examined following reflection of the dura, gentle separation of the hemispheres, and elevation of the falx cerebri. Callosal fractures typically involve the posterior third and are generally accompanied by minimal or petechial hemorrhages. Olfactory bulbs and tracts should also be elevated with care and left attached to the brain; contusions may be limited to these structures in infants.

The location and volume of clots adjacent to the brain or cord, in situ distortions, and weight of the unfixed brain should be recorded. Extent of brain swelling, pressure cones, herniation phenomena, and external lesions require documentation. Since the rostral cervical spinal cord is at greatest risk in whiplash-shaken injuries, this portion should be removed with special care, and a posterior approach is often desirable. The orbital roofs should be elevated for removal of the eyes with attached optic nerves. Hemorrhages into the dural sheath and periorbital fat become obvious, if present.

Routine coronal sections of the cerebrum and transverse sections of the brain stem, cerebellum, and spinal cord may or may not uncover obvious lesions. In any case, sections for microscopic study should include the following: cortex and white matter of superior frontal gyrus at several levels, gyrus rectus, olfactory bulbs and tracts, centrum ovale at several levels; midportion of corpus callosum through genu, anterior, middle, and posterior body and splenium, hippocampal formation; corpus striatum; thalamus, midbrain, pons at the level of the locus ceruleus and through the level of the middle cerebellar peduncles; medulla; cerebellar vermis, sections through all levels of cervical spinal cord, and representative sections of thoracic, lumbar, and sacral cord. Blood clots and dural hemorrhages or membranes should also be studied. The eyes must be evaluated for presence and location of hemorrhages (i.e., epidural, subdural, or retinal).

Lesions at the microscopic level may be subtle and easily missed, especially if the victim died shortly after the injury was inflicted. (See below for details.)

Timing

One of the major aims of forensic necropsy is to establish the time of injury which, in turn, enables law enforcement officers to focus attention on specific caretakers of the pediatric decedent during that period. Determination of timing should be based on both clinical and pathologic data, and may be as much dependent on correlation of the location of the lesion in the central nervous system

(CNS) as on its gross or microscopic characteristics. For example, acute damage of the locus ceruleus generally leads to death within an hour or so. Infants who are shaken, on the other hand, may die soon thereafter if the cervical cord injury is severe and medical care is not administered. However, they may survive for hours before cerebral swelling becomes sufficiently severe to cause death.

The Perpetrator

Infants and children are most often lethally abused by an adult caretaker, rarely do older children inflict the injury. The adult may or may not be the parent, and frequently is the mother's paramour. The abuse often occurs when an infant is cranky or irritable because of a minor illness and the previously benevolent caretaker loses patience with the continuously crying infant.

The person(s) in whose care the decedent was at the time of the injury are presumed by law to be the perpetrator(s) of the crime.

The Lesions

Sixty-two cases of childhood homicide were evaluated at the Office of the Medical Examiner of Philadelphia from 1981 through 1986. Death resulted from a variety of injuries but was often attributable to CNS lesions. The type and frequency of external and internal injuries are listed in Table 30-1. One or more types of lesions were found in about two-thirds of the victims. The incidence is even higher in abused children studied radiographically; Cohen found abnormalities in three-fourths of such cases. Important features of the lesions are described below.

Table 30-1. Type and Frequency of Central Nervous System Lesions in Childhood Homicidal Abuse, 1981–1986, N = 62

Type of Lesion	Number	%
Scalp injury	31	50
Skull fracture	16	25
Brain swelling	41	66
Epidural hemorrhage	5	8
Subdural hemorrhage	31	50
Subarachnoid hemorrhage	29	46
Contusions and lacerations	13	20
Tissue necrosis (gray and/or white matter)	23	37

Scalp and Skull

Lethal head trauma may occur in the absence of observable damage to scalp or skull or, conversely, injury to these tissues may not cause death. Scalp injuries occurred in 50 percent of the 62 child homicides. Whereas burns or lacerations are immediately apparent, ecchymoses resulting from blunt trauma may not appear until several hours afterward. For this reason, clinicians suspecting abuse should examine the child repeatedly during hospitalization. It may be necessary to shave the hair, and even then, ecchymoses may be difficult to discern in dark complexioned individuals. While evidence of blunt trauma may be located anywhere over the scalp, face, or ears, it is often found over the posterior parietal and occipital regions.

Injury may not be apparent until the scalp is reflected to reveal variable galeal and periosteal bleeding or hemorrhages in the temporalis muscles.

One-fourth of the pediatric homicidal victims studied had skull fractures (Table 30-1).

Fracture lines are usually associated with bleeding but may not be obvious unless the periosteum and dura are stripped

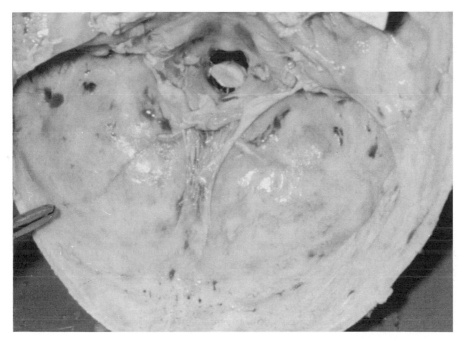

Fig. 30-1. Note linear fracture in left occipital bone (hemostat points to fracture). Dura has been removed. Victim was a 7 month old infant with multiple head injuries.

(Fig. 30-1). Sutural diastasis may occur when brain swelling is severe, or fractures may be of diastatic type.

The noncalcified, somewhat elastic, skull bones of infants are difficult to fracture; hence, this type of injury may be absent. If seen, it suggests that significant force was applied to the head. In babies, the fractures are often in the parietal or occipital bones.

Dural and Leptomeningeal Tears and Hematomas

Tears of the meninges or associated arteries and veins are found in about one-half of the victims at necropsy. As in adults, epidural hematomas are much less common than subdural hematomas, 8 versus 50 percent, respectively (Fig. 30-2). Pathogenesis and features of epidural and subdural hematomas are basically similar in both adults and children, with one major exception. Subdural bleeding in shaken infants most often accumulates in the posterior portion of the interhemispheric fissure, and the volume of blood is not typically large (Fig. 30-3). Since these hemorrhages result from venous bleeding, the blood may accumulate slowly and hence not be apparent on radiologic scans taken soon after injury.

Supratentorial subdural hematomas in infants and young children are infrequently large enough to cause death as a result of tentorial and brain stem herniation (Fig. 30-4). However, large posterior fossa hemorrhages associated with basal or occipital fractures may lead to death by brain stem compression.

Organized hemorrhages, formation of subdural membranes or effusions indicating previous injury, may be associated with acute hemorrhages, may be found if the victim survives for weeks or months following injury, or may be an unexpected finding in an otherwise mysteri-

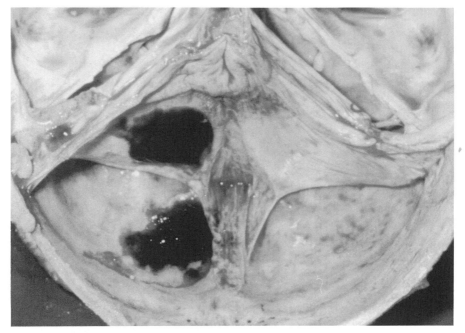

Fig. 30-2. Posterior fossa epidural hemorrhage in same infant whose fracture is pictured in Figure 30-1. Hemorrhage obscures fracture line.

ous death. It suggests previous battering in a child who dies of non-CNS trauma. Standard textbooks should be consulted for criteria used in aging these lesions.

Subarachnoid bleeding may accompany subdural hemorrhages, but it is also seen in isolation. Typically, these hemorrhages are small, although large ones are occasionally seen (Fig. 30-5). They were found in one-half of the childhood homicide victims (Table 30-1). They are not found in any one location but should be sought most carefully at the vertex or base of the brain, primarily over the gyrus rectus.

In some instances, the only intracranial abnormality may be a small amount of blood in the subarachnoid space adjacent to the pons and/or medulla. Blood accumulates at this site when high cervical-vertebral artery injury has occurred, and documentation of such damage requires careful dissection of the region.

An insignificant amount of blood may overlie the brain stem at the junction of the pons and medulla when partial transection occurs in violent hyperextension injuries of the neck.

Brain Lesions

Brain Swelling—Edema. The most common significant CNS lesion of childhood homicide is cerebral edema, seen in two-thirds of the victims at necropsy. Some pediatric victims with fatal CNS injuries, such as severe brain stem or cervical cord trauma, die before edema develops. Infants and young children are especially susceptible to brain swelling, and treatment is a major medical problem during the hospital course. It is a characteristic feature of shaken babies and may be the only finding at necropsy.

In infants, fontanels are generally tense, sutures are widened, and the brain may ooze forth as soon as the skull is

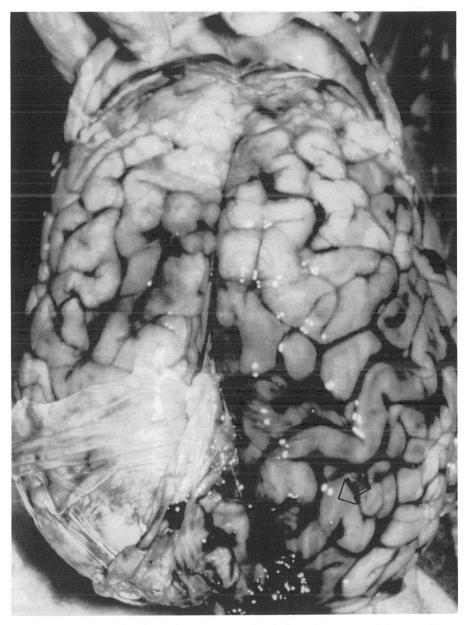

Fig. 30-3. Swollen brain of infant who was severely shaken. Dura over right posterior parietal region is reflected to expose small collection of subdural blood (arrow).

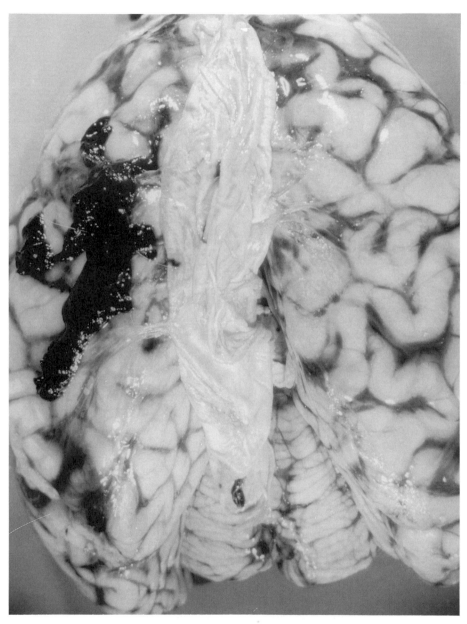

Fig. 30-4. Brain of 6-week-old shaken infant. Note subdural hematoma over left midconvexity region and small posterior subarachnoid hemorrhage.

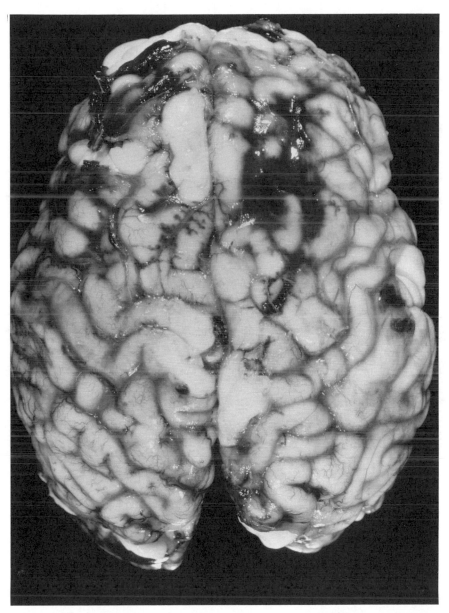

Fig. 30-5. Brain of 2-month-old infant whose mother shook him 12 hours before death. The infant had seizures, was irritable, and breathed with difficulty after the shaking episode. Note brain swelling and small subarachnoid hemorrhages.

opened. Although the swelling is fatal, uncal and parahippocampal grooves may not be dramatic; secondary Duret hemorrhages (in brain stem) do not occur in infants and young children, but tonsillar coning and brain stem swelling are found and tonsils may even be necrotic.

In spite of swelling, the tissue often appears somewhat dry. Section typically shows compression of the ventricular system, which has been emptied of spinal fluid (Fig. 30-6).

Contusions and Lacerations.   Contusions and lacerations (C/L) may be seen on external examination or only after the brain has been sectioned. External lesions are often minimal or absent in shaken infants and, in fact, may be diffi-cult to find internally as well. On the other hand, severe head trauma in babies produces extensive external lacerations, which may be of varying ages (Fig. 30-7). Occasionally, the injury is limited to the olfactory bulbs or tracts (Fig. 30-8).

Almost one-half of the pediatric victims of homicidal abuse had C/L of some type; the corpus callosum was lacerated in 20 percent (Table 30-1).

Callosal injuries are easily missed if the brain is not handled gently, especially in infants. As noted above, examination for callosal injury should always be performed in situ following careful retraction of the falx cerebri. Fibers in the posterior one-third of the body and splenium are most often torn (Fig. 30-9). Some of the interhemispheric subdural clots may ov-

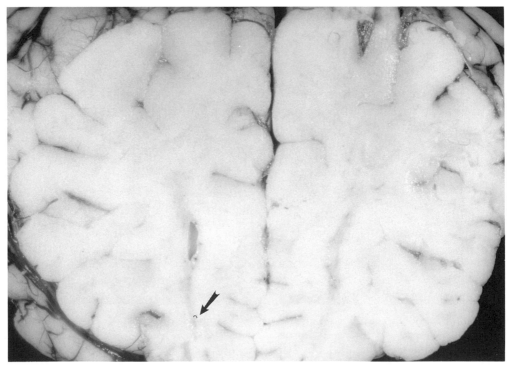

Fig. 30-6. Coronal section through frontal lobes of 4-month-old shaken baby who had retinal hemorrhages but no fractures. Brain is diffusely swollen and cortex of gyrus rectus is necrotic (arrow).

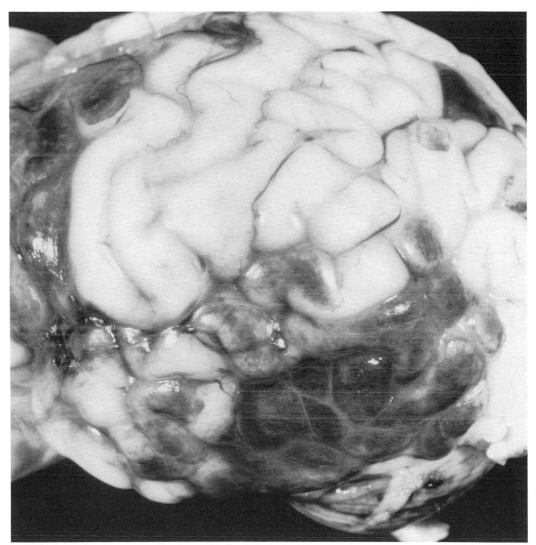

Fig. 30-7. Extensive contusions in brain of 8-week-old infant who was battered repeatedly throughout life. Note gyral swelling and hemorrhage into cortex.

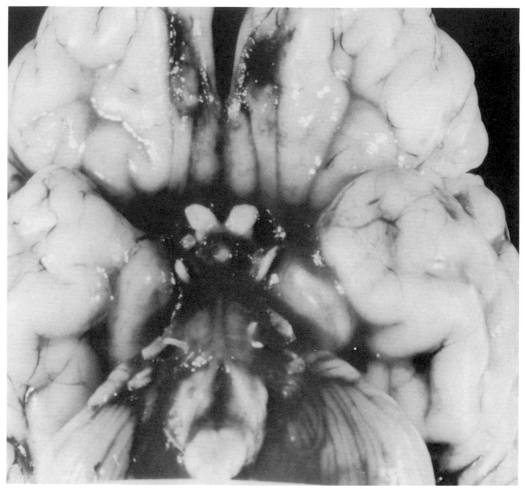

Fig. 30-8. Ventral surface of brain of 2-month-old infant showing hemorrhagic contusions of olfactory bulbs and tracts, gyrus rectus, and a small amount of basal subarachnoid hemorrhage.

erlie the damaged callosum, or petechial hemorrhages may be apparent along the edges of the fractured fibers. On the other hand, the petechiae are only obvious after sectioning or on microscopic examination in some cases.

Contusions/lacerations are most commonly located in the cerebral hemispheres and are relatively rare in the cerebellum. Aside from those on the surface and in the callosum, they characteristically appear as paramedial, linear cavities with the long axis directed dorsoven-

trally, or as small, focal, or confluent hemorrhages in the white matter in the same distribution. These lesions are typically located in the frontal lobes, and the cavitary lesions with or without hemorrhage are most often found in infants. They occasionally occur also in lateral ventral white matter of the frontal lobes (Fig. 30-10). These are the "gliding" contusions, originally described by Lindenberg and Freytag and considered by them to result from falls. However, studies by Adams et al. have shown that this type of contusion

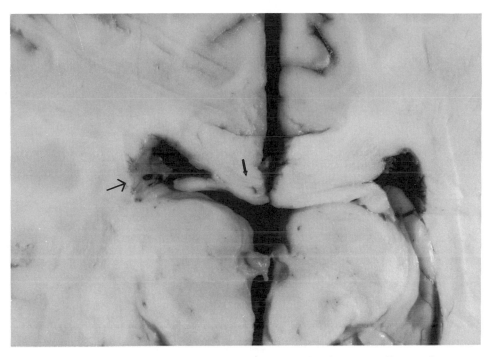

Fig. 30-9. Complete transection of posterior portion of body of corpus callosum from severely battered 2-year-old child. Note petechial hemorrhages just to left of tissue fracture and adjacent intraventricular clot (arrows).

is caused by acceleration/deceleration shear and tensile strains. Violent shaking or battering of an unsupported infant head subjects the brain to this type of acceleration/deceleration strain. Lesions may be acute or of varying ages if battering has been recurrent. Occasionally, chronic cavities are found in children who die months or years after abuse (Fig. 30-11).

If shaking or battering is unusually severe, the white matter fracture extends through the ependyma and communicates with the lateral ventricles; these occur typically at the dorsal angle. Necrotic brain tissue is displaced into the ventricular system and is identified at necropsy in the third or fourth ventricle, and in the aqueduct.

Focal hemorrhages or tears are also sometimes located in the corpus callosum, either midline or laterally, or in the centrum ovale. However, lesions at these sites are occasionally identified only on microscopic study. They appear as petechial hemorrhages, small foci of necrosis or axonal damage. The latter is most easily recognized by presence of retraction balls, which, with routine hematoxylin and eosin staining, appear as pink snowball-like structures (Fig. 30-12). They are seen to better advantage if a silver stain such as the Bodian stain is applied, and other axonal abnormalities are also more clearly delineated. These lesions, generally referred to as diffuse axonal injury, characteristically occur in severe acceleration/deceleration strain but may not be identified morphologically if death occurs within 12 to 24 hours of the injury. Changes that are seen immediately after injury include hemor-

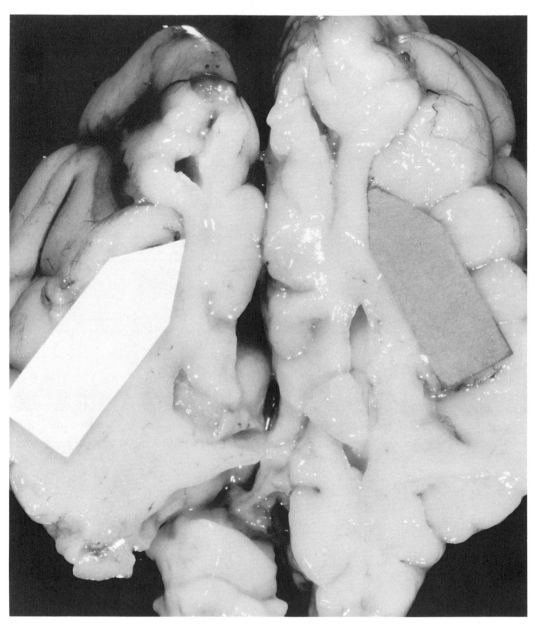

Fig. 30-10. Section through frontal lobes of 3-month-old infant who was starved and repeatedly beaten by the mother. Note fragmenting gelatinous character of tissue. Arrows point to linear clefts in subcortical white matter of superior frontal gyri, typical gliding contusions. Cleft on right more ventrally placed is the anterior horn of the lateral ventricle.

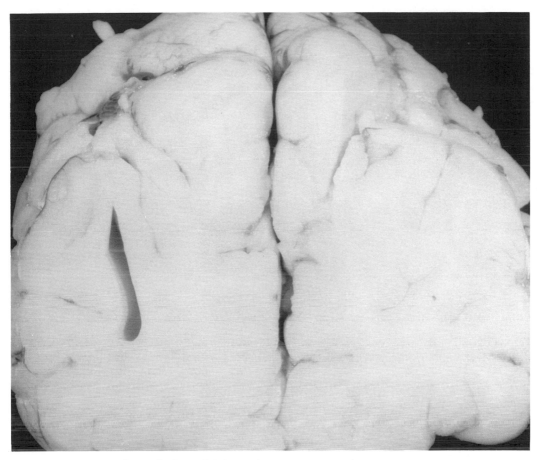

Fig. 30-11. Section through frontal lobes of 2-year-old infant who was shaken at 3 months. Note sharply demarcated subcortical white matter cavity on left side of photograph (in right hemisphere).

rhages, foci of necrosis, acute swelling of oligodendroglia, and often, acute necrosis of oligodendroglia. Inflammatory cell response is variable. If death occurs quickly or if rapid onset of malignant cerebral swelling cuts off blood flow, only the tissue fractures or hemorrhages are found. Thus, even if the victim is maintained on a respirator for days after the injury occurred, expected cellular infiltrations are inconspicuous or absent altogether. On the other hand, astrocytic proliferation may proceed (Fig. 30-13).

The rostral brain stem is particularly vulnerable to injury in severe acceleration/deceleration strain, lesions occurring most typically in the dorsolateral quadrant of the pons at the level of the locus ceruleus. Hemorrhage and necrosis damaging the locus ceruleus are generally life-threatening, since the structure, fibers, and neurons in the vicinity are important brain stem centers involved in control of cardiorespiratory functions. Axons of long fiber tracts at all brain stem levels are also vulnerable to injury and thus require careful microscopic assessment.

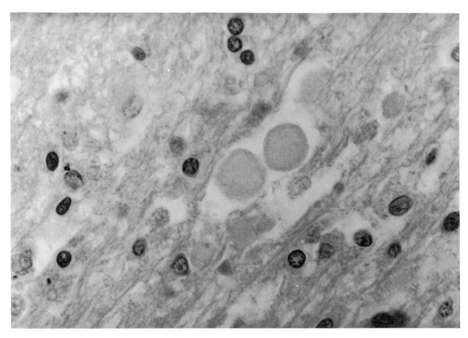

Fig. 30-12. Photomicrograph of white matter illustrating two typical retraction balls in center of field characteristic of acute axonal injury. (Hematoxylin and eosin stain.)

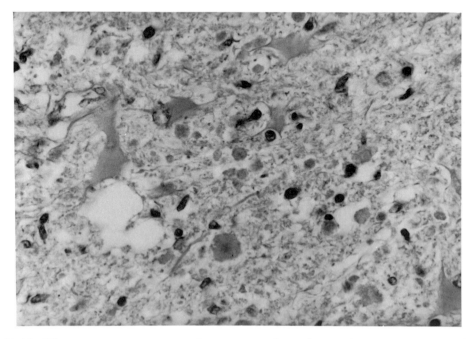

Fig. 30-13. White matter necrosis in infant surviving for 24 hours after injury. Note rarefaction-fragmentation of tissues, activation of large gemistocytic fiber-forming astrocytes, and retraction balls of various sizes. (Hematoxylin and eosin stain.)

Anoxic Encephalopathy. Traumatized pediatric victims frequently sustain cardiorespiratory dysfunction which, if of sufficient length or severity, leads to hypoxic-ischemic encephalopathy. Lesions may be apparent on gross inspection or diagnosable only after careful microscopic study.

The hypoxic-ischemic state probably contributes, in part, to the cerebral swelling, and the swelling, in turn, may complicate the injuries, the depth of fissure infarctions serving as an excellent example of secondary cortical lesions resulting from malignant edema with increased tissue pressure (Fig. 30-14).

Contusional necrosis must be separated from laminary necrosis resulting from hypoperfusion or tissue infarction in a vascular distribution, that is, anterior, middle, or posterior cerebral arteries.

Clear-cut morphologic features of the hypoxic-ischemic damage at both the gross and microscopic levels may not be discernible if death occurs within a few hours of injury. Otherwise, the lesions do not differ from those in older individuals and are easily diagnosable.

Specifically, characteristic tissue swelling and discoloration (generally unassociated with subarachnoid hemorrhage) are seen acutely, or later tissue retraction and sclerosis with or without cyst formation of cortex and/or white matter and/or deep ganglionic structures and/or cerebellar cortex are found. If parenchymal hemorrhage has accompanied or followed tissue necrosis, deposition of blood pigments contributes to the tissue changes.

It is not unusual to find lesions of varying ages in some of these pediatric decedents, reflecting previous episodes of trauma.

Identification of chronic lesions, how-

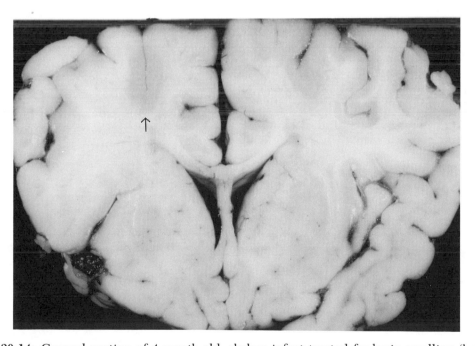

Fig. 30-14. Coronal section of 4-month-old, shaken infant treated for brain swelling (hence ventricles are not compressed). However, there is a typical depth of fissure cortical infarction, an established complication of severe cerebral edema (arrow).

ever, requires separation of those secondary to trauma from other types that may have had genesis in utero, perinatally, or during a difficult postnatal course. Pathologic characteristics and clinical features of this group of lesions in both premature and term infants have been described at length, and can usually be distinguished from postnatal trauma if careful attention is given to the clinical history of the decedent and to the analysis of the lesions present at autopsy.

Lesions of the Vertebral Column and Spinal Cord

Complete necropsy of infants and children suspected to be victims of abuse should always include careful dissection and evaluation of the back, specifically the paravertebral muscles, vertebral column, spinal cord, and its covering. This examination must be done using a posterior approach. Fractures are best identified on the postmortem radiographs, but subluxation occurring at the time of injury is not necessarily fixed.

Soft tissue hemorrhages, particularly into epidural fat, and epidural and subdural hemorrhages tend to be localized to the cervical region in infants who have been shaken. They may be located at any level if beating, pummelling, whipping, or strangulation has occurred or if the victim had been thrown from a height or down stairs.

The volume of blood may not be large in whiplash-shaken injuries, but since bleeding into parameningeal spaces is not ordinarily found after the neonatal period, hemorrhage in these sites must be regarded with suspicion.

Damage to the cord itself is often, but not always, associated with a variable amount of subarachnoid hemorrhage.

It is especially important to examine the *entire* cervical spinal cord in infants who may have been shaken, as cardiorespiratory irregularities may have re-sulted from severe whiplash leading to cord necrosis. If the infant is resuscitated and survives for hours or several days thereafter, vital changes, including evidence of axonal damage with or without retraction balls, may be seen. Although cerebral blood flow consequent to brain swelling is compromised in such infants, circulation to the spinal cord is generally not impaired, thus allowing the expected reactive processes following injury to proceed.

Tissue fractures, small parenchymal hemorrhages, and, occasionally, avulsion of nerve roots are generally identifiable when death occurs shortly after injury. If survival is more prolonged, infiltration of reactive inflammatory cells, retraction balls, and axonal injury may also be documented.

Fragments of necrotic cerebellar tissue are often found in the spinal subarachnoid space in infants/children whose brains have undergone autolysis during respirator therapy.

The Eyes

Complete examination of all unnatural deaths of infants and children should include examination of optic nerves throughout their course, the globe and periorbital fat, and muscles. Acute hemorrhages in the soft tissues and epidural, subdural, and subarachnoid spaces surrounding the optic nerves and in the retinal layer of the eyes are commonly found in pediatric homicides, but they may also occur following accidental/vehicular head trauma. Hemorrhages are usually most extensive in the portion of the nerve within 1 or 2 cm of the globe (Fig. 30-15).

Subhyaloid, retinal, vitreous, and subarachnoid hemorrhages occur in association with natural disease but epidural, subdural, and intradural hemorrhages around the nerve reflect traumatic injury.

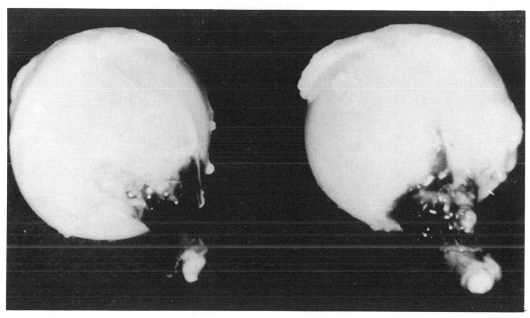

Fig. 30-15. Eyeballs with attached optic nerves from 7-week-old, severely battered infant. Note hemorrhage into epidural and posterior scleral tissue.

SUGGESTED READINGS

1. Adams JH, Doyle D, Graham DI et al: Gliding contusions in nonmissile head injury in humans. Arch Pathol Lab Med 110:485, 1986
2. Bruce DA, Alavi A, Bilaniuk L et al: Diffuse cerebral swelling following head injuries in children: the syndrome of "malignant brain edema." J Neurosurg 54:170, 1981
3. Calder IM, Hill I, Scholtz CL: Primary brain trauma in nonaccidental injury. J Clin Pathol 17:1095, 1984
4. Cohen RA: Cranial computed tomography in the abused child with head injury. Am J Radiol 146:97, 1986
5. Duhaime AC, Gennerelli TA, Thibault LE et al: The shaken baby syndrome: a clinical, pathological and biomechanical study. J Neurosurg 66:409, 1987
6. Friede RL: Developmental Neuropathology. Springer Verlag, New York, 1989
7. Hirsch CS: Craniocerebral trauma. p. 181. In Froede RC (ed): Handbook of Forensic Pathology. College of American Pathologists, Northfield, IL, 1990
8. Lindenberg R: Trauma. p. 1705. In Minckler J (ed): Pathology of the Nervous System. McGraw-Hill, New York, 1971
9. Lindenberg R, Freytag E: Morphology of brain lesions from blunt trauma in early infancy. Arch Pathol 87:298, 1969
10. McClellan NJ, Prasad R, Punt J: Spontaneous subhyaloid and retinal haemorrhages in an infant. Arch Dis Child 61:1130, 1986
11. Pilz P: Axonal injury in head injury. Acta Neurochir Suppl (Wein) 32:119, 1983
12. Rorke LB: Pathology of Perinatal Brain Injury. Raven Press, New York, 1982
13. Vowles GH, Scholtz CL, Cameron JM: Diffuse axonal injury in early infancy. J Clin Pathol 40:185, 1987
14. Weingeist TA, Goldman EJ, Folk JC et al: Terson's syndrome. Clinicalpathological correlations. Ophthalmology 93:1435, 1986

31

Civil and Criminal Judicial Intervention

Mimi Rose
Robert Schwartz

The effort to protect children has led state legislatures and courts to struggle with balancing parental and family autonomy against the need to protect children. The struggle has led to a calibration of child maltreatment along a continuum that begins with mild neglect and ends with serious physical and sexual abuse. The nature of modern state intervention varies, depending on where the maltreatment falls on the continuum.

While families have always been able to obtain help on a voluntary basis from government and charitable organizations, the law regulates when government can intervene without parental consent. Thus, there has developed a legal grid over the continuum of maltreatment that has roughly marked the points at which agencies may intervene in the family to protect children. "Involuntary" intervention by government occurs in the most serious cases through the use of criminal law. Intervention that falls short of characterizing child maltreatment as "criminal" is the "civil" side of child protection.

Every state permits intervention by the civil and criminal courts (Table 31-1). While intervention by the criminal justice system is usually limited to serious, well defined offenses against children, civil intervention can take place in any situation involving allegations of child maltreatment. Civil intervention involves a complex relationship between the public child protection agencies, which are regulated by state and federal law, and state juvenile courts, which are charged with limiting unnecessary state intrusion into families while ensuring that children receive necessary services and protection.

In 1989, the United Nations General Assembly adopted the Convention on the Rights of the Child. This written document proposes to consolidate existing international law on children and to establish new minimal standards for survival, health, and education, as well as explicit protection against physical and mental abuse, neglect, and sexual exploitation. This historic legal codification recognizes the particular vulnerability of children

423

Table 31-1.   Comparison of Civil and Criminal Child Abuse Proceedings

	Civil	*Criminal*
Laws	State child protection law	State criminal codes for specific crimes (e.g., rape, assault, endangerment)
Focus	Child welfare	Offender accountability
Need to prove	Nonaccidental injury to child caused by caretaker's act or omission	Criminal act on a child by any individual
Fact finder	Judge	Judge or judge and jury
Maximum penalty	Removal of the child from parents	Sentence of incarceration for offender
Rules of evidence and formality of proceedings	Relaxed	Strict
Burden of proof	Clear and convincing evidence (75%)	Beyond a reasonable doubt (95%)

and society's responsibility to protect, nurture, and acknowledge the basic human rights of our young.

The Convention not only acknowledges the rights of children, but for countries who ratify this treaty, the Convention on the Rights of the Child becomes binding law. Child advocates in ratifying nations can cite this document as legal precedent to ensure basic services for children. As Bremner notes, the Convention acknowledges children's welfare in terms of international justice rather than charity.

While the United States has not ratified the Convention, perhaps the new world attitude toward children expressed in this legal document will someday be incorporated into the laws of all nations.

CIVIL SYSTEM INTERVENTION

Civil actions to protect children from maltreatment have been around since 1874, when the Society for the Prevention of Cruelty to Animals, in the first documented proceeding, brought an action to protect a child from her stepmother's daily beatings. The early to mid-20th century saw expansion of state protection of children under the *parens patriae* theory, in which the state, through its child protection agencies and the juvenile courts, exercised its "wide range of power for limiting parental freedom and authority in things affecting the child's welfare." Modern civil action became commonplace, however, only after the appearance of *The Battered Child Syndrome* in 1962 and, in particular, after the federal government provided funding incentives to states to expand the reach of their child abuse laws.

The current civil legal arrangement includes (1) state child protection laws that define child abuse, require reporting of child abuse by mandated reporters, and regulate the manner in which state child protection agencies investigate reports and maintain records about child abuse, and which permit the agency to intervene on an emergency basis by removing a child temporarily from the family; (2) state juvenile court laws, which govern the circumstances under which state agencies obtain continued authority to supervise children and families, whether or not the parents agree to such intervention; and (3) federal funding laws, which have contoured the ways in which state agencies and courts operate.

CHILD ABUSE REPORTING LAWS

Federal law shapes the structure of almost all state child abuse reporting laws. Since the following* is a prerequisite to qualifying for federal assistance under the 1974 Child Abuse Prevention and Treatment Act (under its most recent amendments), almost all states have systems that

(1) have in effect a State law relating to child abuse and neglect law, including—
  (A) provisions for the reporting of known and suspected instances of child abuse and neglect; and
  (B) provisions for immunity from prosecution under State or local laws for persons reporting instances of child abuse and neglect arising from such reporting;
(2) provide that upon receipt of a report of known or suspected instances of child abuse or neglect an investigation shall be initiated promptly to substantiate the accuracy of the report, and, upon a finding of abuse or neglect, immediate steps shall be taken to protect the health and welfare of the abused or neglected child and of any other child under the same care who may be in danger of abuse or neglect;
(3) demonstrate that there are in effect

throughout the State, in connection with the enforcement of child abuse and neglect laws and with the reporting of suspected instances of child abuse and neglect, such—
  (A) administrative procedures;
  (B) personnel trained in child abuse and neglect prevention and treatment;
  (C) training procedures;
  (D) institutional and other facilities (public and private); and
  (E) such (sic) related multidisciplinary programs and services as may be necessary or appropriate to ensure that the state will deal effectively with child abuse and neglect cases in the state;
(4) provide for methods to preserve the confidentiality of all records to protect the rights of the child and of the child's parents or guardians;
(5) provide for the cooperation of law enforcement officials, courts of competent jurisdiction, and appropriate State agencies providing human services;
(6) provide that in every case involving an abused or neglected child which results in a judicial proceeding a guardian ad litem shall be appointed to represent the child in such proceedings;
    * * *
(10) have in place for the purposes of responding to the reporting of medical neglect (including instances of withholding of medically indicated treatment from disabled infants with life-threatening conditions), procedures or programs, or both (within the State child protective services system), to provide for—
  (A) coordination and consultation with individuals designated by and within appropriate health-care facilities;
  (B) prompt notification by individuals designated by and within appropriate health care facilities of cases of suspected med-

---

* From the Child Abuse Prevention and Treatment Act of 1974, 42 U.S.C. §5106a (1989 Supp).

ical neglect (including instances of withholding of medically indicated treatment from disabled infants with life-threatening conditions); and

(C) authority, under State law, for the State child protective service system to pursue any legal remedies, including the authority to initiate legal proceedings in a court of competent jurisdiction, as may be necessary to prevent the withholding of medically indicated treatment from disabled infants with life-threatening conditions.

Most state child abuse reporting laws have used the definitions of child abuse found in federal law. Thus, while physicians must know the specific definitions used in their own states, most jurisdictions have some version of the following:

> Child abuse and neglect is "the physical or mental injury, sexual abuse or exploitation, negligent treatment, or maltreatment of a child by a person who is responsible for the child's welfare, under circumstances which indicate that the child's health or welfare is harmed or threatened thereby. . . ."

In every state, child abuse, for purposes of the mandatory reporting requirements, includes abuse "by a person who is responsible for the child's welfare." Many states also include abuse by members of the household, including paramours. Abuse by persons who are strangers to the child does not generally fall within the scope of laws that require reports to child protection agencies. Stranger abuse will invariably result in intervention by law enforcement, while abuse by a person responsible for the child *may* result in law enforcement intervention, but always will involve intervention by the civil child protection system.

"Dependent child" proceedings, as discussed below, are designed to protect children from any kind of maltreatment, of which child abuse is a subcategory. (For example, a parent may place a child with a relative but fail to transfer a medical assistance card to ensure appropriate medical care. Such parental conduct may lead to a "dependent child" proceeding under the state's juvenile court law, but it would not alone constitute the kind of action that would mandate reporting under a state's child protection laws.)

Child abuse reporting laws are designed to trigger quick investigations of the four major categories set forth in the federal law: physical abuse, sexual abuse, mental abuse, or neglect. The bulk of juvenile court proceedings involve neglected children. Some of those children are seriously neglected and enter the system after a child abuse report is filed. Others enter through the filing of a "dependent child" petition (see below). Although the system itself makes distinctions about definitions, and about how a case will proceed, the mandated reporter's duty is to report if abuse is "suspected." The reporter need not be certain that the child is abused. If a mandated reporter has doubts about whether parental conduct meets the definition of abuse, it is best to err on the side of reporting the abuse. The child protection agency will resolve issues of definition and will take the case to its next level of scrutiny.

Typically, state child abuse reporting laws mandate that required reporters inform the state or local child welfare agency—and in some states, law enforcement—of any "suspected" abuse. (Some states require mandated reporters to report if they have "reason to believe" that the child is abused.) Medical professionals are included in every state's list of required reporters. Communications that are usually privileged, such as those between a physician and patient, do not provide an exemption from filing a mandated child abuse report.

When a report is filed, the county or state child protective services—or law enforcement, in those jurisdictions that require reporting to law enforcement agencies—must do a preliminary investigation, usually within 24 to 48 hours.

Child abuse reports are kept in a state's central registry, which receives every report of abuse, and maintains records of substantiated reports. These registries are used to identify patterns of abuse in a family and to ensure that abused children are not concealed by a parent's movement within a state.

If there is reason to believe that the report is accurate, the child protective service has the option of protecting the child through an offer of services to the family on a voluntary basis. During the last decade, child welfare agencies have developed a wide array of services designed to protect children in their own homes in this manner.

If the parents are unwilling or unable to protect the child by voluntarily accepting services, the child protection agency has the option of bringing the case to court. In addition, state law permits hospitals to take custody of a child for a brief period of time if discharge would place the child in imminent danger. When hospitals take a child into protective custody, the law requires that judicial authorization be quickly obtained, and that juvenile court proceedings be initiated.

CIVIL COURT INVOLVEMENT

The state's juvenile or family court is the civil court that hears cases of children who are alleged to be abused, neglected, or otherwise "dependent." Cases are initiated in juvenile court when a petition is filed. Petitions are usually brought by the child protective service, although many states permit any person, including a physician, to file a petition.

Petitions allege facts that give the juvenile court authority (jurisdiction) to hear the case. Petitions generally must contain the child's name, address, and enough facts which, if true, would meet the state's definition of "dependent" child.* Facts that describe child abuse, as defined above, usually meet the state's definition of "dependent" child for purposes of starting juvenile court proceedings.

The juvenile court proceeding has a number of stages. If a child is taken into custody by the child protection agency, state laws require that there be a speedy judicial review, usually within 3 days. The court at this relatively informal "detention" hearing determines whether there is reason to believe that the child (1) falls within the definition of dependent child and (2) must be separated from the parents until the next hearing because the risk to the child is so great that it cannot be managed in the home.

Adjudicatory Hearing

Unlike criminal proceedings, civil protection proceedings are designed to be speedy, recognizing both that the child's sense of time requires speedy intervention, and that families are likely to respond to intervention most receptively at times of crisis. Thus, the trial, or "adjudicatory hearing," will be held in less than 30 days. The hearing will usually be held more quickly if the court at the detention hearing has ordered that the child remain outside the home in protective custody.

At the adjudicatory hearing, the peti-

---

* States use varying terminology to describe the child who is the subject of civil juvenile court proceedings. Usually the child is called "dependent"; sometimes statutes speak of "abused," "neglected," or "deprived" children.

tioner, usually the county or state child protection agency, introduces evidence that the child meets the definition of dependent child. The judge sits without a jury. The parents and child are represented by an attorney (in some states the child has a guardian ad litem who can be an attorney or lay advocate).

Less evidence is required in civil child protection adjudicatory hearings than in criminal trials, where proof of guilt must be "beyond a reasonable doubt." The adjudicatory hearing requires that the petitioner prove the facts in the petition either by a "preponderance" of evidence or by "clear and convincing" evidence. Either standard of proof is easier to meet than the "beyond a reasonable doubt" standard. (This is one reason that civil intervention is used more often than criminal prosecution.)

Physicians are most likely to testify at the adjudicatory hearing. It is here that the judge will take evidence about the nature of the injury to the child, and will hear testimony about whether an injury could have been inflicted accidentally, or in the manner described by the child's caretaker.

Courts have admitted certain expert medical testimony at the adjudicatory hearing. For example, expert testimony has been universally accepted in civil proceedings when it has concerned such widely accepted diagnoses as the battered child syndrome, failure-to-thrive, or fetal alcohol syndrome.

Hospital reports and records will usually be admissible at the adjudicatory hearing. Such evidence includes photographs and radiographs of the child, as well as records routinely kept as part of the hospital's records.

It is at the adjudicatory stage that the court decides whether parental action or inaction falls within acceptable norms (such as in cases of corporal punishment), or whether that conduct is beyond what society is prepared to accept as normal childrearing. In the latter case, a child will be adjudged "dependent."

If the court finds that the allegations in the petition have been proved, and that they meet the state's definition of dependent child, then the court has jurisdiction, or legal authority, to proceed to disposition. If the facts in the petition have not been proved (or, even if proved they do not meet the required definition), then the court has no authority to proceed with the case, and it must dismiss the petition. Under such circumstances, custody must be returned to the parent, and the child protection agency has no continued authority to provide services to the family without its consent.

In a substantial number of cases, the court has authority to proceed because the parties have stipulated, or agreed, that the child is dependent. Under those circumstances, the court does not take testimony. Instead, it enters the adjudication of dependency, and either orders an agreed upon disposition, or moves to a dispositional hearing.

Dispositional Hearing

The dispositional hearing is akin to the sentencing in a criminal proceeding. The difference is that the court has a wide array of alternatives from which to choose. Although the court's direct authority at disposition is limited to decisions about the child (e.g., should the child be left home or be placed in substitute care?), in practice the court may order from a menu of options that is akin to a matrix. The options include leaving the child at home or placing the child in substitute care, but each of those options may involve a large number of services.

At disposition, the court is charged with balancing the child's right to protection with the child's right to be raised by family. The court must include in the balance society's interest in promoting a strong family unit. Thus, courts first look to see if the child can be protected in the home. Courts are also enjoined from separating children from parents merely because of parental poverty or illiteracy.

Physicians' testimony may be required at dispositional hearings. A physician can alert the court to a child's special medical needs, and the level of cooperation that would be required by the parent to meet those needs in the home. A court has authority, for example, to order at disposition that a parent ensure that an infant receives a complete series of immunizations. A physician's subsequent report of noncompliance could lead the court to order more intensive in-home supervision or to order that the child be placed in substitute care.

Many states require medical screens for all children entering foster care. Thus, children with special needs can have included in the court's dispositional order or in the child's case plan a list of services required to meet the child's out-of-home needs. These services might include specialized foster care, special nursing services, or routine transportation to a treating physician by the child protection agency or foster parent.

CHANGES IN CHILD PROTECTIVE AGENCY PRACTICE AND JUDICIAL DECISION-MAKING IMPOSED BY FEDERAL LAW

In the last decade, federal law has aimed to ensure that children are maintained in permanent, nurturing homes. To that end, states have been given federal funding incentives to promote the protection of children in their own homes, to promote efforts at reunifying children with parents when children must be placed in substitute care, and to promote adoption when a child cannot be

returned home. Federal law has affected the manner in which child protection agencies and courts behave at every stage of civil child protection proceedings.

Reasonable Efforts to Prevent Placement*

In 1980, after 5 years of public hearings, Congress amended the Social Security Act to provide fiscal incentives to states to reduce unnecessary placement of children in foster care and to ensure periodic review of the cases of children in placement. The amendments were codified as the Adoption Assistance and Child Welfare Act of 1980, Public Law 96-272.

In order for states to receive matching federal funds for their child welfare programs, P.L. 96-272 imposes on states a number of requirements. One is known as the "reasonable efforts" requirement, which is really two requirements. First, each state in the plan it submits to the federal government must agree to make "reasonable efforts" to prevent placement and to reunify a family once placement has occurred. Second, in order for any individual child to be eligible for federal foster care payments, there must be a judicial determination that "reasonable efforts" have been made to prevent placement. If no such judicial determination is made, a state cannot legally seek federal funding for the cost of foster care for that child.

Despite its importance, the "reasonable efforts" language in P.L. 96-272 is one of the least understood requirements of the Act. While P.L. 96-272 does not define the meaning of "reasonable efforts,"

* From Magdovitz S, Barber R, Mangold SV: A Guide to Judicial Decisions Affecting Dependent Children: a Pennsylvania Judicial Deskbook, pp. 2–4. Juvenile Law Center, Philadelphia, 1990, with permission.

the structure of the Act and its legislative history make it clear that the provision is intended to require children and youth agencies to offer a full range of services as an alternative to foster care placement. It is this requirement that makes the "reasonable efforts" language so critical, providing a legal handle on which to place an order for a range of services, including those that the agency claims are not available.

The aim of P.L. 96-272 was to shift the direction of federal funds from foster care programs to preventive and reunification services. States are to examine closely alternatives to foster care and services that may keep families together or reunite them after separation has taken place.

Federal fiscal incentives were thought to be the best control mechanism for instituting substantive reform of the child welfare system. Congress placed state court judges in the position of guardian of the federal purse. Accordingly, the Act provides that unless a judicial determination that "reasonable efforts" to prevent placement or to reunify children with their families (where separation has occurred) has been made, federal reimbursement will not be forthcoming. Additionally, as will be discussed below, case plans and semiannual case reviews must take place for each child for whom states claim federal reimbursement.

Judicial Reasonable Efforts Determination[†]

In any dependency proceeding, the court must make all of the required findings under state law governing the adju-

---

† From Magdovitz S, Barber R, Mangold SV: A Guide to Judicial Decisions Affecting Dependent Children: a Pennsylvania Judicial Deskbook. pp. 6–10. Juvenile Law Center, Philadelphia, 1990, with permission.

dication of dependency or establishing whether the child was abused. In addition, the court must make the "reasonable efforts" determination.

The court's "reasonable efforts" finding must be very specific, and it would seem impossible for the court to make that determination without at least answering the following:

1. What is the harm that removal is designed to prevent?
2. Can less intrusive measures than placement prevent that harm?

To determine if less intrusive measures can prevent the harm, the judge must ask:

1. Which services other than placement have been considered and rejected and why?
2. Which services have been offered to the family and rejected?
3. Which services have been used but failed?

If after answering the preceding questions, it appears that there remain services either available or presently unavailable that have not been tried, the judge cannot make a finding that "reasonable efforts" have been made *unless* it is found that those services could not prevent the harm that necessitated placement.

While it is the agency's burden to prove that "reasonable efforts" to prevent placement have been made, the lawyer for child or parent can rebut the agency's determination by offering expert social worker testimony establishing that specific services would enable the child to remain at home without further risk of harm to that child. The court cannot make a finding that "reasonable efforts" to prevent placement have been made unless and until those services are provided.

The inquiries that are the foundations for the two central questions in every case are: what are "reasonable efforts?" and has the agency made them? While these determinations are obviously case specific, there are certain parameters that should help define what is reasonable.

First, is it reasonable to provide only what an agency usually provides? The answer to this is clearly no. It may be reasonable to provide a service, different in either nature or intensity, from what the agency has offered. For instance, if an agency has a policy of only providing a homemaker once a week or at hours that do not coincide with a family's need, it would be unreasonable to place the children in substitute care instead of providing the homemaker as needed.

As certain types of neglect become more prevalent, the reasonableness of agency conduct may change. For example, while it may have been reasonable 10 years ago for an agency to exclude home nurses from its menu of services, the crack epidemic of the late 1980s may render such an exclusion unreasonable if that is the service required to protect the child in the home.

Dispositional Reviews*

Federal law requires states to review the status of children in foster care at least every 6 months. Reviews can be conducted by the juvenile court or by an administrative review panel. Those reviews must examine "the continuing necessity for and appropriateness of the placement, the extent of compliance with the case plan, and the extent of progress that has been made toward alleviating or mitigating the causes necessitating placement in

---

* Adapted from Magdovitz S, Barber R, Mangold SV: A Guide to Judicial Decisions Affecting Dependent Children: a Pennsylvania Judicial Deskbook. pp. 12–15. Juvenile Law Center, Philadelphia, 1990, with permission.

foster care, and to project a likely date by which the child may be returned to the home or placed for adoption or legal guardianship[.]"

Sometimes the "reasonable efforts" requirement obligates a county agency to ensure the provision of services that are normally the province of other agencies. For example, a schoolphobic child can become suicidal or seriously ill if forced to attend the regular school program. Such a child may well be "socially and emotionally disturbed" and entitled to special education services from the local school district. If such a child were the subject of a dependency petition on the grounds of being "habitually and without justification truant," a court could determine that the county must work with the parent to obtain in-home special education for the child, thereby avoiding both an adjudication of dependency and an unnecessary and damaging placement.

Another example is a child and family who need mental health services traditionally provided by the mental health/mental retardation system. If individual or family psychotherapy would allow the family of a child to meet the child's needs and avoid placement, the "reasonable efforts" requirement would dictate that the county agency ensure the provision of such services.

While federal law does not define "reasonable efforts," federal regulations do require that states, in their state plans, list available preplacement prevention and reunification services. Such services include, but are not limited to "24-hour emergency caretaker, and homemaker services; day-care; crisis counseling; individual and family counseling; emergency shelters; procedures and arrangements for access to available emergency financial assistance; arrangements for the provision of temporary child care to provide respite to the family for a brief period, as part of a plan for preventing children's removal from home; other services which the agency identifies as necessary and appropriate such as home-based family services, self-help groups, services to unmarried parents, provision of, or arrangements for, mental health, drug and alcohol abuse counseling, and vocational counseling or vocational rehabilitation(.)"

CRIMINAL SYSTEM INTERVENTION

The law criminalizes intentional or reckless acts that harm a child. The majority of criminal prosecutions for physical abuse of children involve severe forms of physical violence from which the child suffers permanent injury or death. Head trauma resulting from direct blows or shaking, immersion burns, and multiple fractures are common forms of criminal physical abuse.

In many of these prosecutions the child either dies or is too young to recount what happened. To determine if the child's injury was accidental, self-inflicted, or inflicted by another person, law enforcement must turn to physicians for guidance. If a caretaker explains a child's injury as accidental (i.e., the child fell off the bed, down the stairs, or into the tub) the opinion of an experienced physician or medical examiner that the caretaker's explanation is inconsistent with the injury is necessary before criminal charges can be filed. Sometimes a caretaker offers no explanation for a child's injuries, which are later determined to be the result of physical abuse. In this situation, criminal charges may be filed if the caretaker had exclusive custody of the child during the period of time the abuse is believed to have occurred.

While the perpetrator of serious physical abuse of a child will face criminal charges, a parent or caretaker who knows that the child is being assaulted and fails to intervene can also be found criminally responsible for the acts of the perpetrator. In most other areas of criminal law, there is no duty to assist someone in peril. Ordinarily, a witness to a crime has no legal obligation to assist the victim; however, a significant exception is found when the onlooker is a parent. Parents have a legal duty to protect their children. Failure to do so constitutes a criminal act. In a Pennsylvania case, a mother witnessed and had full knowledge of a continuing pattern of severe beatings inflicted on her child by her boyfriend over several weeks. She took no steps to stop the abuse of her child, who ultimately died of the injuries. The mother, as well as her boyfriend, were convicted of homicide. Serious injury or death caused by a parent's or guardian's failure to seek conventional medical treatment for a child may also give rise to criminal charges. However, it should be noted that in several states a parent or guardian who elects remedial treatment by spiritual means from a recognized religious denomination is exempt from criminal responsibility if the child dies.

Not all instances of child physical maltreatment result in criminal charges. A gray area exists with regard to corporal punishment. While spanking with a hand, belt, or strap may be inappropriate and emotionally harmful to a child, our society permits parents to physically discipline their children. Whether this parental prerogative triggers the intervention of police and criminal courts will depend on both the extent of the injury and the intent of the parent. As one court tells us:

> Parents or guardians may use corporal punishment to discipline their children so long as the force used is not designed or known to create a substantial risk of death, serious bodily injury, disfigurement, extreme pain or mental distress or

gross degradation. At some point, however, permissible corporal punishment is no longer such, but becomes malicious abuse. This point is reached when the parent or guardian acts with malicious intent in so punishing the child.

A finding of malicious intent sufficient to justify criminal charges is dependent on a careful review of the location of injury, whether the punishment is chronic, and other surrounding circumstances.

SEXUAL ABUSE

Sexual contact between adults and children is a criminal offense. The type of contact, ranging from fondling to penetration, and the age of the child, determine the type of crime and the potential criminal penalty imposed for its violation. The issue of the victim's consent, so often a defense to an allegation of sexual assault where an adult is the victim, is much less available to the adult charged with sexual contact with a child.

In most states the law presumes that preadolescent children are incapable of informed consent to adult sexual contact. While children may acquiesce to an adult's sexual demands, the law distinguishes between compliance and consent. In the case of an adolescent incest victim subjected to years of sexual submission, lack of consent can be established by evidence that the parent exercised psychological, moral, or intellectual force over the child.

As a general rule, when criminal charges are filed, the accused must be informed of the specific date or dates of the alleged criminal activity. This specificity requirement enables the defense to elect an alibi defense to the charges and to establish through witnesses or documents that the alleged perpetrator was elsewhere during the commission of the crime. While this requirement is reasonable for most criminal offenses, when the crime is intrafamilial sexual abuse occurring over many years, it is often impossible for a child to isolate discrete dates and times when the abuse occurred. Accordingly, most courts relax specificity requirements when a child is the victim of abuse, particularly intrafamilial sexual abuse. An example of one court's analysis of this issue appeared in a case where a child was sexually abused by her stepfather from age 11 until she disclosed the abuse at age 16. The defense maintained that the state could not bring charges since the child could not furnish specific dates when the abuse occurred. The court balanced the equities finding in favor of the victim, stating:

> "We do not believe that it would serve the ends of justice to permit a person to rape and otherwise sexually abuse his child with impunity simply because the child has failed to record in a daily diary the unfortunate details of her childhood."

THE CRIMINAL PROCESS

Allegations of child abuse reach the criminal justice system in various ways. Sometimes a child discloses abuse to a relative or neighbor who directly contacts police. In other cases, abuse complaints come to the attention of law enforcement by protocols set forth in state child abuse reporting laws. Each state has laws requiring health care and other specified professionals to report suspicions of child maltreatment to the county child welfare agency, which is legally mandated to investigate these reports for social service intervention. Simultaneous to its own investigation, the child welfare agency is required to contact law enforcement. After police have completed their investigation, the prosecutor reviews the case and decides whether to file criminal charges against the suspect.

Once charges are filed, the suspect, now called the defendant, is arrested. He is required to hire an attorney or, if indigent, legal counsel is appointed at government expense. The victim of a crime (the complaining witness or complainant) is represented by the prosecutor (also known as the state's attorney or assistant district attorney). Unlike lawsuits brought by private individuals for breach of contract or personal injury for example, criminal prosecutions are initiated by the state since, theoretically, criminal acts are offenses committed against the community. While the complainant is certainly the most important witness in a criminal trial, a crime is an affront to the community at large, and the community's interests are represented by the prosecutor.

A criminal trial is an adversarial proceeding designed to determine whether a crime was committed and whether the defendant was the perpetrator. The prosecutor introduces evidence to prove the defendant's guilt. The defense attorney challenges that evidence through cross-examination and sometimes by introducing other evidence. While the adversarial process is designed to ferret out the truth, the prosecution and the defense do not stand on equal footing. The defendant is not required to testify or offer any evidence in support of his innocence; the law presumes his innocence. It is the job of the prosecution to establish guilt beyond a reasonable doubt. A verdict of acquittal is not equivalent to a finding of innocence; it is a conclusion that the state's evidence has failed to persuade a unanimous jury of the defendant's guilt beyond a reasonable doubt.

A criminal case is proved by direct or circumstantial evidence. Direct evidence is testimony from a witness who saw or heard something based on personal knowledge or observation that tends to support or disprove an aspect of a case. A crime victim or an eyewitness would give direct evidence. Circumstantial evidence is not based on actual personal knowledge or observation of the commission of a crime. Rather, it is used to establish links in a chain of circumstances tending to support or refute the defendant's culpability. For example, a preverbal child diagnosed with gonorrhea and vaginal trauma lives alone with her father who is also found to have gonorrhea. While the state has no direct evidence to establish that the father sexually assaulted the child, circumstantial evidence of the father's sole custody of the child and medical testimony as to the physical findings can be used to prove the state's case.

THE EXPERT WITNESS

Legal rules of evidence ordinarily do not permit a witness to testify to personal opinions or conclusions about disputed facts in a criminal case, since it is for the jury to ultimately decide these matters. When an examining physician, nurse, or other medical witness is subpoenaed to court, it is to give information about an event they have witnessed or overheard, not to give an opinion about the significance of the event or their personal belief or disbelief. An examining physician may be asked to testify about physical findings or a social worker or nurse may be questioned about a child's demeanor or statements made by the child, or by the accused, heard in their presence. The law does not permit these witnesses to interpret their observations.

An important exception to this "no opinion" rule is the expert witness. An expert witness is an individual who, by education, training, and experience, has expertise in a particular field beyond the common knowledge of the jury. That witness, after a judge's finding of expertise, may assist the jury by giving an opinion about the significance of facts in a criminal case. Before a witness is permitted to give an opinion, a qualification hearing is held. At this hearing, the witness is asked about training and experience in a particular field. The judge then rules whether the witness has sufficient credentials to be deemed an expert.

In a criminal child abuse trial a physician who qualifies as an expert witness plays a critical role. In a case involving allegations of sexual abuse, for example, a physician with significant experience may be called to court to give an opinion as to whether the physical findings of a child giving a history of sexual contact are consistent with the child's complaint. In a physical assault of a preverbal child, a qualified physician may be asked to review medical records, x-rays, or photographs of injury to express an opinion as to whether the injury could be self-inflicted, accidental, or consistent or inconsistent with the caretaker's explanation of how the injury occurred.

An expert witness is an educator. A physician, qualified to share professional opinions with the jury, helps to dispel unlikely explanations often put forth by attorneys or witnesses to account for signs of abuse. Expert physicians often testify to explain the low probability that a sexually transmitted disease was transmitted by a toilet seat or washcloth; that a particular burn based on the pattern and location of injury would not be consistent with a child falling into a tub; that a type of fracture is inconsistent with the caretaker's explanation of injury; or that a normal genital examination of a child giving a history of sexual contact would not be inconsistent with the child's report of molestation. While an expert witness cannot give an opinion as to whether the accused committed the crime, the physician may

have an opinion about the force required to inflict a particular injury and whether a young sibling of the victim could have applied the amount of force required.

While expert testimony from a physician who practices physical medicine is an accepted form of evidence in child abuse prosecutions, the law is more restrictive in permitting mental health professionals to testify about psychological factors impacting on a child's response to molestation. Where state law permits, a mental health professional may be called to court as an expert witness to help the jury understand why a child might delay in reporting abuse or initially deny abuse. Expert witnesses have also been called on to explain aspects of child development and to give an opinion that the child victim displayed inappropriate sexual knowledge, which could be attributed to sexual abuse. While state laws vary in this area, the growing trend is to restrict or, in some locales prohibit, expert testimony of a psychiatrist, psychologist, or social worker. Convictions in some states have been overturned where a clinician has expressed a view that the child's psychological profile or behavior is consistent with the dynamics of child sexual abuse. Reviewing courts in these states have concluded that this testimony either expressly or implicitly buttresses the credibility of the child's allegations, thus improperly intruding on the jury's function to decide the credibility of the child.

THE CHILD'S HISTORY AS EVIDENCE

A physician is permitted to testify to statements made by a patient in the course of diagnosis and treatment. The admissibility of this evidence is a longstanding exception to the hearsay rule that generally prohibits a third party from testifying to what someone else has said. The diagnosis and treatment exception is based on the belief that statements made to a physician in the course of treatment are inherently reliable, since a patient has a strong interest in telling the truth to a doctor. Accordingly, in a child abuse trial, the history given by a child to the treating physician is admissible, and often powerful, evidence to corroborate the child's testimony.

In a child abuse prosecution, the scope of the diagnosis and treatment exception differs among states. Courts are divided as to whether the identity of the perpetrator as part of the history is admissible evidence. Some state courts have concluded that the identity of the perpetrator is irrelevant to diagnosis and treatment and is therefore inadmissible hearsay. Other jurisdictions have adopted a more liberal view, concluding that the child's disclosure of the identity of the assailant is an essential aspect of a physical examination of a young victim. The more liberal view has been successfully argued in cases where the child is diagnosed with a sexually transmitted disease or where physical injury is found, under the rationale that physicians have a legal duty to prevent an abused child from returning to an abusive environment. In this context, information as to whether the perpetrator was a household member has been found to be pertinent to the diagnosis and treatment of the child.

When the victim of abuse is a child, there are rarely eyewitnesses other than the victim. In physical abuse cases involving preverbal children, medical testimony is crucial to the jury's understanding of the injury and its cause. In sexual assault trials, it is essential that the jury understands the significance of physical findings to corroborate the child's testimony. Since most child victims of sexual and physical assault are examined at a hospital before trial, social workers and nurses have the opportunity to witness interactions between parent and child, or to hear statements concerning the abuse by the child or a suspect. The testimony of doctors, nurses, and hospital social workers is often essential to convince 12 jurors of the accused's culpability beyond a reasonable doubt.

LEGISLATIVE REFORM

In the past decade, state legislatures have given increased attention to the problem of child abuse, yielding many legal reforms protective of children. In several states, penalties for sexual assault, physical abuse, and homicide are enhanced when the victim is a child. Most states now permit young victims of sexual abuse to testify in court with the assistance of anatomically correct dolls or drawings. In some jurisdictions, cases of child abuse are required to receive priority docketing and speedy resolution. Some states require training for judges and other professionals involved in child protection. Multidisciplinary review teams are mandated to review cases of child maltreatment and death. As the pressures on a young child to conceal sexual abuse and the corresponding delay in reporting become better understood, an increasing number of states have expanded the statute of limitations to allow for criminal prosecution years after the abuse has occurred.

Awareness that child witnesses present special evidentiary problems in criminal court, traditional rules of criminal law and procedure have also been modified by many state legislatures to accommodate these child victims. A young child may be developmentally unable to satisfy legal requirements to qualify as a witness. A child threatened with harm or abandonment by the accused if the abuse is disclosed may be psychologically unable or unwilling to testify in the accused's presence. This awareness has led to new laws permitting children to testify by closed circuit television or video deposition, laws creating an exception to the hearsay rule permitting out of court statements of child abuse victims, and abolishment of testimonial competency requirements for children. While these innovative measures permit an increased number of abused children to seek justice through our courts, many of these reforms must be balanced against the accused's constitutional right to confront witnesses.

The threshold requirement in many states, before a witness is permitted to testify in criminal court, is a judicial determination, before trial, that the witness is able to give an accurate and truthful account of events. This requirement is called legal competency. Legal competency requires that the potential witness demonstrate the ability to recall and relate events, to distinguish the concepts of truth and lie, and that the witness understands the moral duty to testify truthfully. While these competency requirements are minimal, and presumptively satisfied when the witness is older than 14, a child under the age of 4 usually lacks the developmental skills to qualify as a witness. A child who has told her mother, a social worker, and police that she was sexually molested, may be precluded from telling the story in criminal court because legal competency requirements cannot be met. Absent other evidence to support a conviction, the accused child abuser may never go to court if the only eyewitness to the crime is the 3-year-old victim or a child who is developmentally disabled.

Frustrated by this frequent dilemma, prosecutors and child advocates from several disciplines called for the repeal of legal competency requirements. Several states and the federal courts have adopted

this approach and permit a child to testify, regardless of age or ability, leaving the accuracy and reliability of the testimony for the jury to decide.

There is often considerable delay between disclosure and trial. As weeks or months pass, the child's memory may dim as to details so critical to assessing the credibility of testimony. In other cases, a child may be overwhelmed by the courtroom environment and may not be able to testify. In each of these situations, the child has probably made several prior out-of-court statements concerning the abuse, possibly to parents, police, a physician, or to a therapist. Child hearsay laws enacted in many states may enable the jury to hear a child's disclosures about sexual abuse when memory or emotional trauma precludes the child from giving courtroom testimony. The Child Hearsay Exception in Pennsylvania states:

> Admissibility of certain statements.
>
> 1. General rule: An out of court statement made by a child victim or witness, who at the time the statement was made was 12 years of age or younger, describing indecent contact, sexual intercourse, or deviate sexual intercourse performed with or on the child by another, not otherwise admissible by statute or rule of evidence, is admissible in evidence in any criminal proceeding if: (a) the court finds, in an in camera hearing, that the evidence is relevant and that the time, content, and circumstances of the statement provide sufficient indicia of reliability. (b) The child either testifies at the proceeding or is unavailable as a witness and there is corroborative evidence of the act.

While the admission of a child's prior statements may seem the obvious solution, one must always keep in mind that a criminal trial is an adversarial proceeding where the accused has the right to test the truthfulness and credibility of witnesses by cross-examination. The Sixth

Amendment to the United States Constitution guarantees that "In all criminal prosecutions the accused shall enjoy the right . . . to be confronted with the witnesses against them." In the case where a child is unable to testify, how does an accused defend against allegations of child abuse when the only testimony comes not from the child, but from a third party to whom the child disclosed? Whether child hearsay laws strike a fair balance between a child's right to justice and the accused's right to confront the witness is an evolving and controversial area of criminal law.

FACE-TO-FACE CONFRONTATION

Another vexing issue is the requirement of face-to-face courtroom confrontation between an accused and the child witness. Our federal constitution affords an accused the right to confront witnesses against him, and many states have given a literal interpretation to this constitutional requirement. Face-to-face confrontation is believed to promote truthful testimony, premised on the idea that a witness will be compelled to speak honestly under the scrutiny of the accused's gaze. Leaving aside the validity of this presumption, our ancestors could not have contemplated child witnesses when fashioning this legal right. To suppose that a frightened young child, threatened with physical harm or abandonment if molestation is disclosed, will testify more truthfully in the presence of the accused is dubious at best. The potential for emotional trauma to some of these children who must face their assailant in a courtroom is of equal concern.

The United States Supreme Court has recently ruled that in appropriate cases, victims of child abuse may testify by way of one-way, closed circuit television rather than in the presence of the abuser. The court held that this procedure does not violate the constitutional right of a defendant to confront his accuser if the prosecution demonstrates in each case that the child witness would be traumatized by having to testify in the defendant's presence.

SUGGESTED READINGS

1. Bremner R (ed): Children and Youth in America. Vol. 2. Harvard University Press, Boston, MA, 1971
2. *Prince v. Massachusetts*, 321 U.S. 158 (1944)
   (upholding state's child labor laws)
3. Kempe, Silverman, Steele et al: The battered child syndrome. JAMA 181:17, 1962
4. Child Abuse Prevention and Treatment Act of 1974, 42 U.S.C. §§5101 *et seq.*
5. Child Abuse Prevention and Treatment Act of 1974, 42 U.S.C. §5106a (1989 supp)
6. Child Abuse Prevention and Treatment Act of 1974, 42 U.S.C. §5106h.
   The same statute defines "sexual abuse" to include rape, molestation, incest, prostitution "or other form of sexual exploitation of children."

   "Withholding of medically indicated treatment" is defined as the failure to respond to the infant's life-threatening conditions by providing treatment (including appropriate nutrition, hydration, and medication) which, in the treating physician's or physicians' reasonable medical judgment, will be most likely to be effective in ameliorating or correcting all such conditions, except that the term does not include the failure to provide treatment (other than appropriate nutrition, hydration, or medication) to an infant when, in the treating physician's or physicians' reasonable medical judgment—
   (A) the infant is chronically and irreversibly comatose;
   (B) the provision of such treatment would—

(i) merely prolong dying;

(ii) not be effective in ameliorating or correcting all of the infant's life-threatening conditions; or

(iii) otherwise be futile in terms of the survival of the infant; or

(C) the provision of such treatment would be virtually futile in terms of the survival of the infant and the treatment itself under such circumstances would be inhumane.

7. Soler MI: Representing the Child Client. Ch. 4, ¶4.03[1] Matthew Bender, Rochester, NY, 1989

One commentator has noted that the grounds for finding dependency generally fall "into the following categories: abuse, abandonment, neglect, parental incapacity, and mental condition of the child."

8. Goldstein J, Freud A, Solnit A: Beyond the Best Interest of the Child, Free Press, New York, 1973

9. Davidson HA, Horowitz RM: Protection of children from family maltreatment. p. 262. In Horowitz RM, Davidson HA (eds): Legal Rights of Children. Shepard's/McGraw-Hill, Colorado Springs, CO, 1984

10. *Rinker Appeal*, 180 Pa.Super. 143, 117 A.2d 780 (1955)

A celebrated Pennsylvania case warned that the laws of child protection were "not intended to provide a procedure to take the children of the poor and given them to the rich, nor to take the children of the illiterate and give them to the educated, nor to take the children of the crude and give them to the cultured, nor to take the children of the weak and sickly and give them to the strong and healthy."

11. The Adoption Assistant and Child Welfare Act of 1980, 42 U.S.C. 620–628, 670–676

12. Code of Federal Regulations, 45 *C.F.R.* *§1357.15(e)(2)*

13. *Commonwealth v. Howard*, 402 A.2d 674 (1979)

14. *Boland v. Leska*, 454 A.2d 75 (1982)

15. *Commonwealth v. Niemetz*, 422 A.2d 1369 (1980)

16. Meyers, John: Expert Testimony in Child Sexual Abuse Litigation. Nebraska Law Review 68:(1&2), 1989

17. *42 PA. Consolidated Statutes* §5985.1 (1990)

18. *Maryland v. Craig* _U.S._, 110 S.ct.3157 (1990)

32

The Physician's Role in Court

Stephen Ludwig
Marylou Barton

For most families, there is a relative balance among the rights of parents, the rights of their children, and the rights of the family unit (Fig. 32-1). The individuals involved usually have overlapping goals, aspirations, and values. However, there are times when the rights of the various family members are in conflict. Child abuse is one clear example of this conflict. In such a situation, the child's rights to be free from physical harm and the parents' rights to "discipline" their child are in conflict. Other examples include rights to health care, education, and, in divorce cases, the right to live with the parent of choice.

In more extreme cases, individuals may commit crimes against children that are subject to criminal penalties, since they are viewed by society as crimes against the state. Such crimes include homicide, aggravated assault, rape, and indecent exposure. These crimes are viewed as more serious or more antisocial, and the perpetrator must be punished as well as possibly rehabilitated.

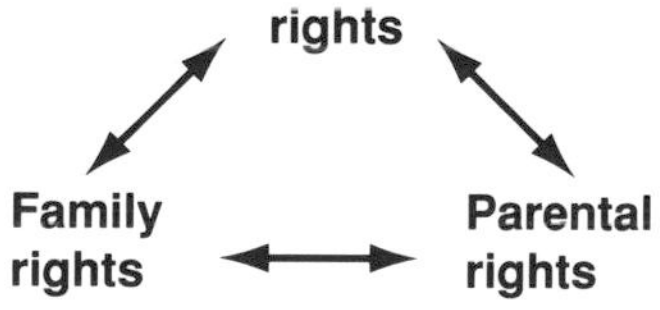

When the rights of the child are in conflict with those of the parent or the family unit, or when a crime has been committed, frequently the physician is asked to provide information to the "resolver of conflict," the family court, or the determiner of guilt or innocence in the criminal court. This chapter reviews some of the principles to be used when appearing in court on behalf of an abused child. Many of the basic concepts may also be applied to other child advocacy situations.

Fig. 32-1. The state of dynamic tension between the rights of the child, rights of the parent, and rights of the family unit.

PREPARING TO APPEAR IN COURT

Define the Purpose

The first step in preparing for a court appearance is to define the reason for going, which is usually in response to a

441

served subpoena. However, once subpoenaed, review your reasons. What do you hope to accomplish? Are you providing simple information or an expert opinion? There are many different goals, such as (1) to effect placement of a child outside the natural home for protective reasons; (2) to establish an official record of facts; (3) to institute or enforce a treatment plan for parents or for the child; (4) to ensure that the perpetrator is punished and possibly incarcerated for crimes committed; and (5) to request that a judge hear the facts of a case and make an impartial decision. In some cases, you may have more than one objective in mind when preparing for court. It is important to have at least one objective in mind, otherwise the experience will be frustrating. You may find yourself leaving the hearing or the trial wondering why you were there.

Know the Setting

Before going to court, it is helpful to know the setting. Will the hearing or trial be in a small conference room with all the parties seated around a conference table, or in a large, imposing courtroom with a jury? Knowing the setting will help you to prepare your testimony and delivery. This is akin to any teaching experience; some techniques work well in a large auditorium, others must be used in a small conference room.

Beyond the physical setting, you will want to know the kind of case in which you are to testify, whether it is civil or criminal. Table 32-1 outlines the differences between the two systems. Chapter 31 details the differences further. There are many legal distinctions; however, in nonlegal terms the differences may be divided into issues, penalties, parties, and rules of evidence. These differences are important in that they determine what you must prove and how you must go about proving it. For the child abuser, these distinctions are also critical. If the case is in criminal court, the perpetrator will also need to decide whether to plead guilty or innocent, and whether to have a jury trial or to waive the right to a jury and have the judge be the finder of fact (waiver trial). The steps of either a civil or a criminal trial and more on the distinctions between the two are presented in Chapter 31.

Table 32-1.   Comparison of Civil Versus Criminal Child Abuse Proceedings

Parameter	Civil	Criminal
Laws	State child protection law	State criminal codes for specific crimes (e.g., assault, endangerment, murder)
Needs to prove	The child was injured by nonaccidental means	That a specific individual injured the child at a particular time
Fact finder	Judge	Judge or judge and jury
Maximum penalty	Removal of the child from parents	Sentence of incarceration or probation dependent on specific crime
Rules of evidence and formality	Lenient	Strict
Burden of proof	Predominance of the evidence	Beyond a reasonable doubt

Understand the Context

It will also be helpful if you can determine from the lawyer(s) involved how they see your testimony as contributing to the overall case. As physicians, we often feel that the entire weight of the case depends on medical findings and opinions. Although this may often be true, it is not always so. The legal counsel should provide the context of the expert's testimony. How will this testimony meld with the testimony of other witnesses when presenting the entire case? Ideally, the attorney will take this to the point of formulating each specific question to be asked in advance of the trial. Others may give a more general overview.

Review Documentation

Nothing will relieve the anxiety of the expert witness more than a thorough review of all existing documents, medical records, radiographs, and pertinent medical literature. The witness who is ill prepared will be easily foiled by an opposing counsel who is prepared. Although medical records may be introduced as evidence to be read in court, the witness will gain a psychological advantage by committing some details to memory. This convinces the judge and jury that this case was important to you and that you remember it distinctly from the many other similar cases you encounter each day. Nothing is more intimidating than an opposing lawyer who has noted something in the medical record that you had not previously seen. If you have written any scientific articles, books, or protocols that are in the public domain, be sure to review these with regard to their impact on this specific case. Your own words may be used against you.

Know the Parties

It is also important to know all the parties involved. You will of course know the child and the parents. However, it is also helpful to know the lawyers and their assistants. In a given case there may be legal counsel for the parents, for the public welfare agency, and for the child. It is expected that the attorney who has subpoenaed you will meet with you in advance of the hearing. One question that is often posed concerns pretrial meetings with opposing counsel. There is fear that such meetings will somehow ruin the case. This is an exaggerated fear because telling the lawyers what will be said under oath during the court session is not harmful. Vague speculation and volunteering more information than is necessary is dangerous and should be avoided. Answer questions briefly and directly.

Establish an On-Call System

The court process is often bogged down by delays, continuances, and out-of-court settlements. Thus, you should try to establish an on-call system so that you can respond promptly when your testimony is needed. This will save you countless hours of wasted time in court waiting rooms. If such arrangements cannot be made, be aware that one of the defense counsel's strategies may be to frustrate you with delays to the point where you will refuse to testify, thus abdicating your role as child advocate. If you are forced to appear at a set time rather than be on-call, take material with you to make your waiting time more profitable.

Special Preparation for First Timers

For interns, residents, and other physicians who are attending court for the first time, special preparation is advised.

Most often an experienced physician or social worker may accompany the novice. Although the "coach" cannot provide specific case information or answers to questions, the new expert witness will be alerted as to what to expect and guided into new territory. Other techniques used include discussion of an article or chapter such as this one or viewing a videotaped mock trial. All of these methods relieve anxiety and help to create a better witness.

PREPARING AN EXPERT REPORT

When serving as an expert witness, it may not be possible or appropriate to have direct contact with the abused child or the parents. The expert's opinion must be drawn from secondary sources, such as hospital records, medical reports, autopsy data, radiographs, and police reports. Many jurisdictions require that an expert prepare and submit a written report before the court appearance. Such a requirement may come under the rules of disclosure that protect a defendant and allow the defense to challenge an expert's testimony. In preparing an expert report, begin by listing the documents reviewed and the contacts you had with any relevant sources. List when and how you were contacted to perform the review. The remainder of the report should include your general findings and some of the major factors that led to your conclusions. The general tone should be concise and factual. An expert must accept the existing facts and come to a conclusion based on the expert's experience, knowledge, and expertise. There is no room for speculation. It is also unwise to go into great detail in the report, since some defense attorneys may choose to discredit the entire report by discrediting one or two of its details. The more detail that is included, the more chance to write something to which exception may be taken. The report should be timed and dated. In review documentation, the lawyer may ask you how much documentation you would like to review. Say that you would like to see all available information; in some cases you may wish to ask for records that have not previously been sought by the prosecutor, for example, birth records that may hold some information about why a child was abused at 2 years of age. As you receive reports, time and date their arrival. Carefully review each document. You want to take the stand confident that you know the contents of the medical records better than anyone else in the courtroom.

THE HEARING OR TRIAL

The typical court hearing or trial consists of three parts: the qualification, direct examination, and cross-examination. Each of these segments will be explored separately.

Qualification

The prosecution or the defense may call you as a fact or expert witness. Usually, it will be the prosecution or the child's counsel who will seek to qualify you as an expert. There may be various kinds of expert testimony. For example, most physicians may be qualified as medical experts based on their completion of formal medical training and licensure. A physician may also be qualified in a particular specialty, for example, pediatrics. Additionally, the physician may be qualified as an expert in "child abuse and neglect." Being qualified as an expert allows the physician not only to report on findings but also to draw conclusions and state opinions as well.

To qualify as an expert witness, the physician will be asked to display training, experience, and qualifications in a specific area. It is helpful to have supplied the lawyers with your curriculum vitae. Opposing counsel may attempt to "stipulate" your qualification. In doing this, the defense agrees to the level of expertise, usually to prevent the judge or jury from hearing the extent of your qualifications. From the psychological perspective, it is better that the fact finders hear just how qualified you are. Be sure to mention previous court experiences. Having been qualified as an expert once, makes it easier the second time. Sometimes physicians are more qualified than they think they are. In sexual abuse cases, the qualification is the physician's previous examination of many normal genitalia, rather than an extensive past experience with sexual abuse. In this example, the primary care physician is far more qualified than the gynecologist who rarely examines the genitalia of normal prepubertal females.

One defense strategy is to make the physician appear overqualified. Qualifications may be used to give the impression that testifying against abusive parents is a full-time job and that some secret pleasure is derived from it. For the experienced expert, the initial qualification statements may just focus on the high points. Then, if challenged, all the details may be exposed.

Another defense question that is likely to be asked is, "Are you being paid for your testimony?" The question is often posed to give your appearance a mercenary quality. The answer is that you are being paid to compensate for your time. You are not being paid to say what someone else wants you to say. This area of questioning is entered purely for the sake of intimidation. Everyone else in the courtroom from the bailiffs to the judge is being paid for work, and there is no reason why you should not be so compensated.

The defense may also attempt to reduce the perception of the witness's qualifications by concentrating on the specifics of the case.

Attorney: "Doctor, how many child abuse cases have you seen?"
Physician: "Approximately 1000."
Attorney: "How many have involved the shaken baby syndrome?"
Physician: "Forty-five cases."
Attorney: "How many were children of the age of Billy White, the subject of today's hearing?"
Physician: "Only three."
Attorney: "So, you have only dealt with two other cases like this one?"

Any expert witness may be reduced to nonexpert status by this technique. However, usually the judge and jury see through the tactic.

Direct Examination

The goal of direct examination is to present all the material that is relevant to the case. With this in mind, the physician should review in advance all the information deemed important. By doing this, the witness can make sure that all the important facts are discussed. Nothing is more frustrating than completing testimony, knowing that the court has not been told all the salient features of the case. For example, lawyers may not appreciate the importance of asking you about the child's development. Although not as tangible as bruises and fractures, the child's developmental delay may be at the heart of a case. By planning in advance what to tell the court, you may include the child's developmental delay in your testimony even when asked a general question about your "findings." During direct examination, the expert will reveal the findings of the case and the conclusions drawn from those findings. In the ideal situation, the lawyer will have informed the expert witness about all the relevant questions that will be asked in court in order to elicit all the important features of the case. It is perfectly acceptable for the expert to know the questions in advance. It is unacceptable for the attorney to suggest answers to those questions. During the testimony, the expert is wise to discuss only prepared issues. Be careful not to delve into areas of speculation or areas of peripheral knowledge. Remember that any area mentioned during direct examination is subject to cross-examination. If a doctor expounds on the mental health status of the parents, this may come back as a line of questioning in the cross-examination. If you are not a mental health expert, do not speculate. Usually, as one crawls out onto an uncomfortable limb, the sound of sawing becomes audible.

Throughout direct examination, remember the psychological aspects of your testimony. A good expert witness is in court to present objective data to the court. The expert must be impartial and fair. The physician in this role must not appear to be "out to get the parents." The expert must appear to have special knowledge and ability. To this end, it may be helpful to use a certain amount of jargon in order to present an air of professionalism. At the same time, translate technical terms into lay terms to be understood. Always keep in mind that the court is a nonmedical arena, with a low level of medical sophistication. Opinions must be firm—honest, but firm.

During direct examination, the expert

may refer to notes and medical records. Usually, the defense will have access to the same medical records. In front of a jury, being a good witness is like being a good teacher. Being clear and concise and using graphs, charts, radiographs, and photographs are important. The old adage that a picture is worth a thousand words is a truism in court. Even the most articulate witness cannot describe the child with multiple lash marks from a beating. It is impossible to describe either the number of marks on the child's body or the quality of the child's pain.

An expert witness should never express a personal opinion about the child victim or the defendant. Such statements have served repeatedly as the basis for reversals.

At any point during the testimony, the lawyers may raise objections. When something is objected to, the witness should immediately stop speaking. This is a signal that there is a legal objection that must be resolved by the lawyers and the judge. The objecting lawyer is not indicating that the witness did or said anything wrong or incorrect. However, there are certain rules of law to which the court must adhere. How strictly these rules of law are followed will vary, depending on the type of hearing, the point of the testimony, and the mind-set and skill of the lawyer and the judge.

At the end of direct examination, the physician will usually be asked about probable cause. The lawyer will ask, "Doctor, to a reasonable degree of medical certainty, what is the cause of these findings?" As physicians, we are trained to always be on the lookout for the one atypical finding or set of circumstances, the one possible cause that is rare. Because of the nature of our training, the answer to this final question may pose a challenge. What the lawyer is asking is, "What is the most likely cause?" The lawyer is not asking for the one and only cause. Thus, the expert must answer in this light. Tell the court the probable cause, the most likely cause. The defense is likely to bring out the other possible, although unlikely, causes. "To a reasonable degree of medical certainty" is that judgment made by a reasonable and prudent physician armed with the facts of the case.

As a last step in the direct examination of many civil cases, the expert may be asked to make recommendations for the case. Frequently, in the turmoil of testifying, the overview is lost. What, in your opinion, should result from your findings? This is the essence of the case and should not be forgotten.

Cross-Examination

The nature of the legal process requires that the attorney representing the alleged perpetrator challenge the statements of the expert. The attorney may do this by attacking the facts or by making it appear that the testimony of the expert has not been objective and fair. By increasing the expert's level of anxiety, these goals may be realized. The first step in preparing for cross-examination is to lower one's anxiety level. The expert will have taken the first step in this regard through careful precourt preparation. The second step is to realize that the expert is not the one on trial. Remember that a rigorous cross-examination is not a personal vendetta against the witness; it is the normal conduct of legal process. The witness must remain uninvolved and firm when testifying. On many occasions, two lawyers who have harassed and objected to one another all day in court shake hands at the conclusion of a trial. Whenever you are asked a question, wait to hear the entire question; think about the question itself

but also the purpose behind the question. If questions are being asked in a rapid-fire manner, they do not have to be answered with equal speed. Take time to consider your answer and how it might affect the purpose behind the question.

There are certain cross-examination techniques of which one should be aware. The defense lawyer may pose a question in a yes-or-no format. However, some questions cannot be answered so briefly; they require some qualification or modification or can be answered "I do not know." Thus, the witness should attempt to make this known by saying, "I cannot answer that yes or no or "Yes, but with the following reservation." There will be times that modification will not be allowed, and the judge will instruct the witness to answer with "yes" or "no." Nonetheless, by protesting you have let the judge and jury know your reservations. There are some questions that will be asked that you simply cannot answer. Not all questions need to be answered. The expert should feel free to say, "I do not know," "I cannot recall," or "That is outside my area." The lawyer may ask a very complex, multifaceted question that is so convoluted that the point is lost. For this type of question or for any question that you do not understand, ask for the question to be repeated.

Whenever you hear the phrase, "In other words . . . ," be very cautious. These words signal that the attorney has taken your words and is about to modify them slightly. In that modification, the essence of what you have said may be lost, and appear completely opposite to your intent. Thus, at the utterance of that phrase, keep your ears open and be sure that you are being paraphrased correctly.

An expert witness may be given a hypothetical situation. This may be used by the defense counsel to make the expert appear as a biased reporter. In the hypothetical case, circumstances will be presented that parallel the real matter before the court, with some important exceptions. For example, the problem is an abused child with a large area of vaginal laceration and positive examination findings for the presence of seminal fluid. The question asked is, "Doctor, is it not true that little girls who fall on the crossbar of their bicycle will sustain a vaginal laceration?" The answer to this must be "Yes." The inexperienced witness can easily be infuriated that an analogy is being drawn. Some will fail to admit to situations that any reasonable layman recognizes as possibilities. Thus, the defense will show the expert in an unflattering prejudiced light. Always recall that the entire case does not rest on the expert's shoulders. The expert is there as a friend of the court to present information and expert interpretation of case material.

Another area that may be used to cross-examine the expert is the written charts and notes. The defense may wish to know why something was written or why another detail was omitted. The answer here is that the interactions we have with patients and their parents are very complex. Even the most meticulous note taker cannot include every detail. Thus, some items will be omitted, others will be weighed disproportionately, and others will be indicated appropriately. Undergoing this part of the cross-examination gives the expert resolve to become more exacting in the use of the medical record. Good record keeping is a skill that is vital to the entire medicolegal process. Its importance cannot be stressed too heavily.

An expert may be asked, "What do you consider an authoritative source of the topic of . . . ?" This is a dangerous question. If the expert answers that a chapter, article, or book is an authoritative source, there is a presumption that the expert agrees with the entire contents of that writer's work. This is another means of discrediting the expert. In a field such as child abuse there are no absolute authoritative sources. Along the same lines, the expert may be asked to read a sentence or a paragraph from an existing publication. Do not read a segment of what has been written without reading the piece in its entirety and getting the author's full intent. Sometimes by reading one sentence, the expert is presenting a concept that is totally opposite to the author's intent. At other times, the expert will simply disagree with what has been written. It is your right as an expert to do so.

CONFLICTS WITHIN THE LEGAL SYSTEM

The civil and criminal court systems are subject to multiple conflicts. There are many problems and dilemmas that the physician must face when entering the foreign territory of the courthouse. These problems go beyond the fact that in court there are foreign policies and procedures and a different technical language is spoken. There are many procedures that make delays and continuances a common problem. In many areas, the courts are so backlogged that cases do not come up for weeks or months. Weeks and months are long times in the life of a child.

Perhaps the most important conflict is that the court system has been established to determine right and wrong, guilt and innocence. Criminal court often seems the wrong place for most child abuse cases. The matters before family (civil) court often cannot be resolved in terms of black or white decisions. The issue is most often what is in the child's best interest. Which parent should have custody of a child is not a matter of right or wrong. Thus, sometimes the system does not fit the purpose to which it is applied. The system is adversarial, and it is being applied to a family in which there is often already too much conflict. There are many situations in which the court process widens the distances between family members rather than resolving the family's crisis.

Many of the concepts (child abuse, neglect, child custody, to name a few) are transitional. Child abuse today is not what it was 500 or even 50 years ago. In the future, we will have even different concepts. This leaves room for differences among what the court believes is abuse, what the expert considers abuse, and what the family would label as abusive. With conflicts, even in our definitions, it is not surprising that conflict ripples through the system. Conflict can lead to frustration and frustration to avoidance. If we avoid our responsibilities as child advocates, who will assume them?

SUGGESTED READINGS

1. Bell C, Mlyniec WJ: Preparing for a neglect proceeding: a guide for the social worker. Public Welfare, Fall 1974

2. Brent RL: The irresponsible expert witness: a failure of biomedical graduate education and professional accountability. Pediatrics 70:754, 1982

3. Davis SM, Schwartz MD: Children's Rights and the Law. Lexington Books, Lexington, 1987

4. Derdeyn AP: Child abuse and neglect: the rights of parents and the needs of children. Am J Orthopsychiatry 47:377, 1977

5. Haialambie AM, Rosenberg DA: The expert witness: social work, medical, psychiatric. p. 396. In Bross DC, Krugman RD, Lenher MR et al (eds): The New Child Protection Team Handbook. Garland Publishing, New York, 1988

6. Kempe HC, Helfer RE: Child abuse and neglect: the family and the community. Ballinger Publishing, Cambridge, MA, 1976

7. Ludwig S, Heiser A, Cullen TR et al: You are subpoenaed.... Clin Proc Child Hosp Natl Med Center 30:133, 1974

8. Torrey S, Ludwig S: Emergency physician's role in the courtroom. Pediatr Emerg Care 3:50, 1987

9. Toth P: Investigation and Prosecution of Child Abuse. American Prosecutors Research Institute, Alexandria VA, 1987

10. Wilkerson AE: Rights of Children. Temple University Press, Philadelphia, 1974

33

Children in Placement

Paul M. Diamond

Children in foster care are a high risk and transient population. Overall, they have a greater number of physical, mental, emotional, and social problems than children in the general population. They require, and often do not receive, comprehensive, well coordinated health care. Studies spanning 18 years show a remarkable consistency in patterns of health care for children in foster care. They all confirm that foster children receive inadequate, poorly organized, fragmented care with erratic documentation and transfer of information. These deficiencies have been repeatedly acknowledged by the American Academy of Pediatrics Committee on Early Childhood, Adoption, and Dependent Care. In 1987 they wrote, ". . . the persistence of these health problems [after placement] suggests major shortcomings in the system of providing health care to foster children." In 1975 they wrote, "In many ways, there is a seeming substitution of community neglect for parental neglect. In one state 40 percent of foster children have health problems and more than 25 percent have not had a recommended treatment program implemented. These figures indicate that priorities given the needs of foster children, in the context of our societal need, are low."

HISTORY

The English Elizabethan Poor Law of 1601 first acknowledged the community's responsibility to care for its poor, especially orphaned, delinquent, or neglected children. Originally, the church or state funded their care in their own homes or with families nearby. Children were also "bound out" as indentured servants, sometimes far from home, working in exchange for their keep until they were of majority age. Many children were thrown into overcrowded, dirty, poor houses, also called almshouses, mixing with the aged, insane, criminal, or physically ill. In the latter part of the 18th century, children began to be separated from adults, and the first public orphanage opened in 1794. Public sentiment was largely against public assistance for children remaining in their own homes, as it was felt that this rewarded and promoted pauperism. In the latter half of the 19th century, interest in child welfare increased, and states began to monitor institutions by requiring annual reports. Institutionalized care and binding out came under criticism by those who favored putting children in foster homes. Beginning in 1868, Massachusetts gave weekly subsidies to families that would take in a foster child.

In 1909, legislation was passed in Massachusetts to protect children deprived of proper physical care because of neglect, crime, cruelty, insanity, drunkeness, or other parental vice. That same year, at the first White House Conference on the Care of Dependent and Neglected Children, sentiment clearly favored home care over institutionalized care, and conference participants resolved that poverty alone was not sufficient cause to remove a child from the home. The seeds from this conference would later blossom into Aid to Families of Dependent Children (AFDC). In 1910, Illinois started giving public assistance to dependent children in their own homes, and by 1935 all but two states had followed suit. Title IV-A, Aid to Dependent Children became law as part of the Social Security Act in 1935 as assistance to widows/widowers to avoid the breakup of families solely for financial reasons. This was later changed to Aid to Families with Dependent Children. Yet, in spite of AFDC, most dependent children were still placed outside their own homes in institutions and foster care.

After the Depression, the number of children in institutions finally began to decrease. Fewer children were being placed for reasons related to parental illness or death. At the same time, more people involved in child welfare were advocating services that would keep families together or allow temporary foster care, with planned services ultimately leading to a family reunion. In 1950, a White House Conference assembly grandly proposed the elimination of slums, (the creation of) programs and facilities for play, learning, and social experiences for all children without prejudice or discrimination, and, most importantly, the preservation of family life. Sadly, the vision of the 1950 conference has failed to materialize. Although Medicaid was created in 1965, Bloch be-

lieves that this and many other federal programs designed to serve dependent children, such as school lunches, food stamps, and vocational training, have failed to keep pace with the increased numbers of children living in poverty. He cited a 1983 report entitled *America's Children: Powerless and in Need of Powerful Friends*, which said, "America's children out of the mainstream have been forgotten. One child in every five, a total of 12 million, live in poverty and unsafe housing. Nine million have no regular health care or have ever seen a dentist. They need education, food, shelter, clothing, and health care."

During the last 30 years, the number of children in foster care has generally increased in the context of deinstitutionalization. The children being placed now more often have special needs. They are physically and emotionally traumatized, commonly the victims of abuse and neglect, rather than orphans or children with parents who are too ill or otherwise unable to care for them. Infants and children of parents with acquired immunodeficiency syndrome (AIDS) are, of course, the exception. Additionally, children with AIDS constitute a growing number of children in foster care. Other factors contributing to the increased number of children in foster care include increased reporting of child abuse, especially sexual abuse, as well as increased poverty and increased parental substance abuse in the face of fewer social supports.

Although often considered a last resort, as many as 5 percent (or more) of children are placed in an institutional or residential setting. This type of placement is often chosen for the child with complex medical or behavioral problems requiring special treatment, such as skilled nursing care or 24-hour supervision, which would be too much for one or two foster parents to provide, even with respite services. This type of setting has one obvious disadvantage; with caretakers changing every 8 hours, it may be difficult to create the bonding and intimacy that some children experience with their foster parents. Also, residential care is expensive and may cost more than twice as much as a child in specialized foster care and possibly as much as 10 times that of a child in regular foster care. Finally, in a residential setting, some children may acquire negative attributes or dysfunctional behaviors as a result of their prolonged contact with other troubled children.

There are also a number of children who are placed with relatives. Placement with relatives is inexpensive and has the obvious advantage of placing the child in a comfortable setting with familiar faces, thus making the adjustment period less traumatic. Theoretically, a relative may take better care of a child who was "their own blood," than a foster parent, "a stranger," would. On the other hand, a relative's parenting skills may have been acquired in the same milieu as the biologic parents, putting the child at continued risk for the same type of maltreatment that had initially led to placement. Of practical consideration is the difficulty in tracking the child, who may drift from one relative to another. Also, a relative may be reluctant to enforce supervised visits when a court orders supervised visitation only for the abusive parent.

FOSTER CHILDREN

There are between 300,000 and 500,000 children in foster care in the United States. The lack of an exact number testifies to the fluid and transient nature of foster placement and the paucity of up-to-date statistics. Foster children are now primarily abused and neglected children (Table 33-1). Victims of physical abuse, especially those who were burned and scalded, are more likely to be placed than are victims of other types of abuse. Recurrent episodes of maltreatment or abuse severe enough to require hospitalization also increase the likelihood of placement. Thus, many foster and abused children have the same characteristics (Table 33-2). Foster children may also be orphans or abandoned children, especially if the child is young. Some children have parents who are incapable of caring adequately for them, owing to parental mental or physical illness or substance abuse. Conversely, other children are placed in foster care when they have a condition that overwhelms the parents'

Table 33-1. Characteristics of Children in Foster Care

Characteristic	% of Foster Children	Suggested Readings
Physically abused	7–42	9, 11, 13, 14
Severely neglected	11–65	9, 11, 13, 14
Sexually abused	3–35	9, 13, 14
Abandoned	17–22	11, 14
Parent mentally ill	23	9, 11
Parent substance abuser	5	11
Parent physically ill	8–12	11, 17
Abused/neglected in previous foster care	3–5	19
Juvenile delinquent	8	19

abilities to be the primary caretaker. The condition may be a serious physical or mental illness or a problem with delinquency, since foster children are at much greater risk for delinquency, especially for violent crimes such as assault.

In the past, children were not only placed in foster care when their parents died or were too ill to care for them, but also to rescue society from juvenile delinquent crimes, which were thought to be an almost inevitable consequence of children growing up in poverty. Schor writes that New York City was plagued with children being arrested for vagrancy and petty crimes and "Charles L. Brace of the New York Children's Aid Society arranged to send nearly 40,000 children to foster homes in the Midwest and Plains States between 1852 and 1879." Conveniently, children were also a source of cheap labor, indentured servants, who worked in exchange for their clothing, room, board, and "care." In retrospect, it is not clear that children were always placed solely according to what was in their own best interest.

In spite of the AFDC, poverty and placement in foster care continue to be

Table 33-2.   Characteristics
of Abused Children

Aggressive, self-destructive behavior

Low self-esteem

Acting out behavior

Adjustment reactions

Enuresis, encopresis

Depression and suicide

Runaway and drug abuse

Sexual molestation of others

Learning disabilities

Impaired social relationships

Attention deficit disorders

Juvenile delinquency

(From Klee and Halfon,[16] with permission.)

Table 33-3.   Factors That Increase
Risk of Placement

Less educated mothers

Abandoned young children

Repeated episodes of maltreatment

Parents who are substance abusers

Parents who believe that severe physical punishment is OK

Victim of physical abuse, especially burns and scalds

Abused severely enough to require hospitalization

Referred from law enforcement agency (police or courts)

(From Runyan et al,[21] with permission.)

intimately related. A family headed by a single female parent is much more likely to be a poor AFDC family than a family with two parents; and an AFDC family is four times more likely to have a child placed in foster care. Having a less educated or teenage mother or other single parent, or being in an immigrant or homeless family or a family which has moved frequently increases the risk of placement, as does a referral to child welfare from the police or courts. Of the list of factors that increases the risk of placement in foster care (Table 33-3) none are predictive, because so many of the risk factors are also found in abused and neglected children left in their own homes. Age and race are not risk factors, in and of themselves, other than how they relate to the issues noted above.

FOSTER PARENTS

Historically, at least in the last two decades, foster parents have typically been middle aged (average age 45 years), working or middle-class adults with a high school education. Many are employed in a skilled trade and own their own homes. They are usually married and have or have had their own children, although the percentage that are married has decreased from 81 percent in 1971 to 66 percent in 1982. It is becoming more common to find nontraditional parents such as single men and women being foster parents, especially for the hard-to-place children, such as those with AIDS. Albeit less common, homosexual and even transvestite adults are also helping to alleviate the chronic shortage of foster parents.

People do not become foster parents for the money. Foster agencies screen such individuals, and financial compensation for foster care expenses hardly seems profitable. In 1985, monthly reimbursements for food, clothing, and other costs of daily living averaged slightly over $250 for a "regular" foster child and somewhat more for a foster child with special needs. Also, all foster children have Medicaid, which is supposed to cover their medical expenses. Nevertheless, Gruber noted in 1977 that 93 percent of foster parents used their own money regularly to cover routine foster care expenses. He also noted that 40 percent of foster parents participated in self-motivated activities to improve their foster parenting skills. A similar number were interested in receiving more specialized foster parent training. It is not surprising that foster parents are seeking more training. They do so much of their work "in the dark." Gruber noted that only 25 percent of foster parents received information on the child's health problems; 27 percent were given some idea of a health problem but were unaware of the extent; and fully 48 percent were given no idea that their foster child had a significant health problem.

For the most part, people become foster parents for the personal satisfaction of providing a needed service and seem to be motivated by an ongoing commitment

to the best interests of the child. Halfon and Klee found that 70 percent of foster parents in California had been foster parents for more than 5 years and 37 percent had been foster parents for more than 10 years. There are scattered reports of children being abused or neglected in foster care, although the risk is five times less than case matched controls who remained in their own homes (5 percent versus 25 percent, respectively).

FOSTER CARE

Modern foster care was designed to be the temporary, short-term placement of a child while intensive services were provided for the family to rectify the situation(s) that made the home unsafe or unfit for the child. Sadly, this ideal is rarely achieved. Placement is usually not short-term, often involves moving from one home to another, and only results in the child being returned to the original home in 55 percent of cases. Consequently, the child cannot be reassured that a foster mommy and daddy will always be there, nor can the child be told that he will soon be returning home. This is the worst of both worlds. Studies in Baltimore by Schor and in New York City by Swire and Kavaler found that foster children spend an average of 1.6 to 5 years in placement and 50 to 68 percent are placed for 4 to 8 years; 42 to 58 percent manage to remain in one foster home but 40 to 60 percent move at least once, and 33 percent move three or more times while in foster care. As noted above, 55 percent ended foster care by returning home, 11 percent were adopted, 9 percent reached majority age, and 3 percent ran away. If children stay in foster care more than 2 years, they are much less likely to leave the system before majority age. Of those who do return home, 20 percent return to foster care.

This statistic reflects the inherent difficulties in placement decisions and the ongoing tug-of-war between a commitment to protect children and a commitment to keep families intact.

HEALTH PROBLEMS OF FOSTER CHILDREN

Virtually every study has revealed a high incidence (40 to 76 percent) of chronic health problems in foster children. Overall, the health problems approximate or exceed those of disadvantaged, low socioeconomic groups. They are 3 to 7 times more likely to have some chronic problem, 3 times as likely to have a hearing problem, 4 times more likely to be anemic, and 7 to 12 times as likely to have a behavioral, emotional, or psychiatric problem than the general population. They are at twice the risk for vision or other eye problems, with an incidence between 9 and 36 percent. Ironically, in one study, 61 percent of foster children with glasses had incorrect prescriptions, and another 29 percent with glasses had unnecessary prescriptions. A significant number have contagious or treatable infections (including sexually transmitted diseases), dental, cardiovascular, pulmonary, dermatologic or speech problems, weight below the fifth percentile, short stature, proteinuria, hematuria, lead poisoning, pregnancy, or iron deficiency anemia or other hematologic problems. Some infants exposed in utero to cocaine or other substances have associated birth defects or test positive for hepatitis B or human immunodeficiency virus (HIV). Evaluating 414 patients for suspected physical abuse, Flaherty and Weiss discovered 19 patients with fractures, seen on radiographs or bone scan, which were unsuspected on physical examination. Many foster children are not up-to-date with their immunizations (Table 33-4). This is not surprising since, in at least one study, 80 percent of foster parents never received any previous provider or immunization information. The realization that many of these problems can be detected during routine well child visits makes it imperative that foster children have access to competent primary care physicians who play a central role, often managing chronic problems, handling day-to-day crises, providing continuity, and coordinating subspecialty intervention(s).

Indeed, a significant number of foster children do require suspecialty intervention (Table 33-5). Most commonly, these include infant stimulation programs for children under 3 years of age, special education classes for children of school age, cardiology, dental, ophthalmology, neurology, speech and physical therapy, and psychiatric interventions of various forms. The high incidence of psychiatric or behavioral problems is not surprising given the multitude of problematic characteristics typical of abused or neglected children in addition to the trauma of repeated separations from biologic and foster families.

The frequency and severity of physical, psychiatric, behavioral, and school-related problems, many of which are treatable, make examining and screening for these problems in foster children a moral imperative, as well as an important and useful exercise. However, the current system is woefully inadequate. Many simple and correctable problems such as dental caries (and others listed in Table 33-6) are often not even evaluated. Many are evaluated incorrectly and the problem(s) continue unrecognized. Chronic disease, subtle health problems, preventive health measures, and behavioral/emotional/psychiatric issues are rarely sought, with children never receiving the proper attention or referral. Major hand-

Table 33-4. Health Problems of Foster Children

Type of Problem	% of Foster Children	Suggested Readings
Overall chronic problems (most identified on first visit)	40–76	9, 11, 14, 17, 28, 31
Vision	9–36	14, 23, 31
Hearing	3–12	23, 31
Speech	8–52	14, 28, 31
School/intellectual/cognitive	4–48	11, 14, 17
Behavior/emotional/psychiatric (overall)	23–96	11, 14, 17, 31, 32
Mild impairment	30	31
Moderate impairment	35	31
Severe to marked impairment	35	31
Dental	13–67	14, 31
Weight below 5%	8–17	14, 17, 31
Deficient immunizations	20–70	17, 23, 32
Abnormal Development screen (DDST)	10–61	14, 28, 31
Cardiovascular	12–19	14, 31
Anemia (hematocrit < 34%)	13	9, 14, 23
Dermatologic	25	14
Hematuria and/or proteinuria	3–4	9

Table 33-5. Patients Requiring Subspecialty Referral

Type of Referral	% of Foster Children
Overall	35
Cardiologist	13
Dental	14
Eye	11
Neurology	10
Various psychiatric interventions	40
Infant stimulation (under 3 years old)	52
Speech	20
Special school/class placement	19
Physical therapy	10

(Data from Hochstadt et al.[14])

Table 33-6. Evaluations That Foster Children Are (Not) Receiving

Problem	% Evaluated	% "Missed" Diagnosis
Vision	40–91	47
Hearing	10–91	93
School/cognitive	75	
Behavior/emotional/psychiatric	70	75
Speech	68	54
Dental	<50	40
Tine test	75	
Anemia	34	

(Data from Swire and Kavaler,[32] and Gruber.[11])

Table 33-7. Children With Identified Problem Who Actually Have Treatment Begun

Type of Problem	% of Foster Children
Vision	82
Hearing	100
School/cognitive	83
Behavior/emotional	66
Speech	76

(Data from Gruber.[11])

icaps and obvious acute problems are usually well recognized and appropriately handled. Yet, of the children who actually have their problems recognized, many still do not receive treatment. In Swire and Kavaler's study in New York City, only 59 percent of referrals were accomplished. Table 33-7 lists the percentage of foster children in a 1977 Massachusetts study who actually had treatment begun after specific common and potentially correctable problems were identified. This may be for a number of reasons, not the least of which is the difficulty of Medicaid patients gaining access to subspecialists and special programs.

MISSED-MISHANDLED HEALTH PROBLEMS

As has already been alluded to, children in foster care have the majority of their health care initiated by foster parents. Some, but certainly not all, agencies require initial or periodic medical evaluations of foster children. The rest of the time it is the foster parent who recognizes health problems. Once a problem is recognized, the foster parent must know which doctor or other health professional to contact for further evaluation and treatment. The professional must accept Medicaid, and the foster parent must be able to get the child to the office for the evaluation. The office may be too far away, or in a high crime section of the city, or the foster parent may not have transportation, or the transportation may be costly compared with how urgent the problem seems to the foster parent. The impression that the placement is temporary and short-term may lead the foster parent to postpone some medical evaluations until the child returns to the regular doctor. Perhaps the foster parent cannot find someone to babysit while keeping the appointment. Perhaps the foster parent cannot get time off from work to go to the appointment or, if a series of ongoing visits are needed, may not be able to get away from work regularly to take the child. All of this assumes that the foster parent recognizes a problem in the first place. This is a major assumption, particularly when foster parents receive little information or training in the area of health care and almost no medical information about their foster child. Will the foster parent be able to find a health care professional who accepts Medicaid, at a time when the number of pediatricians accepting Medicaid is decreasing and the number of pediatricians restricting Medicaid caseloads is increasing (Table 33-8). Schor noted in his 1979 Baltimore study that more than one-half of the foster

Table 33-8. National Trends for Pediatricians' Participation in Medicaid

	1978 (%)	1989 (%)
Pediatricians accepting Medicaid	85	77
Pediatricians restricting Medicaid caseloads	26	39.4

(Data from Yudkowsky et al.[33])

agencies surveyed reported difficulty finding psychiatric testing and treatment, that Medicaid would pay for only two therapy sessions per month, and that there was no Medicaid allowance for group or foster family therapy. He also noted that 54 percent of agencies stated they had trouble finding medical services, and 50 percent had difficulty getting orthodontal services.

Agencies are largely lacking in specific guidelines for medical evaluations. Table 33-9 shows that foster agencies give little information or direction to foster parents regarding health matters, particularly concerning mental health. Only 50 to 75 percent of foster agencies require an initial medical evaluation, and even those that do are often not specific regarding who, when, where, or what should be evaluated or who should perform the evaluation. Consequently, some children get checked before placement, some within 72 hours, some within 1 month of placement, and some not at all. Some agencies require that all children be medically evaluated, some require only those with an acute problem (as recognized by the agency caseworker or foster parent) be evaluated. Recently, the Child Welfare League of America issued recommendations for medical, dental, and mental health evaluations that should be

performed for all foster children within 1 month of placement.

Children may be seen in the emergency department, community clinic, private physician's office, or emergency shelter. They may be checked by the emergency department or shelter nurse, or an emergency, local, or agency doctor. Evaluations can range from a quick general screening to a comprehensive Early Periodic Screening and Development Testing (EPSDT) examination. In spite of the high incidence of mental health problems in foster children, most mental health evaluations are performed on an "as needed" basis, resulting in less than 10 percent of children being evaluated for mental health problems during their initial checkups. Almost all of these evaluations are for obvious or extreme states, and almost all that are evaluated are referred for ongoing therapy. Undoubtedly, many "less than extreme" cases are missed when the system depends on the ability of foster parents and caseworkers to recognize mental health and other medical problems and initiate evaluations.

Not only do many agencies lack detailed guidelines for initial evaluations but most (59 percent) also lack guidelines for routine or ongoing medical care. In agencies with guidelines there is marked variation in the degree to which workers

Table 33-9. Health Information Reported by Foster Parents (California, 1985)

Information Reported	Always (%)	Sometimes (%)	Never (%)
Initial medical screenings	13	57	22
Initial mental health screenings	0	41	39
Medical records received	0	74	26
Immunization records received	0	54	39
Name of previous physician received	0	65	28

(Modified from Halfon and Klee,[13] with permission.)

follow the guidelines. Equally lacking are guidelines regarding documentation of medical care, necessary consents, and the transfer of information among health care providers, foster parents, the foster agency, and the state child welfare agency. Medical, dental, and mental health records may be separate from each other or separate from the "case" file. Agencies may receive medical information from foster parents using standard forms (54 percent), letters, notes, memos, and telephone calls from physicians or foster parents. Recently, the American Academy of Pediatrics (AAP) adopted a resolution recommending the use of a model form for the transfer of medical data to include diagnosis, history, immunizations, pertinent laboratory studies, past and present therapy, and a recommended date for the next medical evaluation.

Many agencies also lack specific guidelines for quality assurance and monitoring of care. Eighty percent of the time the caseworker, who is already overworked and is also undertrained in health matters, is responsible for monitoring the child's health care. To make matters even worse, there is generally a high rate of turnover among caseworkers, making supervision of cases more difficult, and the number of professionally trained social workers being used as caseworkers is decreasing (51 percent in 1958 to 9 percent in 1977).

The guidelines that do exist may come from the AAP, social service or child welfare boards, foster parents' associations, or agency medical care committee. Many agencies do not use AAP or state guidelines and make up their own instead. Yet not all agencies have a medical director or health care consultant to write their policies. Those that do may use nurses or physicians from any number of disciplines, for example, public health, pediatrics, and family medicine.

Without clear lines of responsibility and accountability and without clear and specific guidelines, caseworkers and nurses or other health care professionals cannot teach, implement, or enforce the guidelines. Foster parents cannot be expected to know as much as trained health care professionals and cannot be expected to carry the whole burden of recognizing problems and initiating medical care. A study in Montreal by Moffatt et al. demonstrated that once guidelines were in place, medical care improved with an increased percentage of children receiving well child checkups, immunizations, and vision screening. This improvement was accomplished without any increase in cost to the foster agency.

Solutions and Recommendations

It seems obvious that without the necessary guidelines and a system to implement these guidelines, many foster children and their health problems will continue to fall between the cracks as has been the case for decades. Physicians and dentists will continue to practice according to their own standards and knowledge of children in foster care, largely neglecting the emotional, social, educational, and preventive issues that plague foster children, and agencies will continue to inadequately document or monitor the services provided and the problems recognized.

Two general systems have been suggested as possible first steps toward resolving the crisis in health care for children in foster care.

1. A centralized or regionalized health care facility (health maintenance organization [HMO] or hospital) with primary care providers and subspecialists who will provide all foster chil-

dren with their initial evaluations as well as acute and routine health care. This would allow for a centralized and more comprehensive method of record keeping, more easily coordinated and available subspecialty referrals, and access to health care providers with special skills in the care of abused and neglected foster children. Such access would increase continuity and, it is hoped, decrease the use of costly and fragmented emergency department services for episodic care or the unnecessary use of subspecialty services. Also, services could be more easily monitored, and neglect or abuse in foster care may be detected earlier. Studies in Baltimore by Schor, and in Chicago by Hochstadt et al., noted that capitated plans such as HMOs may pay more attention to psychosocial and preventive needs. However, foster children, as noted previously, have many chronic health problems and are therefore fiscally unattractive to capitated plans without some adjustments to compensate. Other disadvantages include the possible lack of integration of foster children's care with the foster family's doctor and increased traveling distances to doctors' appointments.

2. The social agency acts as the centralized coordinating agency that arranges and monitors all health care for children in placement according to detailed standards written by their health care consultants or staff. The agency would keep centralized records and have a system for communicating medical and other information to caseworkers, foster parents, police, legal officials, and health care providers. A designated person in the agency, perhaps the caseworker (with special training in health care), would be responsible for periodic review and monitoring of health services. This system would allow foster children to

be better integrated into the foster family's community as well as potentially save traveling time for foster parents. However, it may also place a large burden for medical decisions on someone, such as the caseworker, who is not primarily medically trained. This system would also involve the agency using a fair amount of time and personnel to arrange and track the health status of placed children and consequently would be fiscally unattractive to the agency.

Regardless of the particular system used, detailed, specific standards and agency policies should be formulated with the help of a trained health care professional and in accordance with guidelines set by the AAP (Table 33-10) and Child Welfare League of America. These should establish guidelines for initial evaluations (including mental health evaluations) for *all* children at (or near) the time of placement, routine medical care, screening and preventive health services, management of problems, and coordination of referrals. Foster parents should also receive more specific and detailed guidelines regarding health care. Further training should be provided to foster parents, caseworkers, and health care professionals to make them more aware and better able to recognize and take care of the health problems of children in foster care.

There should be standardized, centralized, and comprehensive medical records, as well as a written system of communicating complete and accurate information among health care providers, caseworkers, schools, police, legal personnel, and foster parents. Records should include psychosocial as well as medical information.

There should be a system of periodic case review with a designated person trained in health care responsible for

Table 33-10.   Immunization Schedule

Age	DTP	Polio	TB Test	Measles	Mumps	Rubella	HBCV[b]	Tetanus-Diphtheria
2 mo	X	X					X	
4 mo	X	X					X	
6 mo	X						X	
12–15 mo			X					
15 mo				X	X	X	X	
15–18 mo	X	X						
4–6 yr	X	X						
11–12 yr[a]				X	X	X		
14–16 yr								X

[a] Except where public health authorities require otherwise.

[b] As of October, 1990, only one HBCV (HBOC) has been approved for use in children younger than 15 months of age.

(From American Academy of Pediatrics and Shelov,[3] with permission.)

monitoring the adequacy, quality, and appropriateness of services. There should be better permanency planning, with adoption or more intensive support services and ongoing involvement of the biologic parents during foster care if returning home is the goal. This includes increased coordination of activities at the state, local, agency, and medical center levels.

Finally, there should be financial incentives to increase the number and quality of foster homes along with better financial coverage for mental health services, especially drug abuse treatment, vocational and rehabilitation programs, and treatment of child abuse victims and abusers. Expanded Medicaid coverage for foster children needs to include not only psychiatric services but educational, nutritional, eye, dental, and orthodontal services, and home visits when appropriate, if the needs of children in foster care are to be truly addressed. Fairer reimbursement for foster child/Medicaid providers would go a long way towards increasing the number of Medicaid providers, therefore increasing access of foster children to health care.

HIV INFECTION AND FOSTER CARE

The institution of foster care has hardly begun to deal with or prepare for the impact of HIV infection. Already stressed beyond its limits, the shortage of foster parents (with adequate training) and the lack of funds to support necessary medical services will be even further stretched as escalating numbers of babies with HIV infection and orphans of AIDS parents enter the sytem. In *American Medical News,* Abraham wrote, "According to the Public Health Service, 3000 children will have AIDS by 1991, almost triple the number stricken as of August 1988 . . . and for every child with AIDS, it is estimated that there are four children infected with HIV who are unknown to the Centers for Disease Control. The majority of these children have mothers who are intravenous (IV) drug abusers. This means that by 1991 there may be 10,000 to 20,000 HIV infected children nationwide with 30 to 70 percent of them ending up in foster care!" Permanent placement or adoption seems unlikely for these children as doing so stops the financial assistance, and Medicaid and private insurance companies will not insure someone already diagnosed with AIDS. In addition to the usual problems of recruiting foster parents, people who are going to care for children with AIDS must, according to the AAP Task Force on Pediatric AIDS, be willing to "bear the physical and emotional burden of caring for a child who will suffer from intermittent bouts of increasingly severe illness, and, in most cases, will ultimately die." Foster parents for AIDS children must also be willing to face that AIDS is a contagious disease as well as the social stigma, isolation, and ridicule that the family may encounter from relatives, friends, schools, and community. Realistically, the AAP Task Force on AIDS states that casual, nonsexual spread of HIV is virtually nonexistent. In studies involving over 17,000 family members in contact with AIDS patients, spread of HIV through normal family activities (such as sharing silverware, plates, toothbrushes, hugging, and kissing) or through contact with body fluids other than blood has not been documented except for once in a household where a 4 year old caught the infection from his younger brother who had acquired HIV via transfusion.

A few successful specialized foster parent programs for children with AIDS, such as the Leake and Watts Children's Home in Yonkers, New York, have been developed. Staff members carry small caseloads while foster parents receive intensive support, including medical services, insurance, cribs, clothes, washing machines (if needed), toys, funds for recreation, and $847 per month, which is continued even when the child is hospitalized. From their experience they realized that AIDS foster parents commonly were "well informed about AIDS, had little fear of transmission, and had some medical background or experience caring for ill people." From its inception in 1985

to 1988, the Leake and Watts AIDS specialized foster program placed 30 children. Albeit successful, the number of children enrolled in these programs is still small compared with the present and projected future demand for services. In New Jersey alone, the Division of Youth and Family Services currently provides services to 231 HIV/AIDS infants and children. Of these infants and children, 44 live with relatives, 84 are in foster homes, and 12 are in one of three group homes (personal communication; Christian Hansen, M.D., March 31, 1990).

The Massachusetts Adoption Resource Exchange, among others, has called for increased public education about HIV transmission to stem the "hysteria and social isolation forced on victims (of AIDS) and their families" as well as to help recruit foster and adoptive parents for HIV infected foster children. The group also noted the need for better financial reimbursement, financial incentives, and respite services for AIDS foster or adoptive parents. Long-term solutions will undoubtedly also depend on preventing the spread of HIV itself. "Safe sex," use of condoms, not sharing hypodermic needles, and the prevention of IV drug abuse in the first place will ultimately decrease the number of AIDS children in foster care, just as programs aimed at decreasing teenage pregnancy, poverty, illiteracy, and child abuse will ultimately decrease the number of all children in foster care.

In the interim, the AAP Task Force on Pediatric AIDS has recommended special support services, education, and counseling for families with HIV infected children, regardless of who the caretakers are. This should include risks and modes of transmission, information on immunizations, and specific guidelines for situations such as lacerations and bleeding, routine childhood illnesses, handling of body fluids other than blood, and disinfection procedures. The Task Force also recommends financial support to cover 100 percent of medical costs plus related mental health and educational expenses. They urge the agencies and community services involved to develop respite services and specialized day care, if needed.

Regarding testing of children for HIV before placement, the Task Force acknowledges that foster placement may be difficult unless the risk of HIV is partially alleviated by HIV antibody testing. Nevertheless, noting the ambiguities in interpreting HIV antibody tests in young children and the variable prevalence of HIV in different populations, the Task Force "does not recommend widespread testing of all infants and children awaiting foster placement or adoption." However, the Task Force continues "in populations with high seropositive prevalence, prospective adoptive or foster parents should have access to HIV antibody status." Sidestepping the number that defines "high seropositive prevalence," the Task Force charges local foster care and adoption agencies with the responsibility of collaborating with health care facilities to come up with appropriate testing protocols.

In contrast to the Task Force's recommendation and in the context of the medical, legal, social, and ethical issues surrounding AIDS, this author and others (e.g., Dix) recommend universal HIV testing before placement (or adoption) if the child's HIV status is not known. This is based on the belief that the true seropositive prevalence in a particular population is often difficult to estimate, given the mobility of people in this country, the high prevalence of drug abuse, and the "unsafe" sexual practices of many people. Of course, this testing should be accompanied by the same appropriate counseling and follow-up recommended by the AAP Task Force on Pediatric AIDS.

CONCLUSION

The foster care system is in a state of ongoing crisis regarding the health and wellbeing of children in its care. However, we should not let the depth of problems and the complexity of the system interfere with our efforts to improve the quality of the lives of foster children. This work, done by individuals and fueled by a personal commitment to children in foster care, ultimately has an impact at the clinic, hospital, local agency, state, and federal levels when individuals work together to accomplish the changes that are so desperately needed.

SUGGESTED READINGS

1. Abraham L: Giving love to children who deserve it, need it. Am Med News 3: August 26, 1988
2. American Academy of Pediatrics: Resolution No. 5. AAP News 6:November, 1989
3. American Academy of Pediatrics, Shelov SP (ed): Caring for Your Baby and Young Child. Bantam Books, New York, 1991
4. American Academy of Pediatrics Task Force on pediatric AIDS: Infant and children with acquired immunodeficiency syndrome: placement in adoption and foster care. Pediatrics 83:609, 1989
5. Bloch H: The plight of deprived children: a lingering problem in American democracy. J Natl Med Assoc 82:119, 1990
6. Committee on Adoption and Dependent Care: Health needs of the child in foster family care. Pediatrics 59:465, 1977
7. Dix D: Infants and children with acquired immunodeficiency syndrome: placement in adoption and foster care. Pediatrics 85:388, 1990
8. Dow B: Foster care system seen ill-equipped for kids with AIDS. Am Med News 6:January 15, 1988
9. Flaherty EG, Weiss H: Medical evaluation of abused and neglected children. Am J Dis Child 144:330, 1990

10. Gruber AR: Children in Foster Care. Human Sciences Press, New York, 1978

11. Gruber AR: Foster home care in Massachusetts. A study of foster children and their biological and foster parents. Commonwealth of Massachusetts, Governors Commission on Adoption and Dependent Care, 1973

12. Gurdin P, Anderson GR: Quality care for ill children: AIDS-specialized foster family homes. Child Welfare 66:291, 1987

13. Halfon N, Klee L: Health services for California's foster children: current practices and policy recommendations. Pediatrics 80:183, 1987

14. Hochstadt NJ, Jaudes PK, Zimo DA et al: The medical and psychosocial needs of children entering foster care. Child Abuse Negl 11:53, 1987

15. Kavaler F, Swire MR: Health services for foster children: an evaluation of agency programs. Child Welfare 53:147, 1974

16. Klee L, Halfon N: Mental health care for foster children in California. Child Abuse Negl 11:63, 1987

17. Moffatt MEK, Peddie M, Stulginskas J et al: Health care delivery to foster children: a study. Health Soc Work 10:129, 1985

18. Mulford R: Protective services for children. p. 1115. In Encyclopedia of Social Work. National Association of Social Workers, Washington DC, 1977

19. Runyan D, Gould CL: Foster care for child maltreatment: impact on delinquent behavior. Pediatrics 75:562, 1985

20. Runyan DK, Gould CL: Foster care for child maltreatment II: impact on school performance. Pediatrics 76:841, 1985

21. Runyan D, Gould CL, Trost D et al: Determinants of foster care placement for the maltreated child. Am J Public Health 71:706, 1981

22. Schor EL: Health care supervision of foster children. Child Welfare 55:313, 1981

23. Schor EL: The foster care system and health status of foster children. Pediatrics 69:521, 1982

24. Schor SL: Foster care. Pediatr Clin North Am 35:1241, 1988

25. Schor EL: Foster care. Pediatr Rev 10:209, 1989

26. Schor EL, Neff JM, LaAsmar J: The Chesapeake Health Plan: an HMO model for foster children. Child Welfare 63:431, 1984

27. Seidel HM: AAP Committee on Adoption and Dependent Care: the needs of foster children. Pediatrics 56:144, 1975

28. Simms MD: The foster care clinic: a community program to identify the treatment needs of children in foster care. J Dev Behav Pediatr 10:121, 1989

29. Stepleton SS: Specialized foster care: families as treatment resources. Children Today 16:27, 1987

30. Sterne GG: AAP Committee on Early Childhood, Adoption and Dependent Care: Health care of foster children. Pediatrics 79:644, 1987

31. Swire MR, Kavaler F: The health status of foster children. Child Welfare 56:635, 1977

32. Swire MR, Kavaler F: Health supervision of children in foster care. Child Welfare 57:563, 1978

33. Yudkowsky BK, Cartland JDC, Flint SS: Pediatrician participation in Medicaid: 1978 to 1989. Pediatrics 85:567, 1990

34

Photography of the Abused and Neglected Child

Brian S. Smistek

Medical institutions involved in the evaluation and treatment of abused and neglected children must follow protocol directives issued by their supervisory state, local, and in-house medical and legal authorities. Some health care facilities have instituted child abuse teams composed of physicians, nurses, and allied health care personnel. These teams compile data and evidence relative to each case.

As in any crime, the timeliness and methods with which evidence is collected may be of great importance in deciding the fate of both the victim and the perpetrator. When abuse and neglect are suspected, a concerted effort must be made by the health care team to assure that all items of proof are properly assembled.

Physical and radiographic examinations and personal interviews should be supported by a series of color photographs when intentional trauma is suspected. Photographs will stand as an accurate representation of the patient's condition, providing they are taken soon after injury or when the areas of trauma reach their peak of visibility.

Many states mandate the taking of color photographs and exempt the photographer from civil or criminal liability, providing such photographs were taken in good faith. Some states do not protect photographers and reporters of child abuse from possible litigation; obtain a copy of your state's policies pertaining to the taking and distribution of patient related photographs.

This chapter provides an in-depth guide to photographic techniques for physicians, medical photographers, and medical support personnel responsible for the detection, treatment, and evidence gathering in cases of child abuse and neglect.

THE PHOTOGRAPHER

Many hospitals are equipped with a medical photography department. In addition to their routine responsibilities, medical photographers should be considered the most dependable source for the proper documentation of trauma sites found on suspected abuse patients.

In the event that your institution does not have a medical photographer on the staff, there are some alternatives to acquiring good photographic recordings.

Law enforcement agencies generally have the manpower and equipment necessary to record personal injuries and evidence, and are usually very cooperative when asked to provide this assistance when the case involves an investigation of child abuse.

The hospital might consider retaining the services of a commercial photographer for an on-call fee basis. Some photographic agencies specialize in medicolegal photographic documentation. Either of these alternative sources may be found by contacting your local bar association.

Many emergency departments are equipped with a photographic system such as a point-and-shoot, totally automatic 35-mm camera, or a Polaroid instant camera with close-up attachments. Colposcopic recording devices are also being used in the emergency department; they are especially useful in photographing extra- and intravaginal or rectal injuries.

EQUIPMENT

Medical photographers prefer to use 35-mm, single lens reflex (SLR) cameras with a variety of interchangeable lenses and an assortment of studio and portable electronic flash units. Many show a preference towards one of the special 35-mm medical camera systems that come equipped with a variable focus telephoto/macro (close-up) lens and a built-in, autoexposure ring flash.

For the amateur, there is a plentiful selection of inexpensive, nearly foolproof point-and-shoot, fully automatic 35-mm cameras. Used in conjunction with a fine grain color film, these simple cameras can be very effective in documenting trauma patients. There are drawbacks, however, should an emergency team decide to equip itself with one of these cameras.

The lack of accurate and variable focusing capabilities greatly limits the photographer's need to faithfully and efficiently record a standard series of court photos. Automatic cameras that lack the ability to accept interchangeable lenses can distort the physical appearance of the face when they are used at their closest focusing distance (usually 3 ft).

Not to be forgotten are the 60-second picture developing cameras that may prove very effective in securing proof of trauma on a patient who needs immediate medical intervention. A second set of more accurately defined 35-mm photos may be taken after the patient has been stabilized.

It may be economical to document abused patients on videotape. As a whole, videotape offers an instant view of the child's overall appearance. Preferably, the videotape recorder used should have auto white balance, auto focus, auto exposure, and macro focus capabilities. Blank videotapes cost less than a roll of film and can be easily displayed in the courtroom. When using a videotape recorder in the documentation process, it is advisable to eliminate the audio during the video recording. This can be done by inserting a mini plug adaptor into the external microphone jack, thereby disabling the recorder's internal audio pickup.

The most adaptable system to use would be either the 35-mm SLR camera with interchangeable lenses and an internal light meter that offers manual and autoexposure readings, or a 35-mm SLR medical camera. These specialized cameras are expensive but offer such features as a built-in motor drive, automatic flash exposure, and the ability to close focus while keeping a fair distance between the photographer and the patient (Table 34-1).

A typical SLR outfit would consist of a camera body and an 80-mm or 105-mm telephoto lens with macro focus for use

Table 34-1. Some Recommendations for Purchase of Photo/Video Equipment

Point-and-shoot automatics with macro focus and flash
    Fuji D400
        Under $200.00
    Minolta Freedom Tele
        Under $200.00
    Pentax IQ Zoom 105
        Under $300.00
    Olympus Infinity Super Zoom 330
        Under $300.00

Single lens reflex auto exposure, auto flash, interchangeable lenses
    Minolta X-370N body with Vivitar, 28–70-mm macro zoom lens and Vivitar 550FD flash
        Under $400.00
    Pentax K1000 body with Vivitar, 28–70-mm macro zoom lens and Vivitar 550 FD flash
        Under $350.00

Specialized medical cameras
    Contax/Yashica eye system with noninterchangeable 55-mm macro lens, built-in auto exposure ring flash and motor winder
        Under $800.00

Contax/Yashica 100 DX medical kit with interchangeable 100-mm macro lens, built-in auto ring flash motor drive and D/C power pack
    Under $1700.00

Lester Dine Inc. Medical System, modified Nikon N2000 body with 105-mm macro lens and both a point light source and ring flash
    Under $1000.00

60-second print only cameras
    Polaroid Impulse Auto focus camera
        Under $80.00
    Polaroid Spectra II System, Autofocus
        Under $100.00

VHS camcorders
    Look for features such as low Lux, auto exposure and focus and a flying erase head. As most camcorders are produced by four companies, try to select one that has a familiar trade name
        Under $1000.00

in photographing the subject so as to provide distortion-free pictures of the face. The macro feature will also enable you to then shoot a close-up view of the area without switching lenses. A 50-mm macro lens should be acquired to document larger areas of trauma, as in the case of a full-body view.

LIGHTING

For accuracy and definition, the subject must be properly lighted. There are two primary ways to illuminate the exposure: (1) a camera-mounted auto exposure electronic flash or (2) standard ceiling or floor-mounted speed lights.

Flash on camera lighting can be somewhat effective when used correctly. Exposures should be bracketed, and the flash should have a swivel and tilt head provision for use in bouncing the light off neutrally colored surfaces. This feature allows the photographer to use the macro lens for close-ups while avoiding light fall-off or glare from the patient's skin. Bounce light provides soft, even lighting with no harsh shadows. A drawback to bounce flash is that this light must travel to the ceiling, fall over the subject, and finally be reflected from the subject to the film. Some compensation must be made on the camera to correct for the loss of light. The result is that the lens aperture must be opened from one to three F stops. This effectively lessens the degree of depth of field (sharpness). Correct illumination of trauma sites is very important. It can mean success or failure in proper photographic documentation. Lighting techniques should be adjusted to the type of injury. Reflectivity of the surface, the variability of skin color, and the degree of texture must all be considered when positioning your flash or series of flashes in preparation for actual photography.

If incorrect lighting is used, it may exaggerate, wash out, or conceal in shadow an area of importance. Shoe-mounted flash units tend to throw a shadow across contours and also create hot spots or washed out areas nearest to the camera (Fig. 34-1A).

Studio lighting usually consists of three or four flash units mounted on movable stands. This type of lighting offers the most control over shadows and texture and is most effective in giving the photograph a three-dimensional appearance. The studio lights should be positioned coaxially at a 45-degree angle to the subject. This will display the patient under even illumination, thereby delineating extremes of light and dark (Fig. 34-1B). Should a highly reflective area be encountered such as a keloid, fresh abrasion, or an area coated with emollient, the lights should be repositioned or the camera should be moved so that a lessening of reflection can be observed.

If the patient must be photographed away from the studio, a camera with a built-in ring flash will provide the most accurate illumination (Fig. 34-1C). Regardless of which lighting technique is chosen, a series of test photos should be tried using a coworker. This will help to establish the working parameters of the equipment. Always carry an extra set of flash batteries when on location. Whenever possible, photographs should be taken against a neutral colored, clutter free background.

FILM

A medium speed (ISO-200), color slide or negative film should be used to record the patient. Black and white film should never be used because of its inability to accurately delineate minor differences in flesh tones.

For reasons of confidentiality, the film should be processed by a well established local vendor or at your institution's in-house photography department. Unexposed film should be kept cool and dry and used before the expiration date. Film stored in a refrigerator should be left in the carton for a period of 2 or 3 hours before it is loaded into the camera. To avoid any color shift on exposed film, it should be developed as soon as possible. After processing, the slides, negatives, and prints should be kept in a secured file area that is cool, dry, and free of pollution.

LENSES

A facial photograph should always be included as part of the photographic record whether or not there is visible facial trauma. This establishes an identity link, and the subsequent areas of proof are recorded on the roll of film.

Essentially, a telephoto lens with a focal length of 80 to 105 mm should be employed for facial identification photos. This enables the photographer to maximize the image on film and to avoid any distortion of features owing to curvature of optics in relation to distance from the patient (Fig. 34-2A). If a facial photo is taken with a standard 50-mm focal length lens at close range, the resulting image will be distorted to the point where the face could be falsely represented as being edematous (Fig. 34-2B).

If the patient exhibits injuries on sev-

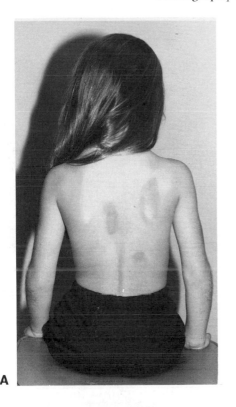

A

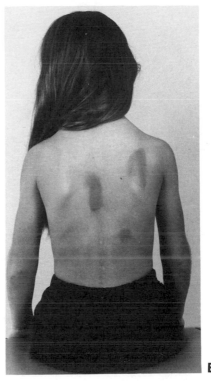

B

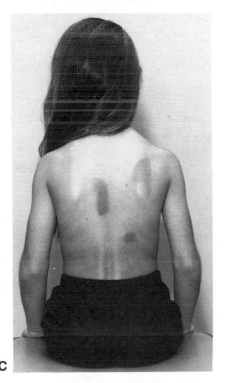

C

Fig. 34-1. (**A**) Incorrect lighting causing washed out areas nearest to the camera. (**B**) Use of studio lighting to delineate extremes of light and dark. (**C**) Accurate illumination from a camera with a built-in ring flash.

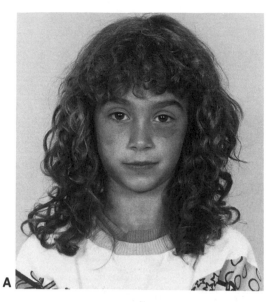 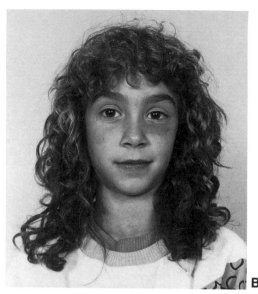

Fig. 34-2. (A) Facial identification photograph taken with a telephoto lens with a focal length of 80 to 105 mm. **(B)** Distortion caused by taking a facial identification photo at close range with a standard 50-mm focal length lens.

eral areas of the body, a full posteroanterior, anteroposterior, or lateral view should be photographed using a multifunctional 50-mm, close-up (macro) lens. The areas of trauma should then be isolated by closer focusing with the macro lens. Two close-up views might be advisable at this point, a picture of the site that includes an anatomic landmark (Fig. 34-3A) and an even closer one concentrating on the color, texture, and pattern of the injury (Fig. 34-3B), if needed. An adhesive centimeter scale should be applied near the close-up area to be photographed, especially in the case of human bite marks.

THE DECISION TO PHOTOGRAPH

The examining physician should be the one to request photography. It is important that the physician provide the photographers with a verbal and anatomic description of the areas of obvious and suspect trauma. In most cases, expedi-

ence in documenting the patient's condition is paramount. The patient should be photographed "as is" whenever possible, so that the entire scope of visible proof is recorded. Bathing and changing of attire may alter proof of physical neglect or destroy evidential connections near a suspected trauma site. In cases where injuries are fresh, consideration should be made for a second series of photographs when the trauma site reaches maturation or has been surgically repaired.

In some cases, the child exhibits prior injuries only. In that event, the photographs need not be taken immediately. Should a patient appear malnourished, as might be found in failure-to-thrive, pictures should be taken before and after medical and nutritional intervention. If dismemberment occurred during an abuse episode or surgical removal of any body part is necessary, the affected specimen and connecting anatomy should also be photographed.

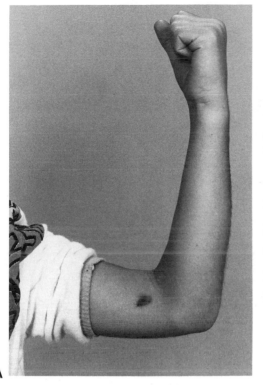
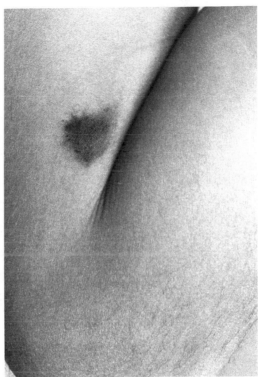

A

B

Fig. 34-3. (A) Photograph of the trauma site that includes an anatomic landmark. (B) A close-up photograph, concentrating on the color, texture, and pattern of the injury.

If your hospital has a medical photographer on staff or if you have established a contract with an outside firm, it would be wise to assign those individuals a remote pager for coverage of emergency cases. Not all reported instances of abuse and neglect are emergent. The attending physician has the option of deciding that photography can wait until the following day, especially if the patient reports to the emergency department outside of office hours and displays obvious signs of healed injuries.

PAPERWORK

A photo requisition form or an emergency department examination sheet containing an anatomic schematic diagram and standard personal data on the patient should be completed and signed by the physician. It should be given to the photographer as a guideline to the areas that need to be photographed (Fig. 34-4). The completed form should contain the patient's name, unit number, date of birth, date and time the photographs were taken, and the physician's and photographer's signatures. These forms become a legal link in the medicolegal chain of evidence. In most states, parental or guardian signatures of consent are not necessary on any of these forms, owing to the "good faith" reporting laws.

PATIENT RAPPORT AND THE PHOTO SESSION

Most often, abused patients exhibit signs of fear, confusion, anxiety, and withdrawal. The photographer should be in-

Request for SorA No. ____________

MEDICAL PHOTOGRAPHY

CHILDREN'S HOSPITAL OF BUFFALO

(please print) Form must be filled out completely

Name ______________________________
Last First

Unit No. ____________ Birth Date ____________

Diagnosis ______________________________

____

Photograph to show ______________________________

____

How patient dressed ______________________________

☐ B&W ☐ Color

Grant or Account No. ____________

Requested by ____________
Physician Signature

Remarks –

Form - 44

Addressograph Plate

Dept use only

No. ____________

Date ____________

AMOUNT CHARGED:

OUTLINE AREAS TO BE PHOTOGRAPHED

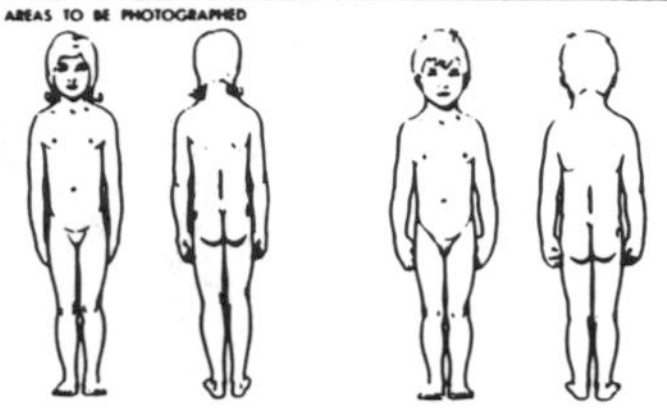

Fig. 34-4. Photo requisition form. (Courtesy of Children's Hospital of Buffalo, Buffalo, New York.)

troduced to the patient and engage in a comforting exchange of dialogue before the session begins. It is important to be supportive of the feelings expressed by the child while maintaining control of the situation. Bending at the knees and avoiding sudden moves towards the child are useful. The photographer needs to remain even tempered, and not to condescend or make any inquiry as to the nature of the injuries. Should total or partial undress of the patient be needed, the photographer should explain this in advance and let the child undress privately or request the help of an assistant or the child's guardian. An explanation of what the session will involve should be given, how the flash unit works shown, and the child given an opportunity to become familiar with the surroundings. It is a good idea to illustrate the position you would like the child to assume before beginning the photography. Try to minimize the degree of physical contact while repositioning the patient, although it is advisable to visually re-examine areas normally concealed by skin folds or clothing for any trauma sites not detected during the emergency department examination.

Infants and toddlers are usually photographed more easily if they are held in lap form by a guardian or an assistant. For full-body views, they are best controlled by being supported under the axillae. This enables them to be rotated and elongated.

For preadolescents and teenagers, allow them to undress while in the company of a person of the same sex, while the photographer waits in another room. Explain to them that the photos are confidential and become a legal document.

Avoid giving the patient a doll or toy unless it can be kept after the session is over. A smile and a toy with words of encouragement help to reinforce the medical team's aim of treatment, caring, and concern.

Two original pictures should be taken of each injury area. This allows for one set for the courts as well as one for the permanent record file.

PHOTOGRAPHS, PHOTOGRAPHERS, AND THE COURT

Very often, photographs of abused children will be ordered to be produced in court as medical evidence. It is imperative that they be clearly and accurately identified as being a true likeness of the patient described in the court's request of records. The prints or slides must be relevant to the injuries described in the medical records as noted by the examining physicians. Consequently, care should be taken in the completion of related forms, correspondence, and the identification of the finished photographs. The original photographs should be identified with the patient's last name, first name, hospital unit number, and the date and time the pictures were taken (Fig. 34-5).

Caution should be used when releasing photographic records to law enforcement officials, court representatives, or social services agents. A sensible approach would be to release them only by subpoena via the medical records department or to present them to a member of a protective or prosecutorial branch of authority when suitable identification and a letter of intent are presented for filing as proof of a records loan.

Before their introduction as evidence, the photographs may be evaluated for

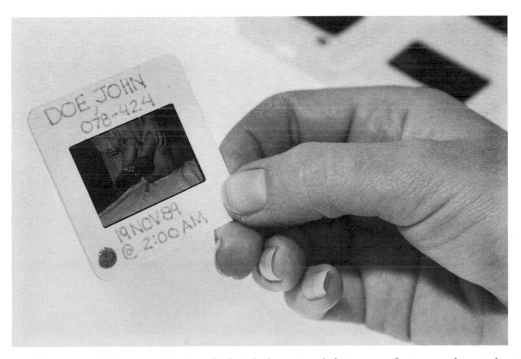

Fig. 34-5. Original photograph identified with the patient's last name, first name, hospital unit number, and the date and time the picture was taken.

their relevance to the medical examination report, their technical merit, and the availability of the photographer as a witness for verification of authenticity. The defense attorney may use this approach as a challenge of the photographic record as admissible or prejudicial evidence.

In the verification process, a witness is called to lay the foundation for the introduction of a series of pictures into evidence, usually the examining physician or the photographer. The witness is asked to provide the court with specifics, such as what prompted the request for photographs and where, who, when, and in what way the pictures were taken. The judge must be the one to decide on relevancy and admissibility of the photographs. If the judge believes that the photographs are overtly prejudicial to the case, they may be withdrawn as evidence. Denial of evidence generally results from pictures considered to be too graphic or upsetting or those of questionable quality and clarity. In cases that go to trial, there is a chance that the photographer alone may be called to offer testimony. The photographer is usually consulted by the prosecutor before a court appearance. The prosecutor will gather information regarding qualifications, experience, and recall of the case in question. Nonprofessional photographers should not claim expert witness status. To do so would leave them open to the defense attorney's attempts to discredit their testimony by asking complex, theoretical questions concerning the formulas of photo optics, chemistry, and the properties of visible light and its effect on different film types. A professional photographer's statements to the court should relate only to the photographs entered as exhibits. There should be no attempt to render any medical opinions unless the photographer is qualified, or is given permission by the judge to offer limited medical testimony. Most states allow for some financial compensation to the expert witness. Contact the disbursement officer for further information.

PHOTOGRAPHIC COSTS

The implementation of photographic documentation for child abuse and neglect patients places an additional financial burden on an institution. Some states allow this service to be underwritten through local or state agencies. The hospital is then reimbursed on a fee-for-service basis or on a retainer payment schedule. If a compensation plan of this type is available, a policy should be drafted spelling out the method for reparation from the government agency.

The establishment of photographic coverage of abused children will cause a substantial increase in the number of service requests made to the institution, increasing operational costs for film, processing, equipment purchase and upkeep, a new series of forms and photos to be handled and catalogued, as well as on-call and travel compensation to the photographer.

CONCLUSION

An administrative policy regarding child abuse photography must be written and posted in the operations manual. Anatomic outline forms should be printed and used for every child photographed. If at all possible, a medical photographer or a free-lance photographer who has experience in personal injury documentation should be used. If this proves to be financially unviable, try to arrange for continued photographic coverage through an equipped law enforcement agency. Should none of these options be available, consider purchasing a point-

and-shoot 35-mm camera for use by emergency department personnel.

Do not try to exaggerate the child's condition. Photograph the child's face for positive relational connection to subsequently photographed trauma sites. Include anatomic landmarks to establish accurately the size and location of the injury. Take at least two pictures of each area. Use an uncluttered background of a neutral color. Use color film only and be certain that the light source is balanced for the type of color film selected.

The photographer should establish an open attitude as an evidence collector. Follow the institution's policies on infection control. Above all, be sincere, understanding, and comforting to the child.

Maintain a cross-reference photo file system using archival quality storage pages, envelopes, or sleeves. Respect confidentiality of the photo files and related paperwork. Policies regarding their distribution and use should also be prepared to protect the child, photographer, and institution.

SUGGESTED READINGS

1. Cantor BJ Esq: The Photographer as an Expert Witness. Industrial Photography, October 1989
2. Cantor BJ Esq: Is it Evidence? Industrial Photography, August 1990
3. Frair J, Ardoin B: Effective Photography. Prentice-Hall, New York, 1982
4. Gill FT: Caring for Abused Children in the Emergency Room. Holistic Nursing Practice, 614:37, 1989
5. Hansell P, Lunnon RJ: Photography for the Scientist. Academic Press, New York, 1984
6. Meadow R, Mitchels B: ABCs of Child Abuse. Br Med J 229:248, 1989
7. Mittleman RE, Mittleman HS: What child abuse really looks like. A J Nurs 87:1185A, 1987
8. Rhodes AM: Identifying and reporting child abuse. Am J Maternal Child Nurs 6:399, 1987
9. Sansone SJ: Police Photography. Anderson Publishing, Cincinnati, OH, 1977
10. Scott CC: Photographic Evidence. 2nd Ed. West Publishing, St. Paul, MN, 1969

Appendix A
Interdisciplinary Glossary on Child Abuse and Neglect*

* From the U.S. Department of Health, Education, and Welfare, Office of Human Development Services, Administration for Children, Youth and Families, Children's Bureau, National Center on Child Abuse and Neglect, DHEW Publication No. (OHDS) 78–30137.

Abandonment   Act of a parent or caretaker leaving children for an excessive period of time without adequate supervision or provision for their needs. State laws vary in defining adequacy of supervision and the length of time a child may be left alone or in the care of another before abandonment is determined. The age of the child also is an important factor. In legal terminology, "abandonment cases" are suits calling for the termination of parental rights.

Abrasion   Wound in which an area of the body surface is scraped of skin or mucous membrane.

Alopecia   Absence of hair from skin areas where it normally appears; baldness.

Anorexia   Lack or loss of appetite for food.

Atrophy   Wasting away of flesh, tissue, cell, or organ.

Battered child syndrome   Term introduced in 1962 by C. Henry Kemp, M.D., in the *Journal of the American Medical Association,* in an article describing a combination of physical and other signs indicating that a child's internal and/or external injuries result from acts committed by a parent or caretaker. In some states, the battered child syndrome has been judicially recognized as an accepted medical diagnosis. Frequently, this term is misused or misunderstood as the only type of child abuse and neglect.

Bruise   (See Intradermal Hemorrhage)

Burn   Wound resulting from the application of too much heat. Burns are classified by the degree of damage caused: first degree—scorching or painful redness of the skin; second degree—formation of blisters; third degree—destruction of outer layers of the skin.

Calcification   Formation of bone. The amount of calcium deposited can indicate via radiograph the degree of healing of a broken bone or the location of previous fractures that have healed prior to the radiograph.

Callus   New bone formed during the healing process of a fracture.

Calvaria   Dome-like portion of the skull.

Cartilage   The hard connective tissue that is not bone but, in the unborn and growing child, may be the forerunner of bone before calcium is deposited.

Child development   Pattern of sequential stages of interrelated physical, psychological, and social development in the process of maturation from infancy and total dependence to adulthood and relative independence. Parents need to understand the level of maturity consistent with each stage of development and should not expect a child to display a level of maturity that the child is incapable of at a particular stage. Abusive or neglectful parents frequently impair a child's healthy growth and development because they do not understand child development or are otherwise unable to meet the child's physical, social, and psychological needs at a given stage(s) of development.

Chip fracture   (See **Fracture**)

Clotting factor   Material in the blood that causes it to coagulate. Deficiencies in clotting factors can cause profuse internal or external bleeding and/or bruising, as in the disease hemophilia. Bruises or bleeding caused by such a disease may be mistaken as abuse.

Colon   The large intestine.

Comminuted fracture   (See **Fracture**)

Compound fracture   (See **Fracture**)

Comprehensive emergency services   A community system of coordinated services available on a 24-hour basis to meet emergency needs of children and/or families in crisis. Components of a comprehensive emergency services system can include 24-hour protection services, homemaker services, crisis nurseries, family shelters, emergency foster care, outreach, and follow-up services.

Concussion   An injury of a soft structure resulting from violent shaking or jarring; usually refers to a brain concussion.

Congenital   Refers to any physical condition present at birth, regardless of its cause.

Conjunctiva   Transparent lining covering the white of the eye and eyelids. Bleeding beneath the conjunctiva can occur spontaneously or from accidental or nonaccidental injury.

Contusion   A wound producing injury to soft tissue without a break in the skin, causing bleeding into surrounding tissues.

Cortex   Outer layer of an organ or other body structure.

Cranium   The skull.

Diaphysis   The shaft of a long bone.

Differential diagnosis   The determination of which of two or more diseases or conditions a patient may be suffering from by systematically comparing and contrasting the clinical findings.

Dislocation   The displacement of a bone, usually disrupting a joint, which may accompany a fracture or may occur alone.

Distal   Far; farther from any point of reference. Opposite of proximal.

Duodenum   The first portion of the small intestine, which connects it to the stomach.

Ecchymosis   (See **Intradermal Hemorrhage**)

Edema   Swelling caused by an excessive amount of fluid in body tissue. It often follows a bump or bruise but may also be caused by allergy, malnutrition, or disease.

Encopresis   Involuntary passage of feces.

Enuresis   Involuntary passage of urine.

Epiphysis   Growth center near the end of a long bone.

Extravasated blood   Discharge or escape of blood into tissue.

Failure-to-thrive syndrome   A serious medical condition most often seen in children younger than 1 year of age. The height, weight, and motor development of a child with failure-to-thrive (FTT) syndrome fall significantly short of the average growth rates of normal children. In about 10 percent of FTT cases, there is an organic cause such as serious heart, kidney, or intestinal disease, a genetic error of metabolism, or brain damage. All other cases are a result of a disturbed parent-child relationship manifested in severe physical and emotional neglect of the child. In diagnosing FTT as child neglect, certain criteria should be considered:

1. The child's weight is below the third percentile, but substantial weight gain occurs when the child is properly nurtured, such as when hospitalized.
2. The child exhibits developmental retardation that decreases when there is adequate feeding and appropriate stimulation.
3. Medical investigation provides no evidence that disease or medical abnormality is the cause of the symptoms.
4. The child exhibits clinical signs of deprivation that decrease in a more nurturing environment.
5. There appears to be a significant environmental psychosocial disruption in the child's family.

Fontanel   The soft spots on a baby's skull where the bones of the skull have not yet fused.

Fracture   A broken bone, which is one of the most common injuries found among battered children. The fracture may occur in several ways.

Chip fracture: A small piece of bone is flaked from the major part of the bone.
Comminuted fracture: Bone is crushed or broken into a number of pieces.
Compound fracture: Fragment(s) of broken bone protrude through the skin, causing a wound.
Simple fracture: Bone breaks without wounding the surrounding tissue.
Spiral fracture: Twisting causes the line of the fracture to encircle the bone like a spiral staircase.
Torus fracture: A folding, bulging, or buckling fracture.

Frontal   Referring to the front of the head; the forehead.

Funduscopic examination   Ophthalmic examination to determine if irregularities or internal injuries to the eye exist.

Gluteal   Related to the buttocks, which are made up of the large gluteus maximus muscles.

Gonorrhea   (See **Venereal disease**)

Hematemesis   Vomiting of blood from the stomach, often resulting from internal injuries.

Hematoma   A swelling caused by a collection of blood in an enclosed space, such as under the skin or the skull.

Hematuria   Blood in the urine.

Hemophilia   Hereditary blood clotting disorder characterized by spontaneous or traumatic internal and external bleeding and bruising.

Hemoptysis   Spitting or coughing blood from the windpipe or lungs.

Hemorrhage   The escape of blood from the vessels; bleeding.

Hyperactive   More active than is considered normal.

Hyperthermia   Condition of high body temperature.

Hyphema   Hemorrhage within the anterior chamber of the eye, often appearing as a bloodshot eye. The cause could be a blow to the head or violent shaking.

Hypoactive   Less active than is considered normal.

Hypothermia   Condition of low body temperature.

Ileum   Final portion of the small intestine, which connects with the colon.

Impetigo   A highly contagious, rapidly spreading skull disorder that occurs principally in infants and young children. The disease, characterized by red blisters, may be an indicator of neglect and poor living conditions.

Infanticide   The killing of an infant(s). Until modern times, infanticide was an accepted method of population control. It often took the form of abandonment. A few primitive cultures still practice infanticide.

Intradermal hemorrhage   Bleeding within the skin; bruise. Bruises are common injuries exhibited by battered children, and are usually classified by size.

> *Petechiae:* Very smll bruises caused by broken capillaries. Petechiae may be traumatic in nature or may be caused by clotting disorders.
> *Purpura:* Petechiae occurring in groups, or a small bruise (up to 1 cm in diameter).
> *Ecchymosis:* Larger bruise.

Jejunum   Middle portion of the small intestine between the duodenum and the ileum.

Laboratory tests   Routine medical tests used to aid diagnosis. The following tests are particularly pertinent to child abuse.

> *Partial thromboplastin time* (PTT): Measures clotting factors in the blood.
> *Prothrombin time* (PT): Measures clotting factors in the blood.
> *Urinalysis:* Examination of urine for sugar, protein, blood, etc.
> *Complete blood count* (CBC): Measure and analysis of red and white blood cells.
> *Rumpel-Leede (tourniquet) test:* Measures fragility of capillaries and/or bruisability.

Laceration   A jagged cut or wound.

Lateral   Toward the side.

Long bone   General term applied to the bones of the leg or the arm.

Lumbar   Pertaining to the part of the back and sides between the lowest ribs and the pelvis.

Malnutrition   Failure to receive adequate nourishment. Often exhibited in a neglected child, malnutrition may be caused by inadequate diet (either lack of food or insufficient amounts of needed vitamins, etc.) or by a disease or other abnormal condition affecting the body's ability to properly process ingested foods.

Maltreatment   Actions that are abusive, neglectful, or otherwise threatening to a child's welfare. Frequently used as a general term for child abuse and neglect.

Marasmus A form of protein/calorie malnutrition occurring in infants and children. It is characterized by retarded growth and progressive wasting of fat and muscle, but it is usually accompanied by the retention of appetite and mental alertness.

Medial Toward the middle or midline.

Menkes kinky hair syndrome Rare, inherited disease resulting in brittle bones and, eventually, death. It is found in infants and, because of the great number of fractures that may be exhibited, can be mistaken for child abuse.

Mesentery Membrane attaching various organs to the body wall.

Metabolism The sum of all physical and chemical processes that maintain the life of an organism.

Metaphysis Wider part of a long bone between the end and the shaft.

Mongolian spots A type of birthmark that can appear anywhere on a child's body, most frequently on the lower back. These dark spots usually fade by age 5. They can be mistaken for bruises.

Moribund Dying or near death.

Occipital Referring to the back of the head.

Ossification Formation of bone.

Osteogenesis imperfecta An inherited condition in which the bones are abnormally brittle and subject to fractures, and that may be mistakenly diagnosed as the result of child abuse.

Pathognomonic A sign or symptom specifically distinctive or characteristic of a disease or condition from which a diagnosis may be made.

Perinatal Around the time of birth, both immediately before and after.

Periosteal elevation The ripping or tearing of the surface layer of a bone (periosteum) and the resultant hemorrhage, occurring when a bone is broken.

Peritonitis Inflammation of the membrane lining the abdomen (peritoneum); caused by infection.

Petechiae (See **Intradermal hemorrhage**)

Polyphagia Excessive or voracious eating.

Proximal Near; closer to any point of reference; opposed to distal.

Purpura (See **Intradermal hemorrhage**)

Radiolucent Permitting the passage of x-rays without leaving a shadow on the film. Soft tissues are radiolucent; bones are not.

Rarefaction Loss of density. On x-ray film, an area of bone that appears lighter than normal is in a state of rarefaction, indicating a loss of calcium.

Retina Inside lining of the eye. Injury to the head can cause bleeding or detachment of the retina, possibly causing blindness.

Rickets Condition caused by a deficiency of vitamin D, which disturbs the normal development of bones.

Sacral area Lower part of the back.

Scurvy Condition caused by a deficiency of vitamin C (ascorbic acid) and characterized by weakness, anemia, spongy gums, and other symptoms.

Seizures Uncontrollable muscular contractions, usually alternating with muscular relaxation and generally accompanied by unconsciousness. Seizures, which vary in intensity and length of occurrence, are the result of some brain irritation that has been caused by disease, inherited condition, fever, tumor, vitamin deficiency, or head injury.

Sequelae Aftereffects; usually medical events following an injury or disease. In child abuse, sequelae is used to refer to psychological consequences of abusive acts and the perpetuation of abusive behavior across generations, as well as specific aftereffects such as brain damage, speech impairment, and impaired physical and/or psychological growth.

Sexually transmitted disease (See **Venereal disease**)

Simple fracture (See **Fracture**)

Skeletal survey   A series of radiographs that show all bones of the body. Such a survey should be done in all cases of suspected abuse to locate any old, as well as new, fractures that may exist.

Spiral fracture   (See **Fracture**)

Subdural hematoma   A common symptom of abused children, consisting of a collection of blood beneath the outermost membrane covering the brain and spinal cord. The hematoma may be caused by a blow to the head or by violently shaking a baby or small child. (See also **Whiplash-shaken infant syndrome**)

Sudden infant death syndrome   A condition that can be confused with child abuse, sudden infant death syndrome (SIDS) affects infants aged 2 weeks to 2 years, but usually occurs in a child younger than 6 months of age. In SIDS, a child who has been healthy except for a minor respiratory infection is found dead, often with bloody, frothy material in the mouth. The cause of SIDS is not fully understood. The confusion with child abuse results from the bloody sputum and occasional facial bruises that accompany the syndrome. However, SIDS parents rarely display the guarded or defensive behavior of many abusive parents.

Suture

1. A type of immovable joint in which the connecting surfaces of the bones are closely united, as in the skull.
2. The stitches made by a physician that close a wound.

Syphilis   (See **Venereal disease**)

Temporal   Referring to the side of the head.

Torus fracture   (See **Fracture**)

Trabecula   A general term for a supporting or anchoring strand of tissue.

Trauma   An internal or external injury or wound brought about by an outside force. Usually, trauma means injury by violence, but it may also apply to the wound caused by any surgical procedure. Trauma may be caused accidentally or, as in a case of physical abuse, nonaccidentally. Trauma is also a term applied to psychological discomfort or symptoms resulting from an emotional shock or painful experience.

Turgor   Condition of being swollen and congested. This can refer to normal or other fullness.

Vascular   Of the blood vessels.

Venereal disease   Any disease transmitted by sexual contact. The two most common forms of venereal disease are gonorrhea and syphilis. Presence of a venereal disease in a child may indicate that the mother was infected with the disease during pregnancy, or it may be evidence of sexual abuse.

Whiplash-shaken infant syndrome   Injury to an infant or child that results from the child having been shaken, usually as a misguided means of discipline. The most common symptoms, which can be inflicted by seemingly harmless shakings, are bleeding and/or detached retinas and other bleeding inside the head. Repeated instances of shaking and resultant injuries may eventually cause mental and developmental disabilities. (See also **Subdural hematoma**)

Work-up   Study of a patient, often in a hospital, in order to provide information for diagnosis. A full work-up includes past medical and family histories, present condition and symptoms, laboratory, and, possibly, radiographic studies.

X-rays   Photographs made by means of x-rays. X-rays are one of the most important tools available to physicians in the diagnosis of physical child abuse or battering. With x-rays, or radiologic examinations, physicians can observe not only the current bone injuries of a child, but also any past injuries that may exist in various stages of healing. This historical information contributes significantly to the assessment of a suspected case of child abuse. Radiologic examination is also essential to distinguish organic diseases that may cause bone breakage from physical child abuse.

Appendix B
State Law Summary

Table B-1. Comparative Criminal Law

States	Special Hearsay Exceptions	Videotaped Statements/ Interviews	Closed-Circuit Television Testimony	Videotaped Testimony	Speedy Disposition	Coordination and Cooperation of Involved Agencies	Leading Questions Permitted	Anatomically Correct Dolls Permitted	Support Persons	Competent to Testify Without Prior Qualifications	Courtroom Closure
Alabama	X		X	X	X	X	X	X		X	
Alaska	X			X							X
Arizona	X	X	X	X						X	
Arkansas	X			X	X	X			X	X	
California	X		X	X	X	X	X		X	X	X
Colorado	X			X	X	X					
Connecticut			X	X						X	
Delaware				X	X	X			X		
DC											
Florida	X		X	X	X	X					X
Georgia	X		X								X
Hawaii		X	X						X		
Idaho	X		X						X		
Illinois	X					X					X
Indiana	X	X	X	X	X	X					
Iowa		X	X	X	X					X	
Kansas	X	X	X	X		X					
Kentucky	X	X	X	X	X						
Louisiana		X	X	X							X
Maine	X										
Maryland			X	X		X					
Massachusetts			X			X					X
Michigan					X						
Minnesota	X	X	X	X	X	X			X		X

State											
Mississippi	X			X		X				X	X
Missouri	X	X		X		X				X	X
Montana				X		X				X	
Nebraska				X		X				X	X
Nevada	X			X	X	X				X	X
New Hampshire			X	X	X						
New Jersey			X			X		X			
New Mexico				X		X				X	
New York	X		X	X	X	X		X	X		
North Carolina						X					
North Dakota			X	X		X					
Ohio	X		X	X		X				X	
Oklahoma	X	X	X	X				X		X	
Oregon											
Pennsylvania	X		X	X		X		X		X	
Rhode Island	X		X	X	X	X			X		X
South Carolina			X	X		X					X
South Dakota	X		X	X		X				X	X
Tennessee	X	X	X	X		X					
Texas	X	X	X	X		X					
Utah	X	X	X	X		X				X	
Vermont	X	X	X	X		X			X		
Virginia						X					
Washington	X								X		
West Virginia					X	X		X		X	
Wisconsin		X	X	X		X				X	X
Wyoming						X				X	X
Total	25	14	25	33	15	30	2	5	10	19	11

(From the American Prosecutors Research Institute, National Center for Prosecution of Child Abuse, Fairfax, VA, with permission.)

Table B-2. Comparative Civil Laws

State	Penalty Fine/ Imprisonment for Failure to Report	Immunity to Reporters	Physician- Patient Privilege Abrogated	Photographs can be Taken by Physicians as Evidence	Child can be Taken Into Protective Custody by Physician
Alabama	X	X	X	—	X
Alaska	X	X	X	X	—
Arizona	X	X	X	X	—
Arkansas	X	X	X	X	X
California	X	X	X	—	X
Colorado	X (petty offense)	X	X	X	X[a]
Connecticut	X	X	—	—	X
Delaware	X	X	X	X	—
DC	X	X	X	X	—
Florida	X	X	X	X	—
Georgia	X	X	—	X	—
Hawaii	X	X	X	—	—
Idaho	—	X	X	—	X
Illinois	—	X	X	X	—
Indiana	X	X	—	X	X
Iowa	X	X	X	X	X
Kansas	X	X	X	X	—
Kentucky	X	X	X	X	X
Louisiana	X	X	X	—	—
Maine	X	X	X	X	—
Maryland	—	X	X	—	—
Massachusetts	X	X	—	—	X[b]
Michigan	X	X	X	X	—
Minnesota	X	X	X	—	—
Mississippi	—	X	X	—	—

State					
Missouri	X	X	X	X	X
Montana	X	X	X	X	X
Nebraska	X	X	—	—	—
Nevada	X	X	X	—	—
New Hampshire	X	X	X[c]	—	X
New Jersey	X	X	—	X	—
New Mexico	X	X	X	—	X
New York	X	X	X	X	—
North Carolina	—	X	X	X[c]	X
North Dakota	X	X	X	X	—
Ohio	X	X	X	—	—
Oklahoma	X	X	X	—	X
Oregon	X	X	X	X	X
Pennsylvania	X	X	X	X	—
Rhode Island	X	X	X	X	X
South Carolina	X	X	X	—	—
South Dakota	X	X	X	—	X
Tennessee	X	X	X	—	—
Texas	X	X	X	X	—
Utah	X	X	X	X	X
Vermont	X	—	X	—	—
Virginia	X	X	X	X	X
Washington	X	X	X	X	—
West Virginia	X	X	X	—	X
Wisconsin	X	X	X	—	—
Wyoming	—	X	X	—	X

[a] With call to court.
[b] With call to hospital supervisor.
[c] With court order.

(From AMA Diagnostic and Treatment Guidelines Concerning Child Abuse and Neglect. American Medical Association, Chicago, 1985, as adapted from Child Abuse Laws File. NCCAN, Washington, D.C., 1984, with permission.)

Table B-3. Mandated Reporters

States	Teachers	Other School Personnel	Social Service Workers	Law Enforcement Officers	Peace Officers	Police Officers	Probation Officers	Parole Officers	Religious Healing Practitioners	Child Care Institution Workers	Clergymen	Attorneys
Alabama	X	X	X	X	X	—	—	—	—	X	—	—
Alaska	X	—	X	—	X	—	—	—	X	—	—	—
Arizona	X	X	X	—	X	—	—	—	—	X	—	—
Arkansas	X	X	X	X	X	—	—	—	—	X	—	—
California	X	X	X	—	X	—	X	—	X	X	X	—
Colorado	X	X	X	—	—	—	—	—	X	X	X	—
Connecticut	X	X	X	—	—	X	—	—	—	X	—	—
Delaware	X	X	X	—	—	—	—	—	—	X	X	—
DC	X	X	X	X	—	—	—	—	—	X	—	—
Florida	X	—	X	—	—	—	—	—	—	—	—	—
Georgia	X	X	X	X	—	—	—	—	—	X	—	—
Hawaii	X	—	X	—	—	—	—	—	—	—	—	—
Idaho	X	—	X	—	—	—	—	—	—	X	—	—
Illinois	X	X	X	X	—	—	—	—	X	X	—	—
Indiana	Any person must report											
Iowa	X	X	X	—	X	—	—	—	—	X	—	—
Kansas	X	X	X	X	X	—	—	—	—	—	—	—
Kentucky	X	X	X	—	X	—	—	—	—	X	—	—
Louisiana	X	—	X	—	—	—	—	—	—	—	—	—
Maine	X	X	X	X	—	—	—	—	X	X	—	—
Maryland	X	X	X	X	—	X	X	X	—	—	—	—
Massachusetts	X	X	X	—	—	X	—	—	—	X	—	—
Michigan	X	X	X	X	—	—	—	—	—	X	—	—
Minnesota	X	X	X	X	—	—	—	—	—	X	—	—

State													
Mississippi	X	X	X	—	—	—	—	—	X	—	X	—	—
Missouri	X	X	X	X	X	X	X	X	X	X	X	X	X
Montana	X	—	X	—	—	—	—	—	X	—	—	—	—
Nebraska	X	X	X	—	—	—	—	—	X	—	X	—	X
Nevada	X	X	X	—	—	—	—	X	X	X	X	X	X
New Hampshire	X	X	X	—	—	—	X	X	X	X	X	X	X
New Jersey	Any person must report												
New Mexico	X	X	X	—	—	—	—	—	—	—	—	—	—
New York	—	X	X	X	—	—	—	X	X	X	X	—	—
North Carolina	X	X	X	—	—	—	—	X	X	—	X	—	—
North Dakota	X	X	X	X	X	—	—	X	X	X	X	—	—
Ohio	X	X	X	—	—	—	—	X	X	X	X	—	X
Oklahoma	—	—	—	—	—	—	—	—	—	—	—	—	—
Oregon	X	X	—	X	—	—	—	X	X	X	X	X	X
Pennsylvania	X	X	X	X	X	—	—	X	X	X	X	—	—
Rhode Island	Any person must report												
South Carolina	X	X	X	X	—	—	—	X	X	X	X	—	—
South Dakota	X	X	X	X	—	—	—	—	—	—	—	—	—
Tennessee	Any person must report												
Texas	Any person must report												
Utah	Any person must report												
Vermont	—	—	—	X	X	—	—	—	—	—	—	—	—
Virginia	X	X	X	—	—	X	—	X	X	X	X	—	—
Washington	X	X	—	—	—	—	—	X	X	X	X	X	X
West Virginia	X	X	X	X	X	—	—	X	X	X	X	X	X
Wisconsin	X	X	X	—	X	—	—	—	—	—	—	—	—
Wyoming	Any person must report												

(From AMA Diagnostic and Treatment Guidelines Concerning Child Abuse and Neglect. American Medical Association, Chicago, 1985, as adapted from Child Abuse Laws File. NCCAN, Washington, D.C., 1984, with permission.)

Table B-4.   State Reporting Agencies

Alabama
Alabama Department of Pensions and
  Security
64 North Union Street
Montgomery, Alabama 36130

Reports made to county 24-hour
emergency telephone services.

Alaska
Department of Health and Social Services
Division of Family and Youth Services
Pouch H-05
Juneau, Alaska 99811

Reports made to Department of Health
and Social Services field offices.

American Samoa
Government of American Samoa
Office of the Attorney General
Pago Pago, American Samoa 96799

Reports made to Department of Medical
Services.

Arizona
Department of Economic Security
P.O. Box 6123
Phoenix, Arizona 85005

Reports made to Department of Economic
Security local offices.

Arkansas
Arkansas Department of Human Services
Social Services Division
P.O. Box 1437
Little Rock, Arkansas 72203

Reports made to statewide toll-free
hotline (800) 482-5964.

California
Department of Social Services
714-744 P Street
Sacramento, California 95814

Reports made to county departments of
welfare and Central Registry of Child
Abuse—(916) 445-7546—maintained by
the Department of Justice.

Colorado
Department of Social Services
1575 Sherman Street
Denver, Colorado 80203

Reports made to county departments of
social services.

Connecticut
Connecticut Department of Children and
  Youth Services
Division of Children and Youth Services
170 Sigourney Street
Hartford, Connecticut 06105

Reports made to (800) 842-2288.

Delaware
Delaware Department of Health and
  Social Services
Division of Social Services
P.O. Box 309
Wilmington, Delaware 19899

Reports made to statewide toll-free
reporting hotline (800) 292-9582.

District of Columbia
Disrict of Columbia Department of
  Human Services
Commission on Social Services
Family Services Administration
Child Protective Services Division
First and I Streets, S.W.
Washington, DC 20024

Reports made to (202) 727-0995.

Florida
Florida Department of Health and
  Rehabilitative Services
1317 Winewood Boulevard
Tallahassee, Florida 32301

Reports made to (800) 342-9152.

Georgia
Georgia Department of Human Resources
47 Trinity Avenue, S.W.
Atlanta, Georgia 30334

Reports made to county departments of
family and children services.

Guam
Child Welfare Services
Child Protective Services
P.O. Box 2816
Agana, Guam 96910

Reports made to state child protective
services agency at 646-8417.

Continued

Table B-4. *(continued)*

Hawaii
Department of Social Services and
Housing
Public Welfare Division
Family and Children's Services
P.O. Box 339
Honolulu, Hawaii 96809
Reports made to hotline operated by
Kapiolani-Children's Medical Center on
Oahu and to branch offices of the Division
of Hawaii, Maui, Kauai, Molokai.

Idaho
Department of Health and Welfare
Child Protection Division of Welfare
Statehouse
Boise, Idaho 83702
Reports made to Department of Health
and Welfare regional offices.

Illinois
Illinois Department of Children and
Family Services
State Administrative Offices
1 North Old State Capitol Plaza
Springfield, Illinois 62706
Reports made to (800) 25-ABUSE.

Indiana
Indiana Department of Public Welfare
Division of Child Welfare–Social Services
141 West Meridian Street, Sixth Floor
Indianapolis, Indiana 46225
Reports made to county departments of
public welfare.

Iowa
Iowa Department of Social Services
Division of Community Programs
Hoover State Office Building, Fifth Floor
Des Moines, Iowa 50319
Reports made to legally mandated toll-free
reporting hotline (800) 362-2178.

Kansas
Kansas Department of Social and
Rehabilitative Services
Division of Social Services
Child Protection and Family Services
Section
Smith-Wilson Building
2700 West Sixth
Topeka, Kansas 66606
Reports made to Department of Social and
Rehabilitative Services area offices.

Kentucky
Kentucky Department for Human
Resources
275 East Main Street
Frankfort, Kentucky 40621
Reports made to county offices within four
regions of the state.

Louisiana
Louisiana Department of Health and
Human Resources
Office of Human Development
Baton Rouge, Louisiana 70804
Reports made to parish protective service
units.

Maine
Maine Department of Human Services
Human Services Building
Augusta, Maine 04333
Reports made to regional office or to state
agency at (800) 452-1999.

Maryland
Maryland Department of Human
Resources
Social Services Administration
300 West Preston Street
Baltimore, Maryland 21201
Reports made to county departments of
social services or to local law enforcement
agencies.

Massachusetts
Massachusetts Department of Social
Services
Protective Services
150 Causeway Street
Boston, Massachusetts 02114
Reports made to regional offices.

Michigan
Michigan Department of Social Services
300 South Capitol Avenue
Lansing, Michigan 48926
Reports made to county departments of
social welfare.

Minnesota
Minnesota Department of Public Welfare
Centennial Office Building
St. Paul, Minnesota 55155
Reports made to county departments of
public welfare.

Continued

Table B-4. (*continued*)

Mississippi
Mississippi Department of Public Welfare
Division of Social Services
P.O. Box 352
Jackson, Mississippi 39216
Reports made to (800) 222-8000.

Missouri
Missouri Department of Social Services
Division of Family Services
Broadway Building
Jefferson City, Missouri 65101
Reports made to (800) 392-3738.

Montana
Department of Social and Rehabilitative
Services
Social Services Bureau
P.O. Box 4210
Helena, Montana 59601
Reports made to county departments of
social and rehabilitative services.

Nebraska
Nebraska Department of Public Welfare
301 Centennial Mall South, Fifth Floor
Lincoln, Nebraska 68509
Reports made to local law enforcement
agencies or to county divisions of public
welfare.

Nevada
Department of Human Resources
Division of Welfare
251 Jeanell Drive
Carson City, Nevada 89710
Reports made to Division of Welfare local
offices.

New Hampshire
New Hampshire Department of Health
and Welfare
Division of Welfare
Bureau of Child and Family Services
Hazen Drive
Concord, New Hampshire 03301
Reports made to Division of Welfare
district offices.

New Jersey
New Jersey Division of Youth and Family
Services
P.O. Box 510
1 South Montgomery Street
Trenton, New Jersey 08625
Reports made to (800) 792-8610. District
offices also provide 24-hour telephone
service.

New Mexico
New Mexico Department of Human
Services
P.O. Box 2348
Sante Fe, New Mexico 87503
Reports made to county social services
offices or to (800) 432-6217.

New York
New York Department of Social Services
Child Protective Services
40 North Pearl Street
Albany, New York 12207
Reports made to (800) 342-3720 or to
district offices.

North Carolina
North Carolina Department of Human
Resources
Division of Social Services
325 North Salisbury Street
Raleigh, North Carolina 27611
Reports made to county departments of
social services.

North Dakota
North Dakota Department of Human
Services
Social Services Division
Children and Family Services Unit
Child Abuse and Neglect Program
Russel Building, Highway 83 North
Bismarck, North Dakota 58505
Reports made to Board of Social Services
area offices and to 24-hour reporting
services provided by human services
centers.

Ohio
Ohio Department of Public Welfare
Bureau of Children's Services
30 East Broad Street
Columbus, Ohio 43215
Reports made to county department of
public welfare.

Oklahoma
Oklahoma Department of Institutions,
Social and Rehabilitative Services
Division of Social Services
P.O. Box 25352
Oklahoma City, Oklahoma 73125
Reports made to (800) 522-3511.

Continued

Table B-4. *(continued)*

Oregon
Department of Human Resources
Children's Services Division
Protective Services
509 Public Services Building
Salem, Oregon 97310

Reports made to local Children's Services
Division offices and to (503) 378-3016.

Pennsylvania
Pennsylvania Department of Public
    Welfare
Office of Children, Youth and Families
Bureau of Family and Community
    Programs
1514 North Second Street
Harrisburg, Pennsylvania 17102

Reports made to toll-free CHILDLINE
(800) 932-0313.

Rhode Island
Rhode Island Department for Children
    and Their Families
610 Mt. Pleasant Avenue
Providence, Rhode Island 02908

Reports made to state agency child
protective services unit at (800) 662-5100
or to district offices.

South Carolina
South Carolina Department of Social
    Services
P.O. Box 1520
Columbia, South Carolina 29202

Reports made to county departments of
social services.

South Dakota
Department of Social Services
Office of Children, Youth and Family
    Services
Richard F. Kneip Building
Pierre, South Dakota 57501

Reports made to local offices.

Tennessee
Tennessee Department of Human
    Services
State Office Building
Room 410
Nashville, Tennessee 37219

Reports made to county departments of
human services.

Texas
Texas Department of Human Resources
Protective Services for Children Branch
P.O. Box 2960
Austin, Texas 78701

Reports made to (800) 252-5400.

Utah
Department of Social Services
Division of Family Services
150 West North Temple, Room 370
Salt Lake City, Utah 84103

Reports made to Division of Family
Services district offices.

Vermont
Vermont Department of Social and
    Rehabilitative Services
Social Services Division
103 South Main Street
Waterbury, Vermont 05676

Reports made to state agency at (802) 828-
3422 or to district offices (24-hour
services).

Virgin Islands
Virgin Islands Department of Social
    Welfare
Division of Social Services
P.O. Box 500
Charlotte Amalie
St. Thomas, Virgin Islands 00801

Reports made to Division of Social
Services.

Virginia
Virginia Department of Welfare
Bureau of Family and Community
    Programs
Blair Building
8007 Discovery Drive
Richmond, Virginia 23288

Reports made to (800) 552-7096 in
Virginia and (804) 281-9081 outside the
state.

Washington
Department of Social and Health Services
Community Services Division
Child Protective Services
Mail Stop OB 41-D
Olympia, Washington 98504

Reports made to local social and health
services offices.

Continued

Table B-4. *(continued)*

West Virginia
  Department of Welfare
  Division of Social Services
  Child Protective Services
  State Office Building
  1900 Washington Street E.
  Charleston, West Virginia 25305

  Reports made to (800) 352-6513.

Wisconsin
  Wisconsin Department of Health and
    Social Services
  Division of Community Services
  1 West Wilson Street
  Madison, Wisconsin 53702

  Reports made to county social services
  offices.

Wyoming
  Department of Health and Social Services
  Division of Public Assistance and Social
    Services
  Hathaway Building
  Cheyenne, Wyoming 82002

  Reports made to county departments of
  public assistance and social services.

(From AMA Diagnostic and Treatment Guidelines Concerning Child Abuse and Neglect. American Medical Association, Chicago, 1985, compiled with the assistance of NCCAN, Washington, D.C., 1984.)

Appendix C
Autopsy Protocol for Child Deaths*

* From The Task Force for the Study of Non-Accidental Injuries and Child Deaths: Protocol for Child Death Autopsies. The Illinois Department of Children and Family Services, 1987, with permission.

Child abuse and neglect are significant problems that involve the entire medical community. The purpose of the protocol is to provide guidelines for establishing a uniform standard for the performance of suspected child abuse/neglect autopsies throughout the state of Illinois. It is expected that a complete autopsy will be performed on all children whose deaths are sudden, unexpected, and/or not due to obvious natural causes. The cause and manner of death may be apparent at autopsy, but frequently these decisions will need to be deferred until all medical records and investigative reports are reviewed and special studies are completed. Consultation with other medical and nonmedical specialists is often necessary and is encouraged. In cases of abuse or neglect, the involved parties may attempt to conceal the true circumstances and mechanism of injury. On the other hand, accusations of abuse or neglect may prove to be unfounded. The personnel responsible for conducting the investigation must collect evidence carefully and present conclusions in a clear manner with the necessary evidence to support conclusions.

There are six major patterns of child abuse: (1) physical abuse, (2) nutritional deprivation, (3) sexual abuse, (4) intentional poisoning or drugging, (5) neglect of medical care or safety, and (6) emotional abuse. It must be understood that frequently the only evidence available will be the results of the autopsy examination. Pathologists must be aware that they will be responsible for answering questions on any of the above forms of abuse:

1. Was death due to neglect, injury, or from complications of neglect or injury?
2. Did a delay in seeking medical care contribute to death; if so, was this an "unreasonable" delay?
3. If related to injury, what was the mechanism of injury?
4. Was the injury consistent with the alleged mechanism of injury; if not, why not?
5. When did the injury occur in relation to the time of death?
6. Did death result from a single episode of injury or as the result of multiple episodes of injury?
7. Were drugs or poisons involved in the death?
8. If neglect was involved, what form did it take?
9. If there has been failure-to-thrive, was this due to metabolic disorder, other disease, or neglect?
10. To what extent did environmental, nutritional, and social factors contribute to death?

FACILITY

The autopsy must be performed in a properly equipped forensic facility or hospital autopsy suite. Where possible, radiography and fluoroscopy should be available on site. A funeral home is not the appropriate place for practicing medicine. The body must not be embalmed before autopsy.

PERSONNEL

The autopsy should be performed by a pathologist experienced in forensic pathology, preferably Board certified in this specialty.

A pathologist who does not routinely deal with death related to injury may lack the necessary experience to interpret the mechanisms of injury in child abuse cases. The following consultants should be available as needed.

1. Experienced forensic odontologist
2. Pediatric radiologist
3. Neuropathologist
4. Pediatrician and pediatric subspecialists
5. Forensic anthropologist
6. Pediatric pathologist

In view of the limited number of such persons throughout the state, a referral list of regional resources can be found under Institutional Resources.

PHOTOGRAPHY

Color photography (preferably 35-mm transparencies) with proper color balance to assure faithful reproduction of lesions is necessary. A ruler and identifying tag should be present in all photographs. It is important that an organized system of photography be in place. Photography by trial and error will not succeed. The body should be photographed as it is received and after it has been cleaned. Photographs of the entire body, various anatomic regions, and individual lesions should be taken.

INVESTIGATION

Review of Records

Before beginning the autopsy all available records should be reviewed and all other necessary records should be ordered. These records should include all investigative reports, Department of Children and Family Services (DCFS) records, police reports, paramedic reports, emergency department records and the previous hospital and/or physician's records, including results of laboratory examinations and radiographs. Medical insurance records might be useful in providing information on previous illness, accident, or medical treatment.

The medical record is likely to be incomplete because of the emergency situation facing a physician when a severely ill or injured child is brought to the emergency department. It is important to discuss with attending physicians, as soon as possible after the death of a child, their recollection of not only the injuries but the general clinical status, history, and family situation. Physicians should also be queried with regard to resuscitation performed.

Family History

Before the autopsy, the pathologist should obtain as much of the child's personal history and family history as possible. This should include developmental, medical, and social history. This history may give important clues to findings at autopsy and their interpretation. More often than not, this information will be obtained by medical personnel, DCFS investigators, or police officers.

Agency Investigation

It is important to have an open line of communication between those agencies responsible for investigation, cause and manner of death determination, and possible prosecution. The medical examiner/coroner, police, DCFS, and State's Attorney's Office should keep each other informed, share data, and otherwise cooperate in all stages of the case, as appropriate for each agency. This is further discussed under Interagency Collaboration.

Scene Investigation

A scene investigation by the pathologist is often essential in evaluating mechanisms of injury. Furthermore, the home environment including cleanliness, safety hazards, neighborhood, pets, quantity and quality of food, medications, etc., may provide important information in making the cause/manner of death determination.

THE AUTOPSY

General Examination

Confirm Identification, if Known

An identification tag should be attached to the body. Identification can be confirmed by a relative or other person who knew the child. If the identification of the child is unknown, footprints should be obtained at the completion of the autopsy. If the body is decomposed or skeletalized, dental, radiologic, or anthropologic identification will be necessary.

Identification of Photographs
As described above, photographs are an essential part of the autopsy record and should be used to document all of the injuries to the child. Each photograph should have a ruler and identification tag present. There should be one photograph of the face for later identification purposes in court. The photographs should systematically cover each region of the body. Individual lesions or groups of lesions must be photographed at close range. A normal focal length lens is not sufficient for proper autopsy photography. A macro lens is essential. Available room light will not provide proper color balance. Either flash or photoflood light must be used, each with the film that will provide proper color balance. Several Kodak publications provide guidance for establishing a photographic facility.

Examination of Clothing and All Items Accompanying Body
It is essential that the body be brought to the autopsy suite with the clothing and other associated items undisturbed. The police must be discouraged from removing the clothing at the scene. The clothing and other personal items should be examined and described. This examination should be done in the presence of an evidence technician from the crime laboratory of the appropriate police jurisdiction. Tears, blood stains, and the general cleanliness of the clothing should be described.

Search for Trace Evidence
A search should be made for hairs, fibers, or other trace evidence that may be on the body or clothing. As appropriate, these should be removed before removal of the clothing, identified, and given to the crime laboratory evidence technicians. The clothing should subsequently be removed and the body again searched for trace evidence. If there is suspicion of sexual abuse, oral, rectal, and vaginal swabs should be taken for antigenic typing of semen and/or microbiologic studies as appro-

priate. The technique to be used should be established in consultation with crime laboratory personnel. Swabs of bite marks should be taken. These specimens must be obtained before the body is washed. Preservation of bite mark evidence is described further under Child Abuse Bite Mark Guidelines.

Radiologic Skeletal Survey
A complete skeletal survey must be done before the start of the autopsy, and the x-ray films must be available for review during the autopsy. Instructions for radiologic examination are contained in Radiographic Guidelines for Suspected Child Abuse.

External Examination

In addition to photographs of the body, body charts, and diagrams should be prepared to document essential findings at autopsy.

General Appearance
The general appearance of the child should be documented. This should include height and weight, body stature, the presence or absence of rigor mortis, and the locations of postmortem lividity if it is present. A general description of the body as appropriate in any autopsy should be given.

The time of death usually cannot be accurately determined. Although drop in body temperature, rise in vitreous potassium, and other postmortem events may give an approximation of the time of death, there are so many biologic variables present in such a determination that it is prudent to be circumspect in one's opinion.

Cleanliness
Is the child's skin clean? Is there dirt present in skin folds? Is this an acute or chronic status? Poor hygiene may be manifested by severe chronic diaper rash, lichenification of the skin, and chronic seborrhea.

Nutrition
Nutritional assessment of the child can be made by comparing height and weight with standard growth curve charts. Head, chest,

and abdominal circumferences should be measured. Poor nutrition or growth retardation reflects a chronic condition. Further information on nutritional assessment is provided in Nutritional Assessment of Diseased Children.

Dehydration

Is dehydration present? In young infants, the fontaneles may be depressed. Sunken eyes, poor skin turgor, and dry mucosal membranes are indicators of dehydration. Vitreous humor electrolyte analysis may show an elevated urea nitrogen and sodium level. Dehydration usually reflects an acute condition.

Failure-to-Thrive

This may be due to metabolic disorders, congenital anomalies, or chronic disease. Chronic abuse, nutritional deprivation, and emotional neglect can also cause failure-to-thrive. Children whose failure-to-thrive is organic are more likely to be abused or neglected.

Congenital Anomalies

Is there evidence of any congenital anomalies? Are there manifestations of a genetic disorder or of fetal alcohol syndrome?

Any Evidence of Neglect/Abuse

If the child is normal size for age, shows no evidence of dehydration or poor hygiene, and has no evidence of cutaneous or sexual injury, then this should be mentioned as an essential negative finding.

Evidence of Sexual Abuse

If there is no physical evidence of sexual abuse then this should be recorded as an essential negative finding. If there is evidence of sexual abuse, this should be described under evidence of injury to the perineal region, rectum, and genitalia.

Evidence of Bite Marks

If injuries suspicious of bite marks are present, a forensic odontologist should be consulted before proceeding with the autopsy. Failure to observe this rule may cause irretrievable loss of evidence. The skin should not be washed before examination of the bite marks,

since this will prevent attempts at recovery of dried saliva for evaluation. Bite marks should not be excised since any attempt will produce tissue distortion.

Evidence of External Injury

Child abuse injuries may be numerous, of different ages, produced by a variety of blunt trauma and other forms of injuries, and involve many parts of the body. As a result describing child abuse injuries can be tedious and confusing to the reader of the protocol, if the description is not given in some organized tabulated form. This can be done by separately describing external injuries and internal injuries, by breaking down the description of injuries into various anatomic regions of the body, and by separately describing recent, healing and healed injuries.

Recent Injuries

These are often best described by anatomic region. The type of injury (contusion, abrasion, or laceration) should be identified and dimensions given.

In suspected beating cases, lengthwise incisions through the skin and subcutaneous tissues of the involved anatomic regions should be made to determine the depth to which hemorrhage extends. This provides an indication of the severity of the blunt force used and may also reveal significant soft tissue injury not apparent from examination of the skin surface.

If the injury is patterned, a description of the pattern should supplement the photograph of the injury. Sections through representative lesions should be taken for microscopic examination.

Healing Injuries

These should be described in a manner similar to the description of the recent injuries. Sections of representative injuries should be taken for microscopic examination.

Healed Injuries

The pattern of scars is frequently characteristic of the type of implements used to produce the injuries. Scars should be recorded in a manner similar to description of other injuries.

Evidence of Internal Injury

These injuries are often best described by anatomic region. It is important to attempt to date the injuries both grossly and by microscopic examination. Where possible, internal injuries should be correlated with external injuries.

Evidence of Skeletal Injury

This description should be based both on radiographic examination and direct examination. Again, it is important to attempt to determine the age of the various lesions. A formal consultation report should be included.

Evidence of Resuscitation

Evidence of resuscitation must be described. Direct injection of epinephrine into the heart may produce pericardial hemorrhage. Lesions such as rib fractures, intra-abdominal hemorrhage, liver lacerations, and other internal injuries should be presumed as not due to resuscitation unless proved otherwise. Even vigorous resuscitation in a young child will rarely, if ever, produce these injuries.

Evidence of Therapy

Prolonged hospitalization may obscure evidence of injury and even brief hospitalization and therapy may alter the appearance of injuries. All findings related to therapy should be described.

General Internal Examination

This examination should mention important positive and negative findings regarding the neck and organs of the chest and abdomen in regard to antecedent disease or abnormality.

Systems Review

Each organ system should be described separately as with a usual medical autopsy. Special procedures include dissection of the posterior neck region in suspected shaken baby autopsies. It may also be necessary to remove the eyes to examine for evidence of retinal hemorrhage.

Microscopic Examination

This should include sections of representative injury sites as well as routine sections of internal organs. The injury process evolves much more rapidly in young children than in adults, and this must be considered when dating the age of injuries. The usual time required for resolution of an injury may be affected by the child's state of nutrition, intercurrent infection, and coma.

Special Studies

Postmortem Chemistry
Vitreous humor should be saved for appropriate electrolyte and chemistry studies. Serum and cerebrospinal fluid should also be saved, as necessary.

Toxicology
Samples of blood, bile, urine, and gastric contents should be saved for toxicologic analysis. Where unusual drugs or poisons are suspected other tissues should be saved as appropriate.

Microbiology
Where appropriate, specimens of blood, lung, brain, or other tissues should be taken for culture.

Neuropathology
The brain should be fixed in formalin and dissected after fixation in cases where head injury is apparent or suspected.

Other Studies

Other types of studies should be considered as appropriate.

Pathological Diagnoses

Pathologic diagnoses should be listed in a clear and concise manner. This should be tabulated so as to be understandable to persons without a medical background.

Comment or Opinion

A brief comment or opinion based on a correlation of history, investigative reports, autopsy findings, and laboratory studies should indicate the cause and manner of death. Frequently, the final opinion in the case must be deferred until after consultation with other involved agencies and a group discussion of the facts in the case. If a decision cannot be reached regarding the cause and/or manner of death, then the death certificate will indicate these to be undetermined. This represents the opinion of the medical examiner/coroner based on all of the information available to him or her. It is not binding on the state's attorney or DCFS.

SUGGESTED DOCUMENTATION

I. The autopsy protocol
1. Written in clear, concise language, understandable by laymen (lawyers, judges, police, etc.)
2. All injuries enumerated individually, not described in paragraph form
3. Pathologic diagnoses
4. Opinion regarding cause of death
II. Photographs
1. All body surfaces
2. All external injuries labeled with case number and date. Include ruler, orientation view, and close-up; hair may have to be shaved to expose wounds

3. Bruises, after incision into wounds
4. Internal injuries
III. Body chart prepared by pathologist
IV. Radiographs and radiologist's report
V. Investigative reports
(Medical examiner/coroner investigator, DCFS, hospital and physician records, police reports, paramedic reports, emergency department records)
VI. Scene investigation with photographs of environment by police, medical examination/coroner, or DCFS.

INTERAGENCY COLLABORATION

Developing good working relationships among personnel from principal agencies is critical to the investigation process as well as to the effectiveness of the roles performed by each of the participating agencies. Important interacting agencies include local law enforcement, DCFS and the Coroner or Medical Examiner's Office. Smooth working relationships among so many agencies do not come about easily and require considerable effort.

1. To begin, key agencies, within each locale should be identified as the "principals" involves in most abuse cases.
2. Agency personnel must develop an understanding of the unique roles and functions of the other agencies. This can take place informally or by means of structured mechanisms.
3. DCFS has appointed several regional multidisciplinary committees throughout the state of Illinois to assist in dealing with complex cases of abuse and neglect. These committees can become the vehicles for education concerning the roles and functions involved in death investigations.
4. It is recommended that every child death case reported as a homicide by a medical examiner or coroner and every case of severe injury to a child reported by a medical facility be reviewed by a "case conference" involving all principal agencies when the DCFS's own investigation has

not produced sufficient "credible evidence" to warrant "indicating" the case.

5. Case conferencing among principal agencies is also recommended in the rare instance where the perpetrator of death or severe injury is a child.
6. Where feasible and appropriate, the safety of surviving and future siblings can be enhanced by notifying and/or involving the family's primary care physician.

Roles and Decisions of Principal Agencies

Any child death thought to have resulted from accident, abuse, neglect, or homicide must be reported to appropriate legal authorities: local police departments; DCFS; or Coroner or Medical Examiner's Office.

For some counties within the state of Illinois, reciprocal agreements regarding notification procedures have been specified. For example, when a suspected case of fatal abuse is reported to the abuse hotline, the local police department is notified by the worker at the Central Registry. In other instances, the police department immediately notifies the Central Registry when called in on a case involving suspected abuse.

During the autopsy process, police collect data, take photographs, and are responsible for ensuring "continuity or chain of custody of evidence."

It is recognized that to establish abuse or neglect at autopsy, the pathologist or medical examiner must determine the cause of death documenting all injuries whether they resulted in whole or in part from physical abuse, neglect, or accident.

In the DCFS *Child Abuse and Neglect Investigation Decision Handbook*, in a section on roles and responsibilities, ". . . a child abuse/neglect investigation is defined as a fact-finding process the purposes of which are (in order of importance): (1) to assure the safety and well-being of children (e.g., surviving siblings) suspected to be abused and/or neglected; (2) to determine the validity of reported allegations; (3) to obtain sufficient information to support DCFS decisions in court (if necessary); (4) to give service delivery staff

adequate information on "indicated" reports to determine if services are appropriate or necessary to ameliorate family dysfunction."

With the information provided by the coroner or medical examiner, the local police department and DCFS notify the State's Attorney's Office. In that office, the decision is made as to whether to prosecute individuals suspected of causing a child's death or inflicting serious injury.

Range of Relevant Information

While there are a number of sources for gathering potential relevant information about a family, three important areas need to be highlighted because of their direct bearing on the success of child injury and death investigations.

The areas include information from paramedics and private ambulance companies, data from other medical professionals (e.g., emergency department hospital records and other outpatient medical personnel, and records kept on file by local police departments and the Illinois DCFS.

Paramedics are often the first professional staff on the scene. Their observations and reports can be critical to the investigation process, contributing information about the injured, the surrounding environment, and verbal exchanges among family members, witnesses, and others. Any form of treatment administered by paramedics during transport is reported and monitored. The nature of the treatment may be important in reaching a decision about the cause of the injuries.

Information pertinent to diagnosis and treatment conducted in the hospital *emergency department* also provides important facts that guide the medical examiner in reaching a conclusion about the cause of death. Obtaining medical history from health professionals (e.g., hospital and clinics), can also do much to clarify the decision reached by the pathologist or medical examiner.

It is important for the investigator to specifically request all documents relevant to the case. It has been shown that requesting information from the medical records department of a hospital may not result in delivery of data covering paramedic or emergency department treatment. Paramedic records may also be subpoenaed from the local fire department or ambulance company.

Finally, the police history of a suspected perpetrator and whether the family has had previous contact with the DCFS or other community services provides important perspectives on what the medical examiner may uncover through the autopsy. It also may be critical in the decision-making process regarding prevention of harm to other family members.

RADIOGRAPHIC GUIDELINES FOR SUSPECTED CHILD ABUSE

Radiographic Views for Suspected Child Abuse During Postmortem Examinations

1. *Skull:* anteroposterior and lateral views of the skull
2. *Torso:* anteroposterior torso, to include chest, abdomen and pelvis, with penetration adequate to visualize the posterior ribs
   A. For these anatomic areas, a single film is used; usually a single 14 × 17 accommodates these areas; occasionally multiple films may be needed
   B. Decubitus views of the chest may be helpful when there is the possibility of pneumothorax
   C. The decubitus view and/or crosstable view of the chest are additional views useful for diagnosing pneumomediastinum and pneumothorax
   D. In cases of possible perforated viscus, free air in the abdominal cavity can be detected with a 10-minute abdominal film in the upright position or left lateral abdominal decubitus film
3. *Anteroposterior of the upper and lower extremities:* arms and forearms should be done individually; because of postmortem flexure contractures, views of the hands and feet are not routinely done

4. *Extremity joints:* right and left shoulder, elbow, wrist, hip, knee, and ankle; individual anteroposterior views of these joints with centering over each joint
5. *Lateral view of the entire spine:* individual views of the cervical, thoracic, and lumbar spine are best for detail; multiple exposures on a single 14 × 17 film can be done; a cone down view of the cervical spine may be necessary
6. *Other studies:* sometimes fractures, especially rib fractures, cannot be identified on preautopsy films; injuries discovered during autopsy are subsequently radiographed; sometimes it is best to remove the skeletal part for radiographic examination

Diagnosis of Skeletal Injuries due to Maltreatment

1. *Age:* usually not the immediate neonatal period; most younger than 2 years of age
2. *Fifty percent fail to show evidence of skeletal injury,* but show evidence of soft tissue injury: bruises, scars, and burns, etc.
3. *Fractures*
   A. Epiphyseal-metaphyseal injuries
      1. Typical Salter-Harris I and II
      2. Bone architecture and mineralization usually normal and this differentiates it from dysplastic, metabolic, and hematologic fractures
   B. Diaphyseal fractures: transverse or oblique
      1. As common and as typical as epiphyseal-metaphyseal fractures
   C. Rib fractures
      1. Common
      2. Difficult for children to obtain other than by abuse; be very suspicious without documented evidence of direct blow or crush injury, that is, automobile accident
      3. Location: posterior, lateral, or anterior
         a. Posterior and lateral fractures show abundant callus
         b. Anterior fractures show exaggerated cuffing of costal chondral junction

D. Skull fractures
1. Etiology: direct blow
2. Type
   a. Linear
   b. Diastatic (split suture) secondary to intracranial bleeding or subdural hematoma
E. Highly suspicious injuries
1. Fracture of distal end of clavicle
2. Fracture of anterior ribs (see above)
3. Fracture of the scapula

4. *Dating injuries*
A. Less than 10 to 14 days: soft tissue changes only; minimal or no signs of healing
B. Two to four weeks: callus and periosteal new bone deposition is evident; periphery calcifies, center lucent; radiolucent space between bone and callus
C. Four to twelve weeks: may still see underlying fracture; callus mature, smooth, and uniformly dense
D. After 12 weeks: may see only thickened cortex; fracture line disappears

5. *Intrauterine abnormalities*
A. Bowing: prenatal
1. Etiology: abnormal fetal position
2. Oligohydramnios
3. Soft bones
   a. Osteogenesis imperfecta
   b. Hypophosphatasia
4. Camptodwarfism
B. Congenital dislocated knee
1. Etiology: faulty intrauterine position

6. *Birth trauma:* most fractures of newborn period occur during delivery
A. Clavicle
1. Most frequently fractured
2. Location
   a. Most common midclavicle, but can occur at either end
B. Long bones: next most common
1. Location
   a. Diaphysis of epiphyseal-metaphyseal junction (Salter-Harris I and II)
   b. Ends of humerus and proximal femur
2. Radiograph: initially soft tissue swelling; cannot see epiphysis as it is not ossified

a. Dislocated joint in neonate rare; think epiphyseal fracture
b. Corner fracture
C. Rib fractures
1. Premature prone to rib fractures 4 to 8 weeks postparturition; often secondary to calcium deficiency or rickets

7. *Differential diagnosis:* birth injury versus abuse
A. Birth injuries show callus between 7 to 11 days
B. Fracture visible after 11 days without signs of callus or subperiosteal bone deposition should *not* be considered related to birth
C. Osteogenesis imperfecta tarda may be present in newborn period
D. Fractures caused by birth trauma
1. Skull fracture
2. Midclavicular fracture
3. Humeral fracture
4. Femoral fracture
5. Femoral epiphyseal fracture—separation

Deprivation Dwarfism

Deprivation or psychosocial dwarfism is a temporary nutritional disorder that simulates pituitary dwarfism. When a child begins taking nutrition, there is rapid growth of the body. The rapid growth of the brain may result in split sutures simulating increased intracranial pressure. These children usually do not have fractures. There are many growth rest lines that help differentiate them from pituitary dwarfism.

Summary of Injuries Detected by Radiographic Techniques

Injuries highly suggestive of abuse†
   Isolated long-bone fracture*
   Corner fracture

---

* In absence of convincing history of accidental trauma.

† (From Hilton SVW, Edwards DK: Radiographic diagnosis of non-accidental trauma. Appl Radiol 14:13, 1985, with permission.)

Acromial fracture
Scapular fracture
Sternal fracture*
Multiple rib fractures
Multiple costovertebral fractures
Incidental compression fracture of the
  spine*
Multiple costochondral fractures
Pancreative pseudocyst*
Duodenal hematoma*
Hepatic laceration or hematoma*
Mesenteric laceration*
Bowel rupture*
Cerebral contusion*
Injuries that are worrisome but are not diag-
nostic of abuse†
  Isolated fracture-separation of distal hu-
    meral epiphysis
  Distal clavicular fracture
  Single rib fracture
  Metatarsal or metacarpal fracture
  Unexplained cerebral atrophy or hydro-
    cephalus
Common accidental trauma†
  Midclavicular fracture
  Distal radiotorus fracture
  Skull fracture
  Spiral tibial fracture (toddler's fracture)
  Amputation or crush injury of distal pha-
    langes
Most common fractures caused by birth
  trauma†
  Skull fracture
  Midclavicular fracture
  Humeral fracture
  Femoral fracture
  Femoral epiphyseal fracture-separation

NUTRITIONAL ASSESSMENT OF DECEASED CHILDREN

1. Calculate child's age to nearest ½ month
   younger than 3 years old, to nearest month
   age 3 years and older. If the child was premature, correct for gestational age up to age
   5 years.
   Example
     Birth date of March 25, 1980, 7 weeks
     premature
     Death date is March 18, 1983
     Calculated age is 3 years

Correcting for prematurity, age is 2
years, 10 months
2. Record weight to nearest ½ pound or 1 kg;
   correct for estimated degree of dehydration, if possible
3. Record length to nearest ½ inch or 1 cm;
   correct for estimated shortening due to
   contractures
4. Plot weight, height, and weight for height
   on standard curves
5. Interpretation
   A. Weight for height
      1. Less than 5th percentile indicates
         nutritional wasting
      2. Fifth to tenth percentile suggests
         nutritional wasting
      3. More than 95th percentile indicates
         obesity
   B. Height
      1. Less than 5th percentile strongly
         suggests nutritional stunting if
         weight for height less than 25th per-
         centile
      2. Fifth to tenth percentile suggests
         nutritional stunting if weight for
         height is less than 25th percentile
   C. Weight
      Less than 5th percentile suggests nu-
      tritional wasting if weight for height is
      less than 10th percentile

CHILD ABUSE BITE MARK GUIDELINES

Identification of a Bite Mark

Teeth are essentially a tool. As such, because of their individual morphologic characteristics, and relationships with each other
in the dental arch, they can leave a unique
mark on the victim that sometimes can be
traced to the perpetrator.

A bite mark will appear as a semicircular
(one arch) or oval (both arches) mark on the
body. Generally, no more than the anterior six
or eight teeth in an arch will mark. Frequently, because of the interspersing of clothing, or nature of the bite, only a few of the
teeth may make a mark. Because of the nature
of a child's skin, bite marks can be very distinct. There may be additional bite marks on

the body, of the same age, or in a partial state of healing, indicating repetitive attacks.

Location of Bite Marks

Bite marks occurring in child abuse are usually found on the chest, abdomen, face, or extremities.

Recovery of Evidence

Since many bite marks are present on victims who have sustained serious other trauma and are covered with dried blood and other debris, a careful examination of the body after removal of the clothing is necessary to preclude loss of serologic evidence from the saliva of the perpetrator when the body is being medically treated or handled in the morgue.

Call Forensic Odontologist

Ideally, a trained forensic odontologist should be called to process the evidence *before* any further disruption of the bite mark. In lieu of this, photographs of the injury should be taken with and without a mm scale in place. A suggested means is a Polaroid "Sonar One Step" camera that focuses automatically, and allows the photographer to see the result immediately. After the evidence is photographed, saliva swabs should be taken from the injury. Moisten the swab in sterile saline and swab the area of the bite from the center outward. Allow the swab to air dry, and place it into an envelope. *Do not lick the envelope to seal it! Use tap water on a gauze pad.* Take a second swab in the same fashion from the other side of the body as a control.

Photography

If a medical photographer is immediately available, the following should be done:

1. Photograph the undisturbed injury
   A. Black and white high contrast
   B. Color negative film (ASA 100)
      1. A KODAK color scale or a gray card along with a mm scale should be used in the frame of the photo
      2. All shots duplicated with and without scale/case ID in place
      3. Long orienting shot of the body
      4. Orienting shot of each bite mark
      5. Close up of each arch of bite with scale and circulate standard in place (a nickel or dime does nicely)
      6. Shot of entire bite in one frame with scales in place.
      7. Scale used in photo *must* become part of patient file.
2. Photograph the injury as above after it has been cleaned.

Impressions of Bite Mark

Impressions of the bite should be made by an odontologist using accepted forensic techniques. Impressions of the victim's own teeth will also be taken as a matter of course to ensure a legally complete procedure.

Police investigators should be advised that bite mark evidence is available, so that if a suspect is located, the State's Attorney Office may prepare a search warrant, court order, etc., to allow impressions to be made of the suspected abuser. Recognition and processing of such evidence may be a critical link to the perpetrator of the abuse.

Appendix D
Diagnostic Imaging Guidelines*†

* From Section on Radiology Executive Committee, 1990–1991 and Haller JO, Kleinman PK, Merten DF et al: Diagnostic imaging of child abuse. Pediatrics 87:262, 1991, with permission.
† From Federation of Pediatric Organizations: Statement of pediatric fellowship training. Pediatrics 87:265, 1991, with permission.

DIAGNOSTIC IMAGING OF CHILD ABUSE

The concept of child abuse as a medical entity has its origins in the radiologic studies of the pediatric radiologist Dr. John Caffey, as well as many other specialists in the field of diagnostic imaging. When all cases of child abuse and neglect are studied, the incidence of physical alterations documentable by diagnostic imaging is relatively small. However, imaging studies are often critical in the infant and young child with evidence of physical injury, and they also may be the first indication of abuse in a child who is seen initially with an apparent natural illness. As most conventional imaging studies performed in this setting are noninvasive and entail minimal radiation risks, recommendations regarding imaging should focus on examinations, which provide the highest diagnostic yield at acceptable costs.

Skeletal Imaging

Although skeletal injuries rarely pose a threat to the life of the abused child, they are the strongest radiologic indicators of abuse. In fact, in the young infant, certain radiologic abnormalities are sufficiently characteristic to allow a firm diagnosis of inflicted injury in the absence of clinical information. This fact mandates that imaging surveys performed to identify skeletal injury be carried out with the same level of technical excellence used in examinations routinely performed to evaluate accidental injuries. The "body gram" or abbreviated skeletal surveys have no place in the imaging of these subtle, but highly specific bony abnormalities.

In general, the radiographic skeletal survey is the method of choice for skeletal imaging in cases of suspected abuse. Modern pediatric imaging systems commonly use special film, cassettes, and intensifying screens to minimize exposure. Certain modifications of such low-dose systems are required to provide the necessary contrast and spatial resolution to image the subtle metaphyseal, rib, and other unusual injuries that frequently elude detection with systems designed for chest and abdominal imaging. Many departments use a so-called extremity system that provides high detail images at modest increases in exposure. This improvement in image quality is obtained primarily by use of a high-detail film and a slower intensifying screen. Maximal detail results with a single emulsion film and a single intensifying screen. Use of cassettes with specially designed front plates using material that allows more lower energy photons to strike the intensifying screen will provide significant improvement in contrast resolution at a lower radiation exposure. Systems of this type are readily available as a result of the technical developments in the field of mammographic imaging, an area where dose considerations are crucial. Knowledgeable radiologists, physicists, and radiologic technologists should choose systems that will perform well clinically, as well as conform to the practical requirements of individual departments.

Once the appropriate imaging system is chosen, a precise protocol for skeletal imaging must be developed to ensure consistent quality. In routine skeletal imaging, an accepted principle is that films must be coned or restricted to the specific area of interest. It is a common practice to encompass larger regions of the skeleton when skeletal surveys are performed. This results in areas of under- and overexposure, as well as loss of resolution due to geometric distortion and other technical factors. The skeletal survey, therefore, must use anteroposterior views of the arms, forearms, hands, femurs, lower legs, and feet, all on separate exposures. Lateral views of the axial skeleton are obtained, along with the routine frontal views in infancy, because of the occurrence of fractures involving the spine and sternum. Anteroposterior and lateral views of the skull are mandatory even when cranial computed tomography (CT) has been obtained, as fractures occurring in the axial plane may be missed with CT. Studies must be monitored by a radiologist for technical adequacy, as well as be assessed for additional lateral or oblique projections.

The skeletal survey is mandatory in all cases of suspected physical abuse in children younger than 2 years of age. A screening skeletal survey in a child older than 5 years of age has little value. Patients in the 2-year to 5-year-old age group must be handled individually, based on the specific clinical indicators of abuse. At any age, when clinical findings point to a specific site of injury, the customary protocol for imaging that region should be used. Application of these guidelines to selected cases of neglect and sexual abuse is appropriate when associated physical maltreatment is suspected.

Radionuclide bone scans, when they are performed by experienced pediatric radiologists in large centers, may offer an alternative to radiography. Clearly, skeletal scintigraphy provides increased sensitivity for rib fractures, subtle shaft fractures, and areas of early periosteal elevation. However, data are limited regarding the sensitivity of scintigraphy for metaphyseal fractures, particularly when they are bilateral, as well as for subtle injuries of the spine, features that carry a high specificity in young infants. Thus, although skeletal scintigraphy plays an important supplementary role to the radiologic skeletal survey, use of this modality as a primary tool should be exercised with extreme caution. Follow-up imaging studies in 1 to 2 weeks may be useful in selected cases, when initial studies are normal or equivocal, or when a repeat study may provide further evidence to allow more precise determination of the age of individual fractures.

Intracranial Injury

All infants and children with suspected intracranial injury must undergo cranial CT and/or magnetic resonance imaging (MRI). Although ultrasonography may reveal intracranial abnormalities, it is inadequate to exclude or to evaluate fully intracranial injury. In cases of suspected acute central nervous system pathology, studies are designed to identify treatable conditions. CT is generally sufficient in this context. However, preliminary studies indicate that MRI is substantially more sensitive than CT in identifying and characterizing most intracranial sequelae of abusive assaults. Subdural hematomas, particularly over the convexities, cortical contusions, cerebral edema, and white matter injuries are well depicted with MRI. Only subarachnoid hemorrhage appears to be detected better with CT. Furthermore, MRI provides better characterization of the age of areas of hemorrhage than does CT. For this reason, MRI should be performed early in all cases of suspected intracranial injury when clinical findings are not explained adequately by CT. A strong argument can be made for a follow-up in all cases of suspected intracranial injury to better characterize the extent of parenchymal injury and to predict clinical outcome. In cases exhibiting chronic central nervous system alterations, and in infants with evidence of the shaken infant syndrome but no clinical evidence of central nervous system injury, MRI should be performed. As MRI becomes more available to the critically ill child, greater application of this elegant imaging modality can be expected.

Thoracoabdominal Trauma

Major blunt and penetrating thoracoabdominal injury is uncommon in the young infant; thus, imaging strategies are the most critical in the toddler and older child. In the massively traumatized patient, protocols similar to those used for accidental injury apply. Initial radiographs in the emergency department include a chest radiograph to evaluate for flail chest, pneumothorax, pleural effusion, and pulmonary parenchymal injury. Abdominal radiographs are insensitive indicators of solid visceral injury, but they will show gross pelvic fractures. It is prudent to obtain a lateral cervical spine radiograph before further diagnostic studies are performed. Once the patient is stabilized, CT is indicated. CT is the most effective and sensitive imaging technique to identify injuries of the lungs, pleura, and solid abdominal organs. Hollow visceral injury may be detected by the presence of small amounts of intraperitoneal air, as well as intramural and mesenteric blood. In particular, pancreatic injury and duodenal hematomas, two characteristic findings in abused children, are assessed well with CT. In children younger than 1 year of age, ultrasonography may be a reasonable preliminary study to perform if abdominal injury is suspected.

In the child exhibiting lesser signs of injury, or a constellation of nonspecific abdominal signs and symptoms that cannot be explained by the history or a unifying diagnosis, ultrasonography is an acceptable initial procedure. Occult duodenal hematomas, pancreatic injury, and renal injuries are studied reasonably well with ultrasonography. The diagnosis of duodenal hematoma, particularly if chronic, may be difficult with ultrasonography or CT. On occasion, an upper gastrointestinal tract series may be required to delineate the injury. Radionuclide scintigraphy plays a relatively small role in visceral injury, but it is of value in cases of renal contusion and myoglobinuria.

To obtain the most thorough diagnostic imaging assessment, caretakers accompanying children to the radiology department must receive advance preparation. Achievement of adequate studies in young children requires restraint and, in cases of skeletal surveys, numerous exposures. Excessive apprehension, hostility, and resistance usually will result in inadequate examinations. Therefore, caretakers should be handled by personnel in a professional and nonjudgmental manner. Questions regarding indications for the study as well as results should be directed to the referring physician. Imaging examinations must be viewed in the clinical context, and the implications of the examinations are best addressed by physicians and other health care workers familiar with the family and skilled in these sensitive interactions.

SUGGESTED READINGS

1. Ball WS Jr: Nonaccidental craniocerebral trauma (child abuse): MR imaging. Radiology 173:609, 1989
2. Caffey J: Multiple fractures in the long bones of infants suffering from chronic subdural hematoma. AJR 56:163, 1946
3. Kempe CH, Silverman FN, Steele BF, et al: The battered-child syndrome. JAMA 181:17, 1962
4. Kleinman PK: Diagnostic Imaging of Child Abuse. Williams & Wilkins, Baltimore, 1987
5. Kleinman PK, Blackbourne BD, Marks SC, et al: Radiologic contributions to the investigation and prosecution of cases of fatal infant abuse. N Engl J Med 320:507, 1989
6. Kleinman PK, Marks SC, Blackbourne BD: The metaphyseal lesion in the abused child: a radiological-histopathologic study. AJR 146:895, 1986
7. Merten DF, Radkowski MA, Leonidas JC: The abused child: a radiological reappraisal. Radiology 146:377, 1983
8. Merten DF, Radkowski MA, Leonidas JC: Craniocerebral trauma in the child abuse syndrome: radiological observations. Pediatr Radiol 14:272, 1984
9. Sato Y, Yuh WTC, Smith WL, et al: Head injury in child abuse: evaluation with MR imaging. Radiology 173:653, 1989
10. Silverman FN: Unrecognized trauma in infants, the battered child syndrome, and the syndrome of Abroise Tardieu: Rigler lecture. Radiology 104:337, 1973
11. Sinal SH, Ball MR: Head trauma due to child abuse: serial computerized tomography in diagnosis and management. South Med J 80:1505, 1987
12. Sivit CJ, Taylor GA, Eichelberger MR: Visceral injury in battered children: a changing perspective. Radiology 173:659, 1989
13. Sty JR, Starshak RJ: The role of bone scintigraphy in the evaluation of the suspected abused child. Radiology 146:369, 1983
14. Trefler M: Radiation exposure reduction using carbon fiber. Radiology 142:751, 1982

Appendix E
Child Abuse/Neglect National Organizations

American Academy of Pediatrics
Section on Child Abuse and Neglect
P.O. Box 927
141 Northwest Point Boulevard
Elk Grove Village, IL 60009
(800)433-9016

Professional organization for pediatricians and others caring for abused children. Promotes professional education and research.

American Humane Association
American Association for Protecting Children
9725 East Hampden Avenue
Denver, CO 80231
(303)695-0811

Collects and reports national statistics on child abuse. Established to promote nationwide availability of child protective services.

C. Henry Kempe National Center for the Prevention and Treatment of Child Abuse and Neglect
1205 Oneida Street
Denver, CO 80220
(303)321-3963

Promotes patient care, education, and research. Provides many publications and audiovisual aids dealing with child abuse.

Center for the Prevention of Sexual and Domestic Violence
1914 North 34th Street
Suite 105
Seattle, WA 98103
(206)634-1903

Provides training and education for professionals on domestic violence.

Child Welfare League of America
440 First Street N.W.
Suite 310
Washington, D.C. 20001
(202)638-2952

Membership is made up from direct service organizations. Provides professional literature.

Children's Defense Fund
122 C Street, N.W.
Washington, D.C. 20001
(202)628-8787

Advocacy group for issues affecting children and families. Publications available.

International Society for Prevention of Child Abuse and Neglect
Pergamon Press
Fairview Park
Elmsford, NY 10523

Publishes the international journal, *Child Abuse and Neglect*.

National Center on Child Abuse and Neglect
Department of Health and Human Services
330 C Street, S.W.
Washington, D.C. 20013
(202)245-0618

Coordinates federal child abuse programs, including funding for research.

National Center for Missing and Exploited Children
2101 Wilson Boulevard
Suite 550
Arlington, VA 22201
(703)235-3900

Assists in the recovery of missing children.

National Center for the Prosecution of Child Abuse
1033 North Fairfax Street
Suite 200
Alexandria, VA 22314
(703)739-0321

Supports education and research regarding child abuse prosecution.

National Clearinghouse on Child Abuse and Neglect
P.O. Box 1182
Washington, D.C. 20013

Provides literature in the field of child abuse and neglect.

National Coalition Against Domestic Violence
P.O. Box 34103
Washington, D.C. 20043
(202)638-6388

Composed of shelters for battered women.

National Committee for the Prevention of Child Abuse
332 South Michigan Avenue
Suite 1600
Chicago, IL 60604
(312)663-3520

Provides advocacy, education, and research. Publications available.

Victims of Child Abuse Laws
P.O. Box 11335
Minneapolis, MN 55411

Advocacy organization supporting those believing they have been wronged by unfair application of child abuse statutes.

Appendix F
Guidelines for Treatment of Sexually Transmitted Diseases*

* From Med Lett 31:5, (issue 810), 1990, with permission.

Bacterial vaginosis

Adolescents and adults: Metronidazole 500 mg PO twice per day for 7 days.

Alternative therapy (limited data): Clindamycin 300 mg PO twice per day for 7 days.

Chlamydia trachomatis

Cervicitis, proctitis, urethritis

Nine years and older: Doxycycline 100 mg PO twice per day for 7 days, or tetracycline 500 mg PO four times per day for 7 days.

Alternative therapy: Erythromycin 500 mg PO four times per day for 7 days.

Younger than 9 years old: Erythromycin 12.5 mg/kg PO four times per day for 7 days.

Neonatal ophthalmia, pneumonia

Erythromycin 12.5 mg/kg PO or IV four times per day for 14 days.

Alternative therapy for pneumonia (after 4 weeks old): Sulfisoxazole 100 mg/kg PO or IV four times per day for 14 days.

Gonorrhea

NOTE: Given the high percentage of women and heterosexual men with gonorrhea who have coexisting chlamydia infection, these patients should also receive a 7-day course of doxycycline or tetracycline, as recommended for treatment of chlamydia.

Urogenital, rectal and pharyngeal

Adults: Ceftriaxone 125 to 250 mg IM once.

Alternative adult therapy: Spectinomycin 2 g IM (not for pharyngeal) or ciprofloxacin 500 mg PO once (may cause joint damage in children).

Children (under 45 kg): Ceftriaxone 125 mg IM once.

Alternative pediatric therapy: Spectinomycin 40 mg/kg IM once (not for pharyngeal) or amoxicillin 50 mg/kg PO plus probenecid 25 mg/kg PO once (if strain known to be susceptible).

Arthritis

Adults: Ceftriaxone 1 g IV daily for 7 to 10 days.

Children: Ceftriaxone 50 mg/kg IV daily (maximum 2 g) for 7 days.

Neonatal ophthalmia

Cefotaxime 25 mg/kg IV or IM two or three times per day for 7 days, plus saline irrigation or ceftriaxone 125 mg IM once, plus saline irrigation.

Alternative therapy: Penicillin-G 100,000 U/kg four times per day for 7 days (if strain known to be susceptible), plus saline irrigation.

Herpes simplex virus

NOTE: The use of acyclovir for genital herpes has been primarily for adults. Experience with children for these non-life-threatening indications is limited.

First genital episode: Acyclovir 400 mg PO three times per day for 7 to 10 days.

Severe recurrence (oral acyclovir is usually not helpful for recurrence): Acyclovir 5 mg/kg IV three times per day for 5 to 7 days.

Prevention of recurrences: Acyclovir 200 mg PO two to five times per day.

Pediculosis pubis

Lindane (Kwell and others), 1% permethrin (NIX), and pyrethrins with piperonyl butoxide (RID and others) applied topically for 10 minutes (4 minutes for lindane) are effective. Lindane may be more toxic.

Syphilis

Early (primary, secondary, or latent less than 1 year): Penicillin-G benzathine 2.4 million U IM once.

Alternative therapy for early: Doxycycline 100 mg PO twice a day for 14 days, tetracycline 500 mg PO four times a day for 14 days, or ceftriaxone 250 mg IM daily for 10 days (limited experience).

Late (more than 1 year's duration, cardiovascular): Penicillin-G benzathine 2.4 million U IM weekly for 3 weeks.

Alternative therapy for late: Doxycycline 100 mg PO twice a day for 4 weeks or tetracycline 500 mg PO four times a day for 4 weeks.

Neurosyphilis: Penicillin-G 2 to 4 million U IV every 4 hours for 10 to 14 days or penicillin-G procaine 2.4 million U IM daily plus probenecid 500 mg PO four times per day for 10 to 14 days.

Congenital: Penicillin-G 50,000 U IM or IV two to three times per day for 10 to 14 days or penicillin-G procaine 50,000 U IM daily for 10 to 14 days.
Alternative therapy for neurosyphilis, congenital syphilis: None known.

Trichomoniasis

Metronidazole 2 g PO once or 500 PO twice per day for 7 days.

Warts, genital

Podophyllin remains the most frequently used therapy; many experts use cryotherapy.

Appendix G
Normal Development Milestones

Table G-1. Developmental Milestones

Age	Motor	Mental	Language	Social
3–6 months	Will bear weight on legs Can roll over stomach to back Engages hands in midline When pulled to sit, head is steady, does not fall back When on abdomen, can lift shoulders off mat When on abdomen, can lift head and look about Will begin to reach for and grasp objects Sits with support	Looks at objects in hand Looks after a toy that is dropped Uses a 2-hand approach to grasp toys Looks at objects as small as a raisin Turns head to voice, follows with eyes	Coos Gurgles Chuckles Laughs aloud Squeals Has expressive noises	Has a social smile Will pat a bottle with both hands Anticipates food on sight
6–9 months	Rolls from back to stomach Gets feet to mouth Sits alone, unsupported, for extended period (over 1 minute) Stands with hands held On back, can lift head up Beginning attempts to crawl or creep When sitting, reaches forward to grasp without falling	Bangs toys in play Transfers objects from hand to hand Reaches for a toy with one hand Picks up a dropped toy Is persistent in obtaining toys Pulls a toy to self by attached string	Responds to name Vocalizes to social stimulus Has single consonants (i.e., ba, ka, ma) Combines syllables (i.e., da-da, ba-ba) Likes to make sounds with toys Imitates sounds	Expects repetition of stimulus Likes frolicky play Discriminates strangers Smiles to mirror image Takes some solid food to mouth Bites and chews toys Beginning to enjoy peekaboo

Age	Gross Motor	Fine Motor / Adaptive	Language	Social
9–12 months	Crawls well Can sit steadily for more than 10 minutes Stands holding on to furniture Can pull to sitting position Walks, holding on to a hand or to furniture	Will uncover a toy seen covered up Can grasp object small as raisin with thumb and one finger Beginning to put things in and out of containers Goes for an object with index finger outstretched Likes to drop objects deliberately Shows interest in pictures	Understands "no," or inflection of "no!" Uses mama, or dada, first inappropriately, then with meaning By 12 months has at least one other word Knows meaning of 1–3 words	Cooperates in games Will try to roll ball to another person Plays patacake and peekaboo Waves goodbye Will offer toy without releasing it Likes to interact in play with adult
12–18 months	By 18 months, walks well alone Creeps up stairs Can get to standing position alone Can stoop and recover an object Walking, pulls a pull-toy Seats self on chair	Looks at pictures in a book Will scribble spontaneously with pencil or crayon Uses spoon Drinks from cup Will follow one or two directions (i.e., take a ball to . . .)	Has 3–5 words Will point to one body part Will point to at least one picture Uses jargon (i.e., unintelligible "foreign" language with inflection) Imitates some words	Cooperates in dressing Holds own bottle or cup Finger feeds Points or vocalizes to make desires known Shows or offers a toy
18–24 months	Can run, albeit stiffly Walks up and down stairs with one hand held Hurls a ball Can kick a ball or object Jumps with both feet Stands on one foot with one hand held	Can tower 2 or more 1-in. blocks Turns pages of a book, even if 2–3 at a time Will try to imitate what an adult draws with pencil Can point to 2–3 body parts	By 2 years, has at least 20 words By 2 years, is combining words in a phrase Jargon, which was elaborate by 18 months, is gone by 24 months Verbalizes desires with words	Uses spoon, spilling very little Removes one piece of clothing Imitates housework more and more Handles a cup quite well

Continued

Table G-1. (continued)

Age	Motor	Mental	Language	Social
2–3 years	Can walk up stairs without hand held Can balance on 1 foot for 1 second Can jump in place Can walk on tiptoe Can jump from the bottom step Kicks ball forward Can throw a ball	Can tower 6 1-in. blocks Can dump a raisin from a bottle to attain it without hints from adult Can imitate a vertical line, possibly a horizontal line, with pencil Can anticipate the need to urinate or defecate If worked with, can toilet self	Uses 2–4 word phrases Uses plurals Names at least one picture Talks incessantly Vocabulary 100–300 words by 3 years Uses some personal pronouns (i.e., I, me, mine) Points to several parts of a doll on request Identifies over 5 parts of own body	Puts on some clothing Washes and dries hands Has parallel play with peers Can pour from a pitcher
3–4 years	Rides a tricycle Alternates feet when going up stairs Can stand on one foot for 2–5 seconds Can broad jump Uses scissors Swings and climbs	Can tower 8–10 1-in. blocks Says full name Can match colors Has sense of round, square, and triangular shaped figures and can match them Copies a circle, line, cross with pencil Can repeat 3 digits	Can answer some questions Knows rhymes and songs Asks questions Has understanding of on, under, and behind	Knows own sex Beginning to play *with* other children Unbuttons Dresses with supervision

Age				
4–5 years	Runs well and turns Can hop on one foot 1–2 times Beginning to skip Stands on one leg for 10 seconds Throws ball well overhand Walks down stairs 1 foot to each step	Can copy a cross with a pencil Can pick the longer of 2 lines Can copy a square with pencil	Vocabular over 1000 words Can match colors, and by 5 years, names 3–4 colors Counts 3 objects with pointing Ninety percent of speech intelligible Can define words in terms of use Can answer questions like what do you do when you are cold . . . hungry . . . . tired. . . ?	Can separate from mother easily Dresses with little supervision Buttons Likes to play "dramatic" play, make-believe Imaginative play with a doll
5–6 years	Skips on both feet alternately Can catch a bounced ball Can walk heel to toe on a line Can hop on 1 foot for 10 feet	Can copy a square or triangle from looking at a copy Gives age Knows morning from afternoon Draws a person with a body, with 3–6 parts Prints simple words	Can repeat 4 digits Asks questions about meaning of words Counts 10 objects Names coins Can tell what some things are made of Can define some words	No supervision necessary for dressing Plays "dress-up" Elaborate dramatic play Does simple chores unattended at home

(From Martin HP: The neuro-psycho-developmental aspects of child abuse and neglect. p. 95. In Ellersteia NS (ed): Child Abuse and Neglect—A Medical Reference. 1st Ed. Churchill Livingstone, New York, 1981, with permission.)

Appendix H
Growth Curves*

* Figures H-1 through H-12 from the Ten State Nutritional Survey, Department of Health, Education, and Welfare, Public Service, Health Resources Administration, National Center for Health Statistics, and Centers for Disease Control. Figures H-13 and H-14 from Tanner JM Davies PSW: Clinical longitudinal standards for height velocity for North American Children, J Pediatr 107:317, 1985, with permission.

527

Fig. H-1. Full-Term Boys—Birth to 36 Months—Weight for Age

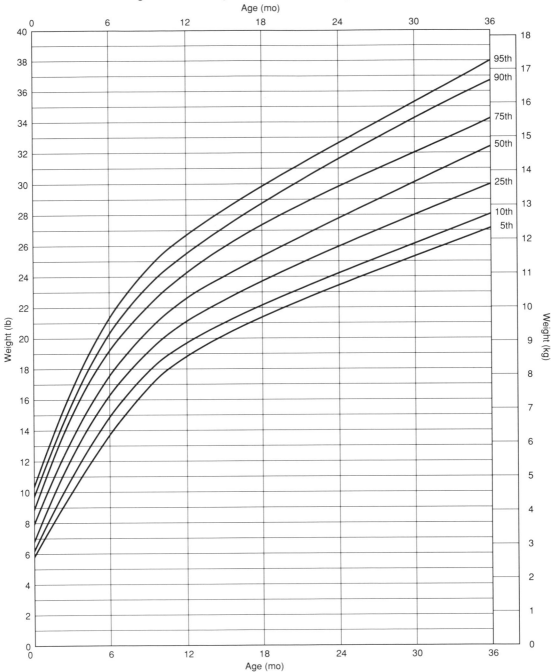

Fig. H-2. Full-Term Boys—Birth to 36 Months—Length for Age

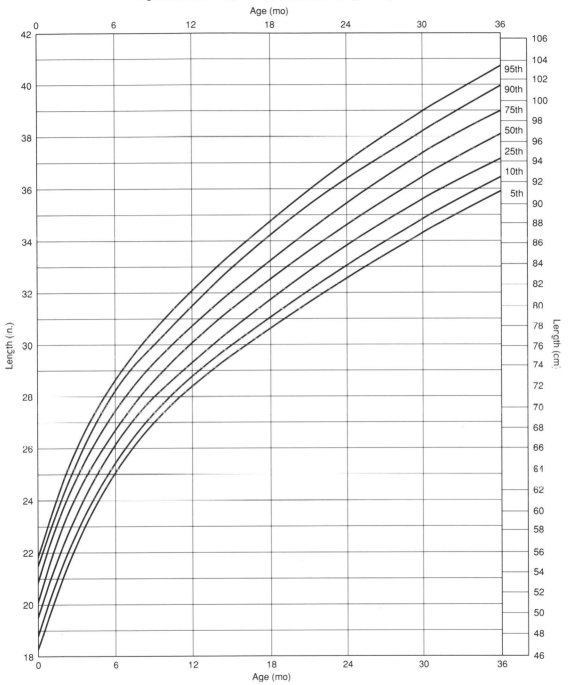

Fig. H-3. Full-Term Boys—Birth to 36 Months—Head Circumference for Age (upper), Weight for Length (lower)

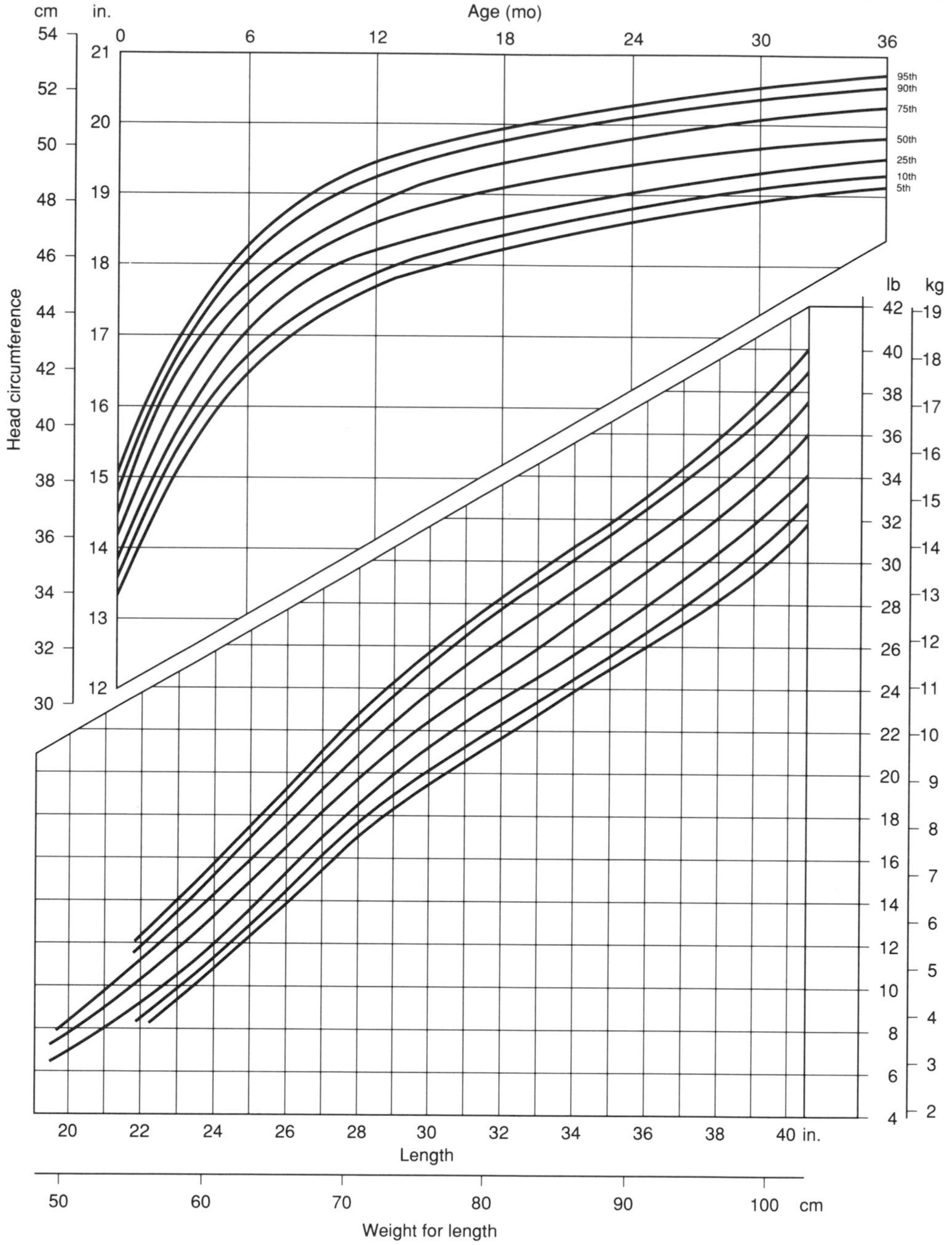

Fig. H-4. Full-Term Girls—Birth to 36 Months—Weight for Age

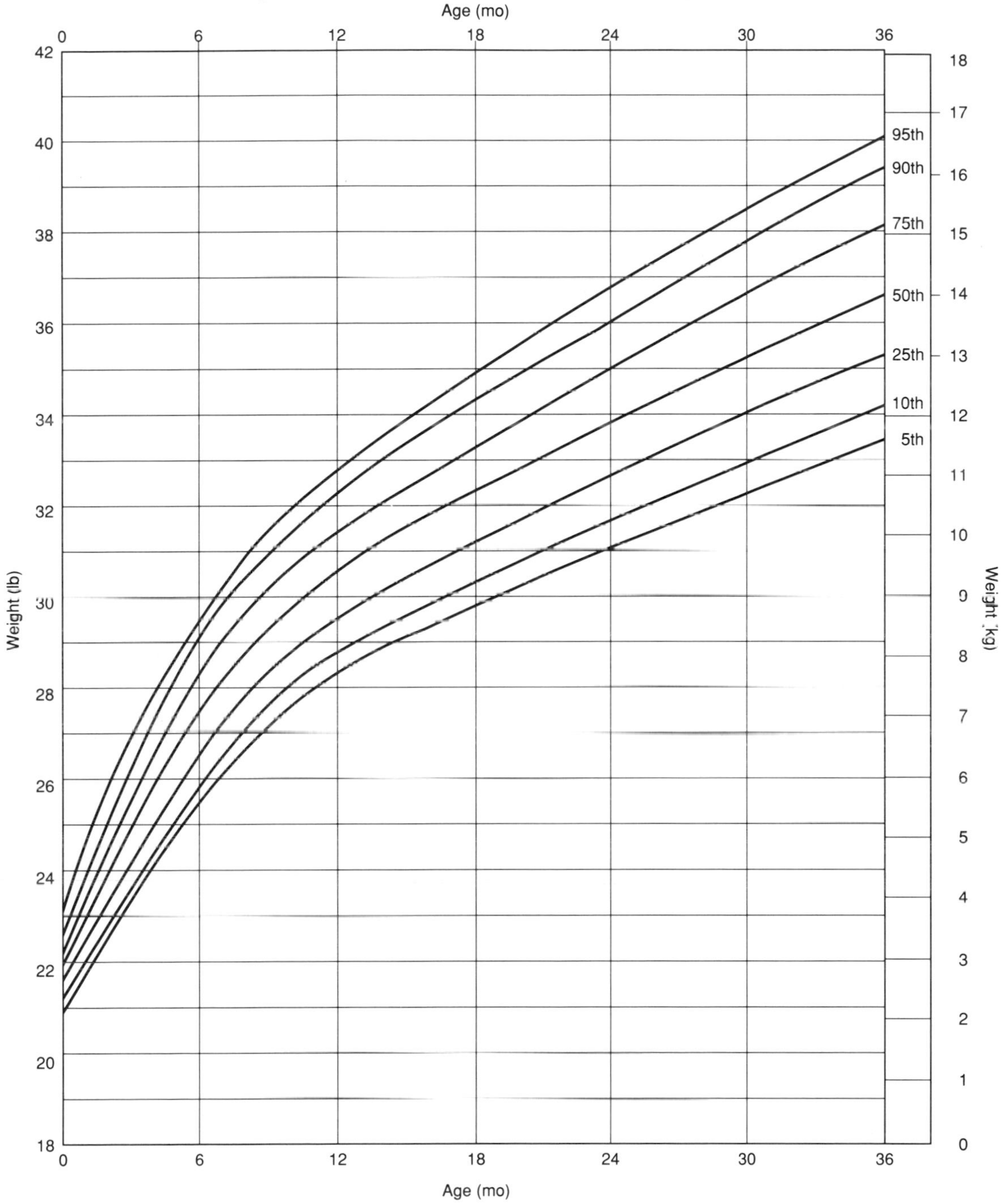

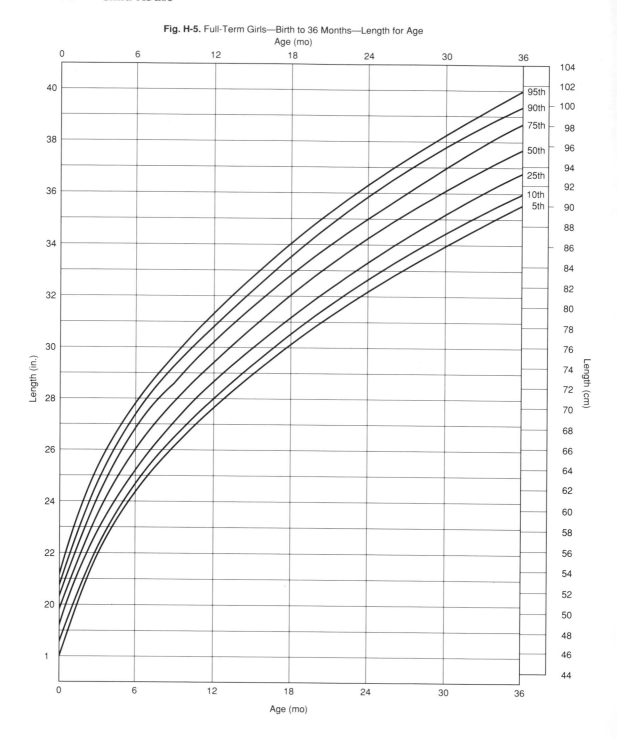

Fig. H-5. Full-Term Girls—Birth to 36 Months—Length for Age

Fig. H-6. Full-Term Girls—Birth to 36 Months—Head Circumference for Age (upper), Weight for Length (lower)

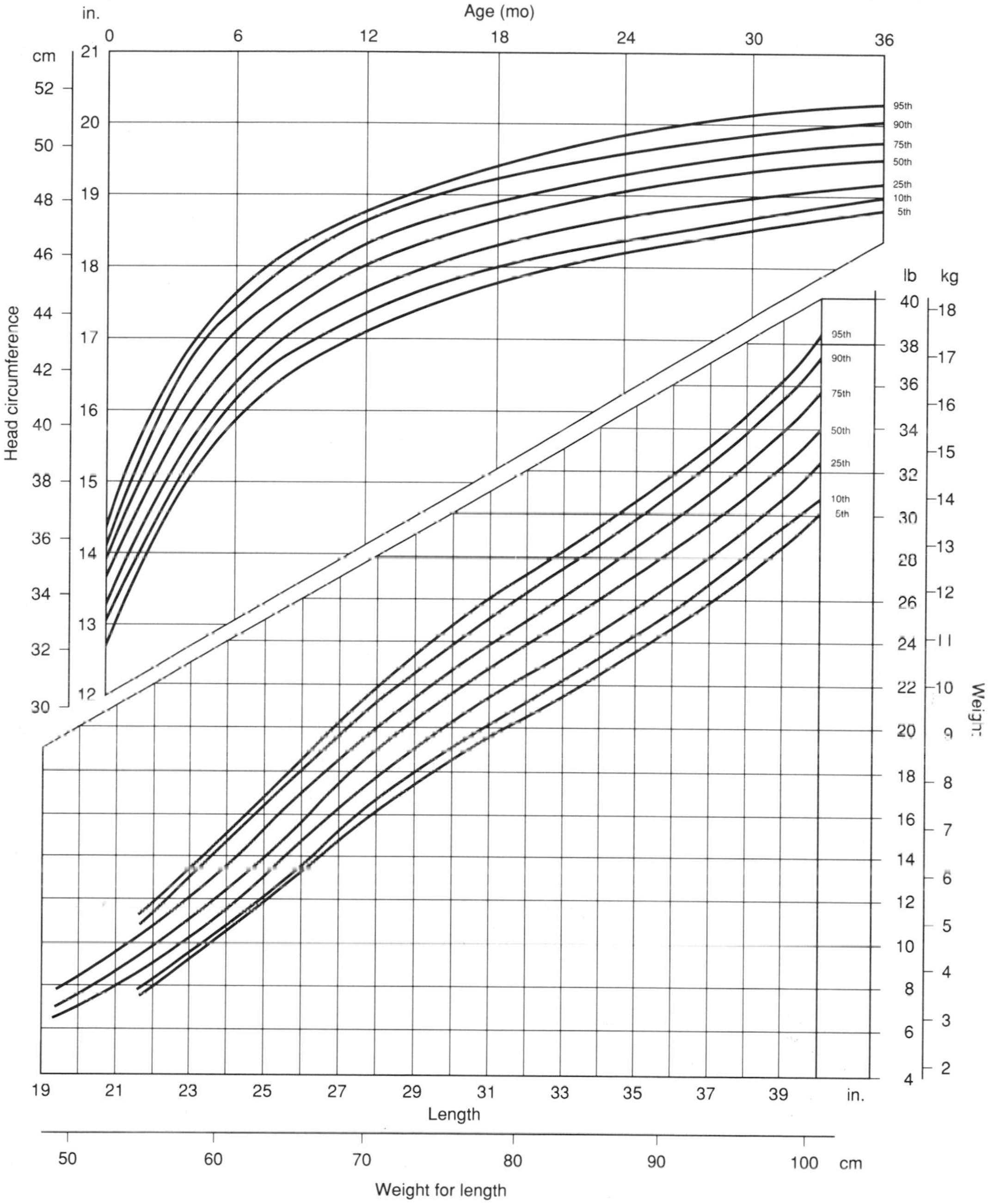

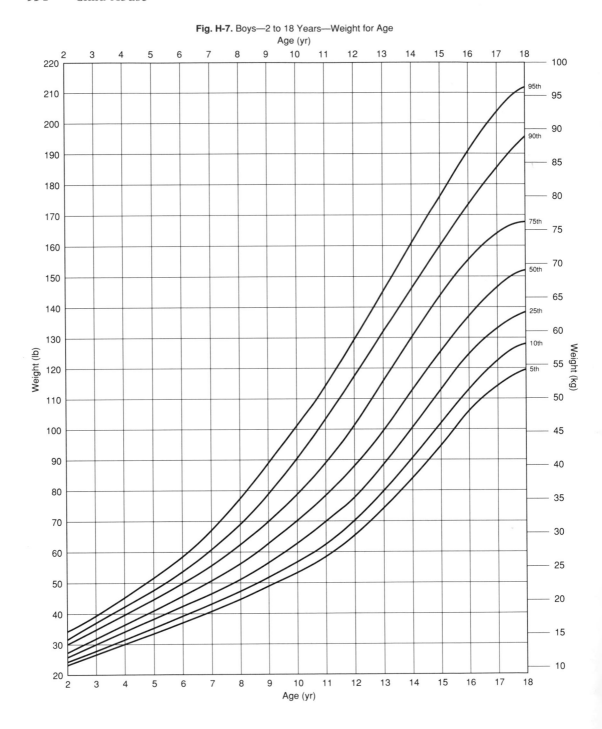

Fig. H-7. Boys—2 to 18 Years—Weight for Age

Fig. H-8. Boys—2 To 18 Years—Height for Stature

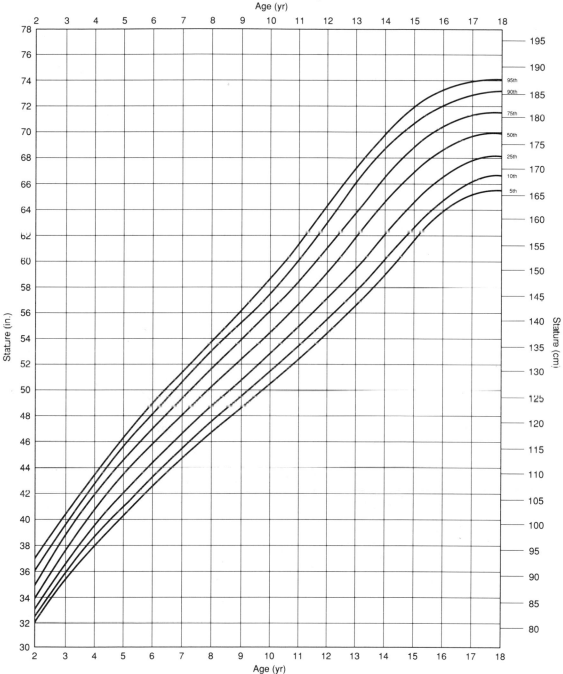

Fig. H-9. Boys—2 to 11¹/₂ Years—Weight for Stature

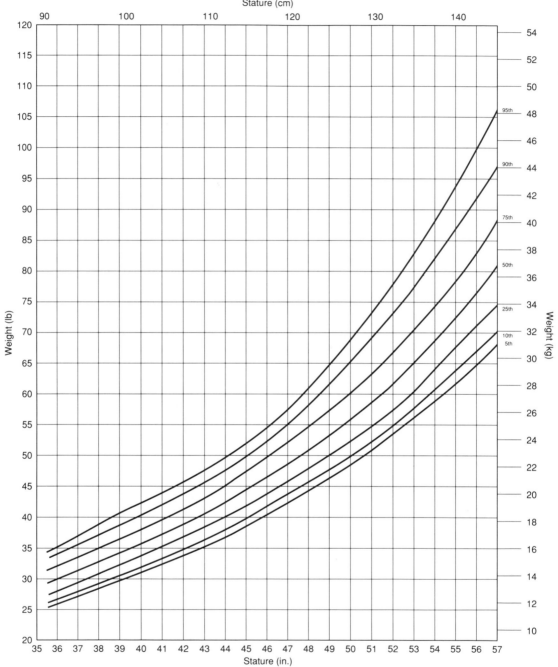

Fig. H-10. Girls—2 to 18 Years—Weight for Age

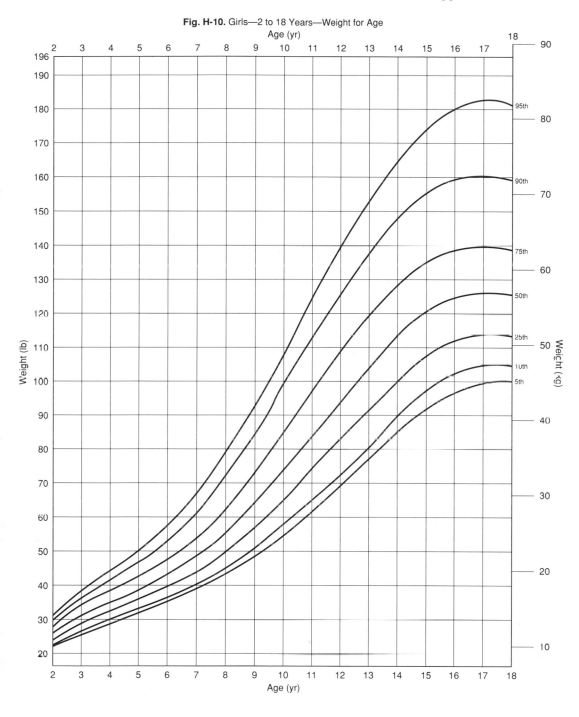

Fig. H-11. Girls—2 to 18 Years—Height for Age

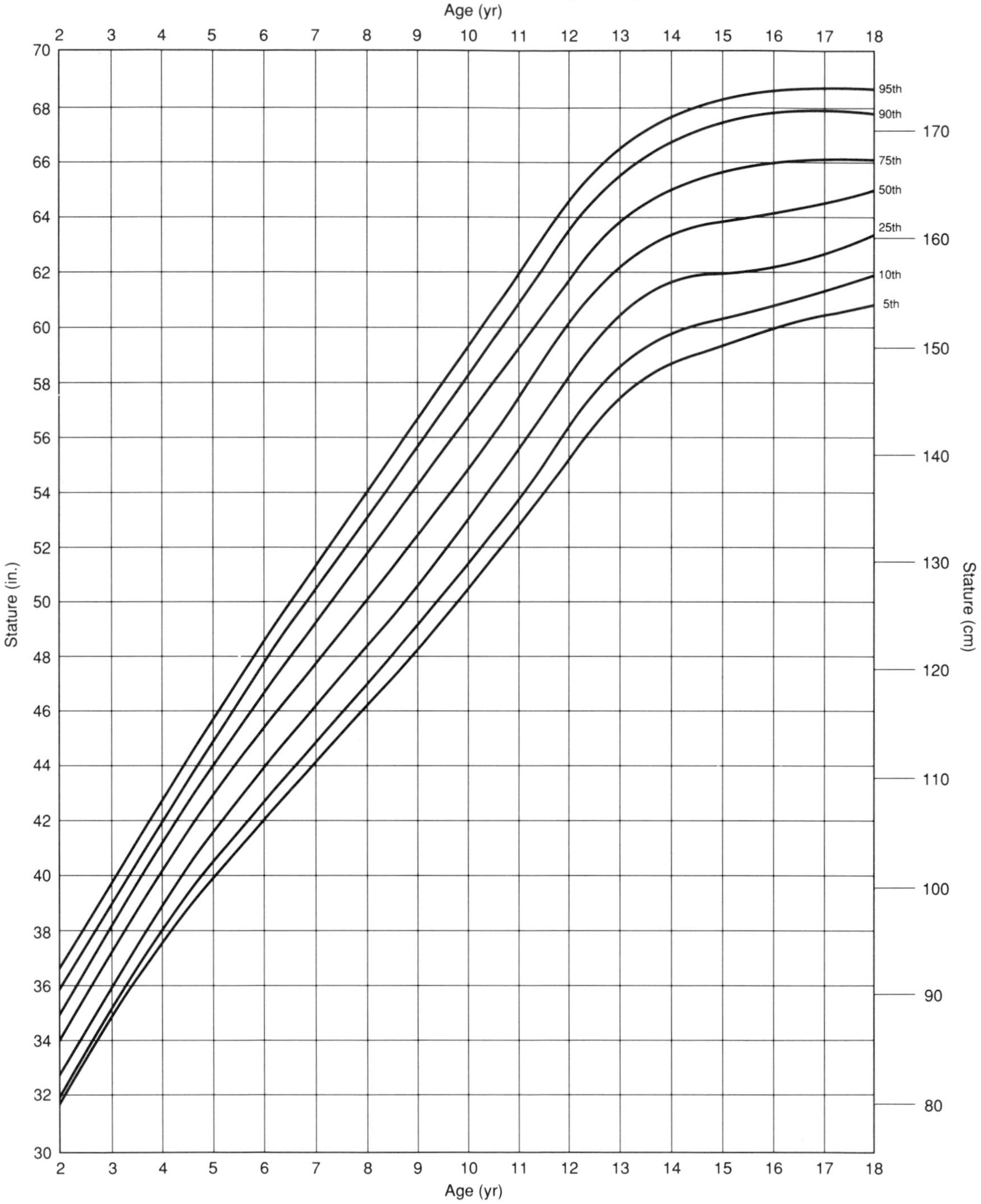

Fig. H-12. Girls—2 To 10 Years—Weight for Stature

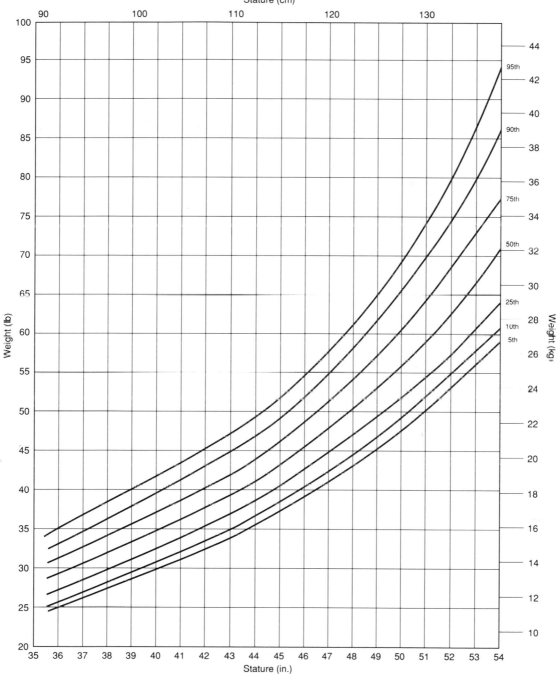

Fig. H-13. Growth Velocity—Boys

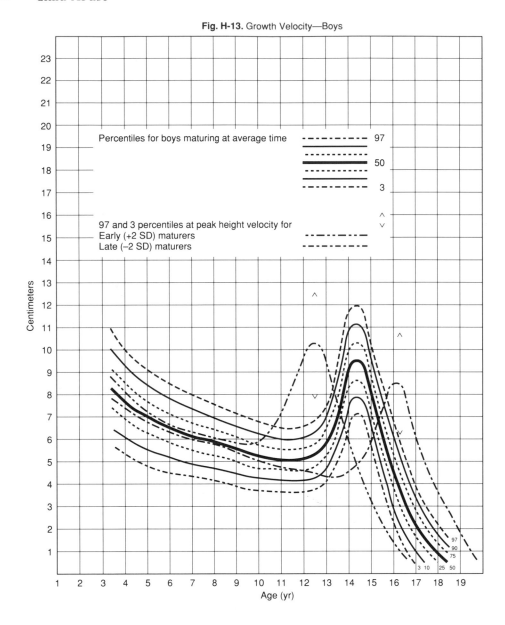

Fig. H-14. Growth Velocity—Girls

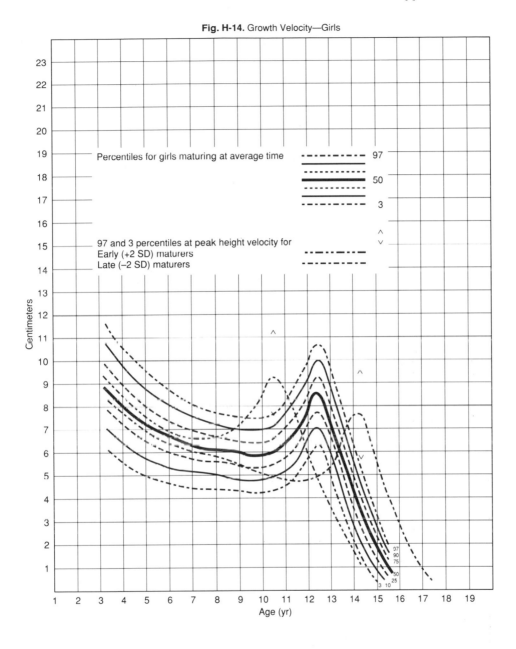

Table H-15. Percentiles for Triceps Skinfold for Whites of the United States: Health and Nutrition Examination Survey I of 1971 to 1974[a]

Triceps Skinfold Percentiles (mm^2)

Age (yr)	Males								Females							
	N	5	10	25	50	75	90	95	N	5	10	25	50	75	90	95
1–1.9	228	6	7	8	10	12	14	16	204	6	7	8	10	12	14	16
2–2.9	223	6	7	8	10	12	14	15	208	6	8	9	10	12	15	16
3–3.9	220	6	7	8	10	11	14	15	208	7	8	9	11	12	14	15
4–4.9	230	6	6	8	9	11	12	14	208	7	8	8	10	12	15	16
5–5.9	214	6	6	8	9	11	14	15	219	6	7	8	10	12	15	18
6–6.9	117	5	6	7	8	10	13	16	118	6	6	8	10	12	14	16
7–7.9	122	5	6	7	9	12	15	17	126	6	7	9	11	13	16	18
8–8.9	117	5	6	7	8	10	13	16	118	6	8	9	12	15	18	24
9–9.9	121	6	6	7	10	13	17	18	125	8	8	10	13	16	20	22
10–10.9	146	6	6	8	10	14	18	21	152	7	8	10	12	17	23	27
11–11.9	122	6	6	8	11	16	20	24	117	7	8	10	13	18	24	28
12–12.9	153	6	6	8	11	14	22	28	129	8	9	11	14	18	23	27
13–13.9	134	5	5	7	10	14	22	26	151	8	8	12	15	21	26	30
14–14.9	131	4	5	7	9	14	21	24	141	9	10	13	16	21	26	28
15–15.9	128	4	5	6	8	11	18	24	117	8	10	12	17	21	25	32
16–16.9	131	4	5	6	8	12	16	22	142	10	12	15	18	22	26	31
17–17.9	133	5	5	6	8	12	16	19	114	10	12	13	19	24	30	37
18–18.9	91	4	5	6	9	13	20	24	109	10	12	15	18	22	26	30
19–24.9	531	4	5	7	10	15	20	22	1060	10	11	14	18	24	30	34
25–34.9	971	5	6	8	12	16	20	24	1987	10	12	16	21	27	34	37
35–44.9	806	5	6	8	12	16	20	23	1614	12	14	18	23	29	35	38
45–54.9	898	6	6	8	12	15	20	25	1047	12	16	20	25	30	36	40
55–64.9	734	5	6	8	11	14	19	22	809	12	16	20	25	31	36	38
65–74.9	1503	4	6	8	11	15	19	22	1670	12	14	18	24	29	34	36

[a] The Lange caliper was used in these studies.
(Adapted from Frisancho AR: New Norms of upper limb fat and muscle areas for assessment of nutritional status. Am J Clin Nutr 34:2540, 1981, with permission.)

Index

Page numbers followed by f *denote figures; those followed by* t *denote tables.*